A+ Guide to Software: Managing, Maintaining, and Troubleshooting
SIXTH EDITION

Jean Andrews, Ph.D.

COURSE TECHNOLOGY
CENGAGE Learning

Australia • Canada • Mexico • Singapore • Spain • United Kingdom • United States

COURSE TECHNOLOGY
CENGAGE Learning

A+ Guide to Software:
Managing, Maintaining, and Troubleshooting
Sixth Edition
Jean Andrews

Vice President, Careers &
  Computing: Dave Garza

Executive Editor: Stephen Helba

Acquisitions Editor: Nick Lombardi

Director, Development – Careers & Computing:
  Marah Bellegarde

Senior Product Manager: Michelle Ruelos Cannistraci

Developmental Editor: Jill Batistick

Editorial Assistant: Sarah Pickering

Director, Market Development: Lisa Lysne

Senior Marketing Manager: Mark Linton

Marketing Coordinator: Benjamin Genise

Director, Brand Management: Jason Sakos

Brand Manager: Kristen McNary

Production Director: Wendy Troeger

Production Manager: Andrew Crouth

Senior Content Project Manager: Andrea Majot

Art Director: GEX

Technology Project Manager: Joe Pliss

Media Editor: Bill Overrocker

Cover image: ©AS_kom/Shutterstock

For product information and technology assistance, contact us at
Cengage Learning Customer & Sales Support, 1-800-354-9706

For permission to use material from this text or product, submit all requests online at **cengage.com/permissions**
Further permissions questions can be emailed to
permissionrequest@cengage.com

Microsoft® is a registered trademark of the Microsoft Corporation.
Library of Congress Control Number: 2012942318

ISBN-13: 978-1-133-13513-5

ISBN-10: 1-133-13513-7

Course Technology
20 Channel Center Street
Boston, MA 02210
USA

Cengage Learning is a leading provider of customized learning solutions with office locations around the globe, including Singapore, the United Kingdom, Australia, Mexico, Brazil, and Japan. Locate your local office at: **international.cengage.com/region**

Cengage Learning products are represented in Canada by Nelson Education, Ltd.

For your lifelong learning solutions, visit **www.cengage.com/coursetechnology**

Purchase any of our products at your local college store or at our preferred online store **www.cengagebrain.com**

Visit our corporate website at **cengage.com**.

Printed in the United States of America
2 3 4 5 6 7 16 15 14 13

Table of Contents

CHAPTER 5

Troubleshooting Windows and Applications 211

CHAPTER 6

Troubleshooting Windows Startup Problems. 255

CHAPTER 7

Connecting to and Setting Up a Network 299

CompTIA A+ 220-802 Exam Mapped to *A+ Guide to Software*

A+ Guide to Hardware and *A+ Guide to Software* when used together fully meet all of the CompTIA A+ exam objectives. If the exam objective is covered in the corresponding textbook, it is referenced in the Chapters and Page Numbers columns.

DOMAIN 1.0 OPERATING SYSTEMS

1.1 Compare and contrast the features and requirements of various Microsoft Operating Systems.

OBJECTIVES	CHAPTERS	PAGE NUMBERS
◢ Windows XP Home, Windows XP Professional, Windows XP Media Center, Windows XP 64-bit Professional	2, Apx C	38–57; 564–566
◢ Windows Vista Home Basic, Windows Vista Home Premium, Windows Vista Business, Windows Vista Ultimate, Windows Vista Enterprise	2, Apx B	38–57; 544–546
◢ Windows 7 Starter, Windows 7 Home Premium, Windows 7 Professional, Windows 7 Ultimate, Windows 7 Enterprise	2	38–57
◢ Features:		
• 32-bit vs. 64-bit	2	38–57
• Aero	2	38–57
• Gadgets	2	38–57
• User Account Control	2	26–28
• BitLocker	9	426–440
• Shadow copy	3	104–116
• System Restore	3	104–116
• Ready Boost	4	118–201
• Sidebar	1	7–8
• Compatibility Mode	2	68–83
• XP Mode	2	68–83
• Easy Transfer	2	68–87
• Administrative tools	4	152–188
• Defender	9	448–466
• Windows Firewall	9	426–440
• Security Center	9	426–440
• Event Viewer	4	152–188
• File structure and paths	3	94–104
• Category view vs. Classic view	1	22–23
◢ Upgrade paths—differences between in-place upgrades, compatibility tools, Windows Upgrade OS Advisor	2	38–68

1.2 Given a scenario, install and configure the operating system using the most appropriate method.

OBJECTIVES	CHAPTERS	PAGE NUMBERS
◢ Boot methods	2	57–68
• USB	2	57-68
• CD-ROM	2	57–68
• DVD	2	57–68
• PXE	2	57–68, 83–87
◢ Type of installations	2	38–68
• Creating image	2, Apx D	38–68; 596–603
• Unattended installation	2	83–87

1.3 Given a scenario, use appropriate command-line tools.

1.4 **Given a scenario, use appropriate operating system features and tools.**

• CMD	3	120–140
• SERVICES.MSC	4	152–188
• MMC	4	152–188
• MSTSC	8	372–377
• NOTEPAD	1	3–16
• EXPLORER	1	3–16
• MSINFO32	1	20–22
• DXDIAG		See online content or *A+ Guide to Hardware, 6e*

1.5 **Given a scenario, use Control Panel utilities** (the items are organized by "classic view/large icons" in Windows).

OBJECTIVES	CHAPTERS	PAGE NUMBERS
◢ Common to all Microsoft Operating Systems		
• Internet options	8	364–372
▪ Connections	8	364–372
▪ Security	8	364–372
▪ General	8	364–372
▪ Privacy	8	364–372
▪ Programs	8	364–372
▪ Advanced	8	364–372
• Display		See online content or *A+ Guide to Hardware, 6e*
▪ Resolution		See online content or *A+ Guide to Hardware, 6e*
• User accounts	2	68–83
• Folder options		
▪ Sharing	8	383–404
▪ View hidden files	1	10–19
▪ Hide extensions	1	10–19
▪ Layout	1	10–19
• System		
▪ Performance (virtual memory)	3	94–104
▪ Hardware profiles		See online content or *A+ Guide to Hardware, 6e*
▪ Remote settings	8	364–383
▪ System protection	3	94–116
• Security center	9	426–440
• Windows Firewall	9	426–440
• Power options		See online content or *A+ Guide to Hardware, 6e*
▪ Hibernate		See online content or *A+ Guide to Hardware, 6e*
▪ Power plans		See online content or *A+ Guide to Hardware, 6e*
▪ Sleep/suspend		See online content or *A+ Guide to Hardware, 6e*
▪ Standby		See online content or *A+ Guide to Hardware, 6e*
• Add/remove programs	2	80–83
• Network connections	7	321–341
• Printers and faxes		See online content or *A+ Guide to Hardware, 6e*

1.6   Set up and configure Windows networking on a client/desktop.

DOMAIN 3.0 MOBILE DEVICES

4.2 **Given a scenario, troubleshoot common problems related to motherboards, RAM, CPU, and power with appropriate tools.**

4.3 **Given a scenario, troubleshoot hard drives and RAID arrays with appropriate tools.**

OBJECTIVES	CHAPTERS	PAGE NUMBERS
• Failure to boot	6	280–294
• Drive not recognized	6	280–294
• OS not found	6	280–294
• RAID not found	6	280–294
• RAID stops working	6	280–294
• BSOD	6	280–294
◢ Tools		See online content or *A+ Guide to Hardware, 6e*
• Screwdriver		See online content or *A+ Guide to Hardware, 6e*
		See online content or *A+ Guide to Hardware, 6e*
• External enclosures		See online content or *A+ Guide to Hardware, 6e*
• CHDKS	6	265–280
• CHKDSK	6	265–280
• FORMAT	6	265–280
• FDISK	6	265–280
• File recovery software	6	291–294

4.4 Given a scenario, troubleshoot common video and display issues.

OBJECTIVES	CHAPTERS	PAGE NUMBERS
◢ Common symptoms		See online content or *A+ Guide to Hardware, 6e*
• VGA mode		See online content or *A+ Guide to Hardware, 6e*
• No image on screen		See online content or *A+ Guide to Hardware, 6e*
• Overheat shutdown		See online content or *A+ Guide to Hardware, 6e*
• Dead pixels		See online content or *A+ Guide to Hardware, 6e*
• Artifacts		See online content or *A+ Guide to Hardware, 6e*
• Color patterns incorrect		See online content or *A+ Guide to Hardware, 6e*
• Dim image		See online content or *A+ Guide to Hardware, 6e*
• Flickering image		See online content or *A+ Guide to Hardware, 6e*
• Distorted image		See online content or *A+ Guide to Hardware, 6e*
• Discoloration (degaussing)		See online content or *A+ Guide to Hardware, 6e*
• BSOD		See online content or *A+ Guide to Hardware, 6e*

4.5 Given a scenario, troubleshoot wired and wireless networks with appropriate tools.

OBJECTIVES	CHAPTERS	PAGE NUMBERS
◢ Common symptoms	8	404–419
• No connectivity	8	404–419
• APIPA address	8	404–419
• Limited connectivity	8	404–419

4.6 **Given a scenario, troubleshoot operating system problems with appropriate tools.**

4.7 **Given a scenario, troubleshoot common security issues with appropriate tools and best practices.**

4.8   **Given a scenario, troubleshoot, and repair common laptop issues while adhering to the appropriate procedures.**

OBJECTIVES	CHAPTERS	PAGE NUMBERS
◢ Common symptoms		See online content or *A+ Guide to Hardware, 6e*
• No display		See online content or *A+ Guide to Hardware, 6e*
• Dim display		See online content or *A+ Guide to Hardware, 6e*
• Flickering display		See online content or *A+ Guide to Hardware, 6e*
• Sticking keys		See online content or *A+ Guide to Hardware, 6e*
• Intermittent wireless		See online content or *A+ Guide to Hardware, 6e*
• Battery not charging		See online content or *A+ Guide to Hardware, 6e*
• Ghost cursor		See online content or *A+ Guide to Hardware, 6e*
• No power		See online content or *A+ Guide to Hardware, 6e*
• Num lock indicator lights		See online content or *A+ Guide to Hardware, 6e*
• No wireless connectivity		See online content or *A+ Guide to Hardware, 6e*
• No Bluetooth connectivity		See online content or *A+ Guide to Hardware, 6e*
• Cannot display to external monitor		See online content or *A+ Guide to Hardware, 6e*
◢ Disassembling processes for proper reassembly		See online content or *A+ Guide to Hardware, 6e*
• Document and label cable and screw locations		See online content or *A+ Guide to Hardware, 6e*
• Organize parts		See online content or *A+ Guide to Hardware, 6e*
• Refer to manufacturer documentation		See online content or *A+ Guide to Hardware, 6e*
• Use appropriate hand tools		See online content or *A+ Guide to Hardware, 6e*

4.9   **Given a scenario, troubleshoot printers with appropriate tools.**   0

OBJECTIVES	CHAPTERS	PAGE NUMBERS
◢ Common symptoms		See online content or *A+ Guide to Hardware, 6e*
• Streaks		See online content or *A+ Guide to Hardware, 6e*
• Faded prints		See online content or *A+ Guide to Hardware, 6e*
• Ghost images		See online content or *A+ Guide to Hardware, 6e*
• Toner not fused to the paper		See online content or *A+ Guide to Hardware, 6e*
• Creased paper		See online content or *A+ Guide to Hardware, 6e*
• Paper not feeding		See online content or *A+ Guide to Hardware, 6e*

- Paper jam

  See online content or
  A+ Guide to Hardware, 6e

- No connectivity

  See online content or
  A+ Guide to Hardware, 6e

- Garbled characters on paper

  See online content or
  A+ Guide to Hardware, 6e

- Vertical lines on page

  See online content or
  A+ Guide to Hardware, 6e

- Backed-up print queue

  See online content or
  A+ Guide to Hardware, 6e

- Low memory errors

  See online content or
  A+ Guide to Hardware, 6e

- Access denied

  See online content or
  A+ Guide to Hardware, 6e

- Printer will not print

  See online content or
  A+ Guide to Hardware, 6e

- Color prints in wrong print color

  See online content or
  A+ Guide to Hardware, 6e

- Unable to install printer

  See online content or
  A+ Guide to Hardware, 6e

- Error codes

  See online content or
  A+ Guide to Hardware, 6e

◢ Tools

  See online content or
  A+ Guide to Hardware, 6e

- Maintenance kit

  See online content or
  A+ Guide to Hardware, 6e

- Toner vacuum

  See online content or
  A+ Guide to Hardware, 6e

- Compressed air

  See online content or
  A+ Guide to Hardware, 6e

- Printer spooler

  See online content or
  A+ Guide to Hardware, 6e

Introduction A+ Guide to Software

A+ Guide to Software, Sixth Edition was written to be the very best tool on the market today to prepare you to support personal computers. Updated to include the most current software technologies with a new chapter on mobile devices and client-side virtualization and new content on supporting Windows 7, this book takes you from the just-a-user level to the I-can-fix-this level for PC software matters. This book achieves its goals with an unusually effective combination of tools that powerfully reinforce both concepts and hands-on, real-world experiences.

Competency in using a computer is a prerequisite to using this book. No background knowledge of electronics is assumed. An appropriate prerequisite course for this book would be a general course in microcomputer applications.

This book includes:

▲ **Several in-depth, hands-on projects** integrated throughout each chapter designed to make certain that you not only understand the material, but also execute procedures and make decisions on your own.

▲ **Comprehensive review and practice end-of-chapter material**, including a chapter summary, key terms, review questions that focus on A+ content, critical thinking questions, and real-world problems to solve.

▲ **Step-by-step instructions** on installation, maintenance, optimization of system performance, and troubleshooting.

▲ **A wide array of photos, drawings, and screen shots** support the text, displaying in detail the exact software features you will need to understand how to manage and maintain your PC.

In addition, the carefully structured, clearly written text is accompanied by graphics that provide the visual input essential to learning. For instructors using the book in a classroom, instructor resources are available online and on the Instructor Resources CD.

Coverage is balanced—while focusing on new hardware and software, the text also covers the real work of PC repair, where some older technology remains in widespread use and still needs support. For example, the book covers how to use a 64-bit operating system to support the latest processors, but also addresses how to get the most out of a 32-bit OS with limited hardware resources. At the writing of this book, Windows 7 is the current Microsoft operating system used on desktop and laptop computers. The book focuses on supporting Windows 7 systems, while also including light coverage of Windows Vista in Appendix B, and XP in Appendix C.

This book provides thorough preparation for the software portions of CompTIA's 2012 A+ Certification examinations. The hardware portions of the A+ 2012 exams are covered in the companion book, *A+ Guide to Hardware*. Both books together map completely to these new exam objectives.

This certification credential's popularity among employers is growing exponentially, and obtaining certification increases your ability to gain employment and improve your salary. To get more information on A+ certification and its sponsoring organization, the Computing Technology Industry Association, see their web site at *www.comptia.org*.

FEATURES

To ensure a successful learning experience, this book includes the following pedagogical features:

- ◢ **Learning Objectives:** Every chapter opens with a list of learning objectives that sets the stage for you to absorb the lessons of the text.
- ◢ **Comprehensive Step-by-Step Troubleshooting Guidance:** Troubleshooting guidelines are included in almost every chapter.
- ◢ **Step-by-Step Procedures:** The book is chock-full of step-by-step procedures covering subjects from operating system installation and maintenance to optimizing system performance.
- ◢ **Art Program:** Numerous detailed photographs, three-dimensional art, and screenshots support the text, displaying hardware and software features exactly as you will see them in your work.
- ◢ **CompTIA A+ Table of Contents:** This table of contents gives the page that provides the primary content for each certification objective on the A+ 2012 exams. This is a valuable tool for quick reference.
- ◢ **Hands-on Projects:** These sections give you practice using the skills you have just studied so that you can learn by doing and know you have mastered a skill.
- ◢ **Applying Concepts:** These sections offer practical applications for the material being discussed. Whether outlining a task, developing a scenario, or providing pointers, the Applying Concepts sections give you a chance to apply what you've learned to a typical PC problem.

A+ Icons: All of the content that relates to CompTIA's 2012 A+ 220-801 and A+ 220-802 Certification exams, whether it's a page or a sentence, is highlighted with an A+ icon. The icon notes the exam name and the objective number. This unique feature highlights the relevant content at a glance, so that you can pay extra attention to the material.

Notes: Note icons highlight additional helpful information related to the subject being discussed.

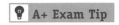

A+ Exam Tip Boxes: These boxes highlight additional insights and tips to remember if you are planning to take the CompTIA A+ Exams.

Caution Icons: These icons highlight critical safety information. Follow these instructions carefully to protect the PC and its data and to ensure your own safety.

Vista Differences: These boxes point the student to Appendix B, *Windows Vista*, where Windows Vista is discussed when it differs from the coverage of Windows 7 in the chapter.

XP Differences: These boxes point the student to Appendix C, Windows XP, where *Windows XP* is discussed when it differs from the coverage of Windows 7 in the chapter.

End-of-Chapter Material: Each chapter closes with the following features, which reinforce the material covered in the chapter and provide real-world, hands-on testing:

⊿ **Chapter Summary:** This bulleted list of concise statements summarizes all major points of the chapter.

⊿ **Key Terms:** The content of each chapter is further reinforced by an end-of-chapter key-term list. The definitions of all terms are included at the end of the book in a full-length glossary.

⊿ **Review Questions:** You can test your understanding of each chapter with a comprehensive set of review questions. The "Reviewing the Basics" questions check your understanding of fundamental concepts focused on A+ content, while the "Thinking Critically" questions help you synthesize and apply what you've learned and also focus on A+ content.

⊿ **Real Problems, Real Solutions:** Each comprehensive problem allows you to find out if you can apply what you've learned in the chapter to a real-life situation.

CertBlaster Test Prep Resources: A+ *Guide to Software, Sixth Edition* includes CertBlaster test preparation questions that mirror the look and feel of CompTIA's A+ 220-802 certificate exam.

Companion web site: To reign in the physical size and weight of the book, most of the content on less significant and older technologies has been placed online at this book's companion web site. To access the A+ 220-802 hardware troubleshooting content, additional course materials, including CourseMate, as well as free study tools, and videos, please visit the texbook's companion web site at *www.cengagebrain.com*. At the CengageBrain.com home page, search for the ISBN of your title (from the back cover of your book) using the search box at the top of the page. This will take you to the product page where these resources can be found.

The textbook's companion web site includes video clips that feature Jean Andrews illustrating key concepts in the text and providing advice on the real world of PC repair. Also included is less significant and older content that still might be important in some PC repair situations. The content includes the following: The Hexademical Number System and Memory Addressing, Introducing the Mac OS, Introducing Linux, Electricity and Multimeters, Facts about Legacy Motherboards, How an OS Uses System Resources, Facts about Legacy Processors, All About SCSI, Behind the Scenes with DEBUG, FAT Details, and Selecting and Installing Hard Drives using Legacy Motherboards. Other helpful online tools include Frequently Asked Questions, Sample Reports, Troubleshooting Flowcharts, and an electronic Glossary. CertBlaster Test Preparation Questions from dtiPublishing are included so that students will have plenty of opportunity to practice, drill, and rehearse for the exam once they have worked through this book. Also included online is the hardware troubleshooting content on the 2012 A+ 220-802 exam that is found in the A+ *Guide to Hardware, Sixth Edition*. Therefore, all the content on the A+ 220-802 exam is included in this book, A+ *Guide to Software, Sixth Edition*, and online at the companion web site.

CompTIA A+ and PC Repair: For additional content and updates to this book and information about our complete line of CompTIA A+ and PC Repair topics, please visit our web site at *www.cengage.com/pcrepair*.

WHAT'S NEW IN THE SIXTH EDITION

Here's a summary of what's new in the *Sixth Edition*:

- Maps to the software content on the CompTIA's 2012 A+ Exams.
- More focus on A+, with non-A+ content moved online to the companion web site or eliminated.
- The chapters focus on Windows 7; Vista content is in Appendix B, and XP content is in Appendix C.
- New content added (all new content was also new to the A+ 2012 exams).
  - Windows 7 is added. Operating systems covered are now Windows 7, Vista, and XP. New content on deploying Windows 7 in an enterprise is added.
  - Supporting mobile devices (including the Android OS and iOS) and client-side virtualization are covered in Chapter 10.
  - Hands-on Projects in several chapters use virtual machines so that students get plenty of practice using this up-and-coming technology.
  - Creating a standard image is added and can be found in Appendix D, *Creating a Standard Image*.
  - Supporting TCP/IP version 6 is added to Chapter 7.
- In an effort to reduce the size of the book, appendices have been reduced to a minimum and extra content has been put on the web site that accompanies the book.
- Mapping to A+ objectives is cleaner and easier to follow.
- Review questions focus on A+ type questions.

ANATOMY OF A PC REPAIR CHAPTER

This section is a visual explanation of the components that make up a PC Repair chapter. The figures identify some of our traditional instructional elements as well as the enhancements and new features we have included for the fifth edition.

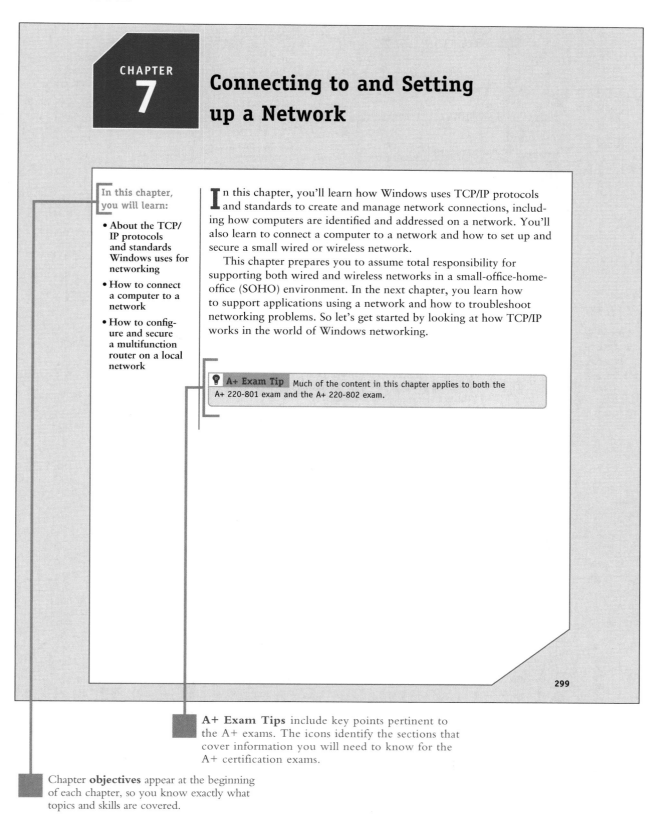

CHAPTER 7

Connecting to and Setting up a Network

In this chapter, you will learn:

• About the TCP/IP protocols and standards Windows uses for networking

• How to connect a computer to a network

• How to configure and secure a multifunction router on a local network

In this chapter, you'll learn how Windows uses TCP/IP protocols and standards to create and manage network connections, including how computers are identified and addressed on a network. You'll also learn to connect a computer to a network and how to set up and secure a small wired or wireless network.

This chapter prepares you to assume total responsibility for supporting both wired and wireless networks in a small-office-home-office (SOHO) environment. In the next chapter, you learn how to support applications using a network and how to troubleshoot networking problems. So let's get started by looking at how TCP/IP works in the world of Windows networking.

💡 **A+ Exam Tip** Much of the content in this chapter applies to both the A+ 220-801 exam and the A+ 220-802 exam.

299

A+ Exam Tips include key points pertinent to the A+ exams. The icons identify the sections that cover information you will need to know for the A+ certification exams.

Chapter **objectives** appear at the beginning of each chapter, so you know exactly what topics and skills are covered.

Cautions identify critical safety information.

A+
220-802
1.1, 1.2

⚡ **Caution**   It's convenient to back up one volume to another volume on a different hard drive. However, don't back up one volume to another volume on the same hard drive, because when a hard drive fails, quite often all volumes on the drive are damaged and you will lose both your data and your backup.

Windows can handle up to four partitions on a drive. In Chapter 3, you learn to use Disk Management to create partitions from unallocated space and to resize, delete, and split existing partitions.

ADMINISTRATOR ACCOUNT

Recall from Chapter 1 that Windows supports two types of accounts, standard accounts and administrator accounts. These accounts are local accounts, meaning they are only recognized by the local computer. Every Windows computer has two local administrator accounts:

▲ During the Windows 7 installation, you are given the opportunity to enter an account name and password to a local user account that is assigned administrator privileges. This account is enabled by default.

▲ A built-in administrator account is created by default. The built-in administrator account is named Administrator, does not have a password, and is disabled by default. In Chapter 8, you learn how to enable this administrator account.

You can log on as an administrator after the OS is installed and create local user accounts that apply to this one computer. How to set up a local account is covered later in the chapter.

A+
220-802
1.1, 1.2,
1.6

NETWORK CONFIGURATION

Three ways Windows supports accessing resources on a network are to use a Windows homegroup, workgroup, or domain.

Windows Workgroup and Homegroup

A homegroup and workgroup are examples of a peer-to-peer (P2P) network, which is a network that is managed by each computer without centralized control. They form a logical group of computers and users that share resources (see Figure 2-12), where administration, resources, and security on a workstation are controlled by that workstation.

📝 **Notes**   When looking at the diagrams in Figure 2-12 and later in Figure 2-13, know that the connecting lines describe the logical connections between computers and not the physical connections. Both networks might be physically connected the same way, but logically, resources are controlled by each computer on the network or by using a centralized database. In network terminology, the arrangement of physical connections between computers is called the **physical topology**. The logical way the computers connect on a network is called the **logical topology**.

Notes indicate additional content that might be of student interest or information about how best to study.

A+
220-802
1.2, 1.6,
4.6

2

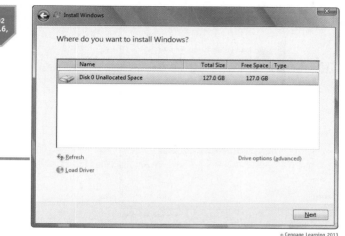

© Cengage Learning 2013

Figure 2-26 Select a partition to install Windows 7 in a clean install or dual-boot environment

6. The installation is now free to move forward. At the end of this process, the window in Figure 2-27 appears asking for a username and computer name. Enter these values and click **Next**. On the next screen, you can enter a password for your user account by entering the password twice followed by a password hint. Then click **Next**.

© Cengage Learning 2013

Figure 2-27 Choose a username and computer name

Full-color screen shots accurately depict computer and software components.

A+ Exam Objectives are highlighted with an icon identifying the exam and objective number to help you identify information tested on the exams. The A+ 220-801 and A+ 220-802 exams are mapped.

A+
220-802
1.2, 1.5

© Cengage Learning 2013

Figure 2-33   Download and install updates for your computer

Windows selects the updates in the order the system can receive them, and will not necessarily list all the updates you need on the first pass. After you have installed the updates listed, go back and start again until Windows Updates tells you there is nothing left to update. If Windows requests a restart after an update, do that before you install more updates. It might take two or more passes to get the PC entirely up to date.

If you see a service pack listed in the updates, install all the updates listed above it. Then install the service pack as the only update to install. It takes about 30 minutes and a reboot to download and install a service pack. Only the latest service pack for an OS will install because the latest service pack includes all the content from previous service packs.

Hands-on | Project 2.7   Updating Windows

On a Windows 7 system connected to the Internet, click **Start**, **All Programs**, and **Windows Update**. Windows Update searches the Microsoft web site and recommends Windows updates. Print the web page showing a list of recommended updates. For a lab PC, don't perform the updates unless you have your instructor's permission.

CONFIGURE AUTOMATIC UPDATES

During the Windows installation, you were asked how you want to handle Windows updates. To verify or change this setting, in the left pane of the Windows Update window, click **Change settings**. From the Change settings window, shown in Figure 2-34, you can decide how often, when, and how you want Windows to install updates. The recommended setting is to allow Windows to automatically download and install updates daily. However,

Hands-On Projects provide practical exercises throughout each chapter so that you can practice the skills as they are learned.

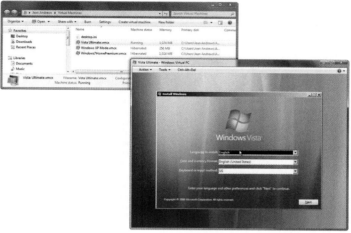

Figure 2-10 A new VM is installing Windows Vista

© Cengage Learning 2013

APPLYING | CONCEPTS

Windows can also be installed in a VM by using an ISO image. An International Organization for Standardization image, also called an ISO image or disc image, contains an image of a disc including the file system used. When downloaded from the web, an ISO image is usually stored in a file with an .iso file extension. An ISO image of the Windows setup DVD can be downloaded as an .iso file. To create a bootable Windows setup DVD from the image, right-click the .iso file and select **Burn disc image** from the shortcut menu. Using a virtual machine, you can mount an ISO image to the VM, which treats the image as though it is a disc. The ISO image file then works like a virtual disc.

To mount an ISO image to a VM, you must change the hardware configuration of the VM. For Virtual PC, first shut down the VM. Then in Explorer, select the VM and click **Settings** in the menu bar. The Settings dialog box appears (see Figure 2-11). To mount an ISO image to the VM, select DVD Drive in the figure and navigate to the ISO file. Make your changes and click **OK**.

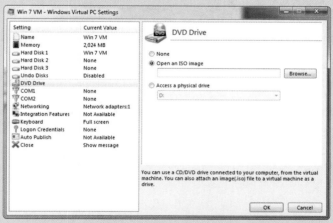

© Cengage Learning 2013

Figure 2-11 Change the hardware configuration for a virtual machine in Virtual PC

Applying Concepts sections provide practical advice or pointers by illustrating basic principles, identifying common problems, providing steps to practice skills, and encouraging creating solutions.

Key Terms are defined as they are introduced and listed at the end of each chapter. Definitions can be found in the Glossary and online.

>> KEY TERMS

For explanations of key terms, see the Glossary near the end of the book.

2

Active Directory
administrator account
answer file
batch file
boot loader menu
Certificate of Authenticity
clean install
client/server
compatibility mode
custom installation
Device Manager
disk cloning
distribution server
distribution share
domain
drive imaging
dual boot
file system
Files and Settings Transfer Wizard
global account
high-touch using a standard image
high-touch with retail media
homegroup
image deployment
ImageX
in-place upgrade
ISO image
lite-touch, high-volume deployment

loadstate
local account
logical topology
Microsoft Assessment and Planning (MAP) Toolkit
multiboot
OEM (Original Equipment Manufacturer) license
partition
peer-to-peer (P2P)
physical topology
Preboot eXecution Environment (PXE, also known as the Pre-Execution Environment)
product activation
Programs and Features
pull automation
push automation
remote network installation
scanstate
setup BIOS
standard image
startup BIOS
system BIOS (basic input/ output system)
unattended installation
upgrade paths
User State Migration Tool (USMT)
virtual machine (VM)

volume
Windows 7 Enterprise
Windows 7 Home Basic
Windows 7 Home Premium
Windows 7 Professional
Windows 7 Starter
Windows 7 Ultimate
Windows Automated Installation Kit (AIK)
Windows Easy Transfer
Windows Preinstallation Environment (Windows PE)
Windows Vista Business
Windows Vista Enterprise
Windows Vista Home Basic
Windows Vista Home Premium
Windows Vista Starter
Windows Vista Ultimate
Windows XP Home Edition
Windows XP Media Center Edition
Windows XP Mode
Windows XP Professional
Windows XP Professional x64 Edition
Windows XP Tablet PC Edition
workgroup
zero-touch, high-volume deployment

>> REVIEWING THE BASICS

1. Which edition of Windows 7 comes only in a 32-bit version?

2. What is the maximum amount of memory a 64-bit version of Windows 7 Home Premium can support?

3. How much free space on the hard drive is required to install a 64-bit version of Windows 7?

4. How do you start the process to reinstall an OS on a laptop computer using the backup files stored on a recovery partition?

5. What are three free applications mentioned in the chapter that can be used to create virtual machines?

Reviewing the Basics sections check understanding of fundamental concepts.

Thinking Critically sections require you to analyze and apply what you've learned.

2

29. Where is the PXE programming code stored that is used to boot a computer when it is searching for an OS on the network?

30. Which boot device should be set as the first boot device in BIOS setup when a technician is configuring a computer to launch Windows PE on the deployment server?

>> THINKING CRITICALLY

1. You are planning an upgrade from Windows Vista to Windows 7. Your system uses a network card that you don't find listed on the Microsoft Windows 7 list of compatible devices. What do you do next?

   a. Abandon the upgrade and continue to use Windows Vista.

   b. Check the web site of the network card manufacturer for a Windows 7 driver.

   c. Buy a new network card.

   d. Install a dual boot for Windows Vista and Windows 7 and only use the network when you have Windows Vista loaded.

2. You have just installed Windows 7 and now attempt to install your favorite game that worked fine under Windows XP. When you attempt the installation, you get an error. What is your best next step?

   a. Purchase a new version of your game, one that is compatible with Windows 7.

   b. Download any service packs or patches to Windows 7.

   c. Reinstall Windows XP.

   d. Install Windows XP Mode to run the game.

3. If you find out that Windows 7 does not support one of your applications and you still want to use Windows 7, what can you do to solve this incompatibility problem?

4. Is it possible to install Windows 7 on a system that does not have a DVD drive? Explain your answer.

>> REAL PROBLEMS, REAL SOLUTIONS

REAL PROBLEM 2-1: A Corrupted Windows Installation

As a PC support technician for a small organization, it's your job to support the PCs, the small network, and the users. One of your coworkers, Jason, comes to you in a panic. His Windows 7 system won't boot, and he has lots of important data files in several locations on the drive. He has no idea in which folder some of the files are located. Besides the applications data he's currently working on, he's especially concerned about losing email addresses, email, and his Internet Explorer Favorites links.

After trying everything you know about recovering Windows 7, you conclude the OS is corrupted beyond repair. You decide there might be a way to remove the hard drive from Jason's computer and connect it to another computer so that you can recover the data. Search the Internet and find a device that you can use to connect Jason's hard drive to another computer using a USB port on that computer. The hard drive uses a SATA hard drive interface. Print the web page showing the device and its price.

Real Problems, Real Solutions allow you to apply what you've learned in the chapter to a real-life situation.

STATE OF THE INFORMATION TECHNOLOGY (IT) FIELD

Most organizations today depend on computers and information technology to improve business processes, productivity, and efficiency. Opportunities to become global organizations and reach customers, businesses, and suppliers are a direct result of the widespread use of the Internet. Changing technology further changes how companies do business. This fundamental change in business practices has increased the need for skilled and certified IT workers across industries. This transformation has moved many IT workers out of traditional IT businesses and into various IT-dependent industries such as banking, government, insurance, and health care.

Millions of individuals are self-employed in this country. The members of this group who are computer specialists will need to keep their skills sharp as they navigate an ever-changing employment and technological landscape.

In any industry, the workforce is important to continuously drive business. Having correctly skilled workers in IT is a struggle with the ever-changing technologies. With such a quick product life cycle, IT workers must strive to keep up with these changes to continue to bring value to their employer.

CERTIFICATIONS

Different levels of education are required for the many jobs in the IT industry. Additionally, the level of education and type of training required vary from employer to employer, but the need for qualified technicians remains constant. As technology changes and advances in the industry continue to rapidly evolve, many employers consistently look for employees who possess the skills necessary to implement these new technologies. Traditional degrees and diplomas do not identify the skills that a job applicant has. With the growth of the IT industry, companies increasingly rely on technical certifications to identify the skills a particular job applicant possesses. Technical certifications are a way for employers to ensure the quality and skill qualifications of their computer professionals, and they can offer job seekers a competitive edge. As you look at certifications, note that there are two types: vendor neutral and vendor specific. Vendor-neutral certifications are those that test for the skills and knowledge required in specific industry job roles and do not subscribe to a specific vendor's technology solution. Vendor-neutral certifications include all of the Computing Technology Industry Association's (CompTIA) certifications, Project Management Institute's certifications, and Security Certified Program certifications. Vendor-specific certifications validate the skills and knowledge necessary to be successful by utilizing a specific vendor's technology solution. Some examples of vendor-specific certifications include those offered by Microsoft, IBM, Novell, and Cisco.

As employers struggle to fill open IT positions with qualified candidates, certifications are a means of validating the skill sets necessary to be successful within an organization. In most careers, salary and compensation are determined by experience and education, but in IT, the number and type of certifications an employee earns also factor into salary and wage increases.

Certifications provide job applicants with more than just a competitive edge over their noncertified counterparts who apply for the same IT positions. Some institutions of higher education grant college credit to students who successfully pass certification exams, moving them further along in their degree programs. Certifications also give individuals who are interested in careers in the military the ability to move into higher positions more quickly. And many advanced certification programs accept, and sometimes require, entry-level certifications as part of their exams. For example, Cisco and Microsoft accept some CompTIA certifications as prerequisites for their certification programs.

CAREER PLANNING

Finding a career that fits a person's personality, skill set, and lifestyle is challenging and fulfilling, but can often be difficult. What are the steps individuals should take to find that dream career? Is IT interesting to you? Chances are that if you are reading this book, this question has been answered. What about IT do you like? The world of work in the IT industry is vast. Some questions to ask include the following: Are you a person who likes to work alone, or do you like to work in a group? Do you like speaking directly with customers or do you prefer to stay behind the scenes? Is your lifestyle conducive to a lot of travel, or do you need to stay in one location? All of these factors influence your decision when faced with choosing the right job. Inventory assessments are a good first step to learning more about your interests, work values, and abilities. There are a variety of web sites that offer assistance with career planning and assessments, and I encourage you to work with your professional network to explore these sites.

WHAT'S NEW WITH COMPTIA A+ CERTIFICATION

In the spring of 2012, CompTIA (*www.comptia.org*) published the objectives for the 2012 CompTIA A+ Certification exams. These exams go live in the fall of 2012. However, you can still become CompTIA A+ certified by passing the older 2009 exams that are to remain available until the summer of 2013.

The A+ 2012 exams include two exams, and you must pass both to become A+ certified. The two exams are the A+ 220-801 exam and the A+ 220-802 exam.

Here is a breakdown of the domain content covered on the two A+ 2012 exams:

CompTIA A+ 220-801 Exam	
PC Hardware	40%
Networking	27%
Laptops	11%
Printers	11%
Operational Procedures	11%
Total	100%

CompTIA A+ 220-802 Exam	
Operating Systems	33%
Security	22%
Mobile Devices	9%
Troubleshooting	36%
Total	100%

HOW TO BECOME COMPTIA CERTIFIED

This training material can help you prepare for and pass a related CompTIA certification exam or exams. In order to achieve CompTIA certification, you must register for and pass a CompTIA certification exam or exams. For information on becoming CompTIA certified, please visit *http://certification.comptia.org/Training/testingcenters*.

CompTIA is a nonprofit information technology (IT) trade association. CompTIA's certifications are designed by subject matter experts from across the IT industry. Each CompTIA certification is vendor neutral, covers multiple technologies, and requires demonstration of skills and knowledge widely sought after by the IT industry.

To contact CompTIA with any questions or comments, please visit *http://certification .comptia.org/contact* or call (866) 835-8020, ext. 2.

A+ TEST PREPARATION MATERIALS

A+ Guide to Software, Sixth Edition includes CertBlaster Online test preparation questions that mirror the look and feel of CompTIA's A+ 220-802 certificate exam. For additional information on the CertBlaster Online test preparation questions, go to *www.dtipublishing.com*. To log in and access the CertBlaster Online test preparation questions for *A+ Guide to Software, Sixth Edition*, please go to *http://www.certblaster.com/login/*

TO ACCESS CERTBLASTER ONLINE:

1. Go to www.certblaster.com/login/

2. If this is your first time using CertBlaster Online, activate your product as follows:

   a. On the registration screen, enter your name, e-mail address and activation code. Click **Submit**.

   b. On the product selection screen, find your product title and expand it to see the tests. Click the test you wish to take.

   c. You will see a confirmation box indicating that your product is activated. Click **OK** to continue.

   d. **Your product is not activated until you see the confirmation.** At this point, your registration information is saved on your computer in a Flash "cookie" (local shared object).

Under normal circumstances, you will not need to enter your registration information again. On subsequent visits to www.certblaster.com/login/, CertBlaster Online will open directly to the product selection screen where you can select the additional tests you wish to take. If you access CertBlaster Online from a different computer, your registration information will not be present on that computer. You will need to re-enter it.

The storage of local shared objects (LSOs) is controlled through the Flash Player Settings Manager **and is enabled by default.** If you have disabled storage of shared objects in Settings Manager, or if you delete the shared object, you will be required to re-enter your registration information.

TO USE THIS BOOK TO PREPARE FOR A+ EXAMS

This book, *A+ Guide to Software, 6th Edition*, covers the software portions on the A+ 220-802 exam. The hardware portions on the exam can be found online and in the *A+ Guide to Hardware, 6th Edition*. The *A+ Guide to Hardware, 6th Edition* fully covers the A+ 220-801 exam and the hardware portions on the A+ 220-802 exam. In addition, *A+ Guide to Managing and Maintaining Your PC, 8th Edition*, covers content on both exams. Diagram 1 shows you three paths you can take to prepare for the A+ exams by using these books.

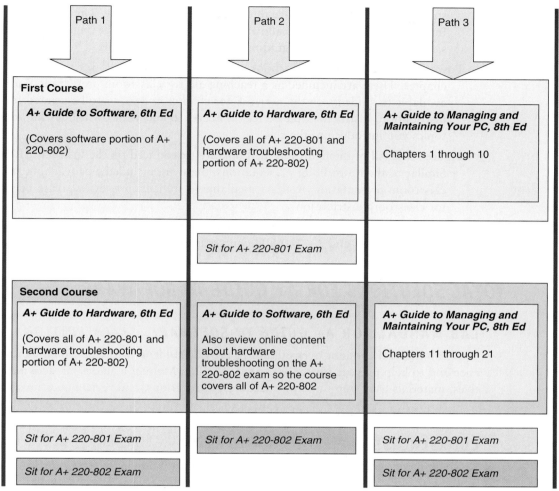

© Cengage Learning 2013

INSTRUCTOR RESOURCES CD (ISBN: 9781133135289)

Please visit login.cengage.com *and log in to access instructor-specific resources.To access additional course materials, please visit* www.cengagebrain.com. *At the CengageBrain.com home page, search for the ISBN of your title (from the back cover of your book) using the search box at the top of the page. This will take you to the product page where these resources can be found.*

The following supplemental materials are available when this book is used in a classroom setting. All of the supplements available with this book are provided to the instructor on a single CD-ROM.

Electronic Instructor's Manual: The Instructor's Manual that accompanies this textbook includes additional instructional material to assist in class preparation, including suggestions for classroom activities, discussion topics, and additional projects.

Solutions: Answers to the end-of-chapter material are provided. These include the answers to the Review Questions and to the Hands-On Projects (when applicable).

ExamView®: This textbook is accompanied by ExamView, a powerful testing software package that allows instructors to create and administer printed, computer (LAN-based), and Internet exams. ExamView includes hundreds of questions that correspond to the topics covered in this text, enabling students to generate detailed study guides that include page references for further review. The computer-based and Internet testing components allow students to take exams at their computers, and also save the instructor time by grading each exam automatically.

PowerPoint Presentations: This book comes with Microsoft PowerPoint slides for each chapter. These are included as a teaching aid for classroom presentation, to make available to students on the network for chapter review, or to be printed for classroom distribution. Instructors, please feel at liberty to add your own slides for additional topics you introduce to the class.

Figure Files: All of the figures in the book are reproduced on the Instructor Resource CD. Similar to the PowerPoint presentations, these are included as a teaching aid for classroom presentation, to make available to students for review, or to be printed for classroom distribution.

A+ 220-801 and A+ 220-802 Syllabus: To help prepare for class, a sample syllabus for the A+ 220-801 and A+ 220-802 courses is provided.

TOTAL SOLUTIONS FOR A+ GUIDE TO SOFTWARE

LAB MANUAL FOR A+ GUIDE TO SOFTWARE, SIXTH EDITION

This Lab Manual contains over 60 labs to provide students with additional hands-on experience and to help prepare for the A+ exam. The Lab Manual includes lab activities, objectives, materials lists, step-by-step procedures, illustrations, and review questions.

- Lab Manual (ISBN: 9781133135159)

COURSENOTES

This laminated quick reference card reinforces critical knowledge for CompTIA's A+ exam in a visual and user-friendly format. CourseNotes will serve as a useful study aid, supplement to the textbook, or as a quick reference tool during the course and afterward.

- A+ Exam# 220-801 CourseNotes (ISBN: 9781133135234)
- A+ Exam# 220-802 CourseNotes (ISBN: 9781133135241)

WEB-BASED LABS

Using a real lab environment over the Internet, students can log on anywhere, anytime via a Web browser to gain essential hands-on experience in security using labs from *A+ Guide to Software, Sixth Edition.*

- Web-Based Labs (ISBN: 9781133135227)

dtiMETRICS

dtiMetrics is an online testing system that automatically grades students and keeps class and student records. dtiMetrics tests against Cengage's textbook as well as against the CompTIA A+ certification exam, including a quiz for each chapter in the book along with a midterm and final exam. dtiMetrics is managed by the classroom instructor, who has 100 percent of the control, 100 percent of the time. It is hosted and maintained by dtiPublishing.

- dtiMetrics for A+ Guide to Software (ISBN: 9781133135197)

LABCONNECTION

LabConnection provides powerful computer-based exercises, simulations, and demonstrations for hands-on, skills courses such as this. It can be used as both a virtual lab and as a homework assignment tool, and provides automatic grading and student record maintenance. LabConnection maps directly to the textbook and provides remediation to the text and to the CompTIA A+ certification exam. It includes the following features:

- ◢ Enhanced comprehension—Through LabConnection's guidance while in the virtual lab environment, learners develop skills that are accurate and consistently effective.
- ◢ Exercises—Lab Connection includes dozens of exercises that assess and prepare the learner for the virtual labs, establishing and solidifying the skills and knowledge required to complete the lab.
- ◢ Virtual labs—Labs consist of end-to-end procedures performed in a simulated environment where the student can practice the skills required of professionals.
- ◢ Guided learning—LabConnection allows learners to make mistakes but alerts them to errors made before they can move on to the next step, sometimes offering demonstrations as well.
- ◢ Video demonstrations—Video demonstrations guide the learners step-by step through the labs while providing additional insights to solidify the concepts.
- ◢ SCORM-compliant grading and record keeping (for online version)—LabConnection will grade the exercises and record the completion status of the lab portion, easily porting to, and compatible with, distance learning platforms.
- ◢ LabConnection Online for A+ Guide to Software (ISBN: 9781133703761).
- ◢ LabConnection On DVD for A+ Guide to Software (ISBN: 9781133703730).

COURSEMATE

To access additional materials (including CourseMate, described in the next section), please visit *www.cengagebrain.com*. At the CengageBrain.com home page, search for the ISBN of your title (from the back cover of your book) using the search box at the top of the page. This will take you to the product page for your book, where you will be able to access these resources.

A+ Guide to Software, Sixth Edition offers CourseMate, a complement to your textbook. CourseMate includes the following:

- ◢ An interactive eBook, with highlighting, note-taking, and search capabilities.
- ◢ Interactive learning tools, including quizzes, flash cards, PowerPoint slides, glossary, and more!
- ◢ Engagement Tracker, a first-of-its-kind tool that monitors student engagement in the course.

Go to *login.cengage.com* to access these resources:

- ◢ CourseMate Printed Access Code with eBook (ISBN: 9781133135531)
- ◢ CourseMate Instant Access Code with eBook (ISBN: 9781133135524)

PC TROUBLESHOOTING POCKET GUIDE

This compact and portable volume is designed to help students and technicians diagnose any computer problem quickly and efficiently. Up to date and current for today's technologies (ISBN: 9781133135166).

COMPTIA A+ PC REPAIR FLASHCARDS

Use the PC Repair flashcards to test knowledge of PC repair concepts and to help prepare for CompTIA's A+ 220-801 and 220-802 exams. (ISBN: 9781133278771)

CREDITS

The screenshots of software programs and operating systems are courtesy of the following companies:

Figure	Company
Throughout	Microsoft, Inc.
1-6, 7-51	Google, Inc.
2-6, 6-26	Award BIOS by Phoenix Technologies
2-7	Lenovo
2-49, 6-2, 8-22, 9-19, 10-59	Intel
5-2	Adobe Systems Incorporated
5-5	Spiceworks, Inc.
7-39	AT&T
7-52, 53, 54, 55, 56, 57, 59, 61, 62, 64, 65, 66	Cisco Systems, Inc.
8-66	Famatech (*www.radmin.com*)
9-27	QUALCOMM Incorporated
9-28	Windstream Communications
9-31	McAfee, Inc.
10-1, 2, 4, 40, 45, 46, 47, 53, 54, 55	Motorola Mobility, Inc.
10-3, 41, 42, 43, 44, 48, 49, 50, 51, 52,	Toshiba America, Inc.
10-5, 6, 7, 8, 16, 17, 18, 19, 20, 21, 22, 23, 24, 25, 26, 27, 28, 29, 30, 31, 32, 33, 34, 35, 36, 37, 38, 39, A-5	Apple Computers, Inc.
A-6	Canonical, Ltd. (*www.ubuntu.com*)

ACKNOWLEDGMENTS

Thank you to the wonderful people at Cengage Course Technology who continue to provide support, warm encouragement, patience, and guidance: Nick Lombardi, Michelle Ruelos Cannistraci, and Andrea Majot. You've truly helped make this sixth edition fun! Thank you, Jill Batistick, Developmental Editor, for your careful attention to detail and your genuine friendship, and to Nancy Lamm, our excellent copy editor. Thank you, Teresa Storch, Serge Palladino, and Susan Pedicini for your careful attention to the technical accuracy of the book. Thank you Abigail Reip for your research efforts. Thank you to Joy Dark and Jill West who were here with me helping with the seemingly endless details associated with the writing process.

Thank you to all the people who took the time to voluntarily send encouragement and suggestions for improvements to the previous editions. Your input and help is very much appreciated. The reviewers of this edition all provided invaluable insights and showed a genuine interest in the book's success. Thank you to:

Lee Cottrell - Bradford School, Pittsburgh, PA;
Humberto Hilario - PC AGE Career Institute;
Carlos Miranda - Mount San Antonio College;
Nancy Severe-Barnett, DeVry University;
Jonathan Weissman - Finger Lakes Community College;
June West - Spartanburg Community College

When planning this edition, Course Technology sent out a survey to A+ and PC Repair instructors for their input to help us shape the edition. Over 150 instructors responded, for which I am grateful. Thank you to each responder. I spent much time poring over your answers to our questions, your comments, and your suggestions. You'll find many of your ideas fleshed out in the pages of this book. Thank you so much for your help!

To the instructors and learners who use this book, I invite and encourage you to send suggestions or corrections for future editions. Please write to me at *jean.andrews@cengage.com*. I never ignore a good idea! And to instructors, if you have ideas for how to make a class in PC Repair or A+ Preparation a success, please share your ideas with other instructors! You can find me on Facebook at *https://www.facebook.com/JeanKnows*, where you can interact with me and other instructors.

This book is dedicated to the covenant of Father God with man on earth.

Jean Andrews, Ph.D.

ABOUT THE AUTHOR

Jean Andrews has more than 30 years of experience in the computer industry, including more than 13 years in the college classroom. She has worked in a variety of businesses and corporations designing, writing, and supporting application software; managing a PC repair help desk; and troubleshooting wide area networks. She has written numerous books on software, hardware, and the Internet, including the bestselling *A+ Guide to Hardware: Managing, Maintaining and Troubleshooting, Sixth Edition* and *A+ Guide to Managing and Maintaining Your PC, Eighth Edition*. She lives in Atlanta, Georgia.

READ THIS BEFORE YOU BEGIN

The following hardware, software, and other equipment are needed to do the Hands-on Projects in each chapter:

- ◢ You need a working PC on which you can install an operating system.
- ◢ Windows 7 is needed for all chapters. Except for a few instances, Windows 7 Professional, Ultimate or Enterprise edition is needed for Chapters 3–9. Windows Vista is needed for Appendix B, and Windows XP is needed for Appendix C.

Introducing Windows Operating Systems

In this chapter, you will learn:

- **How to use Windows to interface with users, files and folders, applications, and hardware**

- **About some Windows tools that you can use to examine and support the system**

Like millions of other computer users, you have probably used your desktop, notebook, or tablet to play games, update your Facebook profile, write papers, or build Excel worksheets. This book takes you from being an end user of your computer to becoming a PC support technician. You'll learn to install and customize an operating system (OS) and applications, troubleshoot and solve problems with the OS, and optimize a system for best performance. The only assumption made here is that you are a computer user—that is, you can turn on your machine, load a software package, and use that software to accomplish a task.

As a PC support technician, you'll want to become A+ certified, which is the industry standard certification for PC support technicians. This book and its accompanying online content at *www.cengagebrain. com* prepare you to pass the A+ 220-802 exam by CompTIA (*www. comptia.org*). See the Preface for more information. This exam is primarily about software but does include some content on troubleshooting hardware problems. The software portions of this exam are here in the book, and the hardware portions of the exam can be found at the accompanying online web site. To access the online content, go to *www.cengagebrain.com*. See the Preface for more information.

The A+ 220-801 exam and the A+ 220-802 exam are required by CompTIA for A+ Certification. The A+ 220-801 exam is about hardware. The companion book, *A+ Guide to Hardware, Managing and Troubleshooting*, 6th edition, covers all the content on the A+ 220-801 exam and also includes the hardware troubleshooting content on the A+ 220-802 exam. This book and the *A+ Guide to Hardware, Managing and Troubleshooting* fully prepare you for both exams needed for CompTIA A+ certification.

In this chapter, you'll learn about Microsoft Windows and how this operating system provides the interface between users and applications and between applications and hardware devices. You'll learn to use several Windows tools and utilities that are useful to change desktop settings, view and manage storage devices, examine a system, and troubleshoot simple problems with hardware and applications.

> **Notes** As a PC support technician, you should be aware of the older and current operating systems and how they have evolved over the years. Appendix A, *Operating Systems Past and Present*, gives you this quick history of operating systems.

USING WINDOWS

An **operating system** (OS) is software that controls a computer. In general, you can think of an operating system as the middleman between applications and hardware, between the user and hardware, and between the user and applications (see Figure 1-1).

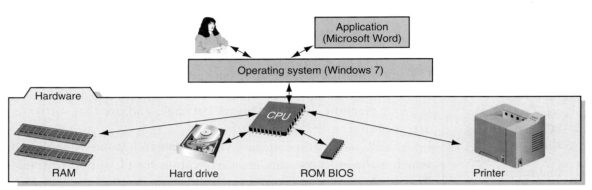

© Cengage Learning 2013

Figure 1-1   Users and applications depend on the OS to relate to all applications and hardware components

Several applications might be installed on a computer to meet various user needs, but a computer really needs only one operating system. Although there are important differences among them, all operating systems share the following four main functions:

▲ *Function 1*: Provide a user interface

- Performing housekeeping procedures requested by the user, often concerning storage devices, such as reorganizing a hard drive, deleting files, copying files, and changing the system date
- Providing a way for the user to manage the desktop, hardware, applications, and data

▲ *Function 2*: Manage files

- Managing files on hard drives, DVD drives, CD drives, USB flash drives, and other drives
- Creating, storing, retrieving, deleting, and moving files

▲ *Function 3*: Manage hardware

- Managing the BIOS (programs permanently stored on hardware devices)
- Managing memory, which is a temporary place to store data and instructions as they are being processed
- Diagnosing problems with software and hardware

1

- Interfacing between hardware and software (that is, interpreting application software needs to the hardware and interpreting hardware needs to application software)

◢ *Function 4*: Manage applications

- Installing and uninstalling applications
- Running applications and managing the interface to the hardware on behalf of an application

Windows 7 is the latest Microsoft operating system, and is an upgrade to Windows XP. Every PC support technician needs to be a power user of Windows 7 and also be familiar with Vista and XP. This part of the chapter covers the two most important tools for using Windows 7/Vista/XP: The Windows desktop and Windows Explorer.

📋 **Notes** This chapter primarily covers Windows 7 and a little about Windows Vista and Windows XP. If you want to know more about Windows Vista, see Appendix B. If you want to learn more about Windows XP, see Appendix C. Vista and XP icons in the margin of a chapter tell you that related content about these OSs can be found in the appendices.

A+
220-802
1.1

THE WINDOWS DESKTOP

The desktop is the initial screen that is displayed after the user logs on and Windows is loaded. The Windows desktop provides a graphical user interface (GUI; pronounced "GOO-ee") that uses graphics as compared to a command-driven interface.

In this section, you will learn about the features of the desktop, including the Start menu and taskbar. You will also learn how to manage shortcuts and icons on the desktop. We use Windows 7 as our primary OS for learning. Minor differences about Vista and XP are noted here in the chapter. But don't forget that additional major differences about Vista are covered in Appendix B, and major differences about Windows XP are covered in Appendix C.

💡 **A+ Exam Tip** The A+ 220-802 exam covers Windows 7, Windows Vista, and Windows XP.

AERO USER INTERFACE

The Windows 7 and Vista desktop provides a 3-D user interface called the Aero user interface that gives a glassy appearance and is sometimes called Aero glass (see Figure 1-2). Windows 7 comes in several editions and each edition offers a different set of features. The Aero interface is not available for the Windows 7 Starter and Home Basic editions and is available on the Home Premium, Business, Enterprise, and Ultimate editions. To support the Aero interface, Windows 7 requires 1 GB of RAM and a video card or on-board video that supports the DirectX 9 graphics standard that has at least 128 MB of graphics memory.

THE START MENU

The Windows 7 Start menu is shown in Figure 1-3. Notice in the figure that the username for the person currently logged on is shown at the top right of the Start menu.

© Cengage Learning 2013

Figure 1-2 The Windows 7 desktop using the Aero interface has a glassy transparent look

© Cengage Learning 2013

Figure 1-3 The Windows 7 Start menu

User-oriented applications that are used often are listed in the white left columns (as shown in the figure) and can change from time to time. Items in the dark right column give access to user libraries and files and to OS utilities.

A+
220-802
1.1, 1.4

HOW TO LAUNCH AN APPLICATION

Let's open a few applications and then see how the Windows desktop can be used to manage these open applications. Four options to open an application are:

- ▲ *Use the Start menu*: Click the **Start** button, select **All Programs**, and then select the program from the list of installed software.
- ▲ *Use the Search box*: Click the **Start** button, and then enter the name of the program file or command in the *Search* box (see Figure 1-4). In Windows 7, the empty box is labeled the *Search programs and files* box. In Vista, the box is labeled the *Search* box, and in Windows XP, it is labeled the *Run* box. Program names you might enter in the *Search* or *Run* box include msinfo32 (to open the System Information window), Notepad (to open the Notepad text editor), and Explorer (to open Windows Explorer.) Incidentally, the Windows 7 and Vista search boxes can also find data files and folders and will search text within document files.

© Cengage Learning 2013

Figure 1-4 Use the Windows 7 *Search* box to launch a program

- ▲ ***Use Windows Explorer or the Computer window.*** Execute a program or launch an application file by double-clicking the icon beside the filename in Windows Explorer or the Computer window. (In Windows XP, the Computer window is called My Computer.) To use the Computer window in Windows 7 or Vista, click **Start, Computer**. The Computer window shown in Figure 1-5 appears. Double-click the drive on which the program file is stored. In our example, we double-clicked **Local Disk (C:)**. Then we drilled down to the program file on the drive. Double-click the program file to launch it.

A+
220-802
1.1, 1.4

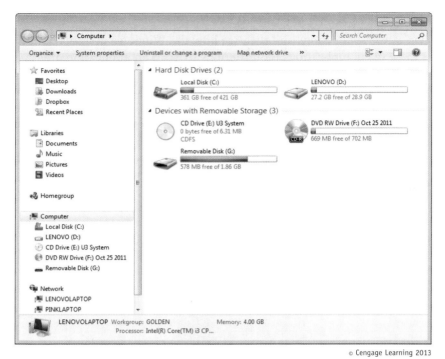

© Cengage Learning 2013

Figure 1-5   If you know the location of a program file, you can drill down to it and launch it from the Computer window

▲ *Use a shortcut icon*: A quick way to open an application you use often is to place a shortcut icon to the program on the desktop or place a program icon in the taskbar. A shortcut icon is a clickable item on the desktop that points to a program you can execute, or to a file or folder. One way to create a shortcut for a program is to right-click the program file in the Computer or Windows Explorer window and select **Create shortcut** from the menu that appears.

> **Notes** The difference between a window and a dialog box is a window can be resized, but a dialog box cannot. A dialog box is sometimes called a box.

When you launch a program, the program window appears on the desktop. You can close, move, or resize the window. Windows 7 Aero Snap and Aero Shake can help:

▲ **Aero Snap** automatically maximizes a window when you drag it to the top of the desktop. To restore a maximized window to its original size, drag the window downward on the screen. Drag a window to the right or left of the screen so that it snaps to the side of the screen to fill half the screen.

▲ Use **Aero Shake** to minimize all other windows except the one you shake. To shake a window, grab the title bar of the window and shake it. Shake again to restore the size of the other windows. You can also use the Maximize, Minimize, and Close buttons on a window.

> **Notes** If you are using the Aero interface, you can get a flip 3D view of applications by pressing **Win+Tab** (the Windows key and the Tab key). Then use the Tab key to move from one open application to another. Windows 7 Starter and Home Basic do not support the Aero interface, and, to conserve system resources, you can turn the feature off using other editions of Windows.

1

A+
220-802
1.1, 1.4

💡 **A+ Exam Tip** The A+ 220-802 exam expects you to be able to use the Aero interface, including using Aero Snap and Shake.

A+
220-802
1.1

The Taskbar and Notification Area (System Tray)

The **taskbar** is normally located at the bottom of the Windows desktop, displaying information about open programs and providing quick access to others. Items displayed in the taskbar can be programs running or not running. An open application displays a program icon in the taskbar. If you are using the Aero interface, when you mouse over the icon, a thumbnail of the open application appears (see Figure 1-6).

© Cengage Learning 2013

Figure 1-6 Mouse over the Internet Explorer icon in the taskbar to see each open tab in IE

When you right-click an icon in the taskbar, the **Jump List** appears, which provides access to some of the major functions of the program (see Figure 1-7). When you mouse over the rectangle to the far right of the taskbar, all windows disappear so you can see the desktop and any gadgets you might have there. This feature is called **Aero Peek** because it gives you a peek at the desktop. Click the rectangle to minimize all windows. Click the rectangle again to restore all windows.

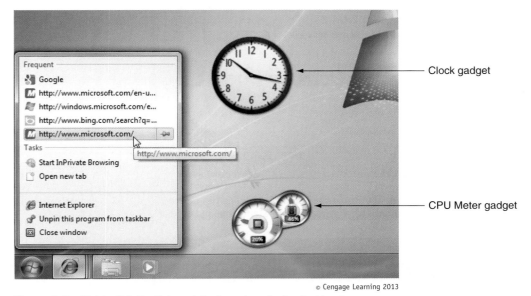

© Cengage Learning 2013

Figure 1-7 Right-click the Internet Explorer icon in the taskbar to see a Jump List of frequently used web pages and quickly access a page

A+
220-802
1.1

> **Notes** A **gadget** is a mini-app that appears on the desktop. Windows 7 gadgets shown in Figure 1-7 can appear anywhere on the Windows 7 desktop. Vista gadgets appear in the Vista **sidebar** on the right side of the Vista desktop. To control Windows 7 gadgets, right-click the desktop and select **Gadgets** from the shortcut menu that appears.

The notification area, also called the system tray or systray, is usually on the right side of the taskbar and displays open services. A service is a program that runs in the background to support or serve Windows or an application. The services in the notification area include the volume control and network connectivity.

To control the Start menu, taskbar, and notification area, right-click the taskbar and click **Properties** from the shortcut menu. The Taskbar and Start Menu Properties dialog box appears (see Figure 1-8). Use it to move the taskbar on the screen, control the icons that appear in the notification area, and control Start menu items.

> **Notes** To pin a program icon to the taskbar so that it's available to quickly launch the program, first locate the program in the Start menu. Then right-click the program and select **Pin to Taskbar** from the shortcut menu.

© Cengage Learning 2013

Figure 1-8   Use the Taskbar and Start Menu Properties box to control what appears in the Start menu and taskbar

> **Notes** If you have a sluggish Windows system, one thing you can do is look at all the running services in the notification tray and try to disable the services that are taking up system resources. How to do that is covered in Chapter 4.

1

A+
220-802
1.1

Hands-on | Project 1.1 Using the Taskbar

You'll find several Hands-on Projects in each chapter that are designed to help you learn by doing. As you read a chapter, take time to do the Hands-on Projects so that you know you have mastered the skills discussed before you move on to learn new skills. Your instructor might require that you submit to him the answers to questions you find in each project.

Using a Windows 7/Vista/XP computer, do the following and answer the following questions about the taskbar:

1. Restart the computer and list the program icons in the taskbar. What is the program name and path to each item? (In Vista, these icons are listed in the Quick Launch area of the taskbar.)

2. List the items in the notification area (system tray) of the taskbar. Don't forget to list the items hidden in this area. Investigate and describe the purpose of each program.

3. Move the taskbar from the bottom of the screen to the left side. List the steps you took to do that.

4. Press **Win+Tab** and describe the results. Are you using the Windows 7/Vista Aero user interface? How do you know?

A+
220-802
1.1, 1.5

PERSONALIZE THE WINDOWS DESKTOP

You can also personalize the desktop. To use the Personalization window, right-click anywhere on the desktop, and choose **Personalize** from the shortcut menu (see Figure 1-9). Using this window, you can personalize the way Windows appears, including the desktop, sounds, mouse action, color themes, and display settings.

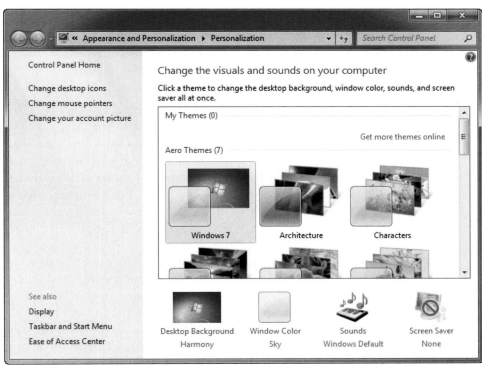

© Cengage Learning 2013

Figure 1-9 Use the Personalization window to change the appearance of Windows

As a support technician, you are often called on to solve problems with display settings. The most common problem with display is a problem with the screen resolution. The **screen resolution** is number of dots or pixels on the monitor screen expressed as two numbers such as 1680 × 1050. To change the resolution, right-click anywhere on the desktop and choose **Screen resolution** from the shortcut menu. In the Screen Resolution window, make your changes and click **Apply**. You can also access the Screen Resolution window from the Control Panel or from the Personalization window.

XP Differences   See Appendix C to learn about the differences in the Windows XP desktop and the Windows 7 desktop.

WINDOWS EXPLORER AND THE COMPUTER WINDOW

The two most useful tools to explore files and folders on your computer are Windows Explorer and the Computer window. (Windows XP calls the Computer window the My Computer window.) You learned to open the Computer window earlier in the chapter. For Windows 7, Windows Explorer is opened in these two ways:

- Click the yellow Windows Explorer icon in the taskbar. If a Windows Explorer window is already open, it becomes the active window.
- Right-click **Start** and select **Open Windows Explorer** from the menu. (For Vista and XP, right-click **Start** and select **Explore** from the menu.) If a Windows Explorer instance is already open, a new instance of Explorer is created. Having two instances of Explorer open makes it easy to drag and drop files and folders from one location to another.

Let's now turn our attention to how to use the Computer and Explorer windows to manage files and folders and other system resources.

FILES AND DIRECTORIES

Every OS manages a hard drive, optical drive, USB drive, or other type drive by using directories (also called folders), subdirectories, and files. The drive is organized with a single **root directory** at the top of the top-down hierarchical structure of subdirectories, as shown in Figure 1-10. The exception to this rule is a hard drive because it can be divided into partitions that can have more than one **volume** such as drive C: and drive D: on the same physical hard drive (see Figure 1-11). For a volume, such as drive C:, the root directory is written as C:. Each volume has its own root directory and hierarchical structure of subdirectories. You can think of volumes as logical drives within the one physical drive.

As shown in Figure 1-10, the root directory can hold files or other directories, which can have names such as C:\Data. These directories, called **subdirectories**, **child directories**, or **folders**, can, in turn, have other directories listed in them. Any directory can have files and other subdirectories listed in it; for example, Figure 1-10 shows one file on drive C: is C:\Data\Business\Letter.docx. In this path to the file, the C: identifies the volume and is called the **drive letter**. Drive letters used for a hard drive, CD, USB drive, or DVD are C:, D:, E:, and so forth. Drive letters used for a floppy drive are A: or B:.

A+
220-802
1.1, 1.4

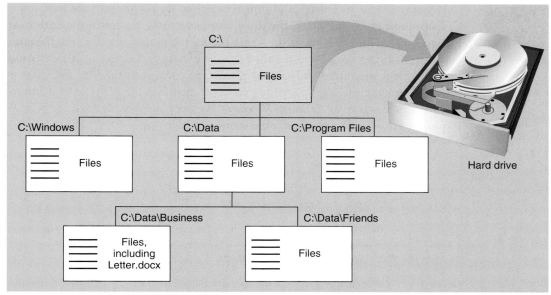

© Cengage Learning 2013

Figure 1-10 Storage devices such as a USB drive, CD, or hard drive, are organized into directories and subdirectories that contain files

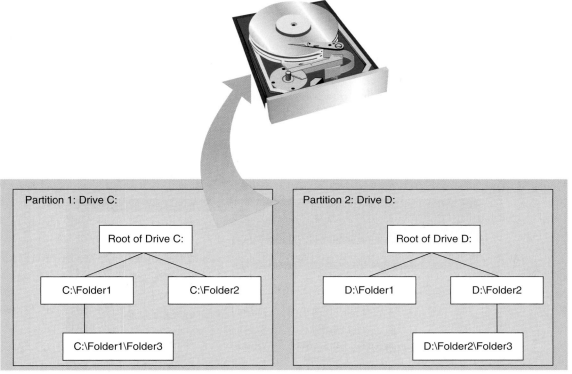

© Cengage Learning 2013

Figure 1-11 A hard drive can be divided into one or more partitions that can each contain a volume such as drive C: or drive D:

Notes Technicians tend to call a directory a folder when working in Windows Explorer, but when working with a command-line interface, they call a directory a directory.

A+
220-802
1.1, 1.4

When you refer to a drive and directories that are pointing to the location of a file, as in C:\Data\Business\Letter.docx, the drive and directories are called the path to the file (see Figure 1-12). The first part of the name before the period is called the filename (Letter), and the part after the period is called the file extension (.docx). A file extension indicates how the file is organized or formatted, the type content in the file, and what program uses the file. For example, the .docx file extension identifies the file type as a Microsoft Word 2010 document file. By default, Windows does not display file extensions in Windows Explorer. How to display these extensions is coming up.

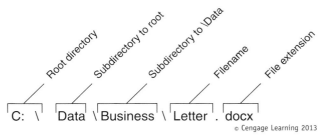

© Cengage Learning 2013

Figure 1-12 The complete path to a file includes the volume letter, directories, filename, and file extension; the colon, backslashes, and period are required to separate items in the path

NAVIGATE THE FOLDER STRUCTURE

When working with the Windows Explorer or Computer window, these tips can make your work easier:

- ◢ *Tip 1*: Click or double-click items in the left pane, called the navigation pane, to drill down into these items. The folders or subfolders appear in the right pane. You can also double-click folders in the right pane to drill down. When you click the white arrow to the left of a folder in the navigation pane, its subfolders are listed underneath it in the pane. (For XP, click the plus sign to the left of a folder.)
- ◢ *Tip 2*: To control how files and subfolders appear in the right pane, click the View icon in the menu bar and select your view (see Figure 1-13).

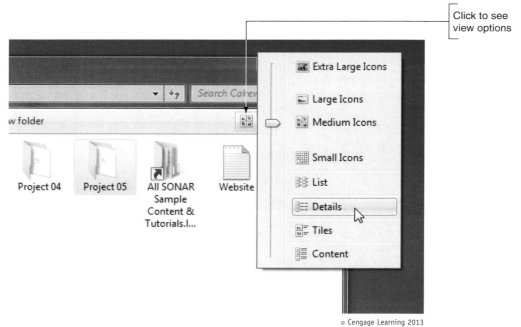

© Cengage Learning 2013

Figure 1-13 Click the View icon to change how files and folders display in the right pane of Windows Explorer

A+
220-802
1.1, 1.4

▲ *Tip 3*: To control the column headings that appear in the Details view, right-click a column heading and select the headings that you want to appear (see Figure 1-14). To control which column is used to sort items in the Details view, click a column heading.

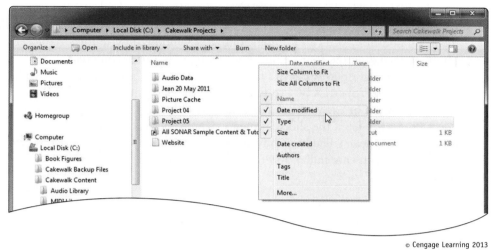

© Cengage Learning 2013

Figure 1-14 Right-click a column heading to select columns to display in the Details view

▲ *Tip 4:* To search for a folder or file, use the Search box in the upper-right corner of the window. (This search box is not available in Windows XP.)

▲ *Tip 5:* Use the forward and back arrows in the upper-left corner to move forward and backward to previous views. (These buttons are not available in Windows XP.)

▲ *Tip 6*: Click a right arrow in the path displayed in the address bar at the top of the Explorer window to see a drop-down list of subfolders (see Figure 1-15). Click one to move to this subfolder.

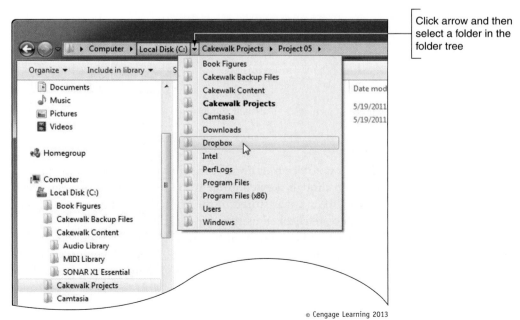

© Cengage Learning 2013

Figure 1-15 Click a right arrow in the address bar to move up the folder tree and down to a new folder

A+
220-802
1.1, 1.4

WINDOWS 7 LIBRARIES

A Windows 7 library is a collection of one or more folders, and these folders can be stored on different local drives or on the network. (Vista and XP do not support libraries.) A library is a convenient way to access several folders in different locations from one central location. When Windows is installed, it creates four default libraries: Documents, Music, Pictures, and Videos. By default, the first three libraries can be accessed from the Start menu. In addition, you can use the Computer window or Windows Explorer to access all libraries, including the four default ones and any libraries you create.

When you first open Windows Explorer, the list of libraries appears (see Figure 1-16). Use a library's Properties box to find out the folders that are contained in the library and the location of each folder. For example, right-click the Documents library and then select **Properties** from the shortcut menu. The Properties box shown on the right side of Figure 1-16 appears. The box shows that the Documents library contains two folders, the user's My Documents folder and the Public Documents folder.

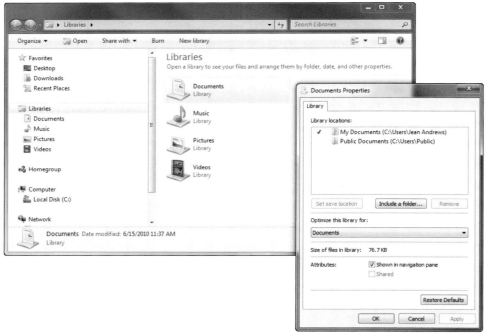

© Cengage Learning 2013

Figure 1-16   Windows 7 includes four default libraries

When you add a new folder to a library, the files in that folder appear as though they are in the library even though they continue to be stored in the original location. When you add a file to the library, it is stored in the library's default save location folder. Which folder is that? It's the one checked as the save location in the library's Properties box. For example, in the Properties box shown in Figure 1-16, you can see the check beside the My Documents folder, indicating it is the save location folder. To create a new library, click in the white space in the right pane of Explorer and then click the **New library** command in the menu bar.

1

A+
220-802
1.1, 1.4,
1.5

CHANGE WINDOWS EXPLORER SETTINGS AND FOLDER OPTIONS

You can view and change options assigned to folders. These options control how users view the files in the folder and what they can do with these files. In Windows Explorer and the Computer window, Windows has an annoying habit of hiding file extensions if it knows which application is associated with a file extension. For example, just after installation, it hides .exe, .com, .sys, and .txt file extensions, but does not hide .docx, .pptx, or .xlsx file extensions until the software to open these files has been installed. Also, Windows really doesn't want you to see its own system files, and it hides these files from view until you force it to show them.

APPLYING | CONCEPTS

A technician is responsible for solving problems with system files (files that belong to the Windows operating system) and file extensions. To fix problems with these files and extensions, you need to see them. To change folder options so you can view system files and file extensions, do the following:

1. To open the Control Panel, click **Start**, **Control Panel**. In the Control Panel, click **Appearance and Personalization**. Then click **Folder Options**. The Folder Options dialog box appears.

2. Use items on the General tab to change the way Windows Explorer works and how items appear in the navigation pane of Explorer. For Windows 7, the General tab is shown on the left in Figure 1-17. The View tab is shown on the right in Figure 1-17. (The Vista and XP Folder Options box looks and works about the same as that of Windows 7.)

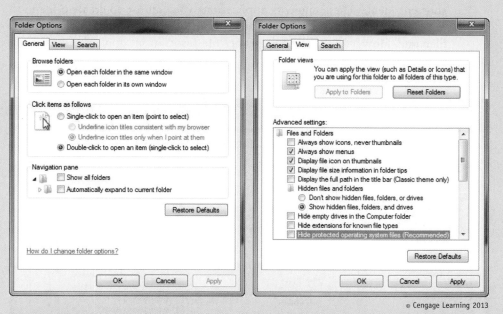

© Cengage Learning 2013

Figure 1-17 Use the Folder Options box to control how Windows Explorer works and displays files and folders

A+
220-802
1.1, 1.4,
1.5

3. On the View tab of the Folder Options box, scroll down in the Advanced settings group and make these selections to show hidden information about files, folders, and drives, as shown on the right in Figure 1-17:

- Select **Show hidden files, folders, and drives**.
- Uncheck **Hide extensions for known file types**.
- Uncheck **Hide protected operating system files (Recommended)** and respond to the Warning box.

4. To display the menu bar in Windows Explorer, check **Always show menus**. (By default, this bar is hidden in Windows 7 and Vista.)

5. To save your changes and close the Folder Options box, click **OK**.

> **A+ Exam Tip** The A+ 220-802 exam expects you to know how to view hidden files and file extensions and to be able to change the layout or view of folders in Windows Explorer.

A+
220-802
1.1, 1.4

CREATE A FILE

You can create a file using a particular application, or you can create a file using Windows Explorer or the Computer window. In Explorer and the Computer window, to create a file, right-click in the unused white area in the right pane of the window and point to **New** in the shortcut menu. The menu lists applications you can use to create a file in the current folder (see Figure 1-18). Click the application and the file is created. You can then rename the filename. However, to keep the proper file association, don't change the file extension.

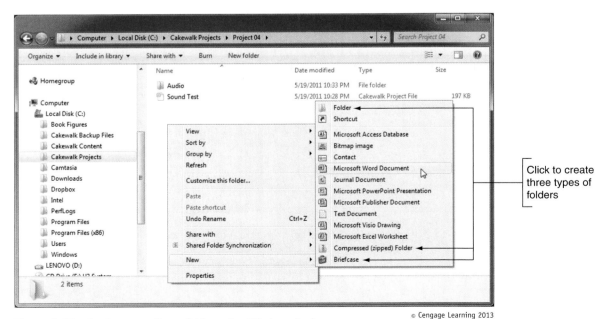

© Cengage Learning 2013

Figure 1-18 Create a new file or folder using Windows Explorer

A+
220-802
1.1, 1.4

CREATE A FOLDER

To create a folder, first select the folder you want to be the parent folder. (Remember that a parent folder is the folder that contains the child folder.) Right-click in the white area of the right pane and point to **New** in the shortcut menu. The menu in Figure 1-18 appears. Notice in the menu that for Windows 7 and Vista, you have three choices for folder types. These choices are explained here:

- ◢ *Folder* creates a regular folder.
- ◢ Compressed (zipped) Folder creates a compressed folder with a .zip extension. Any file or folder that you put in this folder will be compressed to a smaller size than normal. A compressed folder is often used to compress files to a smaller size so they can more easily be sent by email. When you remove a file or folder from a compressed folder, the file or folder is uncompressed back to its original size.
- ◢ Briefcase creates a Briefcase folder, which is a folder that can be used to sync up files in this folder with its corresponding Briefcase folder on another computer. (Windows offers two ways to sync files on different computers: Briefcase and Offline Files.)

Make your selection and the folder is created and highlighted so that you can rename it (see Figure 1-19).

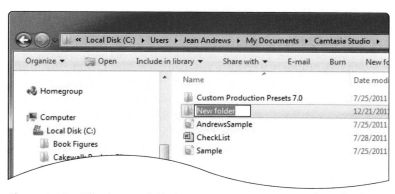

Figure 1-19 Edit the new folder's name   © Cengage Learning 2013

You can create folders within folders within folders, but there is a limitation as to the maximum depth of folders under folders; how deep you can nest folders depends on the length of the folder names themselves. The maximum length of a path and filename cannot exceed 260 characters.

> 📝 **Notes** The Windows desktop is itself a folder and, for Windows 7 and Vista, is located at C:\Users\ *username*\Desktop. For example, if the user, Anne, creates a folder on her desktop named Downloads, this folder is located at C:\Users\Anne\Desktop\Downloads.

COPY, MOVE, RENAME, OR DELETE FILES OR FOLDERS

Use these handy tips to copy, move and delete files or folders using Windows Explorer:

- ◢ To copy a file or folder, right-click it and select **Copy** from the shortcut menu. Then click in the white area of the folder where the copied item is to go and select **Paste** from the shortcut menu. You can also use the Cut and Paste commands to move an item to a new location.

A+
220-802
1.1, 1.4

◢ Drag and drop an item to move or copy it to a new location. If the location is on the same drive as the original location, the file or folder will be automatically deleted from its original location. If you don't want it deleted, hold down the **Ctrl** key while you drag and drop the item.

◢ To rename a file or folder, right-click it and select **Rename** from the shortcut menu. Change the name and click off the file or folder to deselect it.

◢ To delete a file or folder, select the item and press the **Delete** key. Or you can right-click the item and select **Delete** from the shortcut menu. Either way, a confirmation dialog box asks if you are sure you want to delete the item. If you click **Yes**, you send the file or folder and all its contents, including subfolders, to the Recycle Bin.

◢ To select multiple items to delete, copy, or move at the same time, hold down the **Shift** or **Ctrl** key as you click. To select several adjacent items in a list, click the first item and Shift-click the last item. To select nonadjacent items in a list, hold down the Ctrl key as you click each item.

> 📝 **Notes** Appendix E lists handy keystrokes to save you time when working with Windows.

Emptying the Recycle Bin will free up your disk space. Files and folders sent to the Recycle Bin are not *really* deleted until you empty the bin. To do that, right-click the bin and select **Empty Recycle Bin** from the shortcut menu.

CHANGE FILE OR FOLDER ATTRIBUTES

Using Explorer or the Computer window, you can view and change the properties assigned to a file or folder; these properties are called the file attributes or folder attributes. Using these attributes, you can do such things as hide a file, make it a read-only file, or flag a file to be backed up. From Explorer or the Computer window, right-click a file or folder and select **Properties** from the shortcut menu. The Properties window shown on the left side of Figure 1-20 opens for the AnimalList.accdb database file.

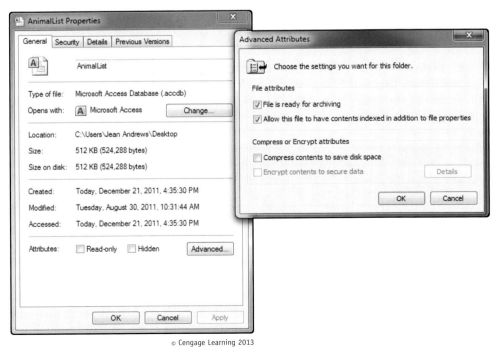

© Cengage Learning 2013

Figure 1-20 Use a file's Properties box to view file properties and edit file attributes

From the Properties window, you can change the read-only, hidden, archive, and indexing attributes of the file or folder. (Indexing is not used in Windows XP.) To make the file a read-only file or to hide the file so that it does not appear in the directory list, check the appropriate box and click **Apply**. The archive attribute is used to determine if a file or folder has changed since the last backup. To change its value, click **Advanced** in the Properties window (see the right side of Figure 1-20). Make your change and click **OK**.

> **Notes** In this chapter, you learn how to use Windows Explorer to create, copy, move, delete, rename, and change the attributes of files and folders. In Chapter 3, you will learn that you can do these same tasks using commands from a command prompt.

Hands-on | Project 1.2   Using Windows Explorer

Do the following to practice using Windows Explorer:

1. Open Windows Explorer and create a folder under the root directory of the hard drive called \Temp. List the steps you took.

2. Add a subfolder to \Temp called **\MyFiles**. List the steps you took.

3. Create a text file in the MyFiles folder named **Text1.txt**. List the steps you took.

4. Create a shortcut to the MyFiles folder on the Windows desktop. List the steps you took.

5. Rename the file **Text2.txt**.

6. Double-click the shortcut on the desktop. What error did you get?

7. The program file for Microsoft Paint is mspaint.exe. Use Windows Explorer to locate the program file and launch the Microsoft Paint program.

8. Create a shortcut to Microsoft Paint on the Windows desktop. Launch Microsoft Paint using the shortcut.

9. To clean up after yourself, delete the \Temp folder and the shortcuts. Close the two Paint windows.

Hands-on | Project 1.3   Practicing Keystrokes

You might be called on to troubleshoot a system when the mouse does not work. In this situation, Appendix E, *Keystroke Shortcuts in Windows*, can help. To prepare yourself to work without a mouse, disconnect your mouse and do the following:

1. Files in the root directory of a computer you are troubleshooting might be corrupted. Open Explorer and display the files in the root directory of drive C. List the steps and keystrokes you used to do this.

2. Seeing hidden files and file extensions might help you to better understand a problem you are facing. Unhide all the files and folders. Using Control Panel, open the **Folder Options** dialog box. Select the **View** tab, and then select **Show hidden files, folders, and drives**. Also uncheck **Hide extensions for known file types** and uncheck **Hide protected operating system files (Recommended)**. List the steps and keystrokes you used.

3. The Pagefile.sys might be corrupted. What is the exact size of the file Pagefile.sys in bytes, and the date and time the file was last modified?

QUICK AND EASY WINDOWS SUPPORT TOOLS

As a PC support technician, you need to be able to sit down at a working computer and within five or ten minutes find the details about what software and hardware is installed on the system and the general health of the system. Within 20 minutes, you should be able to solve any minor problems the computer might have such as a broken network connection.

In this part of the chapter, you learn about the tools you need to quickly find these answers and solve some common problems. You'll learn to use the System window, System Information window, Control Panel, Action Center, User Account Control dialog box, and Windows Help and Support. In other chapters, you'll learn to use more Windows tools.

A+
220-802
1.1, 1.5

SYSTEM WINDOW

The System window is your friend. It can give you a quick look at what hardware and software is installed and can get you to other useful Windows tools. To open the System window, click **Start**, right-click **Computer**, and select **Properties** from the shortcut menu. (Alternately, you can open Control Panel, click System and Security, and then click System.) Figure 1-21 shows the resulting System window for one laptop.

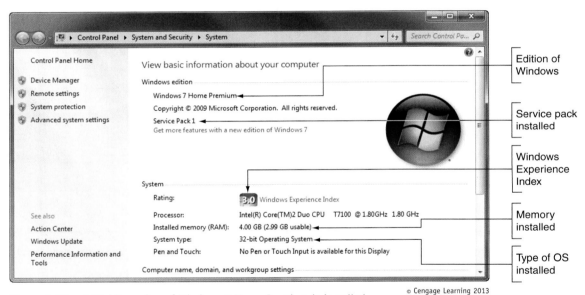

Figure 1-21 A 32-bit version of Windows 7 Home Premium is installed

So what technical information are you looking at? Here is the rundown:

- Windows 7 comes in several editions and you can see this system has the Windows 7 Home Premium edition installed.
- You can see that Service Pack 1 is installed. (A service pack is a major update or fix to an OS occasionally released by Microsoft. Minor updates or fixes that are released more frequently are called patches.)
- The type of OS installed is a 32-bit OS. A 32-bit operating system processes 32 bits at a time, and a 64-bit operating system processes 64 bits at a time. The Starter edition of Windows 7 comes in the 32-bit version and other editions come in either 32-bit or 64-bit versions. A 64-bit OS performs better than a 32-bit OS, but requires more memory. A 32-bit OS can support up to 4 GB of memory, and a 64-bit OS can support much more. The details of how much memory each edition of Windows 7 can support are covered in Chapter 2.

A+
220-802
1.1, 1.5

◢ The amount of installed memory is 4 GB. For a 32-bit OS, this is all the memory the system can use. If the user of this computer is thinking about upgrading RAM, you can tell him to not waste his money so long as he has a 32-bit OS installed.

◢ The Windows Experience Index is 3.0. That index is a rating of the system's overall performance on a scale from 1.0 to 7.9. Immediately, you know this system is not a snail or a blazing torch, but somewhere in the middle and probably toward the low range of performance.

That's a lot of useful information for a first look at a computer.

A+
220-802
1.4

SYSTEM INFORMATION WINDOW

Turn to the System Information (msinfo32.exe) window for more details about a system, including installed hardware and software, the current system configuration, and currently running programs. For example, you can use it to find out what BIOS version is installed on the motherboard, how much RAM is installed, the directory where the OS is installed, the size of the hard drive, the names of currently running drivers, a list of startup programs, print jobs in progress, currently running tasks, and much more. Because the System Information window gives so much useful information, help desk technicians often ask a user on the phone to open it and read to the technician information about the computer.

When strange error messages appear during startup, use the System Information window to get a list of drivers that loaded successfully. Device drivers are small programs stored on the hard drive that tell the computer how to communicate with a specific hardware device such as a printer, network card, or scanner. If you have saved the System Information report when the system was starting successfully, comparing the two reports can help identify the problem device.

To run System Information, click **Start**, and enter **Msinfo32.exe** in the *Search* box and press **Enter**. The System Information window for one computer is shown in Figure 1-22. To drill down to more information in the window, click items in the left pane.

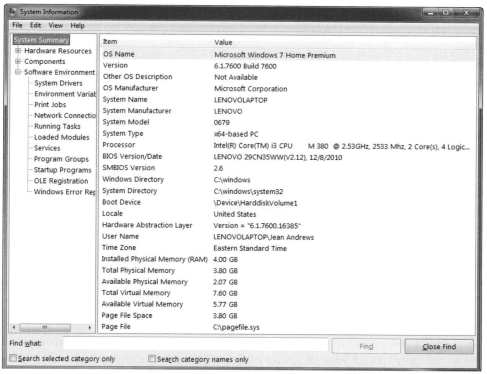

© Cengage Learning 2013

Figure 1-22 Use the System Information utility to examine details about a system

A+
220-802
1.4

> **💡 A+ Exam Tip** The A+ 220-802 exam expects you to be familiar with and know how to use the Windows 7/Vista/XP desktop, Computer, My Computer, Windows Explorer, System, System Information, Control Panel, Action Center, and Network and Sharing Center windows. All these tools are discussed in this section. If the utility can be accessed by more than one method, you are expected to know all of the methods.

Hands-on | Project 1.4 Using the System Information Utility

Do the following to run the System Information utility and gather information about your system:

1. Use the **Msinfo32.exe** command to launch the System Information window.

2. Browse through the different levels of information in this window and answer the following questions:

   a. What OS and OS version are you using?
   b. What is your CPU speed?
   c. What is your BIOS manufacturer and version?
   d. How much video RAM is available to your video adapter card? Explain how you got this information.
   e. What is the name of the driver file that manages your network adapter? Your optical drive?

A+
220-802
1.1

THE CONTROL PANEL

The Control Panel is a window containing several small utility programs called applets that are used to manage hardware, software, users, and the system. (In general, a utility program is a program used to maintain a system or fix a computer problem.) To access the Control Panel, click **Start** and then click **Control Panel**.

Figure 1-23 shows the Windows 7 Control Panel in Category view. To switch to the Large icons or Small icons view, click **Category** and make your selection. (In Vista and XP, you can switch Control Panel between Category view and Classic View. Classic View looks similar to the icon views in Windows 7.) Use the search box in the title bar to help find information and utilities in Control Panel.

You can also access the utilities using one of these methods:

◢ If you know the name of the utility program file, click **Start** and type the program name in the *Search* box. For example, to open the Mouse Properties applet, type **Main.cpl** in the box, and then press **Enter**. (An applet in Control Panel sometimes has a .cpl file extension.)

◢ Type a description or title of the utility in the *Search* box. For example, type **Network and Sharing Center** to open that window.

◢ Find another path to the utility. For example, to open the System window in the System and Security group of Control Panel, click **Start**, right-click **Computer** and select **Properties**.

A+
220-802
1.1

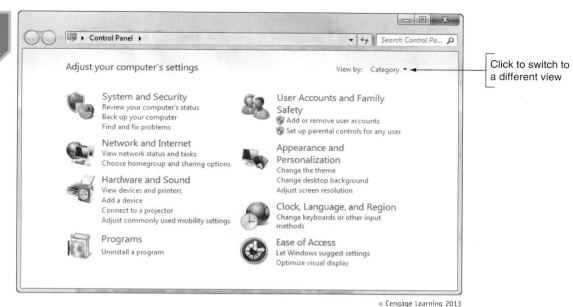

© Cengage Learning 2013

Figure 1-23 The Control Panel is organized by category, although you can easily switch to a list of selections

---

💡 A+ Exam Tip The A+ 220-802 exam expects you to be familiar with the Control Panel and its utilities. You should also know how to use the Large icons view in Windows 7 and the Classic View in Vista and XP. You are also expected to know more than one method of opening a Windows utility program.

A+
220-802
1.1, 1.5

ACTION CENTER

The Action Center is the tool to use when you want to make a quick jab at solving a computer problem. If a hardware or application problem is easy to solve, the Action Center can probably do it in a matter of minutes. The Action Center is new to Windows 7 and lists errors and issues that need attention. The Action Center flag appears in the notification area of the taskbar. If the flag has a red X beside it, as shown in Figure 1-24, Windows considers the system has an important issue that needs resolving immediately.

© Cengage Learning 2013

Figure 1-24 A red X on the Action Center flag in the taskbar indicates a critical issue needs resolving

To open the Action Center, use one of these methods:

▲ Click the **flag icon** in the taskbar. A list of issues appears (see Figure 1-25). Click **Open Action Center**.

▲ Click **Start** and type **Action Center** in the search box and press **Enter**.

▲ Click **Start** and click **Control Panel**. The Control Panel opens. Under the System and Security group, click **Review your computer's status**.

A+
220-802
1.1, 1.5

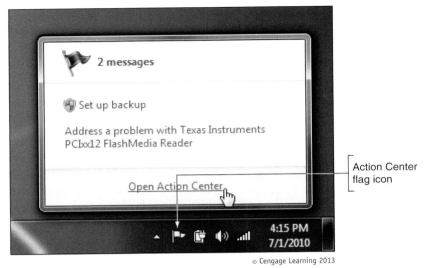

© Cengage Learning 2013

Figure 1-25   Click the Action Center flag to see a list of current issues and to open the Action Center

Using either method, the Action Center for one computer shown in Figure 1-26 appears. Notice the colored bar to the left of a problem. The red color indicates a critical problem that needs immediate attention. In this example, antivirus software is not installed on the system. The orange color indicates a less critical problem, such as no backups are scheduled. Click the button to the right of a problem to find a recommended solution.

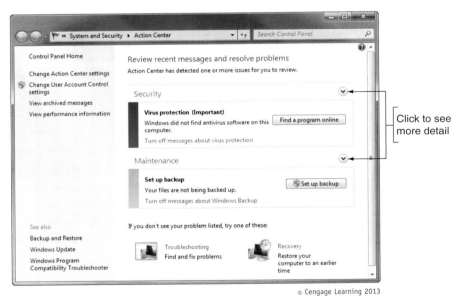

© Cengage Learning 2013

Figure 1-26   The Action Center shows a critical problem that needs a resolution

When you first open the Action Center, any problem that needs addressing is displayed. Looking back at Figure 1-25, you can see the Action Center reports a problem with a Texas Instruments FlashMedia Reader. When you click **View message details** in the Action Center, the screen shown in Figure 1-27 appears. Looking at Figure 1-27, you can see that the device does not have a Windows 7 driver and Windows is suggesting the problem might

A+
220-802
1.1, 1.5

be solved by installing a Vista driver using compatibility mode. By clicking the links on the window, you can attempt the solution. Chapter 2 covers more about the possibility of using a Vista driver in a Windows 7 system.

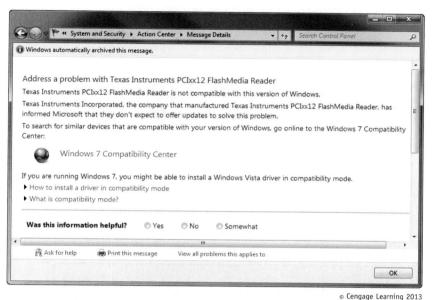

© Cengage Learning 2013

Figure 1-27 A problem reported in the Action Center with a possible solution

To see other information available under the Security and Maintenance groups, click the down arrow to the right of a group. For example, after the arrow to the right of Security is clicked, detailed information about Windows Firewall, Windows Update, and other security settings appears.

To see a complete list of past and current problems on this computer, click **View archived messages** in the left pane of the Action Center. This report helps understand the history of problems on a computer that you are troubleshooting. The problems in this list might or might not have a solution.

Hands-on | Project 1.5   Using the Action Center

Using Windows 7, follow these steps to explore and use the Action Center:

1. Open the Action Center and list any problems it reports.

2. If a problem is listed, click **View message details**. Investigate possible solutions to the problem. If appropriate for your system, apply any solutions not yet applied. Make notes regarding the solutions you applied and the results of applying these solutions.

3. In the left pane of the Action Center, click **View archived messages**. Do you find a previous problem with this computer that already has a solution applied? If so, double-click the problem to read about the solution. Describe the problem and the solution that was applied.

A+
220-802
1.1, 1.5

USER ACCOUNT CONTROL BOX

At some point while working with a computer to maintain or troubleshoot it, the User Account Control (UAC) dialog box, shown in Figure 1-28, will pop up. In Vista, this box was disruptive for power users and administrators because it appears each time a user attempts to perform an action that can be done only with administrative privileges. Windows 7 made the box less annoying and gives more options for configuring it.

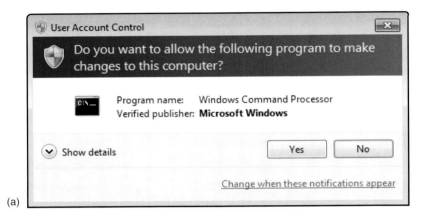

(a)

(b)

© Cengage Learning 2013

Figure 1-28 (a) and (b)   (a) The User Account Control box of an administrator does not require an administrative password; (b)The UAC box of a standard user requires an administrative password

In Windows, there are two types of user accounts: An administrator account and a standard account. An administrator account has more privileges than a standard account and is used by those responsible for maintaining and securing the system. When the UAC box appears, if you are logged on as an administrator, all you have to do is click Yes to close the box and move on, as shown in Figure 1-28(a). If the user account does not have administrative privileges, you'll have the opportunity to enter a password of an administrative account to continue, as shown in Figure 1-28(b).

The purposes of the UAC box are: (1) to prevent malicious background tasks from gaining administrative privileges when the administrator is logged on, and (2) to make it easier

A+
220-802
1.1,1.5

for an administrator to log in using a less powerful user account for normal desktop activities, but still be able to perform administrative tasks while logged in as a regular user.

For example, suppose you're logged on as an administrator with the UAC box turned off and click a malicious link on a web site. Malware can download and install itself without your knowledge and might get admin privileges on the computer. If you're logged on as a standard user and the UAC box is turned off, the malware might still install without your knowledge but with lesser privileges. The UAC box stands as a gatekeeper to malware installing behind your back because someone has to click the UAC box before the installation can proceed.

APPLYING | CONCEPTS   Using Windows 7, you can control how the UAC box works. Do the following:

1. Open the Control Panel and click **User Accounts** in the User Accounts and Family Safety group.

2. In the User Accounts window, click **Change User Account Control settings**. The User Account Control Settings window appears (see Figure 1-29).

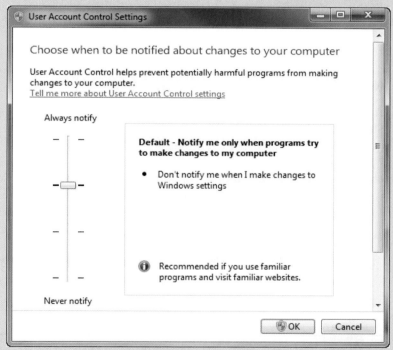

© Cengage Learning 2013

Figure 1-29   Windows 7 provides options to control the UAC box

3. Change when the UAC box appears. Here is a description of the four options shown in Figure 1-29:

   ◢ Always notify me when programs are trying to install software or make other changes to the computer and when I am making changes to Windows settings. (This is the Vista default option.)

A+
220-802
1.1, 1.5

▲ Notify me when programs are trying to make changes, but don't notify me when I am changing Windows settings. (This option is new to Windows 7 and causes the UAC box to be less annoying.)

▲ Same as the second option above but, in addition, do not dim the Windows desktop. Dimming the Windows desktop can alarm a user and take up resources. (In the Vista Business and Ultimate editions, a setting can be used to disable dimming the desktop.)

▲ Never notify me when a program is trying to change the computer or I am changing it. (This option is also available in Vista.)

4. Click **OK** and respond to the UAC box. Close the Action Center window.

Vista Differences To find out how to control the Vista User Account Control box, see Appendix B.

💡 A+ Exam Tip The A+ 220-802 exam expects you to know how to change the settings that control when the UAC box appears.

A+
220-802
1.5

NETWORK AND SHARING CENTER

A failed network connection can sometimes quickly be resolved using the Network and Sharing Center available in Windows 7 and Vista. Use the Control Panel or the taskbar to access the center. To use the taskbar, do the following:

1. Look for the networking icon in the taskbar. Wired networks show the icon on the left side of Figure 1-30 and wireless networks show the icon on the right side of Figure 1-30. Click the icon to see more information. An icon that indicates a problem has a red X and is shown on the left side of Figure 1-31. If wireless networks are available, the icon has a yellow star, as shown on the right side of Figure 1-31. In the pop-up bubble, click a wireless network to connect to it. If the network is secured, you must enter the wireless security key.

📄 Notes If you don't see the networking icon in the taskbar, you can add it using the Taskbar and Start Menu Properties box you learned about earlier in the chapter. You can also access the Network and Sharing Center from the Control Panel.

Wired network icon

Wireless network icon

© Cengage Learning 2013

Figure 1-30   Wired and wireless networking icons in the taskbar

Red X indicates a problem

Yellow star indicates wireless networks are available

© Cengage Learning 2013

Figure 1-31 The network icon in the taskbar indicates a problem or a possible new connection to a wireless network

2. To get more information about a problem, click **Open Network and Sharing Center**.

3. The Network and Sharing Center window opens (see Figure 1-32). A red X indicates a problem. Click the X to get help and resolve the problem. Windows Network Diagnostics starts looking for problems, applying solutions, and making suggestions. You can also check these things:

- For wired networks, is the network cable connected at both ends?

- Are status light indicators next to the network port on your computer lit or blinking appropriately to indicate connectivity and activity?

- Is the wireless switch on a laptop turned on?

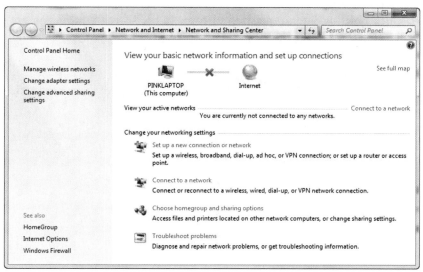

© Cengage Learning 2013

Figure 1-32 The Network and Sharing Center reports a problem connecting to the network

4. After Windows has resolved the problem, you should see a clear path from the computer to the Internet, as shown in Figure 1-33. To verify the problem is resolved, use Windows Explorer to try to access resources on the local network, and use Internet Explorer to try to access the Internet.

A+
220-802
1.5

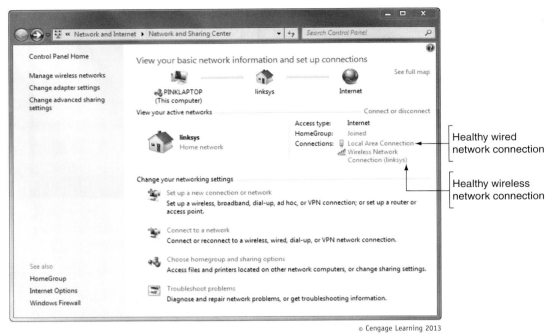

© Cengage Learning 2013

Figure 1-33 The Network and Sharing Center reports two healthy network connections

In Chapter 7, you learn more about the Networking and Sharing Center.

A+
220-802
1.1

WINDOWS HELP AND SUPPORT AND THE WEB

The best PC support technicians are the ones continually teaching themselves new skills. You can teach yourself to use and support Windows by using the web and the Windows Help and Support utility (see Figure 1-34). To start the utility, click **Start** and click **Help and Support**. Click links or enter a question or topic in the search box. If you are connected to the Internet, links can take you to the Microsoft web site where you can find information and watch videos about Windows.

© Cengage Learning 2013

Figure 1-34 Use the Help and Support tool to teach yourself about Windows

1

A+
220-802
1.1

Here are some tips for using the web and Help and Support:

◢ The Microsoft web site (*support.microsoft.com*, *windows.microsoft.com*, and *technet.microsoft.com*) has tons of useful information. Search for a device, an error message, a Windows utility, a symptom, a software application, an update version number, or keywords that lead you to articles about problems and solutions.

◢ Using a search engine such as Google (*www.google.com*), enter the error message, software application, symptom, or Windows utility in the search box to search the web for answers, suggestions, and comments. Beware, however, that you don't bump into a site that does more harm than good. Some sites are simply guessing, offering incomplete and possibly wrong solutions, and even offering a utility the site claims will solve your problem but really contains only pop-up ads or a virus. Use only reputable sites you can trust. You'll learn about several of these excellent sites in this book.

◢ To limit a Google search to the Microsoft web site, use the **site:microsoft.com** text in the search string. A Google search of the Microsoft site often gives better results than the search box on the Microsoft web site.

Other sources of help are user and installation manuals for applications and hardware devices, training materials, and the web sites of application and device manufacturers.

📝 **Notes** If you are serious about learning to provide professional support for Windows, each OS has a resource kit, including support software and a huge reference book containing inside information about the OS. Check out *Microsoft Windows 7 Resource Kit*, *Microsoft Windows Vista Resource Kit*, or *Microsoft Windows XP Professional Resource Kit*. All three are put out by Microsoft Press.

As you work your way through this book, try to learn to teach yourself about Windows by searching for information on the web, in Windows Help and Support, and in Microsoft documentation. The more independent a learner you are, the better support technician you will be.

Hands-on | Project 1.6   Using Windows Help and Support and the web to Research a Topic

Do the following to learn to research a topic so you can become an independent learner about Windows 7:

1. Use Windows Help and Support to find out how to add a folder to an existing library. Using your own user account on a Windows 7 computer, add your Desktop folder to your Documents library. List the steps you took to do that. Verify that items on your desktop are now included in your Documents library.

2. Windows 7 Home Premium, Professional, Enterprise, and Ultimate editions all support the Aero interface. If you are using one of these editions, find out how to turn the Aero interface off and on. Describe the difference in the appearance of Windows when using Aero and not using it.

3. The Windows 7 Snipping Tool can help you take screen shots of the Windows desktop. These screen shots are useful when documenting computer problems and solutions. Use Windows Help and Support to find out how to use the Snipping Tool. Use it to take a screen shot of your Windows desktop. Save the screen shot into a file on a USB flash drive or on the hard drive. Print the file contents.

4. Access the *support.microsoft.com* web site for Windows 7 support. Print one article from the Knowledge Base that addresses a problem when installing Windows 7.

5. Search the web for the purpose of the Pagefile.sys file that you found in the root directory of drive C: while doing Hands-on Project 1-3. What web site did you use to find your answer? Why is the Microsoft.com web site considered the best source for information about the Pagefile.sys file?

>> CHAPTER SUMMARY

Using Windows

◢ An operating system manages hardware, runs applications, provides an interface for users, and stores, retrieves, and manipulates files.

◢ The Windows 7 and Vista desktop offers the Aero user interface. Vista includes the sidebar with gadgets. Gadgets are placed directly on the Windows 7 desktop.

◢ Four ways to launch an application are to use the Start menu, the search box, Windows Explorer, or a shortcut icon on the desktop or taskbar.

◢ Use Windows 7 Aero Snap and Aero Shake to manage open windows on the desktop.

◢ The right side of the taskbar is called the notification area, which some call the system tray.

◢ Windows Explorer and the Computer window are used to manage files, folders (also called directories), and libraries. Windows Vista and XP do not support libraries, and Windows XP calls the Computer window the My Computer window.

◢ The file extension indicates how the file contents are organized and formatted and what program uses the file.

◢ Use the Control Panel Folder Options box to change the way Windows Explorer works and displays files and folders.

Quick and Easy Windows Support Tools

◢ The System window gives a quick overview of the system, including which edition and version of Windows is installed and the amount of installed memory.

◢ The System Information window gives much information about the computer, including hardware, device drivers, the OS, and applications.

◢ Control Panel gives access to a group of utility programs used to manage the system.

◢ The Windows 7 Action Center is a centralized location used to solve problems with security and computer maintenance issues.

▲ The User Account Control (UAC) box is used to protect the system against malware or accidental changes to a system done by inexperienced users.

▲ Use the Network and Sharing Center to manage, secure, and troubleshoot network connections.

▲ Use the web and the Windows Help and Support utility to teach yourself about Windows and how to support it.

>> KEY TERMS

For explanations of key terms, see the Glossary near the end of the book.

32-bit operating system	filename	screen resolution
64-bit operating system	folder attributes	service pack
Action Center	folder	sidebar
administrator account	gadget	standard account
Aero Peek	graphical user interface (GUI)	subdirectory
Aero Shake	Jump List	System Information
Aero Snap	library	system tray
Aero user interface	navigation pane	System window
child directories	Network and Sharing Center	systray
Compressed (zipped) Folder	notification area	taskbar
Control Panel	operating system (OS)	User Account Control (UAC) dialog box
desktop	patches	volume
device driver	path	Windows Experience Index
file attributes	root directory	
file extension	service	

>> REVIEWING THE BASICS

1. List four major functions of an OS.

2. Using Aero Snap, what happens when you drag a window to the top of the Windows 7 desktop?

3. How can you add a program icon to the Windows 7 taskbar so the program can quickly be launched at any time?

4. What might happen to the Windows system if too many services are running, as indicated by multiple icons in the notification area of the taskbar?

5. What is the keyboard shortcut to the flip 3D view?

6. What are the four libraries that Windows 7 creates by default?

7. What part of a file name does Windows use to know which application to open to manage the file?

8. What file extension is used to name a compressed folder?

9. Which folder does Windows use to store files a user puts in the Documents library?

10. Which Windows 7 edition(s) come only in a 32-bit version?

11. What is the memory limitation for a 32-bit operating system?

12. How do you access the Properties box for a file to change a file attribute?

13. What is the program name for the System Information utility?

14. Which Windows 7 window can be used to get a report of the history of problems on a computer?

15. When does a user need to enter a password into the UAC box in order to continue?

>> THINKING CRITICALLY

1. What Windows tool can you use to know how much RAM is installed on your system?

2. Mary wants her 32-bit installation of Windows 7 Professional to run faster. She has 4 GB of memory installed on the motherboard. She decides more memory will help. She installs an additional 2 GB of memory for a total of 6 GB, but does not see any performance improvement. What is the problem and what should you tell Mary?

   a. She should use Control Panel to install the memory in Windows 7. After it is installed, performance should improve. Tell Mary how to open the Control Panel.

   b. A 32-bit OS cannot use more than 4 GB of memory. Tell Mary she has wasted her money.

   c. A 32-bit OS cannot use more than 4 GB of memory. Tell Mary to upgrade her system to the 64-bit version of Windows 7 Professional.

   d. A 32-bit OS cannot use more than 4 GB of memory. Explain to Mary the problem and discuss with her the possible solutions.

3. Jack needs to email two documents to a friend but the files are so large his email server bounced them back as undeliverable. What is your advice?

   a. Tell Jack to open the documents and break each of them into two documents and then email the four documents separately.

   b. Tell Jack to put the two documents in a compressed folder and email the folder.

   c. Tell Jack to put each document in a different compressed folder and email each folder separately.

   d. Tell Jack to put the documents on a USB drive and snail mail the drive to his friend.

4. For each of the following programs, identify if the program is an operating system, application, device driver, or utility program: Internet Explorer, Norton Antivirus, Windows 98, Adobe Photoshop.

>> REAL PROBLEMS, REAL SOLUTIONS

REAL PROBLEM 1-1: Becoming a PC Support Technician

You've just been hired as a PC support technician in the IT department of your university. At the job interview, you were promised a two-week training period, but by noon on your first day on the job it dawns on you that "training period" means you gotta train yourself *really quick*! Listed below are some problems you encounter that day. How do you solve these problems and what Windows tools do you use?

1. A history professor calls you into his office and tells you he thinks the memory on his Windows 7 computer needs upgrading. He wants you to tell him how much RAM is currently installed. What do you do?

2. A PE instructor discovers the history professor has Windows 7 on his desktop. She thinks she has Windows XP on her computer and wants you to tell her exactly which OS she has installed. What do you do?

3. Your boss asks you to go down the hall to the Windows 7 computer in the break room and find out the path and name of the device driver for the optical drive (CD drive or DVD drive) that is installed. What steps do you use? What is the path and name of the optical drive device driver on your Windows XP/Vista/7 system?

4. The Office Administrator for Career Education often uses MS Word and wants you to place a shortcut on her desktop to launch this application. List the steps to do that.

5. A student in a computer lab is trying to answer a question in the lab about the Windows 7 desktop. She needs to add a gadget to the desktop to show the current temperature in Seattle. What steps do you give her to find the answer? Print the screen showing the gadget. List the steps you took to print the screen.

6. The Biology professor's Windows 7 system is slow and you decide to turn off the Aero user interface to save on resources. List the steps to do that and the source of information you used.

Installing Windows

Windows 7, Vista, and XP all share the same basic Windows architecture, and all have similar characteristics. Windows 7 is available for purchase, but you can no longer purchase Vista or XP. However, because many individual users and corporations still rely on Vista and XP, you need to know how to support them.

At the time this book went to print, Windows 8 Beta is available. Microsoft releases beta versions of software so that the user community can test the software before retail versions become available. How to install and support Windows 8 is not covered in this book.

This chapter discusses how to plan a Windows installation and the steps to perform a Windows 7 installation, including what to do after the OS is installed. You also learn about what to expect when installing Windows on computers in a large enterprise.

Vista Differences The details of a Windows 7 installation are covered in this chapter. For details about a Vista installation, see Appendix B, and for details about installing XP, see Appendix C.

HOW TO PLAN A WINDOWS INSTALLATION

A+
220-802
1.1, 1.2

As a PC support technician, you can expect to be called on to install Windows in a variety of situations. You might need to install Windows on a new hard drive, after an existing Windows installation has become corrupted, or to upgrade from one OS to another. Many decisions need to be made before the installation. Decisions to consider about Windows 7 are covered in this part of the chapter and most of these decisions apply to any Windows operating system.

CHOOSE THE EDITION, LICENSE, AND VERSION OF WINDOWS 7

When buying Windows 7, know the price is affected by the Windows edition and type of license you purchase. You also need to decide between the 32-bit and 64-bit version. In this part of the chapter, you learn about your options when purchasing Windows 7 and how to make sure your computer qualifies for Windows 7.

EDITIONS OF WINDOWS 7

Microsoft has produced several editions of Windows 7 designed to satisfy a variety of consumer needs:

- ◢ **Windows 7 Starter** has the most limited features and is intended to be used on netbooks or in developing nations. In the United States, it can only be obtained preinstalled by the manufacturer on a new netbook computer. Windows 7 Starter comes only in the 32-bit version. All other editions of Windows 7 are available in either the 32-bit or 64-bit version.
- ◢ **Windows 7 Home Basic** has limited features and is available only in underdeveloped countries and can only be activated in these countries.
- ◢ **Windows 7 Home Premium** is similar to Windows 7 Home Basic, but includes additional features.
- ◢ **Windows 7 Professional** is intended for business users. You can purchase multiple site licenses (also called volume licensing) using this edition.
- ◢ **Windows 7 Enterprise** includes additional features over Windows 7 Professional. The major additional features are BitLocker Drive Encryption used to encrypt an entire hard drive and support for multiple languages. The edition does not include Windows DVD Maker. Multiple site licenses are available.
- ◢ **Windows 7 Ultimate** includes every Windows 7 feature. You cannot purchase multiple licenses with this edition.

📝 **Notes** An antitrust ruling (a ruling to break up monopolies) in Europe required that Microsoft must offer editions of Windows that do not include multimedia utilities. Windows 7, therefore, comes in N and KN editions that do not include Windows Media Player, Windows Media Center, and Windows DVD Maker. For example, Windows 7 Home Premium N, Windows 7 Ultimate N, and Windows 7 Professional KN do not include these multimedia utilities. If you have an N or KN edition of Windows 7, you can, however, legally download the utilities from the Microsoft web site.

A+
220-802
1.1, 1.2

The major features for all editions are listed in Table 2-1. You will learn how to use and support many of these features later in the book.

> **A+ Exam Tip** Before you sit for the A+ 220-802 exam, take a little time to memorize the features included in each edition of Windows 7 that are listed in Table 2-1.

Feature	Starter	Home Basic	Home Premium	Professional	Enterprise	Ultimate
Aero user interface			X	X	X	X
Create homegroups			X	X	X	X
Scheduled backups	X	X	X	X	X	X
Backup to network				X	X	X
BitLocker Drive Encryption					X	X
Encrypting File System (EFS)				X	X	X
Windows DVD Maker			X	X		X
Windows Media Center			X	X	X	X
Join a domain				X	X	X
Group Policy				X	X	X
Remote Desktop host				X	X	X
Multiple languages					X	X
Windows XP Mode				X	X	X
Processor: 32-bit or 64-bit		X	X	X	X	X

© Cengage Learning 2013

Table 2-1 Windows 7 editions and their features

> **Notes** The Windows 7 setup DVD contains only one edition of Windows 7. When you install Windows 7, setup knows which edition to install even if you do not enter the product key during the installation. On the other hand, the Vista setup DVD includes all editions of Vista. The edition of Vista that you can install depends on the product key you use.

OEM, FULL RETAIL, OR UPGRADE RETAIL LICENSE

When buying Windows 7, know that you can purchase a retail license or an OEM (Original Equipment Manufacturer) license. The OEM license costs less but can only be installed on a new PC for resale. The boxed retail package contains the 32-bit DVD and 64-bit DVD (see Figure 2-1). You can also purchase and download Windows 7 from the Microsoft online store at *microsoftstore.com*. The retail license costs less if you purchase a license to upgrade from Vista or XP to Windows 7. You are required to purchase the Windows 7 full license for a new computer or any computer that has an OS other than Vista and XP installed.

A+
220-802
1.1, 1.2

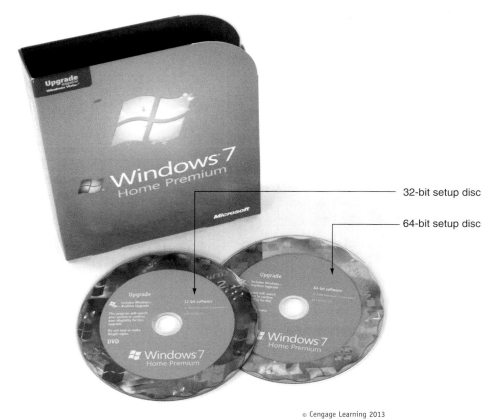

32-bit setup disc

64-bit setup disc

© Cengage Learning 2013

Figure 2-1   A Windows 7 DVD contains either a 32-bit version or a 64-bit version of Windows

Notes   The Windows 7 setup DVD is the same regardless of the full or upgrade license you purchase. This DVD can be used to perform a clean installation or an upgrade. The difference is in the product key, which is tied to the full or upgrade license you purchase. When installing Windows 7, if you use a product key purchased for an upgrade license, setup will verify that the system qualifies to use this license. You cannot use an OEM disc for an upgrade installation.

32-BIT OR 64-BIT VERSIONS

Recall that an operating system can process 32 bits or 64 bits. A 64-bit installation of Windows generally performs better than a 32-bit installation if you have enough RAM. Table 2-2 shows how much RAM each edition and version of Windows 7 can support. Another advantage of 64-bit installations of Windows is they can support 64-bit applications, which run faster than 32-bit applications. Even though you can install 32-bit applications in a 64-bit OS, for best performance, always choose 64-bit applications. Keep in mind that 64-bit installations of Windows require 64-bit device drivers.

Notes   All processors (CPUs) used in personal computers today are hybrid processors and can handle a 32-bit or 64-bit OS. However, the Intel Itanium and Xeon processors used in high-end workstations and servers are true 64-bit processors and require a 64-bit OS.

Operating System	32-bit Version	64-bit Version
Windows 7 Ultimate	4 GB	192 GB
Windows 7 Enterprise	4 GB	192 GB
Windows 7 Professional	4 GB	192 GB
Windows 7 Home Premium	4 GB	16 GB
Windows 7 Home Basic	4 GB	8 GB
Windows 7 Starter	2 GB	NA

Table 2-2   Maximum memory supported by Windows 7 editions and versions   © Cengage Learning 2013

> **Notes** How much memory or RAM you can install in a computer depends not only on the OS installed but also on how much memory the motherboard can hold. To know how much RAM a motherboard can support, see the motherboard documentation.

VERIFY YOUR SYSTEM QUALIFIES FOR WINDOWS 7

The minimum hardware requirements for Windows 7 are listed in Table 2-3. (These minimum requirements are also the Microsoft recommended requirements.) The requirements are the same as those for Windows Vista. Know, however, that Microsoft occasionally changes the minimum and recommended requirements for an OS.

Hardware	For 32-bit Windows 7	For 64-bit Windows 7
Processor	1 GHz or faster	1 GHz or faster
Memory (RAM)	1 GB	2 GB
Free hard drive space	16 GB	20 GB
Video device and driver	DirectX 9 device with WDDM 1.0 or higher driver	DirectX 9 device with WDDM 1.0 or higher driver

Table 2-3   Minimum and recommended hardware requirements for Windows 7   © Cengage Learning 2013

The simplest way to find out if a system can be upgraded to Windows 7 is to download, install, and run the Windows 7 Upgrade Advisor. You can find the software and instructions on how to use it at *windows.microsoft.com/en-US/windows/downloads/upgrade-advisor*. Microsoft also offers the Windows 7 Compatibility Center at *www.microsoft.com/windows/compatibility* (see Figure 2-2). You can search under both software and hardware to find out if they are compatible with Windows 7. The site sometimes offers links to patches or fixes for a program or device so that it will work with Windows 7.

A+
220-802
1.1, 1.2

© Cengage Learning 2013

Figure 2-2 Use the Windows 7 Compatibility Center to find out if your hardware and software qualify for Windows 7

To understand if your system qualifies for Windows 7, it helps to understand how Windows relates to hardware by using device drivers and system BIOS, as shown in Figure 2-3. (In the figure, the kernel is that part of Windows responsible for relating to hardware.)

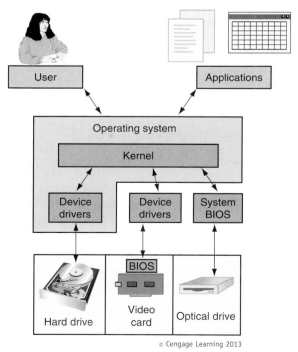

© Cengage Learning 2013

Figure 2-3 Windows relates to hardware by way of device drivers or system BIOS

A+
220-802
1.1, 1.2

When a computer is first turned on, it uses some devices such as the keyboard, monitor, and hard drive before the OS starts up. The motherboard BIOS is contained on a chip on the motherboard (see Figure 2-4) and manages these essential devices. This chip is called a firmware chip because it holds programs.

Coin battery

Firmware chip

© Cengage Learning 2013

Figure 2-4   A chip on a motherboard contains BIOS used to start the computer, hold motherboard settings, and run essential devices. The chip retains power from a nearby coin battery when the computer is turned off.

The motherboard BIOS provides three main functions:

▲ The **system BIOS (basic input/output system)** contains instructions for running essential hardware devices before an operating system is started. After the OS is started, it might continue to use system BIOS or use device drivers to communicate with these devices.

▲ The **startup BIOS** starts the computer and finds a boot device (hard drive, CD drive, or USB flash drive) that contains an operating system. It then turns the startup process over to this OS.

▲ The **setup BIOS** is used to change motherboard settings. You can use it to enable or disable a device on the motherboard (for example, network port, video port, or USB ports), change the date and time that is later passed to the OS, and select the order of boot devices for startup BIOS to search when looking for an operating system to load.

Recall that device drivers are small programs stored on the hard drive that tell the computer how to communicate with a specific hardware device such as a printer, network card, or scanner. These drivers are installed on the hard drive when the OS is first installed, or when new hardware is added to the system. A device driver is written to work for a specific OS, such as Windows 7 or Vista. In addition, a 32-bit OS requires 32-bit drivers, and a 64-bit OS requires 64-bit drivers.

Windows provides some device drivers, and the manufacturer of the hardware device provides others. When you purchase a printer, video card, digital camera, scanner, or other hardware device, a CD that contains the device drivers is usually bundled with the device along with a user manual (see Figure 2-5). You can also download the drivers for a device from the manufacturer's web site.

A+
220-802
1.1, 1.2

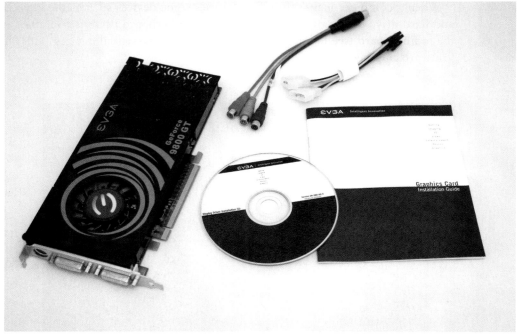

© Cengage Learning 2013

Figure 2-5   A device such as this video card comes packaged with its device drivers stored on a CD

Be sure you have Windows 7 device drivers for all your critical devices such as your network card or motherboard. To find the drivers, look on the CD that came bundled with the device or check the web site of the device manufacturer. Remember that a 64-bit OS requires all 64-bit drivers.

If you are not sure if your devices will work with Windows 7, one solution is to set up a dual boot. A **dual boot**, also called a **multiboot**, allows you to install the new OS without disturbing the old one so you can boot to either OS. After the installation, you can test your software or hardware. If they work under the new OS, you can delete the old one. If they don't work, you can still boot to the old OS and use it. How to set up a dual boot is covered later in the chapter.

If you have applications written for Vista or XP that are not compatible with Windows 7, you can use compatibility mode or Windows XP Mode to solve the problem. **Compatibility mode** is a group of settings that can be applied to older drivers or applications that might cause them to work in Windows 7. **Windows XP Mode** is a Windows XP environment installed in Windows 7 that can be used to support older applications. You learn more about compatibility mode and Windows XP Mode later in the chapter.

Hands-on | Project 2.1   Preparing for an Upgrade

On a PC with Windows Vista or XP installed, access the Microsoft web site (*www.microsoft.com*) and locate and run the Windows 7 Upgrade Advisor to find out if the PC is ready for a Windows 7 installation. Make a list of any hardware or software components found incompatible with Windows 7, and draw up a plan for getting the system ready for a Windows 7 upgrade.

2

INSTALLATIONS WITH SPECIAL CONSIDERATIONS

Depending on the circumstances and the available hardware, you might be faced with an installation on a computer that does not have a DVD drive, a computer that needs a factory recovery, and an installation in a virtual computer. All these special considerations are discussed next.

WHEN THE COMPUTER DOES NOT HAVE A DVD DRIVE

You can buy Windows 7 on DVD or download it from the Internet. If the computer does not have a DVD drive, consider these options:

▲ *Download Windows 7 from the Microsoft web site*: Purchase Windows 7 on the Microsoft web site (*www.microsoftstore.com*) and download it to your computer's hard drive and install it from there. This option assumes the computer already has a working OS installed.

▲ *Use an external DVD drive.* Use an external DVD drive that will most likely connect to the PC by way of a USB port. If the PC does not already have an OS installed, you must boot from this USB port. To do so, access BIOS setup and set the boot order for the USB as the first boot device. The boot order is the order of devices that startup BIOS looks to for an OS. To enter BIOS setup, you press a key, such as F2 or Del, as the computer is booting and before the OS begins to load. To know which key to press, look for a message on-screen during the boot, such as *Press DEL to enter setup*. Then locate the appropriate BIOS setup screen. For example, the BIOS setup screen shown in Figure 2-6 shows a removable device as the first boot device. You can then boot from the external DVD drive and install Windows.

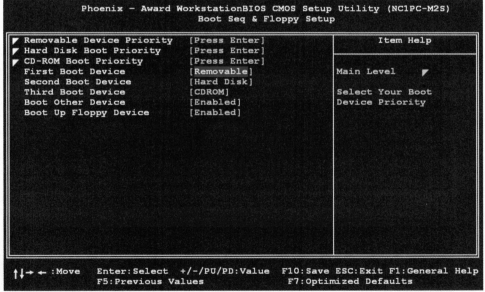

Figure 2-6   Set the boot order in BIOS setup

© Cengage Learning 2013

▲ *Copy the installation files to a USB flash drive.* This method is easy to use if you don't need to boot from the flash drive. If you do need to boot from the flash drive, you need to install software that makes the USB flash drive bootable and also copy Windows setup files to the drive.

A+
220-802
1.1, 1.2

◢ *Use a DVD drive on another computer on the network.* Share the DVD drive on another computer on the network. Then go to the computer that is to receive the Windows installation and locate the DVD drive on the network. Double-click the setup.exe program to run the installation across the network. Alternately, you can copy the files on the DVD from the other computer to your hard drive. Again, this option assumes the computer already has a working OS installed. How to share folders and drives on a network is covered in Chapter 8.

If you are upgrading many computers to Windows 7 in a large enterprise, more automated methods are used. Installation files are made available over the network or on bootable USB flash drives or DVDs. These automated methods are discussed later in the chapter.

FACTORY RECOVERY PARTITION

If you have a notebook computer or a brand-name computer, such as a Dell, IBM, or Gateway, and you need to reinstall Windows, follow the recovery procedures given by the computer manufacturer. A hard drive is divided into one or more **partitions**, and the hard drive on a brand-name computer is likely to have a hidden recovery partition that contains a recovery utility and installation files.

To access the utilities on the hidden partition, press a key during startup. The key to press is displayed on the screen early in the boot before the OS is loaded. If you don't see the message, search the web site of the computer manufacturer to find the key combination. For one Dell laptop, you press Ctrl and F11 to start the recovery. One Gateway computer displays the message *Press F11 to start recovery.* When you press these keys, a menu displays, giving you the opportunity to reinstall Windows from setup files kept in the hidden partition.

Sometimes a manufacturer puts a utility in this hidden partition that can be used to create recovery discs (see Figure 2-7). However, the discs must have already been created if they are to be there to help you in the event the entire hard drive fails. You might also be able to purchase these CDs or DVDs on the notebook manufacturer's web site.

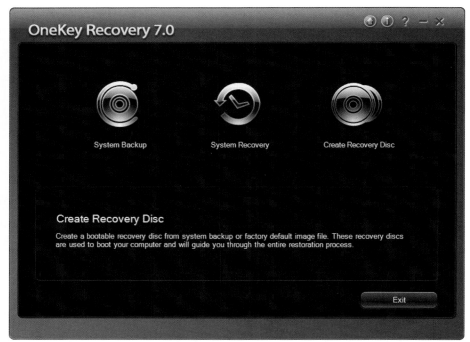

© Cengage Learning 2013

Figure 2-7 Use the recovery utility on this laptop to create DVDs that can be used to recover the system in the event the hard drive fails

A+
220-802
1.1, 1.2

Notes In general, it's best to not upgrade an OS on a notebook unless you want to use some feature the new OS offers. For notebooks, follow the general rule, "If it ain't broke, don't fix it." Many hardware components in a notebook are proprietary, and the notebook manufacturer is the only source for these drivers. If you are considering upgrading a notebook to Windows 7, check the notebook manufacturer web site for advice and to download Windows 7 drivers. It's very important you have a Windows 7 driver for your network port available without having to depend on the network or Internet to get one after Windows 7 is installed. Also know that many Vista drivers also work with Windows 7.

INSTALLATION IN A VIRTUAL COMPUTER

Another type of Windows installation is when you install Windows in a virtual computer. A virtual computer or **virtual machine (VM)** is software that simulates the hardware of a physical computer. Using this software, you can install and run multiple operating systems at the same time on a PC. These multiple instances of operating systems can be used to train users, run legacy software, and support multiple operating systems. For example, help-desk technicians can run a virtual machine for each OS they support on a single PC and quickly and easily switch from one OS to another by clicking a window. Another reason to use a virtual machine is that you can capture screen shots of the boot process in a virtual machine, which is the way the screen shots during the boot were made for this book.

Some popular virtual machine programs for Windows are Virtual PC by Microsoft (*www.microsoft.com*), VirtualBox by Oracle (*www.virtualbox.org*), and VMware by VMware, Inc. (*www.vmware.com*). Virtual PC, VirtualBox, and VMware Player are freeware. Be aware that virtual machine programs require a lot of memory and might slow down your system. Figure 2-8 shows two virtual machines running under Virtual PC.

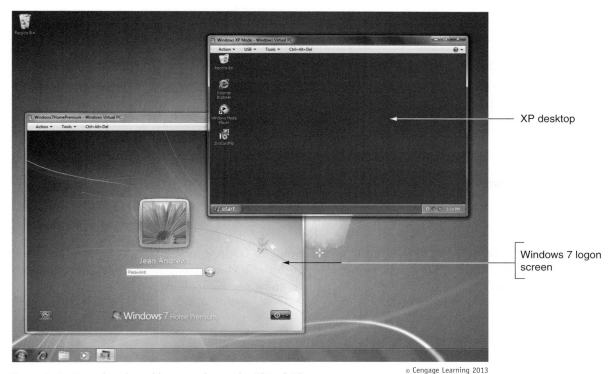

XP desktop

Windows 7 logon screen

© Cengage Learning 2013

Figure 2-8 Two virtual machines running under Virtual PC

A+
220-802
1.1, 1.2

Windows XP Mode is a Windows XP installation that runs under Virtual PC, and can be installed on a Windows 7 Professional, Enterprise, or Ultimate computer. When you install an OS in Virtual PC, normally you must have a valid product key for the installation, but an XP product key is not required for Windows XP Mode.

To use Virtual PC, go to the Microsoft web site and download and install the software. If you plan to use Windows XP Mode, you need to download this software at the same time. To set up a new virtual machine in Virtual PC, click **Start, All Programs**, and **Windows Virtual PC**. (You might need to click Windows Virtual PC a second time.) The Explorer window shown at the top of Figure 2-9 appears. In the menu bar, click **Create virtual machine**. A wizard launches and steps you through the process of creating a new machine. During the process, you can select the name of the virtual machine, how much memory the machine has installed, and the hard drive size. The bottom of Figure 2-9 shows one window in the wizard where you select how much RAM the machine will have. When you complete the wizard, the new virtual machine is listed in the Explorer window.

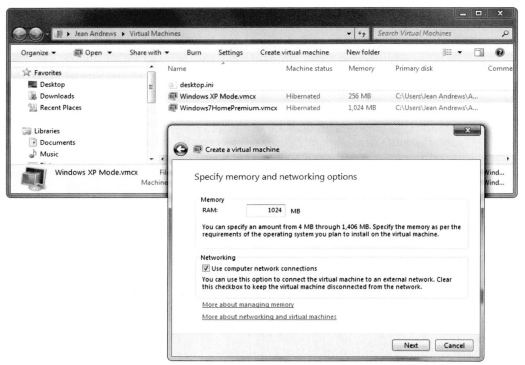

Figure 2-9 Using Virtual PC to set up a new virtual machine

© Cengage Learning 2013

To start this virtual machine and install an OS in it, first insert the operating system setup disc in the DVD drive. Then double-click the VM in Explorer. The VM boots up, finds the DVD, and starts the OS installation, as shown in Figure 2-10.

2

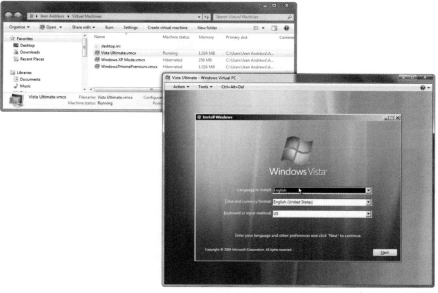

Figure 2-10 A new VM is installing Windows Vista

© Cengage Learning 2013

APPLYING | CONCEPTS

Windows can also be installed in a VM by using an **ISO image.** An International Organization for Standardization image, also called an ISO image or disc image, contains an image of a disc including the file system used. When downloaded from the web, an ISO image is usually stored in a file with an .iso file extension. An ISO image of the Windows setup DVD can be downloaded as an .iso file. To create a bootable Windows setup DVD from the image, right-click the .iso file and select **Burn disc image** from the shortcut menu. Using a virtual machine, you can mount an ISO image to the VM, which treats the image as though it is a disc. The ISO image file then works like a virtual disc.

To mount an ISO image to a VM, you must change the hardware configuration of the VM. For Virtual PC, first shut down the VM. Then in Explorer, select the VM and click **Settings** in the menu bar. The Settings dialog box appears (see Figure 2-11). To mount an ISO image to the VM, select DVD Drive in the figure and navigate to the ISO file. Make your changes and click **OK.**

© Cengage Learning 2013

Figure 2-11 Change the hardware configuration for a virtual machine in Virtual PC

A+
220-802
1.1, 1.2

Hands-on | Project 2.2 Installing and Running Microsoft Virtual PC

Go to the Microsoft web site (*www.microsoft.com*) and download Virtual PC. Install Virtual PC on your computer. Later in the chapter, in Project 2-6, you install Windows in a VM.

CHOOSE THE TYPE OF INSTALLATION: IN-PLACE UPGRADE, CLEAN INSTALL, OR DUAL BOOT

If you are installing Windows on a new hard drive, you must perform a clean install. If an OS is already installed on the hard drive, you have three choices:

▲ *Clean install*: You can perform a clean install, overwriting the existing operating system and applications. In the Windows 7 setup program, a clean install is called a custom installation. The main advantage of a clean install is that problems with the old OS are not carried forward and you get a fresh start. During the installation, you will have the option to reformat the hard drive, erasing everything on the drive. If you don't format the drive, the data will still be on the drive, but the previous operating system settings and applications will be lost. After Windows is installed, you will need to install the applications.

▲ *In-place upgrade*: If the upgrade paths allow it, you can perform an in-place upgrade installation. An in-place upgrade is a Windows installation that is launched from the Windows desktop and the installation carries forward user settings and installed applications from the old OS to the new one. A Windows OS is already *in place* before you begin the new installation. An in-place upgrade is faster than a clean install and is appropriate if the system is generally healthy and does not have problems.

In order to perform an in-place upgrade, Microsoft requires that certain editions and versions of Windows be installed. These qualifying OSs are called upgrade paths. Table 2-4 outlines the acceptable upgrade paths for Windows 7. Notice in the table that there is no upgrade path from Windows XP to Windows 7 or for certain editions and versions of Vista to Windows 7. Even though you can purchase an upgrade license to install Windows 7 on these systems, you must perform a clean install.

From OS	To OS
Vista Home Basic	Windows 7 Home Basic, Home Premium, or Ultimate
Vista Home Premium	Windows 7 Home Premium or Ultimate
Vista Business	Windows 7 Professional, Enterprise, or Ultimate
Vista Enterprise	Windows 7 Enterprise
Vista Ultimate	Windows 7 Ultimate
Windows 7 any edition	Can be repaired by performing an in-place upgrade of the same OS
Windows 7 Starter	Anytime Upgrade to Windows 7 Home Premium, Professional or Ultimate
Windows 7 Home Basic	Anytime upgrade to Windows 7 Home Premium, Professional or Ultimate
Windows 7 Premium	Anytime upgrade to Windows 7 Professional or Ultimate
Windows 7 Professional	Anytime upgrade to Windows 7 Ultimate

© Cengage Learning 2013

Table 2-4 In-place upgrade paths to Windows 7

2

◢ *Dual boot:* You can install Windows in a second partition on the hard drive and create a dual-boot situation with the other OS. Don't create a dual boot unless you need two operating systems, such as when you need to verify that applications and hardware work under Windows 7 before you delete the old OS. Windows 7/Vista/XP all require that they be the only operating system installed on a partition. So to set up a dual boot, you'll need at least two partitions on the hard drive or a second hard drive.

> **Notes** An Anytime Upgrade is used to upgrade an edition of Windows 7 to another edition, such as when you upgrade Windows 7 Starter to Windows 7 Home Premium. The upgrade is easy to do and does not require your going through the entire upgrade process.

In addition to the information given in Table 2-4, keep in mind these tips:

◢ A 64-bit version of Windows can only be upgraded to a 64-bit OS. A 32-bit OS can only be upgraded to a 32-bit OS. If you want to install a 64-bit version of Windows on a computer that already has a 32-bit OS installed, you must perform a clean install.

◢ You can only upgrade Windows Vista to Windows 7 after Vista Service Pack 1 or later has been installed in Vista.

UNDERSTAND THE CHOICES YOU'LL MAKE DURING THE INSTALLATION

While Windows is installing, you must choose which drive and partition to install Windows, the size of a new partition, and how Windows will connect to the network. These three choices are discussed next.

THE SIZE OF THE WINDOWS PARTITION

A hard drive is divided into one or more partitions. When a partition is formatted with a file system and assigned a drive letter (such as drive C:), it is called a **volume**. A **file system** is the overall structure an OS uses to name, store, and organize files on a volume, and Windows is always installed on a volume that uses the NTFS file system. For most installations, you install Windows on the only hard drive in the computer and allocate all the space on the drive to one partition that Windows setup calls drive C: and installs Windows in the C:\Windows folder.

For a clean install or dual boot, you can decide to not use all the available space on the drive for the Windows partition. Here are reasons to not use all the available space:

◢ You *plan to install more than one OS on the hard drive, creating a dual-boot system*: For example, you might want to install Windows 7 on one partition and leave room for another partition where you intend to later install Windows 8, so you can test software under both operating systems. (When setting up a dual boot, always install the older OS first.)

◢ *Some people prefer to use more than one partition or volume to organize data on their hard drives*: For example, you might want to install Windows and all your applications on one partition and your data on another. Having your data on a separate partition makes backing up easier. In another situation, you might want to set up a volume on the drive that is used exclusively to hold backups of data on another computer on the network. The size of the partition that will hold Windows 7 and its applications should be at least 20 GB, but a larger volume is preferred.

A+
220-802
1.1, 1.2

> ⚡ **Caution**   It's convenient to back up one volume to another volume on a different hard drive. However, don't back up one volume to another volume on the same hard drive, because when a hard drive fails, quite often all volumes on the drive are damaged and you will lose both your data and your backup.

Windows can handle up to four partitions on a drive. In Chapter 3, you learn to use Disk Management to create partitions from unallocated space and to resize, delete, and split existing partitions.

ADMINISTRATOR ACCOUNT

Recall from Chapter 1 that Windows supports two types of accounts, standard accounts and administrator accounts. These accounts are local accounts, meaning they are only recognized by the local computer. Every Windows computer has two local administrator accounts:

◢ During the Windows 7 installation, you are given the opportunity to enter an account name and password to a local user account that is assigned administrator privileges. This account is enabled by default.

◢ A built-in administrator account is created by default. The built-in administrator account is named Administrator, does not have a password, and is disabled by default. In Chapter 8, you learn how to enable this administrator account.

You can log on as an administrator after the OS is installed and create local user accounts that apply to this one computer. How to set up a local account is covered later in the chapter.

A+
220-802
1.1, 1.2,
1.6

NETWORK CONFIGURATION

Three ways Windows supports accessing resources on a network are to use a Windows homegroup, workgroup, or domain.

Windows Workgroup and Homegroup

A homegroup and workgroup are examples of a peer-to-peer (P2P) network, which is a network that is managed by each computer without centralized control. They form a logical group of computers and users that share resources (see Figure 2-12), where administration, resources, and security on a workstation are controlled by that workstation.

> **Notes**   When looking at the diagrams in Figure 2-12 and later in Figure 2-13, know that the connecting lines describe the logical connections between computers and not the physical connections. Both networks might be physically connected the same way, but logically, resources are controlled by each computer on the network or by using a centralized database. In network terminology, the arrangement of physical connections between computers is called the **physical topology**. The logical way the computers connect on a network is called the **logical topology**.

2

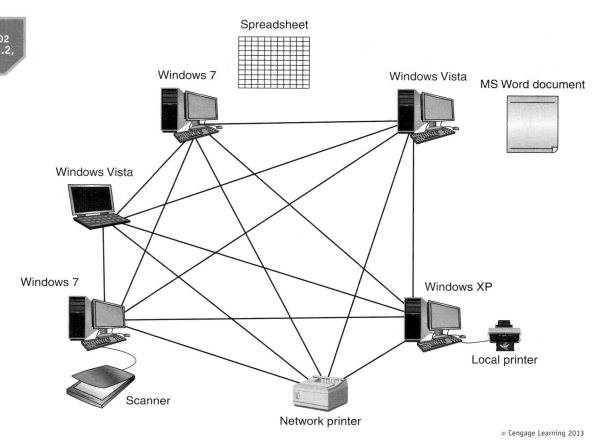

Spreadsheet

Windows 7

Windows Vista MS Word document

Windows Vista

Windows 7

Windows XP

Local printer

Scanner

Network printer

© Cengage Learning 2013

Figure 2-12 A Windows workgroup is a type of peer-to-peer network where no single computer controls the network and each computer controls its own resources

In a Windows **workgroup**, each computer maintains a list of users and their rights on that particular PC. The computer allows a user on the network to access local resources based on these rights she has been given. In a **homegroup**, each computer shares files, folders, libraries, and printers with other computers in the homegroup. A homegroup provides less security than a workgroup because any user of any computer in the homegroup can access homegroup resources.

A homegroup is new to Windows 7 and cannot be used with earlier versions of Windows. If you need to share resources with Windows Vista or XP computers or you need better security so you can share resources with specific users, use workgroup sharing rather than a homegroup. You can also use a combination of homegroup and workgroup sharing on the same computer.

During the Windows installation, if you set the network location to a home network, you are given the opportunity to create or join a homegroup. If the homegroup already exists on the network, you will need the homegroup password to join.

Notes Windows 7 Starter and Home Basic can join a homegroup, but they cannot create one.

A+
220-802
1.1, 1.2,
1.6

Windows setup automatically joins the computer to a workgroup named WORKGROUP. If necessary, you can change the workgroup name after the installation. How to change a workgroup name is covered later in the chapter. Using workgroup sharing, you must set up a user account for each user and share resources with these users. Chapter 8 covers the details of securing and managing homegroups, workgroups, user accounts, and shared resources.

Windows Domain

A Windows **domain** is a logical group of networked computers that share a centralized directory database of user account information and security for the entire group of computers (see Figure 2-13). A Windows domain is a type of **client/server** network, which is a network where resources are managed by centralized computers. Using the client/server model, the directory database is controlled by a Network Operating System (NOS). Examples of network operating systems are Windows Server 2011, UNIX, and Linux.

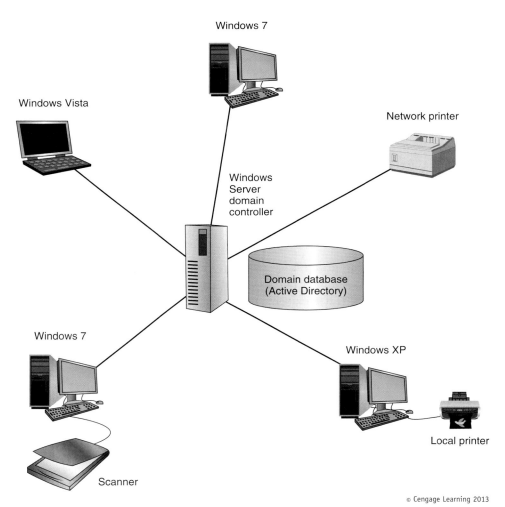

© Cengage Learning 2013

Figure 2-13 A Windows domain is a type of client/server network where security on each PC or other device is controlled by a centralized database on a domain controller

Notes Windows Home Editions do not support joining a domain. If you plan to join a domain on your network, install Windows 7 Professional, Enterprise, or Ultimate editions.

A+
220-802
1.1, 1.2,
1.6

Windows Server controls a network using the directory database called **Active Directory**. Each user on the network must have his own domain-level account called a **global account**, global username or network ID, which is kept in Active Directory and assigned by the network or system administrator. If you are installing Windows on a PC that belongs to a domain, the administrator will tell you the domain name and computer name so you can join the domain during the installation. You will also need a network ID and password to the domain that you can use to log onto the network after Windows is installed.

> 📝 **Notes** If your computer is part of a domain, when Windows starts up, press Ctrl+Alt+Del to display a logon screen, and then enter your network ID and password.

The Windows installation process usually has no problems connecting to the network and the Internet without your help. However, you might need to know how the IP address is assigned. An IP address uniquely identifies a computer on the network. It might be assigned dynamically (IP address is assigned by a server each time it connects to the network) or statically (IP address is permanently assigned to the workstation). If the network is using static IP addressing, you need the IP address for the workstation.

A+
220-802
1.1, 1.2

FINAL CHECKLIST BEFORE BEGINNING THE INSTALLATION

Before you begin the installation, complete the final checklist shown in Table 2-5 to verify that you are ready.

Questions to Answer	Further Information
Does the PC meet the minimum or recommended hardware requirement?	CPU: RAM: Hard drive partition size: Free space on the partition:
Do you have in hand the Windows device drivers for your hardware devices and application setup CDs?	List hardware and software that need to be upgraded:
Do you have the product key available?	Product key:
How will users be recognized on the network?	Homegroup password: Workgroup name: Domain name: Computer name:
How will the PC be recognized on the network?	Static or dynamic IP addressing: IP address (for static addressing):
Will you do an upgrade or clean install?	Current operating system: Does the old OS qualify for an upgrade?

For a clean install, will you set up a dual boot?	List reasons for a dual boot:
	 For a dual boot
	     Size of the second partition:
	     Free space on the second partition:

Have you backed up important data on your hard drive?	Location of backup:

© Cengage Learning 2013

Table 2-5 Checklist to complete before installing Windows

A+
220-802
1.1, 1.2

📝 **Notes** For new installations, look for the product key written on the cover of the Windows setup DVD or affixed to the back of the Windows documentation booklet, as shown in Figure 2-14. If you are reinstalling Windows on an existing system, look for the product key displayed in the System window. Click **Start**, right-click **Computer**, and select **Properties** from the shortcut menu. If Windows will not start, look for the product key sticker mounted on the side of a desktop or bottom of a laptop.

Product key for OEM version

Product key for retail version

© Cengage Learning 2013

Figure 2-14   The Windows 7 product key found on the inside of a retail package or on the outside of an OEM

Before we get into the step-by-step instructions of installing an OS, here are some general tips about installing Windows:

- ◢ Verify that you have all application software CDs or DVDs available and all device drivers.
- ◢ Back up all important data on the drive. How to perform backups is covered in Chapter 3.
- ◢ For upgrade installations and clean installs where you do not plan to reformat the hard drive, run antivirus software to make sure the drive is free from malware. If Windows will not start and you suspect malware might be a problem, plan to reformat the hard drive during the installation so you know the hard drive is clean of malware.
- ◢ If you want to begin the installation by booting from the Windows DVD or other media such as a USB device, use BIOS setup to verify that the boot sequence is first the optical drive or USB device, and then the hard drive.
- ◢ In BIOS setup, disable any virus protection setting that prevents the boot area of the hard drive from being altered.
- ◢ For a notebook computer, connect the AC adapter and use this power source for the complete OS installation, updates, and installation of hardware and applications. You don't want the battery to fail in the middle of the installation process.

📝 **Notes** If your current installation of Windows is corrupted, you might be able to repair the installation rather than reinstalling Windows. Chapter 6 covers what to do to fix a corrupted Windows installation.

A+
220-802
1.1, 1.2

Hands-on | Project 2.3 Preparing for Windows 7

Use the Windows 7 Compatibility Center at *www.microsoft.com/windows/compatibility/windows-7/en-us/default.aspx* to research whether a home or lab PC that does not have Windows 7 installed qualifies for Windows 7. Fill in the following table and print the web pages showing whether each hardware device and application installed on the PC qualifies for Windows 7.

Hardware Device or Application	Specific Device Name or Application Name and Version	Does It Qualify for Windows 7?
Motherboard or BIOS		
Video card		
Modem card (if present)		
Sound card (if present)		
Printer (if present)		
Network card (if present)		
CD-ROM drive (if present)		
DVD drive (if present)		
SCSI hard drive (if present)		
Other device		
Application 1		
Application 2		
Application 3		

INSTALLING WINDOWS 7

A+
220-802
1.2, 1.6,
4.6

In this part of the chapter, you learn the steps to install Windows 7 as an in-place upgrade, clean install, and dual boot, and what to do after the installation. As you install and configure software, be sure to document what you did. This documentation will be helpful for future maintenance and troubleshooting. In a project near the end of this chapter, you will develop a documentation template.

Let's begin with how to perform an in-place upgrade of Windows Vista to Windows 7.

STEPS TO PERFORMING A WINDOWS 7 IN-PLACE UPGRADE

Recall that an in-place upgrade begins after you have booted the system to the Windows desktop. An upgrade from Windows Vista to Windows 7 carries applications and user settings forward into the new installation. Follow these steps:

1. Close any open applications. If you have not already backed up important data and used antivirus software to scan the system for viruses, do so now. After the scan is finished, close the antivirus software so that it does not run in the background. Close other third-party software such as backup software that might be running in the background.

A+
220-802
1.2, 1.6,
4.6

2. Insert the Windows 7 DVD in the DVD drive. You can then launch Windows setup from the AutoPlay dialog box that appears (see Figure 2-15). If it does not appear, enter this command in the search box: **D:\setup.exe**, substituting the drive letter for your DVD drive for D. Respond to the Vista UAC (User Account Control) box.

© Cengage Learning 2013

Figure 2-15 Begin the Windows 7 installation from the AutoPlay box

> **Notes** Figure 2-16 shows the error message that appears when you try to upgrade a 32-bit OS to a 64-bit version of Windows 7.

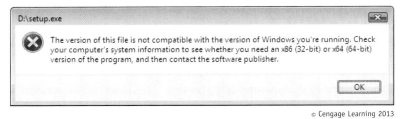

© Cengage Learning 2013

Figure 2-16 Error when running the 64-bit Windows 7 setup program from within a 32-bit operating system

3. The opening menu shown in Figure 2-17 appears. If you have not yet performed the Windows 7 Upgrade Advisor process, you can do so now by clicking *Check compatibility online*. To proceed with the installation, click **Install now**.

> **Notes** If your computer refuses to read from the DVD, verify that your optical drive is a DVD drive. Perhaps it is only a CD drive. If this is the case, refer to the section "When the Computer Does Not Have a DVD Drive" earlier in the chapter.

A+
220-802
1.2, 1.6,
4.6

Figure 2-17 Opening menu when you launch Windows 7 setup from within Windows

4. On the next screen, you can choose to allow the setup program to download updates for the installation (see Figure 2-18). If you have Internet access, click **Go online to get the latest updates for installation (recommended)**. Setup will download the updates. When using this option, you'll need to stay connected to the Internet throughout the installation.

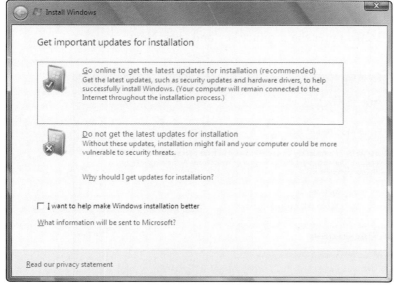

Figure 2-18 Allow setup to download updates for the installation process

5. On the next screen, accept the license agreement and click **Next**.

6. On the next screen, shown in Figure 2-19, select the type of installation you want, either Upgrade or Custom (advanced). The Upgrade option is only available when an existing version of Windows Vista or 7 is running. The Custom installation is a clean install. Select **Upgrade**.

A+
220-802
1.2, 1.6,
4.6

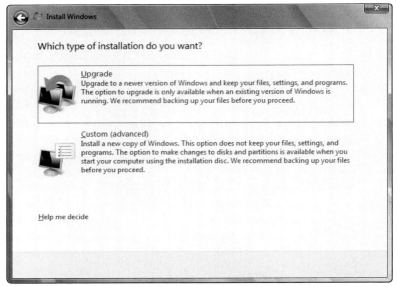

Figure 2-19 Select the type of installation you want

© Cengage Learning 2013

7. Setup will check for any compatibility issues. It will verify that the edition of Vista installed can be used as an upgrade path to the edition of Windows 7 you are installing according to the rules outlined earlier in Table 2-4. It will also verify that Windows Vista has a service pack applied. If setup finds a problem, an error message or a warning message appears. An error message requires that you end the installation and resolve the problem. A warning message allows you to click **Next** to continue with the installation.

8. The installation is now free to move forward. The PC might reboot several times. At the end of this process, a screen appears asking you for the product key (see Figure 2-20). Enter the product key and click **Next**.

Figure 2-20 Enter the product key

© Cengage Learning 2013

2

A+
220-802
1.2, 1.6,
4.6

Notes Notice in Figure 2-20 the check box *Automatically activate Windows when I'm online*. Normally, you would leave this option checked so that Windows 7 activates immediately. However, if you are practicing installing Windows 7 and intend to install it several times using the same DVD, you might choose to uncheck this box and not enter the product key during the installation. You can later decide to enter the product key and activate Windows after the installation is finished. You have 30 days before you must activate Windows.

9. On the following screen, you are asked how you want to handle Windows updates (see Figure 2-21). Unless your company has a different policy, click **Use recommended settings**.

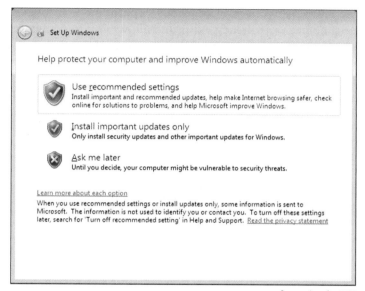

© Cengage Learning 2013

Figure 2-21   Decide how to handle Windows Updates

10. On the next screen, verify the time and date settings are correct and click **Next**.

11. On the next screen, select the network location (see Figure 2-22). Click the option that is appropriate to your network connection. If you need to change this setting later, use the Network and Sharing Center that you learned about in Chapter 1.

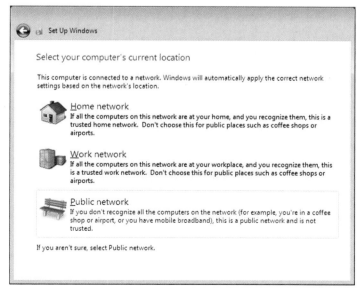

© Cengage Learning 2013

Figure 2-22   Select network settings

A+
220-802
1.2, 1.6,
4.6

Here is an explanation of each option:

▲ **Home network.** Network Discovery is turned on and you can join a homegroup. Network Discovery is a setting that allows this computer to see other computers on the network and other computers can see this computer.

▲ **Work network.** Network Discovery is turned on, you can join a domain, but you cannot join a homegroup.

▲ **Public network.** Network Discovery is turned off and you cannot join a homegroup or domain. This option is the most secure.

12. If you selected Home network in the previous step, the screen shown in Figure 2-23 appears when a homegroup already exists and allows you to configure your homegroup settings. In the figure, you are told that the user, Jean Andrews, has assigned a homegroup password on the computer BLUELIGHT. If setup does not find a homegroup on the network, it suggests a password for the new homegroup. Check what you want to share with others in the homegroup. Enter the password for an existing homegroup or verify/change the password for the new homegroup. Then click **Next** to create or join the homegroup. If you don't want to use a homegroup, click **Skip** to continue.

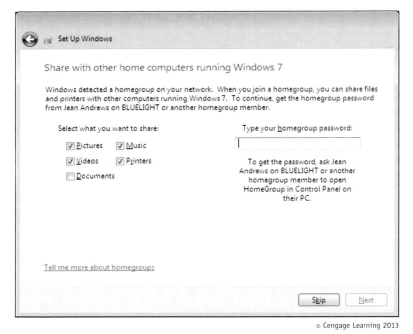

© Cengage Learning 2013

Figure 2-23 Configure your homegroup settings and password

> 📄 **Notes** To know what password has been assigned to an existing homegroup, go to a computer on the network that belongs to this homegroup. Open Control Panel and click **Choose homegroup and sharing options** under the Network and Internet group. On the next screen, click **View or print the homegroup password.**

13. Near the end of the installation, Windows Update downloads and installs updates and the system restarts. Finally, a logon screen appears. Log in with your user account and password. The Windows 7 desktop loads and the installation is complete.

A+
220-802
1.2, 1.6,
4.6

STEPS TO PERFORM A CLEAN INSTALL OR DUAL BOOT

To perform a clean install of Windows 7 or a dual boot with another OS, you can begin the installation from the Windows 7 DVD or from the Windows desktop:

◢ *If no operating system is installed on the PC, begin the installation by booting from the Windows 7 DVD*: Using this method, the Upgrade option is not available and you are forced to do a Custom installation, also called a clean install.

◢ *If an operating system is already installed on the PC, you can begin the installation from the Windows desktop or by booting from the Windows 7 DVD*: Either way, you can perform a Custom installation. If you are using an upgrade license of Windows 7, setup will verify that a Windows OS is present, which qualifies you to use the upgrade license. This is the method to use when upgrading from Windows XP to Windows 7; you are required to perform a clean install even though setup verifies that Windows XP is present.

◢ *If you are installing a 64-bit OS when a 32-bit OS is already installed or vice versa, you must begin the installation by booting from the DVD*: Setup still allows you to use the less expensive upgrade license even though you are performing a clean install because it is able to verify a Windows installation is present.

> **Notes** When setting up a dual boot, you might need to shrink a partition to make room for a second partition to hold Windows 7. If so, use Disk Management in Windows Vista to shrink the partition before you begin the Windows 7 installation. You can also use Disk Management to create a new partition to hold the Windows 7 installation and format that partition. The Windows 7 volume must be formatted using the NTFS file system. How to use Disk Management is covered in Chapter 3.

Follow these steps to begin the installation by booting from the Windows 7 DVD:

1. Insert the Windows 7 DVD in the DVD drive and start the system, booting directly from the DVD. If you have trouble booting from the disc, go into BIOS setup and verify that your first boot device is the optical drive. On the first screen (see Figure 2-24), select your language and other preferences and click **Next**.

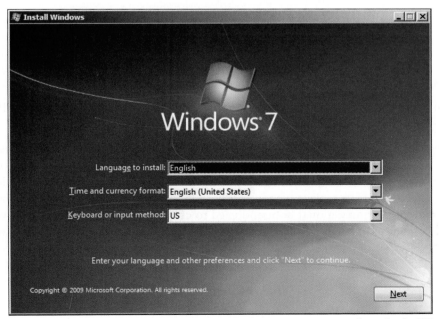

© Cengage Learning 2013

Figure 2-24   Select language, time, and keyboard options

Notes When installing Windows XP, you have to install third-party drivers at the beginning of the XP installation if your computer is using an array of hard drives working together (called RAID) or a hard drive with a SCSI hardware interface. However, Windows 7 or Vista setup has its own drivers for these situations, so no extra third-party drivers are needed. If you encounter a problem when installing Windows 7 using RAID or SCSI drives, such as a RAID or SCSI hard drive is not detected, know that the problem is a hardware or firmware problem and not a Windows setup problem.

2. The opening menu shown in Figure 2-25 appears. Click **Install now**.

Figure 2-25 Screen to begin the Windows 7 installation

© Cengage Learning 2013

3. On the next screen, accept the license agreement.

4. On the next screen, shown earlier in Figure 2-19, select the type of installation you want. Choose **Custom (advanced)**.

5. On the next screen, you will be shown a list of partitions on which to install the OS. For example, the computer shown in Figure 2-26 has one partition on one hard drive. If you want to use this partition for a clean install, click **Next**, which will cause Windows 7 to replace whatever other OS might be installed on this partition. If you are performing a dual boot and need to create a new partition, click **Drive options (advanced)**; setup will step you through the process of creating a new partition.

A+
220-802
1.2, 1.6,
4.6

2

Figure 2-26   Select a partition to install Windows 7 in a clean install or dual-boot environment

6. The installation is now free to move forward. At the end of this process, the window in Figure 2-27 appears asking for a username and computer name. Enter these values and click **Next**. On the next screen, you can enter a password for your user account by entering the password twice followed by a password hint. Then click **Next**.

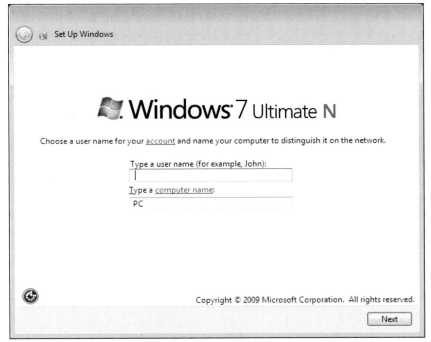

Figure 2-27   Choose a username and computer name

A+
220-802
1.2, 1.6,
4.6

7. The installation now continues the same way as an upgrade installation. You are asked to enter the product key, Windows update settings, time and date settings, and network settings. Windows Update downloads and installs updates and you are asked to restart the system. After the restart, the logon screen appears. After you log in, the Windows 7 desktop loads and the installation is complete.

After the installation, when you boot with a dual boot, the boot loader menu automatically appears and asks you to select an operating system, as shown in Figure 2-28.

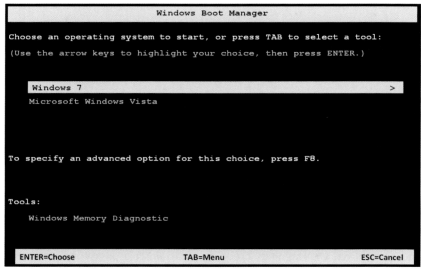

© Cengage Learning 2013

Figure 2-28 Boot loader menu in a dual-boot environment

When using a dual boot, you can execute an application while Windows 7 or Vista is loaded even if the application is installed under the other OS. If the application is not listed in the Start menu, locate the program file in Windows Explorer. Double-click the application to run it from Windows 7 or Vista. You should not have to install an application twice under each OS.

A+
220-802
1.2

USE THE WINDOWS 7 UPGRADE DVD ON A NEW HARD DRIVE

Windows 7 setup expects that an old OS is installed if you use the upgrade license DVD. This requirement presents a problem when you are replacing a hard drive. You have two options in this situation:

▲ *Install Vista or XP first and then install Windows 7*: You must also install a service pack under Vista or XP before you install Windows 7. This first option takes a long time!
▲ *Install Windows 7 twice*: Follow these steps:

1. Use the Windows 7 upgrade DVD to perform a clean install. When you get to the installation window that asks you to enter your product key, don't enter the key and uncheck **Automatically activate Windows when I'm online**. Complete the installation.

A+
220-802
1.2

2. From the Windows 7 desktop, start the installation routine again, but this time as an upgrade. Enter the product key during the installation and Windows 7 will activate with no problems.

> **Notes** If you have problems installing Windows, search the Microsoft web site (*support.microsoft.com*) for solutions. Windows 7 setup creates several log files during the installation that can help you solve a problem. The list can be found in the Microsoft Knowledge Base Article 927521 at this link: *support.microsoft.com/kb/927521*.

> **Vista Differences** Editions of Windows Vista are **Windows Vista Starter, Windows Vista Home Basic, Windows Vista Home Premium, Windows Vista Business, Windows Vista Enterprise**, and **Windows Vista Ultimate**. A Vista installation works the same as a Windows 7 installation. To find out about the editions of Vista and the differences in planning a Vista installation, see Appendix B.

> **XP Differences** Windows XP comes in **Windows XP Home Edition, Windows XP Professional, Windows XP Professional x64 Edition, Windows XP Media Center Edition**, and **Windows XP Tablet PC Edition**. An XP installation begins by booting from the XP setup CD or executing the Winnt32.exe program from the Windows desktop. To find out more about the features of XP editions and how to install and configure XP, see Appendix C.

Hands-on | Project 2.4   Using the Internet for Problem Solving

Access the *support.microsoft.com* web site for Windows 7 support. Print one article from the Knowledge Base that addresses a problem when installing Windows 7.

Hands-on | Project 2.5   Installing Windows 7

Follow the instructions in the chapter to install Windows 7 as either an upgrade or clean install. Write down each decision you had to make as you performed the installation. If you get any error messages during the installation, write them down and list the steps you took to recover from the error. How long did the installation take? If you have virtual machine software installed on your computer, you can do this project in the VM.

A+
220-802
1.2

Hands-on | Project 2.6 Installing Windows 7, Vista, or XP in a VM

Earlier in the chapter, in Hands-on Project 2-2, you installed Virtual PC on your computer. Use it to install a 32-bit version of Windows 7, Vista, or XP. (Virtual PC does not support a 64-bit OS.) You do not have to activate the OS and you will have 30 days to use it before it will not work. You can use this VM installation of Windows 7 in a project in the next chapter.

WHAT TO DO AFTER A WINDOWS INSTALLATION

A+
220-802
1.2, 1.5

After you have installed Windows, you need to do the following:

- Verify that you have network access.
- Activate Windows.
- Install updates and service packs for Windows
- Verify automatic updates are set as you want them.
- Install hardware.
- Install applications, including antivirus software.
- Set up user accounts and transfer or restore from backup user data and preferences to the new system.
- Turn Windows features on or off.

> **Notes** To protect your computer, don't surf the web for drivers or applications until you have installed Windows updates and service packs and also installed and configured antivirus software.

In addition, if you are installing Windows on a laptop, you will want to use Control Panel to configure power management settings. If you are installing an OEM (Original Equipment Manufacturer) version of Windows 7, look for a sticker on the outside of the DVD case. This sticker contains the product key and is called the Certificate of Authenticity. Put the sticker on the bottom of a laptop or the side or rear of a desktop computer (see Figure 2-29).

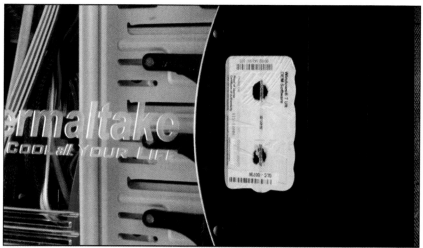

© Cengage Learning 2013

Figure 2-29 Paste the Windows 7 Certificate of Authenticity sticker on a new desktop

Now let's look at the details of the items in the preceding list.

VERIFY THAT YOU HAVE NETWORK ACCESS

When you install Windows 7, the setup process should connect you to the local network and to the Internet, if available. If you are working on a computer in a corporate environment using a Windows domain, follow these steps to join the computer to a domain:

1. Click the **Start** button, right-click **Computer**, and select **Properties** from the shortcut menu. The System window opens (see the left side of Figure 2-30).

© Cengage Learning 2013

Figure 2-30 Use the System window to change computer settings

2. Scroll down to the *Computer name, domain, and workgroup settings* group. Click **Change settings**. The System Properties dialog box displays, as shown in the right side of Figure 2-30. (If you are installing a Windows 7 Home edition, the Network ID button in the figure will be missing because these editions cannot join a domain.)

3. To join a domain, click **Network ID** and follow the directions on-screen to join the domain. To join the domain, you will need your username and password on the domain, the computer name, and the name of the domain. Your network administrator will have all that information. You will need to restart the computer before your changes will take effect.

> **Notes** If your computer is part of a Windows domain, when Windows starts up, it displays a blank screen instead of a logon screen. To log onto the domain, press Ctrl+Alt+Del to display the logon screen. If you want to log onto the local machine instead of the domain, type **.*username***. For example, to log onto the local machine using the local user account "Jean Andrews," type **.\\Jean Andrews**.

A+
220-802
1.2, 1.5

To verify that you have access to the local network and to the Internet, do the following:

1. Open Windows Explorer and verify that you can see other computers on the network (see Figure 2-31). Try to drill down to see shared resources on these computers.

© Cengage Learning 2013

Figure 2-31 Use Windows Explorer to access resources on your network

2. To verify that you have Internet access, open Internet Explorer and try to navigate to a couple of web sites.

3. If Windows Explorer does not show other computers on your network or you cannot access the Internet, use the Network and Sharing Center that you learned about in Chapter 1 to resolve the problem.

If the problem persists after you have tried the simple things suggested in Chapter 1, consider the problem might be the IP address, wireless network, or Network Discovery settings are wrong. How to configure network settings and troubleshoot network connections are covered in Chapters 7 and 8.

ACTIVATE WINDOWS 7

In order to make sure a valid Windows license has been purchased for each installation of Windows, Microsoft requires **product activation**. If you don't activate Windows 7 during the installation, you have 30 days to do so. To view the activation status and product key, open the System window. From this window, you can also change the product key before you activate the installation. If you fail to activate Windows after 30 days, the Windows desktop will not load and an error message appears forcing you to activate the OS.

To activate Windows 7, click the **Start** button and enter **activate** in the *Search* box and press **Enter**. The Windows Activation window opens (see Figure 2-32). Click **Activate Windows online now** to begin the process. If you have not yet entered a product key, the next screen allows you to do that.

2

© Cengage Learning 2013

Figure 2-32 The system has 30 days left before you must activate the installation

> **Notes** If you change the product key after Windows is activated, you must activate Windows again because the activation is tied to the product key and the system hardware. If you replace the motherboard or replace the hard drive and memory at the same time, you must also reactivate Windows.
>
> If you install Windows from the same DVD on a different computer, and you attempt to activate Windows from the new PC, a dialog box appears telling you of the suspected violation of the license agreement. You can call a Microsoft operator and explain what caused the discrepancy. If your explanation is reasonable (for example, you uninstalled Windows from one PC and installed it on another), the operator can issue you a valid certificate. You can then type the certificate value into a dialog box to complete the boot process.

INSTALL WINDOWS UPDATES AND SERVICE PACKS

The Microsoft web site offers patches, fixes, and updates for known problems and has an extensive knowledge base documenting problems and their solutions. It's important to keep these updates current on your system to fix known problems and plug up security holes that might allow viruses and worms in. Be sure to install updates before you attempt to install software or hardware.

To download and apply Windows updates, click **Start, All Programs**, and **Windows Update**. The Windows Update window appears, as shown in Figure 2-33. If important updates are available, a message displays. Click **important updates** to select updates to install. A list of updates appears. Select the ones you want to install.

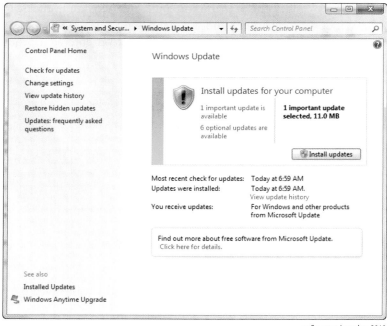

© Cengage Learning 2013

Figure 2-33 Download and install updates for your computer

Windows selects the updates in the order the system can receive them, and will not necessarily list all the updates you need on the first pass. After you have installed the updates listed, go back and start again until Windows Updates tells you there is nothing left to update. If Windows requests a restart after an update, do that before you install more updates. It might take two or more passes to get the PC entirely up to date.

If you see a service pack listed in the updates, install all the updates listed above it. Then install the service pack as the only update to install. It takes about 30 minutes and a reboot to download and install a service pack. Only the latest service pack for an OS will install because the latest service pack includes all the content from previous service packs.

Hands-on | Project 2.7   Updating Windows

On a Windows 7 system connected to the Internet, click **Start**, **All Programs**, and **Windows Update**. Windows Update searches the Microsoft web site and recommends Windows updates. Print the web page showing a list of recommended updates. For a lab PC, don't perform the updates unless you have your instructor's permission.

CONFIGURE AUTOMATIC UPDATES

During the Windows installation, you were asked how you want to handle Windows updates. To verify or change this setting, in the left pane of the Windows Update window, click **Change settings**. From the Change settings window, shown in Figure 2-34, you can decide how often, when, and how you want Windows to install updates. The recommended setting is to allow Windows to automatically download and install updates daily. However,

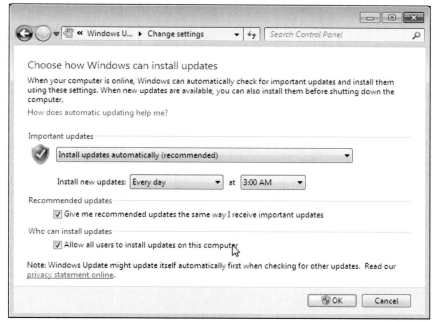

A+
220-802
1.2, 1.5

if you are not always connected to the Internet, your connection is very slow, or you want more control over which updates are installed, you might want to manage the updates differently.

Figure 2-34 Manage how and when Windows is updated

© Cengage Learning 2013

INSTALL HARDWARE

A+
220-802
1.2, 1.4,
1.5

You're now ready to install the hardware devices that were not automatically installed during the installation. As you install each device, reboot and verify that the software or device is working before you move on to the next item. Most likely, you will need to do the following:

▲ *Install the drivers for the motherboard*: If you were not able to connect to the network earlier in the installation process, it might be because the drivers for the network port on the motherboard are not installed. Installing the motherboard drivers can solve the problem. These drivers might come on a CD bundled with the motherboard, or you can use another computer to download them from the motherboard manufacturer web site. To start the installation, double-click a setup program on the CD or a program that was previously downloaded from the web.

▲ *Even though Windows has embedded video drivers, install the drivers that came with the video card so that you can use all the features the card offers*: These drivers are on disc or downloaded from the video card manufacturer web site.

▲ *Install the printer*: For a network printer, run the setup program that came with the printer and this program will find and install the printer on the network. Alternately, you can click **View devices and printers i**n Control Panel to open the Devices and Printers window (see Figure 2-35). Then click **Add a printer** and follow the directions on-screen. To install a local USB printer, all you have to do is plug in the USB printer, and Windows will install the printer automatically.

A+
220-802
1.2, 1.4,
1.5

▲ *For other hardware devices, always read and follow manufacturer directions for the installation*: Sometimes you are directed to install the drivers before you connect the device, and sometimes you will first need to connect the device.

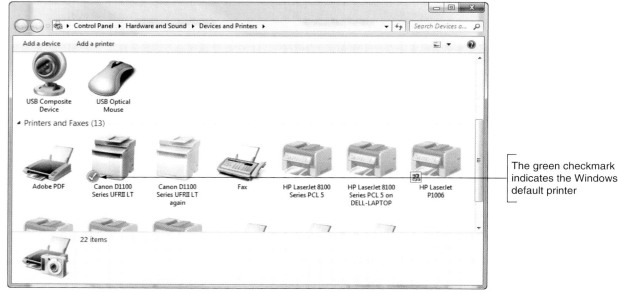

The green checkmark indicates the Windows default printer

© Cengage Learning 2013

Figure 2-35 Installed devices and printers

If a problem occurs while Windows is installing a device, it automatically launches the Action Center to help find a solution. For example, Figure 2-36 shows the error message window that appeared when a USB keyboard and USB printer were connected to a computer following a Windows 7 installation.

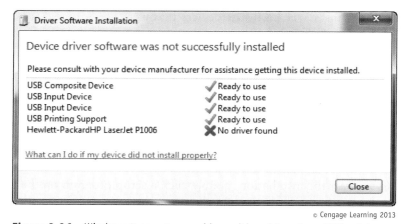

© Cengage Learning 2013

Figure 2-36 Windows 7 reports a problem with a driver for a USB printer

Immediately after this first window appeared, the window in Figure 2-37 appeared that is provided by the Action Center. When the user clicked **Click to download and install the new driver from the Hewlett-Packard Company website**, the driver was immediately downloaded and installed with no errors.

Recall from Chapter 1 that you can also open the Action Center at any time to see a list of problems and solutions. If the problem is still not resolved after following the solutions offered by the Action Center, turn to Device Manager.

A+
220-802
1.2, 1.4,
1.5

2

© Cengage Learning 2013

Figure 2-37 Windows offers to find the missing USB printer driver

USE DEVICE MANAGER

Device Manager (its program file is named devmgmt.msc) is your primary Windows tool for managing hardware. It lists all installed hardware devices and the drivers they use. Using Device Manager, you can disable or enable a device, update its drivers, uninstall a device, and undo a driver update (called a driver rollback).

> **A+ Exam Tip** The A+ 220-802 exam expects you to know in what scenario it is appropriate to use Device Manager. You also need to know how to use the utility and how to evaluate its results.

To access Device Manager, use one of these methods:

▲ Click **Start**, right-click **Computer**, and select **Properties**. The System window appears. Click **Device Manager**. The Device Manager window opens.
▲ Enter **Device Manager** or **Devmgmt.msc** in the search box and press **Enter**. A Device Manager window is shown in Figure 2-38.

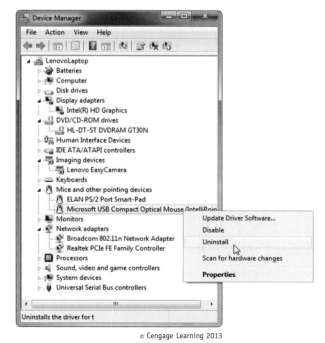

© Cengage Learning 2013

Figure 2-38 Use Device Manager to uninstall, disable, or enable a device

A+
220-802
1.2, 1.4,
1.5

Click a white arrow to expand the view of an item, and click a black arrow to collapse the view. Here are ways to use Device Manager to solve problems with a device:

◢ **Try uninstalling and reinstalling the device**: To uninstall the device, right-click the device and click **Uninstall** on the shortcut menu, as shown in Figure 2-38. Then reboot and reinstall the device, looking for problems during the installation that point to the source of the problem. Sometimes reinstalling a device is all that is needed to solve the problem. Notice in Figure 2-38 that the device selected is a USB mouse. Sometimes USB devices are listed in Device Manager and sometimes they are not.

◢ **Look for error messages offered by Device Manager**: To find out more information about a device, right-click the device and select **Properties** on the shortcut menu. The left side of Figure 2-39 shows the Properties box for the onboard wireless network adapter. Many times, a message shows up in this box reporting the source of the problem and suggesting a solution.

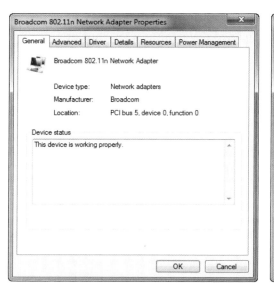 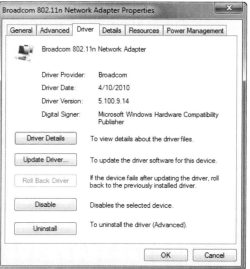

© Cengage Learning 2013

Figure 2-39 Use the device Properties box to solve problems with device drivers

◢ **Update the drivers**: Click the **Driver** tab (see the right side of Figure 2-39) to update the drivers and roll back (undo) a driver update.

APPLYING | CONCEPTS

Follow these steps to use Device Manager to update device drivers:

1. For best results, locate and download the latest driver files from the manufacturer's web site to your hard drive. Be sure to use 64-bit drivers for a 64-bit OS and 32-bit drivers for a 32-bit OS. If possible, use Windows 7 drivers for Windows 7, and Vista drivers for Vista.

2. Using Device Manger, right-click the device and select **Properties** from the shortcut menu. The Properties window for that device appears. Select the **Driver** tab and click **Update Driver**. The Update Driver Software box opens (see Figure 2-40).

2

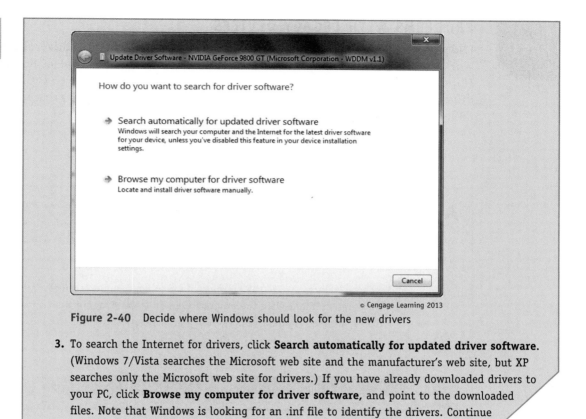

© Cengage Learning 2013

Figure 2-40 Decide where Windows should look for the new drivers

3. To search the Internet for drivers, click **Search automatically for updated driver software**. (Windows 7/Vista searches the Microsoft web site and the manufacturer's web site, but XP searches only the Microsoft web site for drivers.) If you have already downloaded drivers to your PC, click **Browse my computer for driver software**, and point to the downloaded files. Note that Windows is looking for an .inf file to identify the drivers. Continue to follow the directions on-screen to complete the installation.

Notes By default, Device Manager hides legacy devices that are not Plug and Play. To view installed legacy devices, click the **View** menu of Device Manager, and check **Show hidden devices** (see Figure 2-41).

© Cengage Learning 2013

Figure 2-41 By default, Windows does not display legacy devices in Device Manager; you show these hidden devices by using the View menu

A+
220-802
1.2, 1.4,
1.5

PROBLEMS WITH LEGACY DEVICES

Older hardware devices might present a problem. A Windows Vista driver is likely to work in the Windows 7 installation because Vista and Windows 7 are so closely related. If the driver does not load correctly or gives errors, first search the web for a Windows 7 driver. If you don't find one, try running the Vista driver installation program in compatibility mode.

APPLYING CONCEPTS In the example that follows, we're using the installation program for a memory card reader/writer that worked under Vista, but did not load correctly when we installed Windows 7. Follow these steps to use compatibility mode with the driver installation program:

1. Using Windows Explorer, locate the program file with an .exe file extension for the driver installation program. Right-click the program file and select **Troubleshoot compatibility** from the shortcut menu (see Figure 2-42). The Program Compatibility utility launches.

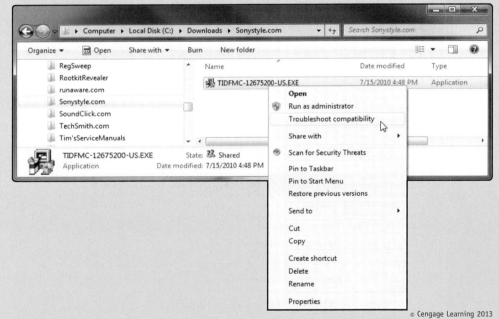

© Cengage Learning 2013

Figure 2-42 Run the Program Compatibility utility from the shortcut menu of the program that is giving a problem

2. On the first screen of the troubleshooter utility (see Figure 2-43), select **Troubleshoot program**.

A+
220-802
1.2, 1.4,
1.5

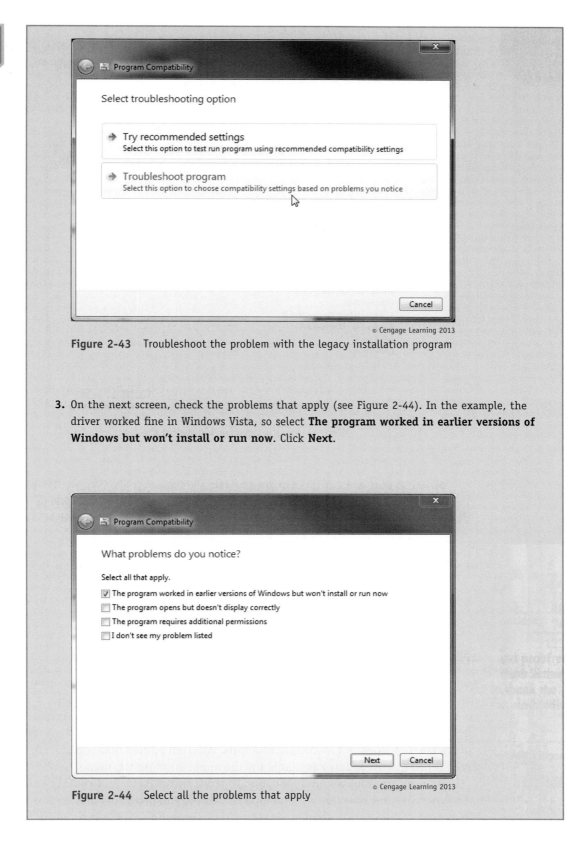

© Cengage Learning 2013

Figure 2-43 Troubleshoot the problem with the legacy installation program

3. On the next screen, check the problems that apply (see Figure 2-44). In the example, the driver worked fine in Windows Vista, so select **The program worked in earlier versions of Windows but won't install or run now**. Click **Next**.

© Cengage Learning 2013

Figure 2-44 Select all the problems that apply

A+
220-802
1.2, 1.4,
1.5

4. On the next screen, the troubleshooter asks for the OS with which the program worked (see Figure 2-45). For this example, you would select **Windows Vista (Service Pack 2)** and click **Next**.

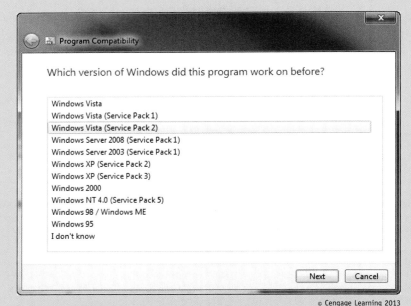

Figure 2-45 shows the Program Compatibility dialog with the question "Which version of Windows did this program work on before?" and the following options:

- Windows Vista
- Windows Vista (Service Pack 1)
- Windows Vista (Service Pack 2)
- Windows Server 2008 (Service Pack 1)
- Windows Server 2003 (Service Pack 1)
- Windows XP (Service Pack 2)
- Windows XP (Service Pack 3)
- Windows 2000
- Windows NT 4.0 (Service Pack 5)
- Windows 98 / Windows ME
- Windows 95
- I don't know

© Cengage Learning 2013

Figure 2-45 Select the operating system with which the program worked

5. On the next screen, click **Start the program** and respond to the UAC box. The program runs and successfully installs the drivers for the memory card device. Checking Device Manager shows no errors with the device. When you test the device, it can both read and write data to a memory card. Compatibility mode worked for this particular driver.

A+
220-802
1.2, 1.5

INSTALL APPLICATIONS

One application you want to be sure to install is antivirus software. To install applications, insert the setup CD or DVD, and follow the directions on-screen to launch the installation routine. For software downloaded from the Internet, open Windows Explorer and double-click the program filename to begin the installation. If you get errors, know that Chapter 5 covers what to do when an installation fails. After an application is installed, you might also need to install any updates available for the application on the manufacturer's web site.

If you need to uninstall an application, open Control Panel and click **Uninstall a program**. The Programs and Features window appears listing the programs installed on this computer where you can uninstall, change, or repair these programs. Select a program from the list. Based on the software, the buttons at the top of the list will change. For example, in Figure 2-46, the Camtasia Studio 7 software offers the option to Uninstall, Change, or Repair the software.

A+
220-802
1.2, 1.5

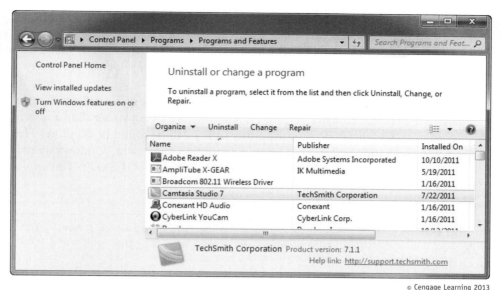

Figure 2-46 Select a program from the list to view your options to manage the software

A+
220-802
1.1, 1.2,
1.5

SET UP USER ACCOUNTS AND TRANSFER USER DATA

To set up a new user account, first log on using an administrator account and then do the following:

1. Open Control Panel and click **Add or remove user accounts**. In the Manage Accounts window, click **Create a new account**.

2. In the next window, enter the username (see Figure 2-47). Select if the account will be a standard user or administrator account. Click **Create Account**.

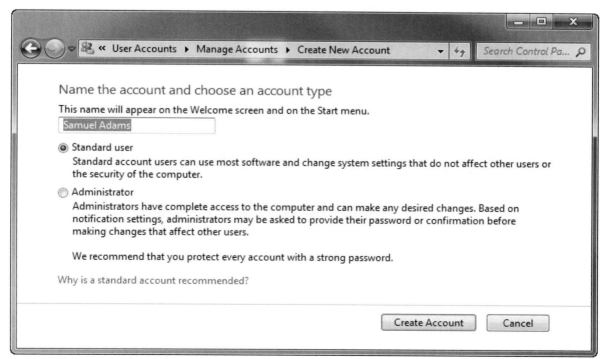

Figure 2-47 Decide the privilege level for the new account

A+
220-802
1.1, 1.2,
1.5

3. To create a password for the account, in the Manage Accounts window, click the account icon and then click **Create a password**. Enter the new password and click **Create password**. The first time a user logs onto the account, user files and folders (called the user profile) are created in the C:\Users folder.

For individuals or small organizations, use Windows Easy Transfer in Windows 7/Vista or Files and Settings Transfer Wizard in Windows XP to copy user data and settings from one computer to another. How to use either utility can be found in Windows Help and Support for each operating system. For large corporations that use a Windows domain, a more advanced tool is required, the User State Migration Tool (USMT). This tool is discussed later in the chapter.

> **Notes** After moving user data and settings from one PC to another, the best practice is to leave the user data and settings on the original PC untouched for at least two months. This practice gives the user plenty of time to make sure everything has been moved over.

A+
220-802
1.2, 1.5

TURN WINDOWS 7 FEATURES ON OR OFF

You can save on system resources by turning off Windows features you will not use, and you might need to turn on some features that are, by default, turned off. To control Windows features, in the left pane of the Programs and Features window, click **Turn Windows features on or off** (refer to Figure 2-46). The Windows Features box opens (see Figure 2-48). Check or uncheck the features you want or don't want and then click **OK**.

© Cengage Learning 2013

Figure 2-48 Turn Windows features on or off

The Windows installation, devices, applications, and user accounts should now be good to go. Restart the computer and make one last check that all is well. Now would be a good time to complete your documentation and make a backup of the entire Windows volume in the event of a hard drive failure or corrupted installation. How to make backups is covered in Chapter 3.

**A+
220-802
1.2, 1.5**

Hands-on | Project 2.8 Creating a Documentation Form

Create a document that technicians can use when installing Windows 7 and performing all the chores mentioned in the chapter that need doing after the installation. The document needs a checklist of what to do before the installation and a checklist of what to do after the installation. It also needs a place to record decisions made during the installation, the applications and hardware devices installed, user accounts created, and any other important information that might be useful for future maintenance or troubleshooting. Don't forget to include a way to identify the computer, the name of the technician doing the work, and when the work was done.

SPECIAL CONCERNS WHEN WORKING IN A LARGE ENTERPRISE

**A+
220-802
1.2, 1.4,
1.5**

Working as a PC support technician in a large corporate environment is different from working as a PC support technician for a small company or with individuals. In this part of the chapter, you will learn how Windows is installed on computers in an enterprise and a little about providing ongoing technical support for Windows in these organizations.

DEPLOYMENT STRATEGIES FOR WINDOWS 7

Earlier in the chapter, you learned how to install Windows 7 using the setup DVD or using files downloaded from the Microsoft web site. You perform the installation while sitting at the computer, responding to each query made by the setup program. Then you must configure Windows and install device drivers and applications. If, however, you were responsible for installing Windows 7 on several hundred PCs in a large corporation, you might want a less time-consuming method to perform the installations. These methods are called deployment strategies. A deployment strategy is a procedure to install Windows, device drivers, and applications on a computer and can include the process to transfer user settings, application settings, and user data files from an old installation to the new installation.

Microsoft suggests four deployment strategies; the one chosen depends on the number of computers to be deployed and determines the amount of time you must sit in front of an individual computer as Windows is installed (this time is called the touch time). As a PC support technician in a large corporation, most likely you would not be involved in choosing or setting up the deployment strategy. But you need to be aware of the different strategies so that you have a general idea of what will be expected of you when you are asked to provide desk-side or help-desk support as Windows is being deployed in your organization.

The four deployment strategies are discussed next.

HIGH-TOUCH WITH RETAIL MEDIA (RECOMMENDED FOR FEWER THAN 100 COMPUTERS)

The high-touch with retail media strategy is the strategy used in the installations described earlier in the chapter. All the work is done by a technician sitting at the computer. To save time doing multiple installations, you can copy the setup files on the Windows setup DVD to a file server on the network and share the folder. Then at each computer, you can execute the Setup program on the server to perform a clean install or upgrade of the OS. A server used in this way is called a distribution server. Except for upgrade installations, applications must be manually installed after the OS is installed.

To transfer (called migrating) user settings, application settings, and user data files to a new installation, you can use Windows 7/Vista Windows Easy Transfer (a manual process that is easy to use) or the User State Migration Tool (more automated and more difficult to set up and use). Windows Easy Transfer is part of Windows 7/Vista, and XP offers a similar tool called the Files and Settings Transfer Wizard. The User State Migration Tool (USMT) is a command-line tool that works only when the computer is a member of a Windows domain. USMT is included in the Windows Automated Installation Kit (AIK) that can be downloaded from the Microsoft web site. The Windows AIK for Windows 7 contains a group of tools used to deploy Windows 7 in a large organization.

HIGH-TOUCH WITH STANDARD IMAGE (RECOMMENDED FOR 100 TO 200 COMPUTERS)

To use the high-touch using a standard image strategy, a system administrator prepares an image, called a standard image that includes Windows 7, drivers, and applications that are standard to all the computers that might use the image. A standard image is hardware independent, meaning it can be installed on any computer. (In Chapter 3, you learn to use Windows Backup and Restore to create another type of image, called a system image that can only be used on the computer that created it.)

> **A+ Exam Tip** The A+ 220-802 exam expects you to know about creating a standard image.

Drive-imaging software is used to clone the entire hard drive to another bootable media in a process called drive imaging or disk cloning. Tools included in the Windows AIK or third-party software can be used. Examples of third-party drive-imaging software are True Image by Acronis (*www.acronis.com*), Norton Ghost by Symantec Corp (*www.symantec.com*), and Clonezilla, freeware managed by NCHC (*www.clonezilla.org*). A standard image is usually stored on an 8 GB or larger bootable USB flash drive (UFD) or on a bootable DVD along with Windows setup files. How to create a standard image using the Windows AIK is covered in Appendix D. The process uses several tools that you will learn to use in Chapters 3 and 6.

> **Notes** To see an introduction to creating a standard image, check out this video at the Microsoft Technet site: *technet.microsoft.com/en-us/windows/ee530017.aspx*.

Installing a standard image on another computer is called image deployment, which always results in a clean install rather than an upgrade. To begin, boot the computer from the bootable UFD or DVD that contains the image. A menu appears to begin the Windows installation. When you finish this Windows installation, the standard image is installed. USMT can then be used to transfer user settings, user data files, and application settings to the new installation.

The high-touch using a standard image strategy takes longer to set up than the previous strategy because a system administrator must prepare the image and must set up USMT, but it takes less time to install on each computer and also assures the administrator that each computer has a standard set of drivers and applications that are configured correctly.

LITE-TOUCH, HIGH-VOLUME DEPLOYMENT (RECOMMENDED FOR 200 TO 500 COMPUTERS)

The lite-touch, high-volume deployment strategy uses a deployment server on the network to serve up the installation after a technician starts the process. The files in the installation include Windows, device drivers, and applications, and collectively are called the distribution share.

2

The technician starts the installation by booting the computer to Windows PE. **Windows Preinstallation Environment (Windows PE)** is a minimum operating system used to start the installation. It is included in the Windows AIK and can be installed on a USB flash drive, CD, or DVD to make the device bootable. The technician boots from the device, which might be configured to display a menu to choose from multiple distribution shares available on the deployment server.

The technician can also boot the PC directly to the network to receive Windows PE from the deployment server. To boot to the network, use BIOS setup to set the first item in the boot device priority to be Ethernet (see Figure 2-49). Then reboot the system. Startup BIOS boots to the **Preboot eXecution Environment (PXE, also known as the Pre-Execution Environment)** that is contained in the BIOS code on the motherboard. PXE searches for a server on the network to provide a bootable operating system (Windows PE on the deployment server).

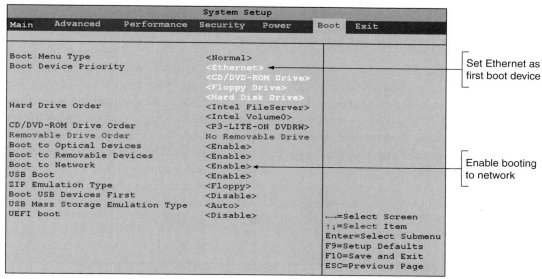

© Cengage Learning 2013

Figure 2-49 Configure BIOS setup to boot to the network

After the installation begins, the technician is not required to respond to prompts by the setup program, which is called an **unattended installation**. These responses, such as the administrator password or domain name, are stored in an **answer file**. The User State Migration Tool is then used to transfer user settings, user data files, and application settings to the new installation.

For high-touch strategies, a technician would normally sit at a computer and use the Windows 7 Upgrade Advisor to determine if the system qualifies for Windows 7 before Windows 7 is installed. Using lite-touch deployments, a more automated method of qualifying a computer is preferred. The **Microsoft Assessment and Planning (MAP) Toolkit** can be used by a system administrator from a network location to query hundreds of computers in a single scan. The software automatically examines hardware and applications on each computer to verify compatibility with Windows 7. The MAP software might also be used by the system administrator before deciding to deploy a new OS to determine what computer hardware upgrades or application software upgrades are required that must be included in the overall deployment budget.

A+
220-802
1.2, 1.4,
1.5

ZERO-TOUCH, HIGH-VOLUME DEPLOYMENT (RECOMMENDED FOR MORE THAN 500 COMPUTERS)

The zero-touch, high-volume deployment strategy is the most difficult to set up and requires complex tools. The installation does not require the user to start the process (called pull automation). Rather, the installation uses push automation, meaning that a server automatically pushes the installation to a computer when a user is not likely to be sitting at it. The entire remote network installation is automated and no user intervention is required. The process can turn on a computer that is turned off and even works when no OS is installed on the computer or the current OS is corrupted.

> **Notes** PC support technicians find that large enterprises appreciate quick and easy solutions to desktop or laptop computer problems. Technicians quickly learn their marching orders are almost always "replace or reimage." Little time is given to trying to solve the underlying problem when hardware can quickly be replaced or a Windows installation can quickly be reimaged.

USING THE USMT SOFTWARE

Let's look briefly at what to expect when using the USMT software. The Windows 7 version of USMT is version 4.0, is much improved over earlier versions, and is included in the Windows AIK software. To prepare to use USMT, a system administrator must first install the AIK software on his computer. In Microsoft documentation, this computer is called the technician computer. The source computer is the computer from which the user settings, application settings, and user data files are taken. The destination computer is the computer that is to receive this data. Sometimes the source computer and the destination computer are the same computer. An example is when you perform a clean installation of Windows 7 on a computer that has Windows XP installed and you want to transfer user files and settings from the XP installation to the Windows 7 installation.

> **Notes** USMT 4.0 is the first version of USMT to use hard-link migration of user files and settings when the source computer and the destination computer are the same computer. Hard-link migration does not actually copy files and settings, but leaves them on the hard drive without copying. This method makes USMT extremely fast when the hard drive is not formatted during the Windows installation.

The USMT software uses two commands: the scanstate command copies settings and files from the source computer to a safe location, and the loadstate command applies these settings and files to the destination computer. Here are the general steps to use USMT:

1. Download and install the AIK software on the technician computer.
2. Copy the USMT program files from the technician computer to the source computer.
3. Run the scanstate command on the source computer to copy user files and settings to a file server or other safe location.
4. Install Windows 7, device drivers, and applications on the destination computer.
5. Run the loadstate command to apply user files and settings from the file server to the destination computer.

2

💡 **A+ Exam Tip** The A+ 220-802 exam expects you to know about the User State Migration Tool (USMT) and the scanstate and loadstate commands.

The details of the parameters for the scanstate and loadstate commands are not covered in this book. Most likely these commands are stored in batch files provided by the system administrator. A batch file has a .bat file extension and contains a list or batch of OS commands that are executed as a group. These batch files might be automatically executed as part of a zero-touch installation or manually executed in a lite-touch or high-touch installation. To manually execute a batch file, you type the name of the batch file at a command prompt.

📑 **Notes** For detailed instructions on using USMT that a system administrator might use, go to *technet.microsoft.com* and search on *using USMT for IT professionals*.

Hands-on | Project 2.9 — Investigating the Windows Automated Installation Kit (AIK)

The Windows Automated Installation Kit (AIK) is a group of tools and documentation that IT professionals can use to deploy Windows and can be downloaded for free from the Microsoft web site. Here are the tools included in the AIK:

◢ User State Migration Tool (USMT) that you learned about in this chapter

◢ **ImageX**, used to create and modify standard images

◢ Deployment Image Servicing and Management (DISM), used to apply updates, drivers, and language packs to an existing Windows image

◢ Windows System Image Manager (SIM), used to create answer files and manage distribution shares and images

◢ Windows Preinstallation Environment (Windows PE), the minimal operating system that is used to install Windows. Place it on a DVD, USB flash drive, or other media to make the media bootable.

Search the Microsoft TechNet Library at *technet.microsoft.com/en-us/library/default.aspx* for information about each tool. Write a short paragraph about each tool that you think would be helpful to someone learning about the tool or how to use it. Share this information with others in your class. As you share with others, everyone gets a better understanding of these tools used to automate a Windows deployment.

>> CHAPTER SUMMARY

How to Plan a Windows Installation

◢ The Windows 7 editions are Windows 7 Starter, Home Basic, Home Premium, Professional, Enterprise, and Ultimate.

◢ Windows can be purchased as the less expensive OEM version or the more expensive retail version. The OEM version can only be installed on a new PC for resale.

◢ Each edition of Windows 7 can be purchased using 32-bit or 64-bit code, except the Starter edition uses 32-bit code.

◢ A 32-bit OS cannot address as much memory as a 64-bit OS. A 64-bit OS performs better and requires more memory than a 32-bit OS.

◢ Before purchasing Windows, make sure your system meets the minimum hardware requirements and all the hardware and applications will work under the OS. A 64-bit OS requires 64-bit drivers.

◢ Windows can be installed from the setup DVD, from files downloaded from the Internet, from a hidden partition on the hard drive (called a factory recovery partition), or in a virtual machine.

◢ Windows can be installed as an in-place upgrade, a clean installation, or in a dual boot environment with another OS.

◢ A hard drive contains one or more partitions or volumes. Normally, Windows is installed on the C: volume in the C:\Windows folder.

◢ Windows supports two types of user accounts. An administrator account has more rights than a standard account.

◢ A Windows computer can use a homegroup, workgroup, or domain configuration to join a network. Using a workgroup or homegroup, each computer on the network is responsible for sharing its resources with other computers on the network. In a domain, the domain controller manages network resources. Windows Home editions cannot join a domain. Windows Starter and Home Basic can join a homegroup but cannot create one.

Installing Windows 7

◢ A technician needs to know how to perform Windows 7 as an in-place upgrade, a clean install, or a dual boot. In addition, you need to know how to install Windows on a new hard drive when using an upgrade license of the Windows setup DVD.

◢ Editions of Windows Vista are Vista Starter, Home Basic, Home Premium, Business, Enterprise, and Ultimate. A Vista installation works the same as a Windows 7 installation.

◢ Editions of XP are Home Edition, XP Professional, XP Professional x64 Edition, Media Center Edition, and Tablet PC Edition.

What to Do After a Windows Installation

◢ After a Windows installation, verify you have network access, activate Windows, install any Windows updates or service packs, verify automatic updates is configured correctly, install hardware and applications, create user accounts, and turn Windows features on or off.

Special Concerns When Working in a Large Enterprise

◢ Four deployment strategies for installing Windows are high-touch with retail media, high-touch with a standard image, lite-touch with high volume, and zero-touch with high volume. Which strategy to use depends on the number of computers to deploy. Zero-touch deployments require the most time to set up, but do not require a technician to be at the computer when the installation happens.

>> KEY TERMS

For explanations of key terms, see the Glossary near the end of the book.

Active Directory
administrator account
answer file
batch file
boot loader menu
Certificate of Authenticity
clean install
client/server
compatibility mode
custom installation
Device Manager
disk cloning
distribution server
distribution share
domain
drive imaging
dual boot
file system
Files and Settings Transfer Wizard
global account
high-touch using a standard image
high-touch with retail media
homegroup
image deployment
ImageX
in-place upgrade
ISO image
lite-touch, high-volume deployment

loadstate
local account
logical topology
Microsoft Assessment and Planning (MAP) Toolkit
multiboot
OEM (Original Equipment Manufacturer) license
partition
peer-to-peer (P2P)
physical topology
Preboot eXecution Environment (PXE, also known as the Pre-Execution Environment)
product activation
Programs and Features
pull automation
push automation
remote network installation
scanstate
setup BIOS
standard image
startup BIOS
system BIOS (basic input/output system)
unattended installation
upgrade paths
User State Migration Tool (USMT)
virtual machine (VM)

volume
Windows 7 Enterprise
Windows 7 Home Basic
Windows 7 Home Premium
Windows 7 Professional
Windows 7 Starter
Windows 7 Ultimate
Windows Automated Installation Kit (AIK)
Windows Easy Transfer
Windows Preinstallation Environment (Windows PE)
Windows Vista Business
Windows Vista Enterprise
Windows Vista Home Basic
Windows Vista Home Premium
Windows Vista Starter
Windows Vista Ultimate
Windows XP Home Edition
Windows XP Media Center Edition
Windows XP Mode
Windows XP Professional
Windows XP Professional x64 Edition
Windows XP Tablet PC Edition
workgroup
zero-touch, high-volume deployment

>> REVIEWING THE BASICS

1. Which edition of Windows 7 comes only in a 32-bit version?

2. What is the maximum amount of memory a 64-bit version of Windows 7 Home Premium can support?

3. How much free space on the hard drive is required to install a 64-bit version of Windows 7?

4. How do you start the process to reinstall an OS on a laptop computer using the backup files stored on a recovery partition?

5. What are three free applications mentioned in the chapter that can be used to create virtual machines?

6. When upgrading from Windows XP to Windows 7, can you perform an in-place upgrade of Windows 7?

7. What must be installed in Windows Vista before you can perform an in-place upgrade from Vista to Windows 7?

8. Which file system is used on the volume where Windows is installed?

9. What is the minimum number of partitions required on a hard drive that is to be set up as a dual boot with Windows 7 and Windows XP?

10. Is the built-in administrator account in Windows 7 enabled or disabled by default? In Windows XP?

11. Which gives better security, workgroup sharing or homegroup sharing? Why?

12. Why will homegroup sharing not work on a network that has a mix of Windows XP, Vista, and 7 computers?

13. During a Windows 7 installation, what network location should you choose when you intend to join the computer to a domain? When you intend to join a homegroup?

14. What is the name of the domain controller database used by Windows Server 2011?

15. If you suspect a PC is infected with a virus, why is it not a good idea to perform an upgrade installation of Windows rather than a clean install?

16. After setting up a dual boot installation with Windows 7 and Vista, how do you boot the system into Vista?

17. What dialog box can you use to change the computer name after Windows 7 is installed?

18. Is the Windows 7 setup disc a CD or DVD? Vista setup disc? XP setup disc?

19. After a Windows installation, what is the easiest way to determine that you have Internet access?

20. How many days do you normally have after a Windows installation to activate the OS?

21. What window in Windows 7 is used to solve connectivity problems on the network?

22. What Windows 7 tool can you use to migrate user data and settings from a Windows Vista installation on one computer to the new Windows 7 installation on a different computer?

23. What is your primary Windows tool for managing hardware devices?

24. What window is used to uninstall an application in Windows 7?

25. Are you required to enter the product key during the Windows 7 installation? During the XP installation?

26. Using an unattended installation of Windows, what is the name of the file that holds the responses a technician would normally give during the installation?

27. What are the two commands used by the User State Migration tool?

28. To use the User State Migration tool, how must a computer join the network?

29. Where is the PXE programming code stored that is used to boot a computer when it is searching for an OS on the network?

30. Which boot device should be set as the first boot device in BIOS setup when a technician is configuring a computer to launch Windows PE on the deployment server?

>> THINKING CRITICALLY

1. You are planning an upgrade from Windows Vista to Windows 7. Your system uses a network card that you don't find listed on the Microsoft Windows 7 list of compatible devices. What do you do next?

   a. Abandon the upgrade and continue to use Windows Vista.

   b. Check the web site of the network card manufacturer for a Windows 7 driver.

   c. Buy a new network card.

   d. Install a dual boot for Windows Vista and Windows 7 and only use the network when you have Windows Vista loaded.

2. You have just installed Windows 7 and now attempt to install your favorite game that worked fine under Windows XP. When you attempt the installation, you get an error. What is your best next step?

   a. Purchase a new version of your game, one that is compatible with Windows 7.

   b. Download any service packs or patches to Windows 7.

   c. Reinstall Windows XP.

   d. Install Windows XP Mode to run the game.

3. If you find out that Windows 7 does not support one of your applications and you still want to use Windows 7, what can you do to solve this incompatibility problem?

4. Is it possible to install Windows 7 on a system that does not have a DVD drive? Explain your answer.

>> REAL PROBLEMS, REAL SOLUTIONS

REAL PROBLEM 2-1: A Corrupted Windows Installation

As a PC support technician for a small organization, it's your job to support the PCs, the small network, and the users. One of your coworkers, Jason, comes to you in a panic. His Windows 7 system won't boot, and he has lots of important data files in several locations on the drive. He has no idea in which folder some of the files are located. Besides the applications data he's currently working on, he's especially concerned about losing email addresses, email, and his Internet Explorer Favorites links.

After trying everything you know about recovering Windows 7, you conclude the OS is corrupted beyond repair. You decide there might be a way to remove the hard drive from Jason's computer and connect it to another computer so that you can recover the data. Search the Internet and find a device that you can use to connect Jason's hard drive to another computer using a USB port on that computer. The hard drive uses a SATA hard drive interface. Print the web page showing the device and its price.

REAL PROBLEM 2-2: Troubleshooting an Upgrade

Your friend, Thomas, has upgraded his Windows Vista laptop to Windows 7. After the installation, he discovers his media card reader does not work. He calls you on the phone asking you what to do. Do the following to plan your troubleshooting approach:

1. List the questions you should ask Thomas to help diagnose the problem.

2. List the steps you would take if you were sitting at the computer solving the problem.

3. What do you think is the source of the problem? Explain your answer.

Maintaining Windows

In the last chapter, you learned how to install Windows. This chapter takes you to the next step in learning how to support a Windows operating system: maintaining the OS after it is installed. Most Windows problems stem from poor maintenance. If you are a PC support technician responsible for the ongoing support of several computers, you can make your work easier and your users happier by setting up and executing a good maintenance plan for each computer you support. A well-maintained computer gives fewer problems and performs better than one that is not maintained. In this chapter, you will learn how to schedule regular maintenance tasks, how to prepare for disaster by setting up backup routines for user data and system files, how to use commands to manage files and folders, how to manage a hard drive, and how to set up Windows to use multiple languages.

In this chapter, we use Windows 7 as our primary OS, but, as you read, know that we'll point out any differences between Windows 7 and Windows Vista/XP so that you can use this chapter to study all three operating systems. As you read, you might consider following the steps in the chapter first using a Windows 7 system, and then going through the chapter again using a Windows Vista or XP system.

Vista Differences For more details about maintaining Windows Vista and Windows XP, see the extra content, "Maintaining Windows Vista and XP," in the online content for this book at *www.cengagebrain.com*. See the Preface for more information.

SCHEDULED PREVENTIVE MAINTENANCE

Regular preventive maintenance can keep a Windows computer performing well for years. At least once a month, you need to verify critical Windows settings and clean up the hard drive. These skills are covered in this part of the chapter. If you notice the system is slow as you do this maintenance, you need to dig deeper to optimize Windows. How to optimize Windows is covered in Chapter 4.

> **Notes** When you're responsible for a computer, be sure to keep good records of all that you do to maintain, upgrade, or fix the computer. When performing preventive maintenance, take notes and include those in your documentation.

VERIFY CRITICAL WINDOWS SETTINGS

Three Windows settings discussed here are critical for keeping the system protected from malware and hackers. Users sometimes change these settings without realizing their importance. Check the three settings and, if you find settings that are incorrect, take time to explain to the primary user of the computer how important these settings are. Here are the critical Windows settings you need to verify:

- *Windows Updates.* Install any important Windows updates or service packs that are waiting to be installed and verify that Windows Updates is configured to automatically allow updating. You learned how to configure Windows Updates in Chapter 2.
- *Antivirus software.* To protect a system against malicious attack, you also need to verify that antivirus software is configured to scan the system regularly and that it is up to date. If you discover it is not scanning regularly, take the time to do a thorough scan for viruses.
- *Network location setting.* To secure the computer against attack from the network, check that the Windows 7 network location is set correctly. How to verify the network location is covered in Chapter 2. Further details of configuring network security are discussed in Chapter 7.

CLEAN UP THE HARD DRIVE

For best performance, Windows needs about 15 percent free space on the hard drive that it uses for defragmenting the drive, for burning CDs and DVDs, and for a variety of other tasks, so it's important to delete unneeded files occasionally. In addition, you can improve drive performance and free up space by defragmenting the drive, checking the drive for errors, compressing folders, and moving files and folders to other drives. All these tasks are discussed in the following subsections. We begin by learning where Windows puts important folders on the drive.

DIRECTORY STRUCTURES

Folder or directory locations you need to be aware of include those for user files, program files, and Windows data. In the folder locations given in this discussion, we assume Windows is installed on drive C:.

User Profile Namespace

When a user first logs onto Windows 7/Vista, a **user profile** is created, which is a collection of user data and settings, and consists of two general items:

- *A user folder together with its subfolders.* These items are created under the C:\Users folder, for example, C:\Users\Jean Andrews. This folder contains a group of subfolders collectively called the **user profile namespace**. (In general, a namespace is a container to hold data, for example, a folder.)
- *Ntuser.data.* Ntuser.dat is a file stored in the C:\Users*username* folder and contains user settings. Each time the user logs on, the contents of this file are copied to a location in the registry.

Program Files

Here is where Windows stores program files unless you select a different location when a program is installed:

- Program files are stored in C:\Program Files for 32-bit versions of Windows.
- In 64-bit versions of Windows, 64-bit programs are stored in the C:\Program Files folder, and 32-bit programs are stored in the C:\Program Files (x86) folder.

Here are folders that applications and some utilities use to launch programs at startup:

- A program file or shortcut to a program file stored in the C:\Users*username*\AppData\Roaming\Microsoft\Windows\Start Menu\Programs\Startup folder launches at startup for an individual user.
- A program file or shortcut to a program file stored in the C:\ProgramData\Microsoft\Windows\Start Menu\Programs\Startup folder launches at startup for all users.

Folders for Windows Data

An operating system needs a place to keep hardware and software configuration information, user preferences, and application settings. This information is used when the OS is first loaded and when needed by hardware, applications, and users. Windows uses a database called the **registry** for most of this information. In addition, Windows keeps some data in text files called **initialization files**, which often have an .ini or .inf file extension.

Here are some important folder locations used for the registry and other Windows data:

- *Registry location.* The Windows registry is stored in the C:\Windows\system32\config folder.
- *Backup of the registry.* A backup of the registry is stored in the C:\Windows\system32\config\RegBack folder.
- *Fonts.* Fonts are stored in the C:\Windows\Fonts folder.
- *Temporary files.* These files, which are used by Windows when it is installing software and performing other maintenance tasks, are stored in the C:\Windows\Temp folder.
- *Offline files.* Offline files are stored in the client-side caching (CSC) folder, which is C:\Windows\CSC. This folder is created and managed by the **Offline Files** utility, which allows users to work with files in the folder when the computer is not connected to the corporate network. Later, when a connection happens, Windows syncs up the offline files and folders stored in the C:\Windows\CSC folder with those on the network.

A+
220-802
1.5, 1.7

Differences for Windows XP

For Windows XP, the user profile is stored in the C:\Documents and Settings folder, for example, C:\Documents and Settings\Jean Andrews. The subfolders under the user folder are organized differently under XP than under Windows 7/Vista.

> **Notes** Most often, Windows is installed on drive C:, although in a dual boot environment, one OS might be installed on C: and another on a different drive. For example, Windows Vista can be installed on C: and Windows 7 installed on E:. If the drive letter of the Windows volume is not known, it is written in Microsoft documentation as *%SystemDrive%*. For example, the location of the Program Files folder is written as *%SystemDrive%*\Program Files.

A+
220-802
1.7

USE THE DISK CLEANUP UTILITY

Begin cleaning up the drive by finding out how much free space the drive has. Then use the Windows Disk Cleanup utility to delete temporary files on the drive.

APPLYING | CONCEPTS Follow these steps for Windows 7/Vista to find out how much free space is on the drive, and use Disk Cleanup. The XP Disk Cleanup utility works about the same as Windows 7/Vista.

1. Open Windows Explorer and right-click the volume on which Windows is installed, most likely drive C:. Select **Properties** from the shortcut menu. The drive Properties box appears, as shown on the left side of Figure 3-1. You can see the free space on this drive C: is 15.2 GB, which is about 11 percent of the volume.

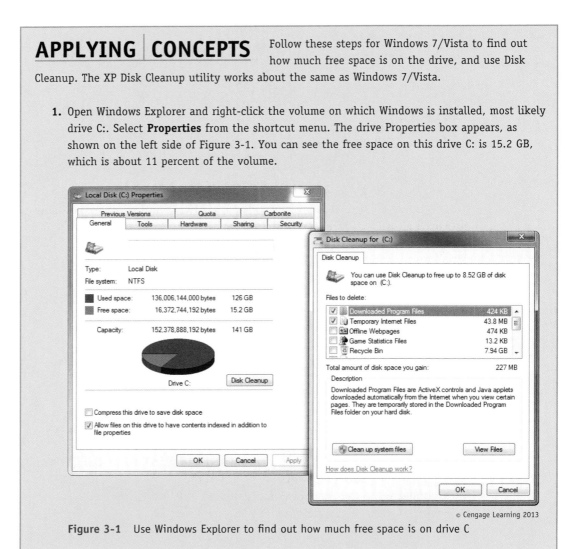

© Cengage Learning 2013

Figure 3-1 Use Windows Explorer to find out how much free space is on drive C

3

2. On the General tab, click **Disk Cleanup**. (You can also access the utility by clicking **Start** and entering **cleanmgr.exe** in the *Search* box.) Disk Cleanup calculates how much space can be freed and then displays the Disk Cleanup box, shown on the right side of Figure 3-1. Select the files you want to delete.

3. Click **Clean up system files** to see temporary system files that you can also delete. The Disk Cleanup box on the left side of Figure 3-2 shows the result for one computer. Notice in the figure the option to delete files from a Previous Windows installation(s), which can free up 30.2 GB of hard drive space. This space is used by the Windows.old folder, which was created when Windows 7 was installed as an upgrade from Vista. Windows 7 setup stored the old Windows, Program Files, and User folders in the Windows.old folder. If the user assures you that no information, data, or settings are needed from the old Windows installation, it's safe to delete these files to free up the 30.2 GB.

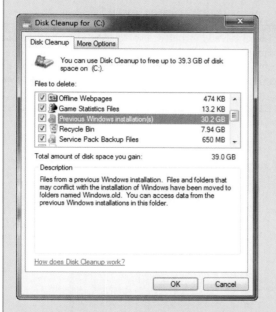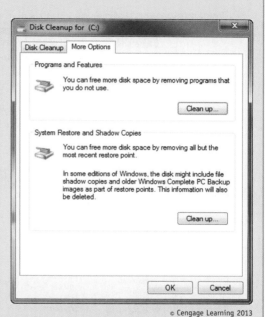

© Cengage Learning 2013

Figure 3-2 Clean up system files no longer needed in order to free up disk space

4. If you still need more free space, click the **More Options** tab (see the right side of Figure 3-2) in the Disk Cleanup box. In the Programs and Features area, click **Clean up**. You are taken to the Programs and Features window where you can uninstall unneeded software to recover that space. Also on the More Options tab in the Disk Cleanup box, when you click **Clean up** under the System Restore and Shadow Copies area, Windows will delete all but the most recent restore points that are created by System Restore. (You will learn more about System Restore later in this chapter.) In Windows XP, the More Options tab offers a third option to delete installed Windows components that you don't need.

DEFRAG THE HARD DRIVE

Two types of hard drives are magnetic hard disk drives (HDDs), which contain spinning platters, and solid-state drives (SSDs), which contain flash memory. For magnetic hard drives, Windows 7/Vista automatically defragments the drive once a week. To **defragment** is to rearrange fragments or parts of files on the drive so each file is stored on the drive in contiguous clusters.

A+
220-802
1.7

In a file system, a cluster, also called a file allocation unit, is a group of whole sectors. The number of sectors in a cluster is fixed and is determined when the file system is first installed. A file is stored in whole clusters, and the unused space at the end of the last cluster, called slack, is wasted free space. As files are written and deleted from a drive, clusters are used, released, and used again. New files written on the drive can be put in available clusters spread over the drive. Over time, drive performance is affected when the moving read/write arm of a magnetic drive must move over many areas of the drive to collect all the fragments of a file. Defragmenting a drive rewrites files in contiguous clusters and improves drive performance.

Because a solid-state drive has no moving parts, defragmenting does not improve read/write time. In fact, defragmenting a solid-state drive can reduce the life of the drive and is not recommended. Windows 7/Vista disables defragmenting solid-state drives.

> **Notes** To find out what type of hard drive is installed, use Device Manager or the System Information window. For example, Figure 3-3 shows the System Information window where we have drilled down to the Storage Disks area, and you can see the model information for two hard drives installed in the system. A quick search on the web shows the first hard drive is an SSD and the second hard drive is a magnetic HDD.

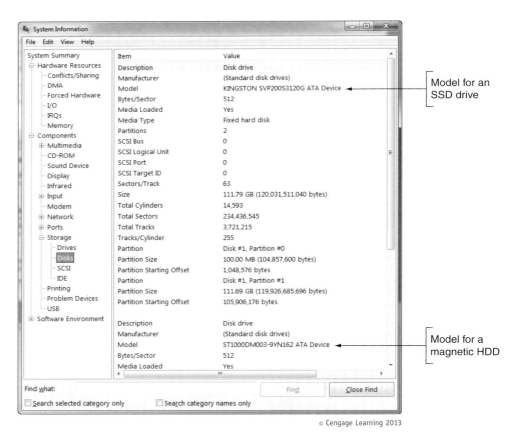

© Cengage Learning 2013

Figure 3-3   Use the System Information window to find the brand and model number for the hard drive

A+
220-802
1.7

APPLYING | CONCEPTS

To verify that Windows 7/Vista is defragmenting a magnetic drive and not defragmenting a solid-state drive, do the following:

1. Use Windows Explorer to open the Properties box for a drive and click the **Tools** tab (see the left side of Figure 3-4), and then click **Defragment now**. In the Disk Defragmenter box (see the right side of Figure 3-4), verify the defrag settings. This system has two hard drives installed. Drive C: in this system is an SSD and is not being defragmented. Drive E: is a magnetic HDD and is scheduled for defragging. To have Windows tell you if a drive needs defragmenting, select a drive and click **Analyze disk**.

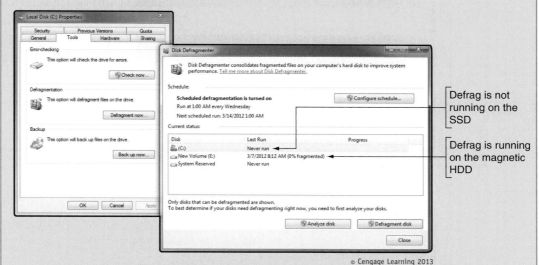

© Cengage Learning 2013

Figure 3-4 Windows is set to automatically defragment a magnetic hard drive once a week

2. If the drive is more than 10 percent fragmented, click **Defragment now** to defrag the drive immediately. The process can take a few minutes to several hours. If errors occur while the drive is defragmenting, check the hard drive for errors and try to defragment again.

Later in the chapter, you will learn to use the Defrag command to defrag the drive from a command prompt window.

For Windows XP, you must manually defragment the drive, and it's a good idea to do so once a week. For Windows XP, first close all open applications. Using Windows Explorer, open the Properties box for the drive. Click the **Tools** tab and then click **Defragment Now**. In the Disk Defragmenter window, click **Defragment** to start the process. Figure 3-5 shows XP defragmenting a volume. You can also use the Defrag command in XP.

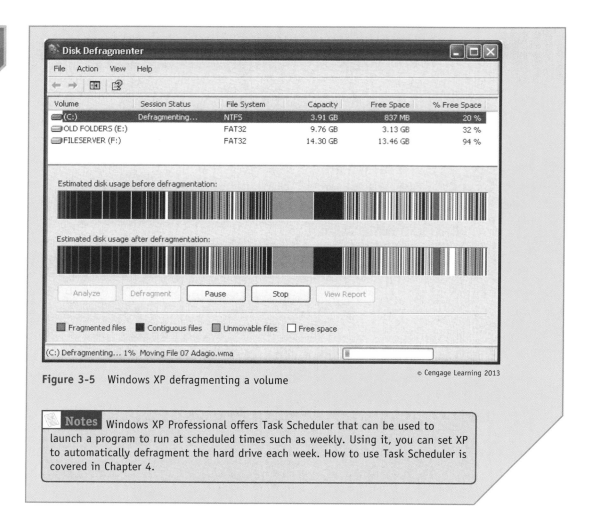

Figure 3-5   Windows XP defragmenting a volume

© Cengage Learning 2013

> **Notes** Windows XP Professional offers Task Scheduler that can be used to launch a program to run at scheduled times such as weekly. Using it, you can set XP to automatically defragment the hard drive each week. How to use Task Scheduler is covered in Chapter 4.

CHECK THE HARD DRIVE FOR ERRORS

Next, to make sure the drive is healthy, you need to search for and repair file system errors. The error checking utility searches for bad sectors on a volume and recovers the data from them if possible. It then marks the sector as bad so that it will not be reused.

To use the error checking utility, in Windows Explorer, right-click the drive, and select **Properties** from the shortcut menu. Click the **Tools** tab, as shown in the left side of Figure 3-6, and then click **Check now**. In the Check Disk dialog box, check **Automatically fix file system errors** and **Scan for and attempt recovery of bad sectors**, as shown in the right side of Figure 3-6, and then click **Start**. For the utility to correct errors on the drive, it needs exclusive use of all files on the drive. When Windows has exclusive use, the drive is called a locked drive. Therefore, a dialog box appears telling you about the problem and asking your permission to scan the drive the next time Windows starts. Reboot the system and let her rip.

A+
220-802
1.7

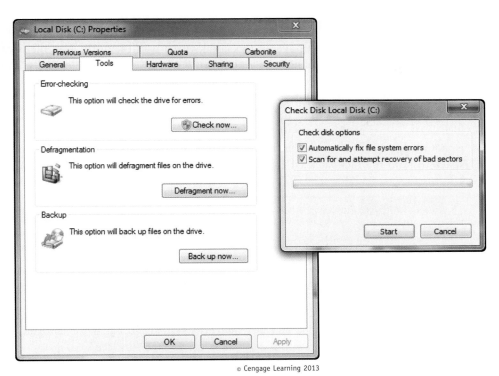

© Cengage Learning 2013

Figure 3-6 Windows repairs hard drive errors under the drive's Properties box using Windows Explorer

Later in the chapter, you learn how to use the Chkdsk command from the command prompt window, which also launches the error checking utility.

FREE UP SPACE ON THE DRIVE

To free up some space on the hard drive, consider these tips:

▲ *Uninstall software you no longer use.* Doing so will free up some space on the hard drive, and, if the software loads a service or program during Windows startup, Windows startup might see performance improvement.

▲ *Move data off the drive.* Consider moving home videos, movies, photos, and other data to an external hard drive or burning them to DVDs or CDs.

▲ **Move programs off the drive.** If your Windows volume needs more free space, you can uninstall a program and reinstall it on a second hard drive installed in the system. An installation routine usually gives you the option to point to another location to install the program other than the default C:\Program Files or C:\Program Files (x86) folder.

▲ *Use drive or folder compression.* Windows offers drive and folder compression that can save on hard drive space. However, it is not recommended that you compress the volume on which Windows is stored. To compress a folder or file on an NTFS drive, open the file or folder **Properties** box and click **Advanced** on the General tab. Then click **Compress contents to save disk space** and click **OK**.

Notes Windows 7/Vista installs on an NTFS volume, but if a second volume on the drive is formatted using the FAT32 file system, you can convert the volume to NTFS. For large drives, NTFS is more efficient and converting might improve performance. NTFS also offers better security and file and folder compression. For two Microsoft Knowledge Base articles about converting from FAT to NTFS, go to *support.microsoft.com* and search for articles 156560 and 314097. The first article discusses the amount of free space you'll need to make the conversion, and the second article tells you how to convert.

A+
220-802
1.5, 1.7

MOVE THE VIRTUAL MEMORY PAGING FILE

Windows uses a file, Pagefile.sys, in the same way it uses memory. This file is called **virtual memory** and is used to enhance the amount of RAM in a system. Normally, the file, Pagefile.sys, is a hidden file stored in the root directory of drive C:. To save space on drive C:, you can move Pagefile.sys to another partition on the same hard drive or to a different hard drive, but don't move it to a different hard drive unless you know the other hard drive is at least as fast as this drive. If the drive is at least as fast as the drive on which Windows is installed, performance should improve. Also, make sure the new volume has plenty of free space to hold the file—at least three times the amount of installed RAM.

> **A+ Exam Tip** The A+ 220-802 exam expects you to know how to configure virtual memory for optimal performance.

APPLYING | CONCEPTS
To change the location of Pagefile.sys in Windows 7/Vista, follow these steps:

1. Open the System window and click **Advanced system settings** in the left pane. The System Properties box appears with the Advanced tab selected (see Figure 3-7).

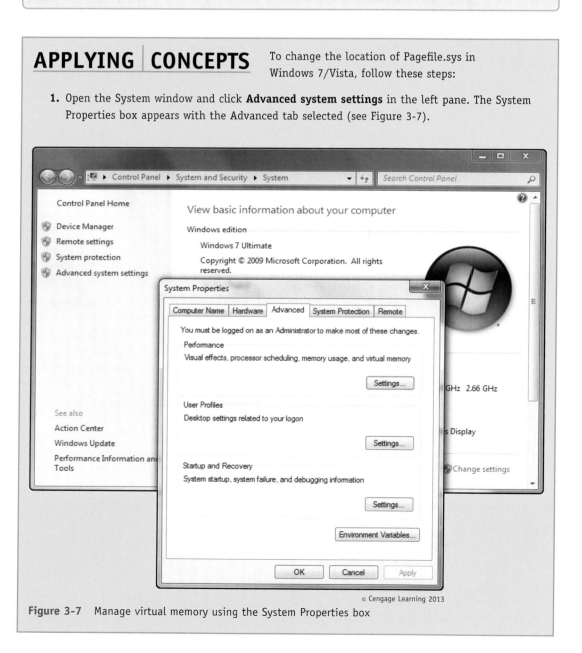

© Cengage Learning 2013

Figure 3-7 Manage virtual memory using the System Properties box

A+
220-802
1.5, 1.7

2. In the Performance section, click **Settings**. In the Performance Options box, select the **Advanced** tab and click **Change**. The Virtual Memory dialog box appears.

3. Uncheck **Automatically manage paging file size for all drives** (see Figure 3-8). Select the drive where you want to move the paging file. For best performance, allow Windows to manage the size of the paging file. If necessary, select **System managed size** and click **Set**.

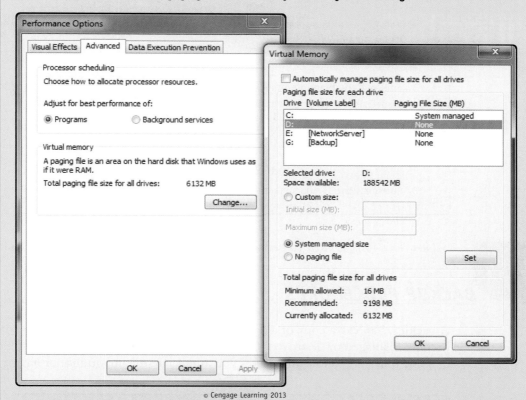

© Cengage Learning 2013

Figure 3-8 Move Pagefile.sys to a different drive

4. Click **OK**. Windows informs you that you must restart the system for the change to take effect. Click **OK** to close the warning box.

5. Click **Apply** and close all boxes. Then restart the system.

For Windows XP, click **Start**, right-click **My Computer**, select **Properties**, and then click the **Advanced** tab. In the Performance section, click **Settings**, click the **Advanced** tab, and then click **Change**. The Virtual Memory box that appears looks and works similarly to the Windows 7 Virtual Memory box in Figure 3-8.

If you still don't have enough free space on the Windows volume, consider adding a second hard drive to the system. In fact, if you install a second hard drive that is faster than the Windows hard drive, know that reinstalling Windows on the faster hard drive will improve performance. You can then use the slower and older hard drive for data.

Notes If the Windows system is still slow and sluggish, know that in Chapter 4 you'll learn more about how to optimize Windows so it performs better.

A+
220-802
1.7

Hands-on | Project 3-1 **Performing Routine Maintenance**

Log onto Windows 7 using a Standard user account. Step through the process described in the chapter to do the following routine maintenance. As you work, note which chores you cannot perform unless you know the password to an administrator account. Do the following:

1. Verify critical Windows settings in Windows Update, antivirus software, and the Network and Sharing Center.

2. Use the Disk Cleanup utility to clean up the hard drive.

3. Find out the brand and model of the hard drive that holds Windows. What is the brand and model? Is the drive a magnetic or solid-state drive? How do you know?

4. Check defrag settings and change them as necessary. Analyze the hard drive and determine if it needs defragmenting. If so, defrag the drive.

5. Check the hard drive for errors.

6. Compress the My Documents folder.

A+
220-802
1.1, 1.7

Now let's look at how to perform on-demand backups and to schedule routine backups.

BACKUP PROCEDURES

A backup is an extra copy of a data or software file that you can use if the original file becomes damaged or destroyed. Losing data due to system failure, a virus, file corruption, or some other problem really makes you appreciate the importance of having backups.

> **Notes** With data and software, here's a good rule of thumb: If you can't get along without it, back it up.

APPLYING | CONCEPTS Dave was well on his way to building a successful career as a PC repair technician. His PC repair shop was doing well, and he was excited about his future. But one bad decision changed everything. He was called to repair a server at a small accounting firm. The call was on the weekend when he was normally off, so he was in a hurry to get the job done. He arrived at the accounting firm and saw that the problem was an easy one to fix, so he decided not to do a backup before working on the system. During his repairs, the hard drive crashed and all data on the drive was lost—four million dollars' worth! The firm sued, Dave's business license was stripped, and he was ordered to pay the money the company lost. A little extra time to back up the system would have saved his whole future. True story!

Because most of us routinely write data to the hard drive, in this section, we focus on backing up from the hard drive to another media. However, when you store important data on any media—such as a flash drive, external hard drive, or CD—always keep a copy of the data on another media. Never trust important data to only one media.

A+
220-802
1.1, 1.7

In this part of the chapter, you will learn how to make a disaster recovery plan and then learn how to use Windows 7 to back up user data, critical Windows system files, and entire volumes.

PLANNING FOR DISASTER RECOVERY

The time to prepare for disaster is before it occurs. If you have not prepared, the damage from a disaster will most likely be greater than if you had made and followed disaster recovery plans. Suppose the hard drive on your PC stopped working and you lost all its data. What would be the impact? Are you prepared for this to happen? Here are decisions you need to make for your backup and recovery plans:

▲ *Decide on the backup destination.* For example, online backup, network drive, CD, DVD, Blu-Ray, SD card, USB flash drive, external hard drive, or other media. Here are points to keep in mind:

- For individuals or small organizations, an online backup service such as Carbonite (carbonite.com) or Mozy (mozy.com) is the easiest, most reliable, and most expensive solution. You pay a yearly subscription for the service, and they guarantee your backups, which are automatically done when your computer is connected to the Internet. If you decide to use one of these services, be sure to restore files from backup occasionally to make sure your backups are happening as you expect and you can recover a lost file.

- Even though it's easy to do, don't make the mistake of backing up your data to another partition or folder on your same hard drive. When a hard drive crashes, most likely all partitions go down together and you will have lost your data and your backup. Back up to another media and, for extra safety, store it at an off-site location.

▲ *Decide on the backup software.* Windows offers a backup utility. However, you can purchase third-party backup software that might offer more features. For example, the external hard drive by Western Digital shown in Figure 3-9 comes with backup software that lets you schedule backups and allows you to select the number of generations of backups you keep. However, before you decide to use an all-in-one backup system such as this one, be certain you understand the risks of not keeping backups at an off-site location and keeping all your backups on a single media.

© Cengage Learning 2013

Figure 3-9 The Western Digital My Passport Essential 750 GB external drive uses USB 3.0 and comes with backup software

◢ *Decide how simple or complex your backup strategy needs to be.* A backup and recovery plan for individuals or small organizations might be very simple. But large organizations might require backups be documented each day, scheduled at certain times of the day or night, and recovery plans tested on a regular basis. Know the requirements of your organization when creating a backup and recovery plan. As a general rule of thumb, back up data for about every 4 to 6 hours of data entry. This might mean a backup needs to occur twice a day, daily, weekly, or monthly. Find out the data entry habits of workers before making your backup schedule and deciding on the folders or volumes to back up.

After you have a backup plan working, test the recovery plan. In addition, you need to occasionally test the recovery plan to make sure all is still working as you expect. Do the following:

◢ *Test the recovery process.* Erase a file on the hard drive, and use the recovery procedures to verify that you can re-create the file from the backup. This verifies that the backup medium works, that the recovery software is effective, and that you know how to use it. After you are convinced that the recovery works, document how to perform it.

◢ *Keep backups in a safe place and routinely test them.* Don't leave a backup disc lying around for someone to steal. Backups of important and sensitive data should be kept under lock and key. In case of fire, keep enough backups off-site so that you can recover data even if the entire building is destroyed. Routinely verify that your backups are good by performing a test recovery of a backed-up file or folder. Backups are useless if the data on the backup is corrupted.

Now let's see how to back up user data, important Windows system files, and entire volumes using Windows 7/Vista/XP tools.

> 💡 **A+ Exam Tip** The A+ 220-802 exam expects you to know how to create and use backups and best practices when scheduling backups.

CREATE AND USE BACKUPS IN WINDOWS 7

Using Windows 7 Backup and Restore, you can back up user data and/or the volume on which Windows is installed. When you set up a backup schedule, you select the folders to back up and you can also choose to back up the Windows volume.

BACK UP THE WINDOWS VOLUME

The backup of the Windows 7 volume is called the system image. Here are points to keep in mind when creating a system image and using it to recover a failed Windows volume:

◢ *A system image includes the entire drive C: or other drive on which Windows is installed.* When you restore a hard drive using the system image, everything on the volume is deleted and replaced with the system image.

◢ *A system image must always be created on an internal or external hard drive.* When using Backup and Restore to back up your data folders, you can include the system

A+
220-802
1.1, 1.7

image in the backup procedure. Even if the files and folders are being copied to a USB drive, CD, or DVD, the system image will always be copied to a hard drive.

▲ *Don't depend just on the system image as your backup.* You should also back up individual folders that contain user data. If individual data files or folders need to be recovered, you cannot rely on the system image because recovering data using the system image would totally replace the entire Windows volume with the system image.

▲ *You can create a system image any time after Windows is installed, and then you can use this image to recover from a failed hard drive.* To create the image, click **Start, All Programs, Maintenance,** and **Backup and Restore.** The Backup and Restore window opens (see Figure 3-10). Click **Create a system image** and follow the directions on-screen. Using the system image to recover a failed hard drive is called reimaging the drive. The details of how to reimage the drive are covered in Chapter 6.

3

> **⚡ Caution** Before creating a system image on a laptop, plug the laptop into an AC outlet so that a failed battery will not interrupt the process.

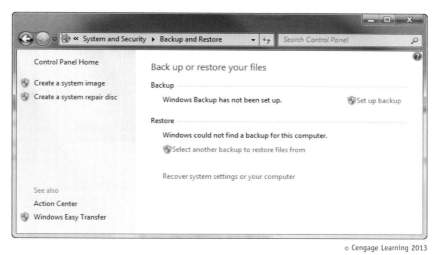

© Cengage Learning 2013

Figure 3-10   Use the Backup and Restore window to create a system image

> **📄 Notes** The system image you create using Backup and Restore can be installed only on the computer that was used to create it. The method used to create a hardware-independent system image, called a standard image, is discussed in Chapter 2 and Appendix D.

BACK UP USER DATA

Because data on a hard drive is likely to change often, it's important to back it up on a regular schedule. Using Backup and Restore, you can create a backup schedule that can include any folder on the hard drive and the system image. The folders and volume are first backed up entirely (called a full backup). Then on the schedule you set, any file or folder is backed up that has changed or been created since the last backup (called an incremental backup). Occasionally, Windows does another full backup.

A+
220-802
1.1, 1.7

APPLYING | CONCEPTS   SET UP A BACKUP SCHEDULE

Follow these steps to learn how to set up a backup schedule using Windows 7 Backup and Restore:

1. Open the Backup and Restore window. If no backup has ever been scheduled on the system, the window will look like the one in Figure 3-10. Click **Set up backup**.

> **Notes** You can open Backup and Restore using the Start, All Programs menu, using the Control Panel (in Control Panel, click **Back up your computer**), or by typing **Backup and Restore** in the *Search* box.

2. In the next dialog box (see Figure 3-11), select the media to hold the backup. In Figure 3-11, choices are volume E: (a second internal hard drive), the DVD drive, and OneTouch (an external hard drive). Make your selection and click **Next**.

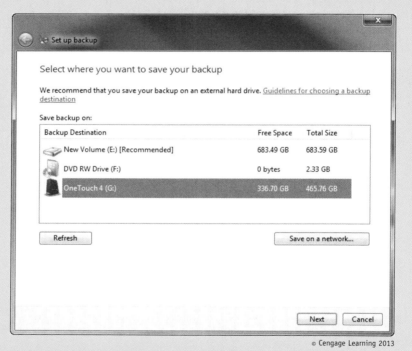

© Cengage Learning 2013

Figure 3-11   Select the destination media to hold the backup

> **Notes** Windows 7 Professional, Ultimate, and Enterprise editions allow you to save the backup to a network location. To use a shared folder on the network for the backup destination, click **Save on a network** (see Figure 3-11). In the resulting box (see Figure 3-12), click **Browse** and point to the folder. Also enter the username and password on the remote computer that the backup utility will use to authenticate to that computer when it makes the backup. You cannot save to a network location when using Windows 7 Home editions. For these editions, the button *Save on a network* is missing in the window where you select the backup destination.

3. In the next box, you can allow Windows to decide what to back up or decide to choose for yourself. Select **Let me choose** so that you can select the folders to back up. Click **Next**.

A+
220-802
1.1, 1.7

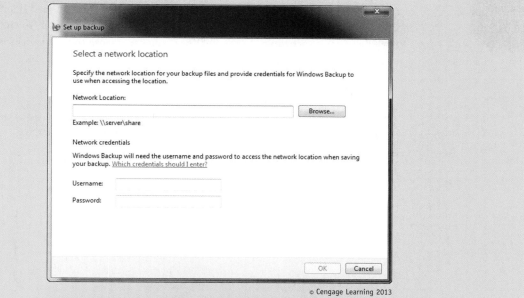

© Cengage Learning 2013

Figure 3-12 Select the folder on the network to hold the backup and enter the username and password for the remote computer

4. In the next box (see Figure 3-13), select the libraries and folders you want to back up. You can click the white triangle beside Local Disk (C:) to drill down to any folder on the hard drive for backup. Check folders or libraries to back up. If the backup media can hold the system image, the option to include the image is selected by default. If you don't want to include the image, uncheck it. Click **Next** to continue. Here are folders that might contain important user data:

▲ Application data is usually found in C:\Users*username*\AppData.

▲ Internet Explorer favorites are in C:\Users*username*\Favorites.

▲ Better still, back up the entire user profile at C:\Users*username*.

▲ Even better, back up all user profiles at C:\Users.

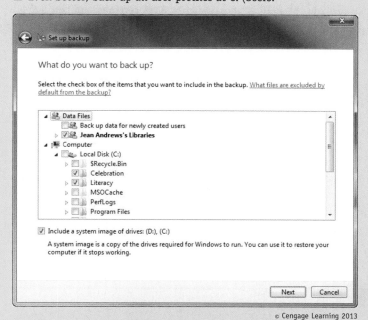

© Cengage Learning 2013

Figure 3-13 Select the folders or libraries to include in the backup

3

A+
220-802
1.1, 1.7

5. In the next box, verify the correct folders and libraries are selected (see Figure 3-14). Notice in the figure, the backup is scheduled to run every Sunday at 7:00 PM. To change this schedule, click **Change schedule**. In the next box, you can choose to run the backup daily, weekly, or monthly and select the time of day. Make your selections and click **OK**.

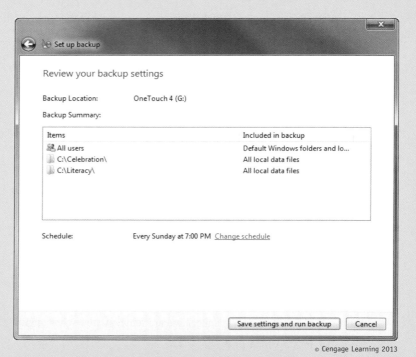

© Cengage Learning 2013

Figure 3-14   By default, Windows runs a backup each week at the same day and time

6. Review your backup settings and click **Save settings and run backup**. The backup proceeds. A **shadow copy** is made of any open files so that files that are currently open are included in the backup.

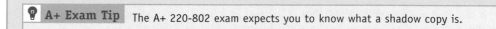 **A+ Exam Tip**   The A+ 220-802 exam expects you to know what a shadow copy is.

If you want to later change the settings for your scheduled backup, open the Backup and Restore window. Notice in Figure 3-15 the window has changed from that shown earlier in Figure 3-10. It now shows the details about the scheduled backup. To change the backup settings, click **Change settings**. Follow the process to verify or change each setting for the backup. Also notice in the left pane of Figure 3-15 that you can turn off the scheduled backup by clicking **Turn off schedule**.

Notes   One limitation of Windows Backup and Restore is that you can have only one scheduled backup routine.

A+
220-802
1.1, 1.7

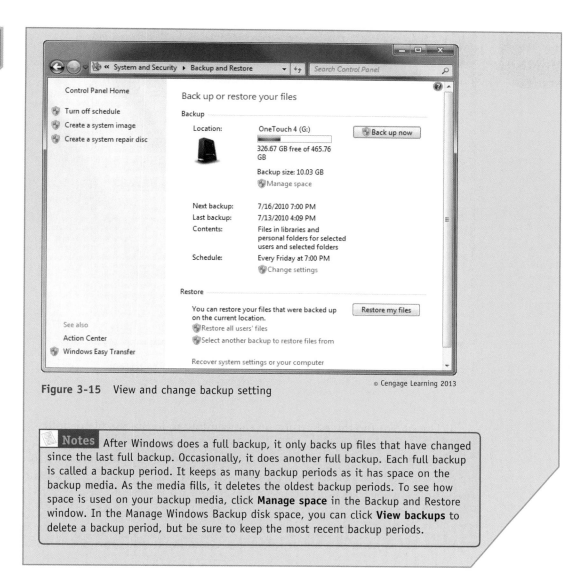

Figure 3-15 View and change backup setting

© Cengage Learning 2013

3

> **Notes** After Windows does a full backup, it only backs up files that have changed since the last full backup. Occasionally, it does another full backup. Each full backup is called a backup period. It keeps as many backup periods as it has space on the backup media. As the media fills, it deletes the oldest backup periods. To see how space is used on your backup media, click **Manage space** in the Backup and Restore window. In the Manage Windows Backup disk space, you can click **View backups** to delete a backup period, but be sure to keep the most recent backup periods.

Recover a Corrupted or Lost File or Folder

If a data file or folder later gets corrupted, you can recover the file or folder using the Backup and Restore window or using the Previous Versions tab of the file or folder Properties box. To use the Backup and Restore window, follow these steps:

1. Make the backup media available to the computer by inserting the backup disc, connecting the external hard drive, or other method.

2. Open the **Backup and Restore** window. Scroll down to the bottom of the window and click **Restore my files**. The Restore Files box appears (see Figure 3-16).

> **Notes** If the *Restore my files* button is missing from the Backup and Restore window, your backup media might not be available to Windows. You might need to plug in the media and then use Windows Explorer to verify you can access the backup folder on the media.

A+
220-802
1.1, 1.7

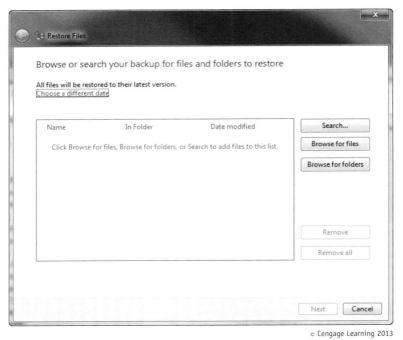

© Cengage Learning 2013

Figure 3-16 Locate the files and folders on the backup media to restore

3. Use one of the three buttons on the window to locate the file or folder. *Search* allows you to search for a file or folder when you only know part of the filename or folder name. *Browse for files* allows you to drill down to the file to restore. *Browse for folders* allows you to search for the folder to restore. You can locate and select multiple files or folders to restore. Then follow the directions on-screen to restore all the selected items.

A previous version of a file or folder is a version that was previously created by the Backup and Restore utility or by System Protection when it created a restore point for the system. To restore a folder or file to a previous version, follow these steps:

1. Use Windows Explorer to copy (do not move) the corrupted folder or file to a new location. When you restore a file or folder to a previous version, the current file or folder can be lost and replaced by the previous version. By saving a copy of the current file or folder to a different location, you can revert back to the copy if necessary.

2. Right-click the file or folder and select **Restore previous versions** from the shortcut menu. The Properties box for the file or folder appears with the Previous Versions tab selected. Windows displays a list of all previous versions of the file or folder it has kept (see Figure 3-17).

3. Select the version you want and click **Restore**. A message box asks if you are sure you want to continue. Click **Restore** and then click **OK**.

4. Open the restored file or folder and verify it is the version you want. If you decide you need another version, delete the file or folder and copy the file or folder you saved in Step 1 back into the original location. Then return to Step 2 and try again, this time selecting a different previous version.

A+
220-802
1.1, 1.7

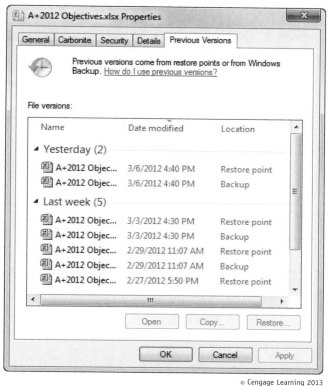

© Cengage Learning 2013

Figure 3-17   Restore a file or folder from a previous version

A+
220-802
1.1, 1.5,
1.7, 1.8

BACK UP WINDOWS SYSTEM FILES

The Windows **System Protection** utility automatically backs up system files and stores them on the hard drive at regular intervals and just before you install software or hardware. These snapshots of the system are called **restore points** and include Windows system files that have changed since the last restore point was made. A restore point does not contain all user data, and you can manually create a restore point at any time.

Make Sure System Protection Is Turned On

To make sure System Protection has not been turned off, open the System window and click **System protection**. The System Protection tab of the System Properties box appears (see the left side of Figure 3-18). Make sure Protection is turned on for the drive containing Windows, which indicates that restore points are created automatically. In Figure 3-18, Protection for drive C: is on and other drives are not being protected. To make a change, click **Configure**. The System Protection box on the right side of the figure appears. If you make a change to this box, click **Apply** and then click **OK**.

Restore points are normally kept in the folder C:\System Volume Information, which is not accessible to the user. Restore points are taken at least every 24 hours, and they can use up to 15 percent of disk space. If disk space gets very low, restore points are no longer made, which is one more good reason to keep about 15 percent or more of the hard drive free.

A+
220-802
1.1, 1.5,
1.7, 1.8

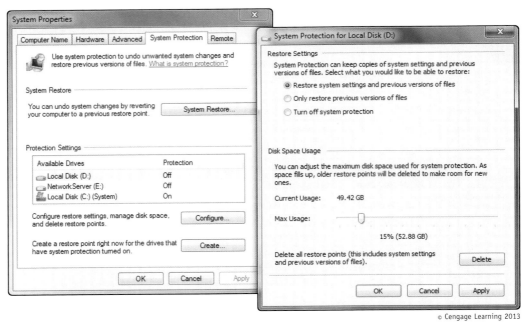

© Cengage Learning 2013

Figure 3-18   Make sure System Protection is turned on for the volume on which Windows is installed

Manually Create a Restore Point

To manually create a restore point, use the System Protection tab of the System Properties box, as shown on the left side of Figure 3-18. Click **Create**. In the System Protection box, enter a name for the restore point, such as "Before I tested software," and click **Create**. The restore point is created.

Apply a Restore Point

System Restore restores the system to its condition at the time a restore point was made. If you restore the system to a previous restore point, user data on the hard drive will not be altered, but you can affect installed software and hardware, user settings, and OS configuration settings. When you use System Restore to roll back the system to a restore point, any changes made to these settings after the restore point was created are lost; therefore, always use the most recent restore point that can fix the problem so that you make the least intrusive changes to the system.

To return the system to a previous restore point, do the following:

1. Click **Start**, **All Programs**, **Accessories**, **System Tools**, and **System Restore**. The System Restore box opens. Click **Next**.

2. In the next box, the most recent restore points appear. For most situations, the most recent is the one to select so as to make the least possible changes to your system. If you want to see other restore points, check **Show more restore points**. Select a restore point (see Figure 3-19) and click **Next**.

3. Windows asks you to confirm your selection. Click **Finish** and respond to the warning box. The system restarts and the restore point is applied.

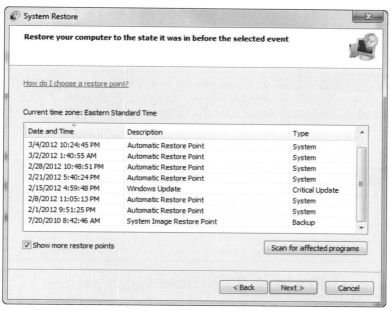

© Cengage Learning 2013

Figure 3-19 Select a restore point

Points to Remember About System Restore

System Restore is a great tool to try to fix a device that is not working, restore Windows settings that are giving problems, or solve problems with applications. Although it's a great tool in some situations, it does have its limitations. Keep these points in mind:

▲ *Point 1:* Restore points replace certain keys in the registry but cannot completely rebuild a totally corrupted registry. Therefore, System Restore can recover from errors only if the registry is somewhat intact.

▲ *Point 2:* The restore process cannot remove a virus or worm infection. However, it might help you start a system that is infected with a virus that launches at startup. After Windows has started, you can then use antivirus software to remove the infection.

▲ *Point 3:* System Restore might create a new problem. I've discovered that whenever I use a restore point, antivirus software gets all out of whack and sometimes even needs reinstalling. Therefore, use restore points sparingly.

▲ *Point 4:* System Restore might make many changes to a system. If you know which change caused a problem, try to undo that particular change first. The idea is to use the least invasive solution first. For example, if updating a driver has caused a problem, first try Driver Rollback to undo that change. Driver Rollback is performed using Device Manager.

▲ *Point 5:* System Restore won't help you if you don't have restore points to use. System Protection must be turned on so that restore points are automatically created.

▲ *Point 6:* Restore points are kept in a hidden folder on the hard drive. If that area of the drive is corrupted, the restore points are lost. Also, if a user turns System Protection off, all restore points are lost.

▲ *Point 7:* Viruses and other malware sometimes hide in restore points. To completely clean an infected system, you need to delete all restore points by turning System Protection off and back on.

A+
220-802
1.1, 1.5,
1.7, 1.8

◢ *Point 8:* If Windows will not start, you can launch System Restore using startup recovery tools, which you will learn to use in Chapter 6.

Vista Differences Windows Vista uses different backup methods than Windows 7 to back up user data, system files, and the Windows volume. The backup of the Vista volume is called the **Complete PC Backup**. To find out more about Vista backups, see Appendix B.

XP Differences Windows XP uses the **Automated System Recovery (ASR)** tool to back up the Windows XP volume. XP calls the backed-up system files that are critical to Windows operation the **system state data**. To find out more about XP backups, see Appendix C.

Hands-on | Project 3-2   Using System Restore

Do the following to find out how System Restore works and how it can affect a system:

1. Create a restore point.

2. Make a change to the display settings.

3. Change the desktop background.

4. Create a new text file in your My Documents folder.

5. Restore the system using System Restore.

Is the text file still in your My Documents folder? Are the other changes still in effect? Why or why not?

MANAGING FILES, FOLDERS, AND STORAGE DEVICES

A+
220-802
1.2

In this part of the chapter, you learn to manage files and folders on the hard drive and other storage devices using commands in a command prompt window and to manage hard drive partitions and volumes using the Disk Management utility. We begin our discussion with how partitions and file systems work in Windows.

HOW PARTITIONS AND FILE SYSTEMS WORK

A hard drive is organized using sectors, partitions, volumes, and file systems. Here's how it all works:

◢ All data is stored on a hard drive in sectors, sometimes called records. Each sector on the drive is the same size, and for most hard drives, that size is 512 bytes. Sector markings used to organize the drive are done before it leaves the factory in a process called low-level formatting. The size of a sector and the total number of sectors on a drive determine the drive capacity. Today's drive capacities are measured in GB (gigabytes, roughly one million bytes) or TB (terabytes, roughly one trillion bytes).

3

A+
220-802
1.2

> **Notes** For magnetic hard drives, each platter is divided into concentric circles called **tracks**, and each track is divided into sectors (see Figure 3-20). Magnetic drive sectors are usually 512 bytes, but sectors on SSD drives can be larger: 4 KB or 16 KB.

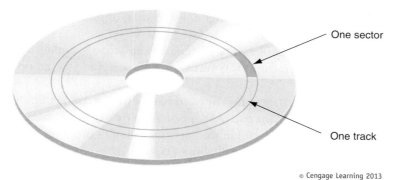

© Cengage Learning 2013

Figure 3-20 A magnetic hard drive is divided into concentric circles called tracks, and tracks are divided into sectors

◢ A drive is further divided into one or more **partitions**. Windows can track up to four partitions on a drive. It keeps a map of these partitions in a **partition table** stored in the very first sector on the hard drive called the **Master Boot Record (MBR)**.

◢ A drive can have one, two, or three **primary partitions**, also called **volumes**. The fourth partition is called an **extended partition** and can hold one or more volumes called **logical drives**. Figure 3-21 shows how a hard drive is divided into three primary partitions and one extended partition.

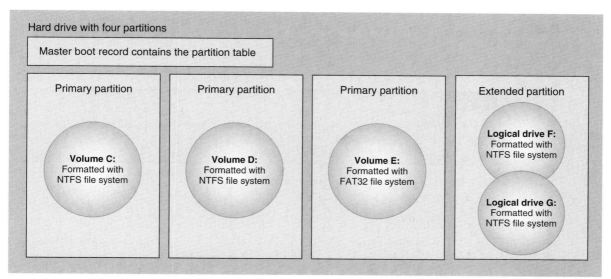

Figure 3-21 A hard drive with four partitions; the fourth partition is an extended partition

© Cengage Learning 2013

> 💡 **A+ Exam Tip** The A+ 220-802 exam expects you to know the difference between a primary and extended partition and between a volume and logical drive.

A+
220-802
1.2

▲ Before a volume or logical drive can be used, it must be assigned a drive letter such as C: or D: and formatted using a file system. A **file system** is the overall structure an OS uses to name, store, and organize files on a drive. Windows 7 supports three types of file systems for hard drives: NTFS, FAT32, and exFAT. NTFS is the most reliable and secure and is used for the volume on which Windows is installed. Installing a drive letter, file system, and root directory on a volume is called **formatting** the drive, also called a **high-level format**, and can happen during the Windows installation.

▲ One of the primary partitions can be designated the **active partition**, which is the bootable partition that startup BIOS turns to when searching for an operating system to start up.

▲ Windows assigns two different functions to hard drive partitions holding the OS (see Figure 3-22). The **system partition**, normally drive C:, is the active partition of the hard drive. This is the partition that contains the OS program to start up Windows. This boot program is called the OS boot manager or boot loader. The other partition, called the **boot partition**, is the partition where the Windows operating system is stored.

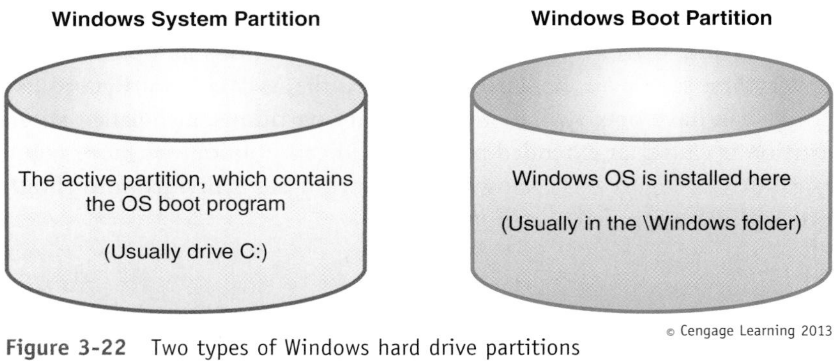

Windows System Partition

Windows Boot Partition

The active partition, which contains the OS boot program

(Usually drive C:)

Windows OS is installed here

(Usually in the \Windows folder)

© Cengage Learning 2013

Figure 3-22 Two types of Windows hard drive partitions

> **Notes** Don't be confused by the terminology here. It is really true that, according to Windows terminology, the Windows OS is on the boot partition, and the boot program is on the system partition, although that might seem backward. The computer starts or boots from the system partition and loads the Windows operating system from the boot partition.

For most installations, the system partition and the boot partition are the same (drive C:), and Windows is installed in C:\Windows. An example of when the system partition and the boot partition are different is when Windows 7 is installed as a dual boot with Windows Vista. Figure 3-23 shows how Windows 7 is installed on drive D: and Windows Vista is installed on drive C:. For Windows 7, the system partition is drive C: and the boot partition is drive D:. (For Windows Vista on this computer, the system and boot partitions are both drive C:.)

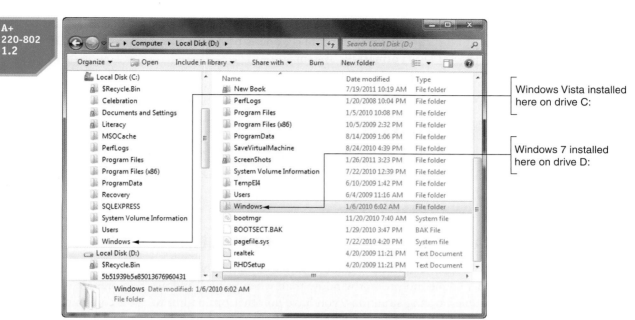

© Cengage Learning 2013

Figure 3-23 Windows 7 and Vista installed on the same system

Here is a list of file systems supported by Windows that you can choose for volumes and drives that don't hold the Windows installation:

▲ *NTFS.* Choose the NTFS file system for hard drives because it uses smaller allocation unit or cluster sizes than FAT32, which means it makes more efficient use of disk space when storing many small files. NTFS is more reliable, gives fewer errors, supports encryption, disk quotas (limiting the hard drive space available to a user), file and folder compression, and offers better security. As an example of the better security with NTFS, if you boot the system from another boot media such as a CD, you can access a volume using a FAT file system. If the volume uses NTFS, an administrator password is required to gain access.

▲ *exFAT.* Choose the exFAT file system for large external storage devices that you want to use with other operating systems. For example, you can use a smart card formatted with exFAT in a Mac or Linux computer or in a digital camcorder, camera, or smart phone. exFAT uses the same structure as the older FAT32 file system, but with a 64-bit-wide file allocation table (FAT). exFAT does not use as much overhead as the NTFS file system and is designed to handle very large files, such as those used for multimedia storage.

▲ *FAT32.* Use FAT32 for small hard drives or USB flash drives because it does not have as much overhead as NTFS.

▲ *FAT16.* The older FAT or FAT16 file system has a 16-bit file allocation table and is only recommended on volumes less than 4 GB.

> 💡 **A+ Exam Tip** The A+ 220-802 exam expects you to know about the FAT, FAT32, NTFS, and CDFS file systems. It also expects you to know the difference between a quick format and a full format.

A+
220-802
1.2

▲ *CDFS and UDF.* CDFS (Compact Disc File System) is an older file system used by optical discs (CDs, DVDs, and BDs), and is being replaced by the newer UDF (Universal Disc Format) file system.

> **Notes** For Windows Vista, the exFAT file system is available if Service Pack 1 is installed. In XP, exFAT is available if Windows XP Service Packs 2 and 3 are installed and you download and install an additional update from Microsoft.

A+
220-802
1.2, 1.3,
4.6

COMMANDS TO MANAGE FILES AND FOLDERS

PC support technicians find it is much faster to manipulate files and folders using commands in a command prompt window than when using Windows Explorer. In addition, in some troubleshooting situations, you have no other option but to use a command prompt window. To open the window, enter **cmd.exe** in the search box and press **Enter**. Alternately, you can click Start, All Programs, Accessories, and Command Prompt. The Command Prompt window is shown in Figure 3-24.

© Cengage Learning 2013

Figure 3-24   Use the exit command to close the command prompt window

Windows 7 and Vista have two levels of command prompt windows: a standard window and an elevated window. The standard window is shown in Figure 3-24. Notice in the figure that the default directory is the currently logged on user's folder. Commands that require administrative privileges will not work from this standard command prompt window. To get an elevated command prompt window, click **Start, All Programs, Accessories,** and right-click **Command Prompt**. Then select **Run as administrator** from the shortcut window. After you respond to the User Account Control (UAC) box, the Administrator: Command Prompt window appears (see Figure 3-25). Notice the word Administrator in the title bar, which indicates the elevated window, and the default directory, which is the C:\Windows\system32 folder.

```
cmd  Administrator: Command Prompt                          ─  □  ✕

Microsoft Windows [Version 6.1.7600]
Copyright (c) 2009 Microsoft Corporation.  All rights reserved.

C:\windows\system32>msinfo32.exe

C:\windows\system32>exit_
```

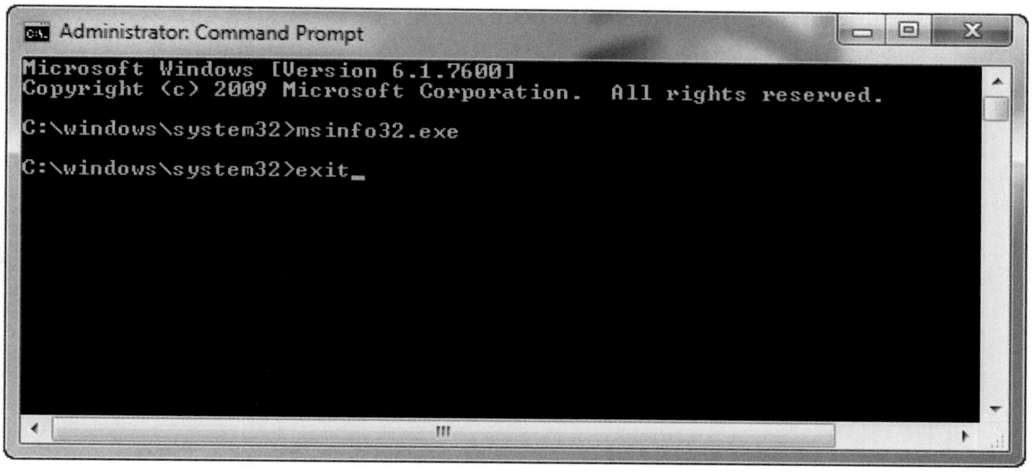

Figure 3-25   An elevated command prompt window has administrative privileges   © Cengage Learning 2013

Here are some tips for working in a command prompt window:

◢ Type **cls** and press **Enter** to clear the window.
◢ To retrieve the last command you entered, press the up arrow. To retrieve the last command line one character at a time, press the right arrow.
◢ To terminate a command before it is finished, press **Ctrl+Break** or **Ctrl+Pause**.
◢ To close the window, type **exit** (see Figure 3-25) and press **Enter**.

> **Notes** Many of the commands you learn about in this section can also be used from the Windows 7/ Vista Recovery Environment or the Windows XP Recovery Console. These operating systems can be loaded from the Windows setup CD or DVD to troubleshoot a system when the Windows desktop refuses to load. How to use the Recovery Environment and the Recovery Console is covered in Chapter 6.

If the command you are using applies to files or folders, the path to these files or folders is assumed to be the default drive and directory. The default drive and directory, also called the current drive and directory, shows in the command prompt. It is the drive and directory that the command will use if you don't give a drive and directory in the command line. For example, in Figure 3-24, the default drive is C: and the default path is C:\Users\Jean Andrews. If you use a different path in the command line, the path you use overrides the default path. Also know that Windows makes no distinction between uppercase and lowercase in command lines.

Now let's look at the filenaming conventions you will need to follow when creating files, wildcard characters you can use in command lines, and several commands useful for managing files and folders.

FILENAMING CONVENTIONS

When using the command prompt window to create a file, keep in mind that filename and file extension characters can be the letters a through z, the numbers 0 through 9, and the following characters:

```
_  ^  $  ~  !  #  %  &  -  {  }  (  )  @  '  `
```

A+
220-802
1.2, 1.3,
4.6

In a command prompt window, if a path or filename has spaces in it, it is sometimes necessary to enclose the path or filename in double quotation marks.

WILDCARD CHARACTERS IN COMMAND LINES

As you work at the command prompt, you can use wildcard characters in a filename to say that the command applies to a group of files or to abbreviate a filename if you do not know the entire name. The question mark (?) is a wildcard for one character, and the asterisk (*) is a wildcard for one or more characters. For example, if you want to find all files in a directory that start with A and have a three-letter file extension, you would use the following command:

```
dir a*.???
```

> **💡 A+ Exam Tip** The A+ 220-802 exam expects you to know how to use the Shutdown, MD, RD, CD, Del, Format, Copy, Xcopy, Robocopy, Defrag, Chkdsk, and Help commands, which are all covered in this section.

> **📝 Notes** Many commands can use parameters in the command line to affect how the command will work. Parameters (also called options, arguments, or switches) often begin with a slash followed by a single character. In this chapter, you will learn about the basic parameters used by a command for the most common tasks. For a full listing of the parameters available for a command, use the Help command. Another way to learn about commands is to follow this link on the Microsoft web site: *technet.microsoft.com/en-us/library/cc772390(WS.10).aspx*.

HELP OR <COMMAND NAME> /?

Use the help command to get help about any command. You can enter help followed by the command name or enter the command name followed by /?. Table 3-1 lists some sample applications of this command:

Command	Result
help xcopy xcopy /?	Gets help about the Xcopy command
help	Lists all commands
help xcopy | more	Lists information one screen at a time

© Cengage Learning 2013

Table 3-1 Sample help commands

DIR [<FILENAME>] [/P] [/S] [/W]

Use the dir command to list files and directories. In Microsoft documentation about a command (also called the command syntax), the brackets [ ] in a command line indicate the parameter is optional. In addition, the parameter included in < >, such as <filename>, indicates that you can substitute any filename in the command. This filename can include a path or file extension. Table 3-2 lists some examples of the dir command.

A+
220-802
1.2, 1.3,
4.6

Command	Result
dir /p	Lists one screen at a time
dir /w	Presents information using wide format, where details are omitted and files and folders are listed in columns on the screen
dir *.txt	Lists all files with a .txt file extension in the default path
dir d:\data*.txt	Lists all files with a .txt file extension in the D:\data folder
dir myfile.txt	Checks that a single file, such as myfile.txt, is present
dir /s	Includes subdirectory entries

Table 3-2 Sample dir commands

© Cengage Learning 2013

3

MD *[DRIVE:]*PATH

The MD command (Make Directory) creates a subdirectory under a directory. Note that in the command lines in this section, the command prompt is not bolded, but the typed command is in bold. To create a directory named \game on drive C:, you can use this command:

```
C:\> MD C:\game
```

The backslash indicates that the directory is under the root directory. If a path is not given, the default path is assumed. This command also creates the C:\game directory:

```
C:\> MD game
```

To create a directory named chess under the \game directory, you can use this command:

```
C:\> MD C:\game\chess
```

Figure 3-26 shows the result of the dir command on the directory game. Note the two initial entries in the directory table: . (dot) and . . (dot, dot). The MD command creates these two entries when the OS initially sets up the directory. You cannot edit these entries with normal OS commands, and they must remain in the directory for the directory's lifetime. The . (dot) entry points to the subdirectory itself, and the .. (dot, dot) entry points to the parent directory, which, in this case, is the root directory.

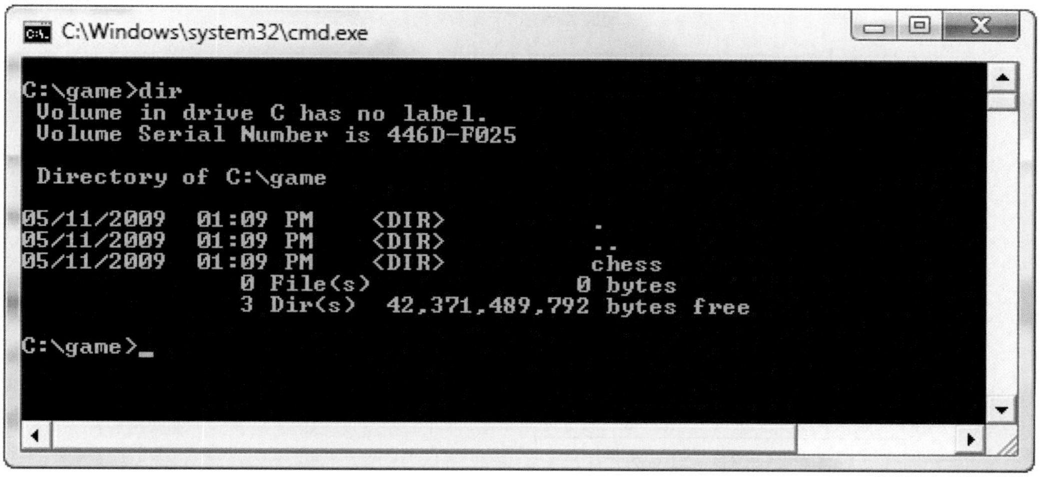

© Cengage Learning 2013

Figure 3-26 Results of the dir command on the game directory

CD *[DRIVE:]PATH OR CD..*

The CD command (Change Directory) changes the current default directory. You enter CD followed by the drive and the entire path that you want to be current, like so:

```
C:\> CD C:\game\chess
```

The command prompt now looks like this:

```
C:\game\chess>
```

To move from a child directory to its parent directory, use the .. (dot, dot) variation of the command:

```
C:\game\chess> CD..
```

The command prompt now looks like this:

```
C:\game>
```

Remember that .. (dot, dot) always means the parent directory. You can move from a parent directory to one of its child directories simply by stating the name of the child directory:

```
C:\game> CD chess
```

The command prompt now looks like this:

```
C:\game\chess>
```

Remember not to put a backslash in front of the child directory name; doing so tells the OS to go to a directory named Chess that is directly under the root directory.

RD *[DRIVE:]PATH [/S]*

The RD command (Remove Directory) removes a directory. Unless you use the /s switch, three things must be true before you can use the RD command:

- ◢ The directory must contain no files.
- ◢ The directory must contain no subdirectories.
- ◢ The directory must not be the current directory.

A directory is ready for removal when only the . (dot) and .. (dot, dot) entries are present. For example, to remove the \game directory when it contains the chess directory, the chess directory must first be removed, like so:

```
C:\> RD C:\game\chess
```

Or, if the \game directory is the current directory, you can use this command:

```
C:\game> RD chess
```

After you remove the chess directory, you can remove the game directory. However, it's not good to attempt to saw off a branch while you're sitting on it; therefore, you must first leave the \game directory like so:

```
C:\game> CD..
C:\> RD \game
```

When you use the /s switch with the RD command, the entire directory tree is deleted, including all its subdirectories and files.

DEL OR ERASE *<FILENAME>*

The del or erase command erases files or groups of files. Note that in the command lines in this section, the command prompt is not bolded, but the typed command is in bold.

To erase the file named Myfile.txt, use the following command:

```
E:\> del myfile.txt
```

To erase all files in the current default directory, use the following command:

```
E:\Docs> del *.*
```

To erase all files in the E:\Docs directory, use the following command:

```
C:\> erase e:\docs\*.*
```

A few files don't have a file extension. To erase all files that are in the current directory and that have no file extensions, use the following command:

```
E:\Docs> del *.
```

REN *<FILENAME1>* *<FILENAME2>*

The ren (rename) command renames a file. *<Filename1>* can include a path to the file, but *<Filename2>* cannot. To rename Project.docx in the default directory to Project_Hold.docx:

```
E:\Docs> ren Project.docx Project_Hold.docx
```

To rename all .txt files to .doc files in the C:\Data folder:

```
ren C:\Data\*.txt *.doc
```

COPY *<SOURCE>* *[<DESTINATION>]* *[/V]* *[/Y]*

The copy command copies a single file or group of files. The original files are not altered. To copy a file from one drive to another, use a command similar to this one:

```
E:\> copy C:\Data\Myfile.txt E:\mydata\Newfile.txt
```

The drive, path, and filename of the source file immediately follow the copy command. The drive, path, and filename of the destination file follow the source filename. If you do not specify the filename of the destination file, the OS assigns the file's original name to this copy. If you omit the drive or path of the source or the destination, then the OS uses the current default drive and path.

To copy the file Myfile.txt from the root directory of drive C: to drive E:, use the following command:

```
C:\> copy myfile.txt E:
```

Because the command does not include a drive or path before the filename Myfile.txt, the OS assumes that the file is in the default drive and path. Also, because there is no destination filename specified, the file written to drive E: will be named Myfile.txt.

To copy all files in the C:\Docs directory to the USB flash drive designated drive E:, use the following command:

```
C:\> copy c:\docs\*.* E:
```

To make a backup file named System.bak of the System file in the \Windows\system32\config directory of the hard drive, use the following command:

```
C:\Windows\system32\config> copy system system.bak
```

If you use the copy command to duplicate multiple files, the files are assigned the names of the original files. When you duplicate multiple files, the destination portion of the command line cannot include a filename.

Here are two switches or parameters that are useful with the copy command:

▲ **/V.** When the /V switch is used, the size of each new file is compared to the size of the original file. This slows down the copying, but verifies that the copy is done without errors.

▲ **/Y.** When the /Y switch is used, a confirmation message does not appear asking you to confirm before overwriting a file.

Notes When trying to recover a corrupted file, you can sometimes use the Copy command to copy the file to new media, such as from the hard drive to a USB drive. During the copying process, if the Copy command reports a bad or missing sector, choose the option to ignore that sector. The copying process then continues to the next sector. The corrupted sector will be lost, but others can likely be recovered. The Recover command can be used to accomplish the same thing.

RECOVER *<FILENAME>*

Use the recover command to attempt to recover a file when parts of the file are corrupted. The command is best used from the Windows 7/Vista Recovery Environment or the XP Recovery Console (discussed in Appendix C). To use it, you must specify the name of a single file in the command line, like so:

```
C:\Data> Recover Myfile.doc
```

XCOPY *<SOURCE>* *[<DESTINATION>]* *[/S]* *[/C]* *[/Y]* *[/D:DATE]*

The xcopy command is more powerful than the copy command. It follows the same general command-source-destination format as the copy command, but it offers several more options. Table 3-3 shows some of these options.

Command	Result
`xcopy C:\docs\*.* E: /S`	Use the /S switch to include subdirectories in the copy; this command copies all files in the directory C:\docs, as well as all subdirectories under \docs and their files, to drive E
`xcopy C:\docs\*.* E: /E`	Same as /S but empty subdirectories are included in the copy
`xcopy C:\docs\*.* E: /D:03/14/12`	The /D switch examines the date; this command copies all files from the directory C:\docs created or modified on or after March 14, 2012
`xcopy C:\docs\*.* E: /Y`	Use the /Y switch to overwrite existing files without prompting
`xcopy C:\docs\*.* E: /C`	Use the /C switch to keep copying even when an error occurs

Table 3-3 Xcopy commands and results

© Cengage Learning 2013

ROBOCOPY *<SOURCE>* *[<DESTINATION>]* *[/S]* *[/E]* *[/LOG:FILENAME]* *[/LOG+:FILENAME]* *[/MOVE]* *[/PURGE]*

The robocopy (Robust File Copy) command is not included in Windows XP and is similar to the xcopy command. It offers more options than xcopy and is intended to replace xcopy. A few options for robocopy are listed in Table 3-4.

Command	Result
`robocopy C:\docs\*.* E: /S`	The /S switch includes subdirectories in the copy but does not include empty directories
`robocopy C:\docs\*.* E: /E`	The /E switch includes subdirectories, even the empty ones
`robocopy C:\docs\*.* E: /LOG:Mylog.txt`	Records activity to a log file and overwrites the current log file
`robocopy C:\docs\*.* E: /LOG+:Mylog.txt`	Appends a record of all activity to an existing log file
`robocopy C:\docs\*.* E: /move`	Moves files and directories, deleting them from the source
`robocopy C:\docs\*.* E: /purge`	Deletes files and directories at the destination that no longer exist at the source

Table 3-4 Robocopy commands and results

© Cengage Learning 2013

CHKDSK *[DRIVE:]* *[/F]* *[/R]*

The chkdsk command (Check Disk) fixes file system errors and recovers data from bad sectors. Earlier in the chapter, you learned to check for errors using the drive properties box, which does so by launching the chkdsk command. Recall that a file is stored on the hard drive as a group of clusters. The FAT, FAT32, and exFAT file systems use a file allocation table (FAT) to keep a record of each cluster that belongs to a file. The NTFS file system uses a database to hold similar information called the master file table (MFT). In Figure 3-27, you can see that each cell in the FAT represents one cluster and contains a pointer to the next cluster in a file.

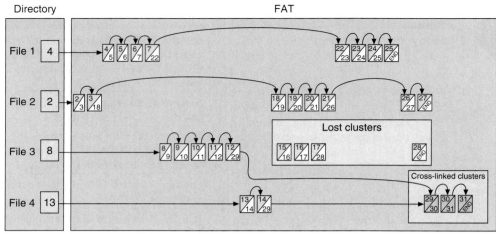

Figure 3-27 Lost and cross-linked clusters

© Cengage Learning 2013

> **Notes** For an interesting discussion of how the FAT works, see the document FAT Details.pdf on the companion web site for this book at *www.cengagebrain.com*. See the Preface for more information.

Used with the /F parameter, chkdsk searches for and fixes two types of file system errors made by the FAT or MFT:

- ◢ *Lost clusters (also called lost allocation units)*—Lost clusters are clusters that are marked as used clusters in the FAT or MFT, but the cluster does not belong to any file. In effect, the data in these clusters is lost.
- ◢ *Cross-linked clusters*—Cross-linked clusters are clusters that are marked in the FAT or MFT as belonging to more than one file.

Used with the /R parameter, chkdsk checks for lost clusters and cross-linked clusters and also checks for bad sectors on the drive. The FAT and MFT keep a table of bad sectors that they normally do not use. However, over time, a sector might become unreliable. If chkdsk determines that a sector is unreliable, it attempts to recover the data from the sector and also marks the sector as bad so that the FAT or MFT will not use it again.

Used without any parameters, the chkdsk command only reports information about a drive and does not make any repairs.

In the following sample commands, we're not showing the command prompt; the default drive and directory are not important. To check the hard drive for file system errors and repair them, use this command:

```
chkdsk C:/F
```

To redirect a report of the findings of the chkdsk command to a file that you can later print, use this command:

```
chkdsk C:>Myfile.txt
```

Use the /R parameter of the chkdsk command to fix file system errors and also examine each sector of the drive for bad sectors, like so:

```
chkdsk C:/R
```

A+
220-802
1.2, 1.3,
4.6

If chkdsk finds data that it can recover, it asks you for permission to do so. If you give permission, it saves the recovered data in files that it stores in the root directory of the drive.

> **Notes** Use either the /F or /R parameter with chkdsk, but not both. Using both parameters is redundant. For the most thorough check of a drive, use /R.

The chkdsk command will not fix anything unless the drive is locked, which means the drive has no open files. If you attempt to use chkdsk with the /F or /R parameter when files are open, chkdsk tells you of the problem and asks permission to schedule the run the next time Windows is restarted. Know that the process will take plenty of time. For Windows 7/Vista, you must use an elevated command prompt window to run chkdsk.

> **Notes** The chkdsk command is also available from the Windows 7/Vista Recovery Environment and the Windows XP Recovery Console.

DEFRAG [*DRIVE:*] [/C]

The defrag command examines a magnetic hard drive for **fragmented files** (files written to a disk in noncontiguous clusters) and rewrites these files to the drive in contiguous clusters. You use this command to optimize a hard drive's performance. Table 3-5 shows two examples of the command. Recall that it's not a good idea to defrag solid-state storage devices such as an SSD, flash drive, or smart card. Doing so can shorten the life of the drive.

Command	Result
defrag C:	Defrag drive C
defrag /c	Defrag all volumes on the computer, including drive C

© Cengage Learning 2013

Table 3-5 Defrag commands and results

The defrag command requires an elevated command prompt window in Windows 7/Vista. It is not available under the Windows 7/Vista Recovery Environment or the XP Recovery Console. Earlier in the chapter, you learned to defrag a drive using the Windows drive properties box.

FORMAT <*DRIVE:*> [/V:*LABEL*] [/Q] [FS:<*FILESYSTEM*>]

You can format a hard drive or other storage device using Disk Management. In addition, you can use the format command from a command prompt window and from the Windows 7/Vista Recovery Environment and the XP Recovery Console. This high-level format installs a file system on the device and *erases all data on the volume*. Table 3-6 lists various sample uses of the Format command.

A+
220-802
1.2, 1.3,
4.6

Command	Description
`Format A: /V:mylabel`	Allows you to enter a volume label only once when formatting several disks; the same volume label is used for all disks. A volume label appears at the top of the directory list to help you identify the disk.
`Format A: /Q`	Re-creates the root directory and FAT to quickly format a previously formatted disk that is in good condition; /Q does not read or write to any other part of the disk
`Format D: /FS:NTFS`	Formats drive D using the NTFS file system
`Format D: /FS:FAT32`	Formats drive D using the FAT32 file system
`Format D: /FS:EXFAT`	Formats drive D using the extended FAT file system

Table 3-6   Format commands and results   © Cengage Learning 2013

One use of the format command is to change the installed file system. For example, in Figure 3-28, the chkdsk command shows a USB flash drive is formatted using the FAT32 file system. The format command reformatted the drive using the exFAT file system.

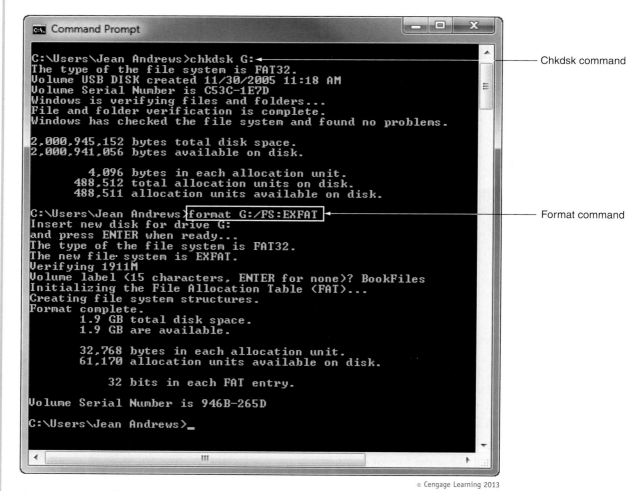

© Cengage Learning 2013

Figure 3-28   The format command uses the exFAT file system to format a flash drive

A+
220-802
1.2, 1.3,
4.6

SHUTDOWN [/M *COMPUTERNAME*] [/I] [/R] [/S] [/F] [/T *XX*]

Use the shutdown command to shut down the local computer or a remote computer. You must be logged on with an administrator account to use this command. By default, the command gives users a 30-second warning before shutdown. To shut down a remote computer on the network, you must have an administrator account on that computer and be logged onto the local computer with that same account and password. Table 3-7 lists some shutdown commands.

Command	Description
shutdown /r	Restart the local computer
shutdown /s /m \\bluelight	Shut down the remote computer named \\bluelight
shutdown /s /m \\bluelight /t 60	Shut down the \\bluelight computer after a 60-second delay
shutdown /i	Displays the Remote Shutdown Dialog box so you can choose computers on the network to shut down

Table 3-7 Shutdown commands and results

© Cengage Learning 2013

Hands-on | Project 3-3 Using a Batch File

A file with a .bat file extension is called a batch file. You can use a batch file to execute a group of commands, sometimes called a script, from a command prompt. Do the following in order to learn to use a batch file:

1. Using a command prompt window, copy the files in your My Documents folder to a folder named \Save on a USB flash drive. Do not include subfolders in the copy.

2. Using Notepad, create a batch file named MyBatch.bat on the USB flash drive that contains the commands to do the following:

   a. Create the C:\Data folder and a subfolder named C:\Data\Documents.
   b. Copy all the files in your \Save folder to the C:\Data\Documents folder.
   c. List the contents of the C:\Data\Documents folder.

3. Using a command prompt window, execute the MyBatch.bat file and fix any problems you see. What happens when you execute the batch file and the C:\Data\Documents folder already exists?

A+
220-802
1.2, 1.4

USE DISK MANAGEMENT TO MANAGE HARD DRIVES

The primary tool for managing hard drives is Disk Management. In Chapter 2, you learned how to install Windows on a new hard drive. This installation process initializes, partitions, and formats the drive. After Windows is installed, you can use Disk Management to install and manage drives. In this part of the chapter, you will learn to use Disk Management to manage partitions on a drive, prepare a new drive for first use, mount a drive, use Windows dynamic disks, and troubleshoot problems with the hard drive.

A+
220-802
1.2, 1.4

> **Notes** In most Microsoft documentation, a partition is called a partition until it is formatted, and then it is called a volume.

RESIZE, CREATE, AND DELETE PARTITIONS

Suppose you have installed Windows 7 on a hard drive and used all available space on the drive for the one partition. Now you want to split the partition into two partitions so you can install Windows 8 in a dual boot installation with Windows 7. You can use Disk Management to shrink the original partition, which frees up some space for the new Windows 8 partition. Follow these steps:

1. To open the Disk Management window, use one of these methods:

   ◢ Click **Start**, right-click **Computer**, and select **Manage** from the shortcut menu. In the Computer Management window, click **Disk Management**.

   ◢ Click **Start**, type **Disk Management** or **diskmgmt.msc** in the search box and press **Enter**.

2. The Disk Management window opens (see Figure 3-29). To shrink the existing partition, right-click in the partition space and select **Shrink Volume** from the shortcut menu (see Figure 3-29). The Shrink dialog box appears showing the amount of free space on the partition. Enter the amount in MB to shrink the partition, which cannot be more than the amount of free space so that no data on the partition will be lost. (For best performance, be sure to leave at least 15 percent free space on the disk.) Click **Shrink**. The disk now shows unallocated space.

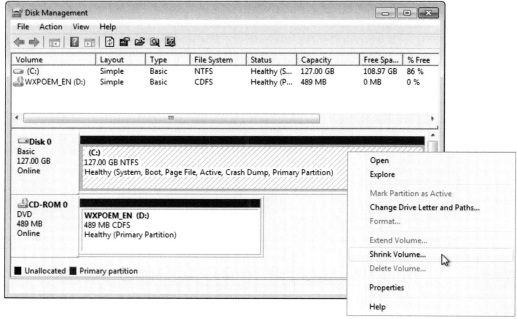

© Cengage Learning 2013

Figure 3-29   Shrink a volume to make room for a new partition

3. To create a new partition in the unallocated space, right-click in that space and select **New Simple Volume** from the shortcut menu (see Figure 3-30). The New Simple Volume Wizard opens.

A+
220-802
1.2, 1.4

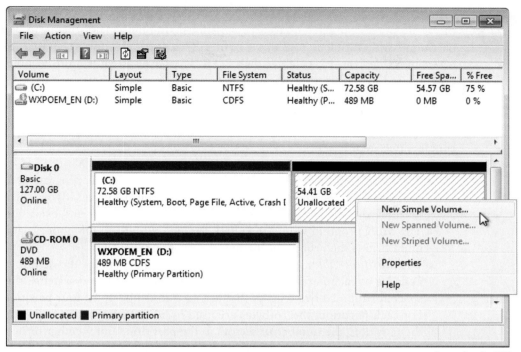

Figure 3-30 Use unallocated space to create a new partition

© Cengage Learning 2013

4. Follow the directions on-screen to enter the size of the volume in MB and select a drive letter for the volume, a file system, and the size for each allocation unit (also called a cluster). It's best to leave the cluster size at the Default value. You can also decide to do a **quick format**, which doesn't scan the volume for bad sectors; use it only when a hard drive has been previously formatted and is in healthy condition. The partition is then created and formatted with the file system you chose.

Notice in Figure 3-29 the options on the shortcut menu that you can use to make the partition the active partition (the one the OS will boot from), change the drive letter for a volume, format the volume (erases all data on the volume), extend the volume (increase the size of the volume), and shrink and delete the volume. An option that is not available for the particular volume and situation is grayed.

> **Notes** The size of a partition or volume cannot be changed in Windows XP unless you use third-party software.

> **A+ Exam Tip** The A+ 220-802 exam expects you to know how to use Disk Management to extend and split partitions and configure a new hard drive in a system.

PREPARE A DRIVE FOR FIRST USE

When you install a new, second hard drive in a computer, use Disk Management to prepare the drive for use. This happens in a two-step process:

Step 1: Initialize the Disk

When the disk is initialized, Windows identifies the disk as a basic disk. A **basic disk** is a single hard drive that works independently of other hard drives. Windows also installs a partitioning system on the hard drive. You can choose the Master Boot Record (MBR)

A+
220-802
1.2, 1.4

system or the **Globally Unique Identifier Partition Table (GUID or GPT)** system. Recall that the MBR system can have up to four partitions, although one of them can be an extended partition with multiple logical drives. The GPT system can support up to 128 partitions and is recommended for drives larger than 2 TB. The GPT system is more reliable, but it can only be used by 64-bit operating systems on computers that have an EFI or UEFI chip rather than the traditional BIOS chip. In this chapter, we focus on the MBR system, which is by far the most common system.

The MBR system writes an MBR record to the first sector of the disk (512 bytes) that contains two items:

▲ *The master boot program (446 bytes).* The purpose of this program is to begin the process of finding and loading an OS installed on the drive. If you were to make this hard drive your boot device, startup BIOS would look for and execute this program. The MBR program would then look for and execute an OS boot program. (This program begins the process of loading the OS.)

▲ *The partition table.* Recall that the partition table contains the description, location, and size of each partition on the drive. For Windows-based systems, this table has space for four 16-byte entries that are used to define up to four partitions on the drive. For each partition, the 16 bytes are used to hold the beginning and ending location of the partition, the number of sectors in the partition, and whether or not the partition is bootable. Recall that the one bootable partition is called the active partition.

When you first open Disk Management after you have installed a new hard drive, the Initialize Disk box automatically appears (see Figure 3-31). If you don't see the box, right-click in the Disk area and select **Initialize Disk** from the shortcut menu (see Figure 3-32). Select the partitioning system and click **OK**. Disk Management now reports the hard drive as a Basic disk.

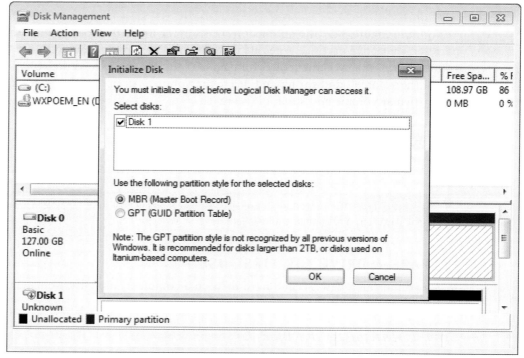

© Cengage Learning 2013

Figure 3-31   Use the Initialize Disk box to set up a partitioning system on a new hard drive

A+
220-802
1.2, 1.4

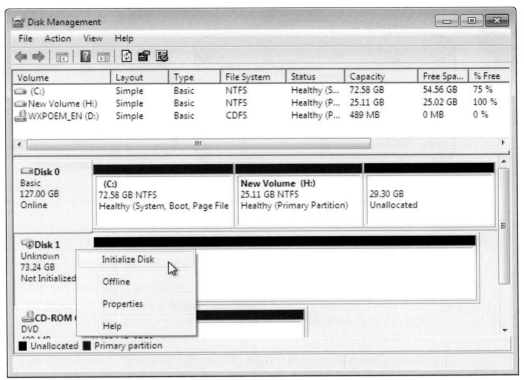

Figure 3-32 The first step to install a new hard drive is to initialize the disk

© Cengage Learning 2013

Step 2: Create a Volume and Format It with a File System

To create a new volume on a disk, right-click in the unallocated space, select **New Simple Volume** from the shortcut menu, and follow the directions on-screen to select the size of the volume, assign a drive letter and name to the volume, and select the file system. When the process is finished, the drive is formatted and ready for use. When you open Windows Explorer, you should see the new volume available for use.

> **Notes** In Chapter 6, you learn to use a command prompt to create and manage partitions on a hard drive.

HOW TO MOUNT A DRIVE

A mounted drive is a volume that can be accessed by way of a folder on another volume so that the folder has more available space. A mounted drive is useful when a folder is on a volume that is too small to hold all the data you want in the folder. In Figure 3-33, the mounted drive gives the C:\Projects folder a capacity of 30 GB. The C:\Projects folder is called the mount point for the mounted drive.

A+
220-802
1.2, 1.4

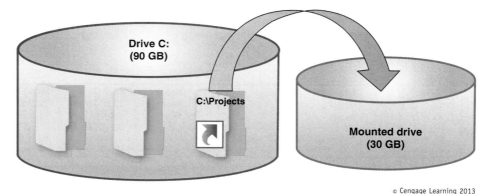

© Cengage Learning 2013

Figure 3-33   The C:\Projects folder is the mount point for the mounted drive

Follow these steps to mount a drive:

1. Make sure the volume that is to host the mounted drive uses the NTFS file system. The folder on this volume, called the mount point, must be empty. You can also create the folder during the mount process. In our example, we are mounting a drive to the C:\Projects folder.

2. Using Disk Management, right-click in the unallocated space of a disk. In our example, we're using Disk 1 (the second hard drive). Select **New Simple Volume** from the shortcut menu. The New Simple Volume Wizard launches. Using the wizard, specify the amount of unallocated space you want to devote to the volume. (In our example, we are using 30 GB although the resulting size of the C:\Projects folder will only show about 29 GB because of overhead.)

3. As you follow the wizard, the box shown on the left side of Figure 3-34 appears. Select **Mount in the following empty NTFS folder,** and then click **Browse.** In the Browse for Drive Path box that appears (see the right side of Figure 3-34), you can drill down to an existing folder or click **New Folder** to create a new folder on drive C:.

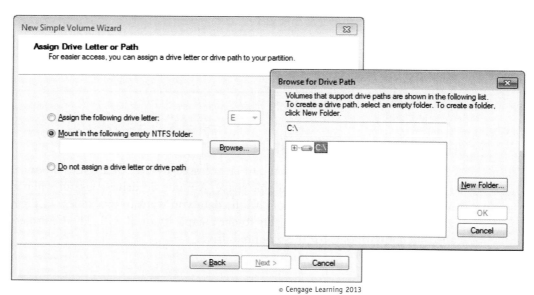

© Cengage Learning 2013

Figure 3-34   Select the mount point for the new volume

A+
220-802
1.2, 1.4

4. Complete the wizard by selecting a file system for the new volume and an Allocation unit size (the cluster size). The volume is created and formatted.

5. To verify the drive is mounted, open Windows Explorer and then open the Properties box for the folder. In our example, the Properties box for the C:\Projects folder is shown in the middle of Figure 3-35. Notice the Properties box reports the folder type as a Mounted Volume. When you click Properties in the Properties box, the volume Properties box appears (see the right side of Figure 3-35). In this box, you can see the size of the volume, which is the size of the mounted volume, less overhead.

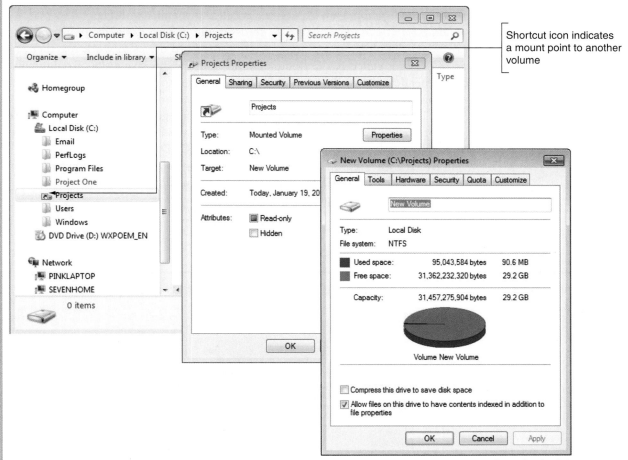

Shortcut icon indicates a mount point to another volume

© Cengage Learning 2013

Figure 3-35 The mounted drive in Windows Explorer appears as a very large folder

You can think of a mount point, such as C:\Projects, as a shortcut to a volume on a second drive. If you look closely at the left window in Figure 3-35, you can see the shortcut icon beside the Projects folder.

WINDOWS DYNAMIC DISKS

A basic disk works independently of other hard drives, but a **dynamic disk** can work with other hard drives to hold data. Volumes stored on dynamic disks are called **dynamic volumes**. Several dynamic disks can work together to collectively present a single dynamic volume to the system.

A+
220-802
1.2, 1.4

When dynamic disks work together, data to configure each hard drive is stored in a disk management database that resides in the last 1 MB of storage space on each hard drive. Home editions of Windows do not support dynamic disks.

Here are four uses of dynamic disks:

- *For better reliability, you can configure a hard drive as a dynamic disk and allocate the space as a simple volume.* This is the best reason to use dynamic disks and is a recommended best practice. Because of the way a dynamic disk works, the simple volume is considered more reliable than when it is stored on a basic disk. A volume that is stored on only one hard drive is called a **simple volume**.
- *You can implement dynamic disks on multiple hard drives to extend a volume across these drives (called spanning).* This volume is called a spanned volume.
- *Dynamic disks can be used to piece data across multiple hard drives to improve performance.* The technology to configure two or more hard drives to work together as an array of drives is called **RAID (redundant array of inexpensive disks or redundant array of independent disks)**. Joining hard drives together to improve performance is called **striping** or **RAID 0**. The volume is called a striped volume (see Figure 3-36). When RAID is implemented in this way using Disk Management, it is called **software RAID**. A more reliable way of configuring RAID is to use BIOS setup on a motherboard that supports RAID, which is called **hardware RAID**.
- *For Windows XP, you can use dynamic disks to mirror two hard drives for fault tolerance (called* **mirroring** *or* **RAID 1***).* This feature is not available in Windows 7/Vista and is not considered a good practice in XP.

**One simple volume
on a single disk**

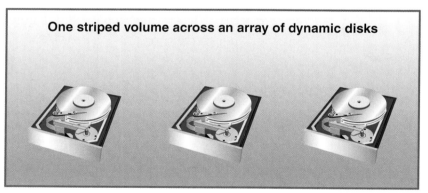

One striped volume across an array of dynamic disks

© Cengage Learning 2013

Figure 3-36   A simple volume is stored on a single disk, but a striped volume is stored on an array of dynamic disks

You can use Disk Management to convert two or more basic disks to dynamic disks. Then you can use unallocated space on these disks to create a simple, spanned, or striped volume. To convert a basic disk to dynamic, right-click the Disk area and select **Convert to Dynamic Disk** from the shortcut menu (see Figure 3-37), and then right-click free space on the disk and select **New Simple Volume**, **New Spanned Volume**, or **New Striped Volume** from the shortcut menu. If you were to use spanning or striping in Figure 3-37, you could make Disk 1 and Disk 2 dynamic disks that hold a single volume. The size of the volume would be the sum of the space on both hard drives.

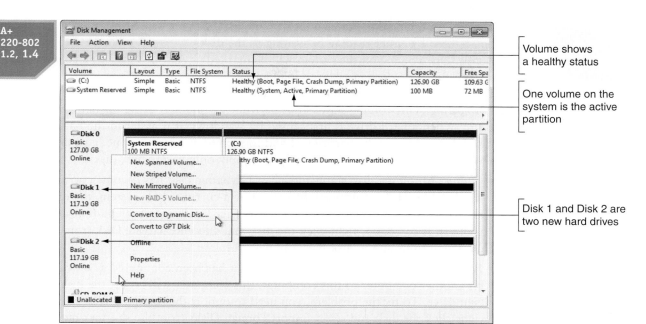

A+
220-802
1.2, 1.4

Volume shows
a healthy status

One volume on the
system is the active
partition

Disk 1 and Disk 2 are
two new hard drives

3

Figure 3-37 Convert a basic disk to a dynamic disk

© Cengage Learning 2013

Now for some serious cautions about software RAID where you use Windows for spanning and striping: Microsoft warns that when Windows is used for software RAID, the risk of catastrophic failure increases and can lead to data loss. Microsoft suggests you only use Windows spanning or striping when you have no other option. In other words, spanning and striping in Windows aren't very safe—to expand the size of a volume, use a mounted drive or use hardware RAID.

> **Notes** When Windows implements RAID, know that you cannot install an OS on a spanned or striped volume that uses software RAID. You can, however, install Windows on a hardware RAID drive.
> Also, after you have converted a basic disk to a dynamic disk, you cannot revert it to a basic disk without losing all data on the drive.

USE DISK MANAGEMENT TO TROUBLESHOOT HARD DRIVE PROBLEMS

Notice in Figure 3-37 that this system has three hard drives, Disk 0, Disk 1, and Disk 2, and information about the disks and volumes is shown in the window. When you are having a problem with a hard drive, it helps to know what the information in the Disk Management window means. Here are the drive and volume statuses you might see in this window:

▲ *Healthy.* The healthy volume status shown in Figure 3-37 indicates that the volume is formatted with a file system and that the file system is working without errors.

▲ *Failed.* A failed volume status indicates a problem with the hard drive or that the file system has become corrupted. To try to fix the problem, make sure the hard drive data cable and power cable are secure. Data on a failed volume is likely to be lost. For dynamic disks, if the disk status is Offline, try bringing the disk back online (how to do that is coming up in this chapter).

A+
220-802
1.2, 1.4

▲ *Online*. An online disk status indicates the disk has been sensed by Windows and can be accessed by either reading or writing to the disk.

▲ *Active*. One volume on the system will be marked as Active. This is the volume that startup BIOS looks to in order to load an OS.

▲ *Unallocated*. Space on the disk is marked as unallocated if it has not yet been partitioned.

▲ *Formatting*. This volume status appears while a volume is being formatted.

▲ *Basic*. When a hard drive is first sensed by Windows, it is assigned the Basic disk status. A basic disk can be partitioned and formatted as a stand-alone hard drive.

▲ *Dynamic*. The following status indicators apply only to dynamic disks:

• *Offline*. An offline disk status indicates a dynamic disk has become corrupted or is unavailable. The problem can be caused by a corrupted file system, the drive cables are loose, the hard drive has failed, or another hardware problem. If you believe the problem is corrected, right-click the disk and select **Reactivate Disk** from the shortcut menu to bring the disk back online.

• *Foreign drive*. If you move a hard drive that has been configured as a dynamic disk on another computer to this computer, this computer will report the disk as a foreign drive. To fix the problem, you need to import the foreign drive. To do that, right-click the disk and select **Import Foreign Disks** from the shortcut menu. You should then be able to see the volumes on the disk.

• *Healthy (At Risk)*. The dynamic disk can be accessed, but I/O errors have occurred. Try returning the disk to online status. If the volume status does not return to healthy, back up all data and replace the drive.

If you are still having problems with a hard drive, volume, or mounted drive, check Event Viewer for events about the drive that might have been recorded there. These events might help you understand the nature of the problem and what to do about it. How to use Event Viewer is covered in Chapter 4.

Hands-on | Project 3-4   Using Disk Management on a Virtual Machine

In Project 2-7 of Chapter 2, you installed Virtual PC software and used it to install Windows 7 in a virtual machine. Use this VM to practice using Disk Management. Do the following:

1. Open Windows Virtual PC, but do not open the virtual machine.

2. With the virtual machine selected, click **Settings**. Use the Settings box to add a new hard drive to the VM.

3. Start up the VM, log on to Windows, and open Disk Management.

4. Use Disk Management to initialize the new disk and partition it. Create two partitions on the disk, one formatted using the NTFS file system and one using the FAT32 file system.

5. View the new volumes using Windows Explorer.

6. Create and save a snip of your screen showing the virtual machine with the new volumes created. Email the snip to your instructor.

REGIONAL AND LANGUAGE SETTINGS

**A+
220-802
1.2**

One more task you might be called on to do as a part of maintaining a computer is to help a user configure a computer to use a different language. Suppose a user needs to see Windows messages in Spanish and wants to use a Spanish keyboard, such as the one in Figure 3-38. Configuring a computer for another language involves downloading and installing the language pack, changing the Windows display language, changing regional settings for dates, time, and numbers, and changing the language used for keyboard input.

3

© Cengage Learning 2013

Figure 3-38 Spanish keyboard

Two ways to install a different language in Windows are:

▲ For Windows 7/Vista Ultimate and Enterprise editions, you can use Windows Update to download and install a language pack that translates most of the Windows user interface. Microsoft offers language packs for many languages.

▲ For all editions of Windows 7/Vista/XP, you can download and install a Language Interface Pack (LIP) that translates only some of the Windows user interface.

A+
220-802
1.2

APPLYING | CONCEPTS

Using Windows 7 Ultimate, follow these steps to configure the computer to use Spanish for the display:

1. To download the Spanish pack using Windows Update, click **Start**, **All Programs**, and **Windows Update**. If important updates are listed in the Windows Update window, first install any of these updates your system needs.

2. In the Windows Update window, if optional updates are not listed, click **Check for updates**. If you see optional updates listed, click **optional updates are available**.

3. In the Select updates to install window (see Figure 3-39), in the list of Windows 7 Language Packs, select the **Spanish Language Pack**. Make sure other updates that you don't want are not selected. Click **OK** and click **Install updates**.

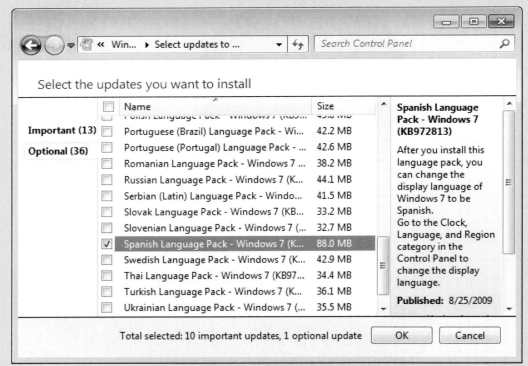

Figure 3-39 Select the language to download and install

© Cengage Learning 2013

4. You are now ready to configure the computer to use the new language. Open Control Panel and click **Clock, Language, and Region**. In the Clock, Language, and Region window, click **Change the date, time, or number format**. The Region and Language box opens (see Figure 3-40).

A+
220-802
1.2

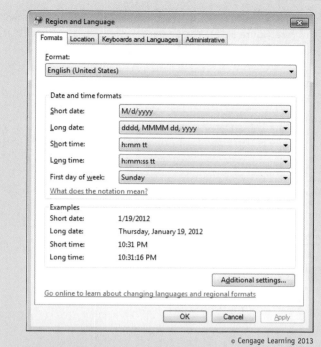

© Cengage Learning 2013

Figure 3-40 Use the Region and Language box to change how dates, times, and numbers display

5. To change the format used to display dates, times, and numbers, select the language from the drop-down list under Format.

6. To change the keyboard layout, select the Keyboards and Languages tab. Click **Change keyboards**. The Text Services and Input Languages box appears. In the list of installed services, only English is listed (see the left side of Figure 3-41). Click **Add**. In the Add Input Language box, select a Spanish keyboard, as shown on the right side of Figure 3-41. Click **OK**. The Spanish keyboard is now added to the list of input languages. Under Default input language, select the Spanish language and click **Apply**. Click **OK** to close the dialog box.

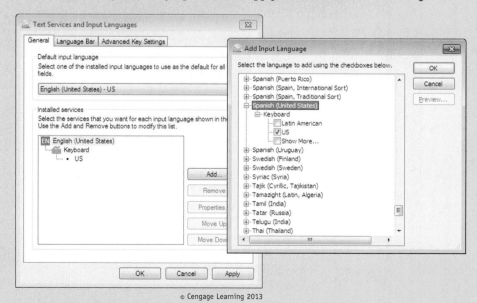

© Cengage Learning 2013

Figure 3-41 Add an input language

A+
220-802
1.2

7. To change the display language on the Keyboards and Languages tab, select **español** from the drop-down menu (see Figure 3-42). The language appears in the list of installed languages because the Spanish language was installed in Step 3.

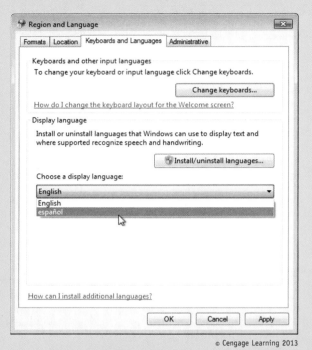

© Cengage Learning 2013

Figure 3-42 Select the display language

8. Click **Apply**. A message appears that says you must log off before changes will take effect. Click **Log off now**. After logging back on the system, the Windows interface is now translated into Español (see Figure 3-43).

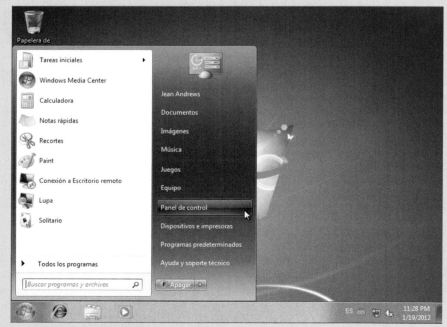

© Cengage Learning 2013

Figure 3-43 Display language in Spanish

Windows 7/Vista Ultimate offers language packs through Windows Update. For other Windows editions, you can go to the Microsoft web site (*www.microsoft.com*) and download the Language Interface Pack (LIP). Then double-click the downloaded file to install the language. After the language pack is installed, use Control Panel to change the Windows display for the installed language. You also need to change the format used for numbers, currencies, dates, and time. And, if a special keyboard is to be used, you need to change the input language.

Hands-on | Project 3-5 Installing Spanish Using Windows 7/Vista Ultimate

Download and install the Spanish language pack on a Windows 7 or Vista computer. If you like, you can use the virtual machine used in Hands-on Project 3-4 for the installation. Configure the machine to use Spanish as the display language and for keyboard input. Print a screen shot of your Windows desktop that appears in Spanish. Return your language settings to English.

>> CHAPTER SUMMARY

Scheduled Preventive Maintenance

◢ Regular preventive maintenance includes verifying Windows settings, cleaning up the hard drive, defragmenting the hard drive, checking the drive for errors, uninstalling unwanted software, and doing whatever else is necessary to free up enough space on the hard drive for Windows to perform well.

◢ Windows 7/Vista stores user profiles in the C:\Users folder, and XP stores them in the C:\Documents and Settings folder.

◢ For best performance, allow at least 15 percent of free space on the Windows volume. The easiest way to clean up temporary files is to use the Disk Cleanup utility in the drive properties box.

◢ You can defrag the hard drive by using the drive properties box or the Defrag command. By default, Windows 7/Vista automatically defrags weekly.

◢ Use the Chkdsk utility to check the drive for errors and recover data. The utility can be accessed from a command prompt or the drive properties box.

◢ Windows 7/Vista supports compressed (zipped) folders and NTFS folder and file compression. You can also compress an NTFS volume.

◢ Virtual memory uses hard drive space as memory to increase the total amount of memory available. Virtual memory is stored in a paging file named Pagefile.sys. To save space on drive C:, you can move the file to another volume.

Backup Procedures

◢ You need a plan for disaster recovery in the event the hard drive fails. This plan needs to include routine backups of data and system files.

◢ A system image of the Windows 7 volume can be created using the Backup and Restore utility. The Complete PC Backup in Vista is a backup of the Vista volume. Windows XP Automated System Recovery can back up the entire hard drive.

◢ Windows 7 Backup and Restore can be used to schedule routine backups of user data files.

Managing Files, Folders, and Hard Drives

▲ Commands useful to manage files, folders, and storage media include Help, Dir, Del, Copy, Recover, Xcopy, Robocopy, MD, CD, RD, Chkdsk, Defrag, and Format.

▲ Use Disk Management to manage hard drives and partitions. Use it to create, delete, and resize partitions, mount a drive, manage dynamic disks, and solve problems with hard drives. XP Disk Management cannot resize a partition.

Regional and Language Settings

▲ A language pack to display and input the Windows user interface in a language other than English can be downloaded and installed in Windows 7/Vista Ultimate and Enterprise editions. A limited Language Interface Pack (LIP) can be downloaded and installed using any edition of Windows 7/Vista.

▲ Change the display and input language and the format used for numbers, currencies, dates, and times using the Regional and Language Options dialog box accessed from Control Panel.

>> KEY TERMS

For explanations of key terms, see the Glossary near the end of the book.

active partition
Automated System Recovery (ASR)
basic disk
boot partition
cluster
Compact Disc File System (CDFS)
Complete PC Backup
defragment
Disk Cleanup
dynamic disk
dynamic volumes
elevated command prompt window
extended partition
file allocation table (FAT)
file allocation unit
file system
formatting
fragmented files
Globally Unique Identifier Partition Table (GUID or GPT)

hardware RAID
high-level format
initialization files
logical drives
low-level formatting
Master Boot Record (MBR)
master file table (MFT)
mirroring
mount point
mounted drive
Offline Files
Pagefile.sys
partition
partition table
primary partition
quick format
RAID (redundant array of inexpensive disks or redundant array of independent disks)
RAID0
RAID1
registry

restore point
sector
shadow copy
simple volume
slack
software RAID
striping
system image
system partition
System Protection
System Restore
system state data
track
Universal Disc Format (UDF)
user profile
user profile namespace
virtual memory
volume
wildcard

>> REVIEWING THE BASICS

1. What are the three Windows settings critical to securing a computer that need to be verified as part of regular maintenance?

2. What folder holds the Windows registry? What folder holds a backup of the registry?

3. What folder holds 32-bit programs installed in a 64-bit installation of Windows?

4. What file in the user account folder stores user settings?

5. What is the purpose of the C:\Windows\CSC folder?

6. What is the purpose of the Windows.old folder?

7. How can you delete the Windows.old folder?

8. By default, how often does Windows 7 automatically defrag a drive?

9. What is another name for a file allocation unit, which is used to hold parts of a file on the hard drive?

10. On what type of hard drive does Windows 7 disable defragmenting?

11. What are two reasons to uninstall software you no longer use?

12. What is the filename and normal path of the Windows paging file used for virtual memory?

13. What type of storage media must be used to create a Windows 7 system image?

14. What two Windows utilities are used to create previous versions of files that can be recovered from the file properties dialog box?

15. Why is it important to not store a backup of drive C on to another partition on the same hard drive?

16. What does Windows XP call a backup of the critical system files it needs for Windows operations?

17. What is the *%SystemRoot%* folder as used in Microsoft documentation?

18. What Windows 7/Vista utility creates restore points?

19. How can you delete all restore points?

20. In what folder are restore points kept?

21. Which dialog box can you use to manually create a restore point?

22. What is the difference between the file allocation table used by the exFAT file system and the one used by the FAT32 file system?

23. List the steps to open an elevated command prompt window.

24. In a command line, what is the purpose of the ? in a filename?

25. What is the purpose of the more parameter at the end of a command line?

26. What is the command to list all files and subdirectories in a directory?

27. Using Windows 7 or Vista, what type of command prompt window is needed to run the Chkdsk command?

28. When you want to use Chkdsk to fix file system errors and the drive is not locked, when does Windows schedule the Chkdsk command to run?

29. What command is intended to replace Xcopy?

30. Which Windows tool can you use to split a partition into two partitions?

31. Which is more stable, RAID implemented by Windows or RAID implemented by hardware?

32. When you move a dynamic disk to a new computer, what status will Disk Management first assign the drive?

33. Which editions of Windows 7 allow you to install a language pack by using Windows Update?

>> THINKING CRITICALLY

1. Write and test commands to do the following:
   (Answers can vary.)

   a. Create a folder named C:\data.

   b. Create a folder named C:\data\test1 and a folder named C:\data\test2.

   c. Copy Notepad.exe to the Test1 folder.

   d. Move Notepad.exe from the Test1 folder to the Test2 folder.

   e. Make C:\ the default folder.

   f. Without changing the default folder, list all files in the Test2 folder.

   g. Delete the Test2 folder.

   h. Delete the C:\data folder.

2. You are trying to clean up a slow Windows 7 system and discover that the 75 GB hard drive has only 5 GB free space. The entire hard drive is taken up by drive C. What is the best way to free up some space?

   a. Compress the entire hard drive.

   b. Move the \Program Files folder to an external hard drive.

   c. Delete the Windows.old folder.

   d. Reduce the size of the paging file.

3. Which is the best first step to protect important data on your hard drive?

   a. Use dynamic disks to set up a striped volume so that the data has redundancy.

   b. Back the data up to another media.

   c. Compress the folder that holds the data.

   d. Put password protection on the data folder.

>> *REAL PROBLEMS, REAL SOLUTIONS*

REAL PROBLEM 3-1: Researching the Winsxs Folder

While cleaning up a hard drive, you begin to look for folders that are excessively large and discover the C:\Windows\winsxs folder is more than 7 GB. That's almost half the size of the entire C:\Windows folder. Use the web to research the purpose of the winsxs folder. What goes in this folder and how does it get there? How can the size of the folder be reduced without causing major trouble with the OS? Write a brief one-page paper about this folder and cite at least three articles you find on the web about it.

REAL PROBLEM 3-2: Using Microsoft SyncToy

You own a small computer service company and have several clients who work out of a home office. Jason is one of them. Jason uses Windows XP on his desktop and Windows 7 on his laptop. He travels with his laptop but uses his desktop computer when he's at home. He keeps all his important data files in a folder, C:\Data, on his desktop computer. When he leaves for a business trip, he copies only the files from the \Data folder to his laptop that he expects to use on the trip. On the trip, some of these files are edited or deleted, and some new files are created. When he gets back home, he copies one file at a time from the laptop to the desktop using his home network. However, he has told you that occasionally he forgets to copy the files from the laptop to the desktop before he makes changes in the desktop files. Therefore, he's concerned that if he copied the entire \Data folder from the laptop to the desktop, he might lose an important change.

He has asked you to help him find a better method to synchronize his \Data folders on these two computers. After a little research, you find the free Microsoft SyncToy utility on the Microsoft web site and decide you need to test it to see if it will meet Jason's needs. Set up a testing situation and then answer the following questions:

1. List the high-level steps (not the keystrokes) you used to test the utility.

2. What test files did you use to test it?

3. What problems, if any, did you encounter in the testing process?

4. Do you think the utility is a good fit for Jason? Why or why not?

REAL PROBLEM 3-3: Cleaning Up a Sluggish Windows System

Do you have a Windows system that is slow and needs optimizing? If not, talk with family and friends and try to find a slow system that can use your help. Using all the tools and techniques presented in this chapter, clean up this sluggish Windows system. Take detailed notes as you go, showing what you checked before you started to solve the problems, what you did to solve the problems, and what were the results of your efforts. What questions did you have along the way? Bring these questions to class for discussion.

Optimizing Windows

In the last chapter, you learned about the tools and strategies to
maintain Windows and about the importance of keeping good
backups. This chapter takes you one step further as a PC support
technician so that you can get the best performance out of Windows.
We begin the chapter learning about the Windows tools you'll need
to optimize Windows. Then we turn our attention to the steps you
can follow to cause a sluggish Windows system to perform at its
best and how to manually remove software that does not uninstall
using normal methods. As you read the chapter, you might consider
following along using a Windows 7 system.

> **Notes** Windows installed in a virtual machine is an excellent environment to use
> when practicing the skills in this chapter.

WINDOWS UTILITIES AND TOOLS TO SUPPORT THE OS

A+
220-802
1.4

Knowledge is power when it comes to supporting Windows. In this part of the chapter, you learn more about how Windows works and to use some Windows tools to poke around under the hood to see what is really happening that is slowing Windows down or giving other problems.

WHAT IS THE SHELL AND THE KERNEL?

Sounds like we're talking about a grain of wheat, but Windows has a shell and a kernel and you need to understand what they are and how they work so you can solve problems with each. A **shell** is the portion of an OS that relates to the user and to applications. The **kernel** is responsible for interacting with hardware. Figure 4-1 shows how the shell and kernel relate to users, applications, and hardware. In addition, the figure shows a third component of an OS, the configuration data. For Windows, this data is primarily contained in the registry.

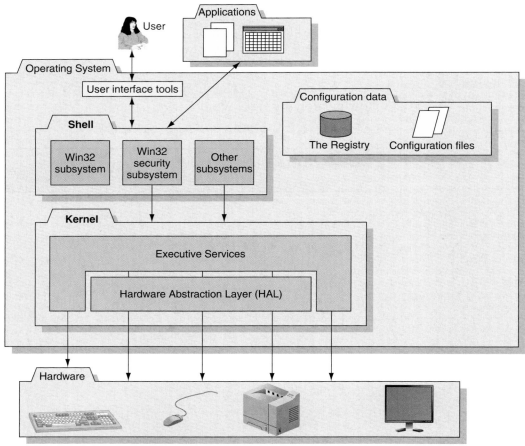

© Cengage Learning 2013

Figure 4-1 Inside an operating system, different components perform various functions

THE WINDOWS SHELL

The shell provides tools such as Windows Explorer or the Windows desktop as a way for the user to do such things as select music to burn to a CD or launch an application. For applications, the shell provides commands and procedures that applications can call on to do such things as print a document, read from a storage device, or display a photograph on-screen.

The shell is made up of several subsystems that all operate in **user mode**, which means these subsystems have only limited access to system information and can access hardware only through other OS services. One of these subsystems, the Win32 security subsystem, provides logon to the system and other security functions, including privileges for file access. All applications relate to Windows by way of the Win32 subsystem.

THE WINDOWS KERNEL

The kernel, or core, of the OS is responsible for interacting with hardware. Because the kernel operates in **kernel mode**, it has more power to communicate with hardware devices than the shell has. Applications operating under the OS cannot get to hardware devices without the shell passing those requests to the kernel. This separation of tasks provides for a more stable system and helps to prevent a wayward application from destabilizing the system.

The kernel has two main components: 1) the **HAL** (hardware abstraction layer), which is the layer closest to the hardware, and 2) the **executive services** interface, which is a group of services that operate in kernel mode between the user mode subsystems and the HAL. Executive services contained in the ntoskrnl.exe program file manage memory, I/O devices, file systems, some security, and other key components directly or by way of device drivers.

When Windows is first installed, it builds the HAL based on the type of CPU installed. The HAL cannot be moved from one computer to another, which is one reason you cannot copy a Windows installation from one computer to another.

HOW WINDOWS MANAGES APPLICATIONS

When an application is first installed, its program files are normally stored on the hard drive. When the application is launched, the program is copied from the hard drive into memory and there it is called a process. A **process** is a program that is running under the authority of the shell, together with the system resources assigned to it. System resources might include other programs it has started and memory addresses to hold its data. When the process makes a request for resources, this request is made to the Win32 subsystem and is called a thread. A **thread** is a single task, such as the task of printing a file that the process requests from the kernel. Figure 4-2 shows two threads in action, which is possible

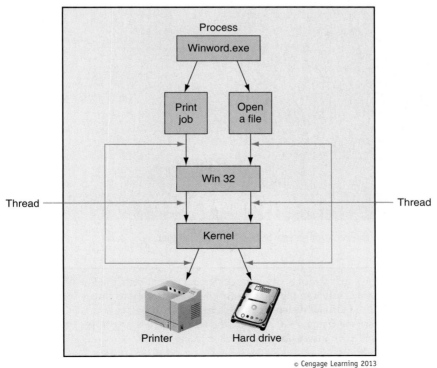

© Cengage Learning 2013

Figure 4-2 A process with more than one thread is called multithreading

A+
220-802
1.4

because the process and Windows support multithreading. Sometimes a process is called an instance, such as when you say to a user, "Open two instances of Internet Explorer." Technically, you are saying to open two Internet Explorer processes.

> **A+ Exam Tip** The A+ 220-802 exam expects you to know how to use Task Manager, MSconfig, the Services console, Computer Management console, MMC, Event Viewer, Task Scheduler, the Registry Editor, and Performance Monitor. All these tools are covered in this part of the chapter.

Now that you are familiar with the concepts of how Windows works, let's see how to use some tools that can help us manage Windows components and processes.

TASK MANAGER

Task Manager (Taskmgr.exe) lets you view the applications and processes running on your computer as well as information about process and memory performance, network activity, and user activity. Several ways to access Task Manager are:

▲ Press **Ctrl+Alt+Delete**. Depending on your system, the security screen (see Figure 4-3) or Task Manager appears. If the security screen appears, click **Start Task Manager**. This method works well when the system has a problem and is frozen.
▲ Right-click a blank area in the taskbar, and select **Start Task Manager** from the shortcut menu.
▲ Press **Ctrl+Shift+Esc**.
▲ Click **Start**, enter **taskmgr.exe** in the search box, and press **Enter**.

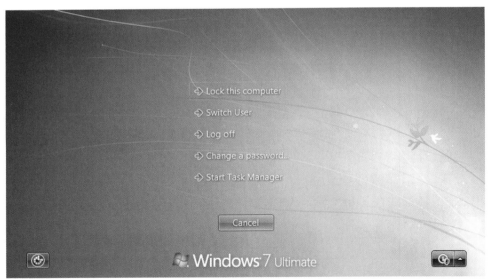

© Cengage Learning 2013

Figure 4-3 Use the security screen to launch Task Manager

> **Notes** When working with a virtual machine, you cannot send the Ctrl+Alt+Delete keystrokes to the guest operating system in the VM because these keystrokes are always sent to the host operating system. To send the Ctrl+Alt+Delete keystrokes to a VM in Windows Virtual PC, click **Ctrl+Alt+Delete** in the VM menu bar (see Figure 4-4a). To send the Ctrl+Alt+Delete keystrokes to a VM in Oracle VirtualBox, click **Machine** and click **Insert Ctrl+Alt+Del** (see Figure 4-4b).

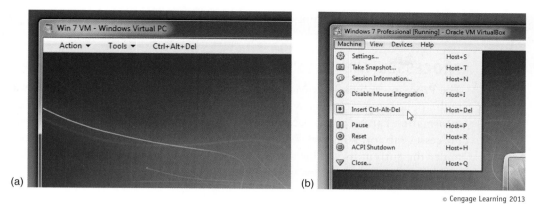

Figure 4-4 Send the Ctrl+Alt+Delete keystrokes to a VM managed by (a) Windows Virtual PC or (b) Oracle VirtualBox

Windows 7/Vista Task Manager has six tabs: Applications, Processes, Services, Performance, Networking, and Users (see Figure 4-5). Let's see how each tab of the Task Manager window works.

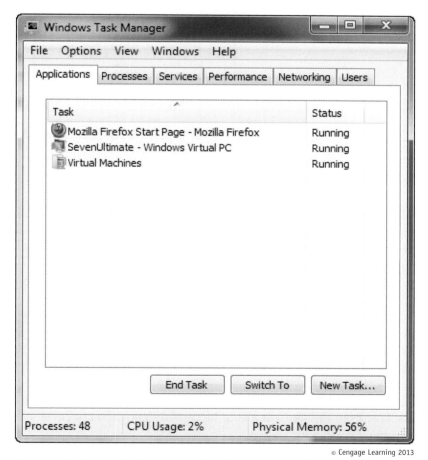

Figure 4-5 The Applications tab in Task Manager shows the status of active applications

APPLICATIONS TAB

On the Applications tab shown in Figure 4-5, each application loaded can have one of two states: Running or Not Responding. If an application is listed as Not Responding, you can end it by selecting it and clicking the **End Task** button at the bottom of the window.

A+
220-802
1.4

The application will attempt a normal shutdown; if data has not been saved, you are given the opportunity to save it.

PROCESSES TAB

The Processes tab of Task Manager lists system services and other processes associated with applications, together with how much CPU time and memory the process uses. This information can help you determine which applications are slowing down your system. The Processes tab for Windows 7 Task Manager (see Figure 4-6a) shows the processes running under the current user. This screen shot was taken immediately after a Windows installation and before any applications were installed.

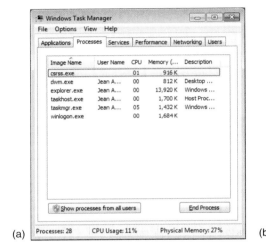
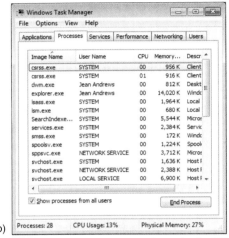

(a) (b)

© Cengage Learning 2013

Figure 4-6 Processes running under (a) the current user and (b) all users, for a new Windows 7 installation

To see all processes running, click **Show processes from all users** (see Figure 4-6b). Task Manager now shows processes running under the current user, System, Local Service, and Network Service accounts. Services running under these last three accounts cannot display a dialog box on-screen or interact with the user. To do that, the service must be running under a user account. Also, a service running under the System account has more core privileges than does a service running under another account.

To stop a process using Task Manager, select the process and click **End Process**. The process is ended abruptly. If the process belongs to an application, you will lose any unsaved information in the application. Therefore, if an application is hung, try using the Applications tab to end the task before turning to the Processes tab to end its underlying process.

If you want to end the process and all related processes, right-click the process and select **End Process Tree** from the shortcut menu. Be careful to not end critical Windows processes; ending these might crash your system.

> **Notes** If your desktop locks up, you can use Task Manager to refresh it. To do so, press **Ctrl+Alt+Del** and then click **Start Task Manager**. Click the **Processes** tab. Select **Explorer.exe** (the process that provides the desktop) and then click **End Process**. Click **End process** in the warning box. Then click the **Applications** tab. Click **New Task**. Enter **Explorer.exe** in the Create New Task dialog box and click **OK**. Your desktop will be refreshed and any running programs will still be open.

APPLYING | CONCEPTS ADJUST THE PRIORITY LEVEL OF AN APPLICATION

Each application running on your computer is assigned a priority level, which determines its position in the queue for CPU resources. You can use Task Manager to change the priority level for an application that is already loaded. If an application performs slowly, increase its priority. You should only do this with very important applications, because giving an application higher priority than certain background system processes can sometimes interfere with the operating system.

To use Task Manager to change the priority level of an open application, do the following:

1. In Task Manager, click the **Applications** tab. Right-click the application and select **Go To Process** from the shortcut menu (see Figure 4-7). The Processes tab is selected and the process that runs the application is selected.

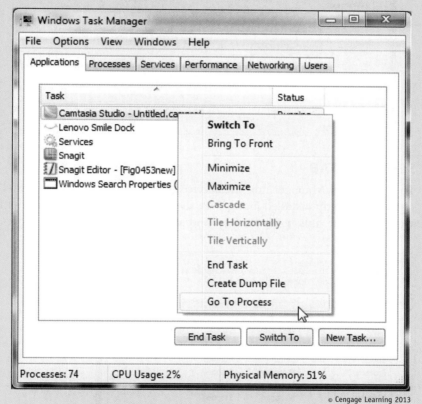

© Cengage Learning 2013

Figure 4-7 Find the running process for this running application

2. Right-click the selected process. From the shortcut menu that appears, point to **Set Priority**, and set the new priority to **Above Normal** (see Figure 4-8). If that doesn't give satisfactory performance, then try **High**.

> 📓 **Notes** Remember that any changes you make to an application's priority level affect only the current session.

A+
220-802
1.4

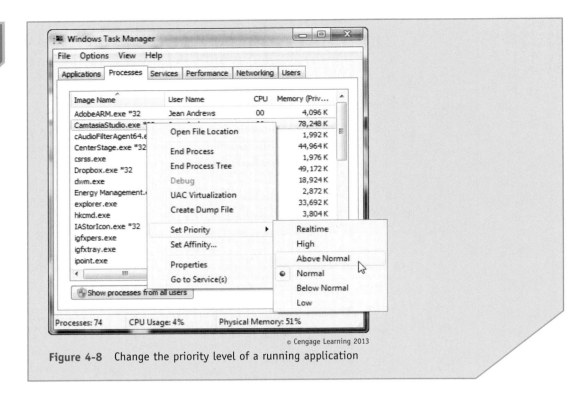

© Cengage Learning 2013

Figure 4-8 Change the priority level of a running application

SERVICES TAB

The third Task Manager tab, the Services tab, is shown in Figure 4-9. This tab lists the services currently installed along with the status of each service. Recall that a service is a program that runs in the background and is called on by other programs to perform a

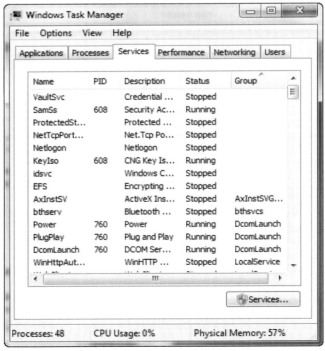

© Cengage Learning 2013

Figure 4-9 The Services tab of Windows 7 Task Manager gives the current status of all installed services

A+
220-802
1.4

background task. Running services are sometimes listed in the notification area of the task-bar. To manage a service, click the **Services** button at the bottom of the window to go to the Services console. How to use this console is discussed later in the chapter.

PERFORMANCE TAB

The fourth Task Manager tab, the Performance tab, is shown in Figure 4-10. It provides graphs that can give you a quick look at how system resources are used.

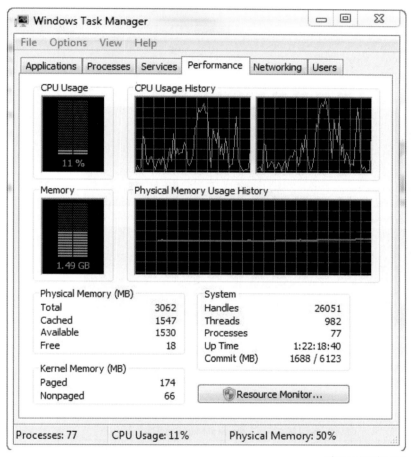

© Cengage Learning 2013

Figure 4-10 The Performance tab window shows details about how system resources are being used

Here is an explanation of the information in the graphs on this tab:

◢ The *CPU Usage* graph indicates the percentage of time the CPU is currently being used. If the graph indicates heavy CPU use, you need to use other tools, such as the Resource Monitor, to investigate the program(s) hogging the CPU. How to use the Resource Monitor is covered later in the chapter.

◢ The *CPU Usage History* graphs show this same percentage of use over recent time.

◢ The left *Memory* graph shows the amount of memory currently used.

◢ The right *Physical Memory Usage History* graph shows how much memory has recently been used. If this blue bar is a flat line near the top of the graph, you defi-nitely need to add more RAM to the system.

A+
220-802
1.4

NETWORKING TAB

The Networking tab lets you monitor network activity and bandwidth used. You can use it to see how heavily the network is being used by this computer. For example, in Figure 4-11, you can see that the wireless connection is running at 144 Mbps, while the local (wired) connection is running at 100 Mbps. The wired connection is slower than the wireless connection, but is used more because it is listed first. In Chapter 7, you learn how to change the order in which network connections are used.

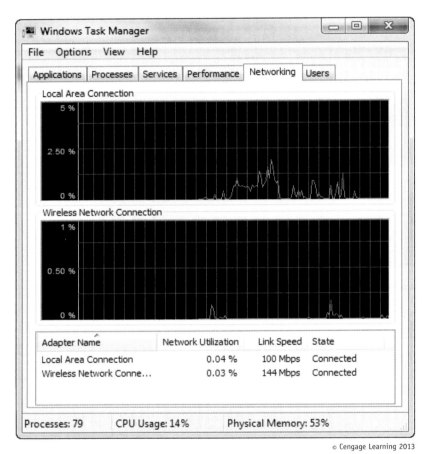

Figure 4-11   Use the Networking tab of Task Manager to monitor network activity

USERS TAB

The Users tab shows all users currently logged on the system. To improve Windows performance or just before you shut down the system, you can log off a user. Before you log off another user, you can select the **Processes** tab and click **Show processes from all users** to verify no applications are running under that user account. Then return to the Users tab, select the user, and click **Logoff**. The dialog box shown in Figure 4-12 appears, warning that unsaved data might be lost. Click **Log off user** to complete the operation.

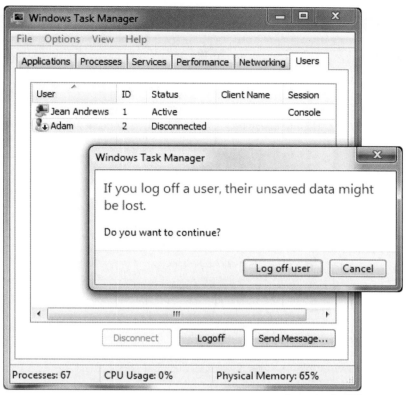

A+
220-802
1.4

Figure 4-12 Use Task Manager to log off a user

© Cengage Learning 2013

Hands-on | Project 4.1 Research Running Processes

Boot to the Windows desktop and then use Task Manager to get a list of all the running processes on your machine. Use the Windows Snipping Tool to save and print the Task Manager screens showing the list of processes. Next, boot the system in Safe Mode with Networking and use Task Manager to list running processes. (Recall you can press F8 during startup to see the Advanced Boot Options menu from which you can start Windows in Safe Mode with Networking.) Which processes that were loaded normally are not loaded when the system is running in Safe Mode?

A+
220-802
1.1, 1.4

ADMINISTRATIVE TOOLS

Windows offers a group of Administrative tools in the Control Panel that are used by technicians and developers to support Windows. To see the list of tools, open Control Panel and then click **Administrative Tools**. Figure 4-13 shows the Administrative Tools window for Windows 7 Ultimate. The Home editions of Windows 7 do not include the Local Security Policy (controls many security settings on the local computer) or Print Management (manages print servers on a network).

A+
220-802
1.1, 1.4

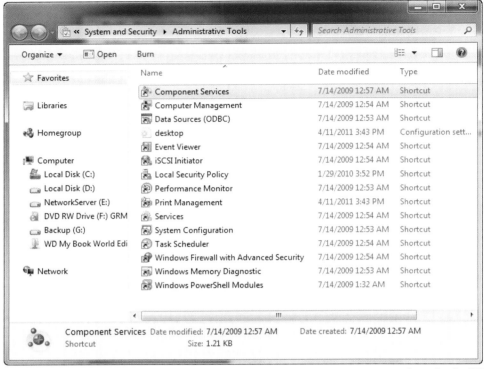

© Cengage Learning 2013

Figure 4-13   Administrative tools available in Windows 7 Ultimate

Several Administrative tools are covered next, including System Configuration, Services console, Computer Management, and Event Viewer. In Chapter 5, you learn to use more Administrative tools.

SYSTEM CONFIGURATION (MSCONFIG)

You can use the System Configuration (Msconfig.exe) utility, which is commonly pronounced "*M-S-config*," to find out what processes are launched at startup and to temporarily disable a process from loading.

Using MSconfig should be a temporary fix to disable a program or service from launching at startup, but it should not be considered a permanent fix. Once you've decided you want to make the change permanent, use other methods to permanently remove that process from Windows startup. For example, you might uninstall a program, remove it from a startup folder, or use the Services console to disable a service. Follow these steps to learn to use MSconfig:

1. To start MSconfig, click **Start**, enter **msconfig.exe** in the search box, and press **Enter**. The System Configuration box opens. Click the **Boot** tab to see information about the boot and control some boot settings. For example, in Figure 4-14, you can see this computer is set for a dual boot and, using this box, you can delete one of the choices for a dual boot from the boot loader menu.

2. Click the **Services** tab to see a list of all services launched at startup (see Figure 4-15). Notice that this tab has a Disable all button. If you use this button, you'll disable all nonessential Windows services as well as third-party services such as virus scan

A+
220-802
1.1, 1.4

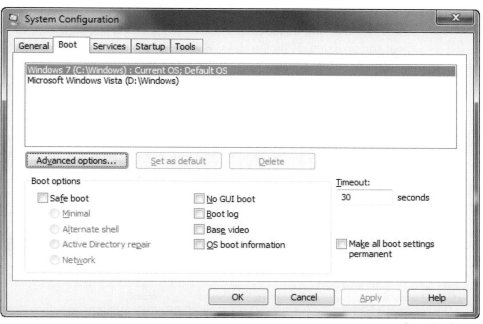

Figure 4-14 Use the Boot tab to control boot settings

© Cengage Learning 2013

4

programs. Use it only for the most difficult Windows problems, because you'll disable some services that you might really want, such as Windows Task Scheduler, Print Spooler, Automatic Updates, and the System Restore service.

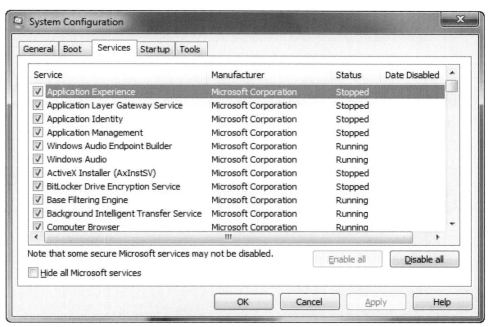

Figure 4-15 Use MSconfig to view and control services launched at startup

© Cengage Learning 2013

3. To view only those services put there by third-party software, check **Hide all Microsoft services**. If you have antivirus software running in the background (and you should), you'll see that listed as well as any service launched at startup and put there

A+
220-802
1.1, 1.4

by installed software. Uncheck all services you don't want. If you don't recognize a service, try entering its name in a search string at *www.google.com* for information about the program. If the program is a service, you can permanently stop it by using the Services console or uninstalling the software.

4. Click the **Startup** tab to see a list of programs that launch at startup (see Figure 4-16). These programs launch at startup by way of a startup folder or a registry key entry. To disable all nonessential startup tasks, click **Disable all**. Or you can check and uncheck an individual startup program to enable or disable it. The Startup tab can be useful when trying to understand how a program is launched at startup because it offers the Location column. This column shows the registry key or startup folder where the startup entry is made.

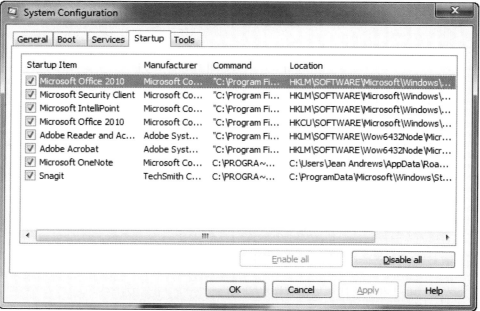

Figure 4-16 Select startup processes to enable or disable

© Cengage Learning 2013

> **Notes** When using MSconfig to troubleshoot startup problems, keep a handwritten list of programs you enable or disable so you can backtrack if necessary.

5. If you made changes, click **Apply**. Now click the **General** tab and you should see *Selective startup* selected, as shown in Figure 4-17. Close the MSconfig box and restart the computer.

6. Watch for error messages during or after the boot that indicate you've created a problem with your changes. For instance, after the boot, you might find out you can no longer use that nifty little utility that came with your digital camera. To fix the problem, you need to find out which service or program you stopped that you need for that utility. Go back to the MSconfig tool and enable that one service and reboot.

The Tools tab in the System Configuration box gives you quick access to other Windows tools you might need during a troubleshooting session (see Figure 4-18).

A+
220-802
1.1, 1.4

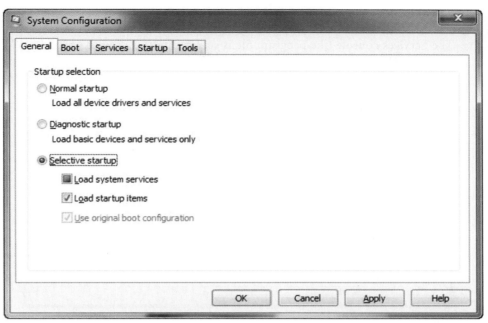

© Cengage Learning 2013

Figure 4-17   MSconfig is set to control the Windows startup programs

© Cengage Learning 2013

Figure 4-18   The Tools tab makes it easy to find troubleshooting tools

Notes MSconfig reports only what it is programmed to look for when listing startup programs and services. It looks only in certain registry keys and startup folders, and sometimes MSconfig does not report a startup process. Therefore, don't consider its list of startup processes to be complete.

Vista Differences Windows Vista uses the System Configuration utility to control startup programs just as does Windows 7. In addition, Vista offers Software Explorer, a user-friendly tool to control startup programs. To learn how to use Software Explorer, see Appendix B.

A+
220-802
1.1, 1.4

SERVICES CONSOLE

The Services console (the program file is services.msc) is used to control the Windows and third-party services installed on a system. To launch the Services console, type **Services.msc** in the search box and press **Enter**. If the Extended tab at the bottom of the window is not selected, click it (see Figure 4-19). This tab gives a description of a selected service.

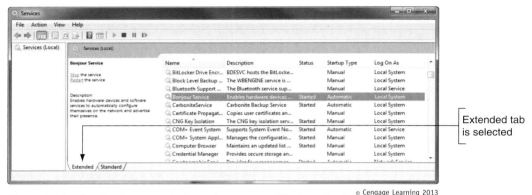

© Cengage Learning 2013

Figure 4-19   The Services console is used to manage Windows Services

When you click a service to select it and the description is missing, most likely the service is a third-party service put there by an installed application. To get more information about a service or to stop or start a service, right-click its name and select **Properties** from the shortcut menu. In the Properties box (see Figure 4-20), the startup types for a service are:

▲ *Automatic (Delayed Start)*. Starts shortly after startup, after the user logs on, so as not to slow down the startup process
▲ *Automatic*. Starts when Windows loads
▲ *Manual*. Starts as needed
▲ *Disabled*. Cannot be started

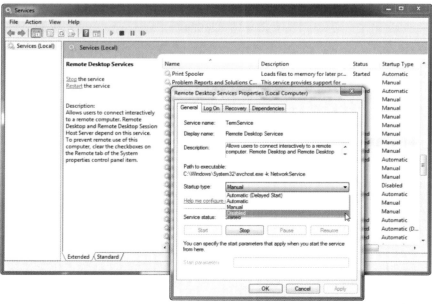

© Cengage Learning 2013

Figure 4-20   Manage a service with the service Properties box

A+
220-802
1.1, 1.4

> **Notes** If you suspect a Windows system service is causing a problem, you can use MSconfig to disable the service. If this works, then try replacing the service file with a fresh copy from the Windows setup DVD.

COMPUTER MANAGEMENT

Computer Management (Compmgmt.msc) contains several tools that can be used to manage the local PC or other computers on the network. The window is called a **console** because it consolidates several Windows administrative tools. To use most of these tools, you must be logged on as an administrator, although you can view certain settings in Computer Management if you are logged on with lesser privileges.

As with most Windows tools, there are several ways to access Computer Management:

◢ Click **Start,** enter **Computer Management** or **compmgmt.msc** in the search box, and press **Enter.**

◢ Click **Start,** right-click **Computer,** and select **Manage** from the shortcut menu.

◢ In Control Panel, look in the **Administrative Tools** group.

The Computer Management window is shown in Figure 4-21. Using this window, you can access Task Scheduler, Event Viewer, performance monitoring tools including the Windows 7 Performance Monitor and the Vista Reliability and Performance Monitor, Device Manager, Disk Management, and the Services console. You can also manage user accounts and user groups (covered in Chapter 8). Several tools available from the Computer Management window are covered in this chapter.

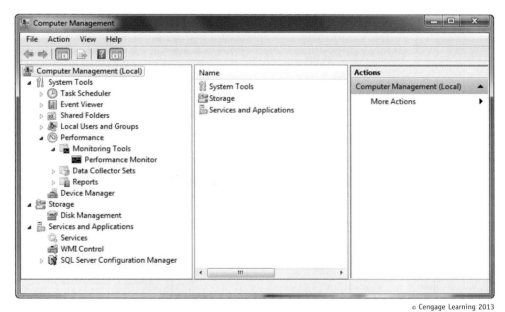

© Cengage Learning 2013

Figure 4-21 Windows Computer Management combines several administrative tools into a single easy-to-access window

MICROSOFT MANAGEMENT CONSOLE (MMC)

Microsoft Management Console (MMC; the program file is mmc.exe) is a Windows utility that can be used to build your own customized console windows. In a console, these individual tools are called **snap-ins.** A console is saved in a file with a .msc file extension, and a

A+
220-802
1.1, 1.4

snap-in in a console can itself be a console. To use all the functions of MMC, you must be logged on with administrator privileges.

> **Notes** A program that can work as a snap-in under the MMC has a .msc file extension.

APPLYING | CONCEPTS CREATE A CONSOLE

If you find yourself often using a few Windows tools, consider putting them in a console stored on your desktop. Follow these steps to create a console:

1. Click **Start**, enter **mmc.exe** in the search box, and press **Enter**. Respond to the UAC box. An empty console window appears, as shown in Figure 4-22.

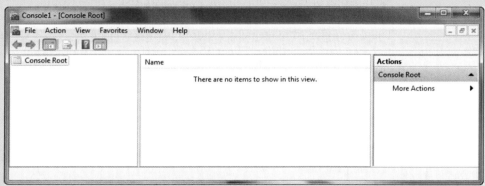

Figure 4-22 An empty console

© Cengage Learning 2013

2. Click **File** in the menu bar and then click **Add/Remove Snap-in**. The Add or Remove Snap-ins box opens, as shown on the left side of Figure 4-23.

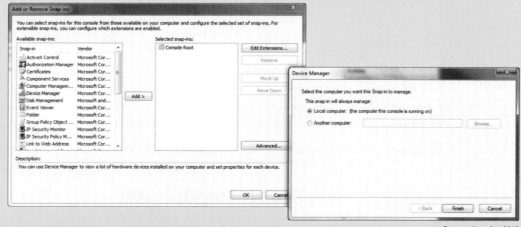

Figure 4-23 Add a snap-in to the new console

© Cengage Learning 2013

A+
220-802
1.1, 1.4

3. Select a snap-in from the list in the Add or Remove Snap-ins box. Notice a description of the snap-in appears at the bottom of the window. The snap-ins that appear in this list depend on the edition of Windows 7/Vista you have installed and what other components are installed on the system. Click **Add** to add the snap-in to the console. (For Windows XP, in the Add/ Remove Snap-In box, click **Add**. A list of snap-ins appears. Select one and click **Add**.)

4. If parameters for the snap-in need defining, a dialog box opens that allows you to set up these parameters. The dialog box offers different selections, depending on the snap-in being added. For example, when Device Manager is selected, a dialog box appears, asking you to select the computer that Device Manager will monitor (see the right side of Figure 4-23). Select **Local computer (the computer this console is running on)** and click **Finish**. The snap-in now appears in the list of snap-ins for this console.

5. Repeat Steps 3 and 4 to add all the snap-ins that you want to the console. When you finish, click **OK** in the Add or Remove Snap-ins box.

6. To save the console, click **File** in the menu bar and then click **Save As**. The Save As dialog box opens.

7. The default location for the console file is C:\Users*username*\AppData\Roaming\Microsoft\ Windows\Start Menu\Programs\Administrative Tools. However, you can save the console to any location, such as the Windows desktop. However, if you save the file to its default location, the console will appear as an option under Administrative Tools in the Start menu. Select the location for the file, name the file, and click **Save**. Then close the console window.

> **Notes** After you create a console, you can copy the .msc file to any computer or place a shortcut to it on the desktop.

Hands-on | Project 4.2   Use the Microsoft Management Console

Using the Microsoft Management Console, create a customized console. Put two snap-ins in the console: Device Manager and Event Viewer. Store a shortcut to your console on the Windows desktop. Copy the console to another computer and install it on the Windows desktop.

EVENT VIEWER

Just about anything that happens in Windows is logged by Windows, and these logs can be viewed using **Event Viewer (Eventvwr.msc)**. You can find events such as a hardware or network failure, OS error messages, a device or service that has failed to start, or General Protection Faults.

Event Viewer is a Computer Management console snap-in, and you can open it by using the Computer Management window, by entering **Event Viewer** or **Eventvwr.msc** in the search box, or by using the Administrative Tools group in Control Panel. The Windows 7/Vista Event Viewer window is shown in Figure 4-24. The XP Event Viewer is shown in Figure 4-25. The XP Event Viewer does not keep as many logs as does the Windows 7/Vista Event Viewer.

A+
220-802
1.1, 1.4

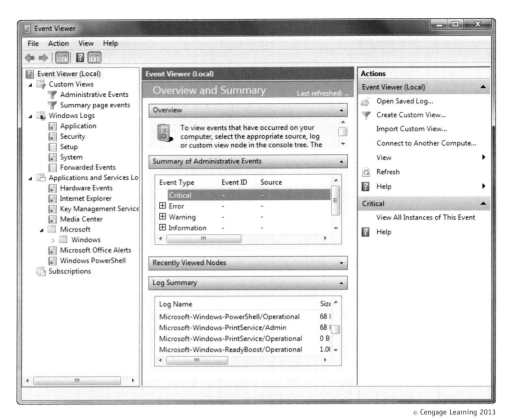

© Cengage Learning 2013

Figure 4-24 Use Event Viewer to see logs about hardware, Windows, security, and applications events

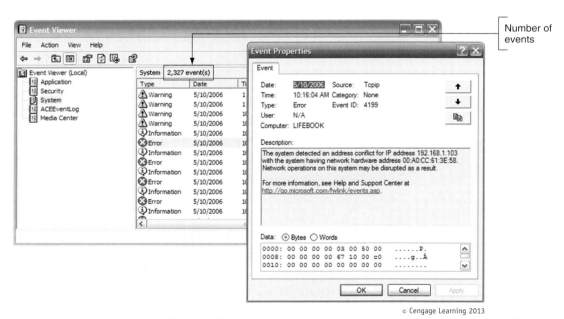

© Cengage Learning 2013

Figure 4-25 Event Viewer in Windows XP works about the same way as the Windows 7/Vista Event Viewer

The different views of logs are listed in the left pane, and you can drill down into sub-categories of these logs. You can filter and sort logs to help find what you need. First select a log in the left pane and then click an event in the middle pane to see details about

A+
220-802
1.1, 1.4

the event. For example, in Figure 4-26, the Administrative Events log shows an event recorded by Windows Backup.

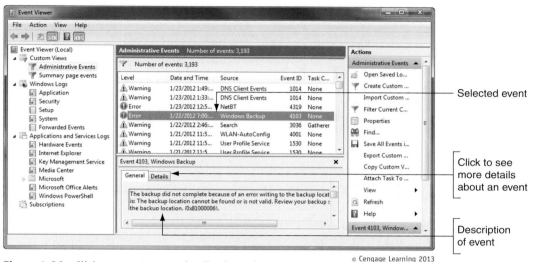

Figure 4-26 Click an event to see details about the event

© Cengage Learning 2013

Three main types of events are Error, Warning, and Information. Error events are the most important and indicate something went wrong with the system, such as a scheduled backup failed to work. Warning events indicate failure might occur in the future.

Here are the views of logs that are the most useful:

▲ *Administrative Events log.* This log is a filtered log that shows only Warning and Error events intended for the administrator. This log is in the Custom Views category and is selected in Figure 4-26.

▲ *Application log.* In the Windows Logs group, look in the Application log for events recorded by an application. This log might help you identify why an application is causing problems.

▲ *Security log.* Events in the Security log are called audits and include successful and unsuccessful logins to a user account and attempts from another computer on the network to access shared resources on this computer.

▲ *Setup log.* Look in the Setup log for events recorded when applications are installed.

▲ *System log.* Look in the System log to find events triggered by Windows components, such as a device driver failing to load or a problem with hardware.

▲ *Forwarded Events log.* This log receives events that were recorded on other computers and sent to this computer.

When you first encounter a Windows, hardware, application, or security problem, get in the habit of checking Event Viewer as one of your first steps toward investigating the problem. To save time, first check the Administrative Events log because it filters out all events except Warning and Error events.

If you want to create your own filtered events log, right-click any log in the left pane and select **Filter Current Log** from the shortcut menu. (For Windows XP, select **Properties** from the shortcut menu and then click the **Filter** tab.) The Filter Current Log box appears (see Figure 4-27).

The Filter Current Log box offers many ways to filter events. To view the most significant events to troubleshoot a problem, check **Critical** and **Error** under the Event level, as shown in Figure 4-27. Critical events are those errors that Windows believes are affecting critical

A+
220-802
1.1, 1.4

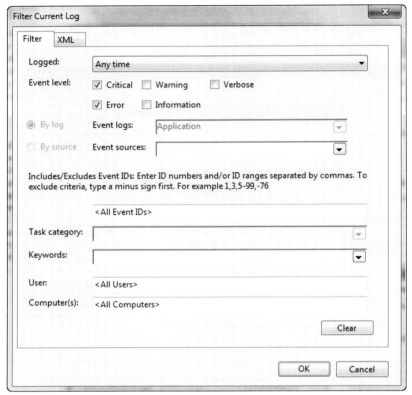

Figure 4-27   Criteria to filter events in Event Viewer   © Cengage Learning 2013

Windows processes. After you select the filters, click **OK**. Only the events that match your filters are listed. To remove the filter, right-click the log and select **Clear Filter**.

Besides filtering a log, here are other useful tips when dealing with logs:

- To sort a list of events, click a column heading in the middle pane.
- To save a filtered log file so you can view it later, right-click the log and select **Save Filtered Log File As** (see Figure 4-28). The log file is assigned a .evtx file extension. When you later double-click this file, it appears in an Event Viewer window. You might want to email a filtered log file to others who are helping you troubleshoot a problem.

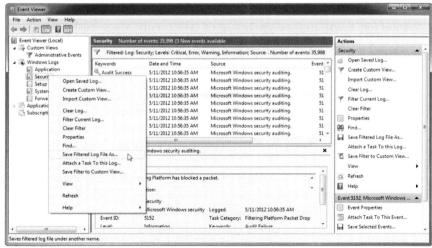

Figure 4-28   Save a filtered log file so that you can view it later   © Cengage Learning 2013

A+
220-802
1.1, 1.4

◢ To control the size of a log file, you can clear it. In the log's shortcut menu, select **Clear Log**. Before clearing the log, Event Viewer gives you a chance to save it.

◢ Select **Properties** in the log's shortcut menu to control the maximum size of the log file and to cause the events to be archived before they are overwritten.

4

APPLYING CONCEPTS

Event Viewer can be useful in solving intermittent hardware problems. For example, I once worked in an office where several people updated Microsoft Word documents stored on a file server. For weeks, people complained about these Word documents getting corrupted. We downloaded the latest patches for Windows and Microsoft Office and scanned for viruses, thinking that the problem might be with Windows or the application. Then we suspected a corrupted template file for building the Word documents. But nothing we did solved our problem of corrupted Word documents. Then one day someone thought to check Event Viewer on the file server. The Event Viewer had faithfully been recording errors when writing to the hard drive. What we had suspected to be a software problem was, in fact, a failing hard drive, which was full of bad sectors. We replaced the drive and the problem went away. That day I learned the value of checking Event Viewer very early in the troubleshooting process.

Hands-on | Project 4.3   Use Event Viewer

Event Viewer can be intimidating to use but is really nothing more than a bunch of logs to search and manipulate. If you have Microsoft Office installed, open a Word document, make some changes in it, and close it without saving your changes. Now look in **Applications and Services Logs**, **Microsoft**, and **Microsoft Office Alerts**. What event is recorded about your actions?

TASK SCHEDULER

Windows Task Scheduler can be set to launch a task or program at a future time, including at startup. When applications install, they might schedule tasks to check for and download their program updates. Task Scheduler stores tasks in a file stored in the C:\Windows\System32\Tasks folder. For example, in Figure 4-29, there are seven scheduled tasks showing and other tasks are stored in four folders.

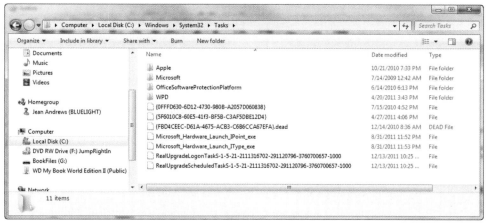

Figure 4-29   The Tasks folder contains tasks that launch at startup

© Cengage Learning 2013

A+
220-802
1.1, 1.4

To open Task Scheduler from the Control Panel, double-click **Task Scheduler** in the Administrative Tools group. Alternately, you can click Start, All Programs, Accessories, System Tools, and Task Scheduler. The Task Scheduler window is shown in Figure 4-30.

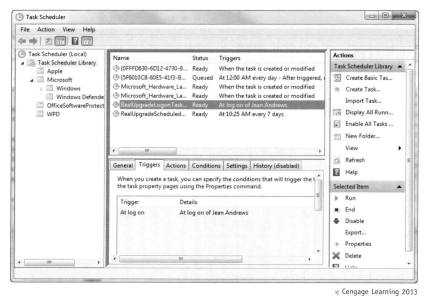

© Cengage Learning 2013

Figure 4-30 View and manage tasks from the Task Scheduler window

Here is what you need to know to use the Task Scheduler window:

- In the left pane, drill down into groups and subgroups. Tasks in a group are listed in the middle pane.
- To see details about a task, including what triggers it, what actions it performs, the conditions and settings related to the task, and the history of past actions, select the task and then click the tabs in the lower-middle pane. For example, in Figure 4-30, you can see that the RealUpgradeLogonTask is scheduled to run when I log on.
- To add a new task, first select the group for the new task and then click **Action**, **Create Basic Task**. A wizard appears to step you through creating the task.
- To delete, disable, or run a task, select it and in the Action menu or in the Actions pane, click Delete, Disable, or Run.

> **Notes** Tasks can be hidden in the Task Scheduler window. To be certain you're viewing all scheduled tasks, unhide them. In the menu bar, click **View**, and then **Show Hidden Tasks**.

Hands-on | Project 4.4 Practice Launching Programs at Startup

Do the following to practice launching programs at startup, listing the steps you took for each activity:

1. Configure Scheduled Tasks to launch Notepad each time the computer starts and any user logs on. List the steps you took.

2. Put a shortcut in a startup folder so that any user launches a command prompt window at startup. See Appendix G for a list of startup folders.

3. Restart the system and verify that both programs are launched. Did you receive any errors?

4. Remove the two programs from the startup process.

A+
220-802
1.1, 1.4

THE REGISTRY EDITOR

Many actions, such as installing application software or hardware, can result in changes to the registry. These changes can create new keys, add new values to existing keys, and change existing values. For a few difficult problems, you might need to edit or remove a registry key. This part of the chapter looks at how the registry is organized, which keys might hold entries causing problems, and how to back up and edit the registry using the **Registry Editor (regedit.exe)**. Let's first look at how the registry is organized, and then you'll learn how to back up and edit the registry.

HOW THE REGISTRY IS ORGANIZED

The most important Windows component that holds information for Windows is the registry. The **registry** is a database designed with a treelike structure (called a hierarchical database) that contains configuration information for Windows, users, software applications, and installed hardware devices. During startup, Windows builds the registry in memory and keeps it there until Windows shuts down. During startup, after the registry is built, Windows reads from it to obtain information to complete the startup process. After Windows is loaded, it continually reads from many of the subkeys in the registry.

Windows builds the registry from the current hardware configuration and from information it takes from these files:

- Five files stored in the C:\Windows\System32\config folder; these files are called hives, and they are named the SAM (Security Accounts Manager), Security, Software, System, and Default hives. (Each hive is backed up with a log file and a backup file, which are also stored in the C:\Windows\System32\config folder.)
- For Windows 7/Vista, the C:\Users*username*\Ntuser.dat file, which holds the preferences and settings of the currently logged-on user.
- Windows XP uses information about the current user stored in two files:
  - C:\Documents and Settings*username*\Ntuser.dat
  - C:\Documents and Settings*username*\Local Settings\Application Data\ Microsoft\Windows\Usrclass.dat

After the registry is built in memory, it is organized into five high-level keys (see Figure 4-31). Each key can have subkeys, and subkeys can have more subkeys and can be assigned one or more values. The way data is organized in the hive files is different from the way it is organized in registry keys. Figure 4-32 shows the relationship between registry keys and hives. For example, in the figure, notice that the HKEY_CLASSES_ROOT key contains data that comes from the Software hive, and this data is also stored in the larger HKEY_LOCAL_MACHINE key.

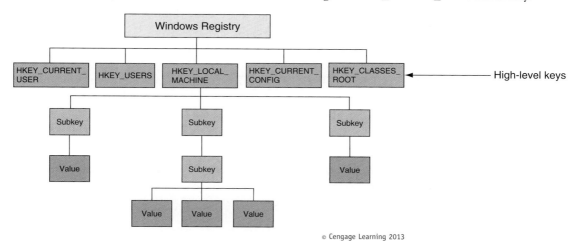

© Cengage Learning 2013

Figure 4-31 The Windows registry is logically organized in five keys with subkeys

A+
220-802
1.1, 1.4

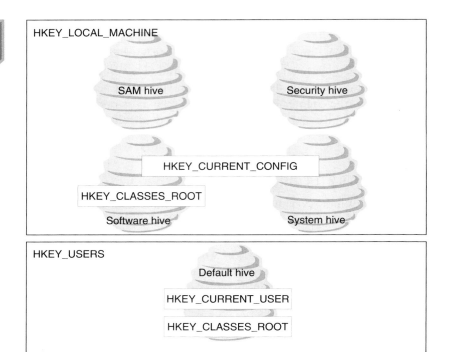

Figure 4-32 The relationship between registry keys and hives

© Cengage Learning 2013

Here are the five keys, including where they get their data and their purposes:

- ◢ **HKEY_LOCAL_MACHINE (HKLM)** is the most important key and contains hardware, software, and security data. The data is taken from four hives: the SAM hive, the Security hive, the Software hive, and the System hive. In addition, the HARDWARE subkey of HKLM is built when the registry is first loaded, based on data collected about the current hardware configuration.
- ◢ **HKEY_CURRENT_CONFIG (HKCC)** contains information that identifies each hardware device installed on the computer. Some of the data is gathered from the current hardware configuration when the registry is first loaded into memory. Other data is taken from the HKLM key, which got its data primarily from the System hive.
- ◢ **HKEY_CLASSES_ROOT (HKCR)** stores information that determines which application is opened when the user double-clicks a file. This process relies on the file's extension to determine which program to load. Data for this key is gathered from the HKLM key and the HKCU key.
- ◢ **HKEY_USERS (HKU)** contains data about all users and is taken from the Default hive.
- ◢ **HKEY_CURRENT_USER (HKCU)** contains data about the current user. The key is built when a user logs on using data kept in the HKEY_USERS key and data kept in the Ntuser.dat file of the current user.

> **Notes** Device Manager reads data from the HKLM\HARDWARE key to build the information it displays about hardware configurations. You can consider Device Manager to be an easy-to-view presentation of this HARDWARE key data.

BEFORE YOU EDIT THE REGISTRY, BACK IT UP!

When you need to edit the registry, if possible, make the change from the Windows tool that is responsible for the key—for example, by using the Programs and Features window in Control Panel. If that doesn't work and you must edit the registry, always back up the registry before attempting to edit it. Changes made to the registry are implemented immediately. *There is no undo feature in the Registry Editor, and no opportunity to change your mind once the edit is made.*

Here are the ways to back up the registry:

- ◢ *Use System Protection to create a restore point.* A restore point keeps information about the registry. You can restore the system to a restore point to undo registry changes, as long as the registry is basically intact and not too corrupted. Also know that, if System Protection is turned on, Windows 7/Vista automatically makes a daily backup of the registry hive files to the C:\Windows\System32\Config\RegBack folder.
- ◢ *Back up a single registry key just before you edit the key.* This method, called exporting a key, should always be used before you edit the registry. How to export a key is coming up in this chapter.
- ◢ *Make an extra copy of the C:\Window\System32\config folder.* This is what I call the old-fashioned shotgun approach to backing up the registry. This backup will help if the registry gets totally trashed. You can boot from the Windows setup DVD and use the Windows 7/Vista Recovery Environment or the XP Recovery Console to restore the folder from your extra copy. This method is drastic and not recommended except in severe cases. But, still, just to be on the safe side, I make an extra copy of this folder just before I start any serious digging into the registry.
- ◢ *For Windows XP, back up the system state.* Use Ntbackup in Windows XP to back up the system state, which also makes an extra copy of the registry hives. Windows XP stores the backup of the registry hives in the C:\Windows\repair folder.

In some situations, such as when you're going to make some drastic changes to the registry, you'll want to play it safe and use more than one backup method. Extra registry backups are always a good thing! Now let's look at how to back up an individual key in the registry, and then you'll learn how to edit the registry.

> **Notes** Although you can edit the registry while in Safe Mode, you cannot create a restore point in Safe Mode.

Backing Up and Restoring Individual Keys in the Registry

A less time-consuming method of backing up the registry is to back up a particular key that you plan to edit. However, know that if the registry gets corrupted, having a backup of only a particular key most likely will not help you much when trying a recovery. Also, although you could use this technique to back up the entire registry or an entire tree within the registry, it is not recommended.

To back up a key along with its subkeys in the registry, follow these steps:

1. Open the Registry Editor. To do that, click **Start** and type **regedit** in the search box, press **Enter**, and respond to the UAC box. Figure 4-33 shows the Registry Editor with the five main keys and several subkeys listed. Click the triangles on the left to see subkeys. When you select a subkey, such as KeyboardClass in the figure, the names of the values in that subkey are displayed in the right pane along with the data assigned to each value.

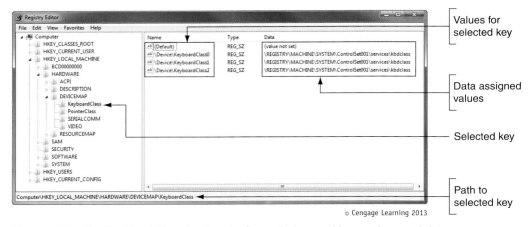

© Cengage Learning 2013

Figure 4-33 The Registry Editor showing the five main keys, subkeys, values, and data

> **Notes** The full path to a selected key display in the status bar at the bottom of the editor window. If the status bar is missing, click **View** in the menu bar and make sure **Status Bar** is checked.

2. Suppose we want to back up the registry key that contains a list of installed software, which is HKLM\Software\Microsoft\Windows\CurrentVersion\Uninstall. (HKLM stands for HKEY_LOCAL_MACHINE.) First click the appropriate triangles to navigate to the key. Next, right-click the key and select **Export** from the shortcut menu, as shown in Figure 4-34. The Export Registry File dialog box appears.

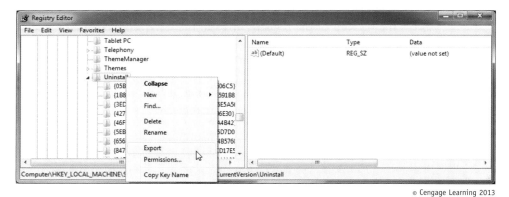

© Cengage Learning 2013

Figure 4-34 Using the Registry Editor, you can back up a key and its subkeys with the Export command

3. Select the location to save the export file and name the file. A convenient place to store an export file while you edit the registry is the desktop. Click **Save** when done. The file saved will have a .reg file extension.

4. You can now edit the key. Later, if you need to undo your changes, exit the Registry Editor and double-click the saved export file. The key and its subkeys saved in the export file will be restored. After you're done with an export file, delete it so that no one accidentally double-clicks it and reverts the registry to an earlier setting.

Editing the Registry

Before you edit the registry, you should use one or more of the four backup methods just discussed so that you can restore it if something goes wrong. To edit the registry, open the **Registry Editor (regedit.exe)**, and locate and select the key in the left pane of the Registry

A+
220-802
1.1, 1.4

Editor, which will display the values stored in this key in the right pane. To edit, rename, or delete a value, right-click it and select the appropriate option from the shortcut menu. For example, in Figure 4-35, I'm ready to delete the value QuickTime Task and its data. Changes are immediately applied to the registry and there is no undo feature. (However, Windows or applications might need to read the changed value before it affects their operations.) To search the registry for keys, values, and data, click **Edit** in the menu bar and then click **Find**.

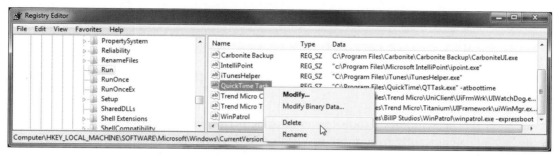

Figure 4-35 Right-click a value to modify, delete, or rename it

© Cengage Learning 2013

> ⚡ **Caution** Changes made to the registry take effect immediately. Therefore, take extra care when editing the registry. If you make a mistake and don't know how to correct a problem you create, then double-click the exported key to recover. When you double-click an exported key, the registry is updated with the values stored in this key.

Hands-on | Project 4.5   Edit and Restore the Registry

Practice editing and restoring the registry by doing the following to change the name of the Recycle Bin on the Windows desktop:

1. Using the Registry Editor, export the registry key HKEY_CURRENT_USER\Software\Microsoft\ Windows\CurrentVersion\Explorer to an export file stored on the desktop.

2. To change the name of the Recycle Bin on the Windows 7/Vista desktop for the currently logged-on user, click the following subkey, which holds the name of the Recycle Bin: HKEY_ CURRENT_USER\Software\Microsoft\Windows\CurrentVersion\Explorer\CLSID\ 645FF040-5081-101B-9F08-00AA002F954E.

3. The data name is (Default), which means the value is not set and the default name, Recycle Bin, is used. To enter a new name for the Recycle Bin, in the right pane, double-click **(Default)**. The Edit String box appears. The Value data text box in the dialog box should be empty. If a value is present, you selected the wrong value. Check your work and try again.

4. Enter a new name for the Recycle Bin, for example, "Trash Can." Click **OK**.

5. Move the Registry Editor window so that you can see the Recycle Bin on the desktop. Don't close the window.

6. Right-click the desktop and select **Refresh** from the shortcut menu. The name of the Recycle Bin changes.

7. To restore the name to its default value, in the Registry Editor window, again double-click **(Default)**, delete your entry, and click **OK**.

A+
220-802
1.1, 1.4

8. To verify the change is made, refresh the Windows desktop. The Recycle Bin name should return to its default value.

9. Exit the Registry Editor and then delete the exported registry key stored on the desktop.

From these directions, you can see that changes made to the registry take effect immediately. Therefore, take extra care when editing the registry. If you make a mistake and don't know how to correct a problem you create, then you can restore the key that you exported by exiting the Registry Editor and double-clicking the exported key.

WINDOWS 7 TOOLS TO MONITOR PERFORMANCE AND OPTIMIZE RESOURCES

The Windows 7 tools for monitoring performance and optimizing resources that differ significantly from those in Vista or XP include the Windows 7 Performance Information and Tools window, Resource Monitor, Reliability Monitor, and Performance Monitor. These Windows 7 tools are covered next.

PERFORMANCE INFORMATION AND TOOLS WINDOW

The Performance Information and Tools window gives information to evaluate the performance of a system and to adjust Windows for best performance.

Use one of the following methods to open the Performance Information and Tools window:

◢ Click **Start**, right-click **Computer**, and select **Properties**. In the System window, click **Performance Information and Tools** (in Vista, click Performance).

◢ In the Action Center, click **View performance information**.

The Performance Information and Tools window for Windows 7 is shown in Figure 4-36, and the Vista window is shown in Figure 4-37.

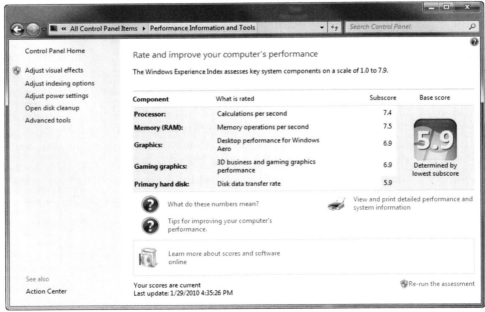

© Cengage Learning 2013

Figure 4-36 The Windows Experience Index gives a rating of key system components in this Windows 7 computer

A+
220-802
1.1, 1.4

> **Notes** To see more detail about the Windows 7 system and to print these details, click **View and print detailed performance and system information**.

4

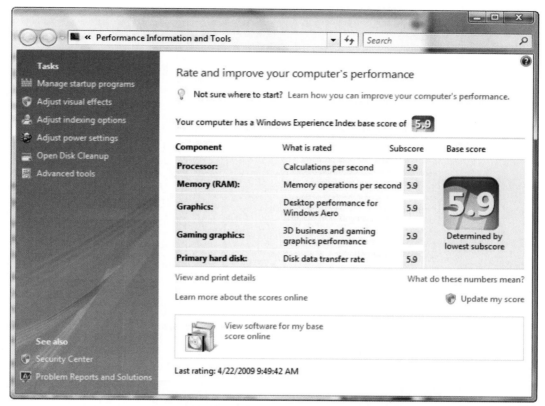

Rate and improve your computer's performance

Not sure where to start? Learn how you can improve your computer's performance.

Your computer has a Windows Experience Index base score of **5.9**

Component	What is rated	Subscore	Base score
Processor:	Calculations per second	5.9	
Memory (RAM):	Memory operations per second	5.9	**5.9**
Graphics:	Desktop performance for Windows Aero	5.9	Determined by lowest subscore
Gaming graphics:	3D business and gaming graphics performance	5.9	
Primary hard disk:	Disk data transfer rate	5.9	

View and print details

What do these numbers mean?

Learn more about the scores online

Update my score

View software for my base score online

Last rating: 4/22/2009 9:49:42 AM

Tasks
- Manage startup programs
- Adjust visual effects
- Adjust indexing options
- Adjust power settings
- Open Disk Cleanup
- Advanced tools

See also
- Security Center
- Problem Reports and Solutions

© Cengage Learning 2013

Figure 4-37 The Windows Experience Index for this Vista system reports no potential bottlenecks

The Windows Experience Index evaluates key system components to give a high-level view of the computer's performance. Five key components are rated on a scale of 1.0 to 7.9. The index is the lowest value of all five ratings because this component is considered the bottleneck component for overall performance.

The left pane contains links to adjusting visual effects, indexing options, and power settings and tools to clean up the hard drive. These utilities can help improve a system's performance and provide more information about the system. Follow these steps to use the tools:

1. Click **Adjust visual effects** to open the Performance Options box (see Figure 4-38). On the Visual Effects tab of this box, you can choose to adjust visual effects for best performance or best appearance. If resources are low on a system, adjusting for best performance can remove a system bottleneck hogging resources. You can also enable or disable individual visual effects to customize the visual effects, creating a balance between best performance and best appearance.

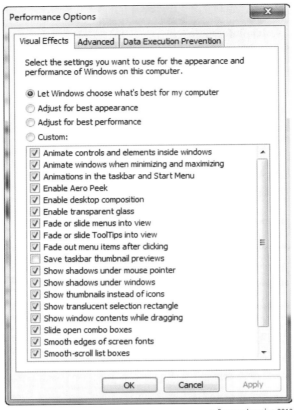

© Cengage Learning 2013

Figure 4-38   Balance visual effects between best performance and best appearance

> **Notes** You can also open the Performance Options box from the System Properties box. In the System Properties box, on the **Advanced** tab, click **Settings** in the Performance area.

2. Click the **Advanced** tab on the Performance Options box to choose how to allocate processor resources, adjusting for best performance between programs running in the foreground and programs running in the background (see Figure 4-39).

> **Notes** Reducing the CPU processing time allowed for programs is called throttling the programs.

3. Also notice on the Advanced tab the ability to adjust virtual memory. Click **Change** to move the file to a different hard drive, which can free up space on the Windows volume and might improve performance.

4. Also in the left pane in the Performance and Information Tools window (refer to Figure 4-36), you can click **Advanced tools** to see a list of performance issues and to open Task Manager, Disk Defragmenter, Event Viewer, Windows 7 Performance Monitor, Windows 7 Resource Monitor, Vista Reliability and Performance Monitor, and other tools.

A+
220-802
1.1, 1.4

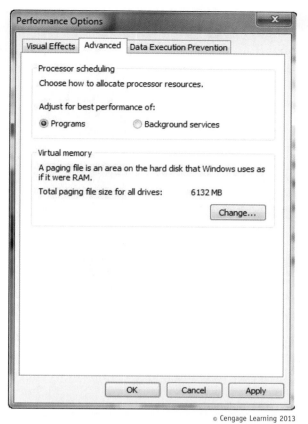

© Cengage Learning 2013

Figure 4-39   Use the Advanced tab of the Performance Options box to adjust how processor resources are allocated to programs and background services

WINDOWS 7 RESOURCE MONITOR

Windows 7 **Resource Monitor** (resmon.exe) monitors the performance of the processor, memory, hard drive, and network. As you learned earlier in the chapter, Task Manager reports some of this information. To access Resource Monitor, use one of these methods:

◢ In Task Manager, click **Resource Monitor** on the Performance tab.
◢ In the Performance Information and Tools window, click **Advanced tools**, and then click **Open Resource Monitor**.
◢ In the Computer Management window, in the System Tools, Performance group, click **Monitoring Tools, More Actions,** and **Resource Monitor**.

The Resource Monitor window is shown in Figure 4-40 with the Memory tab selected.
  The bar graphically showing how memory is used accounts for all the memory installed in a system. The graph shows these five ways memory is used:

◢ Hardware Reserved memory is used by BIOS and certain drivers such as the video drivers. Windows does not have access to this memory. For example, compare total memory reported by Task Manager in Figure 4-10 earlier in the chapter to installed memory reported by Resource Monitor in Figure 4-40 for the same system.
◢ In Use memory is used by other drives, the OS, and applications.
◢ Modified memory will be available as soon as its contents are written to disk.
◢ Standby memory is holding data and code that is ready to use.
◢ Free memory will be used as the system needs it.

A+
220-802
1.1, 1.4

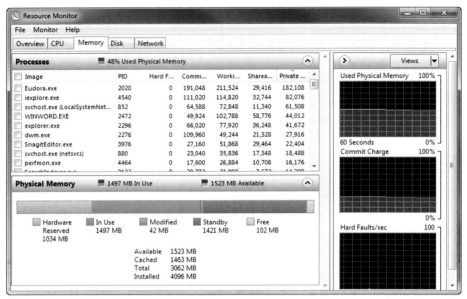

Figure 4-40 The Resource Monitor shows how memory is currently used

© Cengage Learning 2013

The easiest way to find out if a system would benefit from a memory upgrade (adding more memory to the system) is to watch this memory bar as a user does her work. If you consistently see Free memory disappear from this graph, the system would benefit from more installed memory.

> **Notes** To best gauge the performance of a system, ask the user to watch the Resource Monitor throughout the workday and note what the monitor shows when the system is busiest.

The Network tab of Resource Monitor is useful if you suspect a program is hogging network resources. If you suspect a worm or other process is slowing down the network with excessive activity, look for the process in the Processes with Network Activity group on the Network tab (see Figure 4-41). (A worm is malware that can bring down a network by overwhelming it with activity.)

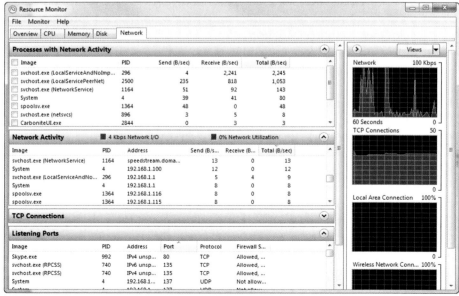

© Cengage Learning 2013

Figure 4-41 Look for a process using excessive networking resources

A+
220-802
1.1, 1.4

WINDOWS 7 RELIABILITY MONITOR

The Windows Reliability Monitor gives information about problems and errors that happen over time. Unless someone has cleared its history log, it reports problems since Windows was installed. To open the Reliability Monitor, open the **Action Center**, click the down arrow to open the Maintenance group, and click **View reliability history**. (You can also enter **Reliability** in the search box.) The Reliability Monitor window is shown in Figure 4-42.

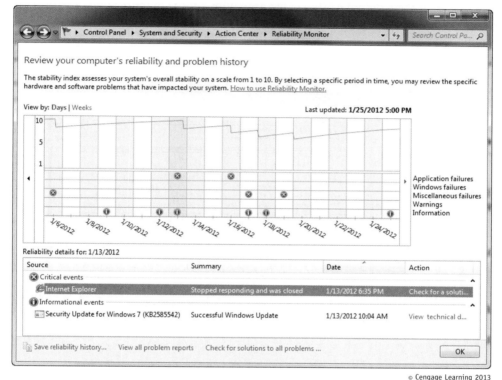

© Cengage Learning 2013

Figure 4-42 Use the Reliability Monitor to search for when a problem began and what else happened about that time

When you click an error in the column graph, the error and other events that happened the same day appear at the bottom of the window. Double-click one of these errors or events to see more information about it.

One important step in troubleshooting a problem is to ask what changes were made to a system at the time a problem began. If you can find out about when a performance problem started, use the Reliability Monitor to find out what happened about that same time. For example, suppose Internet Explorer locks up and the problem started around the day selected in Figure 4-42. You can see from this window that Windows received a security update on this day. The next task would be to research this security update on the Microsoft web site to see if it might be the source of the problem.

WINDOWS 7 PERFORMANCE MONITOR

Windows 7 Performance Monitor is a Microsoft Management Console snap-in (Perfmon.msc or Perfmon.exe) that can track activity by hardware and software to measure performance. Whereas Resource Monitor monitors activities in real time, Performance

A+
220-802
1.1, 1.4

Monitor can monitor in real time and can save collected data in logs for future use. Software developers might use this tool to evaluate how well their software is performing and to identify software and hardware bottlenecks.

Use one of these methods to open the Performance Monitor window shown in Figure 4-43:

◢ Click **Start,** enter **perfmon.msc** in the search box, and press **Enter.**
◢ In the Performance Information and Tools window, click **Advanced tools,** and click **Open Performance Monitor.**
◢ In the Computer Management window in the System Tools, Performance, Monitoring Tools group, click **Performance Monitor.**

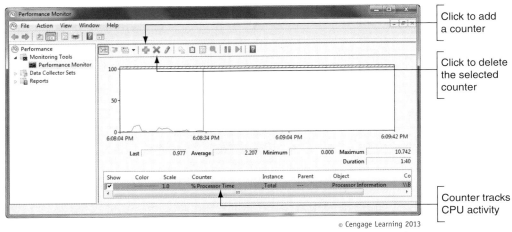

Click to add a counter

Click to delete the selected counter

Counter tracks CPU activity

© Cengage Learning 2013

Figure 4-43 Performance Monitor uses counters to monitor various activities of hardware and software

Performance Monitor offers hundreds of counters used to examine many aspects of the system related to performance. The Windows default setting is to show the %Processor Time counter the first time you open the window (see Figure 4-43). This counter appears as a red line in the graph and tracks activity of the processor.

To keep from unnecessarily using system resources, only use the counters you really need. For example, suppose you want to track hard drive activity. You first remove the %Processor Time counter. To delete a counter, select the counter from the list so that it is highlighted and click the red **X** above the graph.

Next add two counters: % Disk Time counter and Avg. Disk Queue Length counter. The % Disk Time counter tracks the percent of time the hard drive is in use, and the Avg. Disk Queue Length counter tracks the average number of processes waiting to use the hard drive. To add a counter, click the green **plus sign** above the graph. Then, in the Add Counters box, select a counter and click **Add.** Figure 4-44 shows the Add Counters box with two counters added. After all your counters are added, click **OK.**

Allow Performance Monitor to keep running while the system is in use, and then check the counters. The results for one system are shown in Figure 4-45. Select each counter and note the average, minimum, and maximum values for the counter.

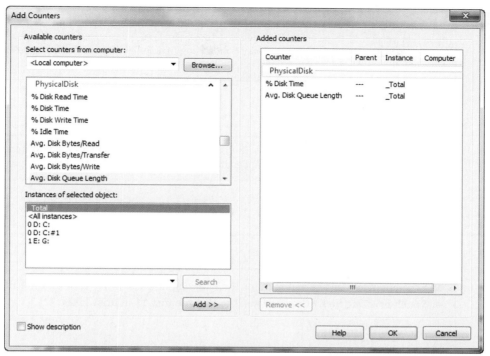

Figure 4-44 Add counters to set up what Performance Monitor tracks

© Cengage Learning 2013

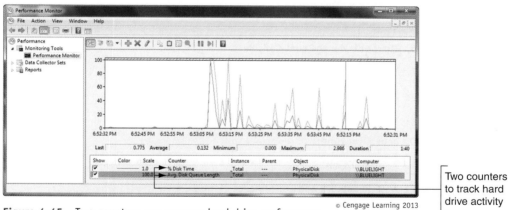

Two counters to track hard drive activity

Figure 4-45 Two counters can measure hard drive performance

© Cengage Learning 2013

If the Avg. Disk Queue Length is above two and the % Disk Time is more than 80%, you can conclude that the hard drive is working excessively hard and processes are slowed down waiting on the drive. Anytime a process must wait to access the hard drive, you are likely to see degradation in overall system performance.

Performance Monitor also offers several data collector sets. A **data collector set** is a set of counters that you can use to collect data about the system and save this data in a report or log file for future use. You can also create your own data collector sets by selecting counters to use in the set and you can decide where to save the log file when you run your customized data collector set. Data collector sets are started, stopped, and customized using the Data Collector Sets group in the left pane of the Performance Monitor window. If you want to know more about using data collector sets, click the Help button in the Performance Monitor window or search the Microsoft web site at *technet.microsoft.com*.

A+
220-802
1.1, 1.4

Vista Differences   The Windows Vista **Reliability and Performance Monitor (Perfmon.msc)** is an earlier version of three separate Windows 7 tools: Windows 7 Resource Monitor, Reliability Monitor, and Performance Monitor. To find out more about the Vista Reliability and Performance Monitor, see Appendix B.

XP Differences   The Windows XP Performance Monitor is also called the **System Monitor**. To find out more about this tool, see Appendix C.

Hands-on │ Project 4.6   Find Windows Utilities

List the program filename and path for the following utilities. (*Hint*: You can use Windows Explorer or Search to locate files.) Use Windows 7 to find the first 11 utilities listed.

1. Task Manager
2. Vista Software Explorer
3. System Configuration
4. Services Console
5. Computer Management
6. Microsoft Management Console
7. Event Viewer
8. Performance Monitor
9. Resource Monitor
10. Reliability Monitor
11. Registry Editor
12. Vista Reliability and Performance Monitor
13. XP Performance Monitor

Now let's turn our attention to the step-by-step procedures using the tools you just learned about to improve Windows performance.

IMPROVING WINDOWS PERFORMANCE

A+
220-802
4.3

In this part of the chapter, you'll learn to search for problems affecting performance and to clean up the Windows startup process. These step-by-step procedures go beyond the routine maintenance tasks you learned about in Chapter 3. We're assuming Windows starts with no errors. If you are having trouble loading Windows, it's best to address the error first rather

A+
220-802
4.3

💡 **A+ Exam Tip** The A+ 220-802 exam expects you to know how to troubleshoot and solve problems with slow system performance.

than to use the tools described here to improve performance. How to handle errors that keep Windows from starting is covered in Chapter 6.

Now let's look at 10 steps you can take to improve Windows performance.

STEP 1: PERFORM ROUTINE MAINTENANCE

It might seem pretty mundane, but the first things you need to do to improve performance of a sluggish Windows system are the routine maintenance tasks that you learned in Chapter 3. These tasks are summarized here:

▲ *Verify critical Windows settings.* Make sure Windows updates are current. Verify that antivirus software is updated and set to routinely scan for viruses. Make sure the network connection is secured. If the system is experiencing a marked decrease in performance, suspect a virus and use up-to-date antivirus software to perform a full scan of the system.

▲ *Clean up, defrag, and check the hard drive.* Make sure at least 15 percent of drive C: is free. For Windows 7/Vista, make sure a magnetic hard drive is being defragged weekly. If you suspect hard drive problems, use Chkdsk to check the hard drive for errors and recover data.

▲ *Uninstall software you no longer need.* Use the Windows 7/Vista Programs and Features window or the XP Add or Remove Programs window to uninstall programs you no longer need.

As always, if valuable data is not backed up, back it up before you apply any of the fixes in this chapter. You don't want to risk losing the user's data.

STEP 2: CLEAN WINDOWS STARTUP

The most important step following routine maintenance to improve performance is to verify that startup programs are kept to a minimum. Before cleaning Windows startup, you can use Safe Mode to set a benchmark for the time it takes to start Windows when only the bare minimum of programs are launched.

OBSERVE PERFORMANCE IN SAFE MODE

To find out if programs and services are slowing down Windows startup, boot the system in Safe Mode and watch to see if performance improves. Do the following:

1. Use a stopwatch or a watch with a second hand to time a normal startup from the moment you press the power button until the wait icon on the Windows desktop disappears.

2. Time the boot again, this time using Safe Mode. To boot the system in Safe Mode, press **F8** while Windows is loading and then select Safe Mode with Networking from the boot options menu (see Figure 4-46).

A+
220-802
4.3

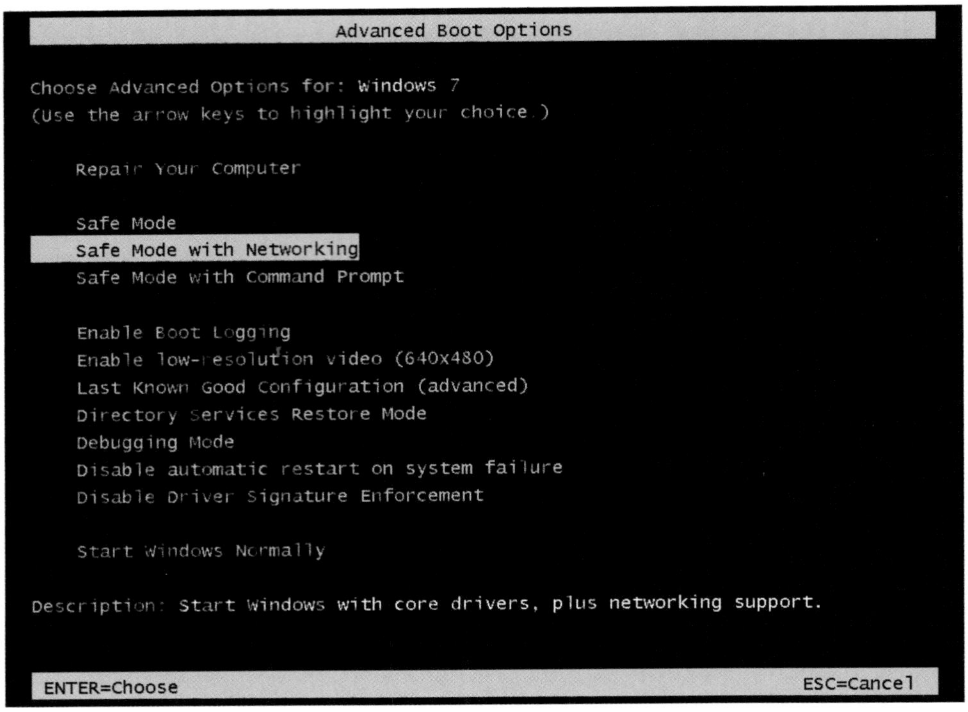

```
                        Advanced Boot Options

Choose Advanced Options for: Windows 7
(Use the arrow keys to highlight your choice.)


    Repair Your Computer


    Safe Mode
    Safe Mode with Networking
    Safe Mode with Command Prompt


    Enable Boot Logging
    Enable low-resolution video (640x480)
    Last Known Good Configuration (advanced)
    Directory Services Restore Mode
    Debugging Mode
    Disable automatic restart on system failure
    Disable Driver Signature Enforcement


    Start Windows Normally

Description: Start Windows with core drivers, plus networking support.


  ENTER=Choose                                           ESC=Cancel
```

© Cengage Learning 2013

Figure 4-46 Windows Advanced Boot Options Menu allows you to launch Safe Mode

If the difference is significant, follow the steps in this part of the chapter to reduce Windows startup to essentials. If the performance problem still exists in Safe Mode, you can assume that the problem is with hardware or Windows settings and you can proceed to *Step 3: Check If the Hardware Can Support the OS.*

INVESTIGATE AND ELIMINATE STARTUP PROGRAMS

To speed up startup, search for unnecessary startup programs you can eliminate. Tools that can help are System Configuration (Msconfig.exe), startup folders, and Task Manager. Follow these steps to investigate startup:

1. Open Msconfig, select the **Startup** tab, and look for specific startup program you don't want. If you're not sure of the purpose of a program, scroll to the right in the Command column to see the name of the startup program file (see Figure 4-47). Then search the web for information on this program. Be careful to use only reliable sites for credible information. Use the Location column to find out how the program was launched. In Figure 4-47, notice the last three items are launched from startup folders.

> ⚡ **Caution** A word of caution is important here: many web sites will tell you a legitimate process is malicious so that you will download and use their software to get rid of the process. However, their software is likely to be adware or spyware that you don't want. Make sure you can trust a site before you download from it or take its advice.

2. If you want to find out if disabling a startup entry gives problems or improves performance, temporarily disable it using Msconfig. To permanently disable a startup item, it's best to uninstall the software or remove the entry from a startup folder. See Appendix G for a list of startup folders.

A+
220-802
4.3

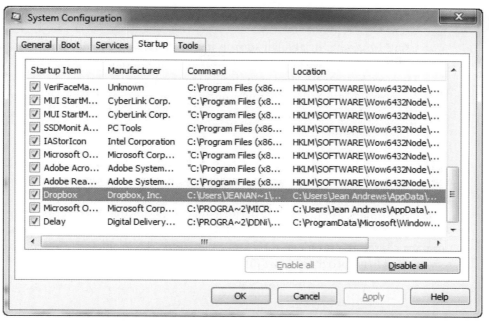

© Cengage Learning 2013

Figure 4-47 Find the path and name of the program file in the Command column of System Configuration

> **Notes** The startup folder for all users is hidden by default. In Chapter 1, you learned how to unhide folders that are hidden.

3. As you research startup processes, Task Manager can tell you what processes are currently running. Open Task Manager and select the **Processes** tab. If you see a process and want to know its program file location, click **View** and click **Select Columns**. In the Select Process Page Columns, check **Image Path Name** and click **OK**. The Image Path Name column is added (see Figure 4-48).

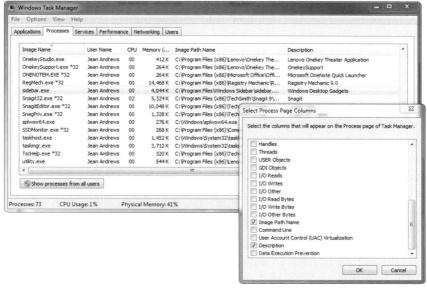

© Cengage Learning 2013

Figure 4-48 Use the Image Path Name column on the Processes tab to locate a program file

A+
220-802
4.3

For extremely slow systems that need a more drastic fix, do the following:

▲ Using Msconfig, disable all startup items on the Startup tab. Then restart the system and see what problems you get into with a program disabled that you really need. Then enable just the ones you decide you need.

▲ An even more drastic approach for extremely slow startups is to disable all non-Microsoft services. On the Services tab, check **Hide all Microsoft services**, and then click **Disable all**.

Regardless of the method you use, be sure to restart the system after each change and note what happens. Do you get an error message? Does a device or application not work? If so, you have probably disabled a service or program you need.

Has performance improved? If performance does not improve by disabling services or startup programs, go back and enable them again. If no non-Microsoft service or startup program caused the problem, then you can assume the problem is caused by a Microsoft service or startup program. Start disabling them one at a time.

> ⚡ **Caution**   You might be tempted to disable all Microsoft services. If you do so, you are disabling Networking, Event Logging, Error Reporting, Windows Firewall, Windows Installer, Windows Backup, Print Spooler, Windows Update, System Protection, and other important services. These services should be disabled only when testing for performance problems and then immediately enabled when the test is finished. Also, know that if you disable the Volume Shadow Copy service, all restore points kept on the system will be lost. If you intend to use System Restore to fix a problem with the system, don't disable this service. If you are not sure what a service does, read its description in the Services console before you change its status.

Remember that you don't want to permanently leave MSconfig in control of startup. After you have used MSconfig to identify the problem, use other tools to permanently remove them from startup. Use the Services console to disable a service, use the Programs and Features window to uninstall software, and remove program files from startup folders. After the problem is fixed, return MSconfig to a normal startup.

Don't forget to restart the computer after making a change to verify that all is well.

CHECK FOR UNWANTED SCHEDULED TASKS

When applications install, they often schedule tasks to check for and download their program updates, and malware sometimes hides as a scheduled task. Scheduled tasks might be unnecessary and can slow a system down. The best way to uninstall a scheduled task is to uninstall the software that is responsible for the task. Open the Task Scheduler window and search through tasks looking for those you think are unnecessary or causing trouble. Research the software the task works with and then you might decide to uninstall the software or disable the task.

Don't forget to restart the system to make sure all is well before you move on.

MONITOR THE STARTUP PROCESS

Now that you have the startup process clean, you will want to keep it that way. You can use several third-party tools to monitor any changes to startup. A good one is WinPatrol by BillP Studios (*www.winpatrol.com*). Download and install the free version of the

A+
220-802
4.3

program to run in the background to monitor all sorts of things, including changes to the registry, startup processes, Internet Explorer settings, and system files. In Figure 4-49, you can see how WinPatrol gave an alert when it detected an Internet Explorer plug-in is placing an entry in the registry. WinPatrol displays a little black Scotty dog in the notification area of the taskbar to indicate it's running in the background and guarding your system. Also, many antivirus programs monitor the startup process and inform you when changes are made.

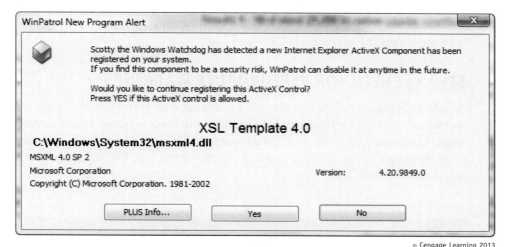

© Cengage Learning 2013

Figure 4-49 WinPatrol by BillP Studios alerts you when a program is making a system change

---

Hands-on | Project 4.7 Monitor Startup Items with WinPatrol

1. Using System Configuration (MSconfig), disable all the non-Windows startup items. Restart your computer.

2. Download and install WinPatrol from *www.winpatrol.com*.

3. Using System Configuration, enable all of the disabled startup items and restart the computer.

4. Are the startup programs able to start? What messages are displayed on the screen?

STEP 3: CHECK IF THE HARDWARE CAN SUPPORT THE OS

The system might be slow because the OS does not have the hardware resources it needs. Use the Windows 7/Vista Windows Experience Index to quickly zero in on a hardware component that might be a bottleneck. If you suspect that the processor, hard drive, or memory is a bottleneck, consider using the Windows 7 Resource Monitor, the Vista Reliability and Performance Monitor, or the XP Performance Monitor to get more detailed information. If the bottleneck appears to be graphics, the problem might be solved by updating the graphics drivers or by updating Windows.

A+
220-802
4.3

> **Notes** Use the System Information Utility (msinfo32.exe) to find information about the installed processor and its speed, how much RAM is installed, and free space on the hard drive. Compare all these values to the minimum and recommended requirements for Windows listed in Chapter 2.

If you find that the system is slow because of a hardware component, discuss the situation with the user. You might be able to upgrade the hardware or install another OS that is compatible with the hardware that is present. Upgrading from Vista to Windows 7 can often improve performance in a computer that has slow hardware components. Better still, perform a clean installation of Windows 7 so that you get a fresh start with installed applications, plug-ins, and background services that might be slowing down the system.

STEP 4: CHECK FOR PERFORMANCE WARNINGS

Windows 7/Vista tracks issues that are interfering with performance. To see these warnings, open the Performance Information and Tools window and click **Advanced tools**. The Advanced Tools window appears, as shown in Figure 4-50. If Windows knows of performance issues, they are listed at the top of this window. Click an issue to see a recommended solution.

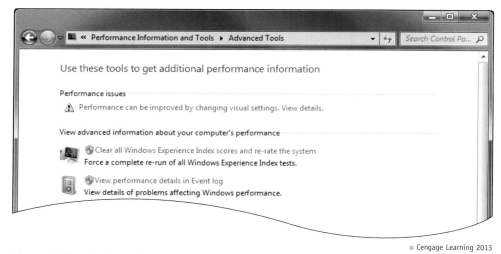

© Cengage Learning 2013

Figure 4-50 Windows 7/Vista provides performance warnings and tools to improve Windows performance

For example, when you click the one issue reported in Figure 4-50, a box appears describing the problem and offering solutions (see Figure 4-51). If you make a change to the system while resolving the issue, restart Windows before tackling the next fix or issue. After you have resolved an issue or have decided to live with it, you can click **Remove from list** so that it will no longer appear in the list of issues. If you need more information about an issue, click **View details in the event log** and Event Viewer opens, displaying the appropriate logs.

Windows XP does not offer the Advanced Tools window. For XP, open Event Viewer and view the System log. Look for events that might indicate a performance problem.

A+
220-802
4.3

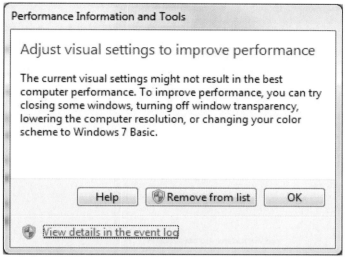

© Cengage Learning 2013

Figure 4-51 Windows reports that current visual settings are affecting performance.

STEP 5: CHECK FOR A HISTORY OF PROBLEMS

Try to identify when the slow performance problem began, and then use the Windows 7 or Vista Reliability Monitor to find out what changes were made to the system around that time and what other problems occurred. If you don't know when the problem started, skim through the line graph at the top of the Reliability Monitor window and look for drops in the graph. Also look for critical events indicated by a red x (refer to Figure 4-42).

STEP 6: DISABLE THE INDEXER FOR WINDOWS SEARCH

The Windows 7/Vista indexer is responsible for maintaining an index of files and folders on a hard drive to speed up Windows searches. The indexing service has a low priority and only works when it senses that the hard drive is not being accessed by a service with a higher priority. However, it might still slow down performance. Do the following to find out if this service is causing a performance problem:

1. Find out if the indexing service is currently indexing the system. To do that, click **Adjust indexing options** in the left pane of the Performance and Information Tools window. (You can also enter **Indexing Options** in the search box.) The Indexing Options box appears (see Figure 4-52).

2. If you see *Indexing speed is reduced due to user activity* at the top of the box, wait while indexing is in progress and the status changes to *Indexing complete*. You can now stop the indexing service.

3. To stop the indexing service, open the Services console. Then stop and disable the **Windows Search** service (see Figure 4-53).

A+
220-802
4.3

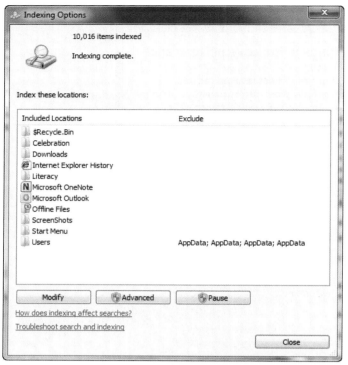

Figure 4-52 Indexing is enabled on this system

© Cengage Learning 2013

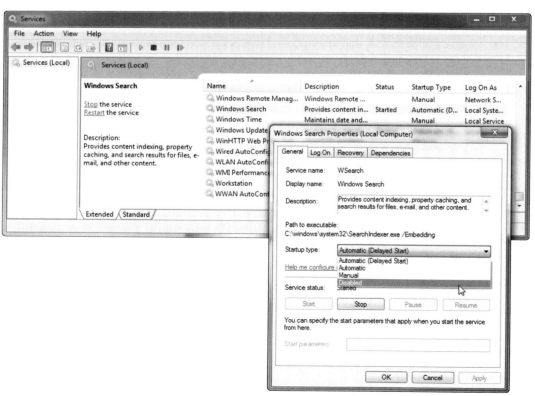

Figure 4-53 Disable the Windows Search service

© Cengage Learning 2013

4. Restart the computer. Run the system for a while and see if performance improves.

5. If performance does not improve, restart the indexing service. To do that, use the Services console to set the status of the Windows Search service to **Automatic (Delayed Start)** and start the service. Then move on to the next section of this chapter, *Step 7: Plug Up Any Memory Leaks.*

6. If performance does improve, it is possible that the problem was caused by a corrupted index database. To rebuild the database, first use the Services console to set the Windows Search service status back to **Automatic (Delayed Start)** and to start the service.

7. Open the Indexing Options box and click **Advanced**. The Advanced Options box opens (see Figure 4-54).

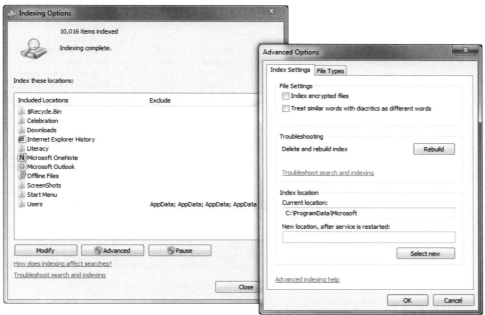

Figure 4-54 Rebuild the indexing database

© Cengage Learning 2013

8. To rebuild the indexing database, click **Rebuild**. A dialog box appears warning you that this can take some time. Click **OK**. Close the Indexing Options box.

9. After running the system for a while, if the performance problem returns, you can disable the Windows Search service and leave it disabled. However, know that searching will not be as fast without indexing.

STEP 7: PLUG UP ANY MEMORY LEAKS

If you notice that performance slows after a system has been up and running without a restart for some time, suspect a memory leak. A memory leak is caused when an application does not properly release memory allocated to it that it no longer needs and continually requests more memory than it needs.

To see how much memory an application has allocated to it that is not available to other programs, open Task Manager and click the **Processes** tab. In the menu bar, click **View**, **Select Columns**. Verify that the Memory Private Working Set, Handles, and Threads columns are checked and click **OK**. If you observe that the values in these three columns increase over time for a particular program, suspect the program has a memory leak. To sort the data by one column, click the column label. For example, the Task Manager window shown in Figure 4-55 is sorted by Memory. It shows the memory-hungry applications on this system are Eudora (an email client) and Skype (an Internet voice and video program).

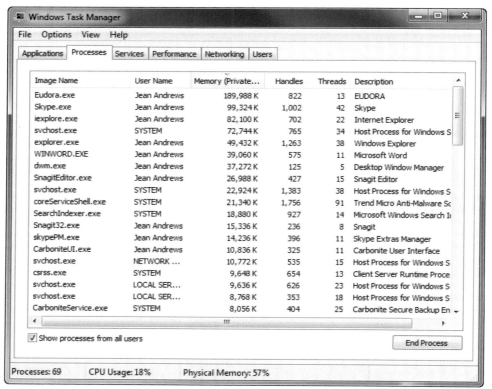

Figure 4-55 Task Manager shows how memory is allocated for an application   © Cengage Learning 2013

Note that the Windows 7 Resource Monitor and the Vista Reliability and Performance Monitor give similar information about how memory is used. If you decide a program has a memory leak, try to get an update or patch from the program manufacturer's web site.

STEP 8: CONSIDER USING READYBOOST

Windows 7/Vista **ReadyBoost** uses a flash drive or secure digital (SD) memory card to boost hard drive performance. The faster flash memory is used as a buffer to speed up hard drive access time. You see the greatest performance increase using ReadyBoost when you have a slow magnetic hard drive (running at less than 7200 RPM). To find out what speed your hard drive is using, use System Information (Msinfo32.exe) and drill down into the Components, Storage group, and select Disks (see Figure 4-56). The model of the hard drive appears in the right pane. Use Google to search on this brand and model; a quick search shows this drive runs at 5400 RPM. It's, therefore, a good candidate to benefit from ReadyBoost.

> 💡 **A+ Exam Tip** The A+ 220-802 exam expects you to know how to use ReadyBoost to improve performance.

A+
220-802
1.1, 4.3

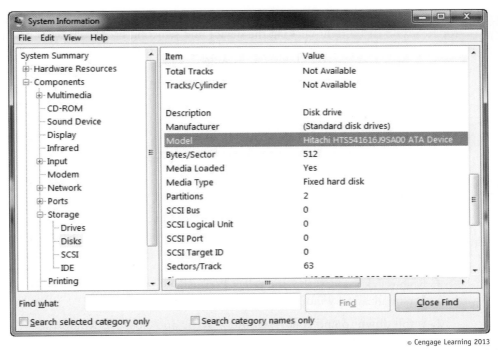

© Cengage Learning 2013

Figure 4-56 Use the System Information window to find out the brand and model of your hard drive

When you first connect a flash device, Windows will automatically test it to see if it qualifies for ReadyBoost. To qualify, it must have a capacity of 256 MB to 4 GB with at least 256 MB of free space, and run at about 2 MB/sec of throughput. If the device qualifies, Windows displays a dialog box that can be used to activate ReadyBoost (see Figure 4-57a). When you click **Speed up my system**, the device properties box appears with the ReadyBoost tab selected (see Figure 4-57b). Here you can decide how much of the device memory to

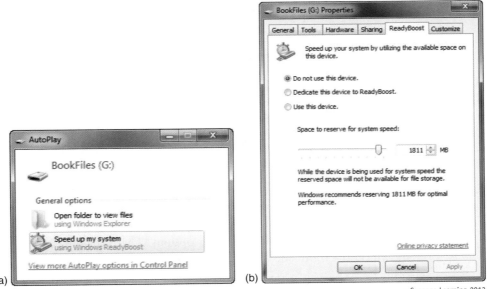

(a) (b)

© Cengage Learning 2013

Figure 4-57 Windows asks permission to use the device for ReadyBoost

A+
220-802
1.1, 4.3

allot for ReadyBoost. You can manually have Windows test a memory card or flash drive for ReadyBoost by right-clicking the device and selecting **Properties** from the shortcut menu. On the device properties window, click the **ReadyBoost** tab.

The best flash devices to use for ReadyBoost are the ones that can take advantage of the faster ports. For example, a SuperSpeed USB (USB 3.0) device and port is about 10 times faster than a Hi-Speed USB (USB 2.0) device and port. Incidentally, when you remove the device, no data is lost because the device only holds a copy of the data.

A+
220-802
4.3

STEP 9: DISABLE THE AERO INTERFACE

The Windows Aero interface might be slowing down the system because it uses memory and computing power. Try disabling it. If performance improves, you can conclude that the hardware is not able to support the Aero interface. At that point, you might want to upgrade memory, upgrade the video card, or leave the Aero interface disabled.

To disable the Aero interface using Windows 7, do the following:

1. Right-click the desktop and select **Personalize** from the shortcut menu. The Personalization window opens (see Figure 4-58).

2. Scroll down to and click **Windows 7 Basic** and close the window.

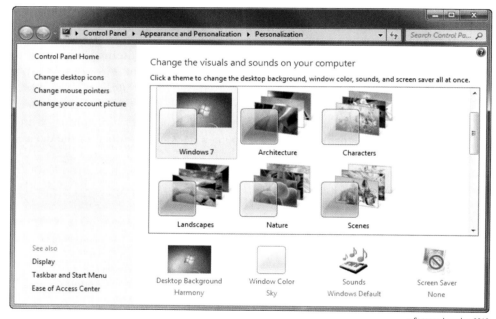

© Cengage Learning 2013

Figure 4-58 Disable the Windows 7 Aero interface to conserve system resources

To disable the Aero interface using Windows Vista, follow these steps:

1. Open the Personalization window and click **Window Color**. Then click **Open classic appearance properties for more color options**. The Appearance Settings box opens, shown on the right side of Figure 4-59.

2. Under Color scheme, select **Windows Vista Basic** and click **Apply**. Close the dialog box and window.

A+
220-802
4.3

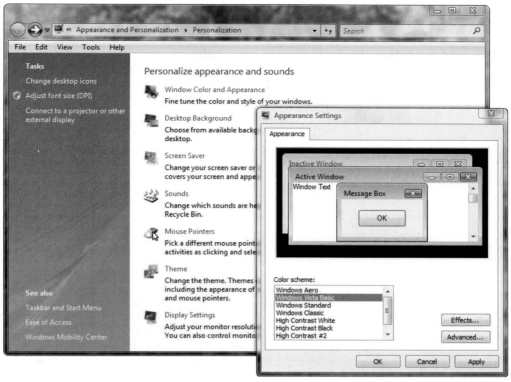

© Cengage Learning 2013

Figure 4-59 Disable the Windows Vista Aero interface to conserve system resources

STEP 10: DISABLE THE VISTA SIDEBAR

Recall that the Vista sidebar appears on the Windows desktop to hold apps called gadgets. The sidebar uses system resources and disabling it can improve performance. To do that, right-click the sidebar and select **Properties** from the shortcut menu. The Windows Sidebar Properties box appears (see Figure 4-60). Uncheck **Start Sidebar when Windows starts**. Then click **Apply** and **OK** to close the box.

© Cengage Learning 2013

Figure 4-60 Disable the Vista sidebar to improve performance

MANUALLY REMOVING SOFTWARE

A+
220-802
4.3

In this part of the chapter, we focus on getting rid of programs that refuse to uninstall or give errors when uninstalling. In these cases, you can manually uninstall a program. Doing so often causes problems later, so use the methods discussed in this section only as a last resort after normal uninstall methods have failed.

This part of the chapter discusses the following steps to manually remove software:

1. First try to locate and use an uninstall routine provided by the software. If this works, you are done and can skip the next steps.

2. Delete the program folders and files that hold the software.

3. Delete the registry entries used by the software.

4. Remove the entries in the Start menu and delete any shortcuts on the desktop.

5. Remove any entries that launch processes at startup.

> **Notes** Before uninstalling software, make sure it's not running in the background. For example, antivirus software cannot be uninstalled if it's still running. You can use Task Manager to end all processes related to the software, and you can use the Services console to stop services related to the software. Then remove the software.

Now let's step through the process of manually removing software.

STEP 1: FIRST TRY THE UNINSTALL ROUTINE

Most programs written for Windows have an uninstall routine that can be accessed from the Windows 7/Vista Programs and Features window, the XP Add Remove Programs window, or an uninstall utility in the All Programs menu. For example, in Figure 4-61, you can see in the All Programs menu that an uninstall item is listed for the Registry Mechanic software installation. (Registry Mechanic is utility software that can clean the registry of unused keys.) Click this option and follow the directions on-screen to uninstall the software. Alternately, you can use the Programs and Features window to uninstall the software.

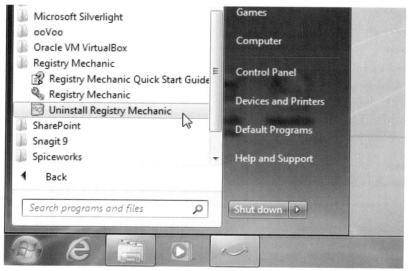

© Cengage Learning 2013

Figure 4-61   Most applications have an uninstall utility included with the software

STEP 2: DELETE PROGRAM FILES

If the uninstall routine is missing or does not work, the next step is to delete the program folders and files that contain the software. In our example, we'll delete the Registry Mechanic software without using its uninstall routine.

Look for the program folder in one of these folders:

◢ C:\Program Files
◢ C:\Program Files (x86)

In Figure 4-62, you can see the Registry Mechanic folder under the C:\Program Files (x86) folder. Keep in mind, however, the program files might be in another location that was set by the user when the software was installed. Delete the **Registry Mechanic** folder and all its contents.

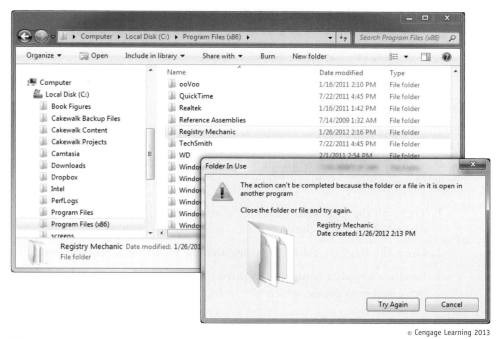

© Cengage Learning 2013

Figure 4-62 Program files are usually found in the Program Files or Program Files (x86) folder

As you do, you might see the warning box shown on the right side of Figure 4-62 saying the program is in use. In this situation, do the following:

1. Look for the program file reported on the Processes tab of Task Manager. If you see it listed, end the process. The Command Line column can help you find the right program.

2. If you don't find the program on the Processes tab, check the **Services** tab. If you find it there, select it and click **Services** (see Figure 4-63). The Services console opens where you can stop the service. (Note in the figure the Registry Mechanic software by PC Tools is running under the PC Tools name.)

3. After the program or service is stopped, try to delete the program folder again. If you still cannot delete the folder, look for other running programs or services associated with the software.

A+
220-802
4.3

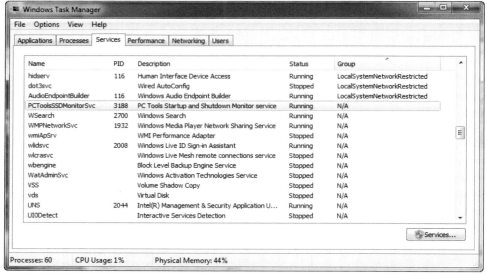

© Cengage Learning 2013

Figure 4-63 Task Manager shows a service is running and needs to be stopped before the program files can be deleted

STEP 3: DELETE REGISTRY ENTRIES

Editing the registry can be dangerous, so do this with caution and be sure to back up first! Do the following to delete registry entries that cause a program to be listed as installed software in the Windows 7/Vista Programs and Features window or the XP Add or Remove Programs window of Control Panel:

1. To be on the safe side, back up the entire registry using one or more of the methods discussed earlier in the chapter.

2. Open the Registry Editor by using the **regedit** command in the search box.

3. Locate a key that contains the entries that make up the list of installed software. Use this criteria to decide which key to locate:

   ◢ For a 32-bit program installed in a 32-bit OS or for a 64-bit program installed in a 64-bit OS, locate this key:
   HKEY_LOCAL_MACHINE\Software\Microsoft\Windows\CurrentVersion\Uninstall

   ◢ For a 32-bit program installed in a 64-bit OS, locate this key:
   HKEY_LOCAL_MACHINE\SOFTWARE\Wow6432Node\Microsoft\Windows\CurrentVersion\Uninstall

> **Notes** Recall that 32-bit programs are installed the \Program Files (x86) folder on a 64-bit system. These 32-bit programs use the Wow6432Node subkey in the registry of a 64-bit OS.

4. Back up the Uninstall key to the Windows desktop so that you can backtrack if necessary. To do that, right-click the Uninstall key and select **Export** from the shortcut menu (see Figure 4-34 earlier in the chapter).

5. In the Export Registry File dialog box, select the **Desktop**. Enter the filename as **Save Uninstall Key**, and click **Save**. You should see a new file icon on your desktop named Save Uninstall Key.reg.

6. The Uninstall key can be a daunting list of all the programs installed on your PC. When you expand the key, you see a long list of subkeys in the left pane, which might have meaningless names that won't help you find the program you're looking for. Select the first subkey in the Uninstall key and watch as its values and data are displayed in the right pane (see Figure 4-64). Step down through each key, watching for a meaningful name of the subkey in the left pane or meaningful details in the right pane until you find the program you want to delete.

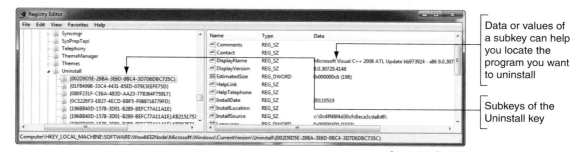

© Cengage Learning 2013

Figure 4-64 Select a subkey under the Uninstall key to display its values and data in the right pane

7. To delete the key, right-click the key and select **Delete** from the shortcut menu (see Figure 4-65) and confirm the deletion. Be sure to search through all the keys in this list because the software might have more than one key. Delete them all and exit the Registry Editor.

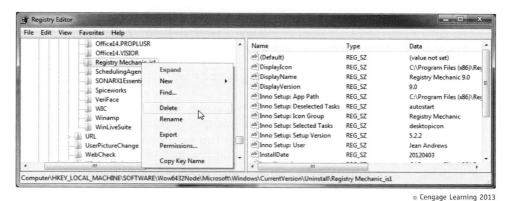

© Cengage Learning 2013

Figure 4-65 Delete the registry key that lists the software as installed software

8. Open the Windows 7/Vista Programs and Features window or the XP Add or Remove Programs window and verify that the list of installed software is correct and the software you are uninstalling is no longer listed.

9. If the list of installed software is not correct, to restore the Uninstall registry key, double-click the **Save Uninstall Key.reg** icon on your desktop.

10. As a last step when editing the registry, clean up after yourself by deleting the Save Uninstall Key.reg file on your desktop. Right-click the icon and select **Delete** from the shortcut menu.

A+
220-802
4.3

STEP 4: REMOVE THE PROGRAM FROM THE ALL PROGRAMS MENU AND THE DESKTOP

To remove the program from the All Programs menu, right-click it and select **Delete** from the shortcut menu (see Figure 4-66). If the program has shortcuts on the desktop, delete these.

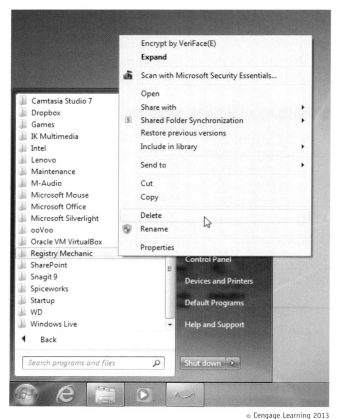

© Cengage Learning 2013

Figure 4-66 Delete the program from the All Programs menu

STEP 5: REMOVE STARTUP PROCESSES

Restart the PC and watch for any startup errors about a missing program file. The software might have stored startup entries in the registry, in startup folders, or as a service that is no longer present and causing an error. If you see an error, use MSconfig to find out how the program is set to start. This entry point is called an orphaned entry. You'll then need to delete this startup entry by editing the registry, deleting a shortcut in a startup folder, or disabling a service using the Services console.

It's unlikely you will be able to completely remove all keys in the registry that the software put there. A registry cleaner can help you find these orphaned keys, but if no errors appear at startup, you can just leave these keys untouched. Also, an installation might put program files in the C:\Program Files\Common Files or the C:\Program Files (x86)\Common Files folder. Most likely you can just leave these untouched as well. Address all error messages you encounter and stop there.

REGISTRY KEYS THAT AFFECT STARTUP AND LOGON EVENTS

You have just seen how you can edit the registry to remove the entries left there by software that you have manually removed. If a system is giving repeated startup errors or you have just removed several programs, you might want to search through registry keys where

A+
220-802
4.3

startup processes can be located. See Appendix G for a list of these registry keys and startup folders. As you read through this list of registry keys to search, know that the list is not exhaustive. With experience, you'll learn that the registry is an ever-changing landscape of keys and values.

Hands-on Project 4.8 Practice Manually Removing Software

To practice your skills of manually removing software, install WinPatrol from *www.winpatrol.com*. (If you did Project 4-2, the software is already installed.) Then, following the directions in the chapter, manually remove the software, listing the steps you used. (Do not use the uninstall routine provided by WinPatrol.) After you have manually removed the software, reboot the system. Did you get any error messages?

>> *CHAPTER SUMMARY*

Windows Utilities and Tools to Support the OS

▲ The Windows OS is made up of two main components, the shell and the kernel. The shell provides an interface for users and applications. The kernel is responsible for interacting with hardware.

▲ A process is a program running under the shell, together with all the resources assigned to it. A thread is a single task that a process requests from the kernel.

▲ Task Manager (Taskmgr.exe) lets you view services and other running programs, CPU and memory performance, network activity, and user activity. It is useful to stop a process that is hung.

▲ Tools listed in the Administrative Tools group of Control Panel are used by technicians and developers to support Windows and applications.

▲ System Configuration (Msconfig.exe) can be used to temporarily disable startup processes to test for performance improvement and find a startup program causing a problem.

▲ The Services console (Services.msc) is used to manage Windows and application services. When and if a service starts can be controlled from this console.

▲ The Computer Management console (Compmgmt.msc) contains a group of Windows administrative tools useful for managing a system.

▲ The Microsoft Management Console (MMC) can be used to build your own custom consoles from available snap-ins.

▲ The Event Viewer (Eventvwr.msc) console displays a group of logs kept by Windows that are useful for troubleshooting problems with software and hardware. You can also use Event Viewer to view security audits made by Windows.

▲ The Registry Editor (Regedit.exe) is used to edit the registry in real time. There is no way to use the Registry Editor to undo changes you make to the registry. Therefore, you should always make a backup before editing it.

◢ The Performance Information and Tools window displays the Windows Experience Index that rates the overall performance of the system. You can reach tools to optimize performance from this window.

◢ Windows 7 Resource Monitor monitors the performance of the process or, memory, hard drive, and network in real time.

◢ The Windows 7 Reliability Monitor can be used to get historical data about problems on the computer since Windows was installed.

◢ The Windows 7 Performance Monitor uses counters to track activity by hardware and software to evaluate performance.

◢ The Vista Reliability and Performance Monitor (Perfmon.msc) is an earlier version of the three separate tools in Windows 7: the Resource Monitor, Reliability Monitor, and Performance Monitor.

◢ The XP Performance Monitor (also called the System Monitor) uses counters and is an earlier version of the Windows 7 Performance monitor.

Improving Windows Performance

◢ The 10 high-level steps to improve Windows performance are (1) routine maintenance, (2) clean Windows startup, (3) check if hardware can support the OS, (4) check for performance warnings, (5) check for a history of problems to find the source of a problem, (6) disable indexing for Windows search, (7) plug up memory leaks, (8) consider using ReadyBoost to improve a slow hard drive's performance, (9) disable the Aero interface, and (10) disable the Vista sidebar.

◢ Tools that can be used to investigate and clean up the Windows start process include Safe Mode, startup folders, MSconfig, Task Scheduler, Task Manager, and Services console.

Manually Removing Software

◢ If software does not uninstall using the Windows 7/Vista Programs and Features window or the XP Add or Remove Programs window, you can manually uninstall the software.

◢ To manually delete software, delete the program files, entries in the Start, All Programs menu, registry keys, and items in startup folders.

>> KEY TERMS

Administrative tools
Computer Management (Compmgmt.msc)
console
data collector set
Event Viewer (Eventvwr.msc)
executive services
HAL (hardware abstraction layer)
HKEY_CLASSES_ROOT (HKCR)
HKEY_CURRENT_CONFIG (HKCC)
HKEY_CURRENT_USER (HKCU)

HKEY_LOCAL_MACHINE (HKLM)
HKEY_USERS (HKU)
kernel
kernel mode
Microsoft Management Console (MMC)
Performance Information and Tools
Performance Monitor
process
ReadyBoost
registry
Registry Editor (regedit.exe)

Reliability and Performance Monitor (Perfmon.msc)
Reliability Monitor
Resource Monitor
Services console
shell
snap-ins
System Configuration (Msconfig.exe)
System Monitor
Task Manager (Taskmgr.exe)
Task Scheduler
thread
user mode

>> REVIEWING THE BASICS

1. List four ways to start Task Manager.

2. If a program is not responding, how can you stop it?

3. If a necessary program is using too much of the system resources and bogging down other applications, what can you do to fix the problem?

4. How can you view a list of users currently logged onto the computer?

5. What is the program filename and extension of System Configuration?

6. Which Windows 7 tool can be used to see a history of problems a computer has had since Windows was installed?

7. What tool in Windows Vista, used to temporarily disable a startup program, is not available in Windows 7 or Windows XP?

8. If a nonessential service is slowing down startup, how can you permanently disable it?

9. What should be the startup type of a service that should not load at startup but might be used later after startup? What tool can you use to set a service's startup type?

10. List three snap-ins that can be found in the Computer Management console that are used to manage hardware and track problems with hardware.

11. What is the file extension of a console that is managed by Microsoft Management Console?

12. Name the program file name and file extension for the Microsoft Management Console.

13. Which log in Event Viewer would you use to find out about attempted logins to a computer?

14. Which log in Event Viewer would you use if you suspect a problem with the hard drive?

15. Which three Windows 7 tools are contained in the Vista Reliability and Performance Monitor?

16. What is the path to the Ntuser.dat file in Windows 7?

17. How is the Ntuser.dat file used?

18. Which registry key contains information that Device Manager uses to display information about hardware?

19. Which Windows 7/Vista tool can give you a quick report of the overall performance of the system expressed as a single number?

20. To improve Windows performance, you decide to disable the indexer used for Windows search. Will Windows search still work?

21. What three indicators in Task Manager can be used to find which program has a memory leak?

22. What key do you press at startup to load the system in Safe Mode?

23. If performance improves when Windows is loaded in Safe Mode, what can you conclude?

24. If performance does not improve when Windows is loaded in Safe Mode, what can you conclude?

25. When using MSconfig to stop startup services including Microsoft services, which service should you not stop so that restore points will not be lost?

26. In what folder does Task Scheduler keep scheduled tasks?

27. What are the two folders where, by default, Windows stores installed software?

28. What must you do first before you can delete the program folder containing software that is running in the background?

29. What is the purpose of the Wow6432Node subkey in the Windows registry?

30. What is the name of the window used to uninstall software in Windows 7/Vista?

>> THINKING CRITICALLY

1. You need to install a customized console on 10 computers. What is the best way to do that?

2. What is the name of the program that you can enter in the search box to execute Event Viewer? What is the process that is running when Event Viewer is displayed on the screen? Why do you think the running process is different from the program name?

3. When cleaning up the startup process, which of these should you do first?

4. Using the Internet, investigate each of the following startup processes. Identify the process and write a one-sentence description.

5. Using Task Manager, you discover an unwanted program that is launched at startup. Of the following items, which ones might lead you to the permanent solution to the problem? Which ones would not be an appropriate solution to the problem? Explain why they are not appropriate.

>> REAL PROBLEMS, REAL SOLUTIONS

REAL PROBLEM 4-1: Using Registry Mechanic

Registry Mechanic by PC Tools can be downloaded free from the registrycleaner.com web site. Download, install, and run the software. How many orphaned registry keys did it find on your computer? Which software installed on your computer is responsible for these orphaned keys? Do you think your system would benefit from allowing Registry Mechanic to clean your registry? If you decide to use Registry Mechanic to clean the registry, be sure to create a restore point first so you can undo the changes to your registry, if necessary.

REAL PROBLEM 4-2: Cleaning Up Startup

Using a computer that has a problem with a sluggish startup, apply the tools and procedures you learned in this chapter to clean up the startup process. Take detailed notes of each step you take and its results. (If you are having a problem finding a computer with a sluggish startup, consider offering your help to a friend, a family member, or a nonprofit organization.)

Troubleshooting Windows and Applications

When a computer gives you problems, a good plan for solving that problem can help you to not feel so helpless. This chapter is designed to give you just that—a plan with all the necessary details and tools so that you can determine just what has gone wrong and what to do about it.

In this chapter, you learn about Windows tools for problem solving and troubleshooting strategies to help solve any computer problem. You learn what to do when a computer freezes or gives a blue screen error (also called the blue screen of death) and when applications give problems. This chapter focuses on problems that occur after the Windows desktop has loaded. In Chapter 6, you'll learn how to solve problems when Windows refuses to start.

OVERVIEW OF WINDOWS TROUBLESHOOTING TOOLS

Table 5-1 is a summary of the Windows tools covered in this and other chapters and is given to you as a quick-and-easy reference of these tools. When you're stuck on a problem, take a quick glance through this list to remind you of tools that might help. In Chapter 6, you learn about more tools that are used to troubleshoot a failed boot.

Tool	Description
Action Center Windows 7	◢ Accessed from the System window or Action Center flag in the taskbar. ◢ Use it to solve problems when installing a device or application, to solve problems with software or hardware, and to get a history of past and current problems.
Advanced Boot Options Menu Windows 7 Windows Vista Windows xp	◢ Accessed by pressing the F8 key when Windows first starts to load. ◢ Use several options on this menu to help you troubleshoot boot problems. ◢ In XP, the menu is called the Boot Options Menu.
Backup and Restore Windows 7 Windows Vista Windows xp	◢ Accessed from the Start menu. In Windows 7, use it to back up and restore user data and the system image and to make a rescue disc. ◢ In Vista, the tool is called the Backup and Restore Center. Use it to back up and restore data and make a Complete PC Backup. ◢ In XP, the program name is ntbackup.exe. Use it to back up and restore data and the system state.
Chkdsk (Chkdsk.exe) Windows 7 Windows Vista Windows xp	◢ At a command prompt, enter Chkdsk with parameters. ◢ Use it to check and repair errors on a drive. If critical system files are affected by these errors, repairing the drive might solve a startup problem.
Cipher (Cipher.exe) Windows 7 Windows Vista Windows xp	◢ At a command prompt, enter Cipher with parameters. ◢ Log in as an administrator and use this command to decrypt a file that is not available because the user account that encrypted the file is no longer accessible.
Compatibility Mode Windows 7 Windows Vista Windows xp	◢ Accessed from the Action Center or the program file's shortcut menu. Use it to resolve issues that prevent legacy applications or drivers from working. ◢ Vista calls the tool the Program Compatibility Wizard.
Component Services Windows 7 Windows Vista Windows xp	◢ A tool in the Administrative Tools list in Control Panel. ◢ Registers a component of an application with the system.
Computer Management (Compmgmt.msc) Windows 7 Windows Vista Windows xp	◢ Accessed from Control Panel, or you can enter Compmgmt. msc at a command prompt. ◢ Use it to access several snap-ins to manage and troubleshoot a system.

Table 5-1 Windows 7/Vista/XP maintenance and troubleshooting tools (continues)

Tool	Description
Data Sources (ODBC) Windows 7 Windows Vista Windows XP	◢ A tool in the Administrative Tools list in Control Panel. ◢ Installs drivers so that an application can open a foreign data source.
Device Driver Roll Back Windows 7 Windows Vista Windows XP	◢ Accessed from Device Manager. ◢ Use it to replace a driver with the one that worked before the current driver was installed.
Device Manager (Devmgmt.msc) Windows 7 Windows Vista Windows XP	◢ Accessed from the System window or XP System Properties window. ◢ Use it to solve problems with hardware devices, to update device drivers, and to disable and uninstall a device.
Disk Cleanup (Cleanmgr.exe) Windows 7 Windows Vista Windows XP	◢ Accessed from a drive's properties box or by entering cleanmgr at a command prompt. ◢ Use it to delete unused files to make more disk space available. Not enough free hard drive space can cause boot problems.
Disk Defragmenter (Dfrg.msc or Defrag.exe) Windows 7 Windows Vista Windows XP	◢ Accessed from a drive's properties box, or use Defrag.exe with parameters at a command prompt. ◢ Use it to defragment a volume on a magnetic hard drive to improve performance.
Disk Management (Diskmgmt.msc) Windows 7 Windows Vista Windows XP	◢ Accessed from the Computer Management console, or enter Diskmgmt.msc at a command prompt. ◢ Use it to view and modify partitions on hard drives and to format drives.
File Signature Verification Tool (Sigverif.exe) Windows 7 Windows Vista Windows XP	◢ At a command prompt, enter Sigverif with parameters. ◢ The tool searches for installed drivers that are unsigned and stores results in \Windows\sigverif.txt. ◢ When a device driver or other software is giving problems, use it to verify that the software has been approved by Microsoft.
Driver Verifier (verifier.exe) Windows 7 Windows Vista Windows XP	◢ Enter verifier.exe at a command prompt. ◢ Use it to identify a driver that is causing a problem. The tool puts stress on selected drivers, which causes the driver with a problem to crash. ◢ The tool can be used to solve system lock-up errors or blue screen errors caused by a corrupted I/O device driver.
Error Reporting or Archived Messages Windows 7 Windows Vista Windows XP	◢ This automated Windows service displays error messages when an application error occurs. In Windows 7, see these messages in the Action Center. ◢ Windows 7 and Vista keep a history of past problems and solutions, but XP does not. ◢ Vista calls the tool Problem Reports and Solutions.

© Cengage Learning 2013

Table 5-1 Windows 7/Vista/XP maintenance and troubleshooting tools (continues)

Tool	Description
Event Viewer (Eventvwr.msc) Windows 7 · Windows Vista · Windows XP	◢ Accessed from the Computer Management console or in Administrative Tools. ◢ Check the Event Viewer logs for error messages to help you investigate all kinds of hardware, security, and system problems.
Group Policy (Gpedit.msc) Windows 7 · Windows Vista · Windows XP	◢ At a command prompt, enter Gpedit.msc, or use the Computer Management console. Only available in Business and Professional editions of Windows. ◢ Use it to display and change policies controlling users and the computer.
Last Known Good Configuration Windows 7 · Windows Vista · Windows XP	◢ Press F8 at startup and select from the Advanced Boot Options menu. ◢ Use this tool when Windows won't start normally and you want to revert the system to before a Windows setting, driver, or application that is causing problems was changed.
Memory Diagnostics (mdsched.exe) Windows 7 · Windows Vista	◢ Enter mdsched.exe in a command prompt window or find it on the System Recovery Options menu after booting the computer into the Windows Recovery Environment (Windows RE). ◢ Use it to test memory.
Network and Sharing Center Windows 7 · Windows Vista	◢ Accessed from the taskbar or Control Panel. ◢ Centralized location to manage network connections and network security.
Performance Monitor (Perfmon.msc) Windows 7 · Windows Vista · Windows XP	◢ At a command prompt, enter Perfmon.msc. Use it to view information about performance to help you identify a performance bottleneck. ◢ Vista embeds the tool in the Reliability and Performance Monitor window.
Programs and Features window Windows 7 · Windows Vista · Windows XP	◢ Accessed from Control Panel. ◢ Use it to uninstall, repair, or update software or certain device drivers that are causing a problem. ◢ XP calls the tool the Add or Remove Programs window.
Registry Editor (Regedit.exe) Windows 7 · Windows Vista · Windows XP	◢ At a command prompt, enter regedit. ◢ Use it to view and edit the registry.
Reliability Monitor Windows 7 · Windows Vista	◢ Accessed in Windows 7 by way of the Action Center, and in Vista, find it in the Reliability and Performance Monitor window. ◢ Use it to get a history of past problems with a computer.
Resource Monitor (Resmon.exe) Windows 7 · Windows Vista	◢ Accessed from Windows 7 Task Manager or Action Center. In Vista, find it in the Reliability and Performance Monitor window. ◢ Use it to view performance of the CPU, memory, hard drive, and network.

Table 5-1 Windows 7/Vista/XP maintenance and troubleshooting tools (continues)

Tool	Description
Runas (Runas.exe) Windows 7 Windows Vista **Windows**^{xp}	◢ At a command prompt, enter Runas with parameters, or press shift-right-click and choose *Run as administrator* or *Run as different user* from the shortcut menu. ◢ Use it to run a program using different permissions from those assigned to the currently logged-on user.
Safe Mode Windows 7 Windows Vista **Windows**^{xp}	◢ At startup, press F8 and select the option from the Advanced Boot Options menu. ◢ Use it when Windows does not start or starts with errors. Safe Mode loads the Windows desktop with a minimum configuration. In this minimized environment, you can solve a problem with a device driver, display setting, or corrupted or malicious applications.
SC (Sc.exe) Windows 7 Windows Vista **Windows**^{xp}	◢ At a command prompt, enter Sc with parameters. ◢ Use it to stop or start a service that runs in the background.
Services (Services.msc) Windows 7 Windows Vista **Windows**^{xp}	◢ At a command prompt, enter Services.msc. ◢ Graphical version of SC.
Software Explorer Windows Vista	◢ Accessed from the Windows Defender window. ◢ Use it to view and change programs launched at startup.
System Configuration (Msconfig.exe) Windows 7 Windows Vista **Windows**^{xp}	◢ Enter Msconfig.exe in the Search box. ◢ Troubleshoot the startup process by temporarily disabling startup programs and services.
System File Checker (Sfc.exe) Windows 7 Windows Vista **Windows**^{xp}	◢ At a command prompt, enter Sfc with parameters. ◢ Use it to verify the version of all system files when Windows loads. Useful when you suspect system files are corrupted, but you can still access the Windows desktop.
System Information (Msinfo32.exe) Windows 7 Windows Vista **Windows**^{xp}	◢ Enter Msinfo32.exe in the Search box. ◢ Use it to display information about hardware, applications, and Windows.
System Information (Systeminfo.exe) Windows 7 Windows Vista **Windows**^{xp}	◢ At a command prompt, enter Systeminfo. ◢ A text-only version of the System Information window. To direct that information to a file, use the command Systeminfo.exe >Myfile.txt. Later the file can be printed and used to document information about the system.
System Restore (Rstrui.exe) Windows 7 Windows Vista **Windows**^{xp}	◢ Accessed from the Start menu, when loading Safe Mode, or from the System Recovery Options menu after booting the computer into Windows RE. ◢ Use it to restore the system to a previously working condition called a restore point; it restores the registry, some system files, and some application files. ◢ Restore points are automatically created when Windows System Protection is turned on.

Table 5-1 Windows 7/Vista/XP maintenance and troubleshooting tools (continues)

Tool	Description
Task Killing Utilities (Tskill.exe or Taskkill.exe) Windows 7 Windows Vista Windows XP	◢ At a command prompt, enter Taskkill or Tskill with parameters. Tskill is available only in business and professional editions of Windows. ◢ Use it to stop or kill a process or program currently running. Useful when managing background services such as an email server or web server.
Task Lister (Tasklist.exe) Windows 7 Windows Vista Windows XP	◢ At a command prompt, enter Tasklist. ◢ Use it to list currently running processes similar to the list provided by Task Manager.
Task Manager (Taskman.exe) Windows 7 Windows Vista Windows XP	◢ Right-click the taskbar and select Start Task Manager. ◢ Use it to list and stop currently running processes. ◢ Useful when you need to stop a locked-up application.
Windows Defender Windows 7 Windows Vista	◢ Accessed from Control Panel. ◢ Monitors activity and alerts you if a running program appears to be malicious or damaging the system.
Windows File Protection Windows 7 Windows Vista Windows XP	◢ Windows service that runs in the background to protect system files and restore overwritten system files as needed.
Windows Firewall Windows 7 Windows Vista Windows XP	◢ Service that runs in the background to prevent or filter uninvited communication from another computer.
Windows Update (Wupdmgr.exe) Windows 7 Windows Vista Windows XP	◢ Accessed from the Start menu. ◢ Use it to update Windows by downloading the latest patches from the Microsoft web site.
Windows XP Mode Windows 7	◢ Download and install on Windows 7 Professional and Ultimate editions to run legacy applications that won't work using Compatibility mode.

© Cengage Learning 2013

Table 5-1   Windows 7/Vista/XP maintenance and troubleshooting tools (continued)

> 💡 **A+ Exam Tip**   If an often-used Windows utility can be launched from a command prompt, the A+ 220-802 exam expects you to know the program name of that utility.

STRATEGIES TO TROUBLESHOOT ANY COMPUTER PROBLEM

A+ 220-802 4.1

When a computer doesn't work and you're responsible for fixing it, you should generally approach the problem first as an investigator and discoverer, always being careful not to compound the problem through your own actions. If the problem seems difficult, see it as an opportunity to learn something new. Ask questions until you understand the source of

A+
220-802
4.1

the problem. Once you understand it, you're almost done because most likely the solution will be evident. If you take the attitude that you can understand the problem and solve it, no matter how deeply you have to dig, you probably *will* solve it.

One systematic method to solve a problem used by most expert troubleshooters is the six steps diagrammed in Figure 5-1, which can apply to both software and hardware problems.

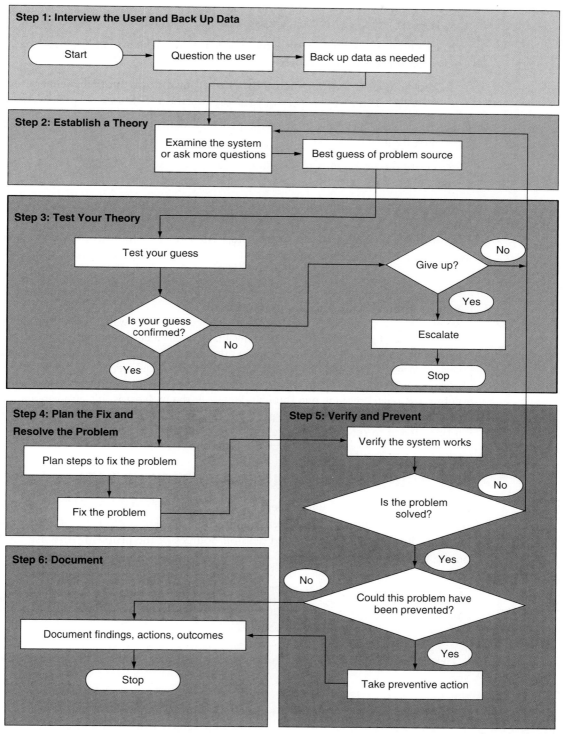

Figure 5-1 General approach to problem solving

© Cengage Learning 2013

> **💡 A+ Exam Tip** The A+ 220–802 exam expects you to know about all the aspects of troubleshooting theory and strategy and how to apply the troubleshooting procedures and techniques described in this section. At the front of the book, read over A+ 220–802 Objective 4.1 and compare it to Figure 5-1.

Here are the steps:

1. Interview the user and back up data before you make any changes to the system.

2. Examine the system, analyze the problem, and make an initial determination of what is the source of the problem.

3. Test your theory. If the theory is not confirmed, form another theory or escalate the problem to someone higher in your organization with more experience or resources.

4. After you know the source of the problem, plan what to do to fix the problem and then fix it.

5. Verify the problem is fixed and that the system works. Take any preventive measures to make sure the problem doesn't happen again.

6. Document activities, outcomes, and what you learned.

Now let's examine the process step by step. As you learn about these six steps, you'll also learn about 13 rules useful when troubleshooting. Here's the first rule.

Rule 1: Approach the Problem Systematically

When trying to solve the problem, start at the beginning and walk through the situation in a thorough, careful way. This one rule is invaluable. Remember it and apply it every time. If you don't find the explanation to the problem after one systematic walkthrough, then repeat the entire process. Check and double-check to find the step you overlooked the first time. Most problems with computers are simple, such as a loose cable or incorrect Windows setting. Computers are logical through and through. Whatever the problem is, it's also very logical. Also, if you are faced with more than one problem on the same computer, work on only one problem at a time. Trying to solve multiple problems at the same time can get too confusing.

STEP 1: INTERVIEW THE USER AND BACK UP DATA

Every troubleshooting situation begins with interviewing the user if he or she is available. If you have the opportunity to speak with the user, ask questions to help you identify the problem, how to reproduce it, and possible sources of the problem. Also ask about any data on the PC that is not backed up.

> **💡 A+ Exam Tip** The A+ 220–801 exam expects you to know how to interact with a user and know what questions to ask, given a troubleshooting scenario.

Here are some questions that can help you learn as much as you can about the problem and its root cause:

1. Please describe the problem. What error messages, unusual displays, or failures did you see? (Possible answer: I see this blue screen with a funny-looking message on it that makes no sense to me.)

2. When did the problem start? (Possible answer: When I first booted after loading this neat little screensaver I downloaded from the web.)

3. What was the situation when the problem occurred? (Possible answers: I was trying to start up my PC. I was opening a document in MS Word. I was using the web to research a project.)

4. What programs or software were you using? (Possible answer: I was using Internet Explorer.)

5. What changes have recently been made to the system? For example, did you recently install new software or move your computer system? (Possible answer: Well, yes. Yesterday I moved the computer case across the room.)

6. Has there been a recent thunderstorm or electrical problem? (Possible answer: Yes, last night. Then when I tried to turn on my PC this morning, nothing happened.)

7. Have you made any hardware, software, or configuration changes? (Possible answer: No, but I think my sister might have.)

8. Has someone else used your computer recently? (Possible answer: Sure, my son uses it all the time.)

9. Is there some valuable data on your system that is not backed up that I should know about before I start working on the problem? (Possible answer: Yes! Yes! My term paper! It's not backed up! You gotta save that!)

10. Can you show me how to reproduce the problem? (Possible answers: Yes, let me show you what to do.)

Based on the answers you receive, ask more penetrating questions until you feel the user has given you all the information he or she knows that can help you solve the problem. As you talk with the user, keep in mind rules 2, 3, and 4.

Rule 2: Establish Your Priorities
This rule can help make for a satisfied customer. Decide what your first priority is. For example, it might be to recover lost data or to get the PC back up and running as soon as possible. When practical, ask the user or customer for help deciding on priorities.

Rule 3: Beware of User Error
Remember that many problems stem from user error. If you suspect this is the case, ask the user to show you the problem and carefully watch what the user is doing.

Rule 4: Keep Your Cool and Don't Rush
In some situations, you might be tempted to act too quickly and to be drawn into the user's sense of emergency. But keep your cool and don't rush. For example, when a computer stops working, if unsaved data is still in memory or if data on the hard drive has not been backed up, look and think carefully before you leap! A wrong move can be costly. The best advice is not to hurry. Carefully plan your moves. Research the problem using documentation or the web if you're not sure what to do, and don't hesitate to ask for help. Don't simply try something, hoping it will work, unless you've run out of more intelligent alternatives!

After you have talked with the user, be sure to back up any important data that is not currently backed up before you begin work on the PC. If the PC is working well enough to boot to the Windows desktop, you can use Windows Explorer to copy data to a flash drive, another computer on the network, or other storage media.

> **💡 A+ Exam Tip** The A+ 220–802 exam expects you to know the importance of making backups before you make changes to a system.

If the computer is not healthy enough to use Windows Explorer, don't do anything to jeopardize the data. If you must take a risk with the data, let it be the user's decision to do so, not yours. Try to boot the system. If the system will not boot to the Windows desktop, know that you can remove the hard drive from the system and use a converter to connect the drive to a USB port on another computer. You can then copy the data to the other computer. Next, return the hard drive to the original computer so you can begin troubleshooting the problem.

If possible, have the user verify that all important data is safely backed up before you continue to the next troubleshooting step. If you're new to troubleshooting and don't want the user looking over your shoulder while you work, you might want to let him or her know you'd prefer to work alone. You can say something like, "Okay, I think I have everything I need to get started. I'll let you know if I have another question."

STEP 2: EXAMINE THE SYSTEM AND MAKE YOUR BEST GUESS

You're now ready to start solving the problem. Rules 5 and 6 can help.

Rule 5: Make No Assumptions
This rule is the hardest to follow because there is a tendency to trust anything in writing and assume that people are telling you exactly what happened. But documentation is sometimes wrong, and people don't always describe events as they occurred, so do your own investigating. For example, if the user tells you that the system boots up with no error messages but that the software still doesn't work, boot for yourself. You never know what the user might have overlooked.

Rule 6: Try the Simple Things First
Most problems are so simple and obvious that we overlook them because we expect the problem to be difficult. Don't let the complexity of computers fool you. Most problems are easy to fix. Really, they are! To save time, check the simple things first, such as whether a power switch is not turned on or a cable is loose. Generally, it's easy to check for a hardware problem before you check for a software problem. For example, if a USB drive is not working, verify the drive works on another computer before verifying the drivers are installed correctly.

Follow this process to form your best guess (best theory) and test it:

1. *Reproduce the problem and observe for yourself what the user has described.* For example, if the user tells you the system is totally dead, find out for yourself. Plug in the power and turn on the system. Listen for fans and look for lights and error messages. As another example, suppose the user tells you that Internet Explorer will not open.

Try opening it yourself to see what error messages might appear. As you investigate the system, refrain from making changes until you've come up with your theory as to what the source of the problem is. Can you duplicate the problem? Intermittent problems are generally more difficult to solve than problems that occur consistently.

2. *Decide if the problem is hardware or software related.* Sometimes you might not be sure, but make your best guess. For example, if the system fails before Windows starts to load, chances are the problem is a hardware problem. If the user tells you the system has not worked since the lightning storm the night before, chances are the problem is electrical. If the problem is that Windows Explorer will not open even though the Windows desktop loads, you can assume the problem is software related. In another example, suppose a user complains that his Word documents are getting corrupted. Possible sources of the problem might be that the user does not know how to save documents properly, the application or the OS might be corrupted, the PC might have a virus, or the hard drive might be intermittently failing. Investigate for yourself, and then decide if the problem is caused by software, hardware, or the user.

3. *Make your best guess as to the source of the problem, and don't forget to question the obvious.* Here are some practical examples of questioning the obvious and checking the simple things first:

   ◢ The video does not work. Your best guess is the monitor cables are loose or the monitor is not turned on.
   ◢ Excel worksheets are getting corrupted. Your best guess is the user is not saving the workbook files correctly.
   ◢ The DVD drive is not reading a DVD. Your best guess is the DVD is scratched.
   ◢ The system refuses to boot and gives the error that the hard drive is not found. Your best guess is internal cables to the drive are loose.

Rule 7: Become a Researcher
Following this rule is the most fun. When a computer problem arises that you can't easily solve, be as tenacious as a bulldog. Search the web, ask questions, read more, make some phone calls, and ask more questions. Take advantage of every available resource, including online help, documentation, technical support, and books such as this one. Learn to perform advanced searches using a good search engine on the web, such as *www.google.com*. What you learn will be yours to take to the next problem. This is the real joy of computer troubleshooting. If you're good at it, you're always learning something new.

If you're having a problem deciding what might be the source of the problem, keep in mind Rule 7 and try searching these resources for ideas and tips:

   ◢ User manuals and installation manuals for a device or software often list symptoms of problems with possible solutions and troubleshooting tips.
   ◢ Use a search engine to search the web for help. Use, in your search string, an error message, symptom, hardware device, or description of the problem. For the most reliable information about a hardware device or application, see the web site of the manufacturer (see Figure 5-2). These sites might offer troubleshooting and support pages, help forums, chat sessions, and email support. For Windows problems, the best web sites to search are *technet.microsoft.com* or *support.microsoft.com*. The chances are always good that someone has had exactly the same problem, presented the problem online, and someone else has presented a step-by-step solution. All you have to do is

A+
220-802
4.1

find it! As you practice this type of web research, you'll get better and better at knowing how to form a search string and which web sites are trustworthy and present the best information. If your first five minutes of searching doesn't turn up a solution, please don't give up! It might take patience and searching for 20 minutes or more to find the solution you need. As you search, most likely you'll learn more and more about the problem, and you'll slowly zero in on a solution.

▰ Training materials, technical books, reference manuals, and textbooks like this one can all be good sources of help.

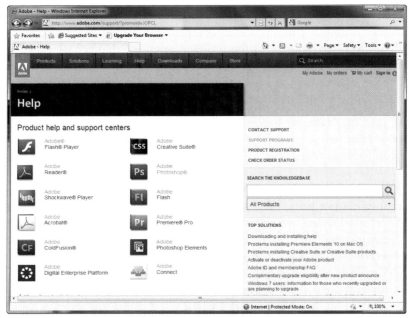

© Cengage Learning 2013

Figure 5-2   Search manufacturer web sites for help with a hardware or software product

> **Notes** To limit your search to a particular site when using *www.google.com*, use the site parameter in the search box. For example, to search only the Microsoft site for information about the defrag command, enter this search string: **defrag site:microsoft.com**.

Hands-on | Project 5.1   Research a Computer Problem

Possibly the most powerful strategy in this entire chapter for troubleshooting is to use a search engine to find insights and solutions on the web. For each of the following research topics, provide the solution, the search string you used to find the solution, and the web site that gave you the solution. Research solutions or answers for the following:

1. Find software that will convert a Windows 7 dynamic disk to a basic disk without destroying its data. Find one good review about this software or a Microsoft recommendation.

2. You are upgrading Vista to Windows 7 and at the beginning of the installation, the setup program halts and gives the error message shown in Figure 5-3. Research this message, describe the source of the problem, and recommend a solution.

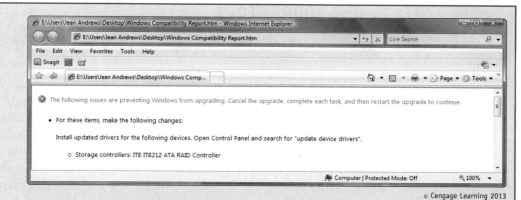

© Cengage Learning 2013

Figure 5-3 Use the web to research a problem and solution that occurs when upgrading to Windows 7

3. The screen resolution on a Windows 7 desktop is causing distortion and blurred text. You go to the Screen Resolution window and see only three choices available under Resolution (see Figure 5-4). Neither of these resolutions solves the problem. You notice the label on the Envision monitor says its native resolution is 1680 × 1050. Device Manager reports the display adapter to be a Standard VGA Graphics Adapter. Research this problem and suggest a solution.

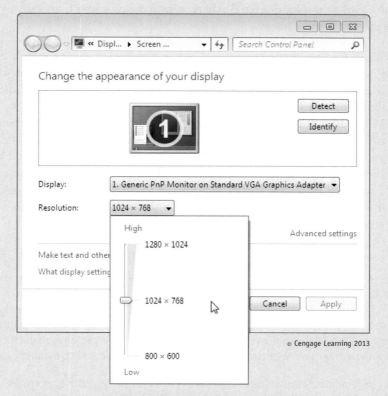

© Cengage Learning 2013

Figure 5-4 Research why the screen resolution needed for your monitor is not listed among the available resolutions

STEP 3: TEST YOUR THEORY

For simple problems, you can zip right through Steps 3, 4, and 5 in Figure 5-1. Here are two examples where Steps 3, 4, and 5 go very fast:

▲ The video does not work and you suspect loose cables or the monitor is not turned on. You check the video cable connection (Step 3) and discover it's loose. As you connect it (Step 4), the video display works. Problem solved. You now can take the time to screw the video cable to the connection (Step 5) so that the problem won't happen again.

▲ Excel worksheets are getting corrupted. As you watch the user save a file, you discover he is saving files in an incorrect format that other software in the office cannot read (Step 3). You step the user through saving the file correctly and then verify that others can open the file (Step 4). You explain to the user which format to use (Step 5). The problem is then solved, and it's not likely to happen again.

Here are two examples of Step 3 that include testing a guess that is not correct:

▲ The CD drive won't read a CD and you suspect the CD is scratched. When you check the disc, it looks fine. Your next guess is the CD drive is not recognized by Windows. You check Device Manager, and it reports errors with the drive. Your next guess is that drivers are corrupted.

▲ The system refuses to boot and gives the error message that the hard drive is not found. Internal cable connections are solid. Your next guess is the drive is not getting power.

Here are two examples of Step 3 where your guess is correct, and then you move on toward Step 4 to plan a solution:

▲ Word files are getting corrupted. After eliminating several simple causes, you guess that the hard drive is going bad. You check Event Viewer and discover Windows has recorded write errors to the drive multiple times (Step 3). Your theory is confirmed that the drive is bad and needs replacing (Step 4).

▲ Video does not work. You check cables and power and verify monitor settings controlled by buttons on the front of the monitor are all okay, but still no video. You guess the video cable might be bad and exchange it with one you know is good, but still no video. Therefore, you guess that the monitor is bad. You move the monitor to a working PC and it still does not work. You try a good monitor on the first PC, and it works fine. Your guess that the monitor is bad has been confirmed (Step 3). Next, you plan how to purchase a new monitor (Step 4).

As you test your guesses, keep in mind rules 8 through 11.

Rule 8: Divide and Conquer

This rule is the most powerful. Isolate the problem. In the overall system, remove one hardware or software component after another until the problem is isolated to a small part of the whole system. As you divide a large problem into smaller components, you can analyze each component separately. You can use one or more of the following to help you divide and conquer on your own system:

▲ In Windows, stop all nonessential services running in the background to eliminate them as the problem.

▲ Boot from a bootable CD or DVD to eliminate the OS and startup files on the hard drive as the problem.

▲ Start Windows in Safe Mode to eliminate unnecessary startup programs as a source of the problem.

Rule 9: Write Things Down
Keep good notes as you're working. They'll help you think more clearly. Draw diagrams. Make lists. Clearly and precisely write down what you're learning. If you need to leave the problem and return to it later, it's difficult to remember what you have observed and already tried. When the problem gets cold like this, your notes will be invaluable.

Rule 10: Don't Assume the Worst
When it's an emergency and your only copy of data is on a hard drive that is not working, don't assume that the data is lost. Much can be done to recover data. If you want to recover lost data on a hard drive, don't write anything to the drive; you might write on top of lost data, eliminating all chances of recovery.

Rule 11: Reboot and Start Over
This is an important rule. Fresh starts are good, and they uncover events or steps that might have been overlooked. Take a break! Get away from the problem. Begin again.

5

By the time you have finished Step 3, the problem might already be solved or you will know the source of the problem and will be ready to plan a solution.

STEP 4: PLAN YOUR SOLUTION AND THEN FIX THE PROBLEM

Some solutions, such as replacing a hard drive or a motherboard, are expensive and time consuming. You need to carefully consider what you will do and the order in which you will do it. When planning and implementing your solution, keep rules 12 and 13 in mind.

Rule 12: Use the Least Invasive Solution First
As you solve computer problems, always keep in mind that you don't want to make things worse, so you should use the least invasive solution. Keep in mind that you want to fix the problem in such a way that the system is returned to normal working condition with the least amount of effort. For example, don't format the hard drive until you've first tried to fix the problem without having to erase everything on the drive. In another example, don't reinstall Microsoft Office until you have tried applying patches to the existing installation.

Rule 13: Know Your Starting Point
Find out what works and doesn't work before you take anything apart or try some possible fix. Suppose you decide to install a Windows 7 service pack to solve a problem with USB devices not working. After the installation, you discover Microsoft Office gives errors and you cannot print to the network printer. You don't know if the service pack is causing problems or the problems existed before you began work. As much as possible, find out what works or what doesn't work before you attempt a fix.

Do the following to plan your solution and fix the problem:

1. Consider different solutions and select the least invasive one. In other words, choose the solution that fixes the problem by making as few changes to the system as possible. Some solutions are obvious, such as updating a device driver, but others might not

be so obvious. For example, if Windows is corrupted and your options are to reinstall Windows or repair it, it's better to repair it so there's less work to do to restore the system to good working order and to return it to the configuration the user had before the problem occurred.

2. Before applying your solution, as best you can, determine what works and doesn't work about the system so you know your starting point.

3. Fix the problem. This might be as simple as plugging up a new monitor. Or it might be as difficult as reinstalling Windows and applications software and restoring data from backups.

STEP 5: VERIFY THE FIX AND TAKE PREVENTIVE ACTION

After you have fixed the problem, reboot the system and verify all is well. Can you reach the Internet, use the printer, or use Microsoft Office? If possible, have the user check everything and verify that the job is done satisfactorily. If either of you find a problem, return to Step 2 in the troubleshooting process to examine the system and form a new theory as to the cause of the problem.

After you and the user have verified all is working, ask yourself the question, "Could this problem have been prevented?" If so, go the extra mile to instruct the user, set Windows to automatically install updates, or do whatever else is appropriate to prevent future problems.

STEP 6: DOCUMENT WHAT HAPPENED

Good documentation helps you take what you learned into the next troubleshooting situation, train others, develop effective preventive maintenance plans, and satisfy any audits or customer or employer queries about your work. Be sure to write down the initial symptoms, the source of the problem, and what you did to fix it. Many companies use call-tracking software to record this type of information. Figure 5-5 shows a window in Spiceworks Help Desk Software, which is popular and free call-tracking software.

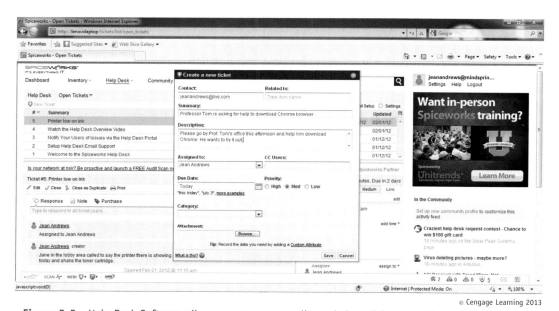

© Cengage Learning 2013

Figure 5-5 Help Desk Software allows you to create, edit, and close tickets used by technicians

A+
220-802
4.1

Hands-on | Project 5.2   Document an Intermittent Problem

Intermittent problems can make troubleshooting challenging. The trick in diagnosing problems that come and go is to look for patterns or clues as to when the problems occur. If you or the user can't reproduce the problem at will, ask the user to keep a log of when the problems occur and exactly what messages appear. Tell the user that intermittent problems are the hardest to solve and might take some time, but you won't give up. Show the user how to take a screenshot of the error messages when they appear. It might also be appropriate to ask him to email the screenshot to you. Do the following:

1. Use the Windows 7 Snipping Tool to take a snip of your Windows desktop showing the Task Manager window open. If you need help using the Snipping Tool, see Windows Help and Support. (Windows Vista and XP don't support the Snipping Tool.)

2. Save the snip and email it to your instructor.

Hands-on | Project 5.3   Research PC Support Sites

The web is an excellent resource to use when problem solving, and it's helpful to know which web sites are trustworthy and useful. Access each of the web sites listed in Table 5-2, and print one web page from each site that shows information that might be useful for a support technician. If the site offers a free email newsletter, consider subscribing to it. Answer the following questions about these sites:

1. Which site can help you find out what type RAM you can use on your computer?

2. Which site explains Moore's Law? What is Moore's Law?

3. Which site offers a free download for data recovery software?

4. Which site gives a review about registry cleaning software?

5. Which two sites allow you to post a question about PC repair to a forum?

6. Which site offers a tutorial to learn C programming?

7. Which site offers free antivirus software published by the site owners?

Organization	Web Site
CNET, Inc.	*www.cnet.com*
Experts Exchange (subscription site)	*www.experts-exchange.com*
F-Secure Corp	*www.f-secure.com*
How Stuff Works	*www.howstuffworks.com*
Kingston Technology (information about memory)	*www.kingston.com*
Michael Karbo	*www.karbosguide.com*
Microsoft Technical Resources	*support.microsoft.com* *technet.microsoft.com*
PC Today Online	*www.pctoday.com*
PC World	*www.pcworld.com*
Tom's Hardware Guide	*www.tomshardware.com*
WebMediaBrands	*www.webopedia.com*
ZDNet (publishes several technical magazines)	*www.zdnet.com*

© Cengage Learning 2013

Table 5-2   Technical information web sites

A+
220-802
4.1

So now let's see how to handle some Windows problems. We'll begin with blue screen stop errors and improper shutdowns.

> 💡 **A+ Exam Tip** This chapter covers how to troubleshoot Windows and applications. Its companion book, *A+ Guide to Hardware*, covers troubleshooting hardware. You can find this hardware troubleshooting content that applies to the A+ 220-802 exam online at this book's companion web site at *www .cengagebrain.com*. See the Preface for more information. This book, *A+ Guide to Software*, and the online content about hardware troubleshooting together cover all the content on the A+ 220-802 exam.

TROUBLESHOOTING BLUE SCREEN ERRORS AND IMPROPER SHUTDOWNS

A+
220-802
4.6

A blue screen error, also called a stop error or a blue screen of death (BSOD), happens when processes running in kernel mode encounter a problem and Windows must stop the system. In such situations, a blue screen appears with a cryptic error message such as the one in Figure 5-6. Look on the blue screen for the stop error at the top and the specific number of the error near the bottom of the screen, as labeled in Figure 5-6.

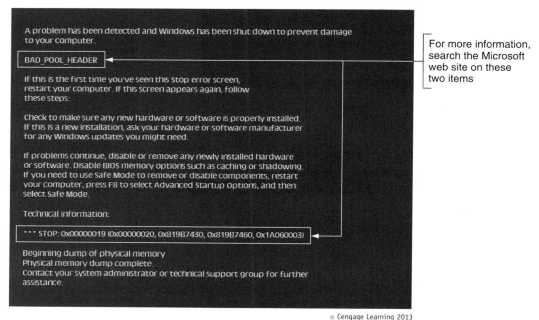

© Cengage Learning 2013

Figure 5-6 A blue screen of death (BSOD) is definitively not a good sign; time to start troubleshooting

How to deal with blue screen errors that happen at startup is covered in Chapter 6. Here's what to do when you get a blue screen error after startup:

1. As for the tools useful in solving blue screen errors, put the web at the top of your list! (But don't forget that some sites are unreliable and others mean you harm.) Search the Microsoft web site on the two items labeled in Figure 5-6.

A+
220-802
4.6

2. If the blue screen names the device driver or service that caused the problem, use Windows Explorer to locate the program file. Driver files are stored in the C:\Windows\System32\drivers folder. Right-click the file and select **Properties** from the shortcut menu. The Details tab of the Properties box tells you the purpose of the file (see Figure 5-7). You can then reinstall the device or program that caused the problem.

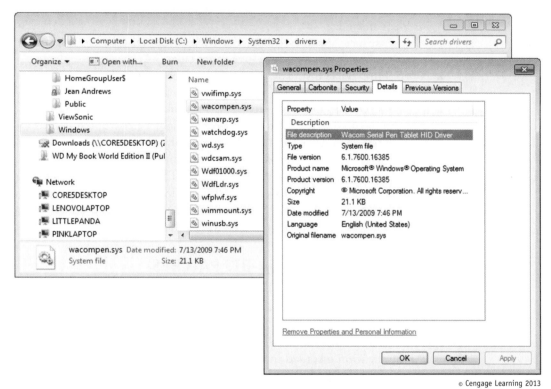

© Cengage Learning 2013

Figure 5-7   Use the Details tab of a driver's Properties box to identify the purpose of the driver

3. Immediately after you restart the system, a Windows error message box or bubble might appear with useful information. Follow the links in the bubble.

4. Check Event Viewer, which might provide events it has logged. Recall that critical errors and warnings are recorded in the Administrative Events log.

5. Also check Archived Messages in the Action Center, and, in Vista, check the Problem Reports and Solutions window for clues.

6. Use Windows Updates to apply patches.

7. Undo any recent changes to the system. If you are not sure which changes to undo, consider using System Restore to restore the system to the point in time before the problem started.

8. Use the Memory Diagnostics tool to check memory and use Chkdsk with the /r parameter to check the hard drive for errors. If the problem is still not resolved, you might need to repair Windows system files by using System File Checker, Safe Mode, or other Windows startup repair tools you will learn about in the next chapter.

Here are some common blue screen errors, the source of the problem, and what to do about it. Following this list, you learn to use the new tools mentioned in the list.

▲ **BAD_POOL_HEADER.** This is the error shown in Figure 5-6 and can occur for a variety of reasons, including a corrupted Windows update, bad memory, or a corrupted application. Start troubleshooting by suspecting the most recent change to the system and try undoing that change. For example, try to roll back a driver or uninstall a Windows update. If there have been several recent changes, you might consider using System Restore to apply a restore point to a point in time just before the problem started.

   Next, suspect memory is bad. Use Memory Diagnostics to test memory. Events logged in Event Viewer might give more clues.

▲ **NTFS_FILE_SYSTEM.** The hard drive is most likely corrupted. Try running Chkdsk with the /r parameter.

▲ **KERNEL_DATA_INPAGE_ERROR.** The immediate problem is Windows could not read the paging file (Pagefile.sys). The file might be corrupted because of bad memory, a corrupted hard drive, or a failing processor. Begin troubleshooting by rebuilding Pagefile.sys. If the error reoccurs, then you must dig deeper to solve the root problem.

▲ **UNEXPECTED_KERNEL_MODE_TRAP.** This error is most likely caused by bad memory. Run Memory Diagnostics to test memory.

▲ **DIVIDE_BY_ZERO_ERROR.** This error is most likely caused by an application. Begin troubleshooting by identifying what application was running when the error occurred.

WINDOWS 32-BIT AND 64-BIT PATCHES

When researching a problem, suppose you discover that Microsoft or a manufacturer's web site offers a fix or patch you can download and apply. To get the right patch, you need to make sure you get a 32-bit patch for a 32-bit installation of Windows, a device driver, or an application. For a 64-bit installation of Windows, make sure you get a 64-bit device driver. An application installed in a 64-bit OS might be a 32-bit application or a 64-bit application.

   The documentation on the Microsoft or other web sites might be cryptic about the type of patch. Follow these guidelines when reading error messages or documentation:

▲ The term x86 refers to 32-bit CPUs or processors and to 32-bit operating systems. For example, you need to download a patch from Microsoft to fix a Windows 7 problem you are having with USB devices. The article on the Microsoft web site that applies to your problem says to download the patch if you are using a Windows 7, x86-based version. Take that to mean you can use this patch if you are using a 32-bit version of Windows 7.

▲ All CPUs installed in personal computers today are hybrid processors that can process either 32 bits or 64 bits. The term x86-64 refers to these processors, such as the Intel Core2 Duo or an AMD Athlon processor. (AMD64 refers specifically to these hybrid AMD processors.) The term x86-64 can also refer to a 64-bit OS. For example, a Windows message might say, "You are attempting to load an x86-64 operating system." Take that to mean you are attempting to load a 64-bit OS onto a computer that has a hybrid 32-bit/64-bit processor installed, such as the Athlon 64 or Intel Core2 Duo.

▲ The term IA64 refers specifically to 64-bit Intel processors such as the Xeon or Itanium used in servers or high-end workstations. For example, you are selecting a utility to download from the Microsoft web site. One choice for the utility specifies an

A+
220-802
4.6

IA64 platform. Only select this choice if you have installed an Itanium or Xeon processor. (By the way, a techie often uses the word *platform* to mean the processor and operating system on which other software is running. However, in this context, the operating system's platform is the processor.)

◢ The term x64 refers to 64-bit operating systems. For example, Microsoft offers two versions of Windows 7 Home Premium: the x86 version and the x64 version.

> **♥ A+ Exam Tip** The A+ 220-802 exam expects you to know the difference between Windows 32-bit and 64-bit versions. You are also expected to be familiar with the terms 32-bit, 64-bit, x86, and x64.

Now let's learn to use the Memory Diagnostics and System File Checker tools, which can be useful when troubleshooting blue screen errors.

A+
220-802
1.4, 4.6

MEMORY DIAGNOSTICS

Errors with memory are often difficult to diagnose because they can appear intermittently and might be mistaken as application errors, user errors, or other hardware component errors. Sometimes these errors cause the system to hang, a blue screen error might occur, or the system continues to function with applications giving errors or data getting corrupted. You can quickly identify a problem with memory or eliminate memory as the source of a problem by using the Windows 7/Vista **Memory Diagnostics** tool. It tests memory for errors and works before Windows is loaded and can be used on computers that don't have Windows 7 or Vista installed. Use one of these three methods to start the utility:

◢ *Method 1:* In a command prompt window, enter **mdsched.exe** and press **Enter**. A dialog box appears (see Figure 5-8) asking if you want to run the test now or on the next restart.

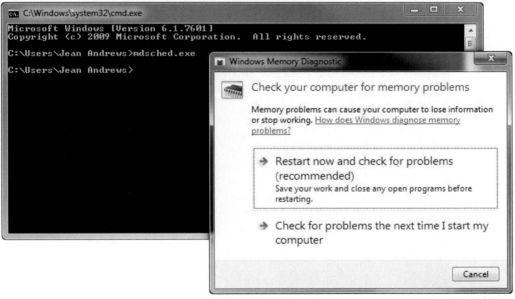

Figure 5-8 Use the mdsched.exe command to test memory

A+
220-802
1.4, 4.6

▲ *Method 2:* If you cannot load the Windows desktop, press the Spacebar during the boot. The Windows Boot Manager screen appears (see Figure 5-9). Select **Windows Memory Diagnostic** and press **Enter**.

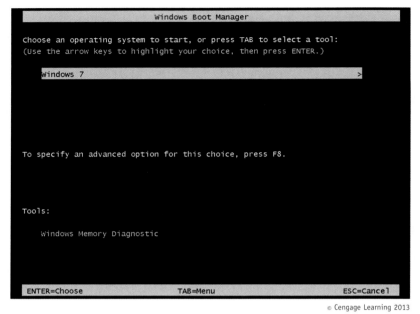

© Cengage Learning 2013

Figure 5-9   Force the Windows Boot Manager menu to display by pressing the Spacebar during the boot

▲ *Method 3:* If you cannot boot from the hard drive, boot the computer from the Windows setup DVD. On the opening screen, select your language. On the next screen (see Figure 5-10), click **Repair your computer**. In the next box, select the Windows installation to repair. The System Recovery Options window appears (see Figure 5-11). Click **Windows Memory Diagnostic** and follow the directions on-screen.

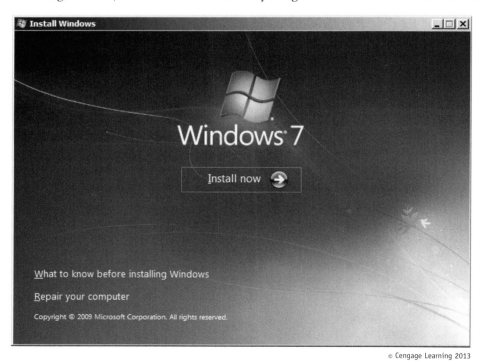

© Cengage Learning 2013

Figure 5-10   Opening menu when you boot from the Windows 7 setup DVD

A+
220-802
1.4, 4.6

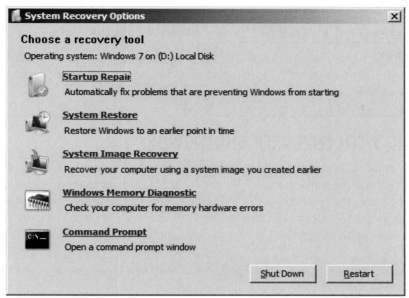

© Cengage Learning 2013

Figure 5-11 Test memory using the System Recovery Options menu

If the tool reports memory errors, replace all memory modules installed on the motherboard.

SYSTEM FILE CHECKER

A+
220-802
1.3, 4.6

A Windows application or hardware problem might be caused by a corrupted Windows system file. That's where System File Checker might help. **System File Checker (SFC)** protects system files and keeps a cache of current system files in case it needs to refresh a damaged file. To use the utility to scan all system files and verify them, first close all applications and then enter the command **sfc /scannow** in an elevated command prompt window (see Figure 5-12). If corrupted system files are found, you might need to provide the Windows setup DVD to restore the files. If you have problems running the utility, try the command **sfc/ scanonce**, which scans files immediately after the next reboot.

© Cengage Learning 2013

Figure 5-12 Use System File Checker to verify Windows system files

Notes Recall from Chapter 3 that you can get an elevated command prompt window in Windows 7/Vista by clicking **Start**, **All Programs**, and **Accessories**. Then right-click **Command Prompt** and select **Run as administrator** from the shortcut menu.

Hands-on | Project 5.4   Rebuild Pagefile.sys

If a blue screen error indicates that Pagefile.sys is corrupted, you can rebuild the file. Search the *support.microsoft.com* web site for the steps to rebuild Pagefile.sys and then practice these steps by rebuilding Pagefile.sys. List the steps you took to rebuild the file.

DEALING WITH IMPROPER SHUTDOWNS

Improper shutdowns and a system lockup that cause a computer to freeze and require that it be restarted are most likely caused by hardware. Hardware that can cause these errors include memory, the motherboard, CPU, video card, or the system overheating. I/O devices such as the keyboard, mouse, or monitor or application errors don't usually cause these types of catastrophic problems.

> **💡 A+ Exam Tip** The 220-802 exam expects you to know how to solve problems when the system shuts down improperly.

When these types of errors occur, try and check these things:

1. Check Event Viewer to see if it has reported a hardware failure.
2. Apply any Windows patches.
3. Use Memory Diagnostics and Chkdsk with the /r parameter to check memory and the hard drive for errors.
4. If you suspect overheating is a problem, immediately after the lockup, go into BIOS setup and check the temperature of the CPU, which should not exceed 38 degrees C. Alternately, you can install a freeware utility, such as SpeedFan by Alfredo Comparetti (*www.almico.com*) to monitor the temperature of the motherboard or hard drive.

When solving problems with any kind of hardware, it's important that you check for physical damage to the device. If you feel excessive heat coming from the computer case or a peripheral device, immediately unplug the device or power down the system. Don't turn the device or system back on until the problem is solved; you don't want to start a fire! Other symptoms that indicate potential danger are strong electrical odors, unusual noises, no noise (such as when the fan is not working to keep the system cool), liquid spills on a device, and visible damage such as a frayed cable, melted plastic, or smoke. In these situations, turn off the equipment immediately.

DEALING WITH ENDLESS SHUTDOWNS AND RESTARTS

With normal Windows settings, if a blue screen error occurs, the system displays the error screen for a moment and then automatically restarts the system, which can result in an endless cycle of restarts. If you're caught in this situation, you can do the following:

1. Try to boot into Safe Mode where the endless shutdowns might not occur. In Safe Mode, you can change the Windows setting to control automatic restarts. Follow these steps:
   a. To boot to Safe Mode, press **F8** before Windows loads. The Advanced Boot Options Menu appears (see Figure 5-13). In the Advanced Boot Options Menu, select **Safe Mode**. The Windows desktop in Safe Mode is shown in Figure 5-14.

A+
220-802
4.6

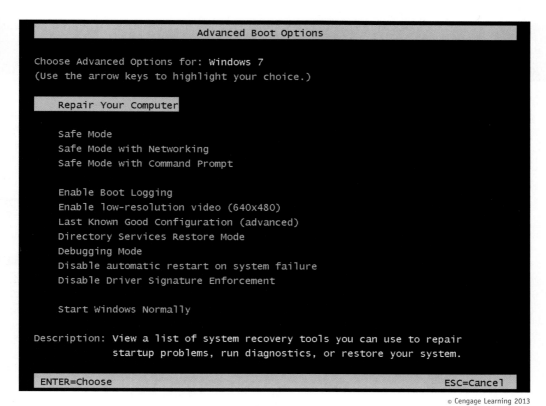

© Cengage Learning 2013

Figure 5-13 Press F8 during the boot to launch the Advanced Boot Options menu

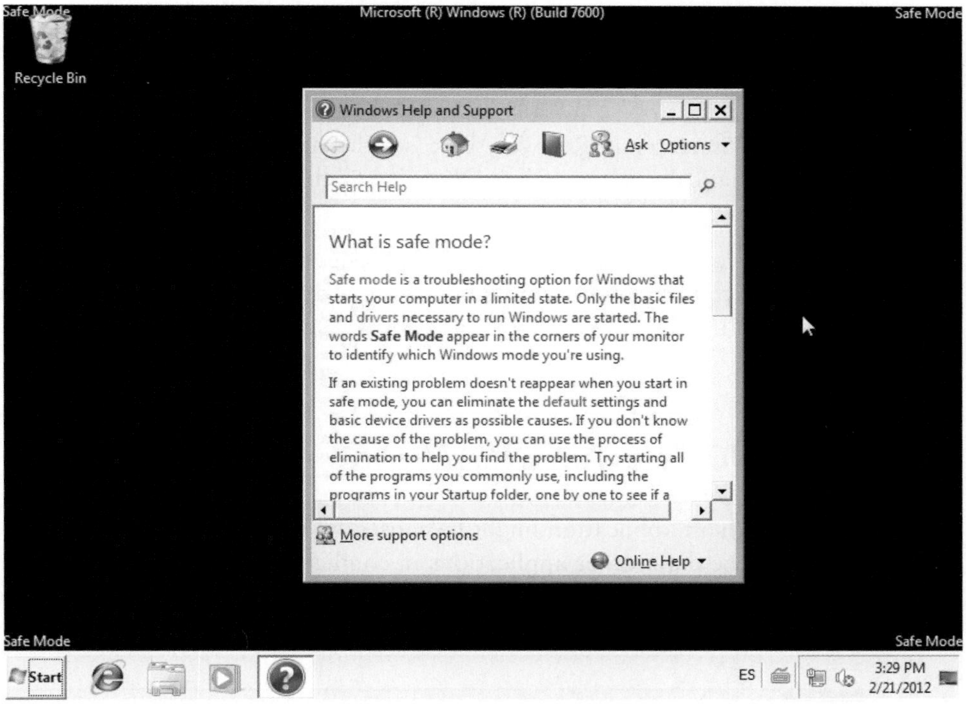

© Cengage Learning 2013

Figure 5-14 The Safe Mode black desktop reminds us that Windows was loaded with a minimum configuration

A+
220-802
4.6

b. Click **Start**, right-click **Computer**, and select **Properties** from the shortcut menu. The System window opens.

c. In the left pane of the System window, click **Advanced system settings**. (For Windows XP, in the System Properties window, click the **Advanced** tab.)

d. In the System Properties box (see the left side of Figure 5-15) in the Startup and Recovery section, click **Settings**.

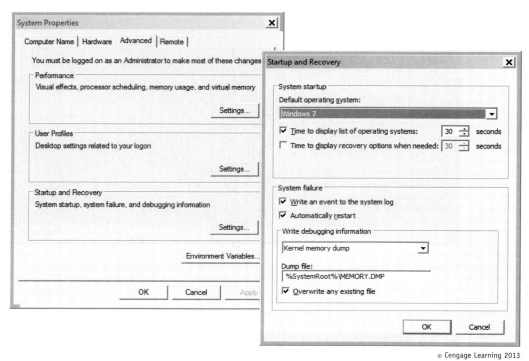

© Cengage Learning 2013

Figure 5-15 Use the Startup and Recovery box to change the way Windows responds to a stop error

e. In the Startup and Recovery box (see the right side of Figure 5-15), uncheck **Automatically restart**. Click **OK** twice to close both boxes. Then close the System window.

2. If you cannot boot the system to Safe Mode, press **F8** at startup and select **Disable automatic restart on system failure** on the Advanced Boot Options menu (refer to Figure 5-13).

TROUBLESHOOTING APPLICATIONS

A problem with an application might be caused by the application, the hardware, the operating system, the data, other applications in conflict with this one, or the user. We begin this part of the chapter by looking at some general steps to help you solve a problem with an application, and then we look at some specific error messages and what to do about them.

> **Notes** As you are troubleshooting a problem and make a change to the system, be sure to restart Windows and check to see if the problem is resolved before you move on to the next fix.

A+ 220-802 4.6

GENERAL STEPS FOR SOLVING APPLICATION ERRORS

Here are a bunch of things to do and try that might solve a problem with an application. As you work your way through these steps, keep in mind where each step fits in the overall strategy given earlier in the chapter for solving any computer problem.

STEP 1: INTERVIEW THE USER AND BACK UP DATA

Worth saying again: Start with interviewing the user:

1. *Interview the user and back up data.* Find out as much information as you can from the user about the problem, when it started, and what happened to the system around the time the problem started. Also ask if valuable data is on the system. If so, back it up.

2. *Ask the user to reproduce the problem while you watch.* Many problems with applications are caused by user error. Watch carefully as the user shows you the problem. If you see him making a mistake, be tactful and don't accuse. Just explain the problem and its solution. It's better to explain and teach rather than fix the problem yourself; that way, the user learns from the experience.

3. *Try a reboot.* Reboots solve a lot of application problems and one might be a shortcut to your solution. If that doesn't work, no harm is done and you're ready to begin investigating the system.

STEP 2: ERROR MESSAGES, THE WEB, AND LOGS MIGHT HELP

Windows might display an error message and offer a solution. Logs kept by Windows can offer clues. Here are a few examples of how to get help from Windows and the web:

◢ *Error messages and the Action Center.* For Windows 7, the Action Center tracks problems with applications, hardware, and Windows (see Figure 5-16). In the Action Center, click **View archived messages** to see a history of past problems (see Figure 5-17). Double-click a problem to read the details about it.

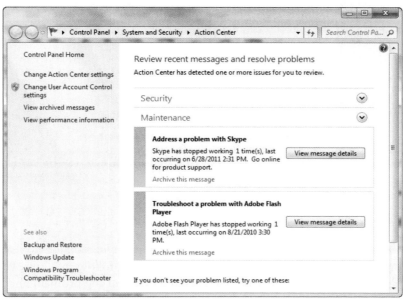

© Cengage Learning 2013

Figure 5-16 Windows 7 reports problems with two applications

A+
220-802
4.6

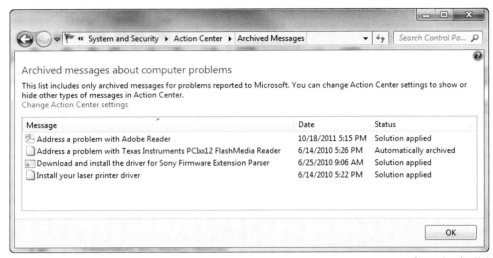

Figure 5-17 Archived messages of past and current problems

© Cengage Learning 2013

▲ *Vista Problem Reports and Solutions window.* For Vista, click **Start**, click **All Programs**, click **Maintenance**, and click **Problem Reports and Solutions**. In the Problem Reports and Solutions window (see Figure 5-18), click **View problem history** to see a list of current and past problems. Click a problem to see details.

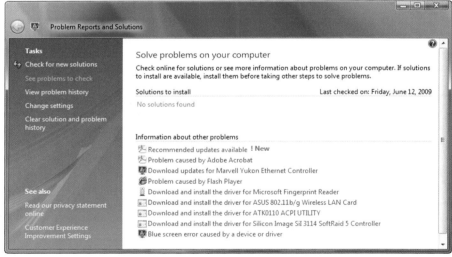

Figure 5-18 Known Vista problems and solutions

© Cengage Learning 2013

▲ *XP error messages.* For XP, an error message appears in a dialog box similar to that in Figure 5-19. When you click Send Error Report and follow the links, your browser opens and displays information from Microsoft about the problem and might offer a solution.

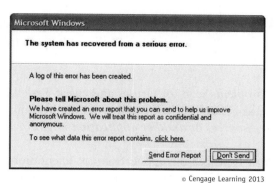

© Cengage Learning 2013

Figure 5-19 A serious Windows XP error sometimes generates this Microsoft Windows error reporting box

A+
220-802
4.6

▲ *Search the web for help.* You might find more information about a problem by searching the web site of the application manufacturer for support and help. Also, search the web on the error message, application, or description of the problem. Look for forums where others have posted the same problem with the same app. Someone else has likely posted a solution. However, be careful and don't take the advice unless you trust the web site.

▲ *Use Event Viewer and Reliability Monitor to look for clues.* The Event Viewer logs might give clues about applications and the system. Hard drive errors often appear as application errors. Use Reliability Monitor to look for errors with other applications or with key hardware components such as the hard drive.

STEP 3: CONSIDER THE DATA OR THE APPLICATION IS CORRUPTED

Now that you've interviewed the user, backed up important data, and examined the system, it's time to come up with a theory as to the cause of the problem. Consider and do these things:

▲ *Consider data corruption.* For applications that use data files such as Microsoft Office, it might appear that the application has a problem when the problem is really a corrupted data file. Try creating an entirely new data file. If that works, then suspect that previous errors might be caused by corrupted data. You might be able to recover part of a corrupted file by changing its file extension to .txt and importing it into the application as a text file.

▲ *Application settings might be wrong.* Maybe a user has made one too many changes to the application settings, which can cause a problem with missing toolbars and other functions. Write down each setting the user has changed and then restore all settings back to their default values. If the problem is solved, restore each setting to the way the user had it until you find the one causing the problem. The process will take some time, but users can get upset if you change their application settings without justification.

▲ *The application might be corrupted.* The application setup might have the option to repair the installation. Look for it in the Programs and Features window, on the setup CD for the application, or on the manufacturer's web site.

▲ *Uninstall and reinstall the application.* Do so with caution because you might lose any customized settings, macros, or scripts. Also know this still might not solve a problem with a corrupted application because registry entries might not be properly reset during the uninstall process.

5

STEP 4: CONSIDER OUTSIDE INTERFERENCE

The problem might be caused by a virus, Windows, other applications, or hardware. Check these things:

- ◢ *Suspect a virus is causing a problem.* Scan for viruses and check Task Manager to make sure some strange process is not interfering with your applications.
- ◢ *You might be low on system resources or another application might be interfering.* Close all other applications.
- ◢ *Maybe a service failed to start.* Research the application documentation and find out if the app relies on a service to work. Use the Services console to make sure the service has started. If the service has failed to start, make sure it has an Automatic or Manual setting.
- ◢ *The problem might be bad memory.* Following the directions given earlier in the chapter, use the Memory Diagnostics tool (mdsched.exe) to test memory. If it finds errors, replace the memory modules.
- ◢ *The problem might be a corrupted hard drive.* To eliminate the hard drive as the source of an application error, use the Chkdsk command with the /r parameter to check the drive and recover data in bad sectors.
- ◢ *A background program might be conflicting with the application.* To eliminate background programs or services as a source of the problem, run the application after booting into Safe Mode. Press **F8** at startup to display the Advanced Boot Options menu, and select **Safe Mode with Networking** from the menu. If the application works in Safe Mode, then you can assume the problem is not with the application but with the operating system, device drivers, or other applications that load at startup and are conflicting with the application.

STEP 5: CONSIDER WINDOWS MIGHT BE THE PROBLEM

A problem with an application can sometimes be solved by updating or restoring Windows system files. Do the following:

- ◢ *Download Windows updates.* Make sure all critical and important Windows updates are installed. Microsoft Office updates are included in Windows updates.
- ◢ *Use System File Checker.* For essential hardware devices, use the System File Checker (SFC) to verify and replace system files. Use the command **sfc /scannow** or **sfc /scanonce**.
- ◢ *Use System Restore.* If you can identify the approximate date the error started and that date is in the recent past, use System Restore. Select a restore point just before the problem started. Reverting to a restore point can solve problems with registry entries the application uses that have become corrupted. However, System Restore can cause problems of its own, so use it with caution.

> 💡 **A+ Exam Tip** The 220-802 exam expects you to know when and how to use System Restore to solve a Windows, hardware, or application problem.

RESPONDING TO SPECIFIC ERROR MESSAGES

In this part of the chapter, we look at some specific error messages that relate to problems with applications.

A+
220-802
1.3, 4.6

WHEN AN APPLICATION HANGS

If an application is locked up and not responding, use Task Manager to end it. If Task Manager can't end a process, use the Tasklist and Taskkill commands. The Tasklist command returns the process identify (PID), which is a number that identifies each running process. The Taskkill command uses the process ID to kill the process. Do the following:

1. Open a Command Prompt window and use the **Tasklist | more** command to get a list of processes currently running. Note the PID of the process you want to end. For example, suppose you see that its PID is 2212.

2. Enter the command **taskkill /f /pid:2212**, using the PID you noted in Step 1. The /f parameter forcefully kills the process. Be careful using this command; it is so powerful that you can end critical system processes that will cause the system to shut down.

> **💡 A+ Exam Tip** For the A+ 220-802 exam, the Kill and Tlist commands are listed in the objectives. These older Windows 2000 commands have been replaced by the Tasklist and Taskkill commands.

5

A+
220-802
4.6

WHEN A FILE FAILS TO OPEN

When you double-click a data file and get an error message that Windows cannot open the file (see Figure 5-20), Windows is unable to identify the application used to read the data file. This problem happens because the application is not installed or the file extension is wrong. The file association between a data file and an application is determined by the file extension. A program associated with a file extension is called its default program.

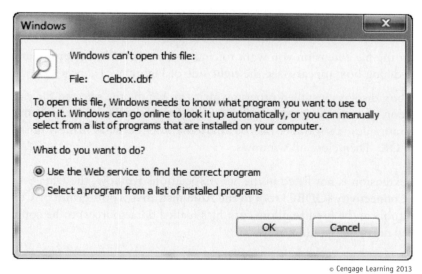

© Cengage Learning 2013

Figure 5-20 Windows does not know which application to use to open the data file

Follow these steps to use the Default Programs window to change the program associated with a file extension:

1. Click **Start** and then click **Default Programs**. The Default Programs window opens. Click **Associate a file type or protocol with a program**. The list of current associations appears in the Set Associations window (see the left side of Figure 5-21).

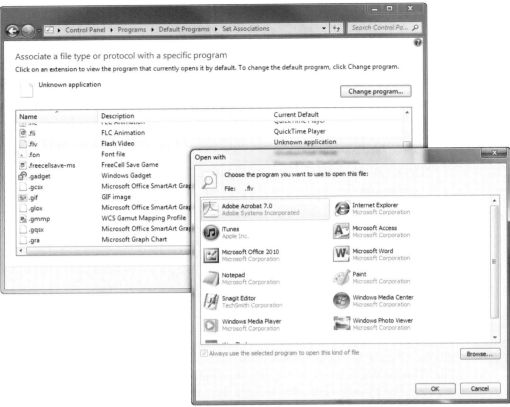

© Cengage Learning 2013

Figure 5-21   Select the default program to associate with a file extension

2. Select the file extension you want to change and click **Change program**. The Open with dialog box appears (see the right side of Figure 5-21).

3. The box displays installed programs that can handle the selected file extension. If you don't see the program you want, click **Browse** to find it in the Program Files or Program Files (x86) folder on your hard drive. Otherwise, make your selection and click **OK**. Then close all windows.

If a file extension is not listed in the Set Associations window, the Data Sources Open Database Connectivity (ODBC) tool in the Administrative Tools group of Control Panel can help. This tool can be used to allow data files (called data sources) to be connected to applications they normally would not use.

APPLYING | CONCEPTS   USING THE ODBC DATA SOURCE TOOL

Suppose a user has some old dBASE database files, which have a .dbf file extension, and she wants to use Microsoft Access installed on her PC to manage these files. Do the following to make this work:

1. In the Administrative Tools group in Control Panel, double-click **Data Sources (ODBC)**. The ODBC Data Source Administrator box opens, as shown in Figure 5-22.

A+
220-802
4.6

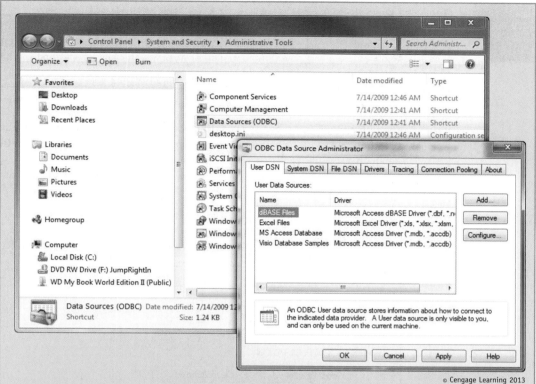

© Cengage Learning 2013

Figure 5-22 Use the Data Sources tool to create a connection between a foreign data source and an application

2. Make sure the **User DSN** tab is selected. (DSN stands for Data Source Name.) The connections made on this tab apply only to the current user. Click **Add**. The Create New Data Source box appears (see Figure 5-23). Select the dBASE driver and click **Finish**.

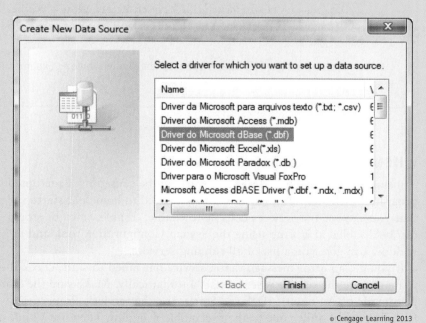

© Cengage Learning 2013

Figure 5-23 Select a driver to interface between the application and the data source

5

Notes If you don't see the driver you need in the Create New Data Source box, close all windows and use Explorer to locate the C:\Windows\SysWOW64\Odbcad32.exe program file. When you double-click this file, the ODBC Data Source Administrator box appears and will have all ODBC drivers available.

3. The ODBC dBASE Setup box appears. Uncheck **Use Current Directory**. Then click **Select Directory** and navigate to the folder that contains the dBASE files and click **OK**. Enter a name for the Data Source Name, as shown in Figure 5-24, and click **OK**. The new data source is now listed in the ODBC Data Source Administrator box, and Windows knows which ODBC driver to use to manage this data source.

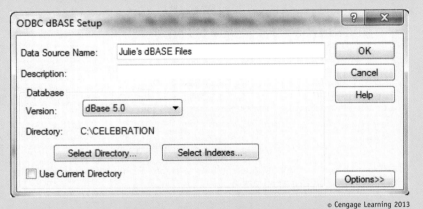

© Cengage Learning 2013

Figure 5-24   Locate the data source files and assign a name to the data source

4. Now you need to establish the file association. Go to the Default Programs window and associate the .dbf file extension with Microsoft Access. Because you have identified an ODBC driver for these .dbf files, this file extension is now listed in the Set Associations box.

5. Test the association by double-clicking a .dbf file in Windows Explorer. The file should open in a Microsoft Access window.

WHEN A SERVICE FAILS TO START

A message about a service failing to start can be caused by a corrupted or missing service program, or the service might not be configured to launch at startup. Recall from Chapter 4 that you can use the Services console to enable, disable, start, or stop a service. A service can be disabled at startup using the System Configuration tool, and the System Information window can give you a list of all running services.

If you get an error message that a service has failed to start, check the Service console to make sure the service is set to start automatically. Make sure the Startup type is set to Automatic or Automatic (Delayed Start). Use the service's Properties box in the console to find the path and filename to the executable program. Then use Windows Explorer to make sure the program file is not missing. You might need to reinstall the service or the application that uses the service.

A+
220-802
1.4, 4.6

WHEN A DLL IS MISSING OR A COMPONENT IS NOT REGISTERED

Most applications have a main program file that uses a collection of many small programs called components or objects that serve the main program. The main program for an application has an .exe file extension and relies on several component services that often have a .DLL file extension. (DLL stands for Dynamic Link Library.) Problems with applications can be caused by a missing DLL program or a broken association between the main program and a component.

If you get an error message about a missing DLL, the easiest way to solve this problem might be to reinstall the application. However, if that is not advisable, you can identify the path and name of the missing DLL file and recover it from backup or from the application installation files.

> 💡 **A+ Exam Tip**   The A+ 220-802 exam expects you to know how to handle missing DLL errors and to know when it's appropriate to use the Component Services, Regsvr32, and Data Sources tools.

5

On the other hand, the file might be present and undamaged, but the application cannot find it because the relationship between the two is broken. Relationships between a main program and its components are normally established by entries in the registry when the application is installed. The process is called registering a component. In addition, the **Component Services** (also called **COM+**) tool, which is a Microsoft Management Console snap-in, can be used to register components. The tool is often used by application developers and system administrators when developing and deploying an application. For example, a system administrator might use COM+ when installing an application on servers or client computers where an application on one computer calls an application on another computer on the network. COM+ is more automated than the older and more manual **Regsvr32_** utility that is also used to register component services.

The Regsvr32.exe program is stored in the C:\Program Files or C:\Program Files (x86) folder and requires an elevated command prompt. Note in Figure 5-25, the first regsvr32 command uses the /u parameter to unregister a component. The second regsvr32 command registers the component again. Also notice that you need to include the path to the DLL file in the command line.

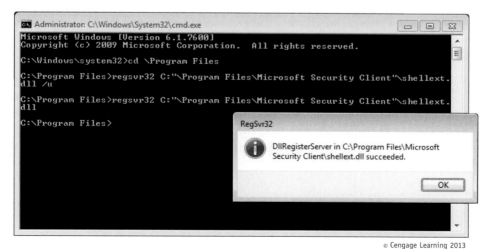

© Cengage Learning 2013

Figure 5-25   Use the regsvr32 command to register or unregister an application component

A+
220-802
1.4, 4.6

As a PC support technician, you might be asked by a system administrator or software provider to use the COM+ or Regsvr32 tool to help solve a problem with an application giving errors. Suppose you get this error when installing an application:

Error 1928 "Error registering COM+ application."

When you contact the help desk of the application provider, you might be instructed to use the COM+ tool to solve the problem. To open the tool, open the **Administrative Tools** group in Control Panel. Then double-click **Component Services**. The Component Services window is shown in Figure 5-26. To learn how to use the tool, click **Help** in the menu bar.

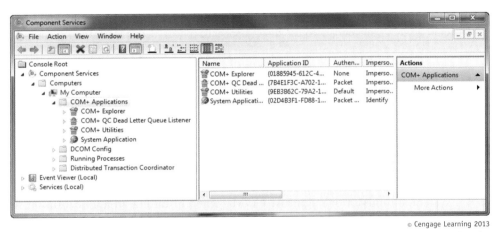

© Cengage Learning 2013

Figure 5-26   Use the Component Services window to register components used by an application

A+
220-802
4.6

WHEN THE APPLICATION HAS NEVER WORKED

If the application has never worked, follow these steps:

1. *Update Windows and search the web.* Installing all important and critical Windows updates can sometimes solve a problem with an application that won't install. Also check the web site of the software manufacturer and the Microsoft support site (*support.microsoft.com*) for solutions. Search on the application name or the error message you get when you try to run it.

2. *Run the installation program or application as an administrator.* The program might require that the user have privileges not assigned to the current user account. Try running the application with administrator privileges, which Windows calls a secondary logon. If the installation has failed, use Windows Explorer to locate the installation executable file. Right-click it and select **Run as administrator** from the shortcut menu (see Figure 5-27).

> **Notes** To run a program using a user account other than administrator, hold down the Shift key and right-click the program file. Then select **Run as different user** from the shortcut menu. You must then enter the username and password of another user account in the Windows Security box.

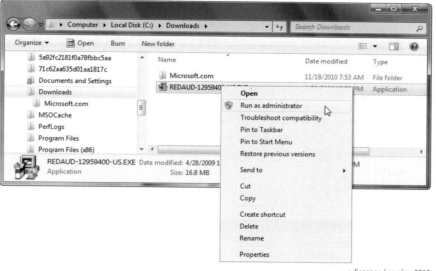

© Cengage Learning 2013

Figure 5-27 Execute a program using administrative privileges

If the application has failed after it is installed, locate the installed program. Look for it in a subfolder of the Program Files or Program Files (x86) folder. If the program works when you run it with administrative privileges, you can make that setting permanent. To do so, right-click it and select **Properties** from the shortcut menu. Then click the **Compatibility** tab and check **Run this program as an administrator** (see Figure 5-28). Click **Apply** and then close the Properties box.

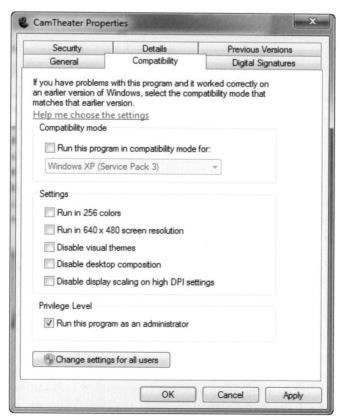

© Cengage Learning 2013

Figure 5-28 Permanently change the privilege level of an application

3. **Consider whether an older application is having compatibility problems with Windows.** Some older applications cannot run under Windows 7 or run with errors. Here are some steps you can take to fix the problem:

a. Go to the Windows 7 Compatibility Center site at *www.microsoft.com/windows/ compatibility* and search for the application. The site reports problems and solutions for known legacy software. For example, when you search on the application WinPatrol, you find that Microsoft recommends Version 16 for Windows 7 (see Figure 5-29). Use the 32-bit or 64-bit type appropriate for your system. If the version and type you are using are not compatible, try to replace or upgrade the software.

© Cengage Learning 2013

Figure 5-29   Microsoft tracks software and hardware compatible with Windows 7

b. Try running the application in compatibility mode. To do that, on the Compatibility tab of the program file Properties box shown earlier in Figure 5-28, check **Run this program in compatibility mode for:**. Then, from the drop-down menu, select the operating system that the application was written to run under. Click **Apply** and close the **Properties** box.

c. For Windows 7 Professional and Ultimate editions, try running the program in Windows XP Mode. Recall from Chapter 2 that Windows XP Mode can be used to install XP in a virtual machine under Windows 7. Applications installed in XP Mode work in the XP environment. Only use this option as a last resort because XP Mode takes up a lot of system resources.

4. **Verify that the application is digitally signed.** Although applications that are not digitally signed can still run on Windows, a digital signature does verify that the application is not a rogue application and that it is certified as Windows-compatible by Microsoft. To view the digital signature, select the **Digital Signatures** tab of the program file's Properties box. Select a signer in the list and click **Details** (see Figure 5-30). If the Digital Signatures tab is missing, the program is not digitally signed.

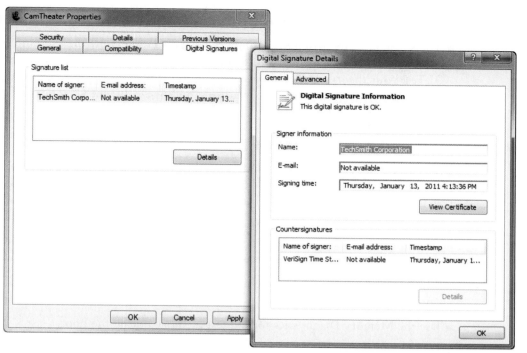

Figure 5-30   This program is digitally signed

© Cengage Learning 2013

5

Hands-on | Project 5.5   Solving Problems with the Microsoft Knowledge Base

You are trying to clean up a hard drive to free some disk space. You notice the hard drive has a C:\Windows.Old folder that takes up 10 GB of valuable hard drive space. However, in the Disk Cleanup dialog box, you don't see the option to delete Previous Windows Installations. Using the Microsoft support site (*support.microsoft.com*), find the Knowledge Base article that allows you to manually delete the folder. Answer these questions:

1. What is the article ID for this article?

2. What are the three command lines needed to delete the folder?

3. Explain the purpose of each of the three commands, and explain the purpose of each parameter in the command line.

>> CHAPTER SUMMARY

Overview of Windows Troubleshooting Tools

◢ In solving Windows problems, it helps to have a handy reference of available Windows tools to remind you of what you might check or do toward finding a solution.

Strategies to Troubleshoot Any Computer Problem

◢ The six steps in the troubleshooting process are: 1) Interview the user and back up data, 2) Examine the system and form a theory of probable cause (your best guess), 3) Test your theory, 4) Plan a solution and implement it, 5) Verify that everything works and take appropriate preventive measures, and 6) Document what you did and the final outcome.

Troubleshooting Blue Screen Errors

◢ To solve blue screen stop errors after Windows startup, use the web to research the error message or symptom, and use Windows error-reporting tools, Event Viewer, Windows updates, System Restore, Memory Diagnostics, and Chkdsk to examine the system and solve the problem.

◢ Operating systems process either 32 bits or 64 bits. Microsoft calls 32-bit operating systems x86-based OSs. The term x64 applies to 64-bit OSs.

◢ 64-bit operating systems require 64-bit drivers and can support 32-bit and 64-bit applications.

◢ Use the Memory Diagnostics tool to test memory during the boot.

◢ Use the System File Checker (SFC) tool to verify and restore system files.

◢ Use the Startup and Recovery section in the System Properties box to keep Windows from automatically restarting after a stop error. Automatic restarts can put the boot into an endless loop.

Troubleshooting Applications

◢ Windows error messages and logs can help you examine a system looking for the source of an application problem.

◢ Applying Windows patches and repairing system files can sometimes solve an application problem. Use System File Checker and System Restore to repair system files.

◢ Other tools that can help you fix a problem with an application include the Default Programs window, Data Sources (ODBC) and Component Services administrative tools, the Services console, a secondary logon, Compatibility Mode, Windows 7 XP Mode, Task Manager, antivirus software, Windows updates, Windows 7 archived messages, Vista Problem Reports and Solutions, XP Error Reporting, Chkdsk, Memory Diagnostics, Safe Mode, and the web site of the application developer.

>> KEY TERMS

blue screen error
blue screen of death (BSOD)
Component Services (also called COM+)
Data Sources Open Database Connectivity (ODBC)

default program
file association
Memory Diagnostics
Problem Reports and Solutions
Regsvr32

secondary logon
System File Checker (SFC)
Taskkill
Tasklist

>> REVIEWING THE BASICS

1. What are the six steps that you can use to solve any computer problem?

2. Blue screen errors happen when which type of processes encounter an error?

3. In what folder are driver files stored?

4. What is the command to use the Memory Diagnostics tool?

5. What method can you use to test memory on a Windows XP system by using the Memory Diagnostics tool without having to install Windows 7 or Vista on the system?

6. What is the command to use the System File Checker to immediately verify system files? To verify system files on the next restart?

7. How many bits does an x86-based operating system process at one time?

8. What GUI tool can you use to stop a program that is hung?

9. What command-line tool can you use to stop a program that is hung?

10. How can you eliminate the possibility that an application error is caused by another application or service running in the background?

11. How does Windows know which application to use to open a file when you double-click the file in Windows Explorer?

12. Which Windows tool can you use to install the drivers needed so that a user can open a data file using an application that is normally not used with the file?

13. Which two tools might a software developer or system administrator use to register a component of an application in the Windows registry?

14. If an application works when the system is loaded in Safe Mode, but does not work when Windows is loaded normally, what can you assume?

15. When an application written for Windows XP does not work in Windows 7, which tool should you attempt to use first to solve the problem, Compatibility Mode or XP Mode? Why?

>> THINKING CRITICALLY

1. Categorize each of the following tasks or decisions into one of the six steps to troubleshoot any computer problem.

   a. Set up a backup schedule.

   b. Reimage Windows 7.

   c. Decide the problem must be a corrupted video driver.

   d. Copy Word documents to a USB flash drive.

   e. Apply a restore point.

2. As a helpdesk technician, list four good detective questions to ask if a user calls to say, "My PC won't boot."

3. Reword the following questions that might be asked when interviewing a user over the telephone. Your new questions should reflect a more positive attitude toward the user.

   a. Did you drop your laptop?

   b. Did you forget to recharge the laptop battery?

   c. You say the problem is that Microsoft Word is giving an error, but do you really know how to use that application?

4. A user tells you that Microsoft Word gives errors when saving a file. What should you do next?

   a. Install Windows updates that also include patches for Microsoft Word.

   b. Ask the user when the problem first started.

   c. Ask the user to save the error message as a screen shot the next time the error occurs and email it to you.

   d. Use Task Manager to end the Microsoft Word program.

>> REAL PROBLEMS, REAL SOLUTIONS

REAL PROBLEM 5-1: Working with DLL Errors

Using Windows 7 installed in a virtual machine or physical machine, follow these steps to learn about what happens when a DLL is missing:

1. Go to *www.winamp.com*, and download and install the free Winamp Media Player program by Nullsoft. (Be careful to not accept the extra software the site offers during the download and installation.) Run the software and verify that you can use it to play an .mp3 audio file. Close the player.

2. Go to the C:\Program Files (x86)\Winamp folder and rename the nde.dll file. Start the Winamp Player. What error message did you get? Return the DLL file to its original name and verify you can now use the player.

A DLL is registered using entries in subkeys of the HKEY_CLASSES_ROOT\CLSID key in the Windows registry. Do the following to find out what happens when a DLL is not registered:

1. Create a restore point so that you can recover from any problems you might have with the registry or installed applications.

2. Open the registry editor and locate the HKCR\CLSID key. Search through the subkeys and write down a list of .dll files you find. Close the registry editor.

3. Search the web and find out which application installed on your system uses each DLL you found. Launch the application to make sure it works. Then open a command prompt window and use the regsvr32 command to unregister its DLL. Try the application again. What error message did you get? If you did not get an error, you might not have used a function of the application that relies on this DLL.

4. Use the regsvr32 command to register the DLL and verify the application is working. If you have a problem with this project, you can undo your changes to the registry by applying the restore point you created.

REAL PROBLEM 5-2: Troubleshooting PC Problems for Friends and Family

You have learned much about PC troubleshooting and repair already in this book. Now it's time to try your hand at some real-life troubleshooting. Make yourself available to family and friends to help them with their computer problems. For the first three problems you tackle, keep notes that describe the initial problem, what you did to solve it or to escalate it to others, and the outcome. Then answer the following questions:

1. What did you learn about Windows or other technologies from these three problems?

2. What did you learn about working with people when you helped them with these three problems?

3. What one thing will you do differently when faced with similar problems?

4. What is something that you recognize you need to know, that you don't yet know, about PC troubleshooting that would have helped you with these three problems?

5

Troubleshooting Windows Startup Problems

In the last chapter, you learned how to deal with Windows and application problems that occur after Windows has started. In this chapter, you take your troubleshooting skills one step further by learning to deal with startup problems. When Windows fails to start, it can be stressful if important data has not been backed up or the user has pressing work to do with the computer. What helps more than anything else is a cool head and a good plan so you don't feel so helpless.

We begin the chapter with a discussion of what happens when you first turn on a computer and Windows starts. The more you understand about startup, the better your chances of fixing startup problems. Then you learn about Windows tools specifically designed to handle startup problems. Finally, you learn a step-by-step strategy for solving startup problems and recovering data on a hard drive when Windows is corrupted beyond repair.

UNDERSTANDING THE BOOT PROCESS

A+
220-802
4.6

Knowledge is power. The better you understand what happens when you first turn on a computer until Windows is loaded and the Windows desktop appears, the more likely you will be able to solve a problem when Windows cannot start. Let's begin by noting the differences between a hard boot and a soft boot.

> **Notes** Most techies use the terms "boot" and "startup" interchangeably. However, in general, the term "boot" refers to the hardware phase of starting up a computer. Microsoft consistently uses the term "startup" to refer to how its operating systems are booted, well, started, I mean.

CHOOSING BETWEEN A HARD BOOT AND A SOFT BOOT

The term **booting** comes from the phrase "lifting yourself up by your bootstraps" and refers to the computer bringing itself up to a working state without the user having to do anything but press the on button. This boot can be a hard boot or soft boot. A **hard boot**, or **cold boot**, involves turning on the power with the on/off switch. A **soft boot**, or **warm boot**, involves using the operating system to reboot.

A hard boot takes more time than a soft boot because in a soft boot, the initial steps of a hard boot don't happen. To save time in most circumstances, you should use the soft boot to restart. A hard boot initializes the processor and clears memory. If a soft boot doesn't work or you want to make certain you get a fresh start, use a hard boot. If you cannot boot from the operating system, look for power or reset buttons on the front or rear of the case. For example, one computer has three power switches: a power button and a reset button on the front of the case and a power switch on the rear of the case (see Figure 6-1).

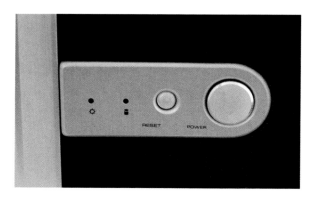 

© Cengage Learning 2013

Figure 6-1   This computer case has two power buttons on the front and one power switch on the rear of the case

They work like this:

▲ The power button in front can be configured as a "soft" power button, causing a normal Windows shutdown and restart.

A+
220-802
4.6

◢ The reset button initializes the CPU so that it restarts at the beginning of the BIOS startup program. The computer behaves as though the power were turned off and back on and then goes through the entire boot process.

◢ The switch on the rear of the case simply turns off the power abruptly and is a "hard" power button. If you use this switch, wait 30 seconds before you press the power button on the front of the case to boot the system. This method gives you the greatest assurance that memory will clear. However, if Windows is abruptly stopped, it might give an error message when you reboot.

How the front two buttons work can be controlled in BIOS setup. Know, however, that different cases offer different options.

STARTUP BIOS CONTROLS THE BEGINNING OF THE BOOT

Recall that the startup BIOS is programming contained on the firmware chip on the motherboard that is responsible for getting a system up and going and finding an OS to load. A successful boot depends on the hardware, the BIOS, and the operating system all performing without errors. If errors occur, they might stall or lock up the boot. Errors are communicated as beeps, as text messages on-screen, or as recorded voice messages.

Startup BIOS is responsible for these early steps in the boot process:

1. *Startup BIOS reads* **motherboard settings** *and runs the POST*. Here are a few important details:

   a. A small amount of RAM on a firmware chip on the motherboard holds an inventory of hardware devices, hardware settings, security passwords, date and time, and startup settings. Startup BIOS reads this information and then surveys the hardware devices it finds present, comparing it to the list kept in this RAM.

   b. Startup BIOS runs POST (power-on self test), which is a series of tests used to find out if startup BIOS can communicate correctly with essential hardware components required for a successful boot.

   c. Before the video controller on the motherboard or video card is tested and configured, startup BIOS communicates any errors as a series of beeps or recorded speech. Short and long beeps indicate an error; the coding for the beeps depends on the BIOS. After startup BIOS has checked the video controller (note that it does not check to see if a monitor is present or working), it can use video to display its progress on-screen.

2. *Setup BIOS might be run*. The keyboard is checked, and if the key is pressed to request BIOS setup, the BIOS setup program is run. For example, for one system, when you press Del, the BIOS setup opening menu shown in Figure 6-2 appears. You can use the menus and items on these screens to verify hardware devices recognized by the system, enable and disable devices, set the date and time, set security passwords to the computer, change the boot device order, and make other changes to BIOS settings. Know that the screens provided by different motherboard manufacturers might be organized differently.

6

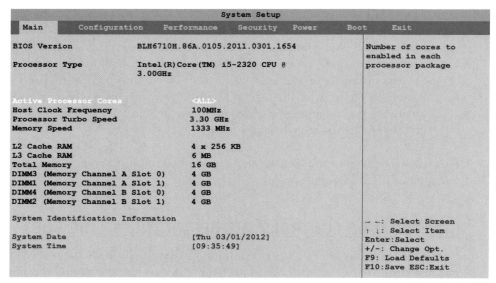

Figure 6-2   Use BIOS setup screens to change the hardware configuration for a system

© Cengage Learning 2013

3. *Startup BIOS searches for a bootable device.* The boot sequence stored in CMOS RAM tells startup BIOS which device to use to launch an OS. Most BIOSs support booting from the hard drive, a CD or DVD, a USB device, or another computer on the network. (Older computers could also boot from a floppy disk.) The BIOS turns to the specified device and turns control over to it. Next let's see what happens if the device is the hard drive.

> **Notes** Future desktop and notebook systems are likely to use replacement technologies for the BIOS firmware on the motherboard. EFI (Extensible Firmware Interface) and UEFI (Unified EFI) are two standards for the interface between firmware on the motherboard and the operating system. The standards replace the legacy BIOS standards and improve on processes for booting, handing over the boot to the OS, and loading device drivers and applications before the OS loads. For more information on either standard, see the UEFI consortium at *www.uefi.org*.

STEPS TO START WINDOWS 7/VISTA

Table 6-1 lists the components and files necessary to start Windows 7/Vista

Component or File	Path*	Description
MBR	First sector of the hard drive called the master boot record	Contains the partition table and the master boot program used to locate and start the BootMgr program.
OS boot record	First sector of the system partition (most likely drive C:)	Windows XP uses this sector, but Windows 7/Vista does not use it.

Table 6-1   Software components and files needed to start Windows 7/Vista (continues)

© Cengage Learning 2013

A+
220-802
4.6

Component or File	Path*	Description
BootMgr	Root directory of system partition (C:\)	Windows Boot Manager manages the initial startup of the OS.
BCD	Boot folder of the system partition (C:\Boot)	The Boot Configuration Data file is organized the same as a registry hive and contains boot settings that control BootMgr, WinLoad.exe, WinResume.exe (when resuming from hibernation), MemTest.exe (when memory is tested), and dual boots.
WinLoad.exe	C:\Windows\System32	Windows Boot Loader loads and starts essential Windows processes.
Ntoskrnl.exe	C:\Windows\System32	Windows kernel.
Hal.dll	C:\Windows\System32	Dynamic link library handles low-level hardware details.
Smss.exe	C:\Windows\System32	Sessions Manager program responsible for starting user sessions.
Csrss.exe	C:\Windows\System32	Win32 subsystem manages graphical components and threads.
Winlogon.exe	C:\Windows\System32	Logon process.
Services.exe	C:\Windows\System32	Service Control Manager starts and stops services.
Lsass.exe	C:\Windows\System32	Authenticates users.
System registry hive	C:\Windows\System32\Config	Holds data for the HKEY_LOCAL_MACHINE key of the registry.
Device drivers	C:\Windows\System32\Drivers	Drivers for required hardware.

*It is assumed that Windows is installed in C:\Windows.

© Cengage Learning 2013

Table 6-1 Software components and files needed to start Windows 7/Vista (continued)

6

> **Notes** Take a moment to distinguish between the system partition and the boot partition. The PC boots from the system partition and loads the Windows operating system from the boot partition. The system partition is the active partition that is used first when finding and loading an operating system. The boot partition contains the \Windows folder where system files are located. Most of the time the boot partition and the system partition are the same partition (drive C:). The only time they are different is in a dual-boot configuration. For example, if Windows 7 has been installed in a dual-boot configuration with Windows XP, the system partition is most likely drive C: (where Windows XP is installed), and Windows 7 is installed on another drive, such as drive E:, which Windows 7 calls the boot partition. The PC boots from drive C: and then loads Windows 7 system files stored on drive E: in the E:\Windows folder.

Now let's look at the steps to start a Windows 7/Vista computer. Several of these steps are diagrammed in Figures 6-3 and 6-4 to help you visually understand how the steps work.

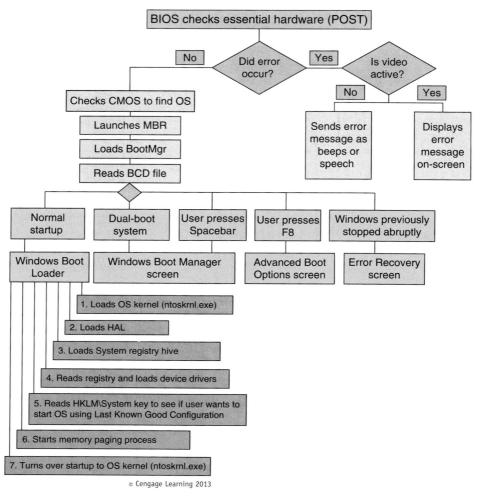

© Cengage Learning 2013

Figure 6-3 Steps to booting the computer and loading Windows 7/Vista

Study these steps carefully because the better you understand startup, the more likely you'll be able to solve startup problems:

1. Startup BIOS turns control over to the MBR program stored in the first sector of the hard drive.

> **Notes** Future desktop and notebook systems are likely to use a different method than the MBR for organizing the hard drive. Even now, in Windows 7/Vista, you can choose between two disk-partitioning systems: MBR and GPT. Using the MBR system, you can have up to four partitions on a hard drive, although one of them can have multiple volumes, which are called logical drives. The GPT (Globally Unique Identifier Partition Table) disk-partitioning system can support up to 128 partitions, and these partitions are more stable and can be larger than MBR partitions. To use the GPT system for your bootable hard drive, your computer motherboard must contain an EFI or UEFI chip rather than the traditional BIOS chip. For more information on the GPT method of organizing a hard drive, go to the *www.microsoft.com* site and search on GPT.

2. The MBR program searches the partition table looking for the active partition, which Windows calls the system partition. It finds and loads the **Windows Boot Manager** (**BootMgr**) program in the root directory of this partition. (Note that the BootMgr

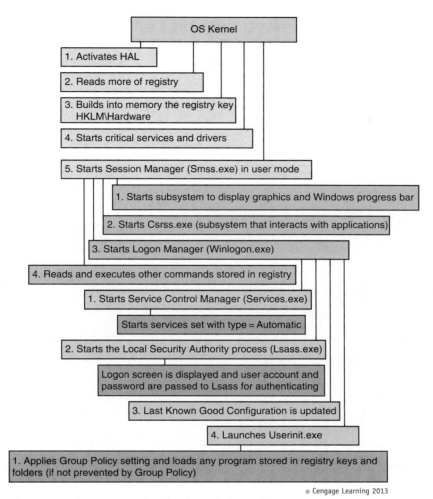

© Cengage Learning 2013

Figure 6-4 Steps to complete loading Windows 7/Vista

program file has no file extension.) If the MBR program cannot find BootMgr or cannot turn over operation to it, one of these error messages appears:

```
Missing operating system
Error loading operating system
Windows failed to load
Invalid partition table
```

> **XP Differences** When starting XP, the MBR looks for the first sector in the active partition, which is called the **OS boot record**. This sector contains a small program that finds the Windows XP boot program named **Ntldr**. Ntldr reads XP settings used for the boot stored in **Boot.ini**. For more detail about starting Windows XP, see Appendix C.

3. BootMgr does the following:

a. It reads the settings in the **Boot Configuration Data (BCD)** file.

b. The next step, one of five, depends on entries in the BCD and these other factors:

◢ *Option 1:* For normal startups that are not dual booting, no menu appears and BootMgr finds and launches **Windows Boot Loader (WinLoad.exe)** stored in the \Windows\System32 folder.

A+
220-802
4.6

▲ *Option 2:* If the computer is set up for a dual-boot environment, BootMgr displays the Windows Boot Manager screen, as shown in Figure 6-5.

▲ *Option 3:* If the user presses the Spacebar, the Windows Boot Manager screen appears.

▲ *Option 4:* If the user presses F8, BootMgr displays the Advanced Boot Options screen, as shown in Figure 6-6.

▲ *Option 5:* If Windows was previously stopped abruptly or another error occurs, the Windows Error Recovery screen (see Figure 6-7) appears.

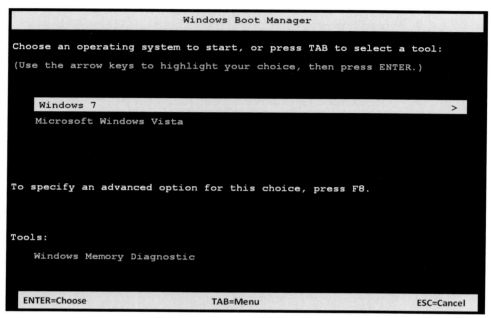

Figure 6-5 Boot loader menu in a dual-boot environment
© Cengage Learning 2013

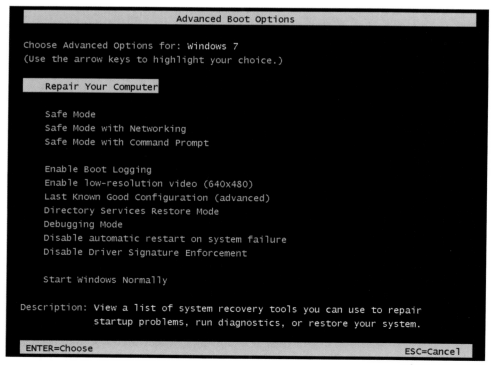

Figure 6-6 Press F8 during the boot to launch the Windows 7 Advanced Boot Options menu
© Cengage Learning 2013

A+
220-802
4.6

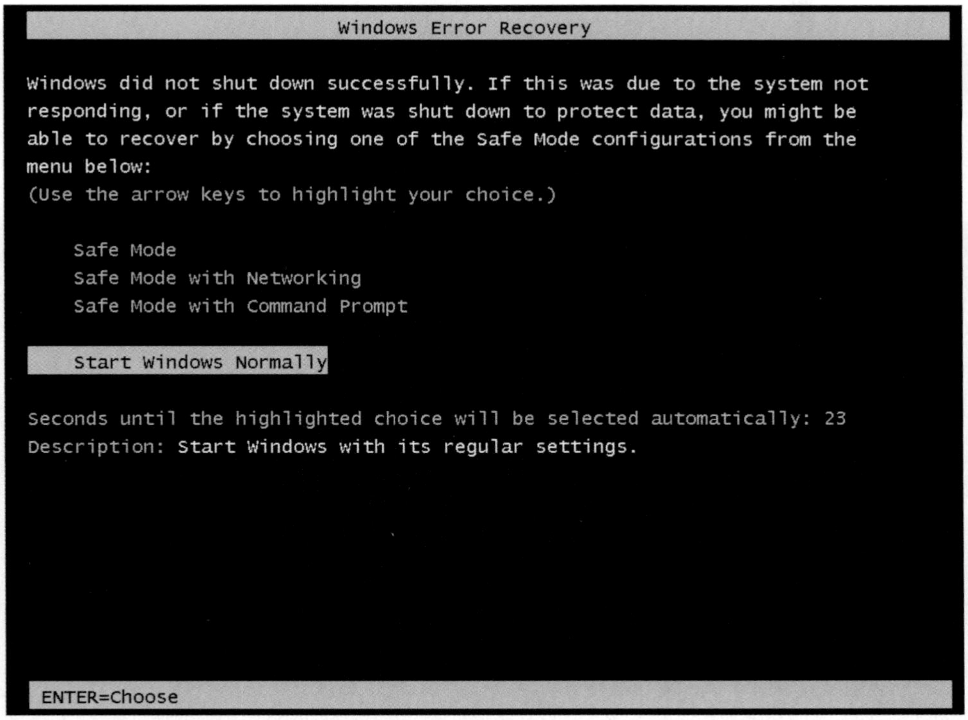

```
                        Windows Error Recovery

Windows did not shut down successfully. If this was due to the system not
responding, or if the system was shut down to protect data, you might be
able to recover by choosing one of the Safe Mode configurations from the
menu below:
(Use the arrow keys to highlight your choice.)


    Safe Mode
    Safe Mode with Networking
    Safe Mode with Command Prompt

    Start Windows Normally

Seconds until the highlighted choice will be selected automatically: 23
Description: Start Windows with its regular settings.




 ENTER=Choose
```
© Cengage Learning 2013

Figure 6-7 This window appears if Windows has been abruptly stopped

6

4. **WinLoad** is responsible for loading Windows components. It does the following:

   a. For normal startups, WinLoad loads into memory the OS kernel, Ntoskrnl.exe, but does not yet start it. WinLoad also loads into memory the Hardware Abstraction Layer (Hal.dll), which will later be used by the kernel.

   b. WinLoad loads into memory the system registry hive (C:\Windows\System32\Config\System).

   c. WinLoad then reads the registry key just created, HKEY_LOCAL_ MACHINE\SYSTEM\Services, looking for and loading into memory device drivers that must be launched at startup. The drivers are not yet started.

   d. WinLoad reads data from the HKEY_LOCAL_MACHINE\SYSTEM key that tells the OS if the user wants to start the OS using the Last Known Good Configuration.

   e. WinLoad starts up the memory paging process and then turns over startup to the OS kernel (Ntoskrnl.exe).

5. The kernel (Ntoskrnl.exe) does the following:

   a. It activates the HAL, reads more information from the registry, and builds into memory the registry key HKEY_LOCAL_ MACHINE\HARDWARE, using information that has been collected about the hardware.

   b. The kernel then starts critical services and drivers that are configured to be started by the kernel during the boot. Recall that drivers interact directly with hardware and run in kernel mode, while services interact with drivers. Most services and drivers are stored in C:\Windows\System32 or C:\Windows\System32\Drivers and have an .exe, .dll, or .sys file extension.

   c. After the kernel starts all services and drivers configured to load during the boot, it starts the Session Manager (Smss.exe), which runs in user mode.

6. The Session Manager (Smss.exe) does the following:

    a. It starts the part of the Win32 subsystem that displays graphics, and the Windows 7 flag or the Vista progress bar is displayed (see Figure 6-8). When you see the flag or progress bar, you know the Windows kernel has loaded successfully.

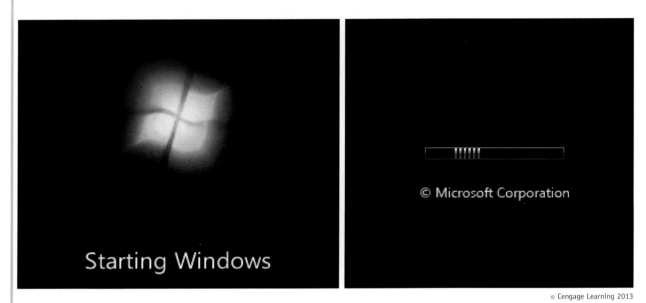

© Cengage Learning 2013

Figure 6-8 The Windows 7 flag on the left or the Vista progress bar on the right indicates that the Windows graphics subsystem is running and the kernel has successfully loaded

    b. Smss.exe then starts the client/server run-time subsystem (Csrss.exe), which also runs in user mode. Csrss.exe is the Win32 subsystem component that interacts with applications.

    c. Smss.exe starts the Logon Manager (Winlogon.exe) and reads and executes other commands stored in the registry, such as a command to replace system files placed there by Windows Update.

7. Winlogon.exe does the following:

    a. It starts the Service Control Manager (Services.exe). Services.exe starts all services listed with the startup type of Automatic in the Services console.

    b. Winlogon.exe starts the Local Security Authority process (Lsass.exe). The logon screen appears (see Figure 6-9), and the user account and password are passed to the Lsass.exe process for authenticating. The Last Known Good Configuration information in the registry is updated.

    c. Winlogon.exe launches Userinit.exe and the Windows desktop (Explorer.exe).

8. Userinit.exe applies Group Policy settings and any programs not trumped by Group Policy that are stored in startup folders and startup registry keys. See Appendix G for a list of these folders and registry keys.

The Windows startup is officially completed when the Windows desktop appears and the wait circle disappears.

With this basic knowledge of the boot in hand, let's turn our attention to the Windows tools that can help you solve problems when Windows refuses to load.

A+
220-802
4.6

Figure 6-9 Windows 7 logon screen

© Cengage Learning 2013

6

WINDOWS 7/VISTA TOOLS FOR SOLVING STARTUP PROBLEMS

Before we begin troubleshooting Windows startup, it helps to first survey the Windows tools so you are familiar with how they can help and how they work. These tools include the Advanced Boot Options menu, the Windows Recovery Environment (Windows RE), and the command prompt window in Windows RE.

As you learn to use each tool, keep in mind that you want to use the tool that makes as few changes to the system as possible to fix the problem.

> ⚡ **Caution** This chapter often refers to the Windows setup DVD. If you have a notebook computer or a brand-name computer such as a Dell, IBM, Lenovo, or Gateway, be sure to use the hidden recovery partition on the hard drive of these computers or the manufacturer's recovery discs rather than the regular Windows setup DVD. These recovery media are likely to contain proprietary drivers needed for installed devices.

ADVANCED BOOT OPTIONS MENU

The Advanced Boot Options menu (refer back to Figure 6-6) appears when a user presses F8 as Windows is loading. You need to be familiar with each option on this menu and know how to use it.

> 💾 **XP Differences** The XP **Advanced Options menu** is similar to the Windows 7/Vista Advanced Boot Options menu and has many of the same items on its menu. See Figure 6-10.

A+
220-802
4.6

```
Windows Advanced Options Menu
Please select an option:

    Safe Mode
    Safe Mode with Networking
    Safe Mode with Command Prompt

    Enable Boot Logging
    Enable VGA Mode
    Last Known Good Configuration (your most recent settings that worked)
    Directory Services Restore Mode (Windows domain controllers only)
    Debugging Mode
    Disable automatic restart on system failure

    Start Windows Normally
    Reboot
    Return to OS Choices Menu

Use the up and down arrow keys to move the highlight to your choice.
```

© Cengage Learning 2013

Figure 6-10 Windows XP Advanced Options menu

REPAIR YOUR COMPUTER

This option is available only in Windows 7 and launches the Windows Recovery Environment (Windows RE) that provides a variety of tools to solve Windows startup problems. You learn to use Windows RE later in the chapter.

SAFE MODE

Safe Mode boots the OS with a minimum configuration and can be used to solve problems with a new hardware installation, a corrupted Windows installation, or problems caused by user settings. Safe Mode boots with the mouse, monitor (with basic video), keyboard, and mass storage drivers loaded. It uses the default system services (it does not load any extra services) and does not provide network access. It uses a plain VGA video driver (Vga.sys) instead of the video drivers specific to your video card.

When you boot in Safe Mode, you will see "Safe Mode" in all four corners of your Windows desktop screen. The screen resolution is 800 × 600 and the desktop wallpaper (background) is black. Figure 6-11 shows Windows 7 in Safe Mode.

© Cengage Learning 2013

Figure 6-11 Safe Mode loads a minimum Windows configuration

Here's what you can do in Safe Mode to recover the system:

1. When Safe Mode first loads, if Windows senses the problem is drastic, it gives you the opportunity to go directly to System Restore. Use System Restore unless you know exactly what it is you need to do to solve your problem. You can also start System Restore from within Safe Mode as you do from the regular Windows desktop.

> **Notes** When using System Restore, you run the risk of undoing *desired* changes to the Windows environment and software installations. Before using one of these fixes, consider what recent changes will be lost when you apply the fix.

2. If you suspect a virus, scan the system for viruses. Use Memory Diagnostics to verify memory and use Chkdsk to fix hard drive problems. Your hard drive might be full; if so, make some free space available.

3. Use Device Manager to uninstall or disable a device with problems or to roll back a driver.

4. Use System Configuration to disable unneeded services or startup processes. If you don't know which one is causing the problem, disable all non-Microsoft services and processes. If the problem goes away, enable one at a time until you discover the one causing the problem.

5. If you suspect a software program you have just installed is the issue, use the Programs and Features window to uninstall it.

6. Use Event Viewer and other error-reporting logs to find information saved during previously failed startups that can help you identify the source of a problem.

> **A+ Exam Tip** The A+ 220-802 exam expects you to know how to use Safe Mode and Chkdsk to help resolve a Windows startup problem.

Here are some tips about loading Safe Mode that you need to be aware of:

- ◢ From the Advanced Boot Options menu, first try Safe Mode with Networking. If that doesn't work, try Safe Mode. And if that doesn't work, try Safe Mode with Command Prompt.
- ◢ Know that Safe Mode won't load if core Windows components are corrupted.
- ◢ When you load Windows in Safe Mode, all files used for the load are recorded in the C:\Windows\Ntbtlog.txt file. Use this file to identify a service, device driver, or application loaded at startup that is causing a problem.

SAFE MODE WITH NETWORKING

Use this option when you are solving a problem with booting and need access to the network to solve the problem. For example, you might need to download updates to your antivirus software. Another example is when you have just attempted to install a printer, which causes the OS to hang when it boots. You can boot into Safe Mode with Networking and download new printer drivers from the network. Uninstall the printer and then install it again from the network. Also use this mode when the Windows installation files are available on the network, rather than the Windows setup DVD, and you need to access those files.

6

A+
220-802
4.6

SAFE MODE WITH COMMAND PROMPT

If the first Safe Mode option does not load the OS, then try Safe Mode with the command prompt. At the command prompt, use the **sfc /scannow** command to verify system files (see Figure 6-12). Also use the **chkdsk /r** command to check for file system errors. If the problem is still not solved, you can use this command to launch System Restore: **C:\Windows\system32\ rstrui.exe**. Then follow the directions on-screen to select a restore point (see Figure 6-13).

© Cengage Learning 2013

Figure 6-12   SFC finds and repairs corrupted system files

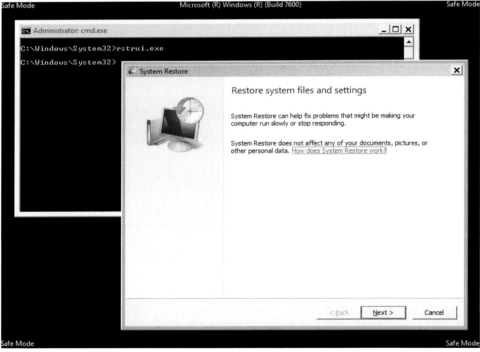

© Cengage Learning 2013

Figure 6-13   Use System Restore after booting to Safe Mode with Command Prompt

ENABLE BOOT LOGGING

When you boot with this option, Windows loads normally and you access the regular desktop. However, all files used during the load process are recorded in a file, C:\Windows\ Ntbtlog.txt (see Figure 6-14). Thus, you can use this option to see what did and did not

**A+
220-802
4.6**

load during the boot. For instance, if you have a problem getting a device to work, check Ntbtlog.txt to see what driver files loaded. Boot logging is much more effective if you have a copy of Ntbtlog.txt that was made when everything worked as it should. Then you can compare the good load to the bad load, looking for differences.

> **Notes** The Ntbtlog.txt file is also generated when you boot into Safe Mode.

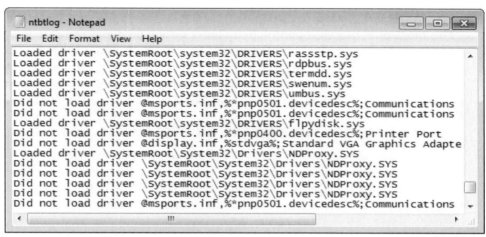

Figure 6-14   Sample Ntbtlog.txt file

© Cengage Learning 2013

> **Notes** If Windows hangs during the boot, try booting using the option Enable Boot Logging. Then look at the last entry in the Ntbtlog.txt file. This entry might be the name of a device driver causing the system to hang.

ENABLE LOW-RESOLUTION VIDEO (640 × 480)

Use this option when the video setting does not allow you to see the screen well enough to fix a bad setting. This can happen when a user creates a desktop with black fonts on a black background, or something similar that makes it impossible to see the desktop. Booting in this mode gives you a very plain, standard VGA video. You can then go to the Display settings, correct the problem, and reboot normally. You can also use this option if your video drivers are corrupted and you need to update, roll back, or reinstall your video drivers. In Windows XP, this option is called "Enable VGA Mode."

LAST KNOWN GOOD CONFIGURATION

Registry settings collectively called the Last Known Good Configuration are saved in the registry each time the user successfully logs onto the system. If your problem is caused by a bad hardware or software installation and you get an error message the first time you restart the system after the installation, using the Last Known Good can, in effect, undo your installation and solve your problem.

6

Remember, the Last Known Good registry settings are saved each time a user logs on to Windows. Therefore, it's important to try the Last Known Good early in the troubleshooting session before it's overwritten. (However, know that if you log onto the system in Safe Mode, the Last Known Good is not saved.)

DIRECTORY SERVICES RESTORE MODE (WINDOWS DOMAIN CONTROLLERS ONLY)

This option applies only to domain controllers and is used as one step in the process of recovering from a corrupted Active Directory. Recall that Active Directory is the domain database managed by a domain controller that tracks users and resources on the domain.

DEBUGGING MODE

This mode gives you the opportunity to move system boot logs from the failing computer to another computer for evaluation. To use this mode, both computers must be connected to each other by way of the serial port. Then, you can reboot into this mode and Windows on the failing computer will send all the boot information through the serial port and on to the other computer. For more details, see the *Windows 7 Resource Kit* by Microsoft Press.

DISABLE AUTOMATIC RESTART ON SYSTEM FAILURE

By default, Windows automatically restarts immediately after a blue screen stop error. The error can cause the system to continually reboot rather than shut down. To stop the rebooting, choose **Disable automatic restart on system failure**. Recall from Chapter 5 that you can use the System Properties box to make this setting permanent.

Hands-on | Project 6.1 — Use Boot Logs and System Information to Research Startup

Boot logs can be used to generate a list of drivers that were loaded during a normal startup and during the Safe Mode startup. Do the following to use boot logs to research startup:

1. Boot to the normal Windows desktop with boot logging enabled. Save the boot log just created to a different name or location so it will not be overwritten on the next boot.

2. Reboot the system in Safe Mode, which also creates a boot log. Compare the two logs, identifying differences in drivers loaded during the two boots. To compare the files, you can print both files and lay them side by side for comparison. An easier method is to compare the files using the Compare tool in Microsoft Word.

3. Use the System Information utility or other methods to identify the hardware devices loaded during normal startup but not loaded in Safe Mode.

As you identify the drivers not loaded during Safe Mode, these registry keys might help with your research:

◢ Lists drivers and services loaded during Safe Mode: HKLM\System\CurrentControlSet\ Control\SafeBoot\Minimal

◢ Lists drivers and services loaded during Safe Mode with Networking: HKLM\ System\CurrentControlSet\Control\SafeBoot\Network

A+
220-802
4.6

Hands-on | Project 6.2   Take Ownership and Replace a Windows System File

The System File Checker tool can be used to find and replace corrupted Windows system files. The tool keeps a log of its actions, and, if it cannot replace a corrupted file, you can find that information in the log file. Then you can manually replace the file. To do so, you can use the takeown command to take ownership of a system file and the icacls command to get full access to the file. The Microsoft Knowledge Base Article 929833 at *support.microsoft.com* explains how to use these two commands.

Do the following to practice manually replacing a system file:

1. Boot the computer into Safe Mode with Command Prompt.

2. Take ownership and gain full access to the C:\Windows\System32\jscript.dll file. What commands did you use?

3. Rename the jscript.dll file to jscript.dll.hold. Run the **sfc /scannow** command. Did SFC restore the jscript.dll file? What is the path and filename of the log file listing repairs?

4. SFC restores a file using files stored on the Windows setup DVD or other folders on the hard drive. If SFC cannot restore a file, you might find a fresh copy in the C:\Windows\winsxs folder or its subfolders. Search these folders. Did you find a version of jscript.dll that is the same file size as the one in C:\Windows\System32? Other than the C:\Windows\winsxs folder, where else can you find a known good copy of a corrupted system file?

> **Notes** To use a command prompt window to search for a file in a folder and its subfolders, use the dir /s command.

THE WINDOWS RECOVERY ENVIRONMENT (WINDOWS RE)

Windows Recovery Environment (Windows RE) is a lean operating system that can be launched to solve Windows startup problems after other tools available on the Advanced Boot Options menu have failed to solve the problem. It provides a graphical and command-line interface.

In Windows 7 or Vista, you can launch Windows RE from the Windows setup DVD. In Windows 7, Windows RE is installed on the hard drive and available on the Advanced Boot Options menu. In addition, you can create a Windows 7 system repair disc and use it to launch Windows RE.

To create a Windows 7 system repair disc, click **Create a system repair disc** in the Windows 7 Backup and Restore window (see Figure 6-15). A 32-bit Windows 7 installation will create a 32-bit version of the repair disc, and a 64-bit Windows 7 installation will create a 64-bit version of the repair disc. A repair disc created on one computer can be used on a different computer even if they are using different editions of Windows 7, but be sure to use a 32-bit disc for a 32-bit installation and a 64-bit disc for a 64-bit Windows installation.

A+
220-802
4.6

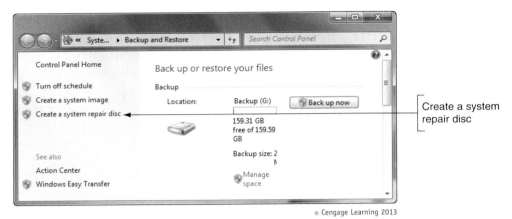

Create a system
repair disc

© Cengage Learning 2013

Figure 6-15   Use Backup and Restore to create a system repair disc to use
instead of the Windows setup DVD

Notes To launch Windows RE from a Windows setup DVD or Windows 7 repair disc, be sure to use a
64-bit DVD for a 64-bit installation of Windows and a 32-bit DVD for a 32-bit installation of Windows.
To boot from a DVD, you might have to change the boot sequence in BIOS setup to put the optical drive
first above the hard drive.

APPLYING | CONCEPTS   EXPLORE WINDOWS RE

Follow these steps to start Windows RE and explore what it has to offer:

1. Use one of the following methods to start Windows RE:

   ◢ For Windows 7 or Vista, boot from the Windows setup DVD. Select your language preference
   and click **Next**. The Install Windows screen appears, as shown in Figure 6-16. Click **Repair
   your computer**.

© Cengage Learning 2013

Figure 6-16   Launch Windows RE after booting from the Windows DVD

◢ For Windows 7, press **F8** during the boot and on the Advanced Boot Options menu, select **Repair Your Computer**. In the dialog box that appears, select your keyboard input method.

◢ For Windows 7, boot from the Windows 7 repair disc. Select your language preference and click **Next**. The Install Windows screen appears, as shown in Figure 6-16. Click **Repair your computer**.

Regardless of the method you use, the System Recovery Options box appears.

2. Depending on the situation, the System Recovery Options box might ask you to select your language preference (when you have booted from a disc) or the Windows installation to repair (in a dual boot system). Make your selection and click **Next**.

3. The System Recovery Options box then asks you to select your user account that has administrative privileges (see Figure 6-17). Select your user account, enter your password, and click **OK**. Without this account and password you will not be allowed to access the volume where Windows is installed.

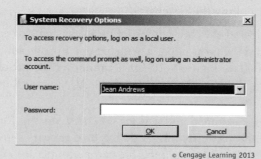

© Cengage Learning 2013

Figure 6-17 Select an account with administrative privileges

4. The System Recovery Options box appears, where you can select a recovery tool (see Figure 6-18).

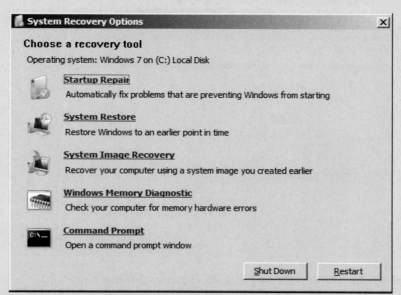

© Cengage Learning 2013

Figure 6-18 Recovery tools in Windows RE for a Windows 7 installation

6

A+
220-802
4.6

When deciding which tool to use in Figure 6-18, always use the least intrusive tool first. In other words, fix the problem while making as few changes to the system as possible.

> **Notes** As you use a tool in the System Recovery Options window, be sure to reboot after each attempt to fix the problem to make sure the problem has not been resolved before you try another tool. To exit the Recovery Environment, click **Shut Down** or **Restart**.

Use the Windows RE tools in the order listed so as to fix the system using the least intrusive method:

1. *Startup Repair.* This option is the least intrusive. It does not change user data or installed applications and can sometimes fix a startup problem, including those caused by corrupted or missing system files. You can't cause any additional problems by using it and it's easy to use. Follow these steps:

    a. Click **Startup Repair** and the tool will examine the system for errors (see Figure 6-19). Based on what it finds, it will suggest various solutions such as using System Restore (see Figure 6-20). If it cannot fix the problem, the box in Figure 6-21 appears. For the system in Figure 6-22, Startup Repair has made repairs and suggests a reboot.

    b. To see a list of items examined and actions taken by Startup Repair, click **Click here for diagnostic and repair details**. A dialog box appears showing the list of repairs accomplished. In addition, a log file can be found at C:\Windows\System32\LogFiles\SRT\SRTTrail.txt.

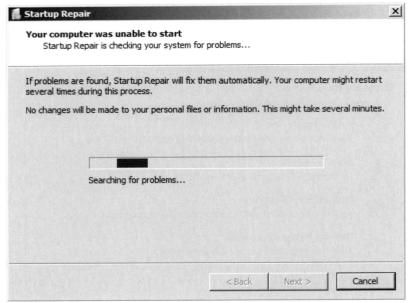

© Cengage Learning 2013

Figure 6-19 Startup Repair searches the system for problems it can fix

© Cengage Learning 2013

Figure 6-20 Startup Repair suggests you use System Restore

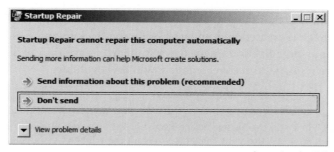

© Cengage Learning 2013

Figure 6-21 Startup Repair has decided it cannot fix the system

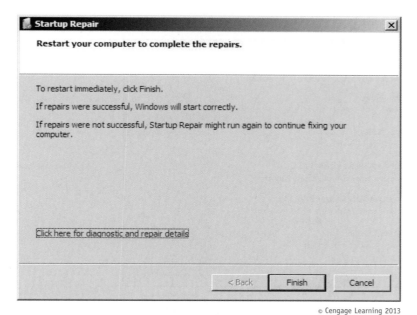

© Cengage Learning 2013

Figure 6-22 Startup Repair has attempted to fix the problem

2. **Windows Memory Diagnostic.** If you suspect memory might be a problem, click this option to identify a corrupted memory module.

3. **System Restore.** Use System Restore to restore the system to a previously saved restore point. This option can sometimes fix a problem with a corrupted device driver,

A+
220-802
4.6

corrupted Windows settings, or corrupted programs. The process will not affect user data. Click **System Restore** and then select a restore point. Select the most recent restore point to make the least intrusive changes to the system.

4. *Command Prompt.* If you suspect the hard drive is corrupted, use the Command Prompt option to open a command prompt window and then use Chkdsk with the /r parameter to check the hard drive for errors. You can also use commands in the Command Prompt window to restore a corrupted registry from a backup. How to use the Windows RE command prompt window is covered later in the chapter.

5. *System Image Recovery.* Use the System Image Recovery as a last resort. It uses a previously created system image to restore the entire Windows volume to this image. Be aware that everything on the Windows volume will be erased and replaced with the system image. Before you use this option, make every attempt to recover from the hard drive any data files that have not yet been backed up. Recall from Chapter 3 that the system image is created and updated using the Backup and Restore window. Also know that your organization might use a standard image or a deployment image rather than a system image to recover a failed Windows volume.

> **Vista Differences** In Vista, the System Image Recovery option is replaced with the Complete PC Restore option (see Figure 6-23). Use it to completely restore the Windows Vista volume and possibly other drives to their state when the last backups of the drives were made. The backups are made using Complete PC Backup, which you learned about in Chapter 3.

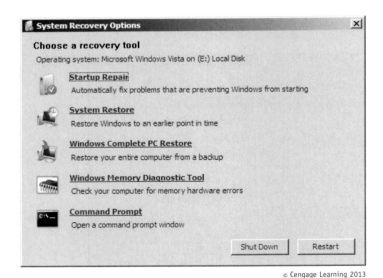

© Cengage Learning 2013

Figure 6-23 Recovery tools in Windows RE for Windows Vista

Now let's see how to use the Windows RE command prompt window.

THE COMMAND PROMPT WINDOW IN WINDOWS RE

A+
220-802
1.3, 4.6

Use the command prompt window in Windows RE when graphical tools available in Windows RE fail to solve the Windows problem. Using this command prompt, you have full read and write access to all files on all drives. Many commands you learned about in

A+
220-802
1.3, 4.6

Chapter 3 can be used at this command prompt. Here are some examples of how to use the Windows RE command prompt to repair a system:

▲ *Repair a hard drive or other drive.* Use the chkdsk and format commands to repair a hard drive. Use the **diskpart** command to manage hard drives, partitions, and volumes. When you enter diskpart at a command prompt, the DISKPART> prompt appears where you can enter diskpart commands. Some important diskpart commands are listed in Table 6-2. Figure 6-24 shows the diskpart commands used to partition and format a USB flash drive. Diskpart can also be used in a normal command prompt window.

Diskpart Command	Description
`list disk`	Lists installed hard disk drives.
`select disk`	Selects a hard disk or other storage device. For example: *select disk 0*
`list partition`	Lists partitions on selected disk.
`select partition`	Selects a partition on the selected disk. For example: *select partition 1*
`clean`	Removes any partition or volume information from the selected disk. Can be useful to remove dynamic disk information or a corrupted partition table or if you just want a fresh start when partitioning a hard disk. All data and partition information on the disk are deleted.
`create partition primary`	Creates a primary partition on the currently selected hard disk.
`assign`	Assigns a drive letter to a new partition. For example: *assign letter=H*
`format`	Formats the currently selected partition. For example: *format fs=ntfs quick* *format fs=fat32*
`active`	Makes the selected partition the active partition.
`inactive`	Makes the selected partition inactive.
`exit`	Exits the Diskpart utility.

Table 6-2   Important diskpart commands used at the DISKPART> prompt

© Cengage Learning 2013

> **Notes**   For a complete list of Diskpart commands, go to the Microsoft support site (*support.microsoft.com*) and search on "DiskPart Command-Line Options."

▲ *Enable networking.* Networking is not normally available from this command prompt. Use the wpeinit command to enable networking.

▲ *Repair the file system and key boot files.* Use the bootrec command to repair the BCD and boot sectors. Use the bcdedit command to manually edit the BCD. Use the bootsect command to repair a dual boot system. Some examples of each command are listed in Table 6-3. To get helpful information about these commands, enter the command followed by /?, such as **bcdedit /?**.

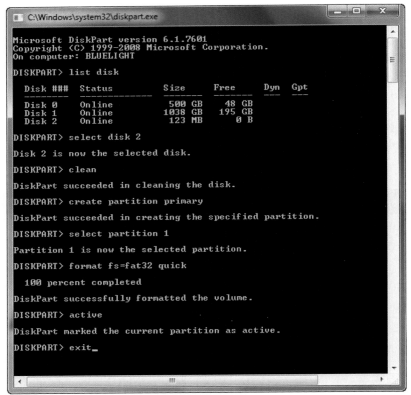

© Cengage Learning 2013

Figure 6-24 Use commands in diskpart to partition and format a USB flash drive

Command Line	Description
bootrec /scanOS	Scans the hard drive for Windows installations not stored in the BCD
bootrec /rebuildBCD	Scans for Windows installations and rebuilds the BCD
bcdedit	Manually edits BCD; be sure to make a copy of the file before you edit it
bootrec /fixboot	Repairs the boot sector of the system partition
bootrec /fixmbr	Repairs the MBR

© Cengage Learning 2013

Table 6-3 Commands used in the command prompt window of Windows RE to repair system files and the file system

> **A+ Exam Tip** The A+ 220-802 exam expects you to know how to use the bootrec and diskpart commands. In addition, it expects you to know about the **FDISK** command, which was part of Windows 9x and was used to create and manage partitions on a hard drive. The FDISK command was launched after booting a computer using a Windows 9x startup floppy disk. The FDISK /MBR command was used to repair a damaged MBR program.

> **XP Differences** The XP **Recovery Console** is similar to the command prompt window in Windows RE. The XP Recovery Console uses the **fixmbr** command to repair the MBR and uses the **fixboot** command to repair the boot sector of the system partition. For more information, see Appendix C.

A+
220-802
1.3, 4.6

◢ *Manage data files and system files.* Use cd, copy, rename, and delete commands to manage data and system files. For example, if key registry files are corrupted or deleted, the system will not start. You can restore registry files using those saved in the C:\Windows\System32\Config\RegBack folder. This RegBack folder contains partial backups of the registry files put there after a successful boot. Use the commands in Table 6-4 to restore the registry files.

Command Line	Description
1. c:	Makes drive C: the current drive.
2. cd \windows\system32\config	Makes the Windows registry folder the current folder.
3. ren default default.save 4. ren sam sam.save 5. ren security security.save 6. ren software software.save 7. ren system system.save	Renames the five registry files.
8. cd regback	Makes the registry backup folder the current folder.
9. copy system c:\windows\system32\config	For hardware problems, first try copying just the System hive from the backup folder to the registry folder and then reboot.
10. copy software c:\windows\system32\config	For software problems, first try copying just the Software hive to the registry folder, and then reboot.
11. copy system c:\windows\system32\config 12. copy software c:\windows\system32\config 13. copy default c:\windows\system32\config 14. copy sam c:\windows\system32\config 15. copy security c:\windows\system32\config	If the problem is still not solved, try copying all five hives to the registry folder and reboot.

Table 6-4 Steps to restore the registry files

© Cengage Learning 2013

After you try each fix, reboot the system to see if the problem is solved before you do the next fix.

XP Differences Windows XP uses an **emergency repair disk** (a floppy disk) to solve problems with missing system files needed for the boot. XP startup error messages that indicate missing system files include "Missing NTLDR" and "Missing Boot.ini." How to create an emergency repair disk and use it to deal with these errors is covered in Appendix C.

A+ Exam Tip The A+ 220-802 exam expects you to know how to use the Windows XP emergency repair disk to repair boot files on an XP system.

6

A+
220-802
1.3, 4.6

Hands-on | Project 6.3 Practice Using the Recovery Environment

Launch Windows RE and then do the following:

1. Execute the Startup Repair process. What were the results?

2. Launch System Restore. What is the most recent restore point? (Do not apply the restore point.)

3. Using the command prompt window, open the Registry Editor. What command did you use? Close the editor.

4. Using the command prompt window, copy a file from your Documents folder to a flash drive. Were you able to copy the file successfully? If not, what error message(s) did you receive?

TROUBLESHOOTING WINDOWS 7/VISTA STARTUP

A+
220-802
4.3, 4.6

This section is written as step-by-step instructions for problem solving, so that you can use it to solve a boot problem with Windows 7/Vista by following the steps. Each step takes you sequentially through the boot process and shows you what to do when the boot fails at that point in the process. Therefore, your first decision in troubleshooting a failed boot is to decide at what point in the boot the failure occurred. Next, you have to decide which tool will be the least invasive to use, yet still will fix the problem. The idea is to make as few changes to your system as possible in order to solve the problem without having to do a lot of work to return the system to normal (such as having to reinstall all your applications). And, as with every computer problem, if user data is at risk, you need to take steps to back up the data as soon as possible in the troubleshooting process.

To determine where in the boot process the failure occurred, we'll focus on these three startup stages of the boot:

▲ *Stage 1: Before the Windows 7 flag or Vista progress bar.* When you see the flag or progress bar appear, you know the Windows kernel, including all critical services and drivers, has loaded. Any problems that occur before this graphic appears are most likely related to corrupt or missing system files or hardware. Your best Windows tools to use for these problems are Startup Repair and System Restore.

▲ *Stage 2: After the flag or progress bar and before logon.* After the flag or progress bar appears, user mode services and drivers are loaded and then the logon screen appears. Problems with these components can best be solved using Startup Repair, the Last Known Good Configuration, System Restore, Safe Mode, Device Manager, and MSconfig.

▲ *Stage 3: After logon.* After the logon screen appears, problems can be caused by startup scripts, applications set to launch at startup, and desktop settings. Use MSconfig to temporarily disable startup programs. Safe Mode can also be useful.

💡 **A+ Exam Tip** The A+ 220-802 exam expects you to know how to deal with errors that occur when the graphical interface fails to load.

Now let's take a closer look at how to address problems at each of the three stages of Windows startup.

PROBLEMS AT STAGE 1: BEFORE THE FLAG OR PROGRESS BAR APPEARS

These problems might be caused by hardware or startup files. Hardware that might be failing includes the power supply, motherboard, CPU, memory, hard drive, video, or keyboard. If any one of these devices is not working, the error is communicated using beep codes, or using on-screen or voice error messages—and then the computer halts.

> **💡 A+ Exam Tip** The A+ 220-802 exam expects you to know how to troubleshoot problems with hardware, including how to replace the motherboard, memory modules, hard drive, CPU, and power supply. This content on troubleshooting hardware is in the companion book, *A+ Guide to Hardware*. You can also find this content online at our textbook's companion web site at *www.cengagebrain.com*. For more information about accessing the site, see the Preface. This book, *A+ Guide to Software,* and the online content about hardware together cover all the content on the A+ 220-802 exam.

As you perform each troubleshooting step, be sure to restart the system to see if the problem is solved before you apply the next step.

IS THE SCREEN BLANK?

If you see absolutely nothing on the screen, check these things:

◢ Is the monitor totally without lights, or is the screen blank but the LED light on front of the monitor is lit? If the LED light is lit, try rebooting the system. If the LED light is not lit, check that power is getting to the monitor. Is it turned on?

◢ Can you hear the spinning fan or hard drive inside the computer case? Are lights lit on the front of the case? If not, suspect that power is not getting to the system or the system might have overheated.

◢ Check that the system is not in standby mode or hibernation: try waking up the system by pressing any key or a special standby key on laptops or by pressing the power-on button.

◢ Try trading the monitor for one you know is good. If you can hear a spinning drive and see lights on the front of the computer case and know the monitor works, the video card might be bad or not seated properly in its slot, the memory might be bad, the video cable might be bad or loosely connected, or a component on the motherboard might have failed.

DOES THE COMPUTER APPEAR TO HAVE POWER?

If you can't hear the spinning drive or see lights on the front of the case, suspect the electrical system. Check power connections and switches. The power supply might be bad or connections inside the case might be loose.

DOES AN ERROR MESSAGE APPEAR BEFORE WINDOWS STARTS?

Recall that when you first turn on a system, startup BIOS takes control, checks essential hardware devices, and searches for an OS to load. If it has a problem while doing all that and the video system is working, it displays an error message on-screen. If video is not working, it might attempt to communicate an error with a series of beep codes or speech (for speech-enabled BIOS). Restart the system and carefully listen for and count the beeps. Then you can look up what they mean on the web site of the motherboard manufacturer.

For messages displayed on-screen that apply to nonessential hardware devices such as a DVD drive, you might be able to bypass the error by pressing a key and moving forward in the boot. However, for errors with essential hardware devices such as the one shown in Figure 6-25, focus your attention on the error message, beep code, or voice message describing the problem. If you don't know what the error message or beep codes mean, you can search the web site of the motherboard manufacturer or do a general search of the web using a search engine such as Google.

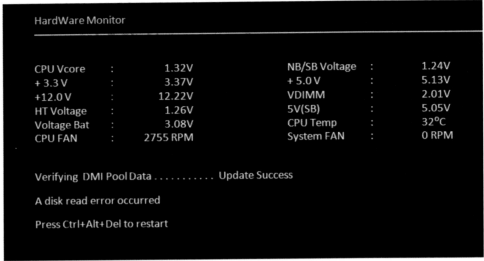

© Cengage Learning 2013

Figure 6-25 This error message at POST indicates a hardware problem

CAN STARTUP BIOS ACCESS THE HARD DRIVE?

Error messages generated by startup BIOS that pertain to the hard drive can be caused by a variety of things. Here is a list of text error messages that indicate that BIOS could not find a hard drive:

- Hard drive not found
- Fixed disk error
- Disk boot failure, insert system disk and press enter
- No boot device available

The problem might be a physical problem with the drive, the data cable, power, or the motherboard. Start with checking BIOS setup to verify that BIOS detected the drive correctly. If the drive was not detected, check the autodetection setting in BIOS setup. If autodetection is turned off, turn it on and reboot. Your problem might be solved. If startup BIOS still doesn't find the drive, power down the system, unplug it, and open the case. Physically check the hard drive power and data cable connections at both ends. Sometimes cables work their way loose. Be careful not to touch circuit boards or the processor as you work, and to protect the system against static electricity, wear an antistatic bracelet that is clipped to the computer case.

Here is a list of error messages that indicate the BIOS was able to find the hard drive but couldn't read what was written on the drive or could not find what it was looking for:

- A disk read error occurred
- Drive not recognized

A+
220-802
4.3, 4.6

◢ Invalid boot disk

◢ Invalid partition table

◢ Inaccessible boot device

◢ Invalid drive specification

◢ Invalid partition table

◢ Operating system not found, No operating system found, Missing operating system, Error loading operating system

◢ Couldn't find bootmgr or bootmgr is missing

> **A+ Exam Tip** The A+ 220-802 exam expects you to be able to resolve a problem that gives the error messages "Drive not recognized" or "OS not found."

For these types of error messages, try the following:

1. Try to press **F8** at startup and launch the Advanced Boot Options menu. This menu cannot load if the system cannot access the hard drive. But at least give it a try before you move on to the tools on the Windows setup DVD.

2. Check BIOS setup to make sure the boot sequence lists the DVD drive before the hard drive, and then boot from the Windows setup DVD.

6

> **Notes** To access BIOS setup, reboot the PC and look on-screen for a message such as "Press DEL for setup," "Press F2 for BIOS settings," or something similar. Press that key and the BIOS setup utility loads. Find the screen, such as the one in Figure 6-26, that lets you set the boot sequence. (If you cannot find the key to press to access BIOS setup, search the web using the computer's brand and model.)

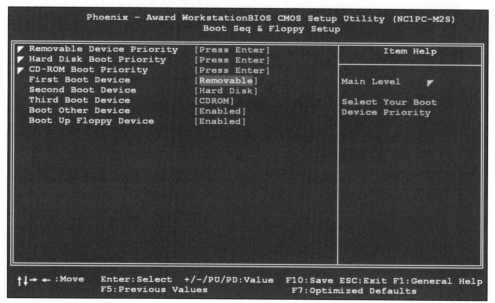

Figure 6-26 Set the boot order in BIOS setup

Hands-on | Project 6.4 Practice Solving Boot Problems

This project is best done on a lab computer rather than your personal computer. Power down the computer, unplug it, open the case, and disconnect the data cable to your hard drive. (If you are not trained to work inside a computer, ask your instructor for assistance opening the case and disconnecting the hard drive data cable.) Turn the computer back on and boot the system. What error message did you see? Now reboot using your Windows setup DVD. Try to load Windows RE. What error messages did you receive, if any? Power down your computer, unplug it, and reconnect your hard drive. Reboot and verify that Windows loads successfully.

CAN YOU BOOT FROM THE WINDOWS SETUP DVD?

Try to boot from the Windows setup DVD. If you cannot boot from this disc, the problem is not just the hard drive. Study the error message and solve the immediate hardware problem. It's possible the hard drive and the optical drive have failed, but a USB port might still work. If you have a bootable USB flash drive, you can try booting from it. If you can boot from the flash drive, you have proven the problem is with both the hard drive and the optical drive.

If you are able to boot from the Windows setup DVD, the window shown in Figure 6-27 appears. If you see this window, you have proven that the problem is isolated to the hard drive. Now the trick is to find out exactly what is wrong with the drive and fix it.

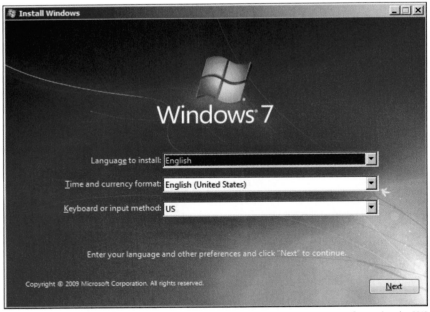

© Cengage Learning 2013

Figure 6-27 Select your language preference

CAN WINDOWS RE FIND THE WINDOWS INSTALLATION?

At this point, click **Next** in Figure 6-27 and then click **Repair your computer** to attempt to launch Windows RE. The first thing Windows RE does is attempt to locate a Windows installation on the hard drive. If it cannot locate the installation, but BIOS setup recognizes the drive, then the drive partitions and file systems might be corrupted. If Windows RE does locate the installation, the problem is more likely to be limited to corrupted or missing system files or drivers.

As you attempt each fix in the following list, be sure to restart the system after each step to find out if the problem still exists or has changed:

1. Run Startup Repair. This process can sometimes fix drastic problems with system files and boot records.

2. Run System Restore. The process won't help if the file system is corrupted.

3. Restart the system and press **F8** during the boot to launch the Advanced Boot Options menu, as shown earlier in Figure 6-6. If the boot menu does not appear, chances are the problem is a corrupted boot sector. If the boot menu appears, chances are the BCD file or other startup files are the problem. If you do see the menu, enable boot logging and reboot. Then check the boot log (\Windows\ntbtlog.txt) for the last entry, which might indicate which system file is missing or corrupt. (If the hard drive is at all accessible, your best chance of viewing the boot log file is to use the command prompt window and the Type command.)

4. If the boot menu does not appear, return to Windows RE, launch the command prompt window, and attempt to repair the boot sector. Try these commands: **bootrec /fixmbr** and **bootrec /fixboot**. Also try the **diskpart** command followed by the **list volume** command. Does the OS find the system volume? If not, the entire partition might be lost.

5. If the boot menu does appear, return to Windows RE, launch the command prompt window, and attempt to repair the BCD file. Try this command: **bootrec /rebuildbcd**.

6. Try to repair a corrupted file system by using the command prompt window and the **chkdsk c: /r** command.

7. When startup files are missing or corrupt, sometimes Windows displays an error message similar to the one shown in Figure 6-28, which names the file giving the problem. You can replace the file by going to a healthy Windows computer and copying the file to a removable media. Then, on the problem computer, boot to Windows RE, open the command prompt window, and rename the original file so you will not overwrite it with the replacement and you can backtrack if necessary. Then copy the replacement file to the hard drive.

6

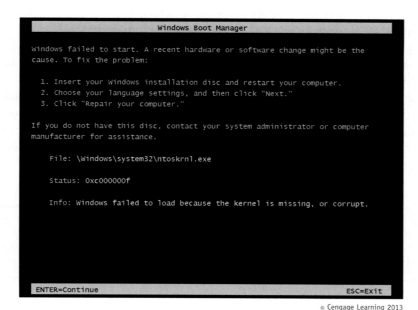

© Cengage Learning 2013

Figure 6-28 Windows might display a screen similar to this one when a critical startup file is missing or corrupt

A+
220-802
4.3, 4.6

8. Try using the command prompt window to access drive C:. If you can get to a C: prompt, use the **dir** command to list folders and files. If you see a good list, check the log file, C:\Windows\System32\LogFiles\SRT\SRTTrail.txt, for clues. (Recall this log file is kept by the Startup Repair process of Windows RE.) If you cannot get a good list of contents of drive C:, most likely the Windows installation is destroyed beyond repair. Before you address the problem of a corrupted Windows installation, make every effort to copy data to another media. You can use copy commands in the Windows RE command prompt window or move the drive to a working computer to copy files.

Hands-on | Project 6.5   Use Windows RE to Solve a Startup Problem

Using Windows Explorer, rename the BootMgr file in the root directory of drive C:. Reboot the system. What error message do you see? Now use Windows RE to restore the BootMgr file. List the steps taken to complete the repair.

A+
220-802
1.7, 4.3
4.6

OPTIONS TO RECOVER FROM A CORRUPTED WINDOWS INSTALLATION

If you are not able to repair the corrupted installation using the techniques in the previous list, your next step is to consider what options are available to restore the system. Your options depend on backups available, including a backup of user data and a backup of the Windows 7 system image or a Vista Complete PC backup. The system image or Complete PC backup is a backup of the Windows volume and is called a recovery image. Here are your choices to restore a corrupted installation:

▲ *Option 1:* If you have a recovery image, use it to restore the system to the last backup. If data is on the hard drive that has not been backed up, make every effort to copy this data to a safe place before you restore the system. To start the recovery, boot into Windows RE. For Windows 7, on the System Recovery Options screen, click **System Image Recovery** and follow the directions on-screen. (For Vista, click **Windows Complete PC Restore** on the System Recovery Options screen.)

▲ *Option 2:* If you don't have a recovery image but you do have backups of the data on the hard drive, reinstall Windows, formatting the hard drive during the installation. You'll need to install all applications again and then restore the data.

▲ *Option 3:* If you don't have a recovery image and you also don't have backups of the data on the drive (worst-case scenario), try to copy the data and then reinstall Windows. Even if you cannot copy the data, you might be able to recover it after the reinstallation. If you have data on the Windows volume, don't format during the Windows installation.

Notes If you cannot start Windows and there is important data on the drive, consider moving the hard drive to another computer and installing it as a second device. Then boot the computer and copy data from the drive to another storage device. You can then return the hard drive to its original computer and reinstall Windows, formatting the drive during the installation process.

A+
220-802
1.7, 4.3,
4.6

XP Differences Windows XP can make a backup of the entire Windows volume using the Automated System Recovery tool. To restore the Windows volume, you need the ASR floppy disk, the ASR backup, and the XP setup CD. For details, see Appendix C.

STEPS TO REINSTALL WINDOWS

Recall from Chapter 2 that you can install Windows from the Windows setup DVD, from a standard image, or from a deployment image. For a network deployment of Windows, recall that you must boot the computer to the network where it finds and loads Windows PE on the deployment server. To boot to the network, go into BIOS setup and set the first boot device to be Ethernet. The PC then boots to the Pre-Execution Environment (PXE) and then PXE searches for a server on the network for Windows PE and the deployment image.

A+ Exam Tip The A+ 220-802 exam expects you to know how to use a pre installation environment and a recovery image to help resolve a Windows startup problem.

6

Follow these steps to reinstall Windows using the Windows setup DVD when the OS refuses to boot and there is important data on the drive:

1. Boot from the Windows setup DVD, and follow the directions on-screen to perform a clean installation of Windows, but do not format the hard drive. Windows setup will move all folders of the old installation into the \Windows.Old folder, including the \Windows, \Users, and \Program Files folders. A fresh, clean installation of Windows is installed in the \Windows folder.

2. If you suspect the hard drive might be failing or need reformatting, immediately save all important data to another media and reinstall Windows a second time, this time reformatting the hard drive. If you believe the hard drive is healthy, then follow these steps to get things back to their original order:

   a. Run Chkdsk to fix errors on the drive.

   b. Install all applications and device drivers.

   c. Create all user accounts and customize Windows settings. How to create user accounts is covered in Chapter 2. Then copy all user data and other folders from the \Windows.Old folder to the new installation.

   d. To free up disk space, delete the \Windows.Old folder. To do that, using the Disk Cleanup utility in the Properties box for drive C:, select **Previous Windows installation(s)** (see Figure 6-29). Note that this option will not be available if the \Windows.Old folder does not exist.

A+
220-802
1.7, 4.3,
4.6

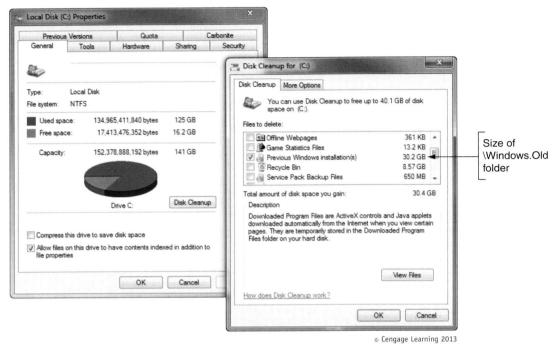

© Cengage Learning 2013

Figure 6-29 Free up disk space by deleting the \Windows.Old folder, which is labeled as Previous Windows installation(s)

> **Notes** Remember that when reinstalling Windows on a laptop or brand-name computer, use the hidden recovery partition on the hard drive or recovery discs so that you have access to proprietary device drivers the system might use.

> **⚡ Caution** When you first become responsible for a laptop computer, it's extremely important that you create or obtain the recovery DVD or CDs that you will need in case the hard drive crashes. Without this recovery media, it's almost impossible to recover the system using a new hard drive. And, laptop manufacturers don't make these media available to customers after the laptop is a few years old. Get the recovery media in hand while it is still available! You might be able to create the media from the hard drive while the system is still healthy. See the laptop documentation for instructions.

A+
220-802
4.3, 4.6

PROBLEMS AT STAGE 2: AFTER THE FLAG OR PROGRESS BAR APPEARS AND BEFORE LOGON

When you see the Windows 7 flag or the Vista progress bar appear during the boot, you know the Windows kernel has loaded successfully and critical drivers and services configured to be started by the kernel are running. You also know the Session Manager (Smss.exe) running in user mode has started the Win32 subsystem necessary to provide the graphics of the flag or progress bar. If the flag or progress bar has appeared and the logon screen has not yet been displayed, most likely the problem is caused by a corrupted driver or service that is started after the kernel has finished its part of the boot. Your general attack plan to fix the problem is to isolate and disable the Windows component, service, or application causing trouble. However, if user data on the hard drive is not backed up, do what you can to copy that data to another media before you focus on the problem at hand.

A+
220-802
4.3, 4.6

Follow these steps:

1. Press **F8** at startup to launch the Advanced Boot Options menu and then try to boot into **Safe Mode**. If you don't know the source of the problem, here are some things you can try in Safe Mode to discover the source and hopefully solve the problem:

   ◢ *Tip 1:* Immediately run antivirus software to eliminate a virus as the problem.

   ◢ *Tip 2:* Run **chkdsk c: /r** to check and repair the hard drive.

   ◢ *Tip 3:* Examine the logs in Event Viewer for errors that might point to the problem.

   > **Notes** The Last Known Good Configuration is updated after you log on normally to Windows. However, logging onto a computer when booting into Safe Mode does not update the Last Known Good.

   ◢ *Tip 4:* Use MSconfig to stop any applications just installed. Then uninstall and reinstall the application. You can also disable all non essential programs and services.

   ◢ *Tip 5:* Use Device Manager to check for hardware errors and disable any devices just installed. If you have just updated a driver, roll back the driver.

   ◢ *Tip 6:* In Safe Mode, use System Information (msinfo32.exe) to find the program filenames of drivers and services. Useful information can be found at these locations: Services in the Software Environment group and Problem Devices in the Components group.

   > **♀ A+ Exam Tip** The A+ 220-802 exam expects you to know how to use System Information to help you resolve a Windows startup problem.

   ◢ *Tip 7:* Open an elevated command prompt window and use the System File Checker (SFC) tool to search for and replace corrupted system files. The command **sfc /scannow** searches for and replaces corrupted system files. Be sure to restart the system after this command is finished.

   ◢ *Tip 8:* If you have an Ntbtlog.txt file from a normal boot, compare the entries in the Ntbtlog.txt file when booting in Safe Mode to the entries when booting normally. Consider that the culprit might be any item that is loaded for a normal boot but not loaded for Safe Mode. Disable each driver one at a time until the problem goes away.

   ◢ *Tip 9:* Rename the Ntbtlog.txt file so it will not be overwritten during a normal boot and you can read it later.

2. If you cannot boot into Safe Mode, select the **Last Known Good Configuration** on the Advanced Boot Options menu. It's important to try this option early in the troubleshooting process because you might accidentally overwrite a good Last Known Good with a bad one as you attempt to log on with the problem still there.

3. Launch Windows RE from the Windows setup DVD and run **Startup Repair** from the System Recovery Options menu shown earlier in Figure 6-18. It can't do any harm, it's easy to use, and it might fix the problem.

4. In Windows RE, run **System Restore**. Select the latest restore point. If that doesn't fix the problem, try an earlier one.

6

5. Boot to the Advanced Boot Options menu and select **Enable Boot Logging**. Windows starts logging information to the log file WindowsNtbtlog.txt. Every driver that is loaded or not loaded is written to the file (see Figure 6-14 shown earlier in the chapter).

6. Compare the Ntbtlog.txt file to one that was created in Safe Mode. If the boot failed, look at the last entry in the Ntbtlog.txt file that was generated. Find that entry in the one created while booting into Safe Mode. The next driver listed in the Safe Mode Ntbtlog.txt file is likely the one giving problems.

7. After you believe you've identified the problem service or device, if you can boot into Safe Mode, first use Device Manager to disable the device or use the Services console to disable the service. Then reboot, and, if the problem goes away, replace the driver or service program file and then enable the driver or service.

8. If you cannot boot into Safe Mode, open the command prompt window in Windows RE. Then back up the registry and open the Registry Editor using the regedit command. Drill down to the service or device key. The key that loads services and drivers can be found in this location:

HKEY_LOCAL_MACHINE\System\CurrentControlSet\Services

9. Disable the service or driver by changing the Start value to 0x4. Close the Registry Editor and reboot. If the problem goes away, use the copy command to replace the service or driver program file, and restart the service or driver.

PROBLEMS AT STAGE 3: AFTER WINDOWS LOGON

Problems that occur after the user logs onto Windows are caused by applications or services configured to launch at startup. Programs can be set to launch at startup by placing their shortcuts in startup folders, by Scheduled Tasks, or by software installation processes that affect registry entries. If you see an error message at startup that gives you a clue as to which service or program is at fault, test your theory by using MSconfig to disable that program. You can also disable all non-Microsoft services and programs and enable them one at a time until you find the one causing the problem.

Table 6-5 summarizes some symptoms and error messages, including blue screen stop errors you might encounter during the boot and what to do about them. Remember that stop errors most likely point to a hardware or driver problem.

Symptom or Error Message	Description and What to Do
A disk read error occurred Non-system disk or disk error Invalid boot disk	Startup BIOS could not communicate with the hard drive. Check BIOS setup for the boot sequence and try to boot from another device. Check drive cables and connections. The drive might be failing. To recover data from the drive, move it to another computer and install it as a second hard drive.
Loud clicking noise	The hard drive is likely failing. Make it your first priority to back up any data on the drive.
Invalid partition table Invalid drive specification Error loading operating system Missing operating system Drive not recognized	MBR record is damaged or the active partition is corrupt or missing. Use the repair commands from the Windows RE command prompt window.

© Cengage Learning 2013

Table 6-5 Error messages during Windows startup and what to do about them (continues)

A+
220-802
4.3, 4.6

Symptom or Error Message	Description and What to Do
Operating system not found Missing operating system Missing bootmgr	Windows system files are missing or corrupted. Boot to Windows RE and use tools there. First try Startup Repair. Use Chkdsk to fix hard drive errors.
RAID not found	Hardware RAID is managed by BIOS on the motherboard. Check the web site of the motherboard manufacturer for help with the exact error message. You might need to update BIOS.
Automatically boots into Safe Mode	This action can occur when Windows recognizes a problem with the registry or other startup files. Attempt to use Last Known Good on the Advanced Boot Options menu, or use System Restore to apply a restore point.
No graphics appear when Windows is started	An error that occurs before the Graphical Interface is started is caused by hardware or the Windows kernel failing to load. To solve problems with critical startup files that load the Windows kernel, use the tools in Windows RE.
An application launched at startup that gives errors or takes up resources	Use Msconfig to remove it from the list of startup programs.
Stop error (BSOD) that occurs during startup	A Stop error can be caused by a corrupted registry, a system file that is missing or damaged, a device driver that is missing or damaged, bad memory, or a corrupted or failing hard drive. Use the Microsoft web site to research the exact error message and error code. Use the Startup Repair tool and then examine the log file it creates at C:\Windows\System32\LogFiles\Srt\Srttrail.txt.

Table 6-5 Error messages during Windows startup and what to do about them (continued) © Cengage Learning 2013

6

HOW TO RECOVER LOST DATA

When data is lost or corrupted, you might be able to recover it using Windows tools, third-party file recovery software, or commercial data recovery services. This section discusses your options to recover lost data.

RECOVER A DELETED OR CORRUPTED DATA FILE

Here are some things to try to recover a deleted or corrupted data file:

◢ If you have accidentally deleted a data file, to get it back, look in the Recycle Bin. Drag and drop the file back to where it belongs, or right-click the file and click **Restore** on the shortcut menu.

◢ If a data file is corrupted, you can restore it from backup using the Backup and Restore window or using the Previous Versions tab on the file's Properties box, as you learned to do in Chapter 3.

◢ You might recover a corrupted file using the Recover command. To use the command, the volume on which the file is located cannot be in use. The easiest way to do that is to boot into Windows RE and open a command prompt window. For example, Figure 6-30 shows the command **recover C:\Data\Mydata.txt**. Notice in the figure that the C: drive is not the current drive. The drive is not used when you load Windows RE, and drive C: is not the current or default drive.

A+
220-802
4.3, 4.6

```
Administrator: X:\windows\system32\cmd.exe - recover C:\data\mydata.txt        _ □ X
Microsoft Windows [Version 6.1.7600]

X:\windows\system32>recover C:\data\mydata.txt
The type of the file system is NTFS.

Press ENTER to begin recovery of the file on drive C:

_
```

© Cengage Learning 2013

Figure 6-30   Use the Recover command to recover a corrupted file while the volume on which
                   it is stored is not in use

▲ If an application's data file gets corrupted, go to the web site of the application
  manufacturer and search the support section for what to do to recover the file. For
  example, if an Excel workbook file gets corrupted, search the Knowledge Base at
  support.microsoft.com for solutions.

▲ Third-party software can help recover deleted and corrupted files. On the Internet, do
  a search on "data recovery" for lots of examples. One good product is GetDataBack
  by Runtime Software (*www.runtime.org*), which can recover data and program files
  even when Windows cannot recognize the drive. It can read FAT and NTFS file
  systems and can solve problems with a corrupted partition table, boot record, or
  root directory.

RECOVER DATA FROM A COMPUTER THAT WILL NOT BOOT

If Windows is corrupted and the system will not boot, recovering your data might be your
first priority. One way to get to the data is to remove your hard drive from your computer
and install it as a second nonbooting hard drive in another system. After you boot up the
system, you should be able to use Windows Explorer to copy the data to another medium.
If the data is corrupted, try to use data recovery software.

For less than $30, you can purchase an IDE to USB converter kit (see Figure 6-31) or a
SATA to USB converter kit (see Figure 6-32) that includes a data cable and power adapter.
(For notebook hard drives, the IDE to USB kit needs to include an adapter for these smaller
drives. This extra adapter is not needed for SATA notebook hard drives because these SATA
connectors are the same size as those used for desktop drives.) You can use one of these

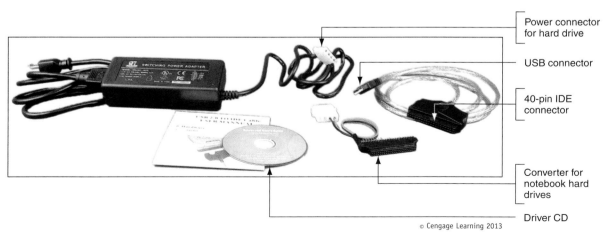

Power connector
for hard drive

USB connector

40-pin IDE
connector

Converter for
notebook hard
drives

Driver CD

© Cengage Learning 2013

Figure 6-31   Use an IDE to USB converter for diagnostic testing and to recover data from a failing IDE hard drive

A+
220-802
4.3, 4.6

kits to temporarily connect a desktop or notebook hard drive to a USB port on a working computer. Set the drive beside your computer and plug one end of the data cable into the drive and the other into the USB port. (For an IDE drive, a jumper on the drive must be set to the master setting.) The AC adapter supplies power to the drive. While power is getting to the drive, be careful to not touch the circuit board on the drive.

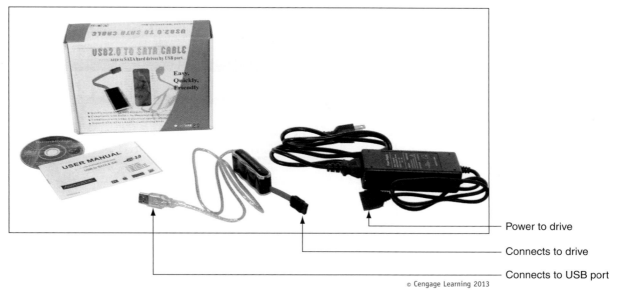

Power to drive
Connects to drive
Connects to USB port

© Cengage Learning 2013

Figure 6-32   Use a SATA to USB converter to recover data from a drive using a SATA connector

Using Windows Explorer, you can browse the drive and copy data to other media. After you have saved the data, use Disk Management to try to repartition and reformat the drive. You can also use diagnostic software from the hard drive manufacturer to examine the drive and possibly repair it.

USE A DATA RECOVERY SERVICE

If your data is extremely valuable and other methods have failed, you might want to consider a professional data recovery service. They're expensive, but getting the data back might be worth it. To find a service, use Google.com and search on "data recovery." Before selecting a service, be sure to read up on reviews, understand the warranty and guarantees, and perhaps get a recommendation from a satisfied customer.

Hands-on | Project 6.6   **Research a Windows Startup Problem**

When you log onto your Windows 7 computer, you notice all the shortcuts on your desktop are missing and a bubble like the one in Figure 6-33 appears. You open Event Viewer and find related errors logged (see Figure 6-34). Using the web for research, suggest the most likely cause of the problem and possible solutions.

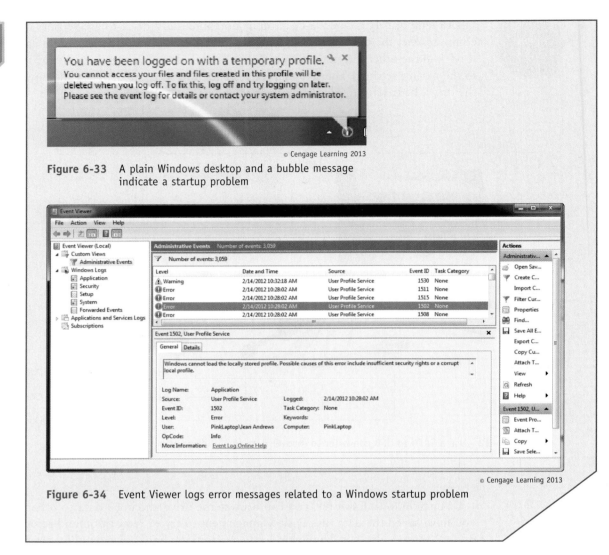

© Cengage Learning 2013

Figure 6-33 A plain Windows desktop and a bubble message indicate a startup problem

© Cengage Learning 2013

Figure 6-34 Event Viewer logs error messages related to a Windows startup problem

>> CHAPTER SUMMARY

Understanding the Boot Process

◢ When you first turn on a system, startup BIOS on the motherboard takes control to examine hardware components and find an operating system to load.

◢ Windows 7/Vista startup is managed by the Windows Boot Manager (BootMgr) and the Windows Boot Loader (WinLoad.exe). The Boot Configuration Data (BCD) file contains Windows startup settings.

Windows 7/Vista Tools for Solving Startup Problems

◢ The Advanced Boot Options menu offers the options to repair your computer, Safe Mode, Safe Mode with networking, Safe Mode with command prompt, enable boot logging, enable low-resolution video (enable VGA mode in Windows XP), Last Known Good Configuration, directory services restore mode, debugging mode, and disable automatic restart on system failure.

◢ The Windows Recovery Environment (Windows RE) can be started from the Windows 7/Vista setup DVD, the Windows 7 Advanced Boot Options menu, and by booting from a Windows 7 repair disc.

◢ Startup Repair in Windows RE can automatically fix many Windows problems, including those caused by a corrupted BCD file and missing system files. You can't cause any additional problems by using it and it's easy to use. Therefore, it should be your first recovery option when Windows refuses to load.

◢ Other tools in Windows RE include Memory Diagnostics, System Restore, a command prompt window, and System Image Recovery. This last tool is used to restore Windows using a system image.

◢ Commands that might be useful when repairing Windows include Bootrec, Bcdedit, Diskpart, Bootsect, and Chkdsk.

Troubleshooting Windows 7/Vista Startup

◢ Windows tools and techniques used to troubleshoot a failed boot include Last Known Good Configuration, Startup Repair, System Restore, Safe Mode, Command Prompt, in-place upgrade of Windows, reimaging the hard drive, and reinstalling Windows.

◢ Last Known Good Configuration can solve problems caused by a bad hardware or software installation by undoing the install.

◢ Use the command prompt window in Windows RE when the other RE tools fail to solve the problem.

◢ Your first decision in troubleshooting a failed Windows boot is to decide at what point in the boot the failure occurred. Determine if the failure occurred before the Windows 7 flag or Vista progress bar appears, after the flag or progress bar and before logon, or after logon.

◢ If a hard drive contains valuable data but will not boot, you might be able to recover the data by installing the drive in another system as the second, nonbooting hard drive in the system.

6

>> KEY TERMS

Advanced Options menu	emergency repair disk	recovery image
bcdedit	FDISK	soft boot
Boot Configuration Data (BCD) file	fixboot	system repair disc
	fixmbr	warm boot
booting	hard boot	Windows Boot Loader (WinLoad.exe)
Boot.ini	Last Known Good Configuration	
bootrec	Ntldr	Windows Boot Manager (BootMgr)
bootsect	OS boot record	
cold boot	POST (power-on self test)	Windows Recovery Environment (Windows RE)
diskpart	Recovery Console	

>> REVIEW QUESTIONS

1. What test does startup BIOS perform when you first turn on a computer to verify it can communicate with essential hardware devices?

2. Where is the partition table on a hard drive found?

3. Is the BootMgr file stored in the boot partition or the system partition?

4. Where is the master boot record (MBR) located?

5. What is the name of the Windows 7 boot loader program? Where is the program located?

6. What is the name of the Windows 7 kernel program?

7. What is the name of the program that manages Windows logon?

8. Which registry hive is loaded first during Windows startup?

9. Where does Windows store device driver files?

10. During Windows 7 startup, how can you know when the Windows kernel has loaded successfully?

11. Blue screen errors happen when which type of processes encounter an error?

12. What method can you use to test memory on a Windows XP system by using the Windows 7 Memory Diagnostics tool without having to install Windows 7 on the system?

13. What is the command to use the System File Checker to immediately verify system files? To verify system files on the next restart?

14. Which key do you press to launch the Advanced Boot Options window during Windows startup?

15. A blue screen error halts the system while it is booting, and the booting starts over in an endless loop of restarts. How can you solve this problem using the Advanced Boot Options screen?

16. What can you assume about the Windows 7 startup when you see the Windows 7 flag on-screen?

17. When is the Windows startup process completed?

18. At what point in Windows startup are the settings that are called the Last Known Good Configuration saved?

19. What command in Windows RE can you use to rebuild the BCD file?

20. What command in Windows RE gives you the opportunity to manage partitions and volumes installed on the system?

21. Which log in Event Viewer only tracks errors and warnings?

22. If you are having a problem with a driver, which of the following is the least invasive solution: update the driver or use System Restore?

23. What are the three stages of the Windows 7/Vista startup process?

24. What is the name of the log file and its location that created when you enabled boot logging from the Advanced Boot Options startup menu?

25. What information is contained in the C:\Windows\System32\LogFiles\SRT\SRTTrail.txt file?

>> THINKING CRITICALLY

1. When the Windows 7 registry is corrupted and you cannot boot from the hard drive, what tool or method is the best option to fix the problem?

   a. Boot into Safe Mode and use System Restore to repair the registry.

   b. Use the Last Known Good Configuration on the Advanced Boot Options menu.

   c. Use commands from the Windows Recovery Environment to recover the registry from backup.

   d. Reinstall Windows 7 using a system image.

2. Your Windows 7 system boots to a blue screen stop error and no desktop. What do you do first?

   a. Reinstall Windows 7.

   b. Attempt to boot into the Advanced Boot Options menu.

   c. Attempt to boot into Windows RE using the Windows setup DVD.

   d. Verify the system is getting power.

3. You have important data on your hard drive that is not backed up and your Windows installation is so corrupted you know that you must repair the entire installation. What do you do first? Explain your answer.

   a. Use System Restore.

   b. Make every attempt to recover the data.

   c. Perform an in-place upgrade of Windows 7.

   d. Reformat the hard drive and reinstall Windows 7.

4. Your computer displays the error message "A disk read error occurred." You try to boot from the Windows setup DVD and you get the same error. What is most likely the problem?

   a. The Windows setup DVD is scratched or damaged in some way.

   b. The hard drive is so damaged the system cannot read from the DVD.

   c. Both the optical drive and the hard drive have failed.

   d. Boot device order is set to boot from the hard drive before the optical drive.

5. When a driver is giving problems in Windows, which tool offers the least intrusive solution?

   a. Device Manager

   b. System Restore

   c. System image recovery

   d. Last Known Good configuration

6. An error message is displayed during Windows 7 startup (before the flag appears) about a service that has failed to start, and then the system locks up. You try to boot into Safe Mode, but get the same error message. What do you try first? Second?

   a. Use the command prompt to edit the registry.

   b. Select the Last Known Good Configuration on the Advanced Boot Options menu.

   c. Perform an in-place upgrade of Windows 7.

   d. Boot to Windows RE and perform a Startup Repair.

>> REAL PROBLEMS, REAL SOLUTIONS

REAL PROBLEM 6-1: Sabotage a Windows 7 System

In a lab environment, follow these steps to find out if you can corrupt a Windows 7 system so that it will not boot, and then repair the system. (This problem can be done using a Windows 7 installation in a virtual machine.)

1. Rename or move one of the program files listed in Table 6-1. Which program file did you select? In what folder did you find it?

2. Restart your system. Did an error occur? Check in Explorer. Is the file restored? What Windows feature repaired the problem?

3. Try other methods of sabotaging the Windows 7 system, but carefully record exactly what you did to sabotage the boot. Can you make the boot fail?

4. Now recover the Windows 7 system. List the steps you took to get the system back to good working order.

REAL PROBLEM 6-2: Building a Standard Image

Now that you know how to install Windows (covered in Chapter 2), use a command prompt window (covered in Chapter 3), and use the Diskpart command (covered in this chapter), you have the skills you need to build a standard image. Recall from Chapter 2 that a standard image can be used to deploy Windows in a corporate environment using a bootable USB flash drive or other bootable media that contains Windows setup files and all the applications and Windows settings that are standard for the organization. Appendix D covers how to create a standard image. Follow the instructions in Appendix D to create a standard image on a bootable USB flash drive.

REAL PROBLEM 6-3: Fixing a Computer Problem

In the last chapter, you began solving computer problems for your friends and family. Helping others and jumping into real computer troubleshooting is the best way to learn. Continue to make yourself available to family and friends who have problems with their computers. For each problem, don't forget to follow the procedures for troubleshooting you have learned in this book, especially the one about backing up user data before you make any changes to a system. For two new problems you face, keep a record that includes this information:

1. Describe the problem as the user described it to you.

2. Briefly list the things you did to discover the cause of the problem.

3. What was the final solution?

4. How long did it take you to fix the problem?

5. What would you do differently the next time you encounter this same problem?

6. Did you learn anything new in solving the problem? If so, briefly describe what you learned.

Connecting to and Setting Up a Network

In this chapter, you'll learn how Windows uses TCP/IP protocols and standards to create and manage network connections, includ- ing how computers are identified and addressed on a network. You'll also learn to connect a computer to a network and how to set up and secure a small wired or wireless network.

This chapter prepares you to assume total responsibility for supporting both wired and wireless networks in a small-office-home- office (SOHO) environment. In the next chapter, you learn how to support applications using a network and how to troubleshoot networking problems. So let's get started by looking at how TCP/IP works in the world of Windows networking.

A+ Exam Tip Much of the content in this chapter applies to both the A+ 220-801 exam and the A+ 220-802 exam.

UNDERSTANDING TCP/IP AND WINDOWS NETWORKING

A+
220-801
2.3

A+
220-802
1.6

When two computers communicate using a local network or the Internet, communication happens at three levels (hardware, operating system, and application). The first step in communication is one computer must find the other computer. The second step is both computers must agree on the methods and rules for communication (called **protocols**). Then one computer takes on the role of making requests from the other computer. A computer making a request from another is called the client and the one answering the request is called the server. Most communication between computers on a network or the Internet uses this **client/server** model. For example, in Figure 7-1, someone uses a web browser to request a web page from a web server. To handle this request, the client computer must first find the web server, the protocols for communication are established, and then the request is made and answered. Hardware, the OS, and the applications on both computers are all involved in this process.

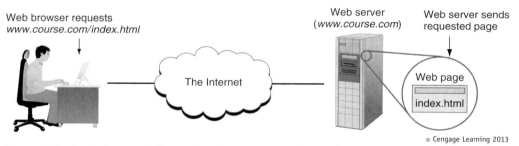

Figure 7-1 A web browser (client software) requests a web page from a web server (server software); the web server returns the requested data to the client

Let's first look at the layers of communication that involve hardware, the OS, and applications and then see how computers are addressed and found on a network or the Internet. Then we'll see how a client/server request is made by the client and answered by the server.

LAYERS OF NETWORK COMMUNICATION

When your computer at home is connected to your Internet Service Provider (ISP) off somewhere in the distance, your computer and a computer on the Internet must be able to communicate. When two devices communicate, they must use the same protocols so that the communication makes sense. For almost all networks today, including the Internet, the group or suite of protocols used is called TCP/IP (Transmission Control Protocol/Internet Protocol).

Before data is transmitted on a network, it is first broken up into segments. Each data segment is put into a **packet**. The packet contains the data (called the payload) and information at the beginning of the packet (called the IP header) that identifies the type of data, where it came from, and where it's going. If the data to be sent is large, it is first divided into several packets, each small enough to travel on the network.

Part of the information included in a packet header is the address information needed to find the computer that is to receive the packet. The address information includes three levels: the address at the hardware level (called a MAC address), the address at the OS level (called an IP address), and the address at the application level (called a port address).

Communication between two computers happens in layers. In Figure 7-2, you can see how communication starts with an application (browser) passing a request to the OS, which

A+
220-801
2.3

A+
220-802
1.6

passes the request to the network card and then onto the network. When the request reaches the network card on the server, the network card passes it on to the OS and then the OS passes it on to the application (the web server).

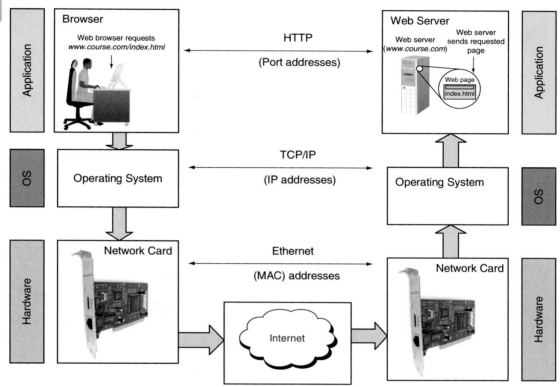

Figure 7-2   Network communication happens in layers

© Cengage Learning 2013

Listed next is a description of each level of communication:

◢ *Level 1: Hardware level.* At the root level of communication is hardware. The hardware or physical connection might be wireless or might use network cables, phone lines (for DSL or dial-up), or TV cable lines (for a cable modem). For local wired or wireless networks, a **network adapter** (also called a network card, a network interface card, or a NIC) inside your computer is part of this physical network. Every network adapter (including a network card, network port on a motherboard, onboard wireless, or wireless NIC) has a 48-bit (6-byte) number hard-coded on the card by its manufacturer that is unique for that device (see Figure 7-3). The number is written in hex, and is called the **MAC (Media Access Control) address**, **hardware address**, **physical address**, **adapter address**, or Ethernet address. Part of the MAC address identifies the manufacturer that is responsible for making sure that no two network adapters have the same MAC address. MAC addresses are used to locate a computer on a local area network (LAN). A **local area network (LAN)** is a network bound by routers or other gateway devices. A **router** is a device that manages traffic between two or more networks and can help find the best path for traffic to get from one network to another. A **gateway** is any device or computer that network traffic can use to leave one network and go to a different network.

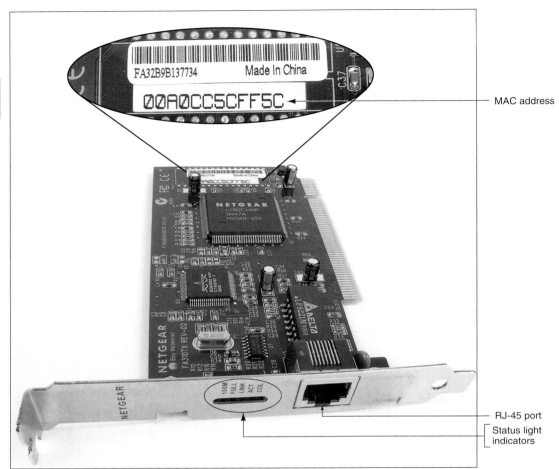

Figure 7-3   Ethernet network card showing its MAC address

© Cengage Learning 2013

▲ *Level 2: Operating system level.* Operating systems use IP addresses to find other computers on a network. An **IP address** is a 32-bit or 128-bit string that is assigned to a network connection when the connection is first made. Whereas a MAC address is only used to find a computer on a local network, an IP address can be used to find a computer anywhere on the Internet (see Figure 7-4) or on an intranet. An **intranet** is

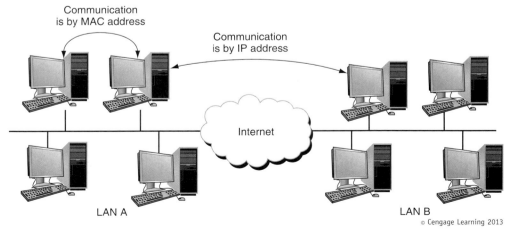

Figure 7-4   Computers on the same LAN use MAC addresses to communicate, but computers on different LANs use IP addresses to communicate over the Internet

© Cengage Learning 2013

A+
220-801
2.3

A+
220-802
1.6

any private network that uses TCP/IP protocols. A large enterprise might support an intranet that is made up of several local networks. When several local networks are tied together in a subsystem of the larger intranet, this group of small local networks is called a subnetwork or **subnet**. IP addresses are used to find computers on subnets, an intranet, or the Internet.

◢ *Level 3: Application level.* Most applications used on the Internet or a local network are client/server applications. Client applications, such as Internet Explorer, Google Chrome, or Outlook, communicate with server applications such as a web server or email server. Each client and server application installed on a computer listens at a predetermined address that uniquely identifies the application on the computer. This address is a number and is called a **port number**, **port**, or **port address**. For example, you can address a web server by entering into a browser address box an IP address followed by a colon and then the port number. These values are known as a socket. For example, an email server waiting to send email to a client listens at port 25, and a web server listens at port 80. Suppose a computer with an IP address of 136.60.30.5 is running both an email server and a web server application. If a client computer sends a request to 136.60.30.5:25, the email server that is listening at that port responds. On the other hand, if a request is sent to 136.60.30.5:80, the web server listening at port 80 responds (see Figure 7-5).

© Cengage Learning 2013

Figure 7-5 Each server running on a computer is addressed by a unique port number

Figure 7-6 shows how communication moves from a browser to the OS to the hardware on one computer and on to the hardware, OS, and web server on a remote computer. As you connect a computer to a network, keep in mind that the connection must work at all three levels. And when things don't work right, it helps to understand that you must solve the problem at one or more levels. In other words, the problem might be with the physical equipment, with the OS, or with the application.

Figure 7-6 How a message gets from a browser to a web server using three levels of communication

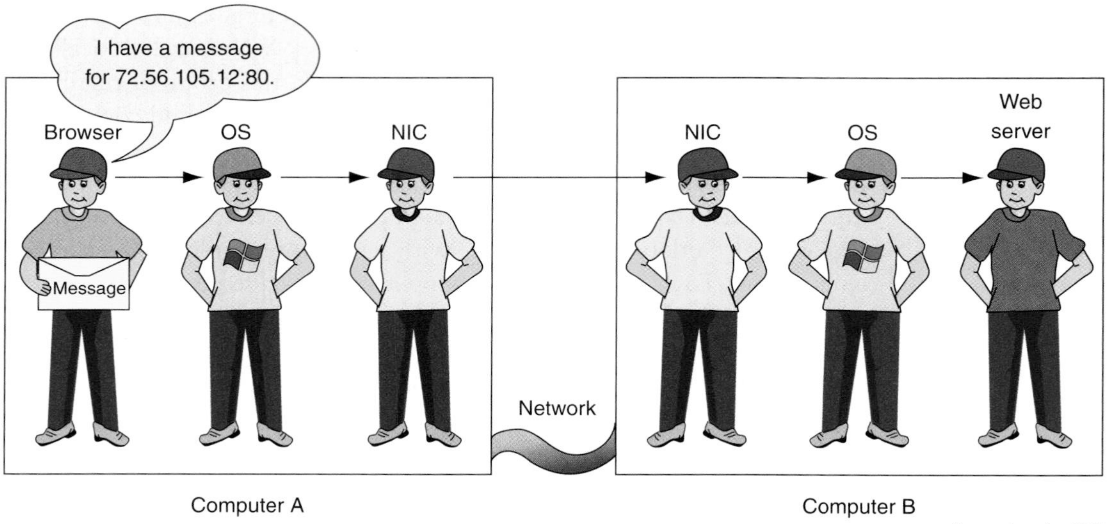

HOW IP ADDRESSES GET ASSIGNED

A MAC address is embedded on a network adapter at the factory, but IP addresses are assigned manually or by software. In Chapter 2, you learned that an IP address can be a dynamic IP address (IP address is assigned by a server each time it connects to the network) or a static IP address (IP address is permanently assigned to the computer or device).

> 💡 **A+ Exam Tip** The A+ 220-801 and A+ 220-802 exams expect you to know what a DHCP server is and understand how to use static and dynamic IP addressing.

For dynamic IP addresses, a DHCP (dynamic host configuration protocol) server gives an IP address to a computer when it first attempts to initiate a connection to the network and requests an IP address. A computer or other device (such as a network printer) that requests address from a DHCP server is called a DHCP client. It is said that the client is leasing an IP address. How to configure a Windows computer to use dynamic or static IP addressing is covered later in the chapter.

An IP address has 32 bits or 128 bits. When the Internet and TCP/IP were first invented, it seemed that 32 bits were more than enough to satisfy any needs we might have for IP addresses because this standard, called Internet Protocol version 4 (IPv4), created about four billion potential IP addresses. Today we need many more than four billion IP addresses over the world. Partly because of a shortage of 32-bit IP addresses, Internet Protocol version 6 (IPv6), which uses an IP address with 128 bits, was developed. Currently, the Internet uses a mix of 32-bit and 128-bit IP addresses. The Internet Assigned Numbers Authority (IANA at *iana.org*) is responsible for keeping track of assigned IP addresses and has already released all its available 32-bit IP addresses. IP addresses leased from IANA today are all 128-bit addresses.

A+
220-801
2.3

📝 **Notes** Now that all of the four billion IPv4 addresses are leased, companies that own these addresses are selling them. Recently, Microsoft purchased over 600,000 IP addresses from Nortel for 7.5 million dollars.

A+
220-802
1.6

Next let's see how IPv4 IP addresses are used, and then you'll learn about IPv6 addresses.

HOW IPV4 IP ADDRESSES ARE USED

A 32-bit IP address is organized into four groups of eight bits each, which are presented as four decimal numbers separated by periods, such as 72.56.105.12. The largest possible 8-bit number is 11111111, which is equal to 255 in decimal, so the largest possible IP address in decimal is 255.255.255.255, which in binary is 11111111.11111111.11111111 .11111111. Each of the four numbers separated by periods is called an octet (for 8 bits) and can be any number from 0 to 255, making a total of about 4.3 billion IP addresses (256 × 256 × 256 × 256). Some IP addresses are reserved, so these numbers are approximations.

The first part of an IP address identifies the network, and the last part identifies the host. When data is routed over the Internet, the network portion of the IP address is used to locate the right network. After the data arrives at the local network, the host portion of the IP address is used to identify the one computer on the network that is to receive the data. Finally, the IP address of the host must be used to identify its MAC address so the data can travel on the host's LAN to that host. The next section explains this in detail.

CLASSES OF IP ADDRESSES

IPv4 IP addresses are divided into three classes: Class A, Class B, and Class C. IP addresses belong in each class according to the scheme outlined in Table 7-1. When IPv4 addresses were available from IANA, a company would lease a Class A, Class B, or Class C license from IANA and from this license could generate multiple IP addresses.

Class	Network Octets*	Approximate Number of Possible Networks or Licenses	Total Number of Possible IP Addresses in Each Network
A	1.x.y.z to 126.x.y.z	126	16 million
B	128.0.x.y to 191.255.x.y	16,000	65,000
C	192.0.0.x to 223.255.255.x	2 million	254

*An x, y, or z in the IP address stands for an octet used to identify hosts.

Table 7-1 Classes of IP addresses

© Cengage Learning 2013

Recall that the first part of an IP address identifies the network, and the last part identifies the host. Figure 7-7 shows how each class of IP addresses is divided into the network and host portions.

Looking back at Table 7-1, you can see that a **Class A** license is for a single octet, which is the network portion of the IP addresses in that license. The remaining octets can be used for host addresses or to identify subnetworks in the larger network. For example, if a company is assigned 87 as its Class A license, then 87 is the network address and is used as the first octet for every host using this license (87.0.0.1, 87.0.0.2, 87.0.0.3, and so forth).

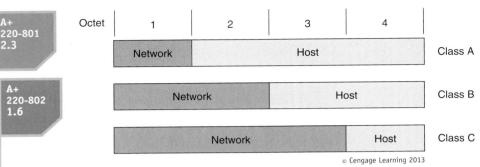

Figure 7-7 The network portion and host portion for each class of IP addresses

(In practice, such a large network is divided into subnets.) Because three octets can be used for Class A host addresses, one Class A license can have approximately 256 × 256 × 254 host addresses, or about 16 million IP addresses. Only very large corporations with heavy communication needs were able to obtain a Class A license.

> **💡 A+ Exam Tip** The A+ 220-801 exam expects you to know how to identify the class of any given IP address. For the exam, memorize these facts: IP addresses that begin with 1 through 126 are class A addresses; addresses that begin with 128 through 191 are class B addresses, and addresses that begin with 192 through 223 are class C addresses.

A Class B license leases the first two octets, and these first two octets are used for the network portion and the last two can be used for the host address or for subnetting the network. An example of a Class B license is 150.35, and examples of IP addresses in this network are 150.35.0.1, 150.35.0.2, and 150.35.0.3. How many host addresses are there in one Class B license? The number of possible values for two octets is about 256 × 254, or about 65,000 host addresses in a single Class B license.

A Class C license assigns three octets as the network address. With only one octet used for the host addresses, there can be only 254 host addresses on a Class C network or its subnetworks. For example, if a company is assigned a Class C license for its network with a network address of 200.80.15, some IP addresses on the network would be 200.80.15.1, 200.80.15.2, and 200.80.15.3.

Class D and Class E IP addresses are not available for general use. Class D addresses begin with octets 224 through 239 and are used for multicasting, in which one host sends messages to multiple hosts, such as when the host transmits a video conference over the Internet. Class E addresses begin with 240 through 254 and are reserved for research.

In addition to classes of IP addresses, a few IP addresses were reserved for special use by TCP/IP and should not be assigned to a device on a network. Table 7-2 lists these reserved IP addresses.

IP Address	How It Is Used
255.255.255.255	Used for broadcast messages by TCP/IP background processes
0.0.0.0	Currently unassigned IP address
127.0.0.1	Indicates your own computer and is called the loopback address

© Cengage Learning 2013

Table 7-2 Reserved IP addresses

A+
220-801
2.3

A+
220-802
1.6

SUBNETS USING IPV4

Looking back at Table 7-1, you can see that a single class license network might have millions of hosts. Managing a network with so many hosts is not practical unless you divide the network into subnets. To divide a network into subnets, you designate part of the host portion of the IP address as a subnet. For example, suppose you have a Class A license of 69. Without using subnets, you have one network: the first octet of all the IP addresses in this network is 69; the last three octets are used for host addresses; and the number of hosts in this one network is about 16 million. Suppose you divide this one network into 256 subnets by using the second octet for the subnet address. (The subnets are 69.0.x.y through 69.255.x.y.) The last two octets are used for host addresses in each subnet with a potential of about 65,000 hosts in each subnet (256 x 254).

The **subnet mask** used with IPv4 identifies which part of an IP address is the network portion and which part is the host portion. Using a subnet mask, a computer or other device can know if an IP address of another computer is on its network or another network (see Figure 7-8).

© Cengage Learning 2013

Figure 7-8 A host (router, in this case) can always determine if an IP address is on its network

A subnet mask is a string of ones followed by a string of zeros. The ones in a subnet mask say, "On our network, this part of an IP address is the network part," and the group of zeros says, "On our network, this part of an IP address is the host part."

If you don't divide a network into subnets, the default subnet mask is used, which is called a **classful subnet mask** because the network portion of the IP address aligns with the class license. For example, Table 7-3 shows the default subnet masks used for three IP addresses. In the table, the green numbers identify the network and the red numbers identify the host.

A+
220-801
2.3

A+
220-802
1.6

Class	Subnet Mask	Address	Network ID	Host ID
Class A	11111111.00000000.00000000.00000000	89.100.13.78	89	100.13.78
Class B	11111111.11111111.00000000.00000000	190.78.13.250	190.78	13.250
Class C	11111111.11111111.11111111.00000000	201.18.20.208	201.18.20	208

© Cengage Learning 2013

Table 7-3 Default subnet masks for classes of IP addresses

These three subnet masks would be displayed in a TCP/IP configuration window like this:

▲ Subnet mask of 11111111.00000000.00000000.00000000 is displayed as 255.0.0.0
▲ Subnet mask of 11111111.11111111.00000000.00000000 is displayed as 255.255.0.0
▲ Subnet mask of 11111111.11111111.11111111.00000000 is displayed as 255.255.255.0

A network is divided into subnets when the subnet mask takes some of the host portion of the IP address for the network ID. This **classless subnet mask** does not align the network ID with the network octets assigned by the class license. Using our earlier example, the classless subnet mask for a Class A license of 69 that uses two octets for the network ID rather than the one octet assigned by the class license would be 11111111.11111111.00000000.00000000 or 255.255.0.0. A classless subnet mask can also have a mix of zeros and ones in one octet such as 11111111.11111111.11110000.00000000, which can be written as 255.255.240.0. These classless subnet masks are used to subnet large corporate networks.

APPLYING | CONCEPTS Larry is setting up a new computer on a network. He creates TCP/IP settings to use static IP addressing. He assigns a subnet mask of 255.255.240.0 and an IP address of 15.50.212.59 to this computer. Suppose this computer wants to communicate with a computer assigned an IP address of 15.50.235.80. Are these two computers in the same subnet? To find out, you can first compare the binary values of the first two octets and determine if they match. Then compare the binary values of the third octet, like this:

```
212 = 11010100
235 = 11101011
```

To be in the same subnet, the first four bits must match, which they don't. Therefore, these two computers are not in the same subnet. However, an IP address that is in the same subnet as 15.50.212.59 is 15.50.220.100 because the first two octets match and the first four bits of the third octet match (comparing 11010100 to 11011100).

> **Notes** Sometimes an IP address and subnet mask are written using a shorthand notation like 15.50.212.59/20, where the /20 means that the subnet mask is written as 20 ones followed by enough zeros to complete the full 32 bits.

A+
220-801
2.3

A+
220-802
1.6

That brings us to a fun way of explaining subnet masks. Suppose all the tall sticks shown in Figure 7-9 belong to the same network, and the short stick is the subnet mask for this network. How many subnets are in the network? Which sticks belong in the same subnet as Stick 5? As Stick 6?

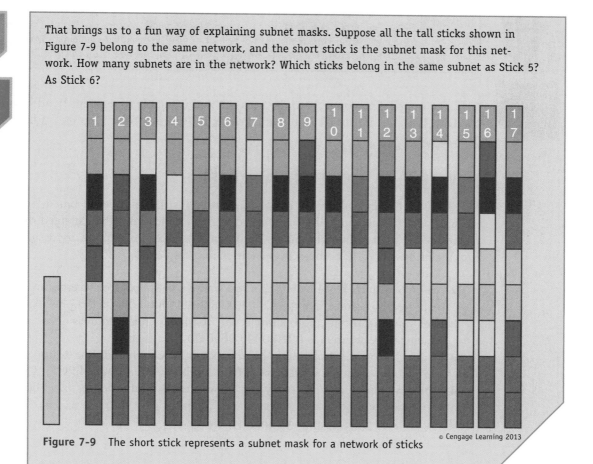

Figure 7-9 The short stick represents a subnet mask for a network of sticks

© Cengage Learning 2013

PUBLIC, PRIVATE, AND AUTOMATIC PRIVATE IP ADDRESSES

When a company applied for a Class A, B, or C license, it was assigned a group of IP addresses that are different from all other IP addresses and are available for use on the Internet. The IP addresses available to the Internet are called public IP addresses.

A company conserves its public IP addresses by using private IP addresses that are not allowed on the Internet. Within the company network, computers communicate with one another using these private IP addresses. A computer using a private IP address on a private network can still access the Internet if a router or other device that stands between the network and the Internet is using NAT (Network Address Translation). NAT is a TCP/IP protocol that substitutes the public IP address of the router for the private IP address of the other computer when these computers need to communicate on the Internet.

Because of NAT, a small company can rely solely on private IP addresses for its internal network and use only the one public IP address assigned to it by its ISP for Internet communication. IEEE recommends that the following IP addresses be used for private networks:

- 10.0.0.0 through 10.255.255.255
- 172.16.0.0 through 172.31.255.255
- 192.168.0.0 through 192.168.255.255

Notes IEEE, a nonprofit organization, is responsible for many Internet standards. Standards are proposed to the networking community in the form of an RFC (Request for Comment). RFC 1918 outlines recommendations for private IP addresses. To view an RFC, visit the web site *www.rfc-editor.org*.

If a computer first connects to the network and is unable to lease an IP address from the DHCP server, it uses an **Automatic Private IP Address (APIPA)** in the address range 169.254.*x.y*.

HOW IPV6 IP ADDRESSES ARE USED

Using the IPv6 standards, more has changed than just the number of bits in an IP address. To improve routing capabilities and speed of communication, IPv6 changed the way IP addresses are used to find computers on the Internet. Let's begin our discussion of IPv6 by looking at how IPv6 IP addresses are written and displayed:

- An IPv6 address has 128 bits that are written as 8 blocks of hexadecimal numbers separated by colons, like this: 2001:0000:0B80:0000:0000:00D3:9C5A:00CC.
- Each block is 16 bits. For example, the first block in the address above is 2001 in hex, which can be written as 0010 0000 0000 0001 in binary.
- Leading zeros in a 4-character hex block can be eliminated. For example, the IP address above can be written as 2001:0000:B80:0000:0000:D3:9C5A:CC.
- If blocks contain all zeros, they can be written as double colons (::). The IP address above can be written two ways:
  - 2001::B80:0000:0000:D3:9C5A:CC
  - 2001:0000:B80::D3:9C5A:CC

To avoid confusion, only one set of double colons is used in an IP address. In this example, the preferred method is the second one: 2001:0000:B80::D3:9C5A:CC because the address is written with the fewest zeros.

The way computers communicate using IPv6 has changed the terminology used to describe TCP/IP communication. Here are a few terms used in the IPv6 standards:

- A link, sometimes called the local link, is a local area network (LAN) or wide area network (WAN) bounded by routers.
- An interface is a node's attachment to a link. The attachment can be a logical attachment or a physical attachment using a network adapter or wireless connection. For example, a logical attachment can be used for tunneling. Tunnels are used by IPv6 to transport IPv6 packets over an IPv4 network.
- The last 64 bits or 4 blocks of an IP address identify the interface and are called the interface ID or interface identifier. These 64 bits uniquely identify an interface on the local link.
- Neighbors are two or more nodes on the same link.

Three tunneling protocols have been developed for IPv6 packets to travel over an IPv4 network:

- ISATAP (pronounced "eye-sa-tap") stands for Intra-Site Automatic Tunnel Addressing Protocol).
- Teredo (pronounced "ter-EE-do") is named after the Teredo worm that bores holes in wood. IPv6 addresses intended to be used by this protocol always begin with the same

A+
220-801
2.3

A+
220-802
1.6

32 bit-prefix (called fixed bits). Teredo IP addresses begin with 2001, and the prefix is written as 2001::/32.

▲ 6TO4 is an older tunneling protocol being replaced by the more powerful Teredo or ISATAP protocols.

IPv6 classifies IP addresses differently from that of IPv4. IPv6 supports these three types of IP addresses:

▲ Using a **unicast address**, packets are delivered to a single node on a network.
▲ Using a **multicast address**, packets are delivered to all nodes on a network.
▲ An **anycast address** is used by routers. The address identifies multiple destinations, and packets are delivered to the closest destination.

A unicast address identifies a single interface on a network. The three types of unicast addresses are global, link-local, and unique local addresses, which are graphically shown in Figure 7-10.

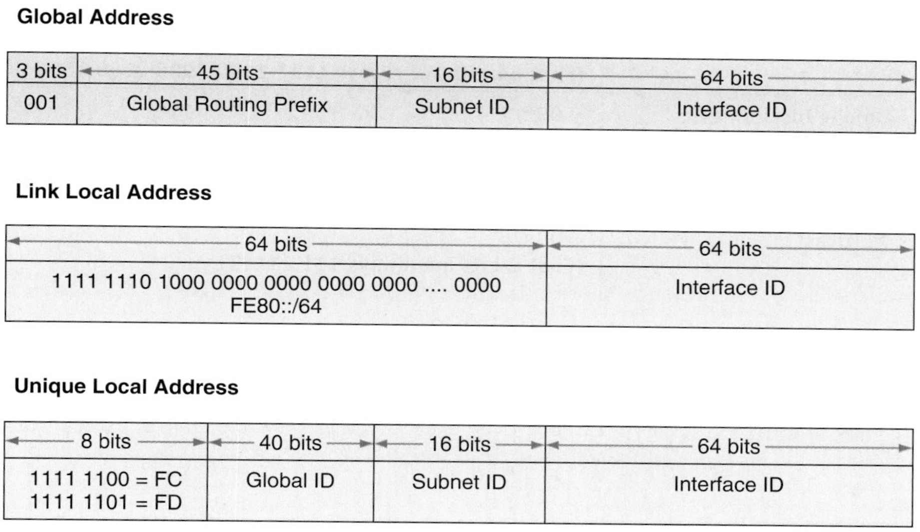

Global Address

3 bits	45 bits	16 bits	64 bits
001	Global Routing Prefix	Subnet ID	Interface ID

Link Local Address

64 bits	64 bits
1111 1110 1000 0000 0000 0000 0000 .... 0000 FE80::/64	Interface ID

Unique Local Address

8 bits	40 bits	16 bits	64 bits
1111 1100 = FC 1111 1101 = FD	Global ID	Subnet ID	Interface ID

Figure 7-10 Three types of IPv6 addresses

© Cengage Learning 2013

Here is a description of each of the three types:

▲ A **global unicast address**, also called a **global address**, can be routed on the Internet. These addresses are similar to IPv4 public IP addresses. Most global addresses begin with the prefix 2000::/3, although other prefixes are being released. The /3 indicates that the first three bits are fixed and are always 001.

▲ A **link-local unicast address**, also called a **link-local address** or local address, can be used for communicating with nodes in the same link. These addresses are similar to IPv4 private IP addresses and are sometimes called link-local addresses or local addresses and most begin with FE80::/64. (This prefix notation means the address begins with FE80 followed by enough zeros to make 64 bits.) Link-local addresses are not allowed on the Internet.

▲ A **unique local unicast address**, also called a **unique local address (ULA)**, is used to identify a specific site within a large organization. For example, an organization might have these two sites: employee.mycompany.com and support.mycompany.com. The address prefixes used for unique local addresses are FC00::/7 and FD00::/8. The Global ID portion of the address is assigned by the organization. Unique local addresses are not allowed on the Internet. They are hybrid addresses between a global unicast address that works on the Internet and a link-local address that works on only one link.

Notice in Figure 7-10 that global and unique local addresses contain a block labeled the Subnet ID, which is the last block in the 64-bit prefix of an IP address. Recall that when using IPv4, the subnet could be identified by any number of bits at the beginning of the IP address. Using IPv6, a subnet is identified using some or all of the 16 bits in the Subnet ID block. Using IPv6, a subnet is, therefore, identified as one or more links that have the same 64 bits in the IP address prefix. This definition implies that a local link is itself a subnet.

Table 7-4 lists the currently used address prefixes for these types of IP addresses. In the future, we can expect more prefixes to be assigned as they are needed.

IP Address Type	Address Prefix
Global unicast	2000::/3 (First 3 bits are always 001)
Link-local unicast	FE80::/64 (First 64 bits are always 1111 1110 1000 0000 0000 0000 ..... 0000)
Unique local unicast	FC00::/7 (First 7 bits are always 1111 110) FD00::/8 (First 8 bits are always 1111 1101)
Multicast	FF00::/8 (First 8 bits are always 1111 1111)

© Cengage Learning 2013

Table 7-4 Address prefixes for types of IPv6 addresses

💡 **A+ Exam Tip** The A+ 220-801 exam expects you to know the prefixes listed in Table 7-4.

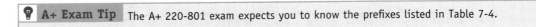

📝 **Notes** An excellent resource for learning more about IPv6 and how it works is the ebook, *TCP/IP Fundamentals for Microsoft Windows*. To download the free PDF, search for it at *www.microsoft.com/download*.

VIEW IP ADDRESS SETTINGS

The Ipconfig command can be used in a command prompt window to show the IPv4 and IPv6 IP addresses assigned to all network connections (see Figure 7-11).

Notice in the figure the four IP addresses that have been assigned to the physical connections:

◢ Windows has assigned the wireless connection two IP addresses, one using IPv4 and one using IPv6.
◢ The Ethernet LAN connection has also been assigned an IPv4 address and an IPv6 address.

The IPv6 addresses are followed by a % sign and a number; for example, %13 follows the first IP address. This number is called the zone ID or scope ID and is used to identify the interface in a list of interfaces for this computer.

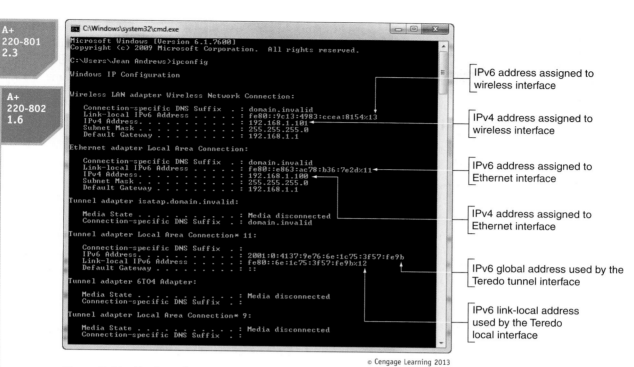

Figure 7-11 The ipconfig command showing IPv4 and IPv6 addresses assigned to this computer

IPv6 addressing is designed so that a computer can autoconfigure its own link-local IP address, which is similar to how IPv4 uses an Automatic Private IP Address (APIPA). Here's what happens when a computer using IPv6 first makes a network connection:

1. The computer creates its IPv6 address by using the FE80::/64 prefix and randomly generating an Interface ID for the last 64 bits.

2. It then performs a duplicate address detection process to make sure its IP address is unique on the network.

3. Next it asks if a router is present on the network to provide configuration information. If a router responds with DHCP information, the computer uses whatever information this might be, such as the IP addresses of DNS servers or its own IP address. Because a computer can generate its own link-local IP address, a DHCPv6 server usually serves up only global IPv6 addresses.

CHARACTER-BASED NAMES IDENTIFY COMPUTERS AND NETWORKS

A+
220-801
2.4

Remembering an IP address is not always easy, so character-based names are used to substitute for IP addresses. Here are the possibilities:

▲ A host name, also called a computer name, is the name of a computer and can be used in place of its IP address. Examples of host names are www, ftp, Jean's Computer, TestBox3, and PinkLaptop. You assign a host name to a computer when you first configure it for a network connection. The name can have up to 63 characters, including letters, numbers, and special characters. On a local network, you can use the computer name in the place of an IP address to identify a computer. To find out and change the computer name in Windows 7/Vista, click **Start**, right-click **Computer**, and select

A+
220-801
2.4

Properties from the shortcut menu. In the System window, click **Advanced system settings**. In the System Properties box, click the **Computer Name** tab (see Figure 7-12). To rename a computer, click **Change**. (For XP, click **Start**, right-click **My Computer**, and select **Properties** from the shortcut menu. Then click the **Computer Name** tab.)

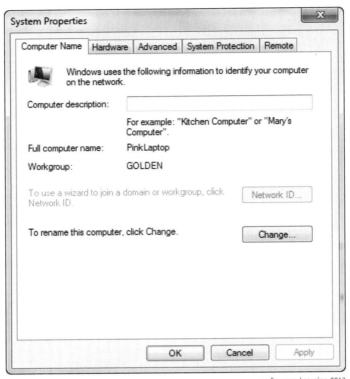

© Cengage Learning 2013

Figure 7-12   View and change the computer name

> ◢ A workgroup is a group of computers on a peer-to-peer network that are sharing resources. The workgroup name assigned to this group is only recognized within the local network.

> ◢ A domain name identifies a network. Examples of domain names are the names that appear before the period in microsoft.com, course.com, and mycompany.com. The letters after the period are called the top-level domain and tell you something about the domain. Examples are .com (commercial), .org (nonprofit), .gov (government), and .info (general use).

> ◢ A fully qualified domain name (FQDN) identifies a computer and the network to which it belongs. An example of an FQDN is www.course.com. The host name is *www* (a web server), *course* is the domain name, and *com* is the top-level domain name of the Course Technology network. Another FQDN is *joesmith.mycompany.com*.

On the Internet, a fully qualified domain name must be associated with an IP address before this computer can be found. This process of associating a character-based name with an IP address is called **name resolution**. The **DNS (Domain Name System or Domain Name Service)** protocol is used by a **DNS server** to find an IP address for a computer when the fully qualified domain name is known. Your ISP is responsible for providing you access to one or more DNS servers as part of the service it provides for Internet access. When a web-hosting site first sets up your web site, IP address, and domain name, it is responsible for entering the name resolution information into its primary DNS server. This server can present the information to other DNS servers on the web and is called the authoritative name server for your site.

> **💡 A+ Exam Tip** The A+ 220-802 exam expects you to be familiar with client-side DNS.

> **📝 Notes** When you enter a fully qualified domain name such as *www.cengage.com* in a browser address bar, that name is translated into an IP address followed by a port number. It's interesting to know that you can skip the translation step and enter the IP address and port number in the address box. See Figure 7-13.

© Cengage Learning 2013

Figure 7-13 A web site can be accessed by its IP address and port number: http://69.32.133.79:80

When Windows is trying to resolve a computer name to an IP address, it first looks in the DNS cache it holds in memory. Information in this cache includes what it loaded at startup from the Hosts file in the C:\Windows\System32\drivers\etc folder. This file, which has no file extension, contains computer names and their associated IP addresses on the local network. An administrator is responsible for manually editing the hosts file when the association is needed on the local network. If the computer name is not found in the hosts file, Windows then turns to a DNS server if it has the IP address of the server. When Windows queries the DNS server for a name resolution, it is called the DNS client.

> **📝 Notes** For an entry in the Hosts file to work, the remote computer must always use the same IP address. One way to accomplish this is to assign a static IP address to the computer. Alternately, if your DHCP server supports this feature, you can configure it to assign the same IP address to this computer each time if you tell the DHCP server the computer's MAC address. This method of computer name resolution is often used for intranet web servers, Telnet servers, and other servers.

TCP/IP PROTOCOL LAYERS

Recall that a protocol is an agreed-to set of rules for communication between two parties. Operating systems and client/server applications on the Internet all use protocols that are supported by TCP/IP. The left side of Figure 7-14 shows these different layers of protocols and how they relate to one another. As you read this section, this figure can serve as your road map to the different protocols.

A+
220-801
2.4

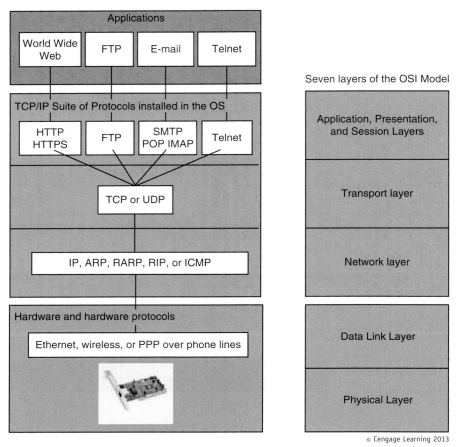

Figure 7-14 How software, protocols, and technology on a TCP/IP network relate to each other

> **Notes** When studying networking theory, the OSI Model is used, which divides network communication into seven layers. In the OSI Model, protocols used by hardware are divided into two layers (data link and physical), and TCP/IP protocols used by the OS are divided into five layers (network, transport, session, presentation, and application). These seven layers are shown on the right side of Figure 7-14.

In the following sections, the more significant applications and operating system protocols are introduced. However, you should know that the TCP/IP protocol suite includes more protocols than just those mentioned in this chapter; only some of them are shown in Figure 7-14.

TCP/IP PROTOCOLS USED BY THE OS

Looking back at Figure 7-14, you can see three layers of protocols between the applications and the hardware protocols. These three layers make up the heart of TCP/IP communication. In the figure, TCP or UDP manages communication with the applications protocols above them as well as the protocols shown underneath TCP and UDP, which control communication on the network.

Remember that all communication on a network happens by way of packets delivered from one location on the network to another. In TCP/IP, the protocol that guarantees packet delivery is **TCP (Transmission Control Protocol)**. TCP makes a connection, checks whether the data is received, and resends it if it is not. TCP is, therefore, called a **connection-oriented protocol**. TCP is used by applications such as web browsers and email. Guaranteed delivery takes longer and is used when it is important to know that the data reached its destination.

A+
220-801
2.4

For TCP to guarantee delivery, it uses protocols at the IP layer to establish a session between client and server to verify that communication has taken place. When a TCP packet reaches its destination, an acknowledgment is sent back to the source (see Figure 7-15). If the source TCP does not receive the acknowledgment, it resends the data or passes an error message back to the higher-level application protocol.

© Cengage Learning 2013

Figure 7-15 TCP guarantees delivery by requesting an acknowledgment

> 💡 **A+ Exam Tip** The A+ 220-801 exam expects you to be able to contrast the TCP and UDP protocols.

On the other hand, UDP (User Datagram Protocol) does not guarantee delivery by first connecting and checking whether data is received; thus, UDP is called a **connectionless protocol** or **best-effort protocol**. UDP is used for broadcasting, such as streaming video or sound over the web, where guaranteed delivery is not as important as fast transmission. UDP is also used to monitor network traffic.

TCP/IP PROTOCOLS USED BY APPLICATIONS

Some common applications that use the Internet are web browsers, email, chat, FTP, Telnet, Remote Desktop, and Remote Assistance. Here is a bit of information about several of the protocols used by these and other applications:

- ◢ *HTTP.* HTTP (Hypertext Transfer Protocol) is the protocol used for the World Wide Web and used by web browsers and web servers to communicate. You can see when a browser is using this protocol by looking for http at the beginning of a URL in the address bar of a browser, such as *http://www.microsoft.com*.
- ◢ *HTTPS.* HTTPS (HTTP secure) is the HTTP protocol working with a security protocol such as Secure Sockets Layer (SSL) or Transport Layer Security (TLS), which is better than SSL, to create a secured socket. HTTPS is used by web browsers and servers to encrypt the data before it is sent and then decrypt it before the data is processed. To know a secured protocol is being used, look for https in the URL, as in *https://www.wellsfargo.com*.
- ◢ *SMTP.* SMTP (Simple Mail Transfer Protocol) is used to send an email message to its destination (see Figure 7-16). An improved version of SMTP is SMTP AUTH (SMTP Authentication). This protocol is used to authenticate a user to an email server when the

email client first tries to connect to the email server to send email. Using SMTP AUTH, an extra dialogue between the client and server happens before the client can fully connect that proves the client is authorized to use the service. After authentication, the client can then send email to the email server. The email server that takes care of sending email messages (using the SMTP protocol) is often referred to as the SMTP server.

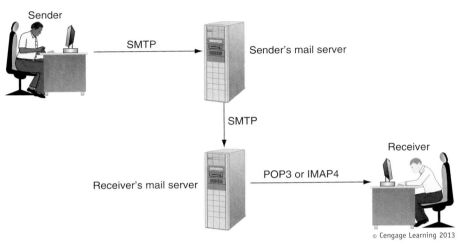

Figure 7-16   The SMTP protocol is used to send email to a recipient's mail server, and the POP3 or IMAP4 protocol is used by the client to receive email

- **POP and IMAP.** After an email message arrives at the destination email server, it remains there until the recipient requests delivery. The recipient's email server uses one of two protocols to deliver the message: **POP3 (Post Office Protocol, version 3)** or **IMAP4 (Internet Message Access Protocol, version 4)**. Using POP, email is downloaded to the client computer. Using IMAP, the client application manages the email stored on the server.
- **Telnet.** The Telnet protocol is used by the Telnet client/server applications to allow an administrator or other user to control a computer remotely. Telnet is not considered secure because transmissions in Telnet are not encrypted.
- **LDAP.** **Lightweight Directory Access Protocol (LDAP)** is used by various client applications when the application needs to query a database. For example, an email client on a corporate network might query a database that contains the email addresses for all employees. Another example is when an application looks for a printer by querying a database of printers supported by an organization on the corporate network or Internet. Data sent and received using the LDAP protocol is not encrypted; therefore, an encryption layer is sometimes added to LDAP transmissions.
- **SMB.** **Server Message Block (SMB)** is the protocol used by Windows to share files and printers on a network.
- **FTP.** **FTP (File Transfer Protocol)** is used to transfer files between two computers. Web browsers can use the protocol. Also, special FTP client software such as CuteFTP by GlobalSCAPE (*www.cuteftp.com*), can be used, which offers more features for file transfer than does a browser. To use FTP in Internet Explorer version 9, enter the address of an FTP site in the address box, for example, *ftp.cengage.com*. A logon dialog box appears where you can enter a username and password (see Figure 7-17). When you click **Log on**, you can see folders on the

FTP site and the FTP protocol displays in the address bar, as in *ftp://ftp.cengage .com*. It's easier to use Windows Explorer to transfer files rather than Internet Explorer. After you have located the FTP site, to use Windows Explorer for file transfers, press **Alt**, which causes the menu bar to appear. In the menu bar, click **View, Open FTP site in Windows Explorer** (see Figure 7-18). Then click **Allow** in the Internet Explorer Security box. Windows Explorer opens, showing files and folders on the FTP site. You can copy and paste files and folders from your computer to the site.

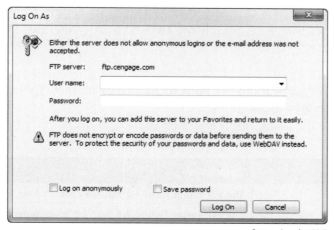

Figure 7-17   Log on to an FTP site
© Cengage Learning 2013

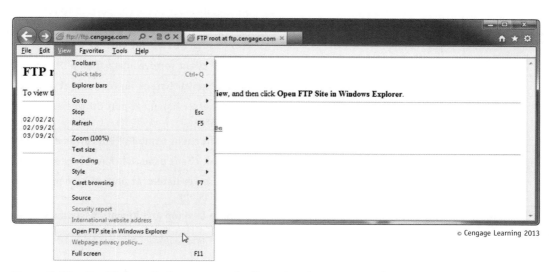

Figure 7-18   Use Windows Explorer to transfer files using the FTP protocol
© Cengage Learning 2013

▲ *SSH.* The **Secure Shell (SSH)** protocol is used to pass login information to a remote computer and control that computer over a network. Transmissions are encrypted so they cannot be intercepted by a hacker.

A+
220-801
2.4

◢ *SFTP.* Secure FTP (SFTP) is used to transfer files from an FTP server to an FTP client using encryption. The encryption layer of the protocol used by Secure FTP is a variation of the SSH (Secure Shell) protocol.

◢ *SNMP.* Simple Network Management Protocol (SNMP) is used to monitor network traffic. It is used by the Microsoft SNMP Agent application that monitors traffic on a network and helps balance that traffic.

◢ *RDP.* Remote Desktop Protocol (RDP) is used by the Windows Remote Desktop and Remote Assistance utilities to connect to and control a remote computer.

> 💡 **A+ Exam Tip** The A+ 220-801 exam expects you to know about the following application protocols: FTP, Telnet, SMTP, DNS, HTTP, POP3, IMAP, HTTPS, RDP, DHCP, LDAP, SNMP, SMB, SSH, and SFTP.

Recall that client/server applications use ports to address each other. Table 7-5 lists the port assignments for common applications.

Port	Protocol and App	Description
20	FTP client	The FTP client receives data on port 20 from the FTP server.
21	FTP server	The FTP server listens on port 21 for commands from an FTP client.
22	SSH server	A server using the SSH protocol listens at port 22.
23	Telnet server	A Telnet server listens at port 23.
25	SMTP email server	An email server listens at port 25 to receive email from a client computer.
53	DNS server	A DNS server listens at port 53.
67	DHCP client	A DHCP client receives data from a DHCP server at port 67.
68	DHCP server	A DHCP server listens for requests at port 68.
80	Web server using HTTP	A web server listens at port 80 when receiving HTTP requests.
110	POP3 email client	An email client using POP3 receives email at port 110.
143	IMAP email client	An email client using IMAP receives email at port 143.
443	Web server using HTTPS	A web server listens at port 443 when receiving HTTPS transmissions.
3389	RDP apps, including Remote Desktop and Remote Assistance	Remote Desktop and Remote Assistance listen at port 3389.

© Cengage Learning 2013

Table 7-5 Common TCP/IP port assignments for client/server applications

> 💡 **A+ Exam Tip** The A+ 220-801 expects you to know the common port assignments of the FTP, Telnet, SMTP, DNS, HTTP, POP3, IMAP, HTTPS, and RDP protocols. Before sitting for this exam, be sure to memorize the ports listed in Table 7-5.

A+
220-801
2.4

Hands-on | Project 7.1 Practice Using FTP

Practice using FTP by downloading the latest version of Firefox, a web browser, using these methods. Do the following:

1. Using your current browser, go to the Mozilla web site at *www.mozilla.org* and download the latest version of Firefox. What is the version number? What is the name of the downloaded file? In what folder on your hard drive did you put the file?

2. Using your current browser as an FTP client, locate the same version of Firefox and the same file at the Mozilla FTP site (*ftp.mozilla.org*) and download it to your PC. What is the path to the Firefox file on the FTP site? In what folder on your hard drive did you put the file?

Now that you have an understanding of TCP/IP and Windows networking, let's apply that knowledge to making network connections.

CONNECTING A COMPUTER TO A NETWORK

A+
220-802
1.5, 1.6

Connecting a computer to a network is quick and easy in most situations. In this part of the chapter, you'll learn to connect a computer to a network using Ethernet, wireless, and dial-up connections.

CONNECT TO A WIRED NETWORK

To connect a computer to a network using a wired (Ethernet) connection, follow these steps:

1. If the network adapter is not yet installed, install it now. These steps include physically installing the card, installing drivers, and using Device Manager to verify that Windows recognizes the adapter without errors.

2. Connect a network cable to the Ethernet port (called an RJ-45 port) and to the network wall jack or directly to a switch or router. Indicator lights near the network port should light up to indicate connectivity and activity. If you connected the cable directly to a switch or router, verify the light at that port is also lit.

3. By default, Windows assumes dynamic IP addressing and automatically configures the network connection. To find out if the connection is working, open Windows Explorer and drill down into the Network group (see Figure 7-19). (For Windows XP, click **Start, My Network Places** to open the My Network Places window.) You should see icons that represent other computers on the network. Double-click a computer and drill down to shared folders and files to verify you can access these resources.

4. To verify you have Internet connectivity, open Internet Explorer and browse to a few web sites.

A+
220-802
1.5, 1.6

© Cengage Learning 2013

Figure 7-19 Windows Explorer shows resources on the network

If the connection does not work, it's time to verify that network settings are configured correctly. Follow these steps using Windows 7:

1. Verify that Device Manager recognizes the network adapter without errors. If you find an error, try updating the network adapter drivers. If that doesn't work, then try uninstalling and reinstalling the drivers. Make sure Device Manager recognizes the network adapter without errors before you move on to the next step.

2. To open the Network and Sharing Center, open **Control Panel** and click **Network and Sharing Center**. (You can also click the network icon in the taskbar.) The Network and Sharing Center window opens (see Figure 7-20).

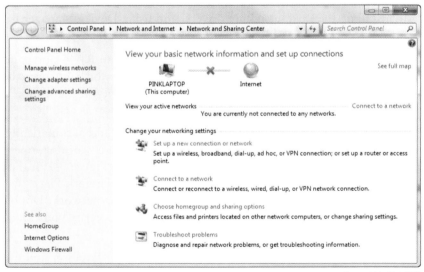

© Cengage Learning 2013

Figure 7-20 The Network and Sharing Center reports a problem connecting to the network

A+
220-802
1.5, 1.6

3. A red X indicates a problem. Click the **X** to get help and resolve the problem. Windows Network Diagnostics starts looking for problems, applying solutions, and making suggestions. You can also check these things:

◢ Is the network cable connected?

◢ Are status light indicators on the network port and router or switch lit or blinking appropriately to indicate connectivity and activity?

4. After Windows has resolved the problem, you should see a clear path from the computer to the Internet, as shown in Figure 7-21. Use Windows Explorer to try again to access resources on the local network, and use Internet Explorer to try to access the Internet.

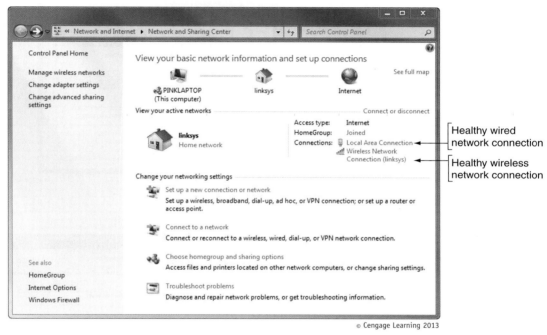

© Cengage Learning 2013

Figure 7-21 The Network and Sharing Center reports two healthy network connections

If you still do not have connectivity, follow these steps to verify and change TCP/IP settings:

1. In the Network and Sharing Center, click **Change adapter settings**. In the Network Connections window, right-click the local area connection and select **Properties** from the shortcut menu. The properties box appears (see Figure 7-22).

2. Select **Internet Protocol Version 4 (TCP/IPv4)** and click **Properties**. The properties box shown in Figure 7-23 (a) appears. Settings are correct for dynamic IP addressing.

> **Notes** Notice in Figure 7-22 that you can uncheck Internet Protocol Version 6 (TCP/IPv6) to disable it. For most situations, you need to leave it enabled. A bug in Windows 7 prevents you from joining a homegroup if IPv6 is disabled.

A+
220-802
1.5, 1.6

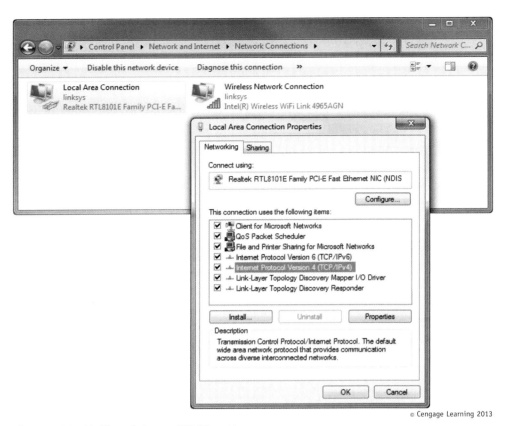

© Cengage Learning 2013

Figure 7-22 Verify and change TCP/IP settings

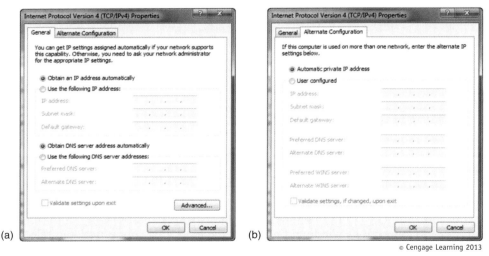

© Cengage Learning 2013

Figure 7-23 Configure TCP/IP settings

3. To change the settings to static IP addressing, select **Use the following IP address**. Then enter the IP address, subnet mask, and default gateway. (A **default gateway** is the gateway a computer uses to access another network if it does not have a better option.)

4. If you have been given the IP addresses of DNS servers, check **Use the following DNS server addresses** and enter up to two IP addresses. If you have other DNS IP addresses, click **Advanced** and enter them on the **DNS** tab of the Advanced TCP/IP Settings box.

A+
220-802
1.5, 1.6

5. If the computer you are using is a laptop that moves from one network to another and one network uses static IP addressing, you can click the **Alternate Configuration** tab and configure an **alternate IP address** (see Figure 7-23 [b]). On this tab, select **User configured**. Then enter a static IP address, subnet mask, default gateway, and DNS server addresses. When you configure the General tab to use dynamic IP addressing, the computer will first try to use dynamic IP addressing. If that is not available on the network, it then applies the static IP address settings entered on the Alternate Configuration tab. If static IP address settings are not available on this tab, the computer uses an automatic private IP address (APIPA). This setup works well for a computer to receive a dynamic IP address while traveling, but use a static IP address when connected to the company network that uses static IP addressing.

> 💡 **A+ Exam Tip** The A+ 220-802 exam expects you to know how to configure an alternate IP address, including setting the static IP address, subnet mask, DNS addresses, and gateway.

6. Close all boxes and windows and again try to access network resources. If you still don't have connectivity, try to disable and enable the network connection. To do that, right-click the connection in the Network Connections window and select **Disable** (see Figure 7-24). For dynamic IP addressing, the IP address is released. Then right-click again and select **Enable**. The connection is remade and a new IP address is leased.

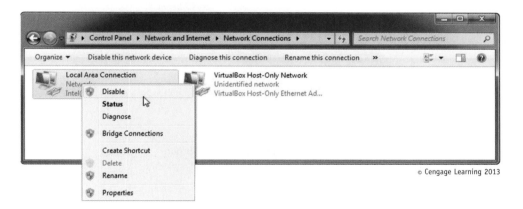

© Cengage Learning 2013

Figure 7-24 To reset a network connection, disable and enable the connection

If you still don't have local or Internet access, it's time to dig a little deeper into the source of the problem. Troubleshooting network connections is covered in Chapter 8.

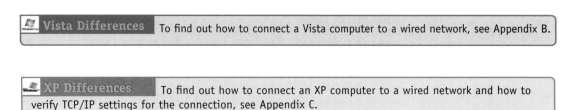

> **Vista Differences** To find out how to connect a Vista computer to a wired network, see Appendix B.

> **XP Differences** To find out how to connect an XP computer to a wired network and how to verify TCP/IP settings for the connection, see Appendix C.

A+
220-802
1.5, 1.6

CONNECT TO A WIRELESS NETWORK

Wireless networks are either unsecured public hotspots or secured private hotspots. Even if you connect to a secured private hotspot, still be careful to protect your data and other Windows resources from attack. In this part of the chapter, you learn how to connect to unsecured and secured wireless networks.

Here are the steps to connect to a wireless network using Windows 7 and how to protect your computer on that network:

1. If necessary, install the wireless adapter. For external adapters such as the one shown in Figure 7-25, be sure to follow the manufacturer's instructions for the installation. Most likely you'll be asked to first install the software before installing the device. During the installation process, you will be given the opportunity to use the manufacturer's configuration utility to manage the wireless adapter or to use Windows to do the job. For best results, use the utility provided by the manufacturer. In the following steps, we're using the Windows utility.

© Cengage Learning 2013

Figure 7-25 Plug the wireless USB adapter into the USB port

2. For embedded wireless, turn on your wireless device. For some laptops, that's done by a switch on the keyboard (see Figure 7-26) or on the side of the laptop. The wireless antenna is usually in the lid of a notebook and gives best performance when the lid is fully raised. For a desktop computer, make sure the antenna is in an upright position (see Figure 7-27).

3. A yellow star in the network icon in the taskbar indicates hotspots are available. Double-click the network icon to see a list of networks. Click one to select it and then click **Connect** (see Figure 7-28).

4. If the network is secured, Windows asks for the security key the first time you connect (see Figure 7-29). Enter the security key or password to the network and click **OK**.

5. If the network is unsecured or you don't trust all the users of the network, verify that Windows has configured the network as a Public network. To do so, open the Network and Sharing Center window (see Figure 7-30). If the network location says

A+
220-802
1.5, 1.6

Figure 7-26 Turn on the wireless switch on your laptop

© Cengage Learning 2013

© Cengage Learning 2013

Figure 7-27 Raise the antenna on a NIC to an upright position

Home network or Work network, click it. The Set Network Location box appears (see Figure 7-31). Click **Public network** and click **Close**. The Network and Sharing Center reports the network location as Public network.

6. Open your browser to test the connection. For some hotspots, a home page appears and you must enter a code or agree to the terms of use before you can use the network.

In addition to a security key used to access a secured wireless network, the network might be set up for even more security. A wireless network is created by a wireless device known

A+
220-802
1.5, 1.6

© Cengage Learning 2013

Figure 7-28   Windows orders the list of wireless
networks in the area from strongest
to weakest signals

© Cengage Learning 2013

Figure 7-29   Enter the security key to connect to a secured
wireless network

as the **wireless access point**. Here is a list of methods that the wireless access point might use
to secure the wireless network:

- ▲ *A security key is required.* This is the most common method of securing a wireless network. A network that uses a security key encrypts data on the network using an
  encryption standard. You learn about these standards later in the chapter.
- ▲ *The SSID is not broadcasted.* The wireless device might not be broadcasting its name,
  which is called the Service Set Identifier (SSID). If the SSID is not broadcasting, the

A+
220-802
1.5, 1.6

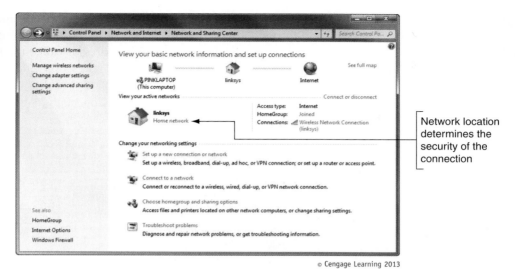

© Cengage Learning 2013

Figure 7-30 Verify that your connection is secure

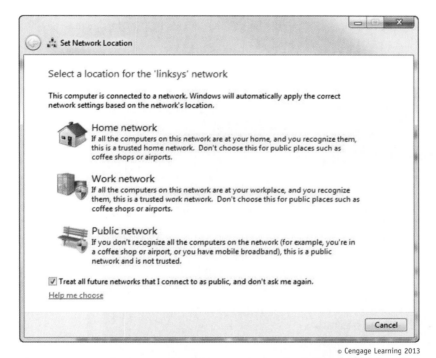

© Cengage Learning 2013

Figure 7-31 For best protection on a network, use the Public network location

name of the wireless network will appear as Unnamed or Unknown Network. When you select this network, you are given the opportunity to enter the name. If you don't enter the name correctly, you will not be able to connect.

◢ *Only computers with registered MAC addresses are allowed to connect.* If MAC address filtering is used, you must give the network administrator the MAC address of your wireless adapter. This address is entered into a table of acceptable MAC addresses kept by the wireless access point.

To know the MAC address of your wireless adapter, for an external adapter, you can look on the back of the adapter itself (see Figure 7-32) or in the adapter documentation.

A+
220-802
1.5, 1.6

Also, if the adapter is installed on your computer, you can open a command prompt window and enter the command **ipconfig /all**, which displays your TCP/IP configuration for all network connections. In the results displayed, the MAC address is called the Physical Address (see Figure 7-33).

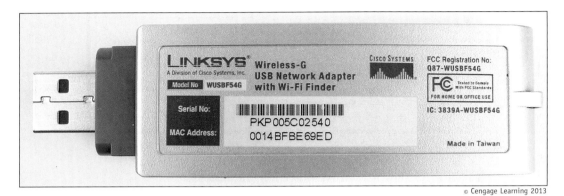

© Cengage Learning 2013

Figure 7-32   The MAC address is printed on the back of this USB wireless adapter

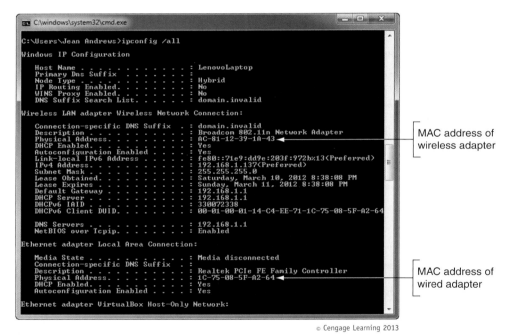

© Cengage Learning 2013

Figure 7-33   Use the ipconfig /all command to display TCP/IP configuration data

If you have problems connecting to a wireless network, here are the steps to follow to verify the network settings:

1. In the left pane of the Network and Sharing Center, click **Manage wireless networks**. The Manage Wireless Networks window appears (see the left side of Figure 7-34).

A+
220-802
1.5, 1.6

2. Using this window, you can change the order of networks that Windows uses to try to make a wireless connection. To view security settings, double-click a network in the list. The Properties box for the wireless network appears.

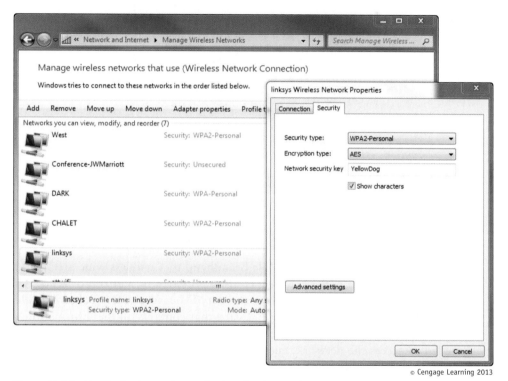

© Cengage Learning 2013

Figure 7-34 Verify the Network security key for the wireless network is correct

3. On the Properties box, click the **Security** tab, which is shown in the right side of Figure 7-34. Check **Show characters** so that you can verify the Network security key is correct. Windows 7 should automatically sense the Security type and Encryption type for the wireless network, and these values should be correct. Change the Network security key if necessary.

4. Click **OK** to close the Properties box. Windows should automatically connect to the network. If you still cannot connect, know that troubleshooting network connections is covered in Chapter 8.

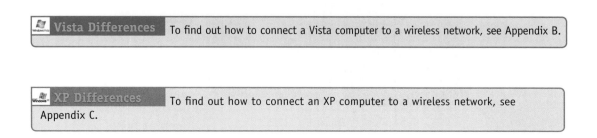

Vista Differences To find out how to connect a Vista computer to a wireless network, see Appendix B.

XP Differences To find out how to connect an XP computer to a wireless network, see Appendix C.

7

A+
220-802
1.5, 1.6

Hands-on | Project 7.2 Investigate a Wireless Connection

Using a computer connected to a wireless network, do the following:

1. In the Network and Sharing Center, click **Manage wireless networks**. Right-click the wireless connection and click Properties to view the Properties box for the wireless network. Is the network secured? If so, what is the security type? What is the encryption type?

2. Open the Properties box for the Wireless Network Connection. Is the connection using TCP/IPv4? TCP/IPv6?

3. View the TCP/IPv4 settings for the wireless adapter. Is the wireless connection using static or dynamic IP addressing?

4. Using the Ipconfig command, what is the IPv4 IP address for the wireless connection? What is the MAC address of the wireless adapter?

CONNECT TO A WIRELESS WAN (CELLULAR) NETWORK

To connect a computer using mobile broadband to a wireless wide area network (WWAN), also called a cellular network, such as those provided by Verizon or AT&T, you need the hardware and software to connect and a SIM card. A **SIM (Subscriber Identification Module)** card is a small flash memory card that contains all the information you need to connect to a cellular network, including a password and other authentication information needed to access the network, encryption standards used, and the services that your subscription includes. SIM cards are used in cell phones, mobile broadband modems, and other devices that use a cellular network (see Figure 7-35).

Back cover of the phone is removed to reveal the SIM card

Battery must be removed to install or remove the SIM card

SIM card installed in slot

© Cengage Learning 2013

Figure 7-35 A SIM card contains proof that your device can use a cellular network

Here are your options for hardware and software:

▲ *Use an embedded mobile broadband modem.* A laptop might have an embedded broadband modem. In this situation, you still need to subscribe to a mobile operator, which will provide you with a SIM card for your laptop.

▲ *Tether your cell phone to your computer.* You can tether your cell phone to your computer by way of a cable that connects your cell phone to a USB port. See Figure 7-36. (Some cell phones don't have a USB port; in this situation, you have to purchase a special cable that works with your proprietary phone connector and a USB port on your computer.) A cell phone with Wi-Fi capabilities can be used to provide a Wi-Fi hotspot that your computer and other devices can connect to. In this situation, the cell phone acts like a wireless router. An app installed on the phone is used to configure the WLAN created by the phone.

© Cengage Learning 2013

Figure 7-36 Tether your cell phone to your laptop using a USB cable

▲ *Use a USB broadband modem.* For any computer, you can use a USB broadband modem (sometimes called an air card), such as the one shown in Figure 7-37. If you purchase the device from your mobile operator, a SIM card is included. If you purchase the modem from another source, you need to go to your mobile operator (for example, AT&T, Verizon, or Sprint) to obtain the SIM card the device will use to verify your subscription to the cellular network. A USB broadband modem is likely to give you access to a cellular network as well as a Wi-Fi network.

Mobile operators and laptop manufacturers with embedded modems provide software and instructions for connecting to the cellular network. Follow those instructions rather than the generic ones presented here. Generally, here's how you can connect to a cellular network:

▲ *Using an embedded broadband modem.* For a laptop with an embedded broadband modem, you must insert the SIM card provided by your mobile operator in the SIM card slot on the laptop. For some laptops, this slot might be in the battery bay, and

A+
220-802
1.5, 1.6

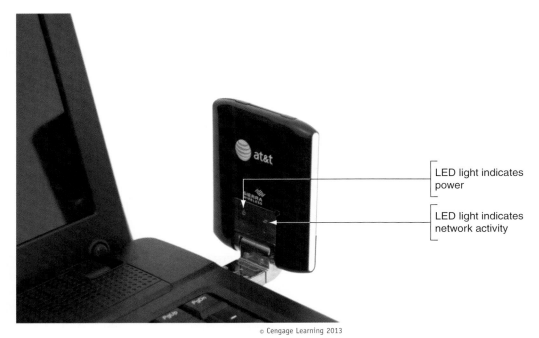

© Cengage Learning 2013

Figure 7-37   A USB broadband modem by Sierra Wireless

you must remove the battery to find the slot. Then use a program installed on the lap-top by the laptop manufacturer to connect to the cellular network. Look for a short-cut on the desktop or a program in the Start menu. In addition, the mobile operator might provide software for you to use.

◢ *Using your cell phone.* To tether your cell phone to your computer to use a cellular network, know that you need a subscription from your mobile operator to use this service. The mobile operator is likely to provide you software on CD, or you can download the software from the operator's web site. Install the software first and then tether your cell phone to your computer. Use the software to make the connection.

◢ *Use a USB broadband modem.* When using a USB broadband modem, make sure the SIM card is inserted in the device (see Figure 7-38). When you insert the modem into a USB port, Windows finds the device, and the software stored on the device automati-cally installs and runs. A window then appears provided by the software that allows you to connect to the cellular network.

Here are more details of how to connect to a WWAN. In this example, we are using the Sierra Wireless modem shown earlier in Figure 7-37. Do the following to make the connection:

1. For best results, connect your computer to a wired network during the first part of the installation.

2. Insert the device into the USB port, and Windows automatically installs the device drivers stored on the device as well as the management software to use the device. Then the management software launches where you must accept the licensing agree-ment. A shortcut is added to your desktop and programs in the Start menu.

3. You must go to the web site of your mobile operator (AT&T in our example) and activate the phone number used by the modem. Then for best results, remove the modem and restart your computer.

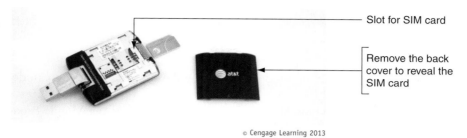

Slot for SIM card

Remove the back cover to reveal the SIM card

© Cengage Learning 2013

Figure 7-38 A SIM card with subscription information on it is required to use a cellular network

4. After your computer restarts, plug in the modem. Wait until LED lights on the modem indicate the modem has found a network and is ready to connect. For this device, a solid blue light on the left indicates power is on, and a blinking green light on the right indicates the device has found a network and is ready to connect.

5. Start the Communication Manager software. When the software starts, it automatically connects to the network (see Figure 7-39). Note that if your computer is connected to a cellular network, it disconnects from a Wi-Fi network.

© Cengage Learning 2013

Figure 7-39 Use the management software to connect and disconnect from the Mobile (cellular) or Wi-Fi network

6. To test the connection, unplug your network cable and try to surf the web. The speed of the connection depends on the type of cellular network you are using, 2G, 3G, or 4G. The 4G networks are the fastest. For the device we are using, the color of the LED indicates the type of network (solid amber is 2G, solid blue is 3G or 4G, solid green is 4G LTE, which currently is the fastest type of cellular network).

A+
220-802
1.5, 1.6

💡 **A+ Exam Tip** The A+ 220-802 exam expects you to know how to connect to a cellular network.

To manage the broadband modem and the WWAN connection, you can do the following:

1. Open the **Network and Sharing Center**. You should see the Mobile Broadband Connection (see Figure 7-40). Make sure the network location is set to Public network.

2. Use Ipconfig to see the IP address assigned to the connection. In Figure 7-41, you can see the IPv4 IP address is a public IP address.

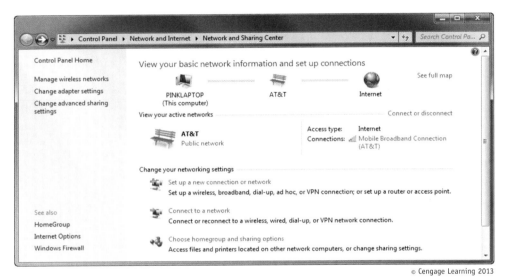

© Cengage Learning 2013

Figure 7-40 Make sure your WWAN connection is secured with a Public network location

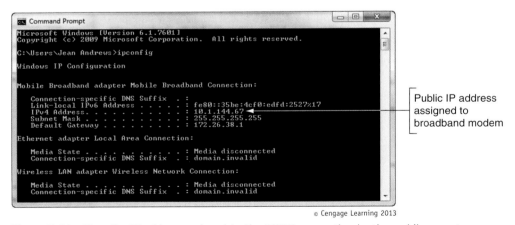

© Cengage Learning 2013

Figure 7-41 View the IP address assigned to the WWAN connection by the mobile operator

3. Device Manager should report the modem is installed with no errors. If you are having problems making the connection, start by checking Device Manager. If errors are reported here, update the device drivers.

A+
220-802
1.5, 1.6

CREATE A DIAL-UP CONNECTION

You never know when you might be called on to support an older dial-up connection. Here are the bare-bones steps you need to set up and support this type of connection:

1. Install an internal or external dial-up modem. Make sure Device Manager recognizes the card without errors.

2. Plug the phone line into the modem port on your computer and into the wall jack.

3. Open the Network and Sharing Center window and click **Set up a new connection or network**. In the dialog box that appears, select **Set up a dial-up connection** and click **Next**.

4. In the next box (see Figure 7-42), enter the phone number to your ISP, your ISP username and password, and the name you decide to give the dial-up connection, such as the name and city of your ISP. Then click **Connect**.

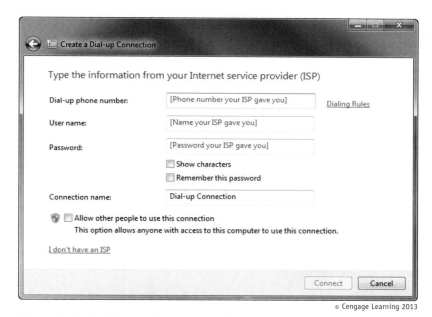

© Cengage Learning 2013

Figure 7-42 Configure a dial-up connection

To use the connection, go to the Network and Sharing Center and click **Connect to a network** (see Figure 7-40). Alternately, you can click your network icon in the taskbar. A bubble appears above your taskbar (see Figure 7-43). Select the dial-up connection, and click **Connect**. The Connect dialog box appears, where you can enter your password (see Figure 7-44). Click **Dial**. You will hear the modem dial up the ISP and make the connection. (For XP, double-click the connection icon in the Network Connections window, and then click **Dial**.)

A+
220-802
1.5, 1.6

© Cengage Learning 2013

Figure 7-43   Select the dial-up connection and then click the Connect button that appears

© Cengage Learning 2013

Figure 7-44   Enter the password to your ISP

A+
220-802
1.5, 1.6

> **A+ Exam Tip** The A+ 220-802 exam expects you to be able to establish a dial-up connection.

If the dial-up connection won't work, here are some things you can try:

- Is the phone line working? Plug in a regular phone and check for a dial tone. Is the phone cord securely connected to the computer and the wall jack?
- Does the modem work? Check Device Manager for reported errors about the modem. Does the modem work when making a call to another phone number (not your ISP)?
- Check the Dial-up Connection Properties box for errors. To do so, click **Change adapter settings** in the Network and Sharing Center, and then right-click the dial-up connection and select **Properties** from the shortcut menu. Is the phone number correct? Does the number need to include a 9 to get an outside line? Has a 1 been added in front of the number by mistake? If you need to add a 9, you can put a comma in the field like this "9,4045661200", which causes a slight pause after the 9 is dialed.
- Try dialing the number manually from a phone. Do you hear beeps on the other end? Try another phone number.
- When you try to connect, do you hear the number being dialed? If so, the problem is most likely with the phone number, the phone line, or the username and password.
- Try removing and reinstalling the dial-up connection.

CREATE A VPN CONNECTION

A **virtual private network (VPN)** is often used by employees when they work away from the corporate network to connect to that network by way of the Internet. A VPN protects data by encrypting it from the time it leaves the remote computer until it reaches a server on the corporate network. The encryption technique is called a tunnel or tunneling (see Figure 7-45).

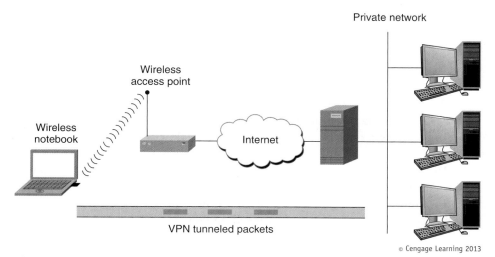

© Cengage Learning 2013

Figure 7-45 With a VPN, tunneling is used to send encrypted data over wired and wireless networks and the Internet

A+
220-802
1.5, 1.6

The VPN is often managed by client/server software such as Citrix Access Gateway by Citrix Systems (*www.citrix.com*). Also, Windows can create a VPN connection rather than using third-party software. A VPN connection is a virtual connection, which means you are really setting up the tunnel over an existing connection to the Internet. When creating a VPN connection on a personal computer, always follow directions given by the network administrator who set up the VPN. The company web site might provide VPN client software to download and install on your PC.

Here are the general steps to use Windows 7 to connect to a VPN:

1. In the Network and Sharing Center, click **Set up a new connection or network**. In the set up box, click **Connect to a workplace** and click **Next**.

2. In the Connect to a Workplace box, click **Use my Internet connection (VPN)**. In the next box, enter the IP address or domain name of the network (see Figure 7-46). Name the VPN connection and click **Next**.

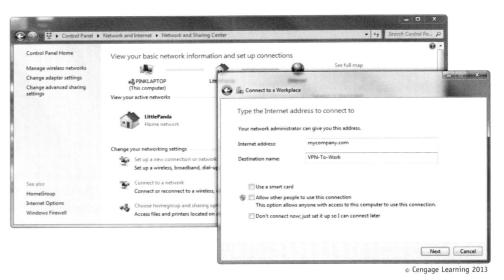

© Cengage Learning 2013

Figure 7-46 Enter login information to the VPN network

3. Enter your username and password to the VPN and click **Connect**. If you want to just set up the connection without connecting to the VPN, in the next box, click **Skip**. The connection is ready to use. Click **Close** to close the wizard.

Whenever you want to use the VPN connection, click the network icon in the taskbar. In the list of available networks, click the VPN connection (see Figure 7-47) and then click **Connect**. A box similar to the one shown earlier in Figure 7-44 appears where you can enter your username and password and click **Connect**. After the connection is made, you can use your browser to access the corporate secured intranet web sites or other resources. The resources you can access depend on the permissions assigned the user account.

A+
220-802
1.5, 1.6

© Cengage Learning 2013

Figure 7-47 Select the VPN connection

Hands-on | Project 7.3 — Investigate TCP/IP Settings

Using a computer connected to a network, answer these questions:

1. What is the hardware device used to make this connection (network card, onboard port, wireless)? List the device's name as Windows sees it in the Device Manager window.

2. What is the MAC address of the wired or wireless network adapter? What command or window did you use to get your answer?

3. What is the IPv4 IP address of the network connection?

4. Are your TCP/IP version 4 settings using static or dynamic IP addressing?

5. What is the IPv6 IP address of your network connection?

6. Disable and enable your network connection. Now what is your IPv4 IP address?

7

SETTING UP A MULTIFUNCTION ROUTER FOR A SOHO NETWORK

A+
220-801
2.6

A PC support technician is likely to be called on to set up a small office or home office network. As part of setting up a small network, you need to know how to configure a multipurpose router to stand between the network and the Internet. You also need to know how to set up and secure a wireless access point. Most SOHO routers are also a wireless access point.

A+
220-802
2.5

💡 **A+ Exam Tip** The A+ 220-801 and A+ 220-802 exams expect you to be able to install, configure, and secure a SOHO wired and wireless router.

FUNCTIONS OF A SOHO ROUTER

Routers can range from small ones designed to manage a SOHO network connecting to an ISP (costing around $75 to $150) to those that manage multiple networks and extensive traffic (costing several thousand dollars). On a small office or home network, a router stands between the ISP network and the local network (see Figure 7-48), and the router is the gateway to the Internet. Note in the figure that computers can connect to the router using wired or wireless connections.

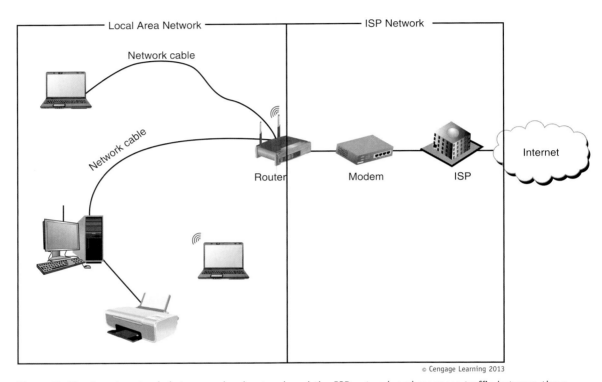

Figure 7-48   A router stands between a local network and the ISP network and manages traffic between them

This router is typical of many SOHO routers and is several devices in one:

  ▲ *Function 1:* As a router, it stands between the ISP network and the local network, routing traffic between the two networks.
  ▲ *Function 2:* As a switch, it manages several network ports that can be connected to wired computers or to a switch that provides more ports for more computers.
  ▲ *Function 3:* As a DHCP server, all computers can receive their IP address from this server.
  ▲ *Function 4:* As a wireless access point, a wireless computer can connect to the network. This wireless connection can be secured using wireless security features.
  ▲ *Function 5:* As a firewall, it blocks unwanted traffic initiated from the Internet and provides Network Address Translation (NAT) so that computers on the LAN can use private or link local IP addresses. Another firewall feature is to restrict Internet access for computers behind the firewall. Restrictions can apply to days of the week, time of day, keywords used, or certain web sites.
  ▲ *Function 6:* As an FTP server, you can connect an external hard drive to the router, and the FTP firmware on the router can be used to share files with network users.

A+
220-801
2.6

A+
220-802
2.5

> **Notes** The speed of a network depends on the speed of each device on the network and how well a router manages that traffic. Routers, switches, and network adapters currently run at three speeds: Gigabit Ethernet (1000 Mbps or 1 Gbps), Fast Ethernet (100 Mbps), or Ethernet (10 Mbps). If you want your entire network to run at the fastest speed, make sure all your devices are rated for Gigabit Ethernet.

An example of a multifunction router is the Linksys E4200 by Cisco shown in Figures 7-49 and 7-50. It has one port for the broadband modem (cable modem or DSL modem) and four ports for computers on the network. The USB port can be used to plug in a USB external hard drive for use by any computer on the network. The router is also a wireless access point having multiple antennas to increase speed and range using Multiple In, Multiple Out (MIMO) technology. The antennas are built in.

© Cengage Learning 2013

Figure 7-49 The Linksys E4200 router by Cisco has built-in wireless antennas and can be used with a DSL or cable modem Internet connection

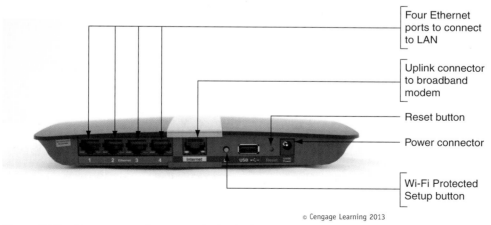

Four Ethernet ports to connect to LAN

Uplink connector to broadband modem

Reset button

Power connector

Wi-Fi Protected Setup button

© Cengage Learning 2013

Figure 7-50 Connectors and ports on the back of the Cisco router

A+
220-801
2.6

A+
220-802
2.5

INSTALL AND CONFIGURE THE ROUTER ON THE NETWORK

To install a router on the network, always follow the directions of the manufacturer rather than the general directions given here. Using the Linksys E4200 as our example router, here is how to install it on the network:

1. On one of your computers on the network (it doesn't matter which one), launch the setup program on the CD that came bundled with the router. The setup program instructs you to use one network cable to connect the computer to the router and a second network cable to connect the router to the DSL or cable modem box using the Internet port on the router. After you have made the connections, click **Next** on the setup screen.

2. On the next screen, you are given the opportunity to change the SSID and password to the router. Be sure to change the password. On the next screen, you can decide to allow or not allow the router to receive automatic updates from Cisco.

3. The setup program says you should be connected to the Internet. Verify the connection by opening your browser and surfing the web. You can then close the router setup program.

> ⚡ **Caution** Changing the router password is especially important if the router is a wireless router. Unless you have disabled or secured the wireless access point, anyone outside your building can use your wireless network. If they guess the default password to the router, they can change the password to hijack your router. Also, your wireless network can be used for criminal activity. When you first install a router, before you do anything else, change your router password and disable the wireless network until you have time to set up and test the wireless security. And, to give even more security, change the default name to another name if the router utility allows that option.

Using any computer on the network, you can use your browser and the firmware on the router to configure it at any time. To do so, follow these steps:

1. Open your browser and enter the IP address of the router, 192.168.1.1, in the address box. The Windows Security box appears (see Figure 7-51). Enter **admin** as the username and the password is the one you set up when installing the router.

© Cengage Learning 2013

Figure 7-51 Enter the username and password to your router firmware utility

A+
220-801
2.6

A+
220-802
2.5

2. The main setup page of the router firmware appears in your browser window (see Figure 7-52). Use the menus near the top of the screen and items on each menu to change your router's configuration. Each router utility is different, but you should be able to poke around and find the setting you need. When finished, click **Save Settings** and close the browser window.

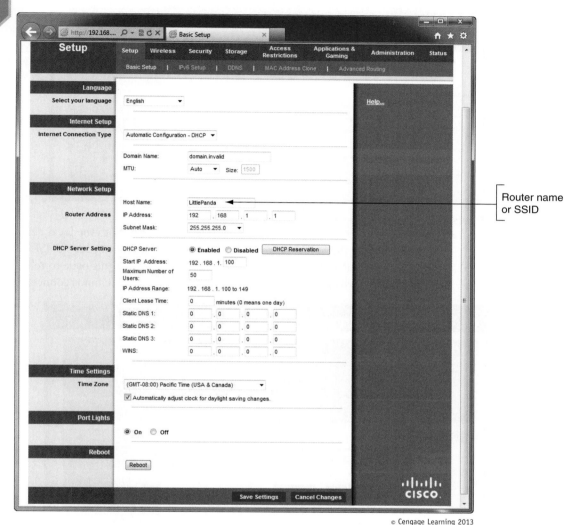

© Cengage Learning 2013

Figure 7-52 Use menus on the router firmware utility screens to configure your router

Following are some changes that you might need to make to the router's configuration. If you make changes on a page, be sure to click **Save Settings** to save your changes. The first setting should always be done:

▲ *Change the router password.* It's extremely important to protect access to your network and prevent others from hijacking your router. If you have not already done so, change the default password to your router firmware. If the firmware offers the option, disable the ability to configure the router from over the wireless network (see Figure 7-53).

▲ *Change the SSID and configure the DHCP server.* On the Basic Setup menu shown earlier in Figure 7-52, you can change the name of the router (the SSID), and you can enable or disable the DHCP server. For the DHCP server, you set the start IP address and set the number of IP addresses DHCP can serve up.

7

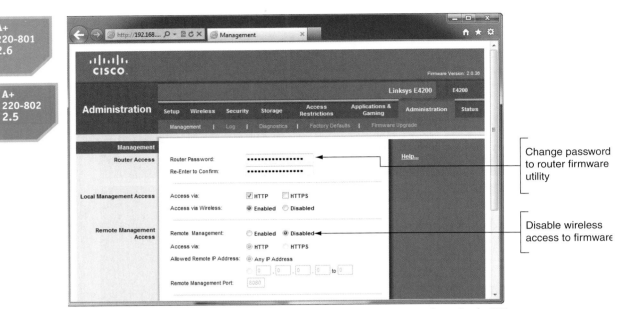

Figure 7-53   Prevent others from hijacking your router

© Cengage Learning 2013

▲ *View assignments made by the ISP.* The router belongs to both the local network and the ISP network. On the Status page shown in Figure 7-54, you can see the ISP has assigned the router a private IP address on its network. You can also use this page to release and renew this IP address, which might help solve a problem when you cannot connect to the ISP.

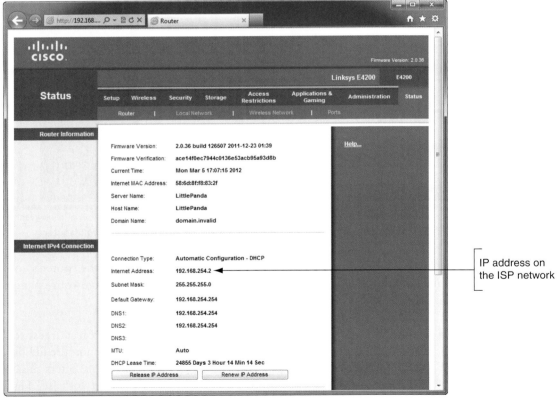

Figure 7-54   The ISP has assigned the router a private IP address

© Cengage Learning 2013

Notes If you are running a web server on the Internet, the web server must use a public and static IP address. For this situation, you can lease a public IP address from your ISP at an additional cost.

A+
220-801
2.6

A+
220-802
2.5

▲ *Assign static IP addresses.* A computer or network printer might require a static IP address. For example, when a computer is running a web server on the local network, it needs a static IP address that you can add to the Hosts file for each computer on the network that needs to access this intranet web site. A network printer also needs a static IP address so computers will always be able to find the printer. To assign a static IP address to a client, click **DHCP Reservation** on the Setup page shown earlier in Figure 7-52. In the DHCP Reservation box, select a client from the DHCP table and click **Add Clients**. Then click **Save Settings**. In Figure 7-55, a Canon network printer is set to receive the IP address 192.168.1.118 each time it connects to the network.

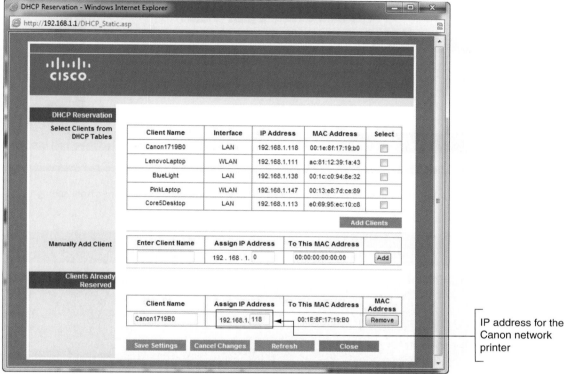

IP address for the Canon network printer

Figure 7-55 Assign a static IP address to a network printer

© Cengage Learning 2013

▲ *Configure the firewall to disable all ports.* On the Security page, you can enable SPI Firewall Protection (see Figure 7-56). SPI (stateful packet inspection) examines each data packet and rejects those unsolicited by the local network. Using this setting, all ports are disabled (closed) and no activity initiated from the Internet can get in. You can allow exceptions to this firewall rule by using port forwarding, port triggering, or a DMZ. How to do so is coming up in the next section.

▲ *Improve QoS for an application.* As you use your network and notice that one application is not getting the best service, you can improve network performance for this application using the Quality of Service (QoS) feature. For example, suppose you routinely use Skype to share your desktop with collaborators over the Internet. To assign a high priority to Skype, go to the **Applications & Gaming** tab (see Figure 7-57). Under Internet Access Priority, select **Enabled**. Under Category, in the drop-down list of Applications, select **Skype**. Under Priority, select **High** and click **Apply**. Skype is added in the Summary area. If you don't see your application listed, you can click **Add a New Application** in the drop-down list of applications and enter its name.

Now let's look at the concepts and steps to allow certain activity initiated from the Internet past your firewall. Then we'll look at how to set up a wireless network.

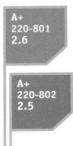

© Cengage Learning 2013

Figure 7-56 Configure the router's firewall to prevent others on the Internet from seeing or accessing your network

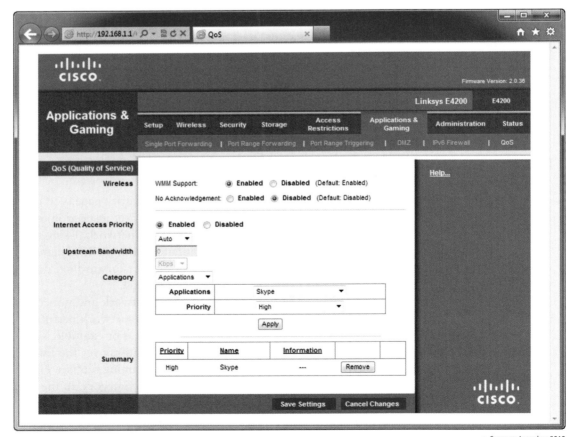

© Cengage Learning 2013

Figure 7-57 Use the QoS feature to assign a high priority to an application to improve its network service

A+
220-801
2.6

A+
220-802
2.5

PORT FORWARDING, PORT TRIGGERING, AND A DMZ

Suppose you're hosting an Internet game or want to use Remote Desktop to access your home computer from the Internet. In both situations, you need to enable (open) certain ports so that activity initiated from the Internet can get past your firewall.

Recall that a router uses NAT redirection to present its own IP address to the Internet in place of IP addresses of computers on the local network. The NAT protocol is also responsible for passing communication to the correct port on the correct local computer.

Here are the ways a router can use NAT to open or close certain ports:

▲ **Port filtering** is used to open or close certain ports so they can or cannot be used. Remember that applications are assigned these ports. Therefore, in effect, you are filtering or controlling what applications can or cannot get through the firewall. For example, in Figure 7-58a, all requests from the Internet to ports 20, 443, 450, and 3389 are filtered or disabled. These ports are closed.

▲ **Port forwarding** means that when the firewall receives a request for communication from the Internet to a specific computer and port, the request will be allowed and forwarded to that computer on the network. The computer is defined to the router by its static IP address. For example, in Figure 7-58a, port 80 is open and requests to

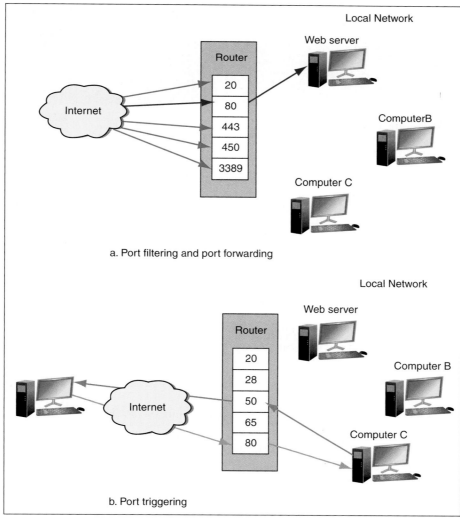

a. Port filtering and port forwarding

b. Port triggering

Figure 7-58   Port filtering, port forwarding, and port triggering

© Cengage Learning 2013

A+
220-801
2.6

A+
220-802
2.5

port 80 are forwarded to the web server that is listening at that port. This one computer on the network is the only one allowed to receive requests at port 80.

⊿ **Port triggering** opens a port when a PC on the network initiates communication
through another port. For example, in Figure 7-58b, Computer C sends data to port
50 to a computer on the Internet. The router is configured to open port 80 for communication from this remote computer. Port 80 is closed until this trigger occurs. Port
triggering does not require a static IP address for the computer inside the network,
and any computer can initiate port triggering. The router will leave port 80 open for a
time. If no more data is received from port 50, then it closes port 80.

> 💡 **A+ Exam Tip** The A+ 220-801 exam expects you to know how to implement port forwarding
> and port triggering.

To configure port forwarding or port triggering, use the Applications & Gaming tab
shown in Figure 7-59. In the figure, the Remote Desktop application outside the network can use port forwarding to communicate with the computer whose IP address is
192.168.1.90 using port 3389. The situation is illustrated in Figure 7-60. This computer is
set to support the Remote Desktop server application. Later in the chapter, you will learn to
use Remote Desktop.

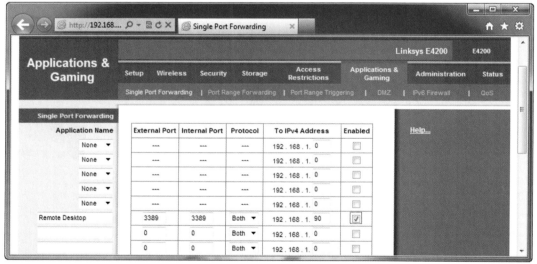

© Cengage Learning 2013

Figure 7-59 Using port forwarding, activity initiated from the Internet is allowed access to a
computer on the network

To configure port triggering, click the **Port Range Triggering** tab and enter the two ranges
of ports. For example, in Figure 7-61, the Triggered Range of ports will trigger the event to
open the ports listed under Forwarded Range.

Here are some tips to keep in mind when using port forwarding or port triggering:

⊿ You must lease a static IP address from your ISP so that people on the Internet can
find you. Most ISPs will provide you a static IP address for an additional monthly fee.

⊿ For port forwarding to work, the computer on your network must have a static IP
address so that the router knows where to send the communication.

⊿ If the computer using port triggering stops sending data, the router might close the triggered port before communication is complete. Also, if two computers on the network
attempt to trigger the same port, the router will not allow data to pass to either computer.

Figure 7-60 With port forwarding, a router allows requests initiated outside the network

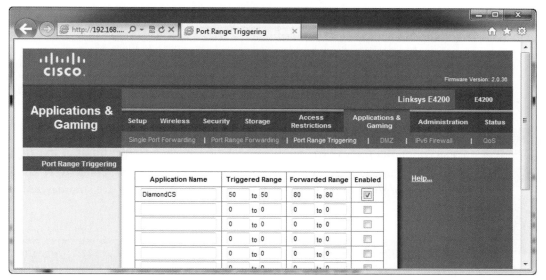

Figure 7-61 Port triggering opens a range of ports when data is sent from inside the network

7

▲ Using port forwarding, your computer and network are more vulnerable because you are allowing external users directly into your private network. For better security, turn on port forwarding only when you know it's being used.

A demilitarized zone (DMZ) in networking is a computer or network that is not protected by a firewall. You can drop all your shields protecting a computer by putting it in a DMZ and the firewall no longer protects it. If you are having problems getting port forwarding or port triggering to work, putting your computer in a DMZ can free it to receive any communication from the Internet. Enter its IP address or MAC address on the DMZ page of the router utility (see Figure 7-62) under Destination. You can also specify that any IP address on the Internet is allowed access or you can limit access to a specific IP address. It goes without saying to not leave the DMZ enabled unless you are using it.

© Cengage Learning 2013

Figure 7-62 Put a computer in a DMZ so that the router firewall does not prevent it from receiving communication from the Internet

> **Notes** By the way, if you want to use a domain name rather than an IP address to access a computer on your network from the Internet, you'll need to purchase the domain name and register it in the Internet name space to associate it with your static IP address assigned by your ISP. Several web sites on the Internet let you do both; one site is by Network Solutions at *www.networksolutions.com*.

SET UP A WIRELESS NETWORK

The standards for a local wireless network are called Wi-Fi (Wireless Fidelity), and their technical name is IEEE 802.11. The IEEE 802.11 standards, collectively known as the 802.11 a/b/g/n standards, have evolved over the years and are summarized in Table 7-6.

> **A+ Exam Tip** The A+ 220-801 exam expects you to know about 802.11 a/b/g/n standards, their speeds, distances, and frequencies.

Wi-Fi Standard	Speeds, Distances, and Frequencies
IEEE 802.11a	• Speeds up to 54 Mbps (megabits per second). • Short range up to 50 meters with radio frequency of 5.0 GHz. • 802.11a is no longer used.
IEEE 802.11b	• Up to 11 Mbps with a range of up to 100 meters. (Indoor ranges are less than outdoor ranges.) • The radio frequency of 2.4 GHz experienced interference from cordless phones and microwaves.
IEEE 802.11g	• Same as 802.11b, but with a speed up to 54 Mbps.
IEEE 802.11n	• Up to 500 Mbps depending on the configuration. • Indoor range up to 70 meters and outdoor range up to 250 meters. • Can use either 5.0 GHz or 2.4 GHz radio frequency.

© Cengage Learning 2013

Table 7-6 Older and current Wi-Fi standards

A+
220-801
2.5, 2.6

A+
220-802
2.5

The latest Wi-Fi standard, 802.11n, uses **multiple input/multiple output (MIMO)**, which means a device can use two or more antennas to improve performance (see Figure 7-63). Most wireless devices today are 802.11 b/g/n compatible.

© Cengage Learning 2013

Figure 7-63   Wireless network adapter with two antennas supports 802.11 b/g/n Wi-Fi standards

When setting up a wireless network, position your router or the stand-alone wireless access point in the center of where you want your hotspot and know that a higher position (near the ceiling) works better than a lower position (on the floor). Be sure to set the device in a physically secure place and not in a public area where it can be stolen.

When configuring an 802.11n network, consider these options:

▲ *The radio frequency (RF) the network will use.* Choices for radio frequency (RF) are 5 GHz and 2.4 GHz. The 5 GHz frequency yields faster speeds than the 2.4 GHz frequency, but the range is shorter. For best performance in a small space, use 5 GHz. Use 2.4 GHz if your hotspot must reach a longer distance. Use both frequencies so they can share the network traffic.

▲ *The older wireless devices that will use the network.* If your network must support older 802.11 b/g wireless devices, you must support the 2.4 GHz frequency.

▲ *The RF interference the network will experience.* Interference for 2.4 GHz frequency might come from cordless phones, microwaves, and other Wi-Fi networks. The 5 GHz frequency is less likely to experience this interference.

▲ *The channel the network will use.* A channel is a specific radio frequency within a broader frequency. For example, two channels in the 5 GHz band are 5.180 GHz and 5.200 GHz channels. In the United States, eleven channels are allowed for 5 GHz or 2.4 GHz bands (Channels 1 through 11). For most networks, you can allow auto channel selection so that any channel in the frequency range (5 GHz or 2.4 GHz) will work. The device scans for the least-busy channel. However, if you are trying to solve a problem with interference from a nearby wireless network, you can set each network to a different channel; make the channels far apart to reduce interference. For example, set one network to Channel 1 and set the other to Channel 11.

▲ *The channel width the network will use.* For a 5 GHz network, choices are 40 MHz and 20 MHz channel widths. For best performance, use 40 MHz. For less interference, use 20 MHz.

7

A+
220-801
2.5, 2.6

A+
220-802
2.5

▲ *The radio power level the device will use.* Some high-end access points allow you to adjust the radio power levels the device can use. To reduce interference, limit the range of the network, or to save on electricity, reduce the power level.

For the firmware utility of the Linksys E4200 wireless router, you can change wireless settings on the Wireless tab when you click **Manual** (see Figure 7-64). Notice in the figure the two wireless setting groups; one is for the 5 GHz range and the other is for the 2.4 GHz range. Unless you have a reason to do otherwise, you can leave the Network Mode for each group set to Mixed, which allows 801.11 b/g/n connections in the 5 GHz or 2.4 GHz band. Notice in the figure that the Channel and Channel Width for each band are set to Auto. If necessary, you can specify a channel or channel width. To force a device to use one band or the other, set a different passphrase for each band.

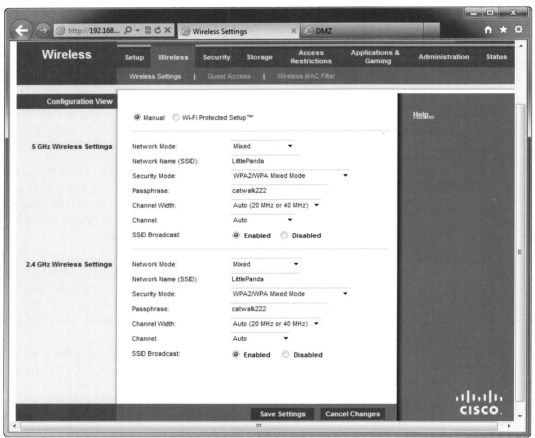

© Cengage Learning 2013

Figure 7-64   Configure settings for the wireless network

It is important to secure a wireless network from outside attack. Recall that securing a wireless network is generally done in three ways:

▲ *Method 1: Requiring a security key and using data encryption*—If encryption is used when you connect to a wireless network, a security key is required. If no security key is required, the data on the wireless network is not encrypted. The three main protocols for encryption for 802.11 wireless networks are:

  o **WEP.** WEP (Wired Equivalent Privacy) is no longer considered secure because the key used for encryption is static (it doesn't change).

A+
220-801
2.5, 2.6

A+
220-802
2.5

o **WPA.** WPA (Wi-Fi Protected Access) also called TKIP (Temporal Key Integrity Protocol) encryption, is stronger than WEP and was designed to replace it. With WPA encryption, encryption keys are constantly changing.

o **WPA2.** WPA2 (Wi-Fi Protected Access 2), also called the 802.11i standard, is the latest and best wireless encryption standard. It is based on the **AES** (Advanced Encryption Standard), which improved on the way TKIP generated encryption keys. All wireless devices sold today support the WPA2 standard.

To configure encryption for the Cisco router, select **Manual** in the Wireless Settings page shown in Figure 7-64 and select the Security Mode from the drop-down menu. For best security, enter a passphrase (security key) to the wireless network that is different from the password you use to the router utility.

> **Notes** To make the strongest passphrase or security key, use a random group of numbers, uppercase and lowercase letters, and, if allowed, at least one symbol. Also use at least eight characters in the passphrase.

▲ *Method 2: Disable SSID broadcasting*—You can disable SSID broadcasting and change the SSID on the Wireless page shown in Figure 7-64. This security method is not considered strong security because software can be used to discovery an SSID that is not broadcasted.

▲ *Method 3: Filter MAC addresses*—A wireless access point can filter the MAC addresses of wireless adapters to either allow or not allow these MAC addresses access to the wireless network (see Figure 7-65). MAC address filtering is considered a weak security measure and does not use encryption.

© Cengage Learning 2013

Figure 7-65 Configure how the router will filter MAC addresses

You also need to know about **Wi-Fi Protected Setup (WPS)**, which is designed to make it easier for users to connect their computers to a wireless network when a hard-to-remember SSID and security key are used. WPS generates the SSID and security key using a random string of hard-to-guess letters and numbers. The SSID is not broadcasted, so both the SSID and security key must be entered to connect. Rather than having to enter these difficult strings,

A+
220-801
2.5, 2.6

a user presses a button on a wireless computer or the router's PIN or computer's PIN is used. All computers on the wireless network must support WPS for it to be used. WPS is enabled on the Wireless page of the router utility shown in Figure 7-66.

A+
220-802
2.5

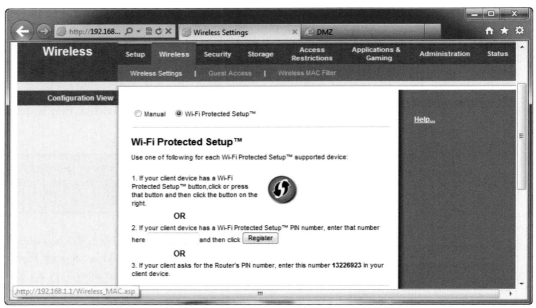

© Cengage Learning 2013

Figure 7-66   Using WPS, it is easy for users to connect to a wireless network with strong security

> **🔆 A+ Exam Tip**   The A+ 220-801 exam expects you to know about installing and configuring a wireless network, including MAC filtering, Wi-Fi channels (1–11), SSID broadcasting, WEP, WPA, WPA2, TKIP, AES, and WPS.
>
>   The A+ 220-802 exam expects you to know about installing and configuring a wireless network, including changing default usernames and passwords, disabling and changing the SSID, using MAC filtering, antenna and access point placements, radio power levels, and assigning static IP addresses.

Hands-on | Project 7.4   Research a Wireless LAN

Suppose you have a DSL connection to the Internet in your home and you want to connect two laptops and a desktop computer in a wireless network to the Internet. You need to purchase a multifunction wireless router like the one you learned to configure in this chapter. You also need a wireless adapter for the desktop computer. (The two laptops have built-in wireless.) Use the web to research the equipment needed to create the wireless LAN and answer the following:

1. Print two web pages showing two different multifunctional wireless routers. What are the brand, model, and price of each router?

2. Print two web pages showing two different wireless adapters a desktop computer can use to connect to the wireless network. Include one external device that uses a USB port and one internal device. What are the brand, model, and price of each device?

3. Which router and wireless adapter would you select for your home network? What is the total cost of both devices?

>> *CHAPTER SUMMARY*

Understanding TCP/IP and Windows Networking

- Networking communication happens at three levels: hardware, operating system, and application levels.

- At the hardware level, a network adapter has a MAC address that uniquely identifies it on the network.

- Using the TCP/IP protocols, the OS identifies a network connection by an IP address. At the application level, a port address identifies an application.

- IP addresses can be dynamic or static. A dynamic IP address is assigned by a DHCP server when the computer first connects to a network. A static IP address is manually assigned.

- An IP address using IPv4 has 32 bits, and an IP address using IPv6 has 128 bits.

- Classes of IPv4 IP addresses used by the public are Class A, Class B, and Class C addresses. Some IP addresses are private IP addresses that can be used only on intranets.

- If a computer is unable to obtain an IP address from a DHCP server, Windows uses Automatic Private IP Addressing (APIPA) to assign the computer an IP address unless an alternate static IP address has been configured for the computer.

- Using IPv6, three types of IP addresses are a unicast address (used by a single node on a network), multicast address (used for one-to-many transmissions), and anycast address (used by routers).

- Three types of unicast addresses are a global unicast address (used on the Internet), a link local unicast address (used on a private network), and a unique local unicast address (used on subnets in a large enterprise).

- A computer can be assigned a computer name (also called a host name), and a network can be assigned a domain name. A fully qualified domain name (FQDN) includes the computer name and the domain name. An FQDN can be used to find a computer on the Internet if this name is associated with an IP address kept by DNS servers.

- TCP/IP uses protocols at the application level (such as FTP, HTTP, and Telnet) and at the operating system level (such as TCP and UDP).

Connecting a Computer to a Network

- A PC support person needs to know how to configure TCP/IP settings and make a wired or wireless connection to an existing network.

- The best method to secure a wireless network is to use encryption (which requires you enter a security key to connect). Two other methods that are sometimes used to secure a network are to not broadcast the SSID (which requires you enter the SSID to connect) and MAC address filtering (which requires the network administrator enter the MAC address of your wireless adapter in a table). These last two methods provide weak security and are not recommended.

- To connect to a wireless WAN or cellular network, you need a mobile broadband modem, a SIM card, and a subscription to the cellular network. The mobile operator provides you a SIM card with your subscription. Your cell phone can serve as the mobile broadband modem when you tether it to your computer.

- A dial-up connection uses a telephone modem to make a connection to an ISP.

7

Setting Up a Multifunction Router for a SOHO Network

▲ A multifunction router for a small-office-home-office network might serve several functions, including a router, a switch, a DHCP server, a wireless access point, a firewall using NAT, and an FTP server.

▲ It's extremely important to change the password to configure your router as soon as you install it, especially if the router is also a wireless access point.

▲ To allow certain network traffic initiated on the Internet past your firewall, you can use port forwarding, port triggering, and a DMZ.

▲ To secure a wireless access point, you can enable MAC address filtering, disable SSID broadcasting, and enable encryption (WPA2, WPA, or WEP).

>> KEY TERMS

6TO4
802.11 a/b/g/n
adapter address
AES (Advanced Encryption Standard)
alternate IP address
anycast address
Automatic Private IP Address (APIPA)
best-effort protocol
channel
Class A
Class B
Class C
classful subnet mask
classless subnet mask
client/server
computer name
connectionless protocol
connection-oriented protocol
default gateway
DHCP (dynamic host configuration protocol)
DHCP client
DMZ
DNS (Domain Name System or Domain Name Service)
DNS client
DNS server
domain name
dynamic IP address
FTP (File Transfer Protocol)
fully qualified domain name (FQDN)
gateway
global address
global unicast address
hardware address

host name
Hosts file
HTTP (Hypertext Transfer Protocol)
HTTPS (HTTP secure)
IMAP4 (Internet Message Access Protocol, version 4)
interface
interface ID
Internet Protocol version 4 (IPv4)
Internet Protocol version 6 (IPv6)
intranet
IP address
ISATAP
Lightweight Directory Access Protocol (LDAP)
link
link-local address
link-local unicast address
local area network (LAN)
local link
loopback address
MAC (Media Access Control) address
multicast address
multicasting
multiple input/multiple output (MIMO)
name resolution
NAT (Network Address Translation)
neighbors
network adapter
octet
packet
physical address

POP3 (Post Office Protocol, version 3)
port
port address
port filtering
port forwarding
port number
port triggering
private IP addresses
protocols
public IP addresses
Quality of Service (QoS)
radio frequency (RF)
Remote Desktop Protocol (RDP)
router
Secure FTP (SFTP)
Secure Shell (SSH)
Server Message Block (SMB)
Service Set Identifier (SSID)
SIM (Subscriber Identification Module) card
Simple Network Management Protocol (SNMP)
SMTP (Simple Mail Transfer Protocol)
SMTP AUTH (SMTP Authentication)
static IP address
subnet
subnet ID
subnet mask
TCP (Transmission Control Protocol)
TCP/IP (Transmission Control Protocol/Internet Protocol)
Telnet

Teredo
TKIP (Temporal Key Integrity Protocol)
UDP (User Datagram Protocol)
unicast address
unique local address (ULA)

unique local unicast address
virtual private network (VPN)
WEP (Wired Equivalent Privacy)
Wi-Fi (Wireless Fidelity)
Wi-Fi Protected Setup (WPS)

wireless access point
wireless wide area network (WWAN)
WPA (Wi-Fi Protected Access)
WPA2 (Wi-Fi Protected Access 2)

>> REVIEWING THE BASICS

1. How many bits are in a MAC address?

2. How many bits are in an IPv4 IP address? In an IPv6 IP address?

3. How does a client application identify a server application on another computer on the network?

4. What are IP addresses called that begin with 10, 172.16, or 192.168?

5. In what class is the IP address 185.75.255.10?

6. In what class is the IP address 193.200.30.5?

7. Describe the difference between public and private IP addresses. If a network is using private IP addresses, how can the computers on that network access the Internet?

8. Why is it unlikely that you will find the IP address 192.168.250.10 on the Internet?

9. In Figure 7-9, the subnet mask is four notches tall and is considered a classless subnet mask for this network of sticks. How many notches tall would be a classful subnet mask for the same network?

10. If no DHCP server is available when a computer configured for dynamic IP addressing connects to the network, what type of IP address is assigned to the computer?

11. If a computer is found to have an IP address of 169.254.1.1, what can you assume about how it received that IP address?

12. What are the last 64 bits of a IPv6 IP address called? How are these bits used?

13. Name at least three tunneling protocols that are used for IPv6 packets to travel over an IPv4 network.

14. How is an IPv6 IP address used that begins with 2000::? That begins with FE80::?

15. How many bits are in the Subnet ID block? What are the values of these bits for a link-local IP address?

16. Which type of IPv6 address is used to create multiple sites within a large organization?

17. What type of server serves up IP addresses to computers on a network?

18. Which TCP/IP protocol that manages packet delivery guarantees that delivery? Which protocol does not guarantee delivery, but is faster?

19. At what port does an SMTP email server listen to receive email from a client computer?

20. Which protocol does a web server use when transmissions are encrypted for security?

21. What type of server resolves fully qualified domain names to IP addresses?

7

22. Which email protocol allows a client application to manage email stored on an email server?

23. What type of protocol is used to present a public IP address to computers outside the LAN to handle requests to use the Internet from computers inside the LAN?

24. Which protocol is used when an application queries a database on a corporate network such as a database of printers?

25. What type of encryption protocol does Secure FTP (SFTP) use to secure FTP transmissions?

26. What two Windows applications use the RDP protocol and port 3389?

27. Which version of 802.11 technologies can use two antennas at both the access point and the network adapter?

28. Which wireless encryption standard is stronger, WEP or WPA?

29. When securing a Wi-Fi wireless network, which is considered better security: to filter MAC addresses, use encryption, or not broadcast the SSID?

30. Would you expect WPS to be used when a wireless network is using strong security, weak security, or no security (as in a public hotspot)?

>> *THINKING CRITICALLY*

1. You have just installed a network adapter and have booted up the system, installing the drivers. You open Windows Explorer on a remote computer and don't see the computer on which you just installed the NIC. What is the first thing you check?

   a. Has TCP/IPv6 been enabled?

   b. Is the computer using dynamic or static IP addressing?

   c. Are the lights on the adapter functioning correctly?

   d. Has the computer been assigned a computer name?

2. Your boss asks you to transmit a small file that includes sensitive personnel data to a server on the network. The server is running a Telnet server and an FTP server. Why is it not a good idea to use Telnet to reach the remote computer?

   a. Telnet transmissions are not encrypted.

   b. Telnet is not reliable and the file might arrive corrupted.

   c. FTP is faster than Telnet.

   d. FTP running on the same computer as Telnet causes Telnet to not work.

3. Your job is to support the desktop computers in a small company of 32 employees. A consulting firm is setting up a private web server to be used internally by company employees. The static IP address of the server is 192.168.45.200. Employees will open their web browser and enter *personnel.mycompany.com* in the URL address box to browse this web site. What steps do you take so that each computer in the company can browse the site using this URL?

>> *REAL PROBLEMS, REAL SOLUTIONS*

REAL PROBLEM 7-1: Setting Up a Small Network

The simplest possible wired network is two computers connected together using a crossover cable. In a crossover cable, the send and receive wires are crossed so that one computer can send and the other computer receive on the same wire. A crossover cable looks just like a regular network cable (also called a patch cable) except for the labeling (see Figure 7-67).

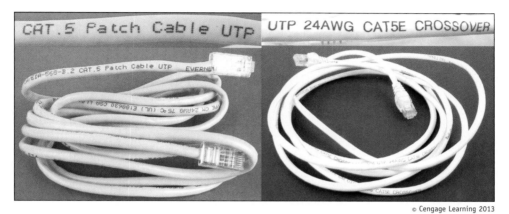

© Cengage Learning 2013

Figure 7-67   A patch cable and crossover cable look the same but are labeled differently

Do the following to set up and test the network:

1. Connect two computers using a crossover cable. Using the Network and Sharing Center, verify your network is up. What is the IP address of Computer A? Of Computer B?

2. Join the two computers to the same homegroup. Then use Windows Explorer to view the files on the other computer shared with the homegroup.

3. Convert the TCP/IP configuration to static IP addressing. Assign a private IP address to each computer. What is the IP address of Computer A? Of Computer B?

4. Verify you can still see files shared with the homegroup on each computer.

7

Windows Resources on a Network

In the last chapter, you learned how to connect to a network and set one up. This chapter focuses on using a network for client/server applications and for sharing files and folders with network users. You also learn how to troubleshoot network connections and what to do when you cannot reach resources on the network.

Security is always a huge concern when dealing with networks. In this chapter, you learn how to share resources on the network and still protect these resources from those who should not have access. In the next chapter, we take security to a higher level and discuss all the many tools and techniques you can use to protect a computer or a SOHO network.

SUPPORTING CLIENT/SERVER APPLICATIONS

Client/server applications you will likely be expected to support include Internet Explorer, Remote Desktop, and other remote applications. You also need to know how to configure network settings to improve performance for client/service applications using Wake on LAN, Quality of Service techniques, and Group Policy. All these skills are covered in this part of the chapter.

> **A+ Exam Tip** The A+ 220-802 exam expects you to know how to install and manage a local printer, network printer, and print server. This content on supporting printers is in the companion book, *A+ Guide to Hardware*. You can also find this content on the textbooks' companion web site at *www .cengagebrain.com*. See the Preface for more information. This book, *A+ Guide to Software*, and the online content together cover all the content on the A+ 220-802 exam.

A+
220-802
1.5, 1.6

INTERNET EXPLORER

By far, the most popular client/server applications on the Internet are a browser and web server. At the time of this writing, Internet Explorer (IE) version 9 is the latest browser released by Microsoft. Windows 7 comes with IE version 8, but you can upgrade to version 9 using Windows Updates. To upgrade, open Windows Updates and find and install the Internet Explorer 9 update. You can also go to the Microsoft.com web site and follow links to download and install IE 9.

If you later have a problem with IE9, you can uninstall it and install it again. Go to the Programs and Features window in Control Panel. Then click **View installed updates**. Select the update (see Figure 8-1) and click **Uninstall**.

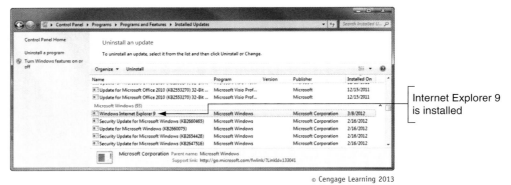

© Cengage Learning 2013

Figure 8-1   Use the Programs and Features window to uninstall Internet Explorer 9, which was installed as a Windows update

Here are some tips when using the Internet Explorer window:

- ▲ To show the menu bar, press the **Alt** key. The menu appears long enough for you to make one selection from the menu. If you want the menu bar to be permanent, right-click a blank area in the title bar and check **Menu bar** from the shortcut menu (see Figure 8-2). Notice in Figure 8-2 you can also add the command bar to the IE window.
- ▲ To get help using IE, press **F1** to open Windows Help and Support. Alternately, you can click **Help** on the menu bar and click **Internet Explorer Help**, or you can click the question mark on the command bar and click **Internet Explorer Help**.

A+
220-802
1.5, 1.6

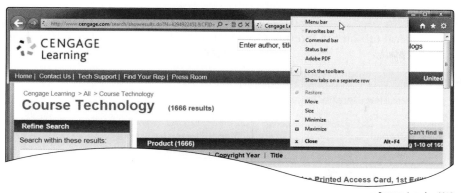

© Cengage Learning 2013

Figure 8-2 Access the shortcut menu from the title bar to control the
Internet Explorer window

Some web servers use the HTTP with SSL or TLS protocols to secure transmissions to
and from the web server. To find out if HTTPS is being used in IE 9, look for https and a
padlock in the browser address box. Click the padlock to get information about the site
security (see Figure 8-3).

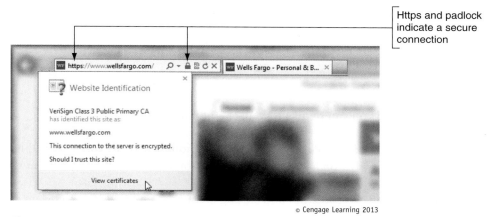

© Cengage Learning 2013

Figure 8-3 A secured connection from browser to web server assures all
transmissions are encrypted

Use the Internet Options box to manage Internet Explorer settings. To open the box,
click the Tools icon on the right side of the IE title bar and click **Internet Options**. Another
method is to press **Alt**, which causes the menu bar to appear; then click **Tools, Internet
Options**. And still a third method is to click **Internet Options** in the Network and Internet
group of Control Panel. The Internet Options box appears. Whenever you make changes in
the box, click **Apply** to apply these changes without closing the box. Alternately, you can
click **OK** to save your changes and close the box.

Now let's see how to use each tab on the Internet Options box.

💡 **A+ Exam Tip** The A+ 220-802 exam expects you to know how to use the General, Security,
Privacy, Connections, Programs, and Advanced tabs on the Internet Options box.

A+
220-802
1.5, 1.6

GENERAL TAB

The General tab on the Internet Options box is shown on the left side of Figure 8-4.

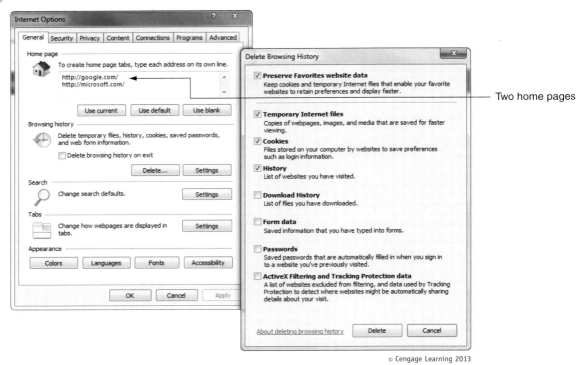

Two home pages

© Cengage Learning 2013

Figure 8-4 Use the General tab of the Internet Options box to delete your browsing history

Here's what you can do using the General tab:

◢ Change the home page or add a second home page. To add a second home page, insert the URL on a second line in the Home page area, as shown on the left side of Figure 8-4.

◢ To protect your identity and surfing records, it's a good idea to delete all your browsing history each time you use IE on a computer that is not your own. To delete this history, click **Delete**. In the Delete Browsing History box (see the right side of Figure 8-4), notice the item at the top. When you leave this item checked, any cookies used by web sites in your Favorites list are *not* deleted. Select the items to delete and click **Delete**.

◢ If you want to delete your browsing history each time you close Internet Explorer, check **Delete browsing history on exit** on the General tab.

◢ Internet Explorer holds a cache containing previously downloaded content in case it is requested again. The cache is stored in several folders named Temporary Internet Files. To manage the IE cache, click **Settings** under Browsing history. The Temporary Internet Files and History Settings box appears (see Figure 8-5). Use this box to change the maximum allowed space used for temporary Internet files and to control the location of these files.

SECURITY TAB

Set the security level on the Security tab (see the left side of Figure 8-6). Medium-high is the default value, which prompts before downloading content and does not download ActiveX controls that are not signed by Microsoft. An **ActiveX control** is a small app or add-on that

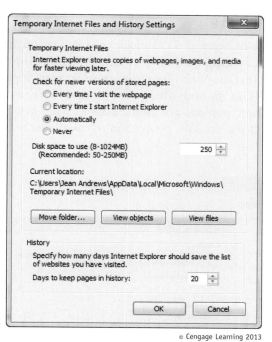

© Cengage Learning 2013

Figure 8-5 Control the size and location of temporary files used by Internet Explorer

can be downloaded from a web site along with a web page and is executed by IE to enhance the web page (for example, add animation to the page). A virus can sometimes hide in an ActiveX control, but IE is designed to catch them by authenticating each ActiveX control it downloads. To customize security settings, click **Custom level**. In the Security Settings box (see the right side of Figure 8-6), you can decide exactly how you want to handle downloaded content. For example, you can disable file downloads.

8

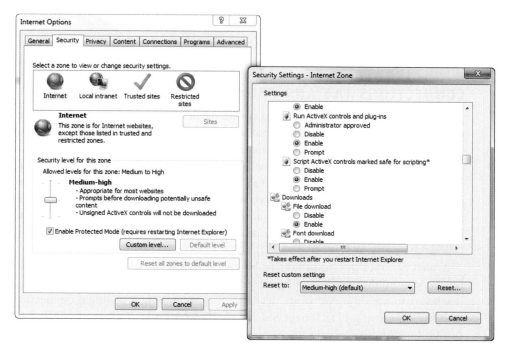

© Cengage Learning 2013

Figure 8-6 Use the Security tab to control what type of content is downloaded and how it is managed

PRIVACY TAB AND CONTENT TAB

Use the Privacy tab (see the left side of Figure 8-7) to block cookies that might invade your privacy or steal your identity. You can also use the tab to control the Pop-up Blocker, which prevents annoying pop-ups as you surf the Web. To allow a pop-up from a particular web site, click **Settings** and enter the URL of the web site in the Pop-up Blocker Settings box (see the right side of Figure 8-7). Some pop-ups are useful, such as when you're trying to download a file from a web site and the site asks permission to complete the download.

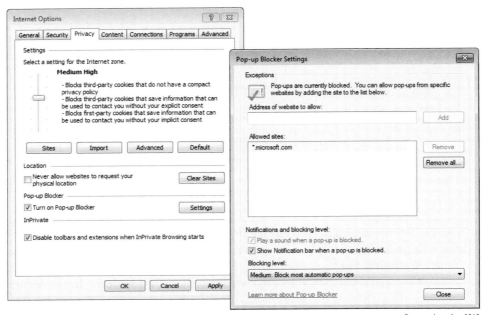

© Cengage Learning 2013

Figure 8-7 Use the Privacy tab to control pop-ups and cookies

The Content tab contains settings for parental controls, allowed content based on ratings, certificates used by web sites, and how AutoComplete and Feeds are handled.

CONNECTIONS TAB AND PROXY SETTINGS

The Connections tab allows you to configure proxy server settings and create a VPN connection. Many large corporations and ISPs use proxy servers to speed up Internet access. A proxy server is a computer that intercepts requests that a browser makes of a server. The proxy server substitutes its own IP address for the request using NAT protocols. Then, when it receives the content, it caches it and passes it on to the browser. If another browser requests the same content, the proxy server can provide the content that it has cached. In addition, proxy servers sometimes act as a gateway to the Internet, a firewall to protect the network, and to restrict Internet access by employees in order to force those employees to follow company policies.

A web browser does not have to be aware that a proxy server is in use. However, one reason you might need to configure Internet Explorer to be aware of and use a proxy server is when you are on a corporate network and are having a problem connecting to a secured web site (one using HTTP over SSL or another encryption protocol). The problem might be caused by Windows trying to connect using the wrong proxy server on the network. Check with your network administrator to find out if a specific proxy server should be used to manage secure web site connections.

A+
220-802
1.5, 1.6

💡 **A+ Exam Tip** The A+ 220-802 exam expects you to know how to configure proxy settings on a client desktop.

If you need to configure Internet Explorer to use a specific proxy server, on the Connections tab, click **LAN settings**. In the settings box, check **Use a proxy server for your LAN** and enter the IP address of the proxy server (see Figure 8-8). If your organization uses more than one proxy server, click **Advanced** and enter IP addresses for each type of proxy server on your network (see Figure 8-9). You can also enter a port address for each server. If you are trying to solve a problem of connecting to a server using HTTP over SSL or other secured protocol, enter the IP address of the proxy server that is used to manage secure connections in the Secure field of this box.

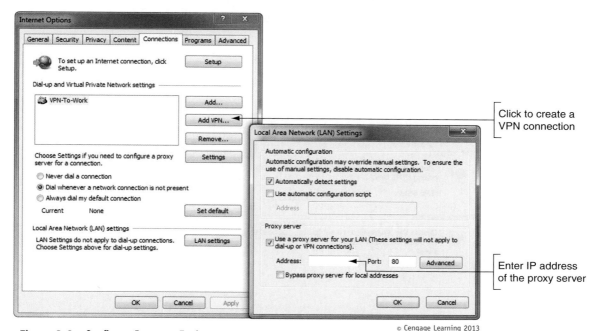

© Cengage Learning 2013

Figure 8-8 Configure Internet Explorer to use one or more proxy servers

© Cengage Learning 2013

Figure 8-9 Enter the IP addresses of all proxy servers on your corporate network

8

A+
220-802
1.5, 1.6

Also notice on the Connections tab of the Internet Options box that you can create a VPN connection. To do so, click **Add VPN** (refer back to the left side of Figure 8-8) and follow the steps of the connection wizard. Recall from Chapter 7 that you can also create a VPN connection using the Network and Sharing Center.

PROGRAMS TAB

Add-ons, also called plug-ins, are small apps that help Internet Explorer to display multimedia content, manage email, translate text, or other actions. The Programs tab (see Figure 8-10) is used to manage add-ons.

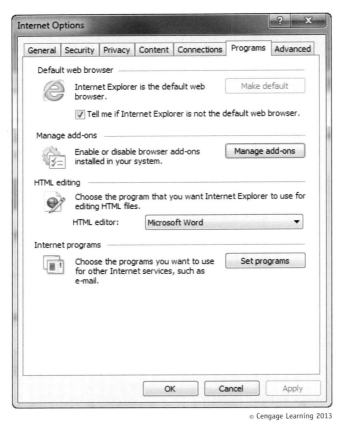

© Cengage Learning 2013

Figure 8-10 Use the Programs tab to manage add-ons and default applications used for Internet services

Click **Manage add-ons** to open the Manage Add-ons box (see the left side of Figure 8-11). In the left pane under Show, you can display All add-ons, Currently loaded add-ons (default view), Run without permission, and Downloaded controls. Click an add-on to select it and see information about it in the lower pane. To disable an add-on, click **Disable**. To enable a disabled one, click **Enable**.

Downloaded ActiveX controls can be uninstalled using this window. To delete a selected ActiveX control, click **More information**. In the More Information box (see the right side of Figure 8-11), click **Remove**. To see only the add-ons you can delete, select **Downloaded controls** in the Show drop-down list of the Manage Add-ons window. You can delete other add-ons using the Programs and Features window in Control Panel.

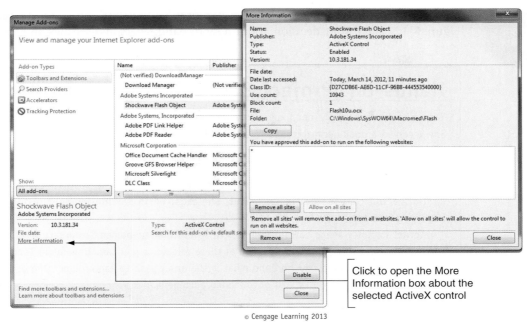

© Cengage Learning 2013

Figure 8-11   Manage Internet Explorer add-ons and delete downloaded ActiveX controls

Notes If you open the Internet Options box through the Control Panel, the box is called the Internet Properties box. Also, when you use the Internet Properties box to open the Manage Add-ons box, the *Currently loaded add-ons* option is missing in the drop-down list under Show.

ADVANCED TAB

The Advanced tab (see the left side of Figure 8-12) contains several miscellaneous settings used to control Internet Explorer. One setting is useful when IE is giving problems. If you suspect problems are caused by wrong settings, you can click **Reset** to return IE to

8

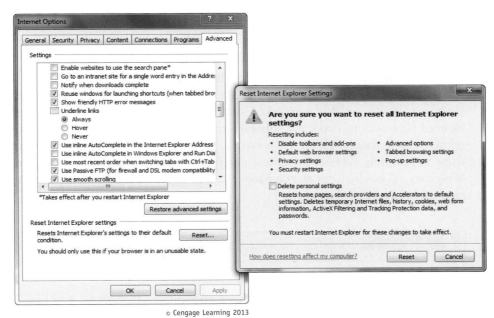

© Cengage Learning 2013

Figure 8-12   Solve problems with Internet Explorer by resetting it to default settings

A+
220-802
1.5, 1.6

all default settings. In the Reset Internet Explorer Settings box shown on the right side of Figure 8-12, make your decision about how to handle personal settings and then click **Reset**.

Hands-on | Project 8.1   Find Lost Downloaded Files

Your friend is using Internet Explorer to send and receive email using her Hotmail account. She received a document attached to an email message from a business associate. She double-clicked the Word document listed as an attachment and spent a couple hours editing it, saving the document as she worked. Then she closed the document. But where's the document? When she later needed it, she searched her email account online and the Documents folder on her hard drive, but cannot find the document. She calls you in a panic asking you to help her find her lost document.

Internet Explorer keeps downloaded files in several folders named Temporary Internet Files. Search your hard drive and find as many of these folders as you can. How many Temporary Internet Files folders did you find and what is the exact path to each folder? One of these folders is certain to contain a lost downloaded document.

Hands-on | Project 8.2   Use Google Chrome

Internet Explorer is not the only browser available, and many users prefer others such as Mozilla Firefox (*www.mozilla.org*) or Google Chrome (*www.google.com*). Go to the Google web site and download and install Google Chrome. Use it to browse the web. How does it compare to Internet Explorer? What do you like better about it? What do you not like as well? When might you recommend to someone that they use Chrome rather than Internet Explorer? What security features does Google Chrome offer? What are the steps to import your favorites list from IE into Chrome?

A+
220-802
1.4, 1.5,
1.6

REMOTE DESKTOP

Remote Desktop gives a user access to a Windows desktop from anywhere on the Internet. As a software developer, I find Remote Desktop extremely useful when I work from a remote location (my home office) and need to access a corporate network to support software on that network. Using the Internet, I can access a file server on these secured networks to make my software changes. Remote Desktop is easy to use and relatively safe for the corporate network. To use Remote Desktop, the computer you want to remotely access (the server) must be running business or professional editions of Windows 7/Vista/XP, but the computer you're using to access it (the client) can be running any version of Windows.

> 💡 **A+ Exam Tip**   The A+ 220-802 exam expects you to know how to use Remote Desktop.

In this section, you'll first see how to set up Remote Desktop for first use, and then you'll learn how to use it.

A+
220-802
1.4, 1.5,
1.6

APPLYING | CONCEPTS HOW TO SET UP REMOTE DESKTOP FOR FIRST USE

The host or server computer is the computer that is serving up Remote Desktop to client computers. To prepare your host computer, you need to configure the computer for static IP addressing and also configure the Remote Desktop service. Here are the steps needed:

1. Configure the computer for static IP addressing. How to assign a static IP address is covered in Chapter 7.

2. If your computer is behind a firewall, configure the router for port forwarding and allow incoming traffic on port 3389. Forward that traffic to the IP address of your desktop computer. You learned how to set up port forwarding in Chapter 7.

3. To turn on the Remote Desktop service, open the System window and click **Remote settings** in the left pane. The System Properties box appears with the Remote tab selected (see Figure 8-13). On this window you can control settings for Remote Assistance and Remote Desktop. In the Remote Desktop area, check **Allow connections from computers running any version of Remote Desktop (less secure)**.

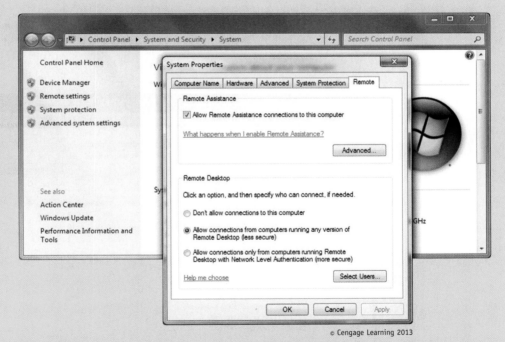

© Cengage Learning 2013

Figure 8-13 Configure a computer to run the Remote Desktop service

4. Users who have administrative privileges are allowed to use Remote Desktop by default, but other users need to be added. If you need to add a user, click **Select Users** and follow the directions on-screen. Then close all windows.

5. Verify that Windows Firewall is set to allow Remote Desktop activity to this computer. To do that, open the **Network and Sharing Center** and click **Windows Firewall**. The Windows Firewall window appears (see Figure 8-14). In the left pane, click **Allow a program or feature through Windows Firewall**.

8

A+
220-802
1.4, 1.5,
1.6

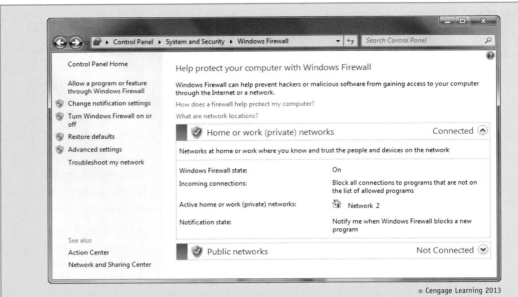

© Cengage Learning 2013

Figure 8-14   Windows Firewall can block or allow activity on the network to your computer

6. The Allowed Programs window appears. Scroll down to Remote Desktop and adjust the settings as needed (see Figure 8-15). Click **OK** to apply any changes. You will learn more about Windows Firewall in Chapter 9.

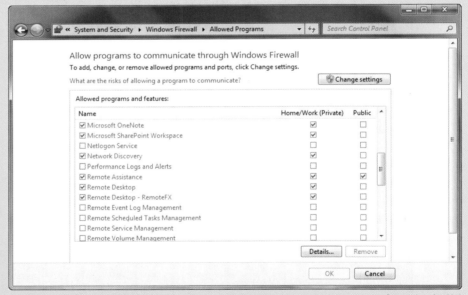

© Cengage Learning 2013

Figure 8-15   Allow Remote Desktop communication through Windows Firewall on your local computer

You are now ready to test Remote Desktop using your local network. Try to use Remote Desktop from another computer somewhere on your local network. Verify you have Remote Desktop working on your local network before you move on to the next step of testing the Remote Desktop connection from the Internet.

A+
220-802
1.4, 1.5,
1.6

HOW TO USE REMOTE DESKTOP

On the client computer, you can start Remote Desktop to remote in to your host computer by using the **mstsc** command in the search box or using the Start, All Programs menu. Follow these steps to use Remote Desktop:

1. Click **Start**, enter **mstsc** in the search box, and press **Enter**. Alternately, you can click **Start**, **All Programs**, **Accessories** and **Remote Desktop Connection**. The Remote Desktop Connection box opens (see Figure 8-16).

© Cengage Learning 2013

Figure 8-16   The IP address of the remote computer can be used to connect to it

> **XP Differences**   To start Remote Desktop in XP, click **Start**, **All Programs**, **Accessories**, **Communications**, and **Remote Desktop Connection**. (After Service Pack 3 is applied to Windows XP, the location of Remote Desktop on the Start menu might change to **Start**, **All Programs**, **Accessories**.)

2. Enter the IP address or the host name of the computer to which you want to connect. If you decide to use a host name, begin the host name with two backslashes, as in \\CompanyFileServer.

> **Notes**   To use the host name when making a Remote Desktop connection on a local network, the host name and IP address of the remote computer must be entered in the Hosts file of the client computer.

3. If you plan to transfer files from one computer to the other, click **Options** and then click the **Local Resources** tab, as shown in the left side of Figure 8-17. Click **More**. The box on the right side of Figure 8-17 appears. Check **Drives**. Click **OK**. Click **Connect** to make the connection. If a warning box appears, click **Connect** again. If another warning box appears, click **Yes**.

8

A+
220-802
1.4, 1.5,
1.6

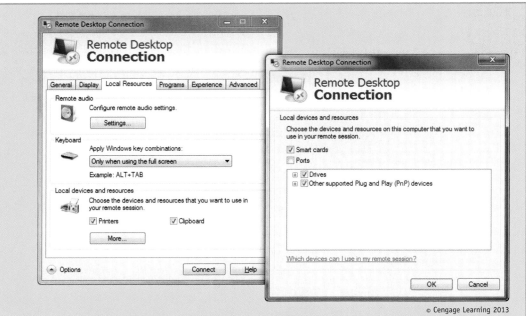

© Cengage Learning 2013

Figure 8-17 Allow drives and other devices to be shared using the Remote Desktop Connection

4. A Windows security box appears that is displayed by the remote computer (see Figure 8-18). Log on using a username and password for the remote computer. If a warning box appears saying the remote computer might not be secure, click **Yes** to continue the connection.

© Cengage Learning 2013

Figure 8-18 Enter your username and password on the remote computer

5. The desktop of the remote computer appears in a window, as shown in Figure 8-19. When you click this window, you can work with the remote computer just as if you were sitting in front of it, except response time is slower. To move files back and forth between computers, use Windows Explorer on the remote computer. Files on your local computer and on the remote computer will appear in Windows Explorer on the remote computer in the Computer group. For example, in Figure 8-19, you can see drive C on each computer labelled in the figure. To close the connection to the remote computer, log off the remote computer or close the desktop window.

A+
220-802
1.4, 1.5,
1.6

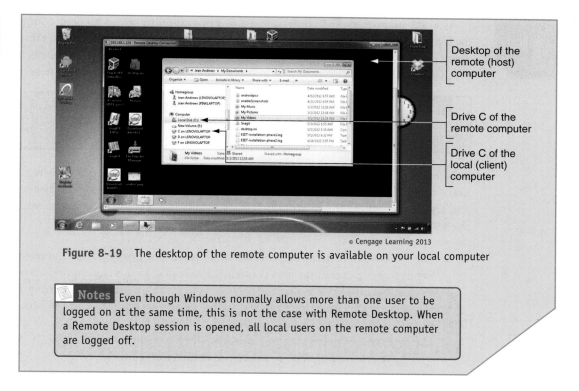

Desktop of the
remote (host)
computer

Drive C of the
remote computer

Drive C of the
local (client)
computer

© Cengage Learning 2013

Figure 8-19 The desktop of the remote computer is available on your local computer

> **Notes** Even though Windows normally allows more than one user to be
> logged on at the same time, this is not the case with Remote Desktop. When
> a Remote Desktop session is opened, all local users on the remote computer
> are logged off.

Is your host computer as safe as it was before you set it to serve up Remote Desktop and enabled port forwarding to it? Actually, no, because a port has been opened, so take this into account when you decide to use Remote Desktop. In a project at the end of this chapter, you'll learn how you can take further steps to protect the security of your computer when using Remote Desktop. Alternately, you can consider using software that does not require you to open ports. Examples of this type of software, some of which are free, are TeamViewer (*www.teamviewer .com*), GoToMyPC by Citrix (*www.gotomypc.com*), and LogMeIn (*www.logmein.com*).

8

Hands-on | Project 8.3 Use Remote Desktop

To use Remote Desktop, you need two networked computers. The computer you will configure as the host computer must be running Windows 7 Professional or Ultimate edition. Configure one computer to be the Remote Desktop host. Use the other computer to remote in to the host computer. Can you view and edit files and folders on the host computer from the remote computer? Try to copy a file from your local computer to the host.

A+
220-802
1.5

REMOTE APPLICATIONS

A **remote application** is an application that is installed and executed on a server and is presented to a user working at a client computer. Windows Server includes the software to manage these remote applications. The software, **Remote Desktop Services** (included in Windows Server 2008 and later) or **Terminal Services** (included in versions of Windows Server prior to 2008), uses the RDP protocol to present the remote app and its data to the client. Remote applications are becoming popular because most of the computing power (memory and CPU speed) and technical support (for application installations and updates and backing up data) are focused on the server in a centralized location, which means the client computers in the field don't require as much computing power or support.

A+
220-802
1.5

As a PC support technician, you need to know how to set up a client computer so that a user sitting at the client computer can access a remote application on a server. Setting the client up is actually pretty easy to do because the client computer only needs a small client program installed that is used to connect to the remote application on the server.

> **Notes** The difference between a client computer using Remote Desktop and using a remote application is that in the first case, the host computer is serving up its entire desktop, and in the second case, the host computer is only serving up a single application.

Windows 7 RemoteApp and Desktop Connection is used to install the small client program using one of two methods. The method used depends on how the system administrator has set up the remote application, which determines what she provides to you to complete the setup on the client end. She might give you a file or a URL:

- *The system administrator provides an application proxy file.* An application proxy file has a .msi file extension and is intended to work on a client computer when the complete application is on a server. If you were given an application proxy file, install the proxy by double-clicking this .msi file in Windows Explorer. In the box that appears, click **Ready to set up the connection** and click **Next**.
- *The system administrator provides a URL to the server application.* If you were given a URL, follow these steps to make the connection to this URL:

  1. Open the Control Panel and in the search box, enter **RemoteApp** and click **Set up a new connection with RemoteApp and Desktop Connections**. A wizard appears to step you through the installation (see Figure 8-20).

  2. In the Connection URL field, enter the URL for the connection provided by your system administrator (include https:// at the beginning). Click **Next** twice and then close all windows.

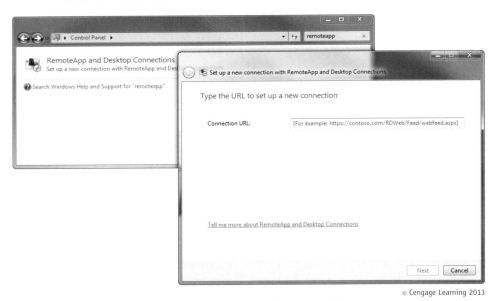

© Cengage Learning 2013

Figure 8-20   Follow the wizard to step through installing the client program to use a remote application

To launch the application, click **Start**, **All Programs**, and **RemoteApp and Desktop Connections**, and then click the name of the remote application. The user must sign onto the remote application using dialog boxes also used by Remote Desktop (refer back to Figures 8-16 and 8-18).

A+
220-802
1.4, 1.6,
1.8, 2.1

NETWORK SETTINGS TO SUPPORT APPLICATIONS

Two network settings that can be used to support client/server applications on the network are Wake on LAN and Quality of Service. Both are discussed in this part of the chapter.

WAKE ON LAN

Server applications such as Remote Desktop listen for network activity from clients. If you want these server applications to be available at all times, you can set your network adapter properties to Wake on LAN. **Wake on LAN (WoL)** causes the host computer to turn on even from a powered-off state when a specific type of network activity happens. When a computer is powered off or asleep, the network adapter retains power and listens for network activity. When it receives a specific type of network activity, it wakes up or powers up the computer. Two types of network activity that can trigger Wake on LAN are a wake pattern and a magic packet.

System administrators might use utilities to remotely wake a computer to perform routine maintenance. In a project at the end of this chapter, you learn to use one of these utilities. Some applications, such as media-sharing apps, can be configured to remotely wake a server that has been configured for Wake on LAN.

Don't use Wake on LAN on a laptop because it can drain the battery. Wake on LAN must be supported by your motherboard and network adapter and must be enabled in both Windows and BIOS setup. To enable Wake on LAN, follow these steps:

1. In Windows, go to the Network and Sharing Center and click **Change adapter settings**. In the Network Connections window, right-click the network connection and select **Properties**. The Properties box for the network connection opens.

2. In the Properties box, click **Configure** on the Networking tab. The Properties box for the network adapter opens. Select the **Power Management** tab (see Figure 8-21).

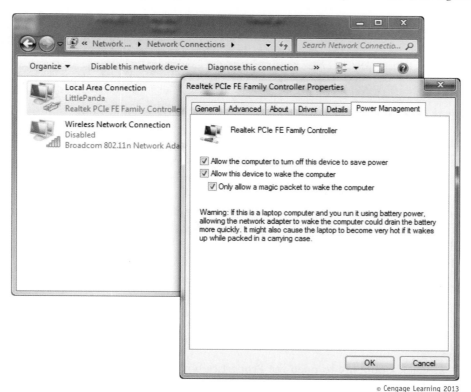

© Cengage Learning 2013

Figure 8-21   Configure Windows for Wake on LAN when the network adapter receives a magic packet

A+
220-802
1.4, 1.6,
1.8, 2.1

> **Notes** Using these steps to enable Wake on LAN, notice you are using two properties boxes: Step 1 uses the Network Connections properties box, and Step 2 uses the network adapter properties box. The network adapter properties box is also available in Device Manager.

3. To enable Wake on LAN, check **Allow this device to wake the computer**. (If this option is not listed, your network adapter does not support WoL.) To limit a wake up only to magic packets, check **Only allow a magic packet to wake the computer**. Click **OK** to close the box. Close all windows.

4. Wake on LAN must also be enabled in BIOS setup. To do so, shut down and boot up the computer. As it boots up, press a key at the beginning of the boot to access BIOS setup. Then locate the screen to manage power. One power management screen to control Wake on LAN is shown in Figure 8-22, but yours might look different. In this BIOS setup, to enable Wake on LAN, choose **Power On – Normal Boot**.

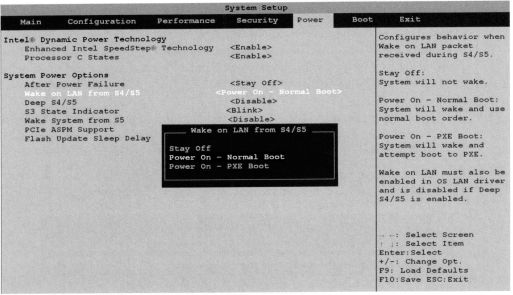

© Cengage Learning 2013

Figure 8-22 Use the Power screen in the BIOS setup to enable Wake on LAN

QUALITY OF SERVICE

Recall from Chapter 7 that Quality of Service (QoS) can improve network performance for an application by raising its priority for allotted network bandwidth. In Chapter 7, you saw how a SOHO router can improve QoS for an application. For Windows to enable QoS for installed applications, the network adapter must support QoS. To configure Windows to provide QoS for applications, you must (1) enable QoS for the network connection and adapter, and (2) set the QoS priority level for applications. Some applications, such as Microsoft Office 365, have QoS priority levels set automatically.

Follow these steps in Windows to enable QoS for the network connection and network adapter:

1. Using the Network and Sharing Center, go to the Network Connections window, and open the Properties box for the network connection. Verify QoS Packet Scheduler is checked (see Figure 8-23).

2. Click **Configure** to open the Properties box for the network adapter, and click the **Advanced** tab (see Figure 8-24). The exact property for QoS might vary by manufacturer. For example, look for Priority & VLAN, Priority, or QoS Packet Tagging and make sure the property is enabled. Click **OK** and close all windows.

A+
220-802
1.4, 1.6,
1.8, 2.1

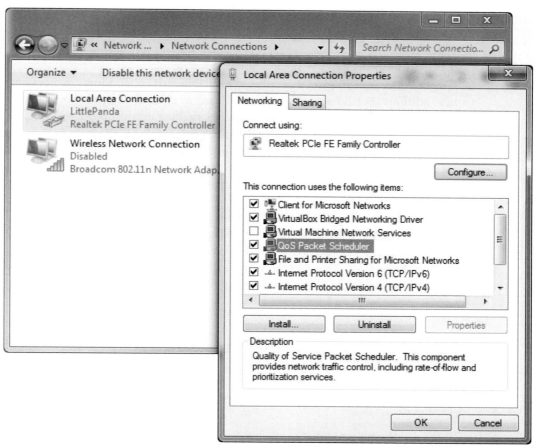

Figure 8-23 QoS Packet Scheduler enabled for the network connection

© Cengage Learning 2013

8

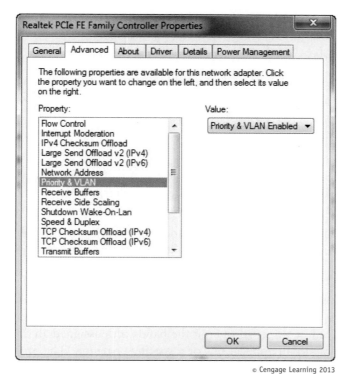

© Cengage Learning 2013

Figure 8-24 Enable the QoS property for the network adapter

A+
220-802
1.4, 1.6,
1.8, 2.1

To set the priority level for applications, you must use Group Policy.

USE GROUP POLICY TO IMPROVE QOS FOR APPLICATIONS

Group Policy (gpedit.msc) is a console available only in Windows professional and business editions (not home editions) that is used to control what users can do and how the system can be used. Group Policy works by making entries in the registry, applying scripts to Windows startup, shutdown, and logon processes, and affecting security settings. Policies can be applied to the computer or to a user. Computer-based polices are applied just before the logon screen appears, and user-based policies are applied after logon.

Follow these steps to use Group Policy to set the QoS level for an application:

1. Click **Start**, type **gpedit.msc** in the search box, and press **Enter**. The Group Policy console opens. On the left side of Figure 8-25, notice the two groups of policies are Computer Configuration and User Configuration. To apply a policy to all users, create it under Computer Configuration. Also notice at the top of the list is Local Computer Policy, which means all policies apply only to the local computer.

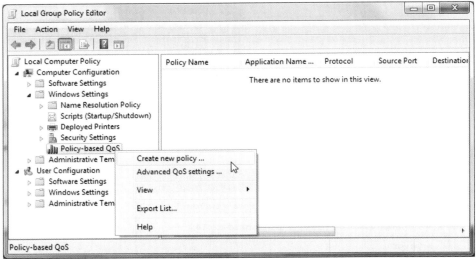

© Cengage Learning 2013

Figure 8-25 Use Group Policy to create a new QoS policy

2. In the Computer Configuration group, expand the Windows Settings group. Right-click **Policy-based QoS** and click **Create new policy,** as shown in Figure 8-25. A wizard opens to step you though the options for the policy (see Figure 8-26).

When creating a policy, here are important options that appear on different screens as you step through the wizard, but know you only need to use the ones that apply to your situation:

- ◢ The priority level is determined by a DSCP (Differentiated Services Code Point) value, which is a number from 0 to 63. The higher the number, the higher the priority.
- ◢ Outbound traffic can be throttled to limit the bandwidth assigned an application.
- ◢ The policy can apply to all applications or a specific program. (The program name must have a .exe file extension.)

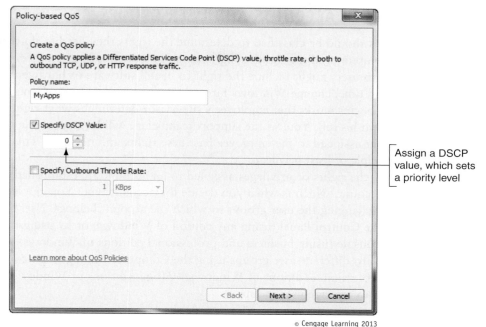

© Cengage Learning 2013

Figure 8-26 Name the QoS policy and enter a DSCP value that determines the priority level of the program(s) to which the policy applies

▲ You can specify the source IP address and/or destination IP address.
▲ You can select the protocol (TCP or UDP) and port numbers for the policy.

3. When the wizard is finished, you are returned to the Group Policy console. Close the console. To apply the new policy, you can restart the computer or enter **gpudate.exe** at a command prompt.

To get the most out of QoS, configure each router and computer on the network to use QoS. Now let's turn our attention to managing another resource on the network: folders and files.

CONTROLLING ACCESS TO FOLDERS AND FILES

Responsibility for a small network can include controlling access to folders and files for users of a local computer and for remote users accessing shared resources over the network. Managing shared resources is accomplished by (1) assigning rights to user accounts and (2) assigning permissions to folders and files.

> **Notes** In Windows, the two terms, rights and permissions, have different meanings. Rights (also called privileges) refer to the tasks an account is allowed to do in the system (for example, installing software or changing the system date and time). **Permissions** refer to which user accounts or user groups are allowed access to data files and folders. *Rights are assigned to an account, and permissions are assigned to data files and folders.*

Let's first look at the strategies used for controlling rights to user accounts and controlling permissions to folders and files. Then you'll learn the procedures in Windows for assigning these rights and permissions.

A+
220-802
1.4, 1.6,
1.8, 2.1

CLASSIFY USER ACCOUNTS AND USER GROUPS

Computer users should be classified to determine the rights they need to do their jobs. For example, some users need the right to log onto a system remotely and others do not. Other rights granted to users might include the right to install software or hardware, change the system date and time, change Windows Firewall settings, and so forth. Generally, when a new employee begins work, that employee's supervisor determines what rights the employee needs to perform his job. You, as the support technician, will be responsible to make sure the user account assigned to the employee has these rights and no more. This approach is called the principle of least privilege.

In Windows, the rights or privileges assigned to an account are established when you first create a user account, which is when you decide the account type. You can later change these rights by changing the user groups to which the account belongs. User accounts can be created from the Control Panel (using any edition of Windows) or by using the Computer Management console (using business and professional editions of Windows). User accounts can be assigned to different user groups using the Computer Management console (using business and professional editions of Windows). (Home editions of Windows, therefore, cannot be used to manage user groups.)

TYPE OF USER ACCOUNT

When you first create a user account, Windows 7/Vista supports these two types of user accounts:

- ▲ *Administrator account.* An administrator account has complete access to the system and can make changes that affect the security of the system and other users. Recall from Chapter 2 that Windows has a built-in administrator account named Administrator. By default, this account is disabled in Windows 7/Vista.
- ▲ *Standard user account.* A standard user account (sometimes called a user account) can use software and hardware and make some system changes but cannot make changes that affect the security of the system or other users.

> **XP Differences**   Windows XP offers two account types for new accounts: an administrator account and a limited account. A **limited account** has read-write access only on its own folders, read-only access to most system folders, and no access to other users' data. Using a Limited account, a user cannot install applications or carry out any administrative responsibilities.

Recall from Chapter 2 that when you use Control Panel to create a user account, you are given the opportunity to select the account type (see Figure 8-27).

When you use Computer Management to create an account, the account type is automatically a standard user account. To create a user account using Computer Management, first open the Computer Management console. Then right-click **Users** under **Local Users and Groups** and select **New User** from the shortcut menu. (Windows Home editions don't include the Local Users and Groups option in the Computer Management console.) Enter information for the new user and click **Create** (see Figure 8-28).

> **A+ Exam Tip**   The A+ 220-802 exam expects you to know about the administrator, standard user, power user, and guest accounts and groups.

A+
220-802
1.4, 1.6,
1.8, 2.1

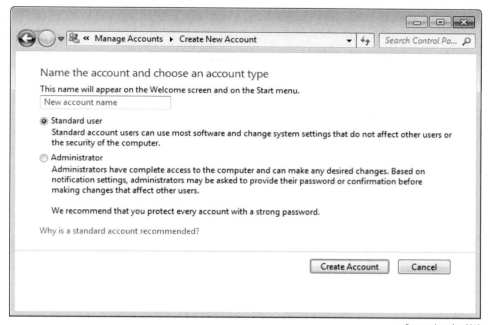

© Cengage Learning 2013

Figure 8-27 Using Control Panel to create a user account, the account type can be Standard user or Administrator

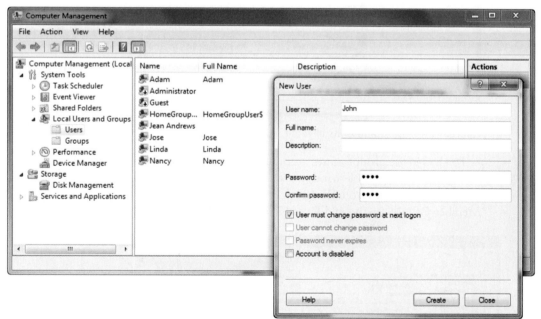

© Cengage Learning 2013

Figure 8-28 Creating a new user

BUILT-IN USER GROUPS

A user account can belong to one or more user groups. Windows offers several built-in user groups and you can create your own. Here are important built-in user groups:

▲ ***Administrators and Users groups.*** By default, administrator accounts belong to the Administrators group, and standard user accounts belong to the Users group. If you want to give administrator rights to a standard user account, use Computer Management console to add the account to the Administrators group.

A+
220-802
1.4, 1.6,
1.8, 2.1

◢ *Guests group.* The Guests group has limited rights on the system and is given a temporary profile that is deleted when the user logs off. Windows automatically creates one account in the Guests group named the Guest account, which is disabled by default.

◢ *Backup Operators group.* An account in the Backup Operators group can back up and restore any files on the system regardless of its access permissions to these files.

◢ *Power Users group.* Windows XP has a Power Users group that can read from and write to parts of the system other than its own user profile folders, install applications, and perform limited administrative tasks. Windows 7/Vista offers a Power Users group only for backward compatibility with XP to be used with legacy applications that were designed to work in XP.

To view user groups installed on a system, open the Computer Management console and click **Groups** under Local Users and Groups (see Figure 8-29).

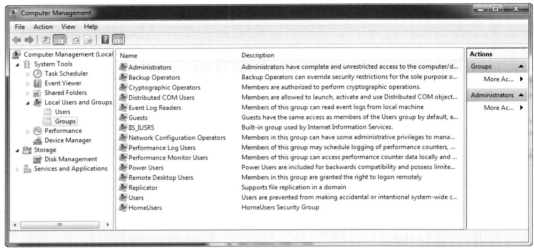

© Cengage Learning 2013

Figure 8-29 Users groups installed on a system

To change the groups a user account is in, click **Users**. The list of user accounts appears in the right pane of the console window (see the left side of Figure 8-30). Right-click the user account and select **Properties** from the shortcut menu. On the user account properties box, click the **Member Of** tab (see the middle of Figure 8-30). Click **Add** and enter the user group name. You

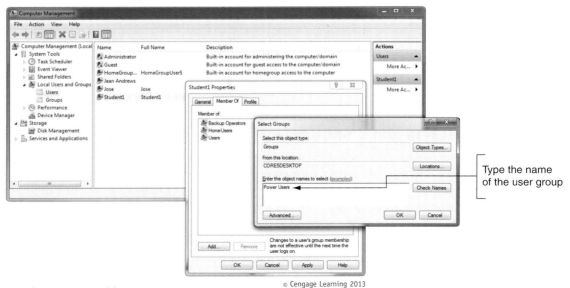

Type the name of the user group

© Cengage Learning 2013

Figure 8-30 Add a user account to a user group

A+
220-802
1.4, 1.6,
1.8, 2.1

must type the user group name exactly as it appears in the list of user groups that you saw earlier in the list of groups (see Figure 8-29). (Alternately, you can click **Advanced**, click **Find Now**, and select the group name from the list of groups that appears.) Click **OK** twice to close both boxes.

In addition to the groups you can assign to an account, Windows might automatically assign one of these built-in user groups to an account when it is determining permissions assigned to a file or folder:

◢ The **Authenticated Users group** includes all user accounts that can access the system except the Guest account. These accounts include domain accounts (used to log onto the domain) and local accounts (used to log onto the local computer). The accounts might or might not require a password. When you create a folder or file that is not part of your user profile, by default, Windows gives access to all Authenticated Users.

◢ The **Everyone group** includes the Authenticated Users group as well as the Guest account. When you share a file or folder on the network or to a homegroup, by default, Windows gives access to the Everyone group.

◢ **Anonymous users** are those users who have not been authenticated on a remote computer. If you log onto a computer using a local account and then attempt to access a remote computer, you must be authenticated on the remote computer. You will be authenticated if your user account and password match on both computers. If you logged onto your local computer with an account and password that do not match one on the remote computer, you are considered an anonymous user on the remote computer. As an anonymous user, you might be allowed to use Windows Explorer to view shared folders and files on the remote computer, but you cannot access them.

CUSTOMIZED USER GROUPS

Using the Management Console in business and professional editions of Windows, you can create your own user groups. When managing several user accounts, it's easier to assign permissions to user groups rather than to individual accounts. First create a user group and then assign permissions to this user group. Any user account that you put in this group then acquires these permissions.

User groups work especially well when several users need the same permissions. For example, you can set up an Accounting group and a Medical Records group for a small office. Users in the Accounting department and users in the Medical Records department go into their respective user groups. Then you only need to manage the permissions for two groups rather than multiple user accounts.

Hands-on | Project 8.4 Manage User Accounts

Using a professional or business edition of Windows, do the following to experiment with managing user accounts:

1. Using Windows 7, create a standard user account and log on using that account. Can you view the contents of the My Documents folder for a user account with administrator privileges?

2. Using the standard account, try to install a program. What message do you receive?

3. What happens if you try to create a new account while logged on under the standard account?

4. Add the standard user account to the Administrator group. Now try to use the account to access the My Documents folder of another administrator account. What happens when you do so?

8

A+
220-802
1.4, 1.5,
1.6, 1.8,
2.1

METHODS TO ASSIGN PERMISSIONS TO FOLDERS AND FILES

Here are the three general strategies for managing shared folders and files in Windows:

▲ ***Windows 7 homegroup sharing.*** When all users on a network require the same access to all resources, you can use a Windows homegroup. Folders, libraries, files, and printers shared with the homegroup are available to all users on the network whose computers have joined the homegroup. You learned how to set up a homegroup in Chapter 2. (Recall that homegroups are not supported by Vista and XP.) After the homegroup is set up, to share a file or folder with the homegroup, use the Sharing Wizard. To do so, right-click the item and select **Share with** from the shortcut menu. The wizard lists four options for sharing (see Figure 8-31). Click **Homegroup (Read)** or **Homegroup (Read/Write)** to assign this permission to the homegroup. To see share permissions, select the folder or file in Windows Explorer. The two-person share icon appears in the status bar (see Figure 8-32). Notice in the status bar the permission is assigned to the Everyone group.

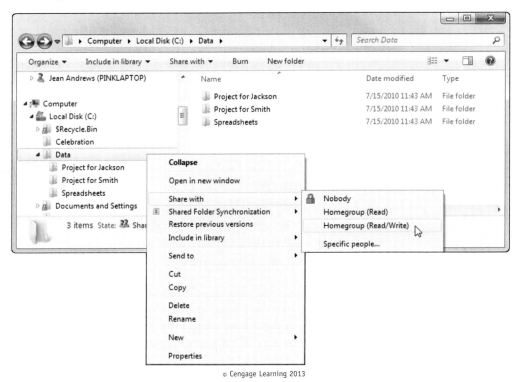

© Cengage Learning 2013

Figure 8-31   Share a folder with the homegroup

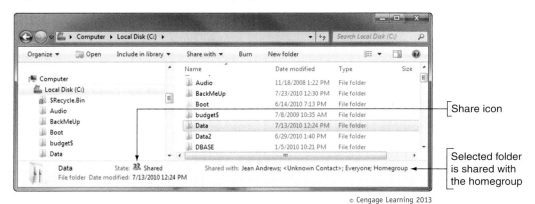

© Cengage Learning 2013

Figure 8-32   A folder shared with the homegroup shows the two-person shared icon in the status bar of Windows Explorer

A+
220-802
1.4, 1.5,
1.6, 1.8,
2.1

📓 **Notes** If the Sharing Wizard is disabled, the four sharing options shown in Figure 8-31 will not appear when you click *Share with*. To enable the Sharing Wizard, using Control Panel, open the Folder Options box and, on the View tab, select **Use Sharing Wizard (Recommended)**. See Figure 8-33. If the Sharing Wizard is not used, you must use advanced sharing methods covered later in the chapter.

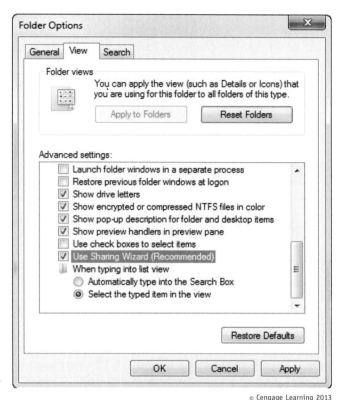

© Cengage Learning 2013

Figure 8-33 The Folder Options box shows the Sharing Wizard is enabled

💡 **A+ Exam Tip** The A+ 220-802 exam expects you to know how to use the Folder Options box to enable or disable the Sharing Wizard.

◢ ***Workgroup sharing.*** For better security than a homegroup, use workgroup sharing. Using this method, you decide which users on the network have access to which shared folder and the type of access they have. All rights and permissions are set up on each local computer so that each computer manages access to its files, folders, and printers shared on this peer-to-peer network.

◢ ***Domain controlling.*** If a Windows computer belongs to a domain instead of a workgroup or homegroup, all security is managed by the network administrator for the entire network.

In this chapter, we focus on workgroup sharing, which might use a file server. A **file server** is a computer dedicated to storing and serving up data files and folders. Here are some tips on which folders to use to hold shared data on a file server or personal computer:

◢ Private data for individual users is best kept in the C:\Users folder or the XP C:\Documents and Settings folder for that user. User accounts with limited or standard privileges cannot normally access these folders belonging to another user account. However, accounts with administrative rights do have access.

8

A+
220-802
1.4, 1.5,
1.6, 1.8,
2.1

▲ The C:\Users\Public folder is intended to be used for folders and files that all users share. It is not recommended you use this folder for controlled access to data.

▲ For best security, create a folder not in the C:\Users or C:\Documents and Settings folder and assign permissions to that folder and its subfolders. You can allow all users access or only certain users or user groups.

Some applications can be shared with others on the network. If you share a folder that has a program file in it, a user on another computer can double-click the program file and execute it remotely on his or her desktop. This is a handy way for several users to share an application that is installed on a single computer. However, know that not all applications are designed to work this way.

Using workgroup sharing, Windows offers two methods to share a folder over the network:

▲ *Share permissions*. Share permissions grant permissions only to network users and these permissions do not apply to local users of a computer. Share permissions work on NTFS, FAT32, and exFAT volumes and are configured using the Sharing tab on a folder's Properties box. Share permissions apply to a folder and its contents, but not to individual files.

▲ *NTFS permissions*. NTFS permissions apply to local users and network users and apply to both folders and individual files. NTFS permissions work on NTFS volumes only and are configured using the Security tab on a file or folder Properties box. (The Security tab is missing on the Properties box of a folder or file on a FAT volume.)

Here are some tips when implementing share permissions and NTFS permissions:

▲ If you use both share permissions and NTFS permissions on a folder, the most restrictive permission applies. For NTFS volumes, use only NTFS permissions because they can be customized better. For FAT volumes, your only option is share permissions.

▲ If NTFS permissions are conflicting, for example, when a user account has been given one permission and the user group to which this user belongs has been given a different permission, the more liberal permission applies.

▲ Permission propagation is when permissions are passed from parent to child. Inherited permissions are permissions that are attained from a parent object. For example, when you create a file or folder in a folder, the new object takes on the permissions of the parent folder.

▲ When you move or copy an object to a folder, the object takes on the permissions of that folder. The exception to this rule is when you move (not copy) an object from one location to another on the same volume. In this case, the object retains its permissions from the original folder.

> **Notes** You can use the xcopy or robocopy command with switches to change the rules for how inherited permissions are managed when copying and moving files. For more information, see the Microsoft Knowledge Base Article 310316 at *support.microsoft.com*.

> **A+ Exam Tip** The A+ 220-802 exam expects you to know about NTFS and share permissions, including how allow and deny conflicts are resolved and what happens to permissions when you move or copy a file or folder.

A+
220-802
1.4, 1.6,
1.8, 2.1

HOW TO SHARE FOLDERS AND FILES

Now that you know about the concepts and strategies for sharing folders and files, let's look at the details of how to use Windows to manage user rights and file and folder permissions.

A+
220-802
1.4, 1.6,
1.8, 2.1

APPLYING | CONCEPTS

Nicole is responsible for a peer-to-peer network for a medical doctor's office. Four computers are connected to the small company network; one of these computers acts as the file server for the network. Nicole has created two classifications of data, Financial and Medical. Two workers (Nancy and Adam) require access to the Medical data, and two workers (Linda and Jose) require access to the Financial folder. In addition, the doctor, John, requires access to both categories of data. Here is what Nicole must do to set up the users and data:

1. Create folders named Financial and Medical on the file server. Create five user accounts, one for John, Nancy, Adam, Linda, and Jose. All the accounts belong to the Windows standard user group. Create two user groups, Financial and Medical.

2. Using NTFS permissions, set the permissions on the Financial and Medical folders so that only the members of the appropriate group can access each folder.

3. Test access to both folders using test data and then copy all real data into the two folders and subfolders. Set up a backup plan for the two folders as you learned to do in Chapter 3.

Let's look at how each of these three steps is done.

> **XP Differences** The steps you're about to see apply to Windows 7/Vista. To find out how to share a folder or file in Windows XP, see Appendix C.

STEP 1: CREATE FOLDERS, USER ACCOUNTS, AND USER GROUPS

Follow these steps to create the folders, user accounts, and user groups on the file server computer that is using Windows 7 Professional:

1. Log onto the system as an administrator.

2. Using an NTFS volume, create these two folders: **C:\Medical** and **C:\Financial**.

3. Open the Computer Management console and create user accounts for **John**, **Nancy**, **Adam**, **Linda**, and **Jose**. The account types are automatically a standard user account.

4. To create the Medical user group, right-click **Groups** under Local Users and Groups and select **New Group** from the shortcut menu. The New Group box appears. Enter the name of the group (**Medical**) and its description (**Users have access to the Medical folder**), as shown in Figure 8-34.

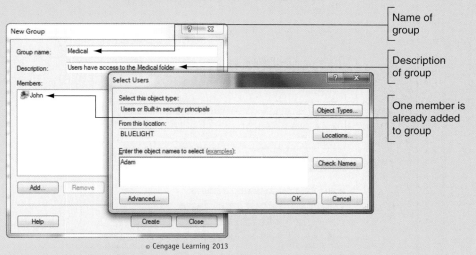

© Cengage Learning 2013

Figure 8-34 Setting up a new user group

8

A+
220-802
1.4, 1.6,
1.8, 2.1

5. Add all the users that need access to medical data (John, Adam, and Nancy). To add members to the Medical group, click **Add**. The Select Users box opens, as shown on the right side of Figure 8-34. Under *Enter the object names to select*, enter the name of a user and click **OK**. As each user is added, his name appears under Members in the New Group box, as shown in Figure 8-34. To create the group, click **Create** in the New Group box.

6. In the same way, create the Financial group and add John, Linda, and Jose to the group. Later, you can use the Computer Management console to add or remove users from either group.

7. Close the Computer Management console.

A+ Exam Tip   The A+ 220–802 exam expects you to be able to set up a user account or group and know how to change the group to which an account is assigned.

XP Differences   By default, when you share a folder in Windows XP, it is shared with Everyone because XP uses **simple file sharing**. Before you can share an XP folder with specific users or user groups, you must turn off simple file sharing. See Appendix C to find out how.

STEP 2: SET FOLDER PERMISSIONS FOR USER GROUPS

Follow these steps to set the permissions for the two folders:

1. Open Windows Explorer, right-click the **Medical** folder, and select **Properties** from the shortcut menu. The Properties box for the folder appears.

2. Click the **Security** tab (see Figure 8-35). Notice in the box that Authenticated Users, SYSTEM, Administrators, and Users all have access to the C:\Medical folder. When you select a user group, the type of permissions assigned to that group appears in the *Permissions for*

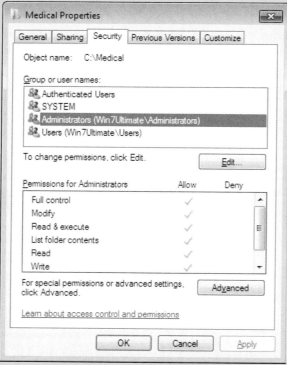

© Cengage Learning 2013

Figure 8-35   Permissions assigned to the Medical folder

A+
220-802
1.4, 1.6,
1.8, 2.1

users area. Table 8-1 gives an explanation of the more significant types of permission. Note that the Administrators group has full control of the folder. Also notice the checks under Allow are dimmed. These permissions are dimmed because they have been inherited from the parent object. In this case, the parent object is Windows default settings.

Permission Level	Description
Full control	Can read, change, delete, and create files and subfolders, read file and folder attributes, read and change permissions, and take ownership of a file or folder.
Modify	Can read, change, and create existing files and subfolders, but cannot delete existing ones. Can read and change attributes. Can view permissions but not change them.
Read & execute	Can read folders and contents and run programs in a folder.
List folder contents	Can read folders and contents and run programs in a folder.
Read	Can read folders and contents.
Write	Can create a folder or file and change attributes, but cannot read data. This permission is used for a drop folder where users can drop confidential files that can only be read by a manager. For example, an instructor can receive student homework in a drop folder.

Table 8-1 Permission levels for files and folders

© Cengage Learning 2013

💡 A+ Exam Tip The A+ 220-802 exam expects you to know that NTFS permissions can customize permissions better than share permissions.

3. To remove the inherited status from these permissions so we can change them, click **Advanced**. The Advanced Security Settings box appears (see the left side of Figure 8-36). Click **Change Permissions**. In the new Advanced Security Settings box (see the middle of Figure 8-36), you can now uncheck **Include inheritable permissions from this object's parent**. A Windows Security warning box appears, also shown in the figure. To keep the current permissions, but remove the inherited status placed on them, click **Add** (in Vista, click **Copy**).

8

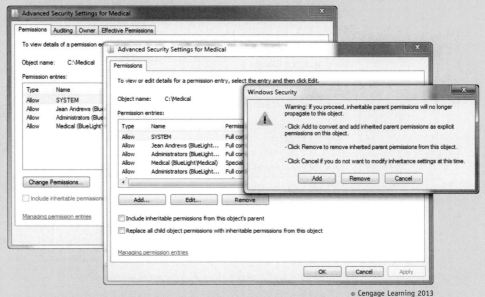

© Cengage Learning 2013

Figure 8-36 Remove the inherited status from the current permissions

A+
220-802
1.4, 1.6,
1.8, 2.1

4. Click **OK** twice to close the Advanced Security Settings box.

5. In the Medical Properties box, notice the permissions are now checked in black, indicating they are no longer inherited permissions and can be changed. Click **Edit** to change these permissions.

6. The Permissions box opens (see Figure 8-37). Select the **Authenticated Users** group and click **Remove**. Also remove the **Users** group. Don't remove the SYSTEM group, which gives Windows the access it needs. Also, don't remove the Administrators group. You need to leave the group as-is so that administrators can access the data.

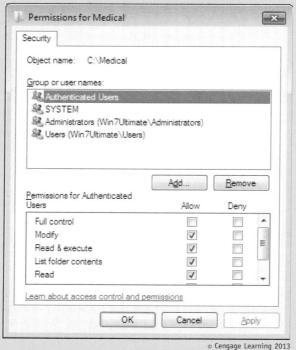

© Cengage Learning 2013

Figure 8-37   Change the permissions to a folder

7. To add a new group, click **Add**. The Select Users or Groups box opens. Under *Enter the object names to select*, type **Medical**, as shown in Figure 8-38, and click **OK**. The Medical group is added to the list of groups and users for this folder.

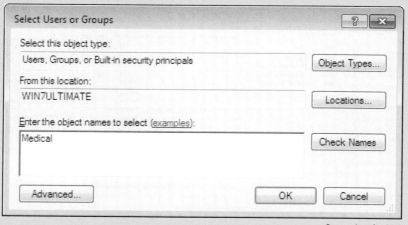

© Cengage Learning 2013

Figure 8-38   Add a user or group to shared permissions

8. Using the check box under Permissions for Medical, check **Allow** under *Full control* to give that permission to this user group. Click **OK** twice to close the Properties box.

A+
220-802
1.4, 1.6,
1.8, 2.1

9. Change the permissions of the C:\Financial folder so that Authenticated Users and Users are not allowed access and the Financial group is allowed full control.

STEP 3: TEST AND GO LIVE

It's now time to test your security measures. Do the following to test the share permissions and implement your shared folders.

1. Test a user account in each user group to make sure the user can read, write, and delete in the folder he needs but cannot access the other folder. Put some test data in each folder. Then log onto the system using an account you want to test and try to access each folder. Figure 8-39 shows the box that appears when an unauthorized user attempts to access a folder. When you click **Continue**, entering an administrator password in the resulting UAC box gives you access.

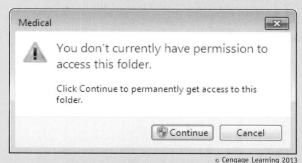

© Cengage Learning 2013

Figure 8-39 Access to a folder is controlled

2. Now that NTFS permissions are set correctly for each local and network user, you are ready to allow access over the network. To do that, both NTFS and share permissions must allow network access. (Share permissions apply only to network access, not local access.) Best practice is to allow full access using share permissions and restrictive access using NTFS permissions. The most restrictive permissions apply. To allow full access using share permissions, click the Sharing tab of the folder properties box, and click Share. In the drop-down list, select Everyone and click Add. Then give Read/Write access to the Everyone group. Click Share and close all boxes.

3. Now that you have the security working on the one computer, go to each computer on the network and create the user accounts that will be using this computer. Then test the security and make sure each user can access or cannot access the \Financial and \Medical folders as you intend. To access shared folders, you can drill down into the Network group in Windows Explorer. Another method is to type the computer name—as in \\bluelight—in the address bar of the Explorer window (see Figure 8-40).

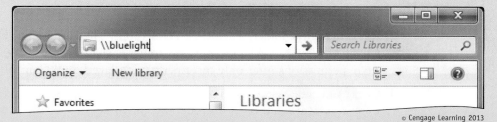

© Cengage Learning 2013

Figure 8-40 Use the computer name to access shared folders on that computer

4. After you are convinced the security works as you want it to, copy all the company data to subfolders in these folders. Check a few subfolders and files to verify that each has the permissions that you expect. And don't forget to put in place on the file server the backup procedures you learned about in Chapter 3.

8

HOW TO USE SHARE PERMISSIONS

Although you can mix NTFS permissions and share permissions on the same system, life is simpler if you use one or the other. For NTFS volumes, NTFS permissions are the way to go because they can be customized better than share permissions. However, you must use share permissions on FAT volumes. To do so, follow these steps:

1. Open the Properties box for the folder (*Financial* in this case) and go to the **Sharing** tab. Then click **Advanced Sharing**. The Advanced Sharing box opens (see Figure 8-41).

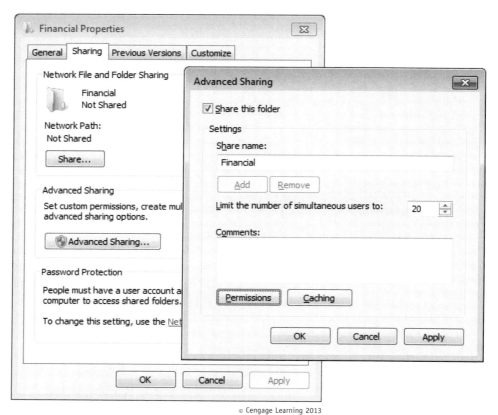

© Cengage Learning 2013

Figure 8-41 Use the Sharing tab of a folder properties box to set up share permissions

2. Click **Share this folder**. Then click **Permissions**. The Permissions box opens (see the left side of Figure 8-42). Initially, the folder is shared with Everyone. Also notice that share permissions offer only three permission levels, Full Control, Change, and Read.

3. Click **Add**. The Select Users or Groups box appears (see the right side of Figure 8-42). Enter a user account or user group and click **OK**.

4. To delete the Everyone group, select it in the Permissions box and click **Remove**. Click **OK** to close each open box in turn.

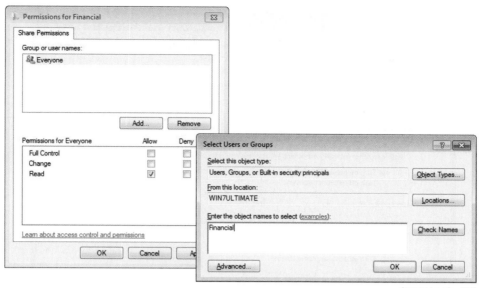

Figure 8-42 Add a user or user group to assign share permissions

© Cengage Learning 2013

SUPPORT AND TROUBLESHOOT SHARED FOLDERS AND FILES

You have just seen how to set up user groups and folder permissions assigned to these groups. If you have problems accessing a shared resource, follow these steps:

1. Open the Network and Sharing Center. Make sure your network location is set to Home or Work.

2. In the left pane, click **Change advanced sharing settings**. The Advanced sharing settings, window opens (see Figure 8-43). Verify the settings here are the default settings for a Home or Work network profile:

   ◢ Select **Turn on network discovery**.

   ◢ Select **Turn on file and printer sharing**.

   ◢ If you want to share the Public folder to the network, under Public folder sharing, select **Turn on sharing so anyone with network access can read and write files in the Public folders**.

   ◢ If you want the added protection of requiring that all users on the network must have a valid user account and password on this computer, select **Turn on password protected sharing**.

   ◢ For a Home network, if you want user accounts and passwords to be required in order to access Homegroup resources, under HomeGroup connections, select **Use user accounts and passwords to connect to other computers**.

   After you have made your changes, click **Save changes** at the bottom of the window.

8

A+
220-802
1.4, 1.6,
1.8, 2.1

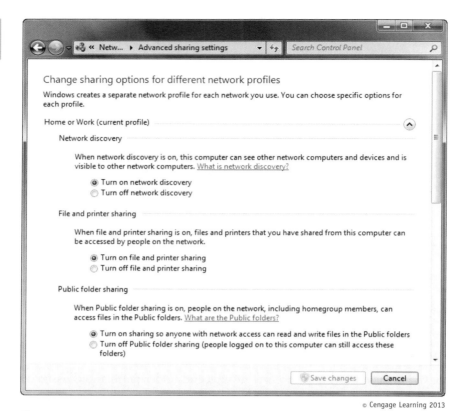

© Cengage Learning 2013

Figure 8-43 Use the Advanced sharing settings window to verify Windows is set to share resources

3. In the Network and Sharing Center, click **Change adapter settings**. Right-click the network connection icon, and select **Properties** from the shortcut menu. In the Properties box, verify that **File and Printer Sharing for Microsoft Networks** is checked (see Figure 8-44).

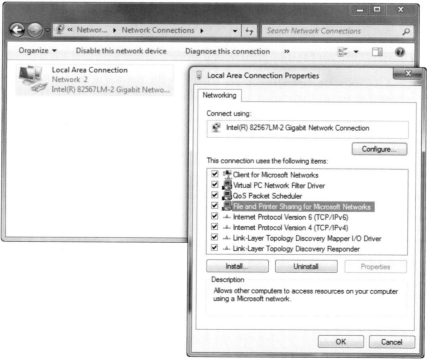

© Cengage Learning 2013

Figure 8-44 Verify the properties for the network connection are set for sharing resources over the connection

A+
220-802
1.4, 1.6,
1.8, 2.1

4. Verify the user account and password on the remote computer match the user account and password on the host computer. If these accounts and passwords don't match, the user is considered an anonymous user and is denied access to resources shared on the remote computer.

> **Vista Differences** The Vista Network and Sharing Center works a little differently from that of Windows 7. To find out how to verify settings that apply to shared files and folders in Vista using its Network and Sharing Center, see Appendix B.

> **XP Differences** For Windows XP to share resources, two services, Client for Microsoft Networks and File and Printer Sharing for Microsoft Networks, must be installed and enabled for the network connection. To find out how to verify these settings using Windows XP, see Appendix C.

Here are a few tips about managing shared folders and files:

▲ *Use advanced permissions settings.* If you need further control of the permissions assigned a user or group, click **Advanced** on the Security tab of a folder's Properties box. The Advanced Security Settings box appears (see the left side of Figure 8-45). On the Permissions tab, click **Change Permissions**. In the next box (see the middle of Figure 8-45), you can see that the Medical user group was given full control. To change these permission details, select the user group and click **Edit**. In our example, we're editing the Medical group. The Permission Entry box opens (see the right side of Figure 8-45).

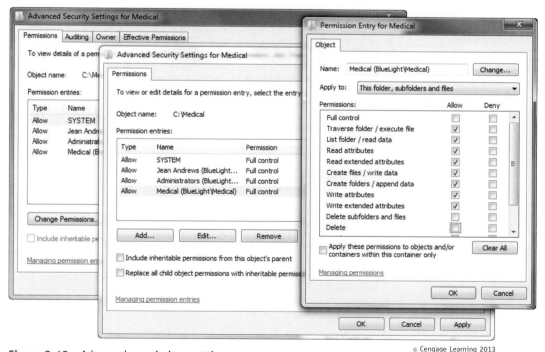

Figure 8-45 Advanced permissions settings

© Cengage Learning 2013

8

We now can change detailed permissions. Notice that the right to delete subfolders and files has been set to Deny, and the right to delete the folder itself has been set to Deny. Click **OK** to close each box. The resulting change means that users of the Medical group cannot delete or move a file or folder. (They can, however, copy the file or folder.)

A+
220-802
1.4, 1.6,
1.8, 2.1

💡 **A+ Exam Tip** The A+ 220–802 exam expects you to be able to implement permissions so that a user can copy but not move a file or folder and understand how to apply Allow and Deny permissions.

▲ *Manage permissions using the parent folder.* When a subfolder is created, it is assigned the permissions of the parent folder. Recall that these inherited permissions appear dimmed, indicating they are inherited permissions. The best way to change inherited permissions is to change the permissions of the parent object. In other words, to change the permissions of the C:\Financial\QuickBooks folder, change the permission of the C:\Financial folder. Changing permissions of a parent folder affects all subfolders in that folder.

▲ *Check the effective permissions.* Permissions manually set for a subfolder or file can override inherited permissions. Permissions that are manually set are called explicit permissions. When a folder or file has inherited an explicit permission set, it might be confusing as to exactly which permissions are in effect. To know for sure exactly which permissions for a file or folder are in effect, see the Effective Permissions tab of the Advanced Security Settings box. (Look back at the left most box in Figure 8-45.)

▲ *Take ownership of a folder.* The owner of a folder always has full permissions for the folder. If you are having a problem changing permissions and you are not the folder owner, try taking ownership of the folder. To do that, click **Advanced** on the Security tab of the folder's Properties box. The Advanced Security Settings box appears. Click the **Owner** tab (see the left side of Figure 8-46). Click **Edit**. The owner can then be edited (see the right side of Figure 8-46). Select a user from the *Change owner to* list and click **Apply** to make that user the new owner. If a user is not listed, click **Other users or groups** and add the user. Close the Advanced Security Settings box and the Properties box, and reopen the Properties box for the change to take effect.

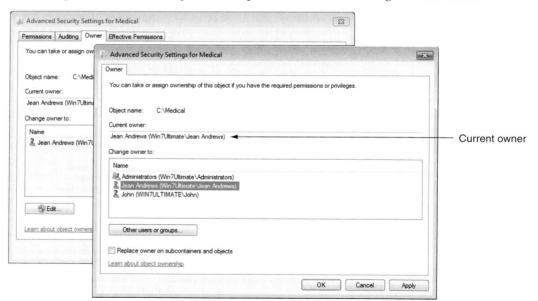

Figure 8-46 Change the owner of a folder

© Cengage Learning 2013

▲ *Use only one workgroup.* It is not necessary that all computers belong to the same workgroup in order to share resources. However, performance improves when they are all in the same workgroup.

▲ *Require passwords for all user accounts.* Don't forget that for best security, each user account needs a password. How to use Group Policy to require that all accounts have passwords is covered in Chapter 9.

▲ *Use a mapped network drive.* For the convenience of remote users, map network drives for shared folders that are heavily used. How to do that is coming up next.

A+
220-802
1.4, 1.6,
1.8, 2.1

HOW TO MAP A NETWORK DRIVE

A network drive map is one of the most powerful and versatile methods of communicating over a network. A network drive map makes one computer (the client) appear to have a new hard drive, such as drive E, that is really hard drive space on another host computer (the server). This client/server arrangement is managed by a Windows component, the Network File System (NFS), which makes it possible for files on the network to be accessed as easily as if they are stored on the local computer. NFS is a type of distributed file system (DFS), which is a system that shares files on a network. Even if the host computer uses a different OS, such as UNIX, the drive map still functions.

> **Notes** A network-attached storage (NAS) device provides hard drive storage for computers on a network. Computers on the network can access this storage using a mapped network drive.

To set up a network drive, follow these steps:

1. On the host computer, share the folder or entire volume to which you want others to have access.

2. On the remote computer that will use the network drive, open Windows Explorer and press **Alt** to display the menu bar. Click the **Tools** menu and select **Map network drive**.

> **Notes** By default, Windows does not show the menu bar in Windows Explorer. To cause the menu to always display, click **Organize** and then click **Folder and search options**. In the Folder Options box, click the **View** tab. Under Advanced settings, check **Always show menus**. Click **OK** to close the box.

3. The Map Network Drive dialog box opens, as shown in Figure 8-47. Select a drive letter from the drop-down list.

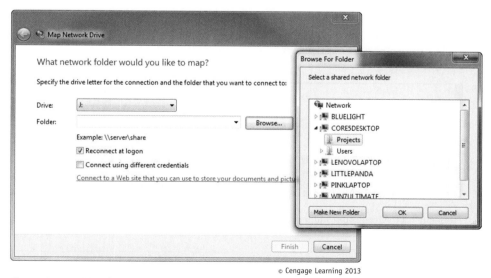

© Cengage Learning 2013

Figure 8-47   Mapping a network drive to a host computer

4. Click the **Browse** button and locate the shared folder or drive on the host computer (see the right side of Figure 8-47). Click **OK** to close the Browse For Folder dialog box, and click **Finish** to map the drive. The folder on the host computer now appears as one more drive in Explorer on your computer.

A+
220-802
1.4, 1.6,
1.8, 2.1

> **Notes** When mapping a network drive, you can type the path to the host computer rather than clicking the Browse button to navigate to the host. To enter the path, in the Map Network Drive dialog box, use two backslashes, followed by the name of the host computer, followed by a backslash and the drive or folder to access on the host computer. For example, to access the Projects folder on the computer named Core5Desktop, enter **\\Core5Desktop\Projects** and then click **Finish**.

If a network drive does not work, go to the Network and Sharing Center, and verify that the network connection is good. You can also use the net use command discussed later in the chapter to solve problems with mapped network drives.

> **Notes** A host computer might be in sleep mode or powered down when a remote computer attempts to make a mapped drive connection at startup. To solve this problem, configure the host computer for Wake on LAN.

HIDDEN NETWORK RESOURCES AND ADMINISTRATIVE SHARES

Sometimes your goal is to assure that a folder or file is not accessible from the network or by other users or is secretly shared on the network. When you need to protect confidential data from users on the network, you can do the following:

- ◢ *Disable File and Printer Sharing.* If no resources on the computer are shared, use the Network and Sharing Center (or the XP Network Connections window) to disable File and Printer Sharing for Microsoft Networks.
- ◢ *Hide a shared folder.* If you want to share a folder, but don't want others to see the shared folder in Windows Explorer, add a $ to the end of the folder name. This shared and hidden folder is called a hidden share. Others on the network can access the folder only when they know its name. For example, if you name a shared folder Financial$ on the computer named Fileserver, in order to access the folder, a user must enter *Fileserver*Financial$ in the search box (see Figure 8-48) on the remote computer and press **Enter**.

Figure 8-48 Accessing a hidden, shared folder on the network

© Cengage Learning 2013

> **XP Differences** To find out how to make your user profile private using Windows XP, see Appendix C.

Folders and files on a computer that are shared with others on the network using local user accounts are called local shares. For computers that belong to a domain, you need to be aware of another way folders are shared, called administrative shares. Administrative shares

A+
220-802
1.4, 1.6,
1.8, 2.1

are the folders that are shared by default that administrator accounts at the domain level can access. You don't need to manually share these folders because Windows automatically does so by default. Two types of administrative shares are:

▲ *The %systemroot% folder.* Enter the path **\\\computername\admin$** to access the *%systemroot%* folder (most likely the C:\Windows folder) on a remote computer. For example, in Figure 8-49, the entry in the Explorer address bar is *\\bluelight\admin$*. Windows requests that the user authenticate with an administrator account to access this administrative share. The admin$ administrative share is called the **Remote Admin** share.

Figure 8-49   Access an administrative share on a domain

© Cengage Learning 2013

▲ *Any volume or drive.* To access the root level of any volume or drive on the network, enter the computer name and drive letter followed by a $, for example, \\bluelight\C$.

> 💡 **A+ Exam Tip**   The A+ 220–802 exam expects you to understand the difference between administrative shares and local shares.

> 📝 **Notes**   To see a list of all shares on a computer, open the **Computer Management** console and drill down to **System Tools**, **Shared Folders**, **Shares** (see Figure 8-50).

8

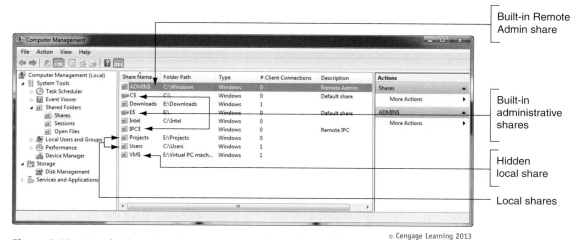

Figure 8-50   Use the Computer Management console to view all shares

© Cengage Learning 2013

When supporting a workgroup, you might be tempted to share all the drives on all computers so that you can have easy access remotely. However, to use local shares in this way is not a good security practice. Don't share the \Windows folder or an entire drive or volume on the network. These local shares appear in everyone's Explorer window. You don't want your system files and folders exposed like this.

A+
220-802
1.4, 1.6,
1.8, 2.1

Hands-on | Project 8.5   Share and Secure a Folder

Using two computers, networked together, do the following to practice sharing and securing folders using Windows 7:

1. Create a user account on Computer 1 named **User1**. In the My Documents folder for that account, create a folder named **Folder1**. Create a text file in the folder named **File1**. Edit the file and add the text **Golden Egg**.

2. On Computer 2, create a user account named **User2**. Try to read the Golden Egg text in File1 on Computer 1. What is the result?

3. Configure the computers so that User1 logged into Computer2 can open File1 and edit the text Golden Egg, but User2 cannot view or access the contents of Folder1. List the steps you took to share and secure the folder and to test this scenario to make sure it works.

4. Now make the folder private so that it cannot be seen from Computer2 in Windows Explorer but it can be accessed if User1 knows the folder name. Describe how you did that.

TROUBLESHOOTING NETWORK CONNECTIONS

A+
220-802
4.5

When troubleshooting network connections, both hardware and software tools can help. Some hardware tools are a cable tester, loopback plug, and wireless locator. Windows offers several TCP/IP utilities that can help you troubleshoot a network problem. Let's first take a look at the tools you'll need, and then we'll discuss troubleshooting strategies using these tools.

CABLE TESTER, LOOPBACK PLUG, AND WIRELESS LOCATOR

A cable tester can be used to test a cable to find out if it is good or to find out what type of cable it is if the cable is not labeled. You can also use a cable tester to trace a network cable through a building. A cable tester has two components, as shown in Figure 8-51.

© Cengage Learning 2013

Figure 8-51   Use a cable tester pair to determine the type of cable and if the cable is good

To test a cable, connect each component to the ends of the cable and turn on the tester. Lights on the tester will show you if the cable is good and what type of cable you have. You'll need to read the user manual that comes with the cable tester to know how to interpret the lights.

You can also use cable testers to trace a network cable through a building. Suppose you see several network jacks on walls in a building, but you don't know

A+
220-802
4.5

which jacks connect. Install a short cable in each of two jacks and then use the cable tester to test the continuity, as shown in Figure 8-52. You might damage a cable tester if you connect it to a live circuit, so before you start connecting the cable tester to wall jacks, be sure that you turn off all devices on the network.

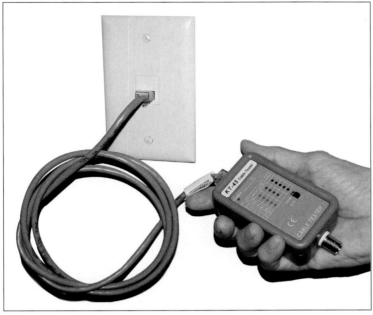

© Cengage Learning 2013

Figure 8-52   Use cable testers to trace network cables through a building

A **loopback plug** can be used to test a network cable or port. Whereas a cable tester works on cables that are not live, a loopback plug works with live cables. To test a port or cable, connect one end of the cable to a network port on a router or computer, and connect the loopback plug to the other end of the cable (see Figure 8-53). If the LED light on the loopback plug lights up, the cable and port are good. Another way to use a loopback plug is to find out which port on a switch in a server closet matches up with a wall jack. Plug the loopback plug into the wall jack. The connecting port on the switch in the closet lights up. When buying a loopback plug, pay attention to the Ethernet speeds it supports. Some only support 100 Mbps; others support 100 Mbps and 1000 Mbps.

8

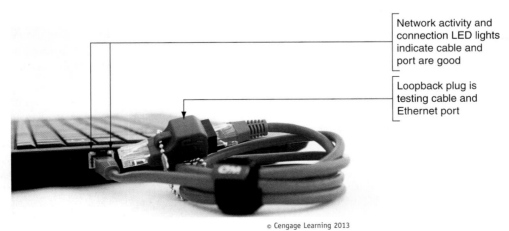

Network activity and connection LED lights indicate cable and port are good

Loopback plug is testing cable and Ethernet port

© Cengage Learning 2013

Figure 8-53   A loopback plug verifies the cable and network port are good

A+
220-802
4.5

A **wireless locator** helps you find a Wi-Fi hotspot and tells you the strength of the RF signal (see Figure 8-54). If you're in a public place looking for a strong hotspot to connect your laptop, walk around with your wireless locator until you find one. Wireless locators are also helpful when mapping out where you need to position your wireless access points so that all areas have a strong RF signal. When buying a wireless locator, look for one that tells you if a hotspot is encrypted (requires a security key to connect) and make sure it supports all the Wi-Fi standards (802.11 b/g/n).

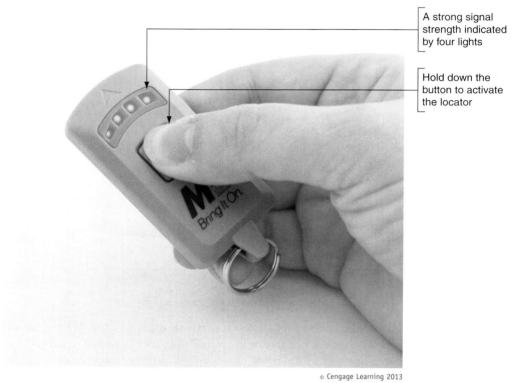

A strong signal
strength indicated
by four lights

Hold down the
button to activate
the locator

© Cengage Learning 2013

Figure 8-54   Use a wireless locator to measure the strength of an RF signal

> **💡 A+ Exam Tip**   The A+ 220-802 exam expects you to know how to use a cable tester, loopback plug, and wireless locator to troubleshoot network problems.

A+
220-802
1.3, 4.5

TCP/IP UTILITIES USED FOR TROUBLESHOOTING

Windows includes several TCP/IP utilities you can use to troubleshoot networking problems. In this part of the chapter, you learn to use ping, ipconfig, nslookup, tracert, net use, net user, nbtstat, and netstat. Most of these program files are found in the \Windows\System32 folder.

> **💡 A+ Exam Tip**   The A+ 220-802 exam expects you to know about these TCP/IP utilities: ping, tracert, netstat, ipconfig, net, nslookup, and nbtstat. You need to know when and how to use each utility and how to interpret results.

> **📝 Notes**   Only the more commonly used parameters or switches for each command are discussed. For several of these commands, you can use the /? or /help parameter to get more help with the command. And for even more information about each command, search the *technet.microsoft.com* site.

Now let's see how to use each utility.

A+
220-802
1.3, 4.5

PING [-A] [-T] [*TARGETNAME*]

The Ping (Packet InterNet Groper) command tests connectivity by sending an echo request to a remote computer. If the remote computer is online, detects the signal, and is configured to respond to a ping, it responds. (Responding to a Ping is the default Windows settings.) Use ping to test for connectivity or to verify name resolution is working. A few examples of ping are shown in Table 8-2. Two examples are shown in Figure 8-55.

Ping Command	Description
Ping 69.32.142.109	To test for connectivity using an IP address. If the remote computer responds, the round-trip times are displayed.
Ping –a 69.32.142.109	The –a parameter tests for name resolution. Use it to display the host name and verify DNS is working.
Ping –t 69.32.142.109	The –t parameter causes pinging to continue until interrupted. To display statistics, press Ctrl+Break. To stop pinging, press Ctrl+C.
Ping 127.0.0.1	A loopback address test. The IP address 127.0.0.1 always refers to the local computer. If the local computer does not respond, you can assume there is a problem with the TCP/IP configuration.
Ping www.course.com	Use a host name to find out the IP address of a remote computer. If the computer does not respond, assume there is a problem with DNS. On the other hand, some computers are not configured to respond to pings.

Table 8-2 Examples of the ping command

© Cengage Learning 2013

8

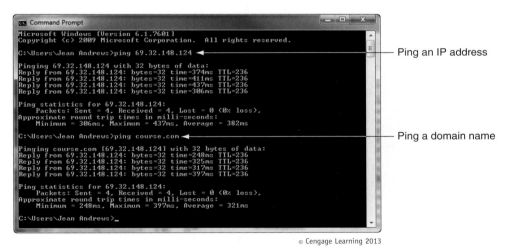

© Cengage Learning 2013

Figure 8-55 Use ping to test for connectivity and name resolution

IPCONFIG [/ALL] [/RELEASE] [/RENEW] [/DISPLAYDNS] [/FLUSHDNS]

The Ipconfig (IP configuration) command can display TCP/IP configuration information and refresh the TCP/IP assignments to a connection including its IP address. Some examples of the command are listed in Table 8-3.

A+
220-802
1.3, 4.5

Ipconfig Command	Description
Ipconfig /all	Displays TCP/IP information.
Ipconfig /release	Releases the IP address when dynamic IP addressing is being used.
Ipconfig /release6	Releases an IPv6 IP address.
Ipconfig /renew	Leases a new IP address from a DHCP server.
Ipconfig /renew6	Leases a new IPv6 IP address from a DHCP IPv6 server.
Ipconfig /displaydns	Displays information about name resolutions that Windows currently holds in the DNS resolver cache.
Ipconfig /flushdns	Flushes the name resolver cache, which might solve a problem when the browser cannot find a host on the Internet.

© Cengage Learning 2013

Table 8-3 Examples of the ipconfig command

NSLOOKUP [*COMPUTERNAME*]

Nslookup (name space lookup) lets you read information from the Internet name space by requesting information about domain name resolutions from the DNS server's zone data. Zone data is information about domain names and their corresponding IP addresses kept by a DNS server. For example, to find out what your DNS server knows about the domain name www.microsoft.com, use this command:

```
nslookup www.microsoft.com
```

Figure 8-56 shows the results. Notice in the figure that the DNS server reports one IP address assigned to *www.microsoft.com*. It also reports that this information is non-authoritative, meaning that it is not the authoritative, or final, name server for the *www .microsoft.com* computer name.

© Cengage Learning 2013

Figure 8-56 The Nslookup command reports information about the Internet name space

A reverse lookup is when you use the Nslookup command to find the host name when you know a computer's IP address, such as:

```
nslookup 192.168.1.102
```

To find out the default DNS server for a network, enter the Nslookup command with no parameters.

A+
220-802
1.3, 4.5

TRACERT *TARGETNAME*

The Tracert (trace route) command can be useful when you're trying to resolve a problem reaching a destination host such as an FTP site or web site. The command sends a series of requests to the destination computer and displays each hop to the destination. (A hop happens when a packet moves from one router to another.) For example, to trace the route to the *www.course.com* site, enter this command in a command prompt window:

```
tracert www.course.com
```

The results of this command are shown in Figure 8-57. A packet is assigned a Time To Live (TTL), which is the number of hop counts it can make before a router drops the packet and sends an ICMP message back to the host that sent the packet (see Figure 8-58). Internet

```
Command Prompt

Copyright (c) 2009 Microsoft Corporation.  All rights reserved.

C:\Users\Jean Andrews>tracert www.course.com

Tracing route to www.course.com [69.32.148.124]
over a maximum of 30 hops:

  1    <1 ms    <1 ms    <1 ms  LittlePanda.domain.invalid [192.168.1.1]
  2    <1 ms     1 ms    <1 ms  192.168.254.254
  3   177 ms   173 ms   173 ms  h1.20.29.71.dynamic.ip.windstream.net [71.29.20.
1]
  4   245 ms   297 ms   237 ms  h228.112.186.173.static.ip.windstream.net [173.1
86.112.228]
  5   318 ms   237 ms   203 ms  h114.72.102.166.static.ip.windstream.net [166.10
2.72.114]
  6   194 ms   199 ms   196 ms  h80.72.102.166.static.ip.windstream.net [166.102
.72.80]
  7   207 ms   203 ms   241 ms  xe-8-0-0.edge4.Atlanta2.Level3.net [4.59.12.41]

  8   218 ms   206 ms   215 ms  vlan52.ebr2.Atlanta2.Level3.net [4.69.150.126]
  9   154 ms   166 ms   171 ms  ae-3-3.ebr2.Chicago1.Level3.net [4.69.132.73]
 10   119 ms   158 ms   195 ms  ae-5-5.ebr2.Chicago2.Level3.net [4.69.140.194]
 11     *      170 ms     *     ae-2-52.edge4.Chicago3.Level3.net [4.69.138.166]

 12   202 ms   203 ms   221 ms  TIME-WARNER.edge4.Chicago3.Level3.net [4.53.98.4
6]
 13    54 ms    54 ms    54 ms  cnc1-ar3-xe-0-0-0-0.us.twtelecom.net [66.192.244
.202]
 14   195 ms   199 ms   196 ms  69.32.144.42
 15   217 ms   223 ms   226 ms  tluser.thomsonlearning.com [69.32.128.159]
 16     *        *        *     Request timed out.
 17   231 ms   229 ms   238 ms  www.course.com [69.32.148.124]

Trace complete.

C:\Users\Jean Andrews>_
```

Figure 8-57   The Tracert command traces a path to a destination computer

© Cengage Learning 2013

8

© Cengage Learning 2013

Figure 8-58   A router eliminates a packet that has exceeded its TTL

A+
220-802
1.3, 4.5

Control Message Protocol (ICMP) messages are used by routers and hosts to communicate error messages and updates, and some routers don't send this information. The tracert command creates its report from these messages. If a router doesn't respond, the *Request timed out* message appears.

THE NET COMMANDS

The net command is several commands in one, and most of the net commands require an elevated command prompt window. In this section, you learn about the net use and net user commands. The net use command connects or disconnects a computer from a shared resource or can display information about connections. For example, the following command makes a new connection to a remote computer and to a shared folder on that computer:

```
net use \\bluelight\Medical
```

> **Notes** Other important net commands are net accounts, net config, net print, net share, and net view. You might want to do a Google search on each of these commands to find out how they work.

Use the following command to pass a username and password to the \\bluelight remote computer and then map a network drive to the \Medical folder on that computer:

```
net use \\bluelight\Medical /user:"Jean Andrews" mypassword
```

```
net use z: \\bluelight\Medical
```

The double quotation marks are needed in the first command above because the username has a space in it.

A persistent network connection is one that happens at each logon. To make the two commands persistent, add the /persistent parameter like this:

```
net use \\bluelight\Medical /user:"Jean Andrews" mypassword
/persistent:yes
```

```
net use z: \\bluelight\Medical /persistent:yes
```

The net user command manages user accounts. For example, recall that the built-in administrator account is disabled by default. To activate the account, use this net user command:

```
net user administrator /active:yes
```

NBTSTAT [-N] [-R] [-RR]

The nbtstat (NetBIOS over TCP/IP Statistics) command is used to display statistics about the NetBT (NetBIOS over TCP/IP) protocol. NetBIOS is an older network protocol suite used before TCP/IP. Occasionally, you find a legacy application still in use that relies on NetBIOS and NetBIOS computer names. The NetBT protocol was developed to allow NetBIOS to work over a TCP/IP network.

Whereas TCP/IP uses a Hosts file on the local computer and a DNS server to resolve computer names, NetBIOS uses an Lmhosts file on the local computer and a WINS

A+
220-802
1.3, 4.5

(Windows Internet Name Service) server to resolve NetBIOS computer names. Table 8-4 lists some nbtstat commands that you might use when a legacy application cannot access resources on the network.

Command	Description
nbtstat -n	Displays the NetBIOS name table on the local computer
nbtstat -r	Purges and rebuilds the NetBIOS name cache on the local computer using entries in the Lmhosts file
nbtstat -RR	Releases and renews the NetBIOS names kept by the WINS server

© Cengage Learning 2013

Table 8-4 Nbtstat commands

NETSTAT [-a] [-b] [-o]

The netstat (network statistics) command gives statistics about TCP/IP and network activity and includes several parameters. Table 8-5 lists a few Netstat commands.

Command	Description
netstat	Lists statistics about the network connection, including the IP addresses of active connections and the ports the computer is listening on.
netstat >>netlog.txt	Directs output to a text file.
netstat -b	Lists programs that are using the connection (see Figure 8-59) and is useful for finding malware that might be using the network. The -b switch requires an elevated command prompt.
netstat -b -o	Includes the process ID of each program listed. When you know the process ID, you can use the taskkill command to kill the process.
netstat -a	Lists statistics about all active connections.

© Cengage Learning 2013

Table 8-5 Netstat commands

8

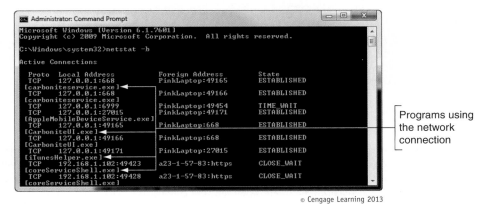

© Cengage Learning 2013

Figure 8-59 Netstat -b lists programs and their ports that are using a network connection

> **Notes** Many commands other than netstat can use the >> parameter to redirect output to a text file. For example, try the ping or tracert command with this parameter.

A+
220-802
4.5

STRATEGIES FOR TROUBLESHOOTING NETWORK CONNECTIONS

With tools in hand, you're now ready to tackle network troubleshooting, including problem-solving when there is no connectivity and limited or intermittent connectivity. Here is how to find out the extent of the problem:

1. To check for local connectivity, use Windows Explorer to try to access shared folders on the network. No connectivity might be caused by the network cable or its connection, a wireless switch not turned on, a bad network adapter, or TCP/IP settings in Windows.

2. Determine whether other computers on the network are having trouble with their connections. If the entire network is down, the problem is not isolated to the computer you are working on.

3. If you can access some, but not all, shared resources on the network, this limited connectivity problem might be caused by cables or a switch on the network or a problem at the computer sharing the resources you're trying to reach.

4. To test for Internet access, use a browser to surf the web. Problems with no Internet access can be caused by cables, a SOHO router, a broadband modem, or problems at the ISP.

5. To find out if a computer with limited or no connectivity was able to initially connect to a DHCP server on the network, check for an Automatic Private IP Address (APIPA). Recall from Chapter 7 that a computer assigns itself an APIPA if it is unable to find a DHCP server at the time it first connects to the network. Use the ipconfig command to find out the IP address (see Figure 8-60). In the results, an APIPA presents itself as the Autoconfiguration IPv4 Address, and the address begins with 169.254.

Indicates an APIPA IP address is assigned

© Cengage Learning 2013

Figure 8-60 The network connection was not able to lease an IP address

> **A+ Exam Tip** This chapter covers how to use Windows and a few hardware tools when troubleshooting network connections. Its companion book, *A+ Guide to Hardware*, gives more information about troubleshooting and repairing hardware when network connections fail. You can find this A+ 220-802 content for hardware troubleshooting on the textbooks' companion web site at *www.cengagebrain.com*. See the Preface for more information. This chapter and the online content on hardware troubleshooting together cover all the network troubleshooting portions on the A+ 220-802 exam.

Now let's see how to handle problems with no or intermittent connectivity and then we'll look at problems with Internet access.

A+
220-802
4.5

PROBLEMS WITH NO CONNECTIVITY OR INTERMITTENT CONNECTIVITY

When a computer has no network connectivity or intermittent connectivity, begin by checking hardware and then move on to checking Windows network settings.

Follow these steps to solve problems with hardware:

1. Check the status indicator lights on the NIC or the motherboard Ethernet port. A steady light indicates connectivity and a blinking light indicates activity (see Figure 8-61). Check the indicator lights on the router or switch at the other end. Try a different port on the device. If the router or switch is in a server closet and the ports are not well labelled, you can use a loopback plug to find out which port the computer is using. If you don't see either light, this problem must be resolved before you consider OS or application problems.

© Cengage Learning 2013

Figure 8-61 Status indicator lights verify connectivity for a network port

2. Check the network cable connection at both ends. Is the cable connected to a port on the motherboard that is disabled? It might need to be connected to the network port provided by a network card. A cable tester can verify the cable is good or if it is the correct cable (patch cable or crossover cable). Try a different network cable.

3. For wireless networking, make sure the wireless switch on a laptop is turned on. If you have no connectivity, limited connectivity, or intermittent connectivity, move the laptop to a new position in the hotspot. Use a wireless locator to find the best position. Rebooting a laptop might solve the problem of not receiving a signal. Problems with a low RF signal can sometimes be solved by moving the laptop or connecting to a different wireless access point with a stronger RF signal.

4. After you've checked cable connections and the wireless switch and the problem still persists, turn to Windows to repair the network connection. Use one of these methods:

   ◢ In an elevated command prompt window, use these two commands: **ipconfig /release** followed by **ipconfig /renew**.
   ◢ For Windows 7, in the Network and Sharing Center, click a yellow triangle or red **X** to launch Windows diagnostics (see Figure 8-62). If that doesn't work, click **Change adapter settings**, right-click the connection, and click **Disable** followed by **Enable**.
   ◢ For Vista, open the Network and Sharing Center window and click **Diagnose and repair**.
   ◢ For XP, in the Network Connections window, right-click the network icon and select **Repair** from the shortcut window.

8

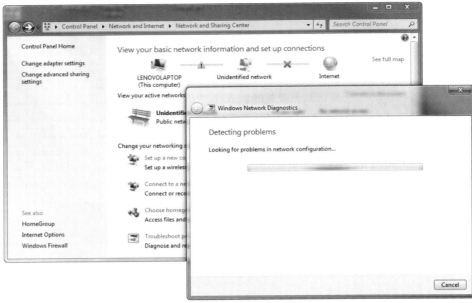

© Cengage Learning 2013

Figure 8-62   Windows indicates a network connectivity problem

If the problem is still not resolved, you need to dig deeper. Perhaps the problem is with the network adapter drivers. To solve problems with device drivers, which might also be related to a problem with the NIC, follow these steps:

1. Make sure the network adapter and its drivers are installed by checking for the adapter in Device Manager. Device Manager should report the device is working with no problems.

2. If errors are reported, try updating the device drivers. (Use another computer to download new drivers to a USB flash drive and then move the flash drive to this computer.) If the drivers still install with errors, look on the manufacturer web site or installation CD that came bundled with the adapter for diagnostic software that might help diagnose the problem.

3. If Device Manager still reports errors, try running antivirus software and updating Windows. Then try replacing your network adapter. If that does not work, the problem might be a corrupted Windows installation.

Intermittent connectivity on a wired network might happen when a network device such as a VoIP phone is sensitive to electrical interference. You can solve this problem by attaching a **ferrite clamp** (see Figure 8-63) on the network cable near the phone port. This clamp helps to eliminate electromagnetic interference (EMI). Some cables come with preinstalled clamps, and you can also buy ferrite clamps to attach to other cables.

> 💡 **A+ Exam Tip**   The A+ 220-802 exam expects you to be able to troubleshoot network problems that present themselves as no connectivity or limited, local, or intermittent connectivity.

A+
220-802
4.5

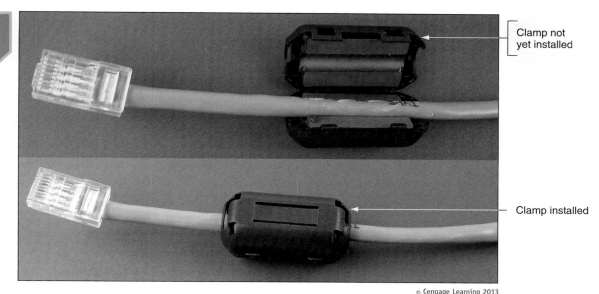

Clamp not
yet installed

Clamp installed

© Cengage Learning 2013

Figure 8-63   Install a ferrite clamp on a network cable to protect against electrical interference

PROBLEMS WITH INTERNET CONNECTIVITY

If you have local connectivity, but not Internet access, do the following:

1. Try recycling the connection to the ISP. Follow these steps:

   a. Unplug from the power source the cable modem, DSL modem, or other device that you use to connect to your ISP. Unplug the router. Wait about five minutes for the connection to break at the ISP.

   b. Plug in the cable modem, DSL modem, or other ISP device. Wait until the lights settle. Then plug in your router.

   c. On any computer on your network, use the Network and Sharing Center to repair the network connection. Open your browser and try to browse some web sites.

2. For a cable modem, check to make sure your television works. The service might be down. For a DSL connection, check to make sure your phone gives a dial tone. The phone lines might be down.

3. To eliminate the router as the source of the problem, connect one computer directly to the broadband modem. If you can access the Internet, you have proven the problem is with the router or cables going to it. Connect the router back into the network and check all the router settings. The problem might be with DHCP, the firewall settings, or port forwarding. Try updating the firmware on the router. If you are convinced all settings on the router are correct, but the connection to your ISP works without the router and does not work with the router, it's time to replace the router.

4. To eliminate DNS as the problem, follow these steps:

   a. Try substituting a domain name for the IP address in a ping command:

   ```
   ping www.course.com
   ```

   If this ping works, then you can conclude that DNS works. If an IP address works, but the domain name does not work, the problem lies with DNS.

   b. Try pinging your DNS server. To find out the IP address of your DNS server, open the firmware utility of your router and look on a status screen.

8

A+
220-802
4.5

5. If you're having a problem accessing a particular computer on the Internet, try using the tracert command, for example:

```
tracert www.course.com
```

The results show computers along the route that might be giving delays.

6. If one computer on the network cannot access the Internet but other computers can, make sure MAC address filtering is disabled or this computer is allowed access.

7. Perhaps the problem is with your router firewall or Windows Firewall. How to verify router firewall settings is covered in Chapter 7, and Windows Firewall is covered in Chapter 9.

8. If you still cannot access the Internet, contact your ISP.

If some computers on the network have both local and Internet connectivity, but one computer does not, move on to checking problems on that computer, which can include TCP/IP settings and problems with applications.

USE TCP/IP UTILITIES TO SOLVE CONNECTIVITY PROBLEMS

No connectivity or no Internet access can be caused by Windows TCP/IP configuration and connectivity. Follow these steps to verify that the local computer is communicating over the network:

1. Using the Network and Sharing Center or the ipconfig command, try to release the current IP address and lease a new address. This process solves the problem of an IP conflict with other computers on the network or your computer's failure to connect to the network.

2. To find out if you have local connectivity, try to ping another computer on the network. To find out if you have Internet connectivity and DNS is working, try to ping a computer on the Internet using its host address. Try **ping www.course.com**. If this last command does not work, try the tracert command to find out if the problem is outside or inside your local network. Try **tracert www.course.com**.

3. In a command prompt window, enter **ipconfig /all**. Verify the IP address, subnet mask, and default gateway. For dynamic IP addressing, if the computer cannot reach the DHCP server, it assigns itself an APIPA, which is listed as an Autoconfiguration IPv4 Address that begins with 169.254 (refer back to Figure 8-60). In this case, suspect that the PC is not able to reach the network or the DHCP server is down.

4. Next, try the loopback address test. Enter the command **ping 127.0.0.1** (with no period after the final 1). Your computer should respond. If you get an error, assume the problem is TCP/IP settings on your computer. Compare the configuration to that of a working PC on the same network.

5. If you're having a problem with slow transfer speeds, suspect a process is hogging network resources. Use the **netstat –b** command to find out if the program you want to use to access the network is actually running.

6. Firewall settings might be wrong. Are port forwarding settings on the router and in Windows Firewall set correctly? You learn to configure Windows Firewall in the next chapter.

A+
220-802
4.5

7. Two computers on the network might have the same computer name. This command reports the error:

```
net view \\computername
```

8. If you can ping a computer, but cannot access it in Windows Explorer, verify the NTFS permissions and share settings on the remote computer. For help, see "Support and Troubleshoot Shared Folders and Files" earlier in the chapter. Also verify that the user account and password are the same on both computers.

9. Use this command to view a list of shared folders on the remote computer:

```
net view \\computername
```

If the command gives an error about access being denied, the problem is with permissions. Make sure the account you are using is an account recognized by the remote computer. Try this command to pass a new account to the remote computer:

```
net use \\computername /user:username
```

In this last command, if there is a space in the username, enclose the username in double quotation marks, as in:

```
net use \\computername /user:"Jean Andrews"
```

10. If the net view command using a computer name does not work, try the command using the remote computer's IP address, as in:

```
net view 192.168.1.102
```

If this command works, the problem is likely with name resolution. Make sure the computer name you are using is correct.

11. If you're having problems getting a network drive map to work, try making the connection with the net use command like this:

```
net use z: \\computername\folder
```

To disconnect a mapped network drive, use this command:

```
net use z: /delete
```

For slow network connections, try these things:

1. If a computer uses both a wireless and wired connection to the network, you can control the priority order of the connections. To see the priority order and find out which connection is faster, use the Networking tab of Task Manager (see Figure 8-64). Notice the wired connection graph is listed first, followed by the wireless connection graph. Windows is using the wired connection at the top the most although it's slower than the wireless connection. (To compare connection speeds, compare 100 Mbps to 144 Mbps in the list at the bottom of the window.)

8

A+
220-802
4.5

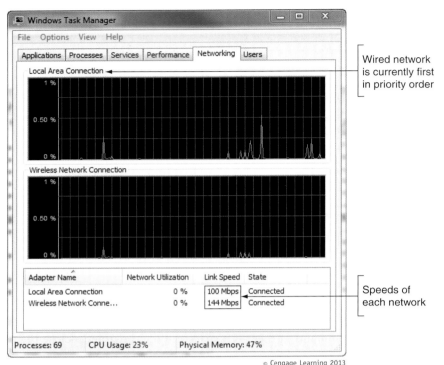

© Cengage Learning 2013

Figure 8-64   Use Task Manager to find out network connection speeds and priority order

2. To change the priority order, open the Network and Sharing Center and click **Change adapter settings** in the left pane. The Network Connections window appears (see the left side of Figure 8-65). Press **Alt** to display the menu bar and, on the menu bar, click **Advanced** and click **Advanced Settings**. The Advanced Settings box appears (see the right side of Figure 8-65). Select the connection you want to move up in the priority order and then click the green up arrow, as shown in the figure. Then return to the Task Manager window and confirm the priority order has changed.

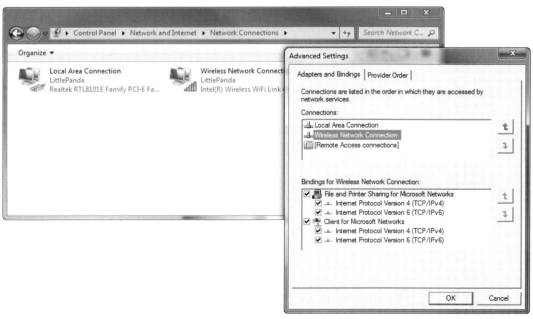

© Cengage Learning 2013

Figure 8-65   Change the priority order of the network connections

A+
220-802
4.5

Notes Figure 8-64 reports the wired network is running at 100 Mbps (called Fast Ethernet), rather than 1000 Mbps (called Gigabit Ethernet). Most network adapters, switches, and routers sold today use Gigabit Ethernet. For best performance, the network adapters, switches, and routers on this network should be converted to Gigabit Ethernet so the entire network runs at the faster speed.

Hands-on | Project 8.6   Use a Port Scanner

Port scanning software can be used to find out how vulnerable a computer is with open ports. This project will require the use of two computers on the same network to practice using port scanning software. Do the following:

1. On Computer 1, download and install Advanced Port Scanner by Famatech at *www.radmin.com*. (Be careful to not accept other software offered while downloading.)

2. On Computer 2, set the network location to **Public network**.

3. On Computer 1, start Advanced Port Scanner and make sure that the range of IP addresses includes the IP address of Computer 2. Change the default port list to 0 through 6000. Then click **Scan**.

4. Browse the list and find Computer 2. List the number and purpose of all open ports found on Computer 2.

5. On Computer 2, set the network location to **Home network**. Open the **System** window, click **Remote settings**, and allow Remote Assistance connections to this computer. Close all windows.

6. On Computer 1, rescan and list the number and purpose of each port now open on Computer 2. Figure 8-66 shows the results for one computer, but yours might be different.

8

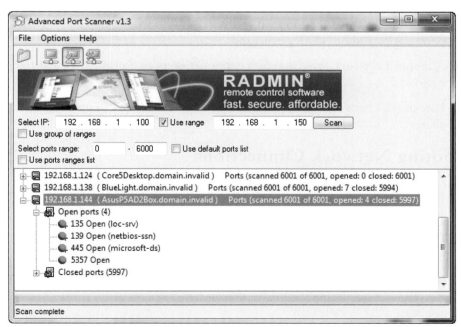

© Cengage Learning 2013

Figure 8-66   Advanced Port Scanner shows open ports on networked computers

>> *CHAPTER SUMMARY*

Supporting Client/Server Applications

▲ The Internet Options dialog box is used to manage many Internet Explorer settings. Proxy settings are managed using the Connections tab, and add-ons are managed using the Programs tab.

▲ Remote Desktop gives you access to your Windows desktop from anywhere on the Internet. To turn on the Remote Desktop service, use the Remote tab on the System Properties box. The service listens at port 3389.

▲ The RemoteApp and Desktop Connection tool in Control Panel is used to install the client portion of a remote application that runs on a server in a corporate environment.

▲ Configure the Windows network adapter properties and BIOS setup to use Wake on LAN so that a computer can be powered up by specific network activity.

▲ A policy can be set using Group Policy to improve Quality of Service (QoS) for an application so that it gets a higher priority on the network.

Controlling Access to Folders and Files

▲ Controlling access to folders and files on a network is done by assigning rights to user accounts and assigning permissions to folders and files.

▲ Apply the principle of least privilege when assigning rights to users. Types of user accounts that can be used when creating a new user account in Windows 7/Vista are administrative and standard accounts. You can change the rights an account has by adding or removing it from a user group.

▲ Customized user groups that you create make it easier to manage rights to multiple user accounts.

▲ Three ways to share files and folders on the network are to use homegroup sharing, workgroup sharing, and domain controllers. With workgroup sharing, you can use share permissions and/or NTFS permissions.

▲ A mapped network drive makes it easier for users to access drives and folders on the network.

▲ Peer-to-peer networks use local shares, and a Windows domain supports administrative shares.

Troubleshooting Network Connections

▲ Cable testers are used to test cables and trace network cables through a building. A loopback plug is used to test network cables and ports. A wireless locator can help find a wireless hotspot with a strong RF signal.

▲ Useful Windows TCP/IP utilities are ping, ipconfig, nslookup, tracert, net use, net user, nbtstat, and netstat.

▲ When troubleshooting network problems, check hardware, device drivers, Windows, and the client or server application, in that order.

>> *KEY TERMS*

ActiveX control
administrative shares
Administrators group
anonymous users
application proxy
Authenticated Users group
Backup Operators
cable tester
Everyone group
ferrite clamp
file server
Group Policy (gpedit.msc)
Guests group
hidden share
inherited permissions
Internet Options
Ipconfig (IP configuration)

limited account
local shares
loopback plug
mstsc
nbtstat (NetBIOS over TCP/IP Statistics)
net use
net user
netstat (network statistics)
network drive map
Nslookup (name space lookup)
NTFS permissions
permission propagation
permissions
Ping (Packet InterNet Groper)
Power Users group
principle of least privilege

proxy server
Remote Admin
remote application
Remote Desktop
Remote Desktop Services
RemoteApp and Desktop Connection
reverse lookup
share permissions
simple file sharing
Terminal Services
Tracert (trace route)
Users group
Wake on LAN (WoL)
wireless locator

>> *REVIEWING THE BASICS*

1. Which editions of Windows can be used to serve up Remote Desktop?

2. What is the listening port for Remote Desktop?

3. Explain the difference when a user sees http:// in a browser address box and when the user sees https:// in the address box.

4. Which has more rights, a standard account or a guest account?

5. What folder in Windows 7/Vista is intended to be used for folders and files that all users share?

6. When using the Control Panel in Windows 7, what two types of user accounts can be created?

7. Which Windows console is used to create a new user group?

8. Why doesn't the Properties box for a file have a Sharing tab?

9. When you view the Properties box for a folder, why might the Security tab be missing?

10. What is the term Windows XP uses to describe sharing files in a way that gives no control over which users have access to a shared file?

11. What type of permission does a folder receive from its parent folder?

12. What type of permissions must be used for a folder on a FAT volume?

13. If a folder has 10 subfolders, what is the easiest way to change the permissions for all 10 folders?

14. If you are having a problem changing the permissions of a folder that was created by another user, what can you do to help solve the problem?

15. A shared folder whose name ends with a $ is called a(n) _____.

8

16. What command do you enter in the Explorer search box to access the Remote Admin share on the computer named Fin?

17. What is the full command line to use ipconfig to release the current IP address?

18. What is the full command line for the loopback address test command?

19. What command can tell you if two computers on the same network have the same computer name?

20. What command lists the shared resources on a remote computer on the network?

21. Which type of net command can be used to map a network drive?

22. Which command tests for connectivity between two computers?

23. Which command is used to find the host name of a computer when you know its IP address?

24. Which command can give you the hop count from your computer to another?

25. What parameter can be added to the netstat command so that you can see what programs are using a network connection?

26. What TCP/IP utility would you use to display the route taken over the Internet by a communication between a web browser and web server?

27. What utility would you use to display information about the name space kept by a DNS server for a particular domain name?

28. How can you physically tell if a network card is not working?

29. To know if Windows recognizes a NIC without errors, which tool do you use?

30. List the steps to recycle the connection to an ISP when using a cable modem and router.

>> *THINKING CRITICALLY*

1. Suppose your SOHO network connects to the Internet using cable modem. When you open your browser and try to access a web site, you get the error, "Internet Explorer cannot display the webpage." What might be the problem(s) and what do you try first? Second?

   a. The cable modem service is down. Recycle the SOHO router and cable modem.

   b. Windows networking has a problem. In the Network and Sharing Center, try to repair the connection.

   c. The network adapter is giving errors. Go to Device Manager and check for reported problems.

   d. The network cable is loose or disconnected. Check the lights near the network port for connectivity.

2. Your organization has set up three levels of data classification accessed by users on a small network:

   - Low security: Data in the C:\Public folder

   - Medium security: Data in a shared folder that some, but not all, user groups can access

   - High security: Data in a shared and encrypted folder that requires a password to access. The folder is shared only to one user group.

Classify each of the sets of data:

    a. Directions to the company Fourth of July party

    b. Details of an invention made by the company president that has not yet been patented

    c. Resumes presented by several people applying for a job with the company

    d. Payroll spreadsheets

    e. Job openings at the company

3. You work in the Accounting Department and have been using a network drive to post Excel workbook files to your file server as you complete them. When you attempt to save a workbook file to the drive, you see the error message: "You do not have access to the folder 'J:\'. See your administrator for access to this folder." What should you do first? Second? Explain the reasoning behind your choices.

    a. Ask your network administrator to give you permission to access the folder.

    b. Check Windows Explorer to verify that you can connect to the network.

    c. Save the workbook file to your hard drive.

    d. Using Windows Explorer, remap the network drive.

    e. Reboot your PC.

>> REAL PROBLEMS, REAL SOLUTIONS

REAL PROBLEM 8-1: More Security for Remote Desktop

When Jacob travels on company business, he finds it's a great help to be able to access his office computer from anywhere on the road using Remote Desktop. However, he wants to make sure his office computer as well as the entire corporate network is as safe as possible. One way you can help Jacob add more security is to change the port that Remote Desktop uses. Knowledgeable hackers know that Remote Desktop uses port 3389, but if you change this port to a secret port, hackers are less likely to find the open port. Search the Microsoft Knowledge Base articles (*support.microsoft.com*) for a way to change the port that Remote Desktop uses. Practice implementing this change by doing the following:

1. Set up Remote Desktop on a computer using Windows 7 Professional or Ultimate. This computer is your host computer. Use another computer (the client computer) to create a Remote Desktop session to the host computer. Verify the session works by transferring files in both directions.

2. Next, change the port that Remote Desktop uses on the host computer to a secret port. Print a screen shot showing how you made the change. Use the client computer to create a Remote Desktop session to the host computer using the secret port. Print a screen shot showing how you made the connection using the secret port. Verify the session works by transferring files in both directions.

3. What secret port did you use? What two or more Microsoft Knowledge Base Articles gave you the information you needed?

REAL PROBLEM 8-2: Use Advanced IP Scanner and Wake on LAN

Advanced IP Scanner by Famatech (*www.radmin.com*) is freeware recommended by Microsoft that can be used to scan for devices on the network and remotely control them. Go to the Famatech web site and watch the video titled *Advanced IP Scanner Video*. Then do the following:

1. On Computer 1, download and install the Advanced IP Scanner utility. Use it to scan for computers or other devices on your network.

2. On Computer 2, configure Wake on LAN and put this computer to sleep. Use Advanced IP Scanner to scan again. Did it find the computer that is asleep?

3. Use Advanced IP Scanner to remotely control Computer 2. Can you use the utility to view the desktop of Computer 2? What software did you have to install on Computer 2 so you could remote control it using Advanced IP Scanner?

4. Remotely shut down Computer 2. Can you power up Computer 2 using Advanced IP Scanner?

5. List three reasons why an administrator might find Advanced IP Scanner useful.

CHAPTER 9

Security Strategies

In Chapter 8, you learned the concepts and principles of classifying users and data and protecting that data by applying appropriate permissions to the data so that only the authorized users can access it. In this chapter, you'll learn about additional Windows tools and techniques to secure a workstation. You'll also learn how to use hardware and other physical security tools and techniques to secure a workstation and small network. Finally, you'll learn how to recognize that a system is infected with malware and how to clean an infected system and keep it clean.

As you learn about these and other security strategies, keep in mind that when implementing a security plan, be sure you know about and follow any security guidelines established by your organization or by government regulations that control your organization.

This chapter gives you the basics of securing a personal computer. Later in your career as a support technician, you can build on the skills of this chapter to implement even more security such as controlling how Windows stores its passwords. However, keep in mind that even the best security will eventually fail. As a thief once said, "Locks are for honest people," and a thief will eventually find a way to break through. Security experts tell us that security measures basically make it more difficult and time consuming for a thief to break through so that she gets discouraged and moves on to easier targets.

SECURING A WINDOWS WORKSTATION

Where you have a choice in the security that you use, keep in mind two goals, which are sometimes in conflict. One goal is to protect resources, and the other goal is to not interfere with the functions of the system. A computer or network can be so protected that no one can use it, or so accessible that anyone can do whatever they want with it. The trick is to provide enough security to protect your resources while still allowing users to work unhindered. Also, too much security can sometimes force workers to find nonsecure alternatives. For example, if you require users to change their passwords weekly, some of them might start writing their passwords down to help remember them.

© Phil Marden/Getty Images

Figure 9-1 Security measures should protect resources without hindering how users work

A+
220-802
2.1

📝 **Notes** The best protection against attacks is layered protection. If one security method fails, the next might stop an attacker. When securing a workstation, use as many layers of protection as is reasonable for the situation and are justified by the value of the resources you are protecting.

USE WINDOWS TO AUTHENTICATE USERS

Recall from Chapter 8 that controlling access to computer resources is done by authenticating and authorizing a user or process. A user is authenticated when he proves he is who he says he is. Recall that when a computer is on a Windows domain, the domain is responsible for authentication. For a peer-to-peer network, authentication must happen at the local computer. Normally, Windows authenticates a user with a Windows password.

As an administrator, when you first create an account, be sure to assign a password to that account. It's best to give the user the ability to change the password at any time. As an administrator, you can control how a user logs on, require a workstation be locked when the user steps away, disable the guest account, and reset a password if a user forgets it. Now let's see how to do all these chores to bring added security to a Windows workstation.

CONTROLLING HOW A USER LOGS ON

Normally, when a computer is first booted or comes back from a sleep state, Windows provides a welcome screen that shows all active user accounts (see Figure 9-2). Malware can sometimes display a false welcome screen to trick users into providing user account passwords. A more secure method of logon is to require the user to press **Ctrl+Alt+Delete** to get to a logon window.

A+
220-802
2.1

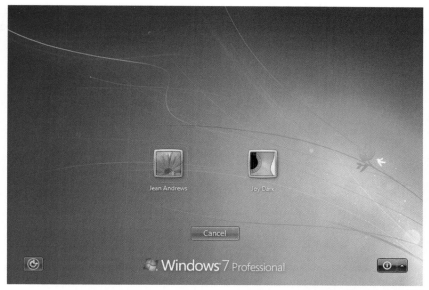

© Cengage Learning 2013

Figure 9-2 Windows 7 Welcome screen

Use the netplwiz command to change the way Windows logon works:

◢ Using Windows 7/Vista, enter **netplwiz** in the search box and press **Enter**. The User Accounts box appears. On the Users tab (see the left side of Figure 9-3), you can add and remove users, change the groups a user is in, and reset a password. Click the **Advanced** tab (see the right side of Figure 9-3). Check **Require users to press Ctrl+Alt+Delete**. Click **Apply** and close the box.

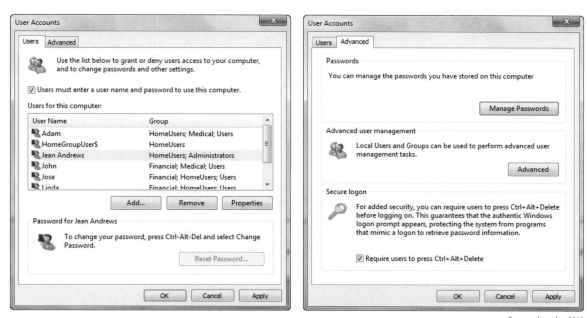

© Cengage Learning 2013

Figure 9-3 Change the way users log onto Windows

9

XP Differences   To find out how to change the way Windows XP users log onto a system, see Appendix C.

A+
220-802
2.1

When Crtl+Alt+Delete is required, the Welcome screen looks like that in Figure 9-4. When a user presses Ctrl+Alt+Delete, the Windows Welcome screen that appears has not been known to be intercepted by malware.

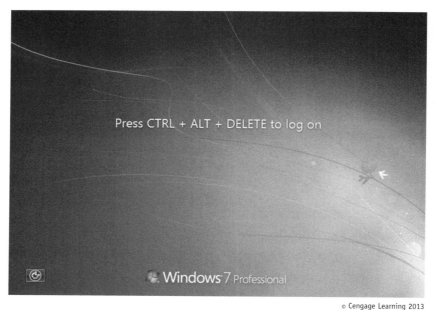

© Cengage Learning 2013

Figure 9-4　Windows 7 screen after the boot or returning from sleep state

A+
220-802
2.1, 2.3

POWER SETTINGS USED TO LOCK A WORKSTATION

To keep a system secure, users need to practice the habit of locking down their workstation each time they step away from their desks. The quickest way to do this is to press the **Windows key + L**. Another method is to press **Ctrl+Alt+Delete**. If the user is already logged on when she presses these keys, the login screen in Figure 9-5 appears. When the user clicks **Lock this computer**, Windows locks down. To unlock Windows, the user must enter her password. For this method to be effective, all user accounts need a password. Later in the chapter, you learn to use Group Policy to make passwords a requirement.

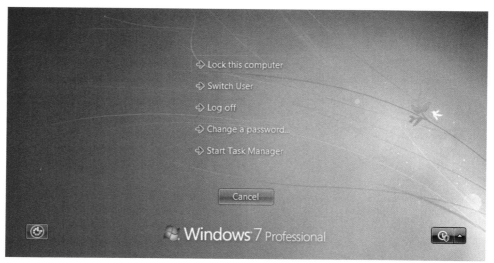

© Cengage Learning 2013

Figure 9-5　Results of pressing Ctrl-Alt-Del when a user is already logged on

A+
220-802
2.1, 2.3

APPLYING | CONCEPTS

REQUIRE A PASSWORD TO WAKE UP A COMPUTER

An unauthorized user might get access to a system when a user steps away from her workstation and forgets to lock it. To better secure the workstation, you can activate the screensaver (turn off the display) after a short period of inactivity and require a password be used to turn on the display and wake up the computer. Follow these steps:

1. In the Control Panel, click **Power Options** in the Hardware and Sound group.

2. In the Power Options window (see Figure 9-6), click **Change when the computer sleeps**.

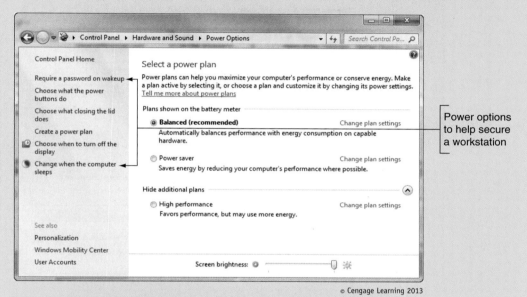

Power options to help secure a workstation

© Cengage Learning 2013

Figure 9-6 Windows power options available on the Power Options window to help lock down a workstation

3. In the Edit Plan Settings window, set when the display turns off and when the computer goes to sleep (see Figure 9-7). Click **Save changes**.

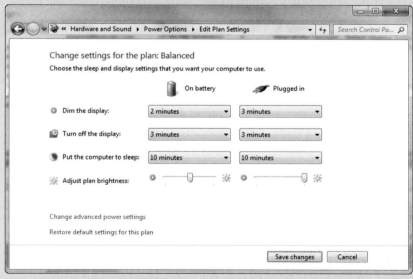

© Cengage Learning 2013

Figure 9-7 To protect the computer's resources from uninvited users, put the computer to sleep after a short period of inactivity

9

A+
220-802
2.1, 2.3

4. In the Power Options window, click **Require a password on wakeup**. In the System Settings window, make sure **Require a password (recommended)** is selected (see Figure 9-8). If you need to change this setting, first click **Change settings that are currently unavailable**. Save your changes and close all windows.

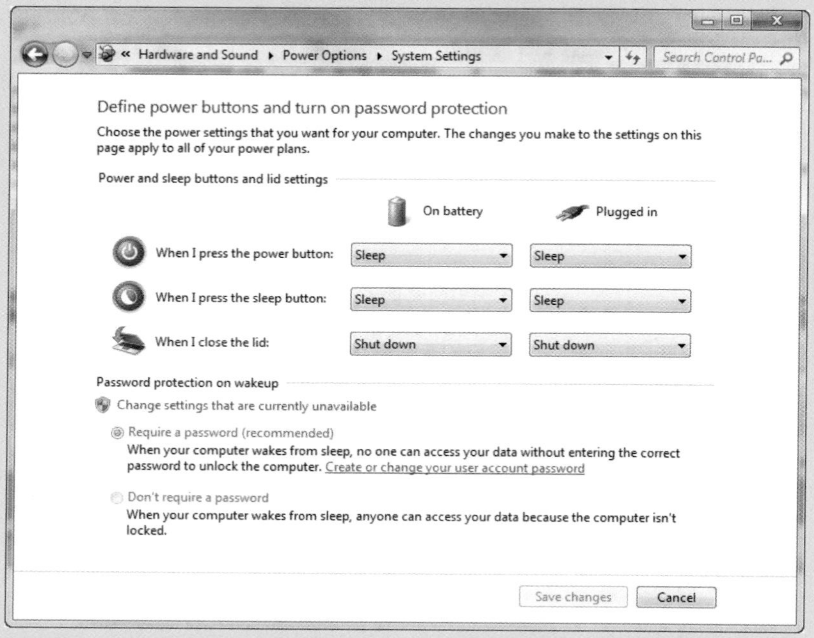

Figure 9-8   Require a password when the computer wakes up

© Cengage Learning 2013

A+
220-802
2.1

DISABLE THE GUEST ACCOUNT

The Guest account is disabled by default and should remain disabled. If you want to set up an account for visitors, create a standard account and name it Visitor. To make sure the Guest account is disabled, in Control Panel, click **Add or remove user accounts** in the User Accounts and Family Safety group. In the list of accounts, verify the Guest account is turned off. If it is not, double-click it and click **Turn off the guest account** (see Figure 9-9).

Figure 9-9   For best security, turn off the Guest account

© Cengage Learning 2013

RESET A USER PASSWORD

Sometimes a user forgets his or her password or the password is compromised. If this happens, as an administrator, you can reset the password. Keep in mind, however, that resetting a password causes the OS to lock the user out from using encrypted files or email and from

A+
220-802
2.1

using Internet passwords stored on the computer. For business and professional editions of Windows, reset a password using the Computer Management console. For all editions of Windows, you can use the netplwiz command or the Control Panel to reset a password for another user. Follow these steps:

1. In Control Panel, click **Add or remove user accounts** in the User Accounts and Family group. Double-click the account and then click **Change the password**. The Change Password window opens (see Figure 9-10).

2. Enter the new password twice and a password hint. Click **Change password**. Close the window.

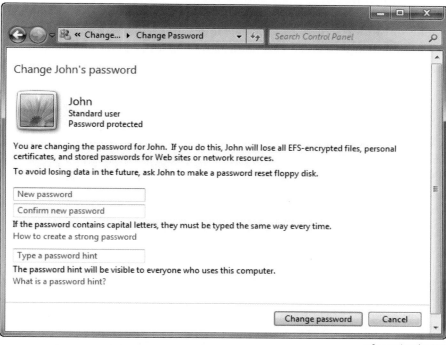

Figure 9-10   Reset a user's password

© Cengage Learning 2013

A+
220-802
2.1, 2.3

CREATE STRONG PASSWORDS

A password needs to be a strong password, which means it should not be easy to guess by both humans and computer programs designed to hack passwords.

A strong password, such as @y&kK1ff, meets all of the following criteria:

- ◢ Use eight or more characters (14 characters or longer is better).
- ◢ Combine uppercase and lowercase letters, numbers, and symbols.
- ◢ Use at least one symbol in the second through sixth position of your password.
- ◢ Don't use consecutive letters or numbers, such as "abcdefg" or "12345."
- ◢ Don't use adjacent keys on your keyboard, such as "qwerty."
- ◢ Don't use your logon name in the password.
- ◢ Don't use words in any language. Don't even use numbers for letters (as in "p@ssw0rd") because programs can now guess those as well.
- ◢ Don't use the same password for more than one system.

> **Notes** To keep from having to write down a password, create one that is easy to remember, for example, mF1dI8iC. The letters in the password stand for "My favorite desert is ice cream." If you must keep track of lots of different passwords, password management software can hold your passwords safely so that you don't forget them.

9

A+
220-802
2.1, 2.3

In some situations, a blank Windows password might be more secure than an easy-to-guess password such as "1234." That's because you cannot authenticate to a Windows computer from a remote computer unless the user account has a password. A criminal might be able to guess an easy password and authenticate remotely. For this reason, if your computer is always sitting in a protected room such as your home office and you don't intend to access it remotely, you might choose to use no password. However, if you travel with a laptop, always use a strong password.

If you write your password down, keep it in as safe a place as you would the data you are protecting. Don't send your passwords over email or chat. Change your passwords regularly, and don't type your passwords on a public computer. For example, computers in hotel lobbies or Internet cafes should only be used for web browsing—not for logging on to your email account or online banking account. These computers might be running keystroke-logging software put there by criminals to record each keystroke. Several years ago, while on vacation, I entered credit card information on a computer in a hotel lobby in a foreign country. Months later, I was still protesting $2 or $3 charges to my credit card from that country. Trust me. Don't do it—I speak from experience.

FILE AND FOLDER ENCRYPTION

In Windows, files and folders can be encrypted using the Windows Encrypted File System (EFS). This encryption works only with the NTFS file system and business and professional editions of Windows. If a folder is marked for encryption, every file created in the folder or copied to the folder will be encrypted. An encrypted file remains encrypted if you move it from an encrypted folder to an unencrypted folder on the same or another NTFS volume. To encrypt a folder or file, right-click it and open its Properties box (see Figure 9-11).

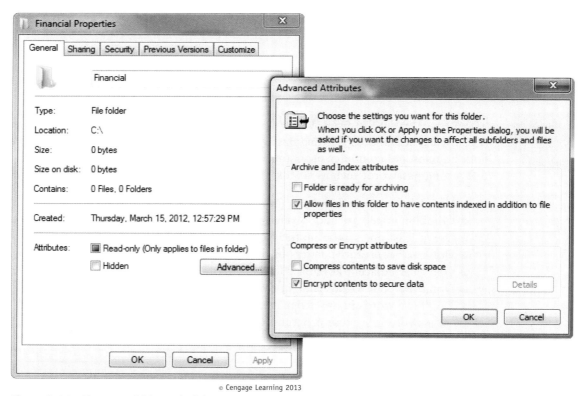

© Cengage Learning 2013

Figure 9-11 Encrypt a folder and all its contents

On the General tab, click **Advanced**. On the Advanced Attributes tab, check **Encrypt contents to secure data** and click **OK**. In Windows Explorer, encrypted file and folder names are displayed in green.

WINDOWS FIREWALL SETTINGS

A+
220-802
1.1, 1.4,
1.5, 1.6,
2.1

Recall from Chapter 7 that a router can serve as a hardware firewall to protect its network from attack over the Internet. Recall that the best protection from attack is layered protection (see Figure 9-12). In addition to a hardware network firewall, a large corporation might use a software firewall, also called a corporate firewall, installed on a computer that stands between the Internet and the network to protect the network. This computer has two network cards installed, and the installed corporate firewall filters the traffic between the two cards.

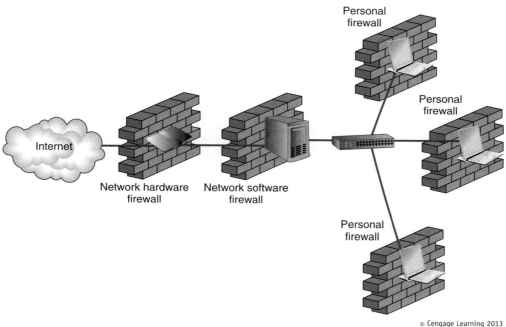

© Cengage Learning 2013

Figure 9-12   Three types of firewalls used to protect a network and individual computers on the network

A personal firewall, also called a host firewall, is software installed on a computer to protect this computer. A personal firewall provides redundant protection from attacks over the Internet and also protects a computer from attack from other computers on the same network. When setting up a SOHO network or a personal computer, configure a personal firewall on each computer.

Windows Firewall is a personal firewall that protects a computer from intrusion and is automatically configured when you set your network location in the Network and Sharing Center. However, you might want to customize these settings. For example, recall from Chapter 8 that you customized Windows Firewall to allow access through Remote Desktop connections.

A+
220-802
1.1, 1.4,
1.5, 1.6,
2.1

APPLYING | CONCEPTS CONFIGURE WINDOWS FIREWALL

Follow these steps to find out how to configure Windows Firewall:

1. Use one of these methods to open Windows Firewall:

   ◢ Open the **Network and Sharing Center** and in the lower part of the left pane, click **Windows Firewall**.

   ◢ In Control Panel, click **System and Security** and then click **Windows Firewall**.

   The Windows Firewall window is shown in Figure 9-13.

© Cengage Learning 2013

Figure 9-13 Windows Firewall shows the computer currently connected to a private network

2. To control firewall settings for each type of network location, click **Turn Windows Firewall on or off** in the left pane. The Windows Firewall Customize Settings window appears (see Figure 9-14). Notice in the figure Windows Firewall is turned on for each network location.

3. To allow no exceptions though the firewall on a home or work (private) network or public network, check **Block all incoming connections, including those in the list of allowed programs**. After you have made your changes, click **OK**.

4. You can allow an exception to your firewall rules. To change the programs allowed through the firewall, in the Windows Firewall window shown in Figure 9-13, click **Allow a program or feature through Windows Firewall**. The Allowed Programs window appears (see Figure 9-15).

5. Find the program you want to allow to initiate a connection from a remote computer to this computer. In the right side of the window, click either **Home/Work (Private)** or **Public** to indicate which type of network location the program is allowed to use. If you don't see your program in the list, click **Allow another program** to see more programs or to add your own. (If the option is gray, click **Change settings** to enable it.) When you are finished making changes, click **OK** to return to the Windows Firewall window.

A+
220-802
1.1, 1.4,
1.5, 1.6,
2.1

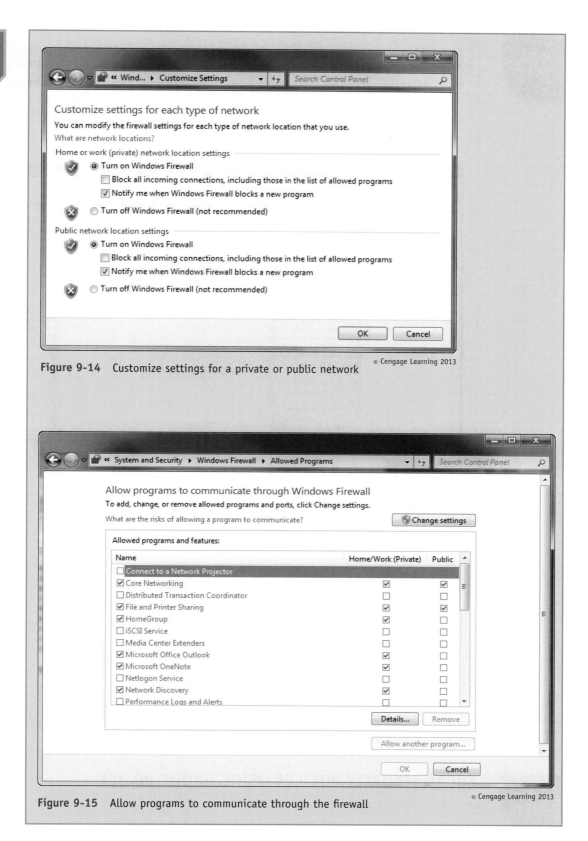

Figure 9-14 Customize settings for a private or public network   © Cengage Learning 2013

Figure 9-15 Allow programs to communicate through the firewall   © Cengage Learning 2013

9

A+
220-802
1.1, 1.4,
1.5, 1.6,
2.1

6. For even more control over firewall settings, in the Windows Firewall window, click **Advanced settings**. The Windows Firewall with Advanced Security window opens. In the left pane, select Inbound Rules or Outbound Rules. A list of programs appears. Right-click a program and select **Properties** from the shortcut menu. Using the Properties box, you have full control of how exceptions work to get through the firewall, including which users, protocols, ports, and remote computers can use it (see Figure 9-16).

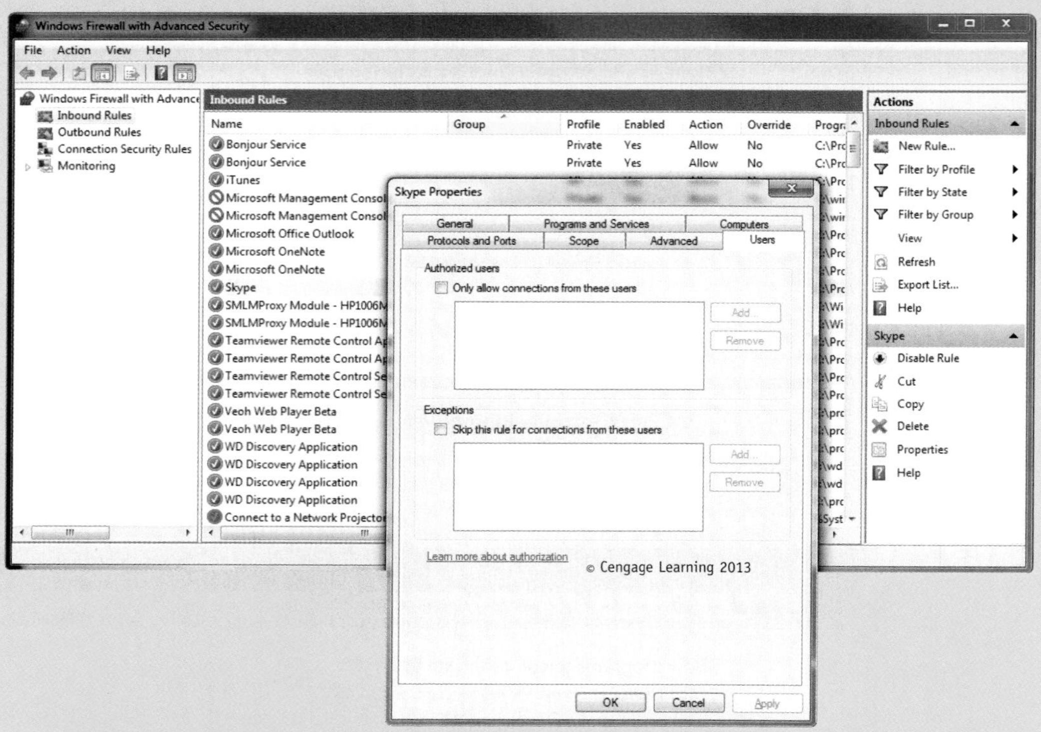

© Cengage Learning 2013

Figure 9-16 Use advanced settings to control exactly how a program can get through Windows Firewall

Vista Differences In Vista, you can allow exceptions to Windows Firewall by program name or port number. To see how the Vista Windows Firewall works differently from Windows 7, see Appendix B.

XP Differences To see how Windows Firewall in Windows XP works differently from Windows 7, see Appendix C.

A+
220-802
1.8, 2.3

LOCAL SECURITY POLICES USING GROUP POLICY

Recall from Chapter 8 that the Group Policy utility controls what users can do with a system and how the system is used and is available with business and professional editions of Windows. Using Group Policy, you can set security policies to help secure a workstation. For example, you can set policies to require all users to have passwords and to rename default user accounts.

A+
220-802
1.8, 2.3

APPLYING | CONCEPTS   APPLY LOCAL SECURITY POLICIES

Follow these steps to set a few important security policies:

1. Log onto Windows using an administrator account on a system using Windows 7 Professional, Ultimate, or Enterprise.

2. To start Group Policy, use the **gpedit.msc** command in the search box. The Local Group Policy Editor console opens.

3. To change a policy, first use the left pane to drill down into the appropriate policy group and then use the right pane to view and edit a policy. Here are important security policies you might want to change:

   ◢ *Change default usernames.* A hacker is less likely to hack into the built-in Administrator account or Guest account if you change the names of these default accounts. To change the name of the Administrator account, drill down in the **Computer Configuration**, **Windows Settings**, **Security Settings**, **Local Policies**, **Security Options** group (see the left side of Figure 9-17). In the right pane, double-click **Accounts: Rename administrator account**. In the Properties box for this policy (see the right side of Figure 9-17), change the name and click **OK**. To change the name of the Guest account, use the policy **Account: Rename guest account**.

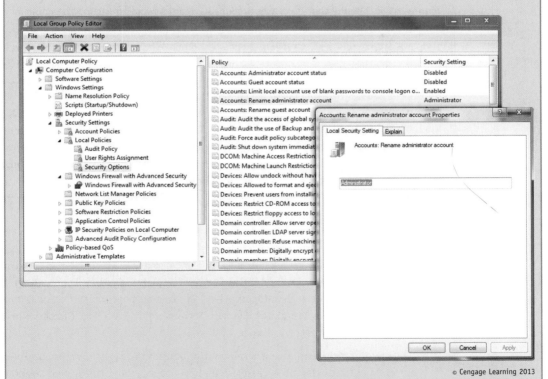

© Cengage Learning 2013

Figure 9-17   Use Group Policy to rename a default user account

> **Notes**   The Properties box for many policies offers the Explain tab. Use this tab to read more about a policy and how it works.

9

A+
220-802
1.8, 2.3

▲ ***Require user passwords.*** To require that all user accounts have passwords, drill down to the **Computer Configuration**, **Windows Settings**, **Security Settings**, **Account Policies**, **Password Policy** group (see the left side of Figure 9-18). Use the **Minimum password length** policy and set the minimum length to six or eight characters (see the right side of Figure 9-18).

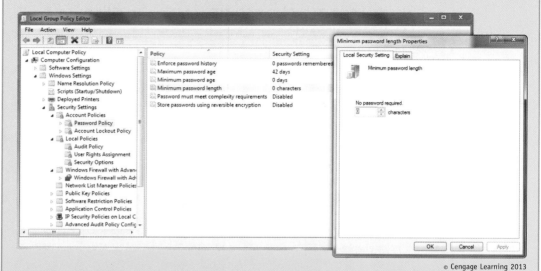

© Cengage Learning 2013

Figure 9-18   Require that each user account have a password by setting the minimum password length policy

▲ ***Allow only a single logon.*** By default, Windows allows fast user switching, which means multiple users can log onto Windows. To disable this feature and allow only a single logon, drill down to the **Computer Configuration**, **Administrative Templates**, **System**, **Logon** group. Then use the **Hide entry points for Fast User Switching** policy. Enable this policy so that the *Switch user* option is dimmed and not available on the Shut down menu on the Start menu.

▲ ***Audit logon failures.*** Group Policy offers several auditing policies that monitor and log security events. These Security logs can then be viewed using Event Viewer. To set an audit policy to monitor a failed logon event, drill down to the **Computer Configuration**, **Windows Settings**, **Security Settings**, **Local Policies**, **Audit Policy** group. Use the **Audit logon events** policy. You can audit logon successes and failures. To keep the log from getting too big, you can select **Failure** to only log these events.

▲ ***Disable logon and shutdown scripts.*** Policies can run scripts for the computer or user during logon or shutdown. These scripts can contain programs, which might contain malware. To manage logon scripts, in the Computer Configuration or User Configuration group, drill down to the **Administrative Templates**, **System**, **Logon** group. Use the **Run these programs at user logon** policy. To manage shutdown scripts, drill down to the **Administrative Templates**, **System**, **Scripts** group. For a list of folders where Group Policy stores these scripts, see Appendix G.

4. When you finish setting your local security policies, close the Local Group Policy Editor console. To put into effect the changes you have made, reboot the system or enter the command **Gpupdate.exe** in a command prompt window.

> **Notes**   Sometimes policies overlap or conflict. To find out the resulting policies for the computer or user that are currently applied to the system, you can use the **Gpresult** command in a command prompt window with parameters. To find out more about this command, search the *technet.microsoft.com* web site.

A+
220-802
1.8, 2.3

Notes The group of policies in the Local Computer Policy, Computer Configuration, Windows Settings, Security Settings group can also be edited from the Control Panel. In the Control Panel, open the **Administrative Tools** and double-click **Local Security Policy**.

Hands-on | Project 9.1   Use Group Policy to Secure a Workstation

Using Windows 7 Professional, Ultimate or Enterprise, set local security policies to allow only single user logons, to require a password for each account, to audit failed logon events, and to create a logon script that displays the message, "The Golden Pineapple Was Here!" when anyone logs onto the system. Test your policies by verifying only one user can log onto a system, a password is required, your script executes when you log on, and a failed logon event using an invalid password is logged and can be viewed in Event Viewer. Answer the following questions:

1. Which policies did you set and what setting was applied to each policy?

2. What software did you use to create your script? What is the exact path and filename (including the file extension) to your script?

3. Which log in Event Viewer shows the logon failure event?

4. List three more policies you find in Group Policy not discussed in this chapter that can make a workstation more secure.

A+
220-802
1.1

USE BITLOCKER ENCRYPTION

BitLocker Encryption in Windows professional and business editions locks down a hard drive by encrypting the entire Windows volume and any other volume on the drive. It's a bit complicated to set up and has some restrictions that you need to be aware of before you decide to use it. It is intended to work in partnership with file and folder encryption to provide data security.

A+ Exam Tip The A+ 220–802 exam expects you to know about the features and benefits of BitLocker Encryption.

9

The three ways you can use BitLocker Encryption depend on the type of protection you need and the computer hardware available:

- ◢ *Computer authentication.* Many notebook computers have a chip on the motherboard called the TPM (Trusted Platform Module) chip. The TPM chip holds the BitLocker encryption key (also called the startup key). If the hard drive is stolen from the notebook and installed in another computer, the data would be safe because BitLocker would not allow access without the startup key stored on the TPM chip. Therefore, this method authenticates the computer. However, if the motherboard fails and is replaced, you'll need a backup copy of the startup key to access data on the hard drive. (You cannot move the TPM chip from one motherboard to another.)
- ◢ *User authentication.* For computers that don't have TPM, the startup key can be stored on a USB flash drive (or other storage device the computer reads before the OS is loaded), and the flash drive must be installed before the computer boots. This method authenticates the user. For this method to be the most secure, the user must never leave the flash drive stored with the computer. (Instead, the user might keep the USB startup key on his key ring.)

A+
220-802
1.1

◢ *Computer and user authentication*. For *best* security, a PIN or password can be required at every startup in addition to TPM. Using this method, both the computer and the user are authenticated.

BitLocker Encryption provides great security, but security comes with a price. For instance, you risk the chance your TPM will fail or you will lose all copies of the startup key. In these events, recovering the data can be messy. Therefore, use BitLocker only if the risks of BitLocker giving problems outweigh the risks of stolen data. And, if you decide to use BitLocker, be sure to make extra copies of the startup key and/or password and keep them in a safe location.

For detailed instructions on how to set up BitLocker Encryption, see the Microsoft Knowledge Base article 933246 at *support.microsoft.com*.

USE BIOS FEATURES TO PROTECT THE SYSTEM

Many motherboards for desktop and laptop computers offer several BIOS security features, including power-on passwords, support for intrusion-detection devices, and support for a TPM chip. Power-on passwords include a supervisor password (required to change BIOS setup), user password (required to use the system or view BIOS setup), and a drive lock password (required to access the hard drive). The drive lock password is stored on the hard drive so that it will still control access to the drive in the event the drive is removed from the computer and installed on another system. Figure 9-19 shows one BIOS setup Security screen where you can set the hard drive password. This screen can also be used to set the supervisor and user passwords to the system.

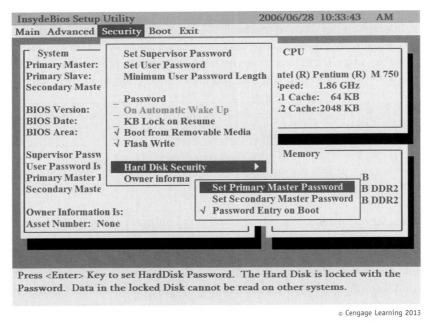

© Cengage Learning 2013

Figure 9-19 Submenu shows how to set a hard drive password that will be written on the drive

Some laptops contain the LoJack technology on the motherboard to support the laptop-tracking software Computrace LoJack by Absolute Software (*www.absolute.com*). When you install the software on your laptop and if the laptop is ever stolen, Absolute can lock down your hard drive and track down the laptop.

ADDITIONAL METHODS TO PROTECT RESOURCES

A+
220-802
2.1

Securing data and other computer resources might seem like a never-ending task. Come to think of it, that's probably true. In this part of the chapter, you'll learn even more ways to securely authenticate users on a large network, physically protect computer resources, destroy data before you toss out a storage device, and educate users to not unintentionally compromise the security measures you've put in place.

AUTHENTICATE USERS FOR LARGE NETWORKS

Normally, Windows authenticates a user with a Windows password. However, the best authentication happens when a user (1) knows something (such as a Windows password) and (2) possesses something, which is called the security token (such as a smart card or biometric data; for example, a fingerprint scan). This extra authentication is sometimes used to secure access to a corporate network. In this part of the chapter, you learn about smart cards and biometric data used to add this extra authentication. One warning to keep in mind is a smart card or biometric data should be used in addition to, and not as a replacement to a Windows password.

SMART CARDS

The most popular type of token used to authenticate a user is a smart card, which is any small device that contains authentication information. The information on the smart card can be keyed into a logon window by a user, read by a smart card reader (when the device is inserted in the reader), or transmitted wirelessly. (You also need to know that some people don't consider a card to be a smart card unless it has an embedded microprocessor.)

> **💡 A+ Exam Tip** The A+ 220-802 exam expects you to know about biometric data, badges, key fobs, RFID badges, retinal scans, and RSA tokens used to authenticate to a computer system or network.

Here are some variations of smart cards:

◢ *Key fob.* A key fob is a smart card that fits conveniently on a keychain. RSA Security (*www.rsasecurity.com*), a leader in authentication technologies, makes several types of smart cards, called SecurIDs or RSA tokens. One SecurID key fob by RSA Security is shown in Figure 9-20. The number on the key fob changes every 60 seconds. When a user logs onto the network, she must enter the number on the key fob, which is synchronized with the network authentication service. Entering the number proves that the user has the smart card in hand. Because the device does not actually make physical contact with the system, it is called a contactless token.

Courtesy of RSA, The Security Division of EMC

Figure 9-20 A smart card such as this SecurID key fob is used to authenticate a user gaining access to a secured network

9

▲ *Wireless token.* Another type of contactless token uses wireless technology to transmit information kept by the token to the computer system. A Radio Frequency Identification (RFID) token transmits authentication to the system when the token gets in range of a query device. For example, an **RFID badge** worn by an employee can allow the employee entrance into a locked area of a building.

▲ *Memory stripe card.* An example of a contact token is an employee badge or other smart card with a magnetic stripe that can be read by a smart card reader (see Figure 9-21). Because these cards don't contain a microchip, they are sometimes called memory cards. They can be read by a smart card reader, such as the one shown in Figure 9-22, which connects to a computer using a USB port. Used in this way, they are part of the authentication process into a network. The magnetic stripe can contain information about the user to indicate their rights on the system. The major disadvantage of this type of smart card is that each computer used for authentication must have one of these smart card reader machines installed. Also, in the industry, because a card with a magnetic stripe does not contain a microchip, some in the industry don't consider it to fit into the category of a smart card, but rather simply call it a magnetic stripe card.

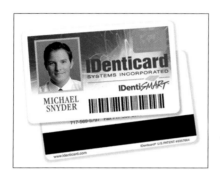 

Courtesy of IDenticard Systems

Figure 9-21   A smart card with a magnetic strip can be used inside or outside a computer network

Courtesy of Athena Smartcard Solutions Inc.

Figure 9-22   This smart card reader by Athena Smartcard Solutions (*www.athena-scs.com*) uses a USB connection

▲ *Cell phone with token.* An app installed on a cell phone can hold the user's token, which includes a digital signature or digital certificate. A **digital certificate** is assigned by a Certification Authority (for example, VeriSign—*www.verisign. com*) and is used to prove you are who you say you are. The authentication can be sent to the network via a USB connection, text message, phone call, or Bluetooth connection. This method is sometimes used when an employee authenticates to a VPN connection to the corporate network.

A+
220-802
2.1

BIOMETRIC DATA

As part of the authentication process, some systems use biometric data to validate the person's physical body, which, in effect, becomes the token. A **biometric device** is an input device that inputs biological data about a person, which can identify a person's fingerprints, handprints, face, voice, retinal, iris, and handwritten signatures. Figure 9-23 shows one biometric input device, an iris reader, that scans your iris. Iris scanning is one of the most accurate ways to identify a person using biological data. **Retinal scanning** scans the blood vessels on the back of the eye and is considered the most reliable of all biometric data scanning. However, the equipment is more expensive and it takes more time to make a retinal scan than other scans. Retinal scanning is used for the highest level of security by the government and military.

Courtesy of Iris ID Systems, Inc.

Figure 9-23 The iCAM7000 iris recognition camera by Iris ID Systems, Inc.

9

PHYSICAL SECURITY METHODS AND DEVICES

Physically protecting your computer and data might be one of the security measures you will implement when on the job. Here are some suggestions:

▲ *If your data is* really *private, keep it behind a locked door or under lock and key.* You can use all kinds of security methods to encrypt, password protect, and hide data, but if it really is that important, one obvious thing you can do is to keep the computer behind a locked door. You can also store the data on a removable storage device such as an external hard drive and, when you're not using the data, put the drive in a fireproof safe. And, of course, keep two copies. Sounds simple, but it works. And don't forget printouts of sensitive documents should also be kept under lock and key.

▲ *Lock down the computer case.* Some computer cases allow you to add a lock so that you can physically prevent others from opening the case (see Figure 9-24). Some motherboards have a BIOS feature that alerts you when an intrusion has been detected.

A+
220-802
2.1

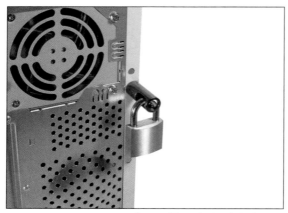

Courtesy of Innovative Security Products Inc.

Figure 9-24 This computer case allows you to use a lock and key to keep intruders from opening the case

▲ *Lock and chain.* You can also use a lock and chain to physically tie a computer to a desk or other permanent fixture so someone can't walk away with it. Figure 9-25 shows a cable lock system for a laptop. Most laptops have a security slot on the case to connect the cable lock.

Courtesy of Kensington Computer Group

Figure 9-25 Use a cable lock system to secure a notebook computer to a desk to help prevent it from being stolen

▲ *Privacy filters.* To keep other people from viewing a monitor screen, you can install a privacy filter that fits over the screen to prevent it from being read from a wide angle.

A+
220-802
2.1

▲ *Theft-prevention plate.* As an added precaution, physically mark a computer case or laptop so it can be identified if it is later stolen. You embed a theft-prevention plate into the case or engrave your ID information into it. The identifying numbers or bar code identify you, the owner, and can also clearly establish to police that the notebook has been stolen. Two sources of theft-prevention plates and cable locks are Computer Security Products, Inc. (*www.computersecurity.com*) and Flexguard Security System (*www.flexguard.com*). To further help you identify stolen equipment, record serial numbers and model numbers in a safe place separate from the equipment.

A+
220-802
2.1, 2.4

DATA DESTRUCTION

Don't throw out a hard drive, CD, DVD, tape, or other media that might have personal or corporate data on it unless you know the data can't be stolen off the device. Trying to wipe a drive clean by deleting files or even using Windows to format the drive does not completely destroy the data. Here are some ways to destroy printed documents and sanitize storage devices:

▲ *Use a paper shredder.* Use a paper shredder to destroy all documents that contain sensitive data.

> 💡 **A+ Exam Tip** The A+ 220-802 exam expects you to know about data-destruction techniques, including a low-level format, drive wipe, shredder, degausser, and drill, which can do physical damage to a hard drive.

▲ *Overwrite data on the drive.* You can perform a low-level format of a drive to overwrite the data with zeroes. (A low-level format is different from a Windows format. A device receives a low-level format at the factory, which writes sector markings on the drive. You can obtain a low-level format utility from the device manufacturer.) You can also use a zero-fill utility that overwrites all data on the drive with zeroes. Either method works for most low-security situations, but professional thieves know how to break through this type of destruction. If you use one of these utilities, run it multiple times to write zeroes on top of zeroes. Data recovery has been known to reach 14 levels of overwrites because each bit is slightly offset from the one under it.

▲ *Physically destroy the storage media.* Use a drill to drill many holes through the drive housing all the way through to the other side of the housing. Break CDs and DVDs in half and do similar physical damage to flash drives or tapes. Again, expert thieves can still recover some of the data.

▲ *For magnetic devices, use a degausser.* A degausser exposes a storage device to a strong magnetic field to completely erase the data on a magnetic hard drive or tape drive (see Figure 9-26). For best destruction, use the degausser and also physically destroy the drive. Degaussing does not erase data on a solid-state hard drive or other flash media because these devices don't use a magnetic surface to hold data.

▲ *For solid-state devices, use a Secure Erase utility.* As required by government regulations for personal data privacy, the American National Standards Institute (ANSI) developed the ATA Secure Erase standards for securely erasing data from solid-state devices such as a USB flash drive or SSD drive. You can download a Secure Erase utility from the manufacturer of the device and run it to securely erase all data on the device.

▲ *Use a secure data-destruction service.* For the very best data destruction, consider a secure data-destruction service. To find a service, search the web for "secure data destruction." However, don't use a service unless you have thoroughly checked its references and guarantees of legal compliance that your organization is required to meet.

9

A+
220-802
2.1, 2.4

Courtesy of VS Security Products, Ltd.

Figure 9-26 Use a degausser to sanitize a magnetic hard drive or tape

A+
220-802
2.1, 2.2

EDUCATE USERS

Generally speaking, the weakest link in setting up security in a computer environment is people. That's because people can often be tricked into giving out private information. Even with all the news and hype about identity theft and criminal web sites, it's amazing how well these techniques still work. Many users naively download a funny screen saver, open an email attachment, or enter credit card information on a web site without regard to security. In the computer arena, social engineering is the practice of tricking people into giving out private information or allowing unsafe programs into the network or computer.

A good support technician is aware of the criminal practices used, and is able to teach users how to recognize this mischief and avoid it. Here is a list of important security measures that users need to follow to protect passwords and the computer system:

▲ Never give out your passwords to anyone, not even a supervisor or tech support person who calls and asks for it.

▲ Don't store your passwords on a computer. Some organizations even forbid employees from writing down their passwords.

▲ Don't use the same password on more than one system (computer, network, application, or web site).

▲ Be aware of shoulder surfing when other people secretly peek at your monitor screen as you work. A privacy filter can help.

▲ Lock down your workstation each time you step away from your desk.

▲ Users need to be on the alert for tailgating, which is when someone who is unauthorized follows the employee through a secured entrance to a room or building. Another form of tailgating is when a user steps away from her computer and another person continues to use the Windows session when the system is not properly locked.

Beware of online social engineering techniques. For example, don't be fooled by scam email or an email hoax such as the one shown in Figure 9-27. When the user who received this email scanned the attached file using antivirus software, the software reported the file contained malware.

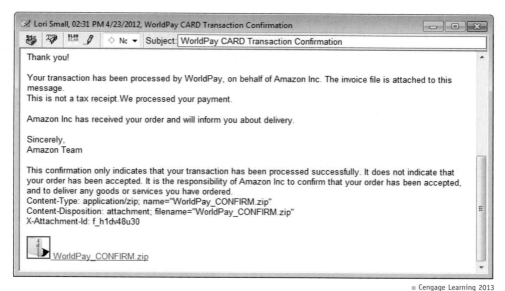

© Cengage Learning 2013

Figure 9-27 This phishing technique using an email message with an attached file is an example of social engineering

> 💡 **A+ Exam Tip** The A+ 220-802 exam expects you to be aware of social engineering situations such as tailgating, phishing, and shoulder surfing that might compromise security.

Here are some good sites to help you debunk a virus hoax or email hoax:

- ◢ *www.snopes.com* by Barbara and David Mikkelson
- ◢ *www.viruslist.com* by Kaspersky Lab
- ◢ *www.vmyths.com* by Rhode Island Soft Systems, Inc.

Don't forward an email hoax. When you get a hoax, if you know the person who sent it to you, do us all a favor and send that person some of these links!

Here are some other types of online social engineering situations:

- ◢ Phishing (pronounced "fishing") is a type of identity theft where the sender of an email message scams you into responding with personal data about yourself. The scam artist baits you by asking you to verify personal data on your bank account, ISP account, credit card account, or something of that nature. Often you are tricked into clicking a link in the email message, which takes you to an official-looking site complete with corporate or bank logos where you are asked to enter your user ID and password to enter the site.
- ◢ An email message might contain a link that leads to a malicious script. To keep the script from running, copy and paste the link to your browser address bar instead.

A study by Dell showed that 65 percent of business travelers have not secured the corporate data on their hard drives, and 42 percent don't back up that data. Here are some commonsense rules to help protect a laptop when traveling:

- ◢ When traveling, always know where your laptop is. If you're standing at an airport counter, tuck your laptop case securely between your ankles. At security checkpoints, pay attention to your belongings; tell yourself to stay focused. When flying, never check in your laptop as baggage, and don't store it in airplane overhead bins; keep it at your feet.

9

A+
220-802
2.1, 2.2

◢ Never leave a laptop in an unlocked car. If you leave your laptop in a hotel room, use a laptop cable lock to secure it to a table.

◢ When at work, lock your laptop in a secure place or use a laptop cable lock to secure it to your desk.

A PC support technician will most certainly be called on to help a user rid a system of malware. Let's turn our attention to how to deal with that problem.

DEALING WITH MALICIOUS SOFTWARE

Malicious software, also called malware, or a computer infestation, is any unwanted program that means you harm and is transmitted to your computer without your knowledge. Grayware is any annoying and unwanted program that might or might not mean you harm. In this part of the chapter, you'll learn about the different types of malware and grayware, what to do to clean up an infected system, and how to protect a system from infection.

WHAT ARE WE UP AGAINST?

You need to know your enemy! Different categories of malicious software and scamming techniques are listed next:

◢ A virus is a program that replicates by attaching itself to other programs. The infected program must be executed for a virus to run. The program might be an application, a macro in a document, a Windows system file, or a boot loader program.

◢ A boot sector virus is a virus that hides in the MBR program in the boot sector of a hard drive or in an OS boot loader program.

◢ Adware produces all those unwanted pop-up ads.

◢ Spyware spies on you to collect personal information about you that it transmits over the Internet to web-hosting sites.

◢ A keylogger tracks all your keystrokes and can be used to steal a person's identity, credit card numbers, Social Security number, bank information, passwords, email addresses, and so forth.

◢ A worm is a program that copies itself throughout a network or the Internet without a host program. A worm creates problems by overloading the network as it replicates and can even hijack or install a server program such as a web server.

◢ A Trojan does not need a host program to work; rather, it substitutes itself for a legitimate program. In most cases, a user launches it thinking she is launching a legitimate program. A Trojan is often downloaded from a web site when a user is tricked into thinking it is legitimate software, or a user is tricked into opening an email attachment (refer back to Figure 9-27).

◢ A rootkit is a virus that loads itself before the OS boot is complete. Because it is already loaded when the antivirus software loads, it is sometimes overlooked by the software. A rootkit can hide folders that contain software it has installed and can hijack internal Windows components so that it masks information Windows provides to user mode utilities such as Task Manager, Windows Explorer, the registry editor, and antivirus software. This last trick helps it remain undetected.

A+ Exam Tip The A+ 220-802 exam expects you to be able to compare and contrast viruses, Trojans, worms, spyware, and rootkits.

A+
220-802
2.1

STEP-BY-STEP ATTACK PLAN

This section is a step-by-step attack plan to clean up an infected system. We'll use **antivirus (AV) software** to remove all types of general malware and then use **antispyware software** to remove spyware and adware. Then we'll use some Windows tools to check out the system to make sure all remnants of malware have been removed and the system is in tip-top order.

> ⚡ **Caution** If a system is highly infected and will later hold sensitive data, consider backing up the data, reformatting the hard drive, and reinstalling the OS and applications. In fact, Microsoft recommends this to be the safest way to deal with highly infected systems.

A+
220-802
2.1, 4.7

STEP 1: IDENTIFY MALWARE SYMPTOMS

A PC support technician needs to know how to recognize that a system is infected with malware and how to clean an infected system. Here are some warnings that suggest malicious software is at work:

▲ Pop-up ads plague you when surfing the web. Your browser home page has changed and you see new toolbars you didn't ask for. Your browser might be redirected to a web site you didn't ask for. This last type of attack is called browser hijacking. Figure 9-28 shows a web page that appeared as the user tried to access another page. This bogus page is phishing for login information to the DSL service or home router. Also notice in the figure the uninvited toolbars.

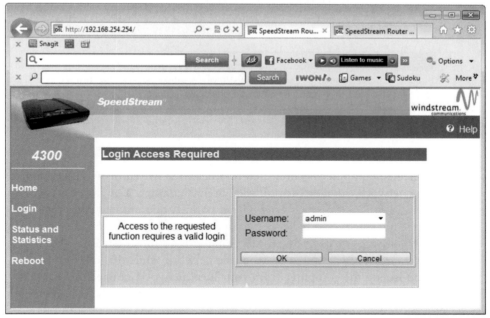

© Cengage Learning 2013

Figure 9-28 Uninvited toolbars and a redirected web page indicate an infected system

▲ Generally, the system works much slower than it used to. Programs take longer than normal to load. Strange or bizarre error messages appear. Programs that once worked now give errors. Task Manager shows unfamiliar processes running.
▲ The number and length of disk accesses seem excessive for simple tasks. The number of bad sectors on the hard drive continues to increase. The system might even lock up.
▲ You have problems making a network connection or accessing the web.
▲ Your antivirus software displays one or more messages.

A+
220-802
2.1, 4.7

◢ Windows updates fail to install correctly or give errors during installation.

◢ The system cannot recognize the CD or DVD drive, although it worked earlier.

◢ In Windows Explorer, filenames now have weird characters or their file sizes seem excessively large. Executable files have changed size or file extensions change without reason. Files mysteriously disappear or appear. Windows system files are renamed. Files constantly become corrupted. Files you could once access now give access denied messages, and file permissions change.

◢ The OS begins to boot, but hangs before getting a Windows desktop.

◢ You receive email messages telling you that you have sent someone spam or an infected message. This type of attack indicates your email address or email client software on your computer has been hijacked.

◢ Even though you can browse to other web sites, you cannot access AV software sites such as *www.symantec.com* or *www.mcafee.com*, and you cannot update your AV software. A window appears telling you that antivirus software you didn't ask for is installed (called rogue antivirus software).

◢ A message appears that a downloaded document contains macros, or an application asks whether it should run macros in a document. (It is best to disable macros if you cannot verify that they are from a trusted source and that they are free of viruses or worms.)

> 💡 **A+ Exam Tip** The A+ 220-802 exam expects you to know about the common symptoms of malware listed previously and how to quarantine and remediate an infected system.

> 📝 **Notes** Malicious software is designed to do varying degrees of damage to data and software, although it does not damage PC hardware. However, when boot sector information is destroyed on a hard drive, the hard drive can appear to be physically damaged.

STEP 2: QUARANTINE AN INFECTED SYSTEM

If an infected computer is connected to a network (wired or wireless), immediately disconnect the network cable or turn off the wireless adapter. You don't want to spread a virus or worm to other computers on your network. A quarantined computer is not allowed to use the regular network that other computers use. If you need to use the Internet to download AV software or its updates, take some precautions first. Consider your options. Can you disconnect other computers from the network while this one computer is connected? Can you isolate the computer from your local network, connecting it directly to the ISP or a special quarantined network? If neither option is possible, try downloading the AV software updates while the computer is booted into Safe Mode with Networking. Malware might still be running in Safe Mode, but is less likely to do so than when the system is started normally.

Always keep in mind that data might be on the hard drive that is not backed up. Before you begin cleaning up the system, back up data to another media.

STEP 3: RUN AV SOFTWARE

Table 9-1 lists popular antivirus software for personal computers and web sites that also provide information about viruses. Before selecting a product, be sure to read some reviews about it and check out some reliable web sites that rate AV software.

A+
220-802
2.1, 4.7

Notes Be aware of web sites that appear as sponsored links at the top of search results for AV software. These sites might make you think they are the home site for the software, but are really trying to lure you into downloading adware or spyware.

Antivirus Software	Web Site
AntiVirus + AntiSpyware by Trend Micro (for home use)	www.trendmicro.com
Avast by ALWIL Software (home edition is free)	www.avast.com
AVG Anti-Virus by AVG Technologies	www.avg.com
Bitdefender Antivirus	www.bitdefender.com
ClamWin Free Antivirus by ClamWin (open source and free)	www.clamwin.com
F-Secure Anti-Virus by F-Secure Corp.	www.f-secure.com
Kaspersky Anti-Virus	www.kaspersky.com
Malwarebytes Anti-Malware (free version available)	www.malwarebytes.org
McAfee AntiVirus Plus by McAfee, Inc.	www.mcafee.com
Norton AntiVirus by Symantec, Inc.	www.symantec.com
Panda Antivirus Pro	www.pandasecurity.com
SUPERAntiSpyware	www.superantispyware.com
Microsoft Security Essentials (free)	windows.microsoft.com

© Cengage Learning 2013

Table 9-1 Antivirus software and web sites

Notes It's handy to have AV software on CD so that you don't need Internet access to download the software, but recognize that this AV software won't have the latest updates. You'll need these updates downloaded from the Internet before the software will catch newer viruses.

Now let's look at different situations you might encounter when attempting to run AV software.

Run AV Software Already Installed

If AV software is already installed and you suspect an infection, update the software and perform a full scan on the system. Do the following:

1. Make sure the AV software is up to date. These updates download the latest **virus definitions**, also called **virus signatures**, which the software uses to define or detect new viruses as they get into the wild.

2. Use the AV software to perform a full scan of the system. As it scans, the software might ask you what to do with an infected program or it might log this event in an event viewer or history log it keeps. The logs are likely to contain a history of quarantined items and programs that you've allowed to run. Use the event viewer and the logs to decide what to do with each item. In most situations, choose to delete any suspicious file. Take notes of any program files the software is not able to delete. You can manually delete them later. Figure 9-29 shows the history of events kept by Microsoft Security Essentials.

9

A+
220-802
2.1, 4.7

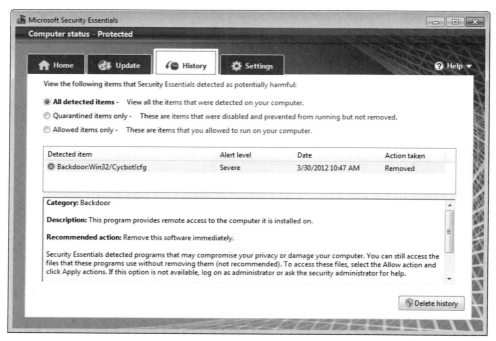

Figure 9-29   History of events kept by Microsoft Security Essentials

© Cengage Learning 2013

3. After the scan is complete and you have decided what to do with each suspicious file, reboot the system and allow the software to update itself again and then scan the system again. Most likely, some new malware will be discovered. Keep rebooting and rescanning until a scan comes up clean.

If you have problems running the AV software, try running it in Safe Mode. In Safe Mode, a virus might not load that is keeping the AV software from working or from detecting the virus.

> **Notes** If you ever encounter a virus that your updated AV software did not find, be sure to let the manufacturer of the software know so they can research the problem.

Run AV Software from a Networked Computer

If AV software is not already installed, the most effective way to clean the computer is to run the software from another computer. Follow these steps:

1. Make sure the remote computer has its software firewall set for maximum protection and its installed AV software is up to date and running.

2. Network the two computers and share drive C on the infected computer. (Don't connect the infected computer to the entire network. If necessary, you can connect the two computers using a crossover cable or using a small switch and network cables.)

3. To make your work easier, you can map a network drive from the remote computer to drive C on the infected computer.

4. Perform a virus scan on the remote computer, pointing the scan to drive C on the infected computer.

A+
220-802
2.1, 4.7

Install and Run AV Software on the Infected Computer

If you don't have another computer available to scan the infected computer, you can purchase the AV software on CD, or use another computer to download the AV software from its web site and then burn the downloaded files to a CD. Don't make the mistake of using the infected PC to purchase and download AV software because keyloggers might be spying and collecting credit card information. During the installation process, the AV software updates itself and performs a scan. You can also run free online AV software without downloading and installing it, but be careful to use only reputable web sites.

Install and Run AV Software in Safe Mode

Some malware prevents AV software from installing. In this situation, try booting the system in Safe Mode with Networking and installing the AV software. Some viruses still load in Safe Mode, and some AV programs will not install in Safe Mode.

In either situation, while you are in Safe Mode, use System Restore to apply a restore point that was taken before the infection. Applying a restore point cannot be counted on to completely remove an infection, but it might remove startup entries the malware is using, making it possible to install the AV software from the normal Windows desktop or run the AV software in Safe Mode.

> **Notes** If viruses are launched even after you boot in Safe Mode and you cannot get the AV software to work, try searching for suspicious entries in the subkeys under HKLM\System\CurrentControlSet\Control\SafeBoot. Subkeys under this key control what is launched when you boot into Safe Mode. How to edit the registry is covered in Chapter 4.

Run AV Software from a Bootable Rescue Disc or Flash Drive

If the system is so infected you cannot install the AV software, know that some AV software products, such as the AVG Rescue CD software, offer the option to create a bootable USB flash drive or CD. You can then use this device to boot the system and run the AV software from the device in this preinstallation environment. Most of the products listed earlier in Table 9-1 offer the option on their web site to download software to create the bootable CD or drive. Be sure to use a healthy computer to create the rescue CD or flash drive. In addition, you might need to create a 32-bit version to scan a 32-bit Windows system or a 64-bit version to scan a 64-bit system. When selecting a product to create a bootable device, find one that can store the latest updates on the CD or flash drive so you don't need Internet access when you scan the infected system.

After you've scanned the system using this method, reboot and install AV software on the hard drive. Update the AV software, and then keep scanning and rebooting until the scan report is clean.

STEP 4: RUN ADWARE OR SPYWARE REMOVAL SOFTWARE

A+
220-802
1.1, 2.1,
4.7

To completely clean a badly infected system, experience says use more than one anti-malware product. Almost all AV software products today also search for adware and spyware. However, software specifically dedicated to removing this type of malware generally does a better job of it than does AV software. The next step in the removal process is to use antispyware software. Table 9-2 lists some products that can catch adware, spyware, cookies, browser hijackers, dialers, keyloggers, and Trojans.

9

A+
220-802
1.1, 2.1,
4.7

Adware and Spyware Removal Software	Description
Ad-Aware by Lavasoft (*www.lavasoft.com*)	One of the most popular and successful adware and spyware removal products. It can be downloaded without support for free.
Spybot Search & Destroy by Safer Networking, Ltd. (*www.safer-networking.org*)	Does an excellent job of removing malicious software and it's free.
Spy Sweeper by Webroot Software, Inc (*www.webroot.com*)	Very good antivirus and antispyware software but does require you pay a yearly subscription.
Windows Defender (*windows.microsoft.com*)	Free antispyware software embedded in Windows.

Table 9-2   Anti-adware and antispyware software

© Cengage Learning 2013

Windows Defender is antispyware included in Windows 7/Vista. To perform a scan using Windows Defender, open Control Panel and enter **Windows Defender** in the Control Panel search box. Then click **Windows Defender**. The Windows Defender window appears (see Figure 9-30). To check for updates, click the down arrow to the right of the help question mark and then click **Check for updates**. After updates are installed, click **Scan** to perform a scan. If Defender is not turned on, when you first open the Defender window you are given the opportunity to turn it on. However, if Microsoft Security Essentials is running, it does not allow Defender to also be on.

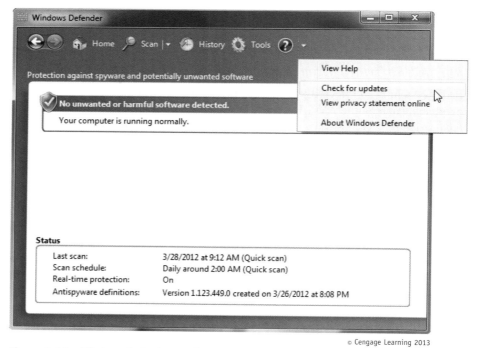

© Cengage Learning 2013

Figure 9-30   Windows Defender can be used to scan for spyware and adware

💡 **A+ Exam Tip**   The A+ 220-802 exam expects you to know how to use Windows Defender.

A+
220-802
2.1, 4.7

STEP 5: PURGE RESTORE POINTS

Some malware hides its program files in restore points stored in the System Volume Information folder maintained by System Protection. If System Protection is on, AV software can't clean this protected folder. To get rid of that malware, you can turn off System Protection and run the AV software again so it can clean the System Volume Information folder (see Figure 9-31). Realize that when you turn off System Protection, all your restore points are lost. To turn off System Protection, open the System window and click **System protection**. After your AV software has scanned the system again, turn System Protection back on. Later, when you are sure the system is clean, create a new restore point that you can use in the future if problems arise.

© Cengage Learning 2013

Figure 9-31 Malware found in a restore point

STEP 6: CLEAN UP WHAT'S LEFT OVER

Next, you'll need to clean up anything the anti-malware software left behind. Sometimes AV software tells you it is not able to delete a file, or it deletes an infected file but leaves behind an orphaned entry in the registry or startup folders. If the AV software tells you it was not able to delete or clean a file, first check the AV software web site for any instructions you might find to manually clean things up. In this section, you'll learn about general things you can do to clean up what might be left behind.

Respond to Any Startup Errors

On the first boot after anti-malware software has declared a system clean, you might still find some startup errors caused by incomplete removal of the malware. Recall from Chapter 4 that you can use Msconfig.exe to find out how a startup program is launched. If the program is launched from the registry, you can back up and delete the registry key. If the program is launched from a startup folder, you can move or delete the shortcut or program in the folder. See Chapter 4 for the details of how to remove unwanted startup programs. Appendix G lists registry keys and folders that are known to contain startup entries.

Research Malware Types and Program Files

Your AV software might alert you to a suspicious program file that it quarantines and then ask you to decide if you want to delete it. Also, Task Manager and other tools might find processes you suspect are malware. The web is your best tool to use when making your

A+
220-802
2.1, 4.7

decision about a program. Here are some web sites that offer virus encyclopedias that are reliable and give you symptoms and solutions for malware:

▲ Process Library by Uniblue Systems Limited at *www.processlibrary.com*
▲ DLL Library by Uniblue Systems Limited at *www.liutilities.com*
▲ All the antivirus software sites listed earlier in the chapter in Table 9-1

Beware of using other sites! Much information on the web is written by people who are just guessing, and some of the information is put there to purposefully deceive. Check things out carefully, and learn which sites you can rely on.

Delete Files

For each program file the AV software told you it could not delete, delete the program file yourself following these steps:

1. First try Windows Explorer to locate a file and delete it. For peace of mind, don't forget to empty the Recycle Bin when you're done.

2. If the file is hidden or access is denied, open an elevated command prompt window and use the commands listed in Table 9-3 to take control of a file so you can delete it. If the commands don't work using an elevated command prompt window, use the commands in a command prompt in Windows RE or the XP Recovery Console.

Command	Description
attrib –h –s filename.ext	Remove the hidden and system attributes to a file.
tasklist |more taskkill /f /pid:9999	To stop a running process, first use the Tasklist command to find out the process ID for the process. Then use the Taskkill command to forcefully kill the process with the given process ID.
takeown /f filename.ext	Take ownership of a file.
icacls filename.ext /GRANT ADMINISTRATORS:F	Take full access of a file.

Table 9-3   Commands used to take control of a malware file so you can delete it

3. To get rid of other malware files, delete all Internet Explorer temporary Internet files. To do so, use the Disk Cleanup process in the Drive C: properties box, or delete the browsing history using the Internet Options box.

Clean the Registry

Appendix G lists registry keys that can affect startup. You can search these keys and delete entries you don't want. You can also use Autoruns at Microsoft TechNet (*technet .microsoft.com*) to help you search for orphaned registry entries. Figure 9-32 shows a screen shot where Autoruns is displaying an orphaned entry in the HKLM\Software\Microsoft\ Windows\CurrentVersion\Run registry key used to launch the OsisOijw.dll malware program. AV software had already found and deleted this DLL file, but it left the registry key untouched.

A+
220-802
2.1, 4.7

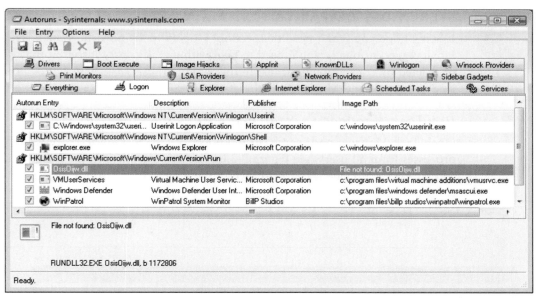

© Cengage Learning 2013

Figure 9-32 Autoruns finds orphan registry entries left there by AV software

Scan through the Autoruns window looking for suspicious entries. Research any entries that you think might be used by malware. To get rid of these entries, back up the registry and then use Regedit to delete unwanted keys or values.

After you have finished cleaning the registry, don't forget to restart the system to make sure all is well before you move on.

Clean Up Internet Explorer

Adware and spyware might install add-ons to Internet Explorer (including toolbars you didn't ask for), install cookie trackers, and change your IE security settings. Antiadware and antivirus software might have found all these items, but as a good defense, take a few minutes to find out for yourself. Chapter 8 covers how to use the Internet Options box to search for unwanted add-ons and delete ActiveX controls. You can uninstall unwanted toolbars and plug-ins using the Programs and Features window (see Figure 9-33).

9

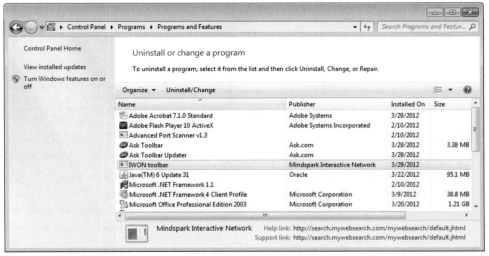

© Cengage Learning 2013

Figure 9-33 Browser toolbars can be uninstalled using the Programs and Features window

STEP 7: DIG DEEPER TO FIND MALWARE PROCESSES

It is my hope you won't need this section! Hopefully, by now the system is malware free. However, occasionally you'll need to deal with a really nasty infection that won't be found or deleted by conventional means. In this situation, use Task Manager or Process Explorer by Sysinternals and Microsoft TechNet to find running malware processes.

Use Task Manager to Search for Malware Processes

Open Task Manager and search for unknown processes. On the Processes tab, check **Show processes from all users** (see Figure 9-34). You can also click in the Image Name column to sort processes alphabetically, as shown in the figure. Recall from Chapter 4 that a process can run under a user (in this case, Jean Andrews), System, Local Service, or Network Service account.

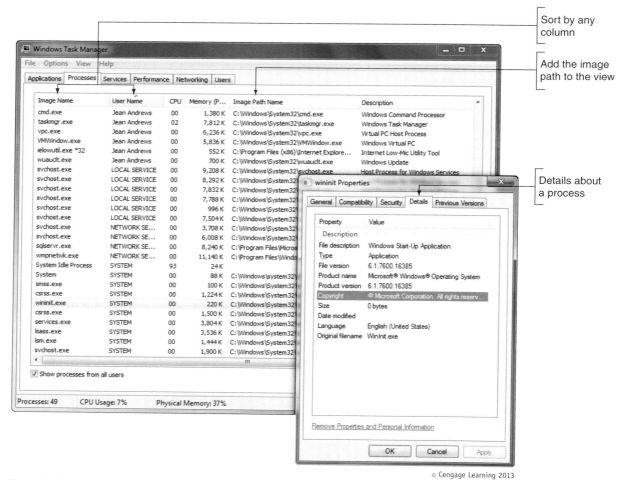

Figure 9-34 Processes currently running under Windows 7 with important information displayed

To find out the path to a process, click **View** on the Task Manager menu and select **Select Columns**. In the Select Process Page Columns dialog box, check **Image Path Name** and click **OK**. In Figure 9-34, the Image Path Name column is showing.

Sometimes a virus will disguise itself as a legitimate Windows core process such as svchost.exe or lsass.exe. Here are some tips to help you find malware processes:

◢ You can recognize a program as a counterfeit process if it's not running under System, Local Service, or Network Service. For example, if you spot a svchost.exe process running under a username, suspect a rat.

A+
220-802
2.1, 4.7

◢ If you notice the svchost.exe program file is located somewhere other than C:\Windows\ system32, this most likely means it's a counterfeit version put there to make trouble.

◢ To find out more about a process, right-click it and select **Properties** from the shortcut menu. In the Properties box for the process, click the **Details** tab. Figure 9-34 shows the details for the Wininit.exe process.

◢ As you research each process listed by Task Manager, know the most reliable sites about Windows processes are the Microsoft support sites (*support.microsoft.com* or *technet.microsoft.com*). A search on a process name, an error message, a description of a process or problem with a process, or other related information can turn up a Knowledge Base article with the information you need.

To help you with researching a process, Table 9-4 lists core Windows processes that are likely to be listed by Task Manager. If you suspect a core Windows process is corrupted or has been hijacked by a virus, use an SFC command to restore the corrupted program. If you suspect a program is masquerading as a Windows program and it is not in the Windows folder or subfolders, kill it and delete it. Stomp that bug.

Process and Path	Description
Csrss.exe (C:\Windows\System32)	Client/server run-time server subsystem; manages many commands in Windows that use graphics.
Explorer.exe (C:\Windows)	Windows graphical shell that manages the desktop, Start menu, taskbar, and file system.
Lsass.exe (C:\Windows\System32)	Manages local security and logon policies.
Lsm.exe (C:\Windows\System32)	Manages user services for the currently logged-on users.
SearchIndexer.exe (C:\Windows\System32)	Manages indexes used for fast searches.
Services.exe (C:\Windows\System32)	Starts and stops services.
Smss.exe (C:\Windows\System32)	Windows sessions manager; essential Windows process.
Spoolsv.exe (C:\Windows\System32)	Handles Windows print spooling. Stopping and starting this process can sometimes solve a print spooling problem.
Svchost.exe (C:\Windows\System32)	Manages each process that is executed by a DLL. One instance of Svchost runs for each process it manages. To see a list of services managed by Svchost, enter this command in a command-prompt window: `tasklist /SVC`
System Idle Process	Appears in the Task Manager window to show how CPU usage is allotted. It is not associated with a program file.
System	Windows system counter that shows up as a process, but has no program file associated with it.
Taskmgr.exe (C:\Windows\System32)	Task Manager utility itself.
Wininit.exe (C:\Windows\System32)	Starts Windows background services and applications.
Winlogon.exe (C:\Windows\System32)	Manages logon and logoff events.

Table 9-4 Core Windows processes and their purposes

9

Use Process Explorer at Microsoft TechNet

Process Explorer by Mark Russinovich, which is available at Microsoft TechNet (*technet .microsoft.com*), works like Task Manager, but takes us to another level of information. When you look at all the processes and services running in Task Manager, it's difficult, if not impossible, to know how these processes are related to each other. Understanding these relationships can help you identify a process that is launching other processes, which is called a process tree. By identifying the original process, which is the one handling other processes, you can lay the axe to the root of the tree rather than swinging at branches.

When you go to the web site *technet.microsoft.com*, search for and download Process Explorer, and run it, the window in Figure 9-35 appears.

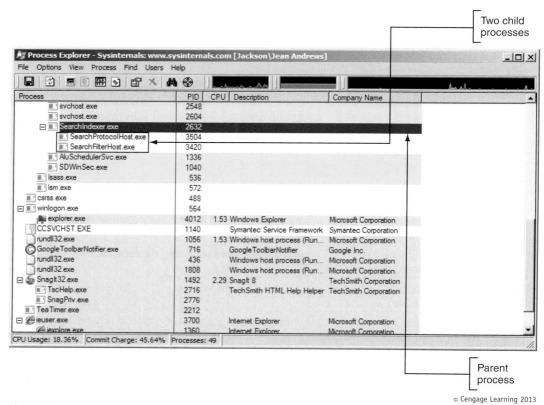

Figure 9-35 Process Explorer color codes child-parent relationships among processes and gives information about processes

On this system monitored by Process Explorer, a browser hijacker is at work changing web pages and producing pop-ups. As I watched the browser jump from one web page to another without my involvement, Process Explorer showed me what was happening with the related processes. From the information in Figure 9-35, we see that the process, SearchIndexer.exe, has called two other processes shown in the figure. As the browser jumped from one web page to another, these two processes completed and started up again. I was watching live malware in action!

As you can see, Process Explorer gives much information about a process and is a useful tool for software developers when writing and troubleshooting problems with their software, installation routines, and software conflicts. You can use the tool to smoke out processes, DLLs, and registry keys that elude Task Manager.

A+
220-802
2.1, 4.7

STEP 8: REMOVE ROOTKITS

A rootkit uses unusually complex methods to hide itself, and many spyware and adware programs are also rootkits. The term rootkit applies to a kit or set of tools used originally on UNIX computers. In UNIX, the lowest and most powerful level of UNIX accounts is called the root account; therefore, this kit of tools was intended to keep a program working at this root level without detection.

Rootkits can prevent Task Manager from displaying the running rootkit process, or may cause Task Manager to display a different name for this process. The program filename might not be displayed in Windows Explorer, the rootkit's registry keys might be hidden from the registry editor, or the registry editor might display wrong information. All this hiding is accomplished in one of two ways, depending on whether the rootkit is running in user mode or kernel mode (see Figure 9-36). A rootkit running in user mode intercepts the API calls between the time when the API retrieves the data and when it is displayed in a window. A rootkit running in kernel mode actually interferes with the Windows kernel and substitutes its own information in place of the raw data read by the Windows kernel.

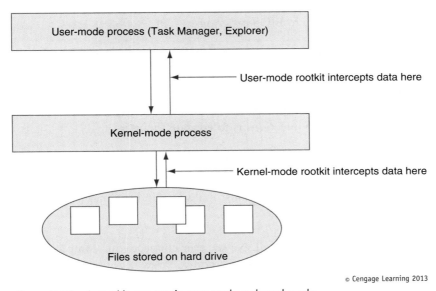

© Cengage Learning 2013

Figure 9-36 A rootkit can run in user mode or kernel mode

Because most AV software to one degree or another relies on Windows tools and components to work, the rootkit is not detected if the Windows tools themselves are infected. Rootkits are also programmed to hide from specific programs designed to find and remove them.

> **Notes** The Windows UAC box has been known to catch a rootkit before it installs itself.

The best-known anti-rootkit product is Blacklight by F-Secure (*www.f-secure.com*). Generally, anti-rootkit software works to identify a rootkit using these methods:

- ◢ The software looks for hidden files and folders or for running processes that don't match up with the underlying program filenames.
- ◢ The software compares files, registry entries, and processes provided by the OS to the lists it generates from the raw data. If the two lists differ, a rootkit is suspected.

If the software suspects a rootkit, it reports that to you. If you believe your system has a rootkit, the best solution is to immediately disconnect the computer from the network (if you have not already done so), back up your important data, format your hard drive, and reinstall Windows.

9

STEP 9: REPAIR BOOT BLOCKS

If an infected computer will not boot, it might be that the boot sectors of the hard drive are infected or damaged or the BIOS code might be corrupted. Here are the methods to deal with these problems:

▲ Launch the Windows RE command prompt and use the command **bootrec /fixmbr** to repair the MBR. The command **bootrec /fixboot** repairs the OS boot record. For Windows XP, launch the Recovery Console and use these two commands: **fixmbr** and **fixboot**. Chapter 6 gives more information about solving boot problems.

▲ A virus is rarely able to attack startup BIOS code stored on the motherboard. BIOS contains a boot block, which is a small program stored on the BIOS firmware chip that attempts to recover the BIOS when updating (flashing) the BIOS has failed. If you see an error at POST, such as "Award BootBlock BIOS ROM checksum error" or a similar error, you can suspect BIOS has become corrupted. The solution is to treat the problem as you would if flashing the BIOS has failed. See the motherboard manufacturer web site for more information. Again, however, know that viruses are unlikely to be able to gain access to BIOS programs.

STEP 10: ENABLE SYSTEM PROTECTION AND EDUCATE THE USER

Now that the system is clean, if System Protection is still turned off, turn it back on and create a restore point. Now would be a good time to go over with the user some tips presented earlier in the chapter to keep the system free from malware. Sometimes the most overlooked step in preventing malware infections is to educate the user.

STEP 11: PROTECT AGAINST MALICIOUS SOFTWARE

Once your system is clean, you'll certainly want to keep it that way. The best practices you need to follow to protect a system against malware are listed next. The first three methods are the most important ones:

▲ **Always use a software firewall.** Never, ever connect your computer to an unprotected network without using a firewall. Windows Firewall is turned on by default. Recall that you can configure Windows Firewall to allow no uninvited communication in or to allow in the exceptions that you specify (see Figure 9-37).

Figure 9-37   A software firewall protecting a computer

© Cengage Learning 2013

A+
220-802
1.1, 1.5,
2.1, 4.7

> **Notes** To avoid conflicts, don't run more than one personal firewall program on the same computer.

◢ **Use anti-malware software.** As a defensive and offensive measure to protect against malware, install and run AV software and keep it current. Configure the AV software so that it (1) runs in the background, (2) automatically scans incoming email attachments, and (3) automatically downloads updates to the software. Most AV software is also antispyware and protects the system from spyware. To avoid conflicts and not slow down performance, it's best to run only one anti-malware program on a computer. Do the following to find out what AV software or antispyware is installed and turned on:

- For Windows 7, open the Security group in the Action Center. Figure 9-38 shows one system that has Microsoft Security Essentials installed, which automatically disabled Windows Defender. When you click **View installed antispyware programs,** you can see three programs installed (see the lower part of Figure 9-38).

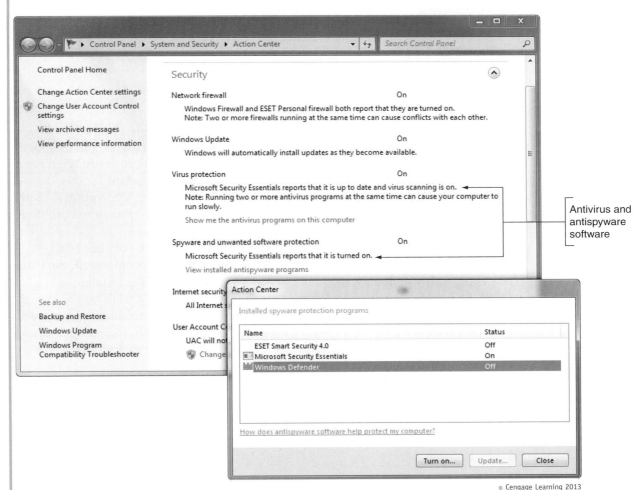

Figure 9-38 Microsoft Security Essentials installed

© Cengage Learning 2013

- For Vista, in the Control Panel, click **Security** and then click **Security Center.** The Vista **Security Center** is shown in Figure 9-39. Using this window, you can confirm Windows Firewall, Windows Update, anti-malware settings, including that of Windows Defender, and other security settings.

9

A+
220-802
1.1, 1.5,
2.1, 4.7

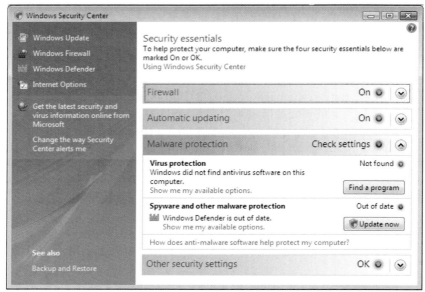

© Cengage Learning 2013

Figure 9-39   Use the Windows Security Center in Vista to confirm security settings
to protect a computer against malware

▲ *Keep Windows updates current.* Windows updates are continually being released to
plug up vulnerable entrances in Windows where malware might attack and to update
Microsoft Security Essentials or Windows Defender. Recall you can verify Windows
Update settings by clicking **Start, All Programs,** and **Windows Update.**

▲ *Keep good backups.* One of the more important tasks in securing a computer is to prepare in advance for disaster to strike. One of the most important things you can do to
prepare for disaster is to make good backups of user data.

▲ *Keep the User Account Control box enabled.* The UAC box is one of your best
defenses against malware installing itself. When software attempts to install, the UAC
box appears. If you don't respond to the box, Windows aborts the installation.

▲ *Limit the use of administrator accounts.* If malware installs itself while you're logged
on as an administrator, it will most likely be running under this account with more
privileges and the ability to do more damage than if you had been logged on under a
less powerful account. Use a standard user account with lesser privileges for your
everyday normal computer activities.

▲ *Set Internet Explorer for optimum security.* Internet Explorer includes the pop-up
blocker, the ability to manage add-ons, the ability to block scripts and disable scripts
embedded in web pages, and the ability to set the general security level. You learned
how to configure IE in Chapter 8.

Notes You might want to consider using an alternate browser other than Internet Explorer and an
alternate email client other than Outlook because these programs are often attacked by malware. Using
an alternate email address might also be wise. When you have to give an email address to companies
that you suspect might sell your address to spammers, use a second email address that you don't use for
normal emailing.

A+
220-802
1.1, 1.5,
2.1, 4.7

Large corporations generally have additional plans in place so that malware is quickly detected and does not take down the entire network. Here is what these plans might look like:

▲ *Use a hard drive image.* Each computer is built using a hard drive image. If a system gets infected, a technician simply reinstalls the image. Reinstalling from a standard image or deployment image is much faster than going through the detailed process of removing malware from a system.

▲ *No data is kept on a personal computer.* Company policy says that all data must be installed on network drives and not on the local hard drive. The purpose of this policy is so that (1) an infected system can be restored from an image without having to deal with data on the hard drive, and (2) data on network drives are backed up on a regular basis and, therefore, safer than when stored on a local hard drive. Recall that reinstalling a hard drive image erases everything on the drive. Because all user data is stored on network drives, no user data is lost when the image is used.

▲ *Use network-monitoring software.* Network-monitoring software (for example, Big Brother Professional at *www.bb4.com*) is constantly monitoring the network for unusual activity. If the software discovers a computer on the network is acting suspiciously, the computer will be quarantined. The monitoring software alerts a technician about the problem. If the technician believes the system is infected, he will reimage the hard drive. All this can take place within an hour of malware becoming active on a computer.

Hands-on | Project 9.2 — Create and Use an AV Software Rescue Disc

When an infected computer does not have AV software installed, one method to clean the infection is to create and use an AV rescue disc. Select AV software that offers a free download to create a bootable USB flash drive or CD. For example, Windows Defender Offline or F-Secure Rescue CD can be used. Create a bootable USB flash drive or CD and use it to scan a computer. Answer the following questions:

1. What is the URL where you found the download to create a rescue disc or drive?

2. List the files in the root directory of the USB flash drive or CD that the software created.

3. Describe the menu or screen that appears when you booted from the rescue media.

9

Hands-on | Project 9.3 — Download and Use AV Software

A free trial of AVG Anti-Virus software is available on the AVG site at *www.avg.com*. Do the following to download, install, and run the software:

1. Download the free trial version of AVG Anti-Virus software from the *www.avg.com* site and install the software.

2. Update the software with the latest virus signatures.

3. Perform a complete scan of the system. Were any suspicious programs found?

4. Set the AV software to scan the system daily.

5. Set the software to scan incoming email.

A+
220-802
1.1, 1.5,
2.1, 4.7

Hands-on | Project 9.4 — Learn to Use Process Explorer

Download and install Process Explorer by TechNet and Sysinternals (*technet.microsoft.com*). Open the Process Explorer window and compare it to the Task Manager window. Describe any differences between the lists each tool provides of running processes.

Hands-on | Project 9.5 — Use the Web to Learn About Malware

One source of information about viruses on the web is F-Secure Corporation. Go to the web site *www.f-secure.com*, and find information about the latest malware threats. Answer the following questions:

1. Name and describe a recent Trojan downloader. How does the Trojan install and what is its payload (the harm it does)?

2. Name and describe a recent rootkit. How does the rootkit install and what is its payload?

3. Name a recent worm. How does it get into the network and what is its payload?

>> CHAPTER SUMMARY

Securing a Windows Workstation

- The netplwiz command can be used to require the user to press Ctl+Alt+Delete to log onto Windows.

- Windows power settings can be used to lock down the workstation after a short period of inactivity and to require a password to unlock the workstation.

- An administrator might be called on to reset a forgotten password.

- A strong password is not easy to guess and contains uppercase and lowercase letters, numbers, and symbols.

- The Encrypted File System (EFS) is used with an NTFS volume for Windows business and professional editions.

- Windows Firewall can block all communication initiated outside the workstation and can allow exceptions for certain programs, protocols, ports, and remote computers.

- Group Policy is used in Windows professional and business editions to set policies that can secure the local computer.

- BitLocker Encryption with Windows professional or business editions can lock down the entire hard drive. It can be set to authenticate the computer, authenticate the user, or authenticate both the computer and the user.

- BIOS security features include passwords, drive lock passwords, and support for a TPM chip and an intrusion-detection device.

Additional Methods to Protect Resources

◢ Large networks might use a security token in addition to a Windows password to authenticate a user.

◢ Tokens include a smart card (key fob, RSA token, or RFID badge) and biometric data (iris scan, retinal scan, or fingerprint scan). The most secure biometric data is a retinal scan.

◢ Physical security can include a locked door, lock and chain, or privacy filter.

◢ Data can be partly or completely destroyed using a paper shredder, low-level format, drill, degausser, or Secure Erase utility.

◢ Security methods include educating users against social engineering and how to best protect a laptop when traveling.

Dealing with Malicious Software

◢ Malware includes a virus, adware, spyware, keylogger, worm, Trojan, and rootkit.

◢ Symptoms that malware is present include pop-up ads, slow performance, error messages, file errors, spam, and strange processes running.

◢ When you suspect a computer is infected, immediately quarantine it. Then scan the system with up-to-date antivirus software. If necessary, you can scan the infected computer using AV software installed on another computer or use a rescue disc for the scan. Some systems become so highly infected, the only solution is to reinstall Windows.

◢ To protect a computer against malware, use a software firewall, keep AV software up to date and running, and maintain Windows updates.

>> KEY TERMS

For explanations of key terms, see the Glossary near the end of the book.

adware	keylogger	smart card reader
antispyware software	LoJack	social engineering
antivirus (AV) software	malicious software	spyware
ATA Secure Erase	malware	strong password
biometric device	phishing	tailgating
BitLocker Encryption	privacy filter	Trojan
boot sector virus	quarantined computer	virus
computer infestation	retinal scanning	virus definition
degausser	RFID badge	virus encyclopedia
digital certificate	rootkit	virus signature
email hoax	RSA tokens	Windows Defender
Encrypted File System (EFS)	Security Center	Windows Firewall
grayware	shoulder surfing	worm
key fob	smart card	

9

>> *REVIEWING THE BASICS*

1. Why is it more secure to require a user press Ctrl+Alt+Delete to log on rather than displaying the Windows Welcome screen?

2. Which window in Control Panel is used to require a Windows password to wake up a sleeping computer?

3. Which two tools can be used to reset a Windows password for another user when using Windows 7 Home Premium?

4. Why is PINE963$&apple not a strong password?

5. Which link in the Windows Firewall window allows you to add a port to the list of exceptions allowed through the firewall?

6. Which policy in Group Policy must be enabled before you can monitor failed attempts at logging onto a Windows system?

7. What hardware component is needed to set up BitLocker Encryption so that you can authenticate the computer?

8. What Windows utility can you use to change the name of the built-in Administrator account?

9. What type of employee badge does not have to be swiped by a card reader to allow the employee through a door?

10. Which type of biometric data is considered the most secure?

11. Which is better to destroy sensitive data on a hard drive, a low-level format, drill, or degausser?

12. What tool is best to use when destroying data on an SSD drive? Where can you get this tool?

13. What device can be installed on a laptop to prevent shoulder surfing?

14. Define and explain the differences between a virus, worm, and Trojan.

15. What are the two best ways to protect a computer or network against worms?

16. What is the best way to determine if an email message warning about a virus is a hoax?

17. What is the first thing you should do when you discover a computer is infected with malware?

18. What does AV software look for to determine that a program or a process is a virus?

19. Which antispyware software is embedded in Windows 7?

20. Why is it helpful to run AV software in Safe Mode?

21. What registry key keeps information about services that run when a computer is booted into Safe Mode?

22. What folder is used by Windows to hold restore points?

23. What must you do to allow AV software to scan and delete malware it might find in the data storage area where restore points are kept?

24. What is the best tool to use to find out the purpose of a program that is running on your system?

25. What software can you use to display a process tree that shows how processes relate, yielding more information than given by Task Manager?

>> *THINKING CRITICALLY*

1. In which policy group of Group Policy is the policy that requires a smart card be used to authenticate a user to Windows?

   a. Computer Configuration, Windows Settings, Security Settings, Local Policies, Biometrics

   b. Computer Configuration, Administrative Templates, System, Logon

   c. Computer Configuration, Windows Settings, Security Settings, Local Policies, Security Options

   d. User Configuration, Administrative Templates, System, Logon

2. Which two of the following program files are likely to be malware? Why?

   a. C:\Windows\Sys\lsass.exe

   b. C:\Windows\SearchIndexer.exe running under a user account

   c. C:\Windows\System32\lsass.exe running under the SYSTEM account

   d. C:\Windows\System32\cmd.exe running under a user account

3. You open a folder Properties box to encrypt the folder, click Advanced, and discover *Encrypt contents to secure data* is dimmed. What is the most likely problem?

   a. Encryption has not been enabled. Use the Computer Management console to enable it.

   b. You are not using an edition of Windows that supports encryption.

   c. Most likely a virus has attacked the system and is disabling encryption.

   d. Encryption applies only to files, not folders.

4. A virus has attacked your hard drive and now when you start up Windows, instead of seeing a Windows desktop, the system freezes and you see the blue screen of death. You have extremely important document files on the drive that you cannot afford to lose. What do you do first? Explain your answer.

   a. Try a data-recovery service even though it is very expensive.

   b. Remove the hard drive from the computer case and install it in another computer.

   c. Try GetDataBack by Runtime Software (*www.runtime.org*) to recover the data.

   d. Use Windows utilities to attempt to fix the Windows boot problem.

   e. Run antivirus software to remove the virus.

5. AV software has removed malware from a highly infected system. After the first reboot, an error message is displayed that contains a reference to a strange DLL file that is missing. Which two options should you use to begin troubleshooting?

   a. Run the AV software again

   b. Run Msconfig and look for startup entries that are launching the DLL

   c. Run Regedit and look for keys that refer to the DLL

   d. Search the web for information about the DLL

9

>> *REAL PROBLEMS, REAL SOLUTIONS*

REAL PROBLEM 9-1: Recovering a Windows Password

You can use freeware to discover a forgotten Windows password, and hackers can use the software to steal a password. The stronger the password, the more difficult it is to discover. Follow these steps to learn more:

1. Using Windows 7, create three user accounts on a system and assign the accounts an easy password (use only lowercase letters), a moderately easy password (use lowercase letters and numbers, but no symbols), and a strong password (see the rules given earlier in the chapter for strong passwords).

2. Go to **ophcrack.sourceforge.net** by Geeknet, Inc. and download the free ISO file that contains ophcrack LiveCD. Use the ISO file to burn the ISO image to a CD-R. Label the CD.

3. Boot from the CD. As it boots, it automatically searches for and lists the user accounts and passwords on the system. Answer the following questions:

   a. What is the name of the operating system the ophcrack software uses on the CD?

   b. Which user account passwords did ophcrack discover?

   c. If ophcrack did not discover a password, perhaps another freeware utility can. List three other password-cracking products that receive positive online reviews.

Keep the ophcrack LiveCD in your PC repair toolkit in case a client in the field asks you to help him recover a forgotten Windows password.

REAL PROBLEM 9-2: Researching a Laptop with a TPM Chip

Many laptops sold today have a TPM chip, and some have encryption-enabled hard drives that don't require encryption software such as BitLocker. Research the web for a laptop that offers a TPM chip and answer these questions:

1. What is the brand and model laptop that has the TPM chip? Print the web page listing the laptop specifications showing the chip.

2. Is the chip optional? If so, what is the cost of including the chip?

3. Does the laptop have an encryption-enabled hard drive?

4. Does the laptop come bundled with encryption software? If so, what is the name of the software?

5. Does the laptop offer a drive lock password?

6. What is the cost of the laptop, including the TPM chip?

CHAPTER

CHAPTER 10

Mobile Devices and Client-side Virtualization

Previous chapters have focused on supporting Windows when it is installed on personal computers. This chapter deviates from this topic as we discuss mobile devices and client-side virtualization. As mobile devices become more common, many people use them to surf the web, access email, and manage apps and data. As a computer support technician, you need to know about the operating systems and hardware used with mobile devices and how to help a user configure and secure a mobile device. The data, settings, and apps stored on mobile devices need to be backed up and synchronized to other storage locations. In this chapter, you learn how you can synchronize content on mobile devices to a personal computer or to storage in the cloud (on the Internet). Finally, in this chapter, you learn about server-side and client-side virtualization and the various ways client-side virtualization is implemented.

OPERATING SYSTEMS USED ON MOBILE DEVICES

The operating system for a mobile device is installed at the factory. Here are the two most popular ones in the United States:

▲ Android OS by Google (*android.com*) is based on Linux and is used on various smart phones and tablets. Currently, Android is the most popular OS for smart phones. About 60% of the smart phones sold today use the Android OS.

▲ iOS by Apple (*apple.com*) is based on Mac OS X and is currently used on the iPhone, iPad, and iPod touch by Apple. About 30% of smart phones sold today are made by Apple and use the iOS.

The remaining 10% of the current market share for smart phones in the U.S. is shared by these mobile OSs:

▲ Blackberry OS by RIM (*rim.com*) is a proprietary OS used on devices built by RIM.

▲ Windows Phone by Microsoft (*microsoft.com*) is based on Windows and is used on devices made by Dell, Fujitsu, Nokia, Samsung, and others.

▲ The Symbian OS from the Symbian Foundation (*symbian.org*) is popular outside the United States and is used on devices made by multiple manufacturers, including Nokia, Samsung, Sony, and others.

This chapter focuses on the Android and iOS operating systems used on smart phones and tablets.

> 💡 **A+ Exam Tip** The A+ 220-802 exam expects you to know how to support the Android and iOS operating systems used with mobile devices.

A+
220-802
3.1

ANDROID OS BY THE OPEN HANDSET ALLIANCE AND GOOGLE

The Android operating system is based on the Linux OS and uses a Linux kernel. Linux and Android are open source, which means the source code for the operating system is available for free and anyone can modify and redistribute the source code. Open source software is typically developed as a community effort by many contributors. Android was originally developed by the Open Handset Alliance (*www.openhandsetalliance.com*), which is made up of many technology and mobile phone companies and led by Google, Inc.

In 2005, Google acquired this source code. Google does not own Android, but it has assumed a leadership role in development, quality control, and distributions of the Android OS and Android apps. Ongoing development of the Android OS code made by Google and other contributors is released to the public as open source code.

GETTING TO KNOW AN ANDROID DEVICE

Releases of Android are named after desserts and include Froyo or frozen yogurt (version 2.2.x), Gingerbread (version 2.3.x), Honeycomb (version 3.x), and Ice Cream Sandwich (version 4.x). (Future releases of Android will follow in alphabetic order: G, H, I, and J.) Most smart phones currently sold use Gingerbread, and most tablets use Honeycomb. It is expected that most new phones and tablets will ship with Ice Cream Sandwich installed.

A+
220-802
3.1

Android supports windows, panes, and 3D graphics. It can use an embedded browser, manage a database using SQLite, and connect to Wi-Fi, Bluetooth, and cellular networks. Current Android phones have four physical buttons on the front of the device for Menu, Home, Go Back, and Search (see Figure 10-1).

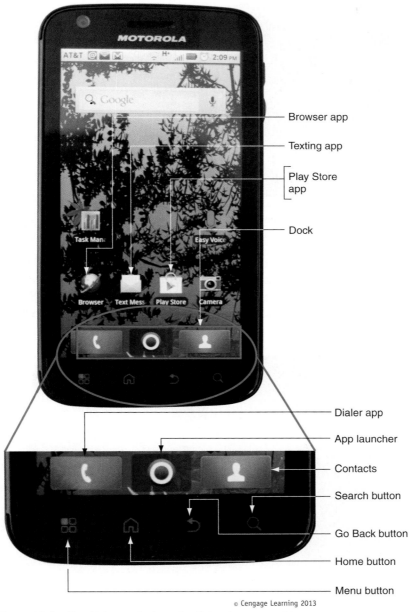

Browser app

Texting app

Play Store app

Dock

Dialer app

App launcher

Contacts

Search button

Go Back button

Home button

Menu button

© Cengage Learning 2013

Figure 10-1 The Atrix smart phone by Motorola comes with Android Froyo installed

The Menu button changes functions (depending on the app in use) to give you settings and options for that app. On Android phones, up to four apps can be pinned to the dock at the bottom of the screen. The pinned apps shown in Figure 10-1 are the Dialer (for making phone calls), the App launcher (lists and manages all your apps), and Contacts. Apps in the dock stay put as you move from home screen to home screen. All but the App launcher

10

A+
220-802
3.1

can be replaced by third-party apps. For example, Figure 10-2 shows the home screen on an Android Gingerbread smart phone. On this phone, the apps pinned to the dock are the Dialer app, Email app, Web app (a browser to surf the web), and App launcher.

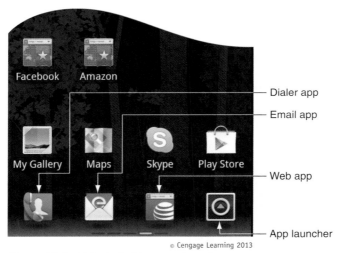

© Cengage Learning 2013

Figure 10-2 This Android smart phone has four apps pinned to the dock

Android tablets have software buttons at the bottom of the screen. For example, the Android Thrive by Toshiba shown in Figure 10-3 in landscape view has the Back button, Home button, and Recent apps button in the bar at the bottom of the screen called the System bar or Action bar. Buttons in the System bar stay put as you move from home screen to home screen (up to seven screens).

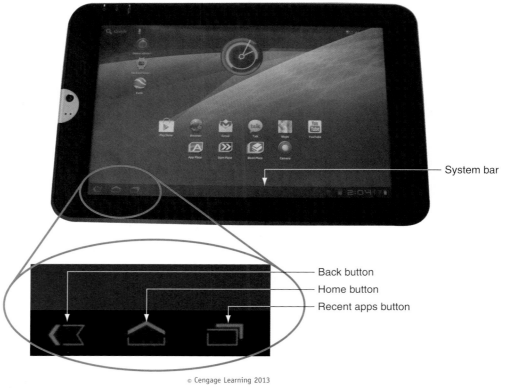

© Cengage Learning 2013

Figure 10-3 The Thrive tablet by Toshiba comes with Android Honeycomb installed

A+
220-802
3.1

ANDROID APPS

Android apps are sold or freely distributed from any source or vendor. However, the official source for apps, called the Android marketplace, is **Google Play** at *play.google.com*. To download content, you need a **Google account**, which you can set up using the web site or your device. The account is associated with any valid email address. Associate a credit card with the account to make your purchases at Google Play. Then you can purchase or download free music, books, movies, and Android apps from Google Play to your mobile device.

Android Market was renamed Google Play in March 2012. To download an app using newer versions of Android, use the Play Store app. For older versions of Android, use the Market app.

To download an app, tap the **Play Store** app or the **Market** app on the home screen of your device. (If you don't see the app icon on your home screen, tap the **App launcher** and then tap **Play Store** or **Market**.) The app takes you to Google Play, where you can search for apps, music, books, and movies (see Figure 10-4). In addition, you can get apps and data from other sources, such as the Amazon Appstore at Amazon.com or directly from a developer.

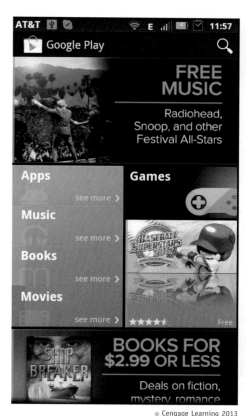

© Cengage Learning 2013

Figure 10-4 Use the Play Store app to search Google Play for apps, music, books, and movies that you can download

10

Google maintains the Android web site at *android.com* where an app developer can download the Android Software Development Kit (SDK) from *developer.android.com*. An SDK is a group of tools that developers use to write apps. The Android SDK is free and is released as open source. Most Android apps are written using the Java programming language.

A+
220-802
3.1

IOS BY APPLE

Apple, Inc. (www.apple.com) owns, manufactures, and sells the Apple iPhone (a smart phone), iPad (a handheld tablet), and iPod touch (a multimedia recorder and player *and* a game player). These devices all use the iOS operating system, also developed and owned by Apple. The iOS is based on OS X, the operating system used by Apple desktop and laptop computers. There have been five major releases of the iOS; the latest is iOS version 5.

GETTING TO KNOW AN IOS DEVICE

Because Apple is the sole owner and distributor of the iOS, the only devices that use it are Apple devices (currently the iPhone, iPad, and iPod touch). Figure 10-5 shows an iPhone and Figure 10-6 shows an iPad. Each device has a Wake/sleep button and a Home button. Apps pinned to the bottom of the iPhone screen are the Phone, Mail, Safari, and Music apps. (The Music app is also called the iPod app.) Apps pinned to the bottom of the iPad screen are the Safari, Mail, Photos, and Music apps.

© Cengage Learning 2013

Figure 10-5 An iPhone by Apple has iOS version 5.1 installed

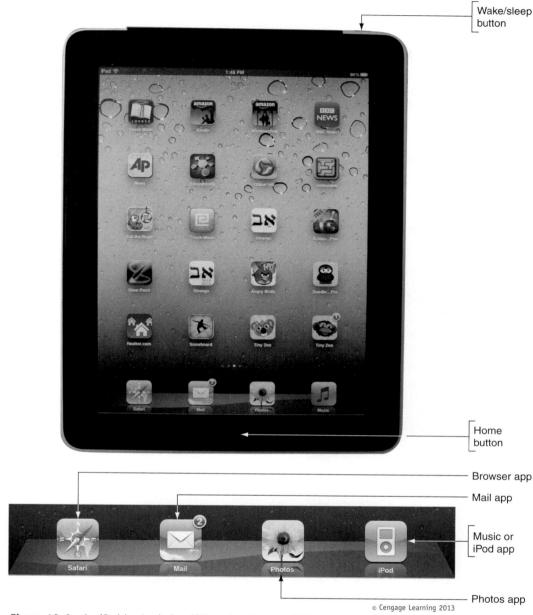

Wake/sleep button

Home button

Browser app

Mail app

Music or iPod app

Photos app

© Cengage Learning 2013

Figure 10-6 An iPad by Apple has iOS version 5.1 installed

Also, because Apple is the sole developer and manufacturer, it can maintain strict standards on its products, which means the iOS is extremely stable and bug free. The iOS is also a very easy and intuitive operating system to use. The iOS can have up to eleven home screens. (Use your finger to swipe screens to the left or right.) As with OS X, the iOS makes heavy use of icons.

IOS APPS AVAILABLE THROUGH ITUNES

You can get Android apps from many sources, but the only place to go for an iOS app is Apple. Apple is the sole distributer of iOS apps at its iTunes App Store (*itunes.apple.com*). Other developers can write apps for the iPhone, iPad, or iPod, but these apps must be sent to Apple for their close scrutiny. If they pass muster, they are distributed by Apple on its web site. One requirement is that an app be written in the Objective-C, C, or C++ programming language.

A+
220-802
3.1

Not only does Apple scrutinize an app for quality, it also filters apps for inappropriate content, such as pornography. What content is judged to be inappropriate? That decision is made solely by Apple.

All downloads of iOS updates and patches, apps, and multimedia content are by way of the iTunes web site. First, you set up an Apple ID or user account using a valid email address and password and associate this account with a credit card number. Then you can use the iTunes web site to:

▲ Use the App Store app on your mobile device (see Figure 10-7 for an iPhone example) to purchase and download (or download for free) content from the iTunes Store, including apps, music, TV shows, movies, books, podcasts, and iTunes U content. (iTunes U contains lectures and even complete courses from many schools, colleges, and universities.)

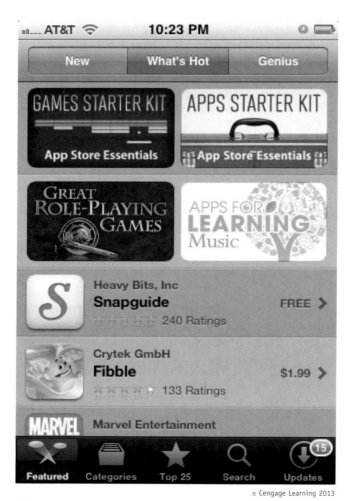

© Cengage Learning 2013

Figure 10-7 Use the App Store app to download content from the iTunes Store

▲ Download and install the iTunes software on a Mac or Windows personal computer. Then connect your mobile device to the computer by way of a USB port. iTunes can then sync the device to iOS updates downloaded from iTunes.com and to content on your computer. You can also purchase content that is downloaded to your device by way of iTunes on your computer. Figure 10-8 shows the iTunes window when an iPhone is connected to the PC. How to use iTunes to sync data and apps on your device is covered later in the chapter.

A+
220-802
3.1

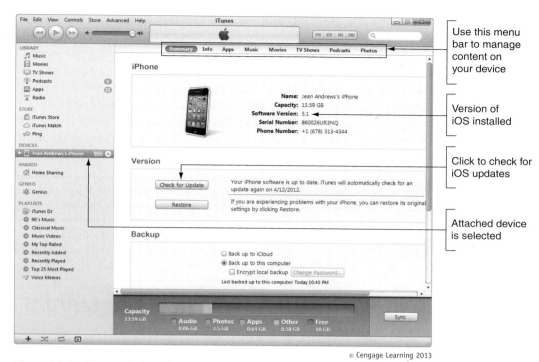

© Cengage Learning 2013

Figure 10-8 iTunes window shows summary information for an attached iPhone

When you first purchase an iPad or an iPod touch, you must activate it by connecting it to a computer that has iTunes installed. iTunes then downloads the latest updates to the iOS and you can then use the device. Therefore, the iPad and iPod touch are considered peripheral devices to a personal computer. iPhone version 5 (not iOS version 5) is to be released in late 2012, and Apple has announced that this iPhone will be capable of activating itself and directly downloading OS updates without your first connecting the device to a computer. (After activation, current iPhones and iPads can receive iOS updates without a PC connection.)

> **Notes** If you ask, a retail associate at an Apple store will activate your new iPad or iPod touch for you before you leave the store.

Recall that apps can be downloaded to an iOS device only from the iTunes Store. People have discovered that it is possible to break through this restriction in a process called jailbreaking. **Jailbreaking** gives you root or administrative privileges to the operating system and the entire file system (all files and folders) and complete access to all commands and features. Jailbreaking was once illegal, but in 2010, the U.S. Copyright Office and the Library of Congress made a copyright ruling that a user has the right to download and use software that will jailbreak his iOS device.

COMPARING OPEN SOURCE AND CLOSED SOURCE OPERATING SYSTEMS

Open source (such as the Android) and closed source (such as the iOS) operating systems have their advantages and disadvantages. Here are some key points to consider about releasing or not releasing source code:

- ◢ Apple carefully guards its iOS source code and internal functions of the OS. Third-party developers of apps only have access to APIs, which are calls to the OS. An app must be tested and approved by Apple before it can be sold in its online App Store. These policies assure users that apps are high quality. It also assures developers they have a central point of contact for users to buy their apps.

10

A+
220-802
3.1

◢ The Android source code and the development and sale of apps are not closely guarded. Apps can be purchased or downloaded from Google Play, but they can also be obtained from other sources such as Amazon.com or directly from a developer. This freedom comes with a cost because users are not always assured of high-quality, bug-free apps, and developers are not always assured of a convenient market for their apps.

◢ Because any smart phone or tablet manufacturer can modify the Android source code, many variations of Android exist. These variations can make it difficult for developers to write apps that port to any Android platform. It can also make it difficult for users to learn to use new Android devices because of these inconsistencies.

> **Notes** Apple iOS does not support Adobe Flash, which is used by many web sites to present graphics, animation, and other multimedia content. By comparison, the Android OS does support Flash.

> **♀ A+ Exam Tip** The A+ 220-802 exam expects you to understand the advantages and disadvantages of open-source and closed-source operating systems on mobile devices.

COMPARING MOBILE DEVICE HARDWARE TO LAPTOPS

A+
220-802
3.1, 3.4

Besides the operating system, you need to know about hardware used with smart phones and handheld tablets and how this hardware differs from that which is used with laptops. A **smart phone** is primarily a cellphone and also includes abilities to send text messages (using a technology called **Short Message Service** or **SMS**), send text messages with photos, videos, or other multimedia content attached (using a technology called **Multimedia Messaging Service** or **MMS**), surf the web, manage email, play games, take photos and videos, and download and use small apps. A smart phone uses a cellular network (for voice or data) and is likely to have the ability to use a Wi-Fi local wireless network or make a Bluetooth wireless connection to other nearby Bluetooth devices. Earlier in the chapter, you saw smart phones that use touch screens. Figure 10-9 shows a smart phone that uses a physical keyboard and a touch screen.

© Oleksiy/www.Shutterstock.com

Figure 10-9 This smart phone uses a physical keyboard and a touch screen

A+
220-802
3.1, 3.4

A handheld tablet is a computing device with a touch screen that is larger than a smart phone and has functions similar to a smart phone. Most tablets can connect to Wi-Fi networks and use Bluetooth to wirelessly connect to nearby Bluetooth devices. Many tablets have the ability to use a cellular network for data transmissions. A few tablets, such as the Samsung Galaxy Tab and the Viewsonic ViewPad 7, have the ability for texting and making phone calls. You can also install apps such as a Skype app on a tablet so that you can make voice phone calls, send text, and make video calls. When you can use your tablet to make a phone call, the distinction between a smart phone and a tablet is almost nonexistent.

You can buy all kinds of accessory devices for smart phones and tablets, such as wireless keyboards, speakers, ear buds, headphones, printers, extra batteries, USB adapters, and chargers. Figure 10-10 shows a wireless keyboard and an iPad that use a Bluetooth connection. Figure 10-11 shows a car dock for a smart phone. Using this car dock, the smart phone is a GPS device giving driving directions.

© Cengage Learning 2013

Figure 10-10 An iPad and a wireless keyboard can connect using Bluetooth

Figure 10-11 A smart phone and a car dock

© Cengage Learning 2013

10

A+
220-802
3.1, 3.4

TOUCH INTERFACE

Mobile devices rely on touch screens more so than do laptops. Mobile device touch screens can work by the touch of a finger or a stylus, and the touch on the screen can be a tap, long-press, slide, or two-finger pinch. A touch screen that can handle a two-finger pinch is called a **multitouch** screen. High Tech Computer (HTC), Inc., a manufacturer of smart phones and tablets, developed one type of multitouch technology called **TouchFLO**. HTC now incorporates the older TouchFLO technology into a more comprehensive user interface called **HTC Sense**.

A touch screen uses resistive or capacitive technologies. A **capacitive touch screen** uses electrodes that sense the conductive properties of skin. A **resistive touch screen** has two sheets of glass covered with a resistive coating (see Figure 10-12). The two sheets are kept from touching by spacers between them. When pressure is placed on the top glass, the glass bends and makes contact with the lower glass.

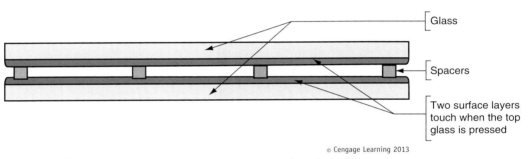

© Cengage Learning 2013

Figure 10-12 Pressure causing contact between two surfaces is used on a resistive touch screen

Capacitive touch screens don't respond to pressure, but resistive touch screens do. The trend for all smart phones and tablets is to move toward capacitive touch screens, which are generally more responsive than resistive touch screens. iPhone, iPad, and iPod touch devices use capacitive touch screens, which is why you should not wear gloves when you use them. With some laptops and monitors, touch screens need to be calibrated so that the software that controls touch input is in alignment with the hardware. Because of the way a touch screen is integrated into a mobile device, screen calibration is not required. When a mobile device appears as though the touch of a finger is not aligned with data input (such as when you touch a P on the touch keyboard and an O appears on-screen), the problem most likely can be resolved by updating the operating system.

STORAGE DEVICES

Most smart phones use a SIM (Subscriber Identity Module) card that contains a microchip to hold data about the subscription you have with your cellular carrier. The SIM card is purchased from the cellular carrier, and the carrier is responsible for loading it with your subscription information. The SIM card must be inserted in the phone or tablet for the device to make a connection to a cellular network. Figure 10-13 shows the slot on the side of the iPad where you can insert a SIM card so that the iPad can send and receive data transmissions (not voice transmissions) over the cellular network.

© Cengage Learning 2013

Figure 10-13   A SIM card is required for a tablet or smart phone to use most cellular networks

> **Notes** Two types of cellular networks are GSM (Global System for Mobile Communication) and CDMA (Code Division Multiple Access). GSM is by far the most popular and is replacing CDMA. GSM networks require that a cellular device have a SIM card, but CDMA networks do not require a SIM card.

The internal storage used by Android and iOS for their apps and data is a solid-state device (SSD), a type of flash memory. In addition, an Android device might have an external slot where you can plug in a smart card such as an SD card to provide extra storage (see Figure 10-14). The iPhone, iPad, and iPod touch don't have these external slots for a smart card.

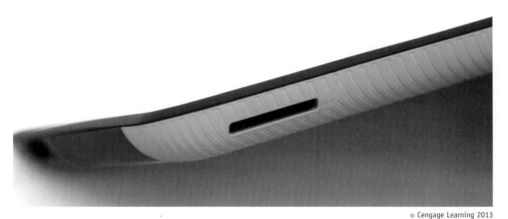

© Cengage Learning 2013

Figure 10-14   An Android device might provide a memory card slot to allow for extra storage

An Android device might also have a USB port that you can use to plug in a USB flash drive to provide extra storage or transfer files and folders to other devices. Apple devices don't have USB ports.

FIELD-SERVICEABLE PARTS

For the purposes of PC support technicians supporting mobile devices, know that there are no field-replaceable units (FRU) in mobile devices, and it is not possible to upgrade or replace internal components. (Although it is possible to replace the screens in some mobile devices, a support technician is not expected to have this skill.) SIM cards and batteries can be replaced, and accessories such as a battery charger or ear buds can be attached.

OTHER HARDWARE COMPONENTS

Other internal hardware components of a mobile device include a small gyroscope, called an accelerometer, and a GPS component. Here are brief details about each:

▲ A **gyroscope** is a device that contains a disc that is free to move and can respond to gravity as the device is moved (see Figure 10-15). Three axes in the device sense how the disc moves and, therefore, can tell the direction of motion. An **accelerometer** is a type of gyroscope used in mobile devices to sense the physical position of the device. The accelerometer is used by the OS and apps to adjust the **screen orientation** from portrait to landscape as the user rotates the device. Apps such as a Compass, Carpenter's Leveler, and some game apps use the accelerometer to sense how the user is moving the device.

© Cengage Learning 2013

Figure 10-15 A gyroscope uses gravity to sense its relative position to the earth

▲ Mobile devices might contain a **GPS (Global Positioning System) receiver**. The Global Positioning System is a system of 24 or more satellites orbiting the earth, and a GPS receiver can locate four or more of these satellites at any time and from these four locations, calculate its own position in a process called triangulation. A smart phone can determine its position by using the GPS satellite data or data from the position of nearby cellular towers in its cellular network. A phone with a GPS receiver is likely to use both types of data to find its position. A mobile device routinely reports its position to Apple or Google at least twice a day, and usually more often, which makes it possible for these companies to track your device's whereabouts, which is called **geotracking**. Law enforcement agencies sometimes use this data to reconstruct a person's travels.

CONFIGURING, SYNCING, AND SECURING IOS DEVICES

In this part of the chapter, you learn to configure network connections, update, secure, and back up data, content, and settings on an iOS device. (We cover the iPad and iPhone but not the iPod touch.) Later in the chapter, you learn similar skills using Android devices.

This chapter is intended to show you how to support a device that you might not own or normally use. Technicians are often expected to do such things! If you don't have an iPhone or iPad to use as you read through these sections, you can still follow along paying careful attention to the screen shots taken on each device. Learning to use an iOS device is fun, and supporting one is equally easy.

Most of the settings you need to know to support an iOS device are contained in the Settings app, which you can find on the home screen (see Figure 10-16a). Basically, you can

A+
220-802
3.2

(a) (b)

© Cengage Learning 2013

Figure 10-16 (a) Use the Settings app to configure the iOS and apps, (b) Airplane mode turns off all three antennas that connect the iPhone to networks

tap the Settings app and search through its menus and submenus until you find what you need. So let's get started.

CONFIGURING NETWORK CONNECTIONS

A mobile device can contain up to four antennas (Wi-Fi, GPS, Bluetooth, and cellular). The device uses a Wi-Fi, Bluetooth, or cellular antenna to connect to each type of network, and settings on the device allow you to enable or disable each antenna. One setting, called airplane mode, disables all three antennas so the device can neither transmit nor receive signals. To use Airplane Mode, tap the **Settings** app and turn **Airplane Mode** on or off (see Figure 10-16b).

A cellular network provided by a carrier (for example, AT&T or Verizon) is used by cell phones for voice communication and text messaging. A smart phone or tablet might also contain the technology to connect to a cellular network for data transmission. These cellular data networks are called 2G, EDGE (an earlier version of 3G), 3G, 4G, or 4G LTE (the latest and fastest version of 4G). For example, the iPad shown earlier in Figure 10-16 contains 3G technology and is able to connect to this type of network for data transmissions (not voice transmissions). To make a cellular data connection, the subscription with your carrier must include an activated cellular data plan.

💡 **A+ Exam Tip** The A+ 220-802 exam expects you to know how to configure a Wi-Fi, cellular data, and Bluetooth connection using the iOS and Android operating systems.

10

A+
220-802
3.2

Here is how to manage connections with the iOS using cellular, Wi-Fi, and Bluetooth:

▲ *Cellular connection.* To enable a cellular data network connection, tap **Settings**, **General**, **Network**. On the Network screen (see Figure 10-17a), enable the Cellular Data connection. The device used in the figure supports 3G. When you enable 3G, data transmissions are faster. Also notice in Figure 10-17a you can enable or disable Data Roaming. Using data roaming might mean additional charges if you are in a foreign country.

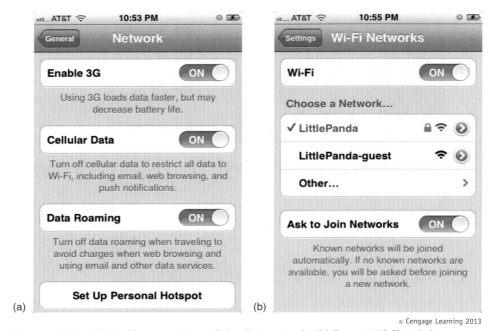

© Cengage Learning 2013

Figure 10-17   (a) Enable access to a cellular data network, (b) Turn on Wi-Fi and show a Wi-Fi network

▲ *Wi-Fi connection.* To configure a Wi-Fi connection, tap **Settings**, **Wi-Fi**. On the Wi-Fi Networks screen (see Figure 10-17b), you can view available Wi-Fi hotspots, see which Wi-Fi network you are connected to, turn Wi-Fi off and on, and decide whether the device needs to ask before joining a Wi-Fi network. When the device is within range of a Wi-Fi network, it displays the list of networks. Select one to connect. If the Wi-Fi network is secured, enter the security key to complete the connection.

▲ *Bluetooth connection.* To configure a Bluetooth connection, first turn on the other Bluetooth device you want to connect to. Then on your mobile device, tap **Settings**, **General**, **Bluetooth**. On the Bluetooth screen, turn on Bluetooth. The device searches for Bluetooth devices. If it discovers a Bluetooth device, tap it to connect. The two Bluetooth devices now begin the **pairing** process. The devices might require a **Bluetooth PIN code** to complete the Bluetooth connection. For example, in Figure 10-18, an iPad and Bluetooth keyboard are pairing. To complete the connection, enter the 4-digit PIN on the keyboard. To test the connection, enter text on the keyboard and make sure the text appears on the iPad screen in the active app.

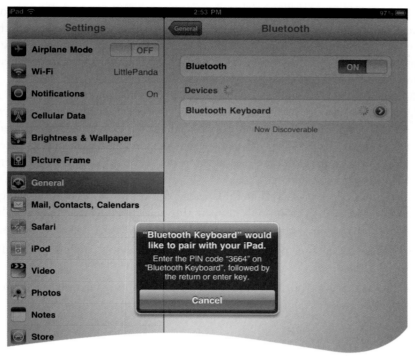

Figure 10-18 A PIN code is required to pair the two Bluetooth devices

If you have a problem connecting to a Bluetooth device, try turning the device off and back on. The device might also offer a pairing button to enable pairing. When you press this button, a pairing light blinks, indicating the device is ready to receive a Bluetooth connection.

CONFIGURING EMAIL

Using a personal computer or mobile device, email can be managed in one of two ways:

◢ *Use a browser.* Using a browser, go to the web site of your email provider and manage your email on the web site. In this situation, your email is never downloaded to your computer or mobile device, and your messages remain on the email server until you delete them.

◢ *Use an email client.* An email client, such as Microsoft Outlook, can be installed on your personal computer, or you can use an email app on your mobile device. The client or app can either download email messages to your device (using the POP protocol) or can manage email on the server (using the IMAP protocol). When the client or app downloads the email, you can configure the server to continue to store the email on the server for later use or delete the email from the server. The built-in Mail app for managing email is available on smart phones and tablets.

Here is the information you'll need to configure the Mail app on an iOS device:

◢ **Your email address and password.** If your email account is with iCloud, Microsoft Exchange, MobileMe (Apple's email service), Gmail, Yahoo!, Hotmail, or AOL, your email address and password are all you need because the iOS can automatically set up these accounts.

A+
220-802
3.2

▲ **The names of your incoming and outgoing email servers.** To find this information, check the support page of your email provider's web site. For example, the server you use for incoming mail might be pop.mycompany.com, and the server you use for outgoing mail might be smtp.mycompany.com. The two servers might have the same name.

▲ **The type of protocol your incoming server uses.** This server will use POP or IMAP. Using IMAP, you are managing your email on the server. For example, you can move a message from one folder to another and that change happens on the server. Using POP, the messages are downloaded to your device where you manage them. Using POP, the Mail app leaves the messages on the server (does not delete them), but you can change this setting if you like.

▲ **Security used.** Most likely, if email is encrypted during transmission using the SSL protocol, the configuration will happen automatically without your involvement. However, if you have problems, you need to be aware of these possible settings:

- An IMAP server uses port 143 unless it is secured and using SSL. IMAP over SSL (IMAPS) uses port 993.

- A POP server uses port 110 unless it is secured and using SSL. POP over SSL uses port 995.

> 💡 **A+ Exam Tip** The A+ 220-802 exam expects you to know about POP, IMAP, SSL, and the ports they use.

Follow these steps to configure the email client on an iOS device:

1. Tap **Settings** and then tap **Mail, Contacts, Calendars**. In the Mail, Contacts, Calendars screen, you can add a new email account and decide how email is handled. To add a new email account, tap **Add Account**. On the next screen, select the type of account (see Figure 10-19a) and enter your email address and password. If your email account type is not in the list, slide the screen up and tap **Other** at the bottom of the list.

2. On the Other screen, tap **Add Mail Account**. On the New Account screen, enter your name, email address, password, and description (optional). Tap **Next**.

3. On the next screen, tap IMAP or POP (see Figure 10-19b). Enter the Host Name for your incoming mail server. Enter your User Name and Password if they are different from your email address and its password. Slide the screen up and enter the Host Name for your outgoing mail server. Tap **Next**.

4. The Mail app assumes it is using SSL (to secure email in transit using encryption) and attempts to make the connection. If it cannot, it asks if you want it to try to make the connection without using SSL. Click **OK** to make that attempt.

5. To use the account, tap the **Mail** app on your Home screen.

A+
220-802
3.2

© Cengage Learning 2013

Figure 10-19 (a) The iOS can automatically set up several types of email accounts
(b) An email account is set up to use IMAP or POP for incoming mail

If you later need to verify the email account settings or delete the account, follow these steps.

1. Tap **Settings**, and then tap **Mail, Contacts, Calendars**. In the list of Accounts, tap the account. On the account screen, you can enable and disable the account and change the account settings.

2. To delete the account, slide the screen up and tap **Delete Account** at the bottom of the screen (see Figure 10-20a).

10

© Cengage Learning 2013

Figure 10-20 (a) Delete an email account or use Advanced settings, (b) Decide how messages are handled on the server after you receive them

A+
220-802
3.2

3. To see advanced settings, tap **Advanced**. On the Advanced screen (see Figure 10-20b), tap **Delete from server** to decide how to handle mail you have downloaded using the POP protocol. Choices are Never, Seven Days, or When removed from inbox.

4. Also notice on the Advanced screen that you can enable and disable SSL. When you do so, notice that the port the app addresses is also changed.

You need to know about an exception in how email is managed when using a Gmail account. **Gmail** is an email service provided by Google at *mail.google.com*. Normally, when you use the Mail app, you can delete a message by selecting it and tapping **Delete** (see Figure 10-21a). However, using Gmail, by default, you archive a message rather than delete it (see Figure 10-21b).

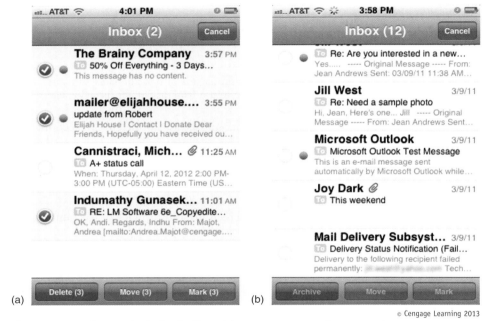

© Cengage Learning 2013

Figure 10-21 Two methods for dealing with messages you no longer need:
a) Using most email, delete a message, or b) Using Gmail, archive a message

Using most email services, a message arrives in your Inbox, which is a folder on the email server. You organize these messages by moving them to other folders or deleting them. Deleted messages are placed in the Trash folder and permanently deleted after a period of time. Using Gmail, a message remains in the Inbox and you organize these messages by assigning each message one or more labels. When you archive a message, you move the message from the Inbox to the All Mail folder out of sight but still accessible. Therefore, when using the Mail app on an Apple device with a Gmail account, the Delete button is replaced with the Archive button.

To change the Gmail account so that you can delete messages, go to the Home screen and tap **Settings** and then tap **Mail, Contacts, Calendars**. Tap the Gmail account. On the account screen (see Figure 10-22), turn off the **Archive Messages** switch. The Mail app will now have a Delete button for Gmail.

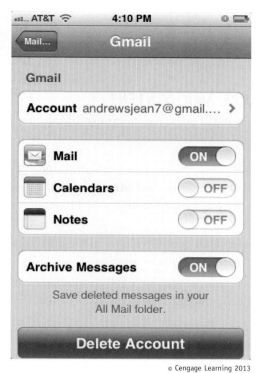

© Cengage Learning 2013

Figure 10-22 Decide if Gmail messages are archived or deleted

Microsoft Exchange is a server application that can handle email, contacts, and calendars, and is a popular application used by large corporations for their employee email, contacts, and calendars. When you set up a Microsoft Exchange email account, the Mail app automatically enables ActiveSync, which causes all email, contacts, and calendar updates made on the Exchange server or on your mobile device to stay in sync. Any changes at either location are automatically and immediately transmitted to the other. You can change the ActiveSync settings by doing the following:

1. On the Home screen, tap **Settings**, and tap **Mail, Contacts, Calendars**.

2. Select your Exchange email account. On the account screen, you can turn on or off the Mail (to sync email), Contacts (to sync contacts) and Calendars (to sync your calendar) settings. You can also set the number of days, weeks, or months of email you want to stay in sync. You can also decide whether you want folders in addition to the Inbox folder to be pushed to you from the Exchange server.

💡 **A+ Exam Tip** The A+ 220-802 exam expects you to know about special considerations when configuring Gmail and Exchange email accounts.

SYNCING, UPDATING, BACKING UP, AND RESTORING FROM BACKUP

To protect your data and apps in the event your mobile device is destroyed, lost, or stolen, you will want to keep backups of this content. For Apple devices, you can back up app data, iOS settings, email, contacts, wallpaper, and multimedia content, including photos,

10

A+
220-802
3.5

music, and videos, by syncing this content using iTunes or iCloud. iTunes backs up to your computer, and iCloud backs up to storage on the Apple web sites at *www.icloud.com*. In the following subsections, you learn to use both iTunes and iCloud to back up your data and to use iTunes to install iOS updates and patches.

USE ITUNES TO SYNC IOS APPS AND CONTENT

To sync data and install iOS updates using iTunes, you first must install the iTunes software on your computer. Follow these steps:

1. Make sure your computer qualifies for iTunes. For a Windows PC, iTunes can install under Windows 7/Vista/XP and needs 200 MB of free hard drive space. Install a 64-bit version of iTunes on a 64-bit OS and a 32-bit version of iTunes on a 32-bit OS.

2. Go to **www.apple.com/itunes/download** and download and install the software. After the software is installed, restart your computer.

3. Connect your device to your computer by way of a USB port. iTunes automatically launches and displays the window shown in Figure 10-23.

© Cengage Learning 2013

Figure 10-23   Opening window when you first connect a new device to iTunes

4. Step through each window to register your Apple device and set up or enter an existing Apple ID (see Figure 10-24).

5. One window in the process asks which types of data to sync (contacts, calendars, bookmarks, notes, and email). After you make your selections, the sync starts and the *Sync in Progress* message appears on your device. If you must interrupt the sync, don't worry. When the device is next connected, syncing picks up where it left off.

A+
220-802
3.5

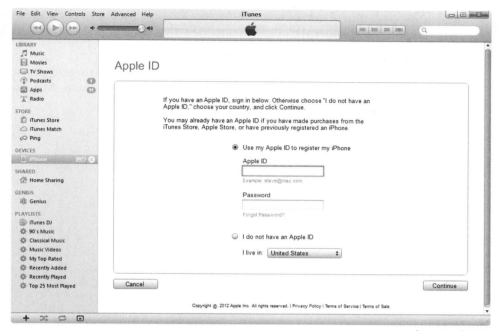

Figure 10-24 An Apple ID is required to sync a device with iTunes

© Cengage Learning 2013

iTunes automatically syncs the contacts, app data and app settings, documents, calendar, call history, photos and videos taken by the iPhone, Wi-Fi and email passwords, Microsoft Exchange information, bookmarks, text messages and pictures, and voice messages. To verify and customize exactly what iTunes is syncing, do the following:

1. With your device connected to your computer, select your device in the DEVICES list in the left pane of the iTunes window. To see what apps are synced, click **Apps** in the menu bar under the apple icon (see Figure 10-25). In this pane, you can view your apps and decide how they are synced.

Click to manage apps on your device

10

© Cengage Learning 2013

Figure 10-25 View apps and configure how apps are synced

2. Also click other types of content (Music, Movies, TV Shows, Podcasts, and Photos) in the menu bar under the apple icon to view that content and to configure how to sync the content.

3. On the Info pane (see Figure 10-26), you can decide how to sync contacts, calendars, email, and bookmarks. This type of content can be synced with Microsoft Outlook and Internet Explorer installed on your computer.

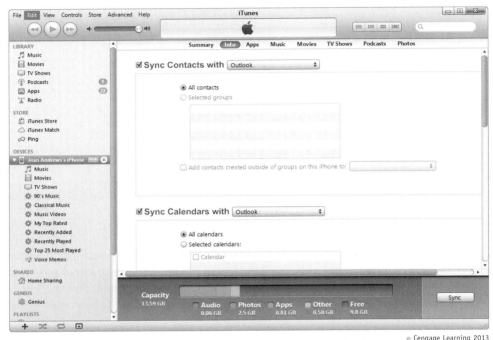

© Cengage Learning 2013

Figure 10-26   Decide how to sync contacts, calendars, email, and bookmarks

4. If you have made changes to the content to sync, click **Sync** at the bottom of the iTunes window to sync content immediately.

When you sync content with iTunes, the backup is stored on your computer at this location using Windows 7/Vista:

C:\Users*username*\AppData\Roaming\Apple Computer\MobileSync\Backup

If you have more than one Apple device, the next time the second device is connected to iTunes, content is synced to it. Using iTunes, any content on any device makes its way to the other devices and to your computer for backup.

> **Notes** For best protection, be sure you make routine backups of the user profile folder. The user profile folder contains user settings and data, and part of this data is your iOS device backups.

After iTunes is set up for your new device, the next time you plug the device into your computer, iTunes does one of the following:

▲ When iTunes recognizes the device, it automatically syncs up unless you have iCloud backup turned on. (If you have iCloud backup turned on, iTunes backup is automatically disabled.)

▲ To manually sync with iTunes, right-click the device in the DEVICES list and click **Back Up** in the shortcut menu.

A+
220-802
3.5

To restore from backup, connect the device to iTunes, right-click the device in the DEVICES list, and select **Restore from Backup** in the shortcut menu (see Figure 10-27). Also, when you are setting up a new device and you first connect it to iTunes on your computer, it will ask if you want to restore from backup.

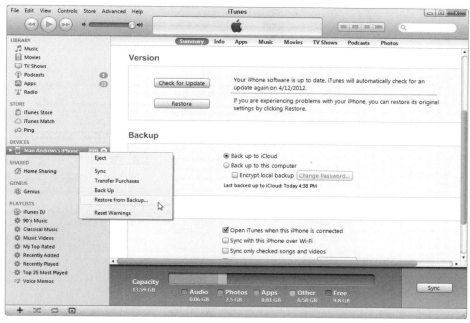

Figure 10-27 iTunes can restore from backup to your iPhone or iPad

© Cengage Learning 2013

USE ITUNES TO INSTALL IOS UPDATES AND PATCHES

The operating system on a mobile device is installed on firmware at the factory. Before iOS version 5, a device must be connected to iTunes to receive iOS updates and patches, which can happen automatically when a device is connected. With iOS version 5, these updates can be received without an iTunes connection. You can use iTunes to upgrade a device to iOS version 5. Follow these steps:

1. For an iPhone, set the device to Airplane Mode so it will not be interrupted while the OS upgrade is in progress.

2. Connect the Apple device to your computer.

3. Select the phone in the DEVICES list and back up all your content and settings.

4. Click the **Summary** tab. iTunes reports new updates are available. To download the updates, click **Update**. A message box appears (see Figure 10-28). To start the update, click **Update**.

5. The update process can take an hour or longer and it's best to not interrupt it. When the process is finished, disconnect your device. When iTunes installs a new version of iOS, you must go through the process of configuring your device for the new OS. Follow the directions on the device screen to do so. One of these setup screens is shown in Figure 10-29a, where you are asked to sign in with your Apple ID.

With iOS version 5, updates can happen at any time. You can manually request updates by tapping **Settings, General**. On the General screen, tap **Software Update**, as shown in Figure 10-29b.

10

A+
220-802
3.5

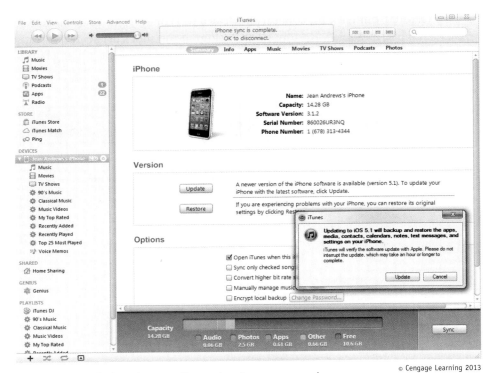

© Cengage Learning 2013

Figure 10-28   Update the operating system to a newer version

© Cengage Learning 2013

Figure 10-29   (a) Each of your Apple devices uses your Apple ID to connect to iTunes and iCloud, (b) Use the General screen to request iOS updates

A+
220-802
3.5

USE ICLOUD TO SYNC IOS CONTENT

Another option for syncing content on your Apple device is to use iCloud storage at *www.icloud.com*. You can set up a free iCloud account to hold all your apps, music, movies, videos, books, and iTunes U course curriculum and push this content to any iOS device you have. The first 5 GB of storage is free. iCloud syncing happens every day if the screen is locked and the device is connected to a cellular or Wi-Fi network and is plugged into an electrical outlet (such as when you recharge your iPhone while you sleep).

To use iCloud, follow these steps:

1. iCloud requires iOS 5 or higher. To verify your Apple device is updated to iOS 5, tap **Settings, General, About** (see Figure 10-30 for an iPhone screen).

© Cengage Learning 2013

Figure 10-30 Verify your iOS is using version 5 or higher

2. To configure iCloud, tap **Settings, iCloud**. Using the iCloud screen (see Figure 10-31 for an iPad screen), you can turn on or off items to sync to iCloud. These items include Mail, Contacts, Calendars, and so forth. Note that iCloud does not back up movies, podcasts, audio books, photos that came from your computer, and music and TV shows not purchased from the iTunes Store. (You can, however, sync these items using iTunes.)

3. To have your device report its position to iCloud, turn on **Find My iPad** or **Find My iPhone**. Later, if you lose your device, sign in to iCloud and there you can see its position on a map.

10

A+
220-802
3.5

© Cengage Learning 2013

Figure 10-31 Decide what type of content to sync to iCloud

4. Tap **Storage & Backup**. On the Storage and Backup screen (see Figure 10-32), make sure iCloud Backup is turned on.

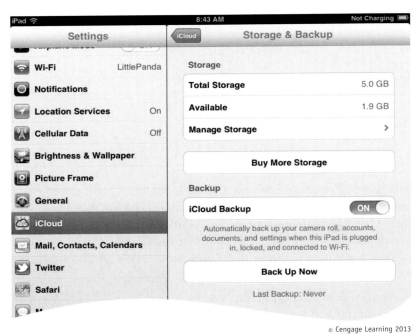

© Cengage Learning 2013

Figure 10-32 Manage iCloud backup and view available storage on iCloud

5. To back up manually to iCloud at any time, on the Storage & Backup screen shown in Figure 10-32, you can tap **Back Up Now**.

6. To view and manage your backups, on the Storage & Backup screen, tap **Manage Storage**. On the Manage Storage screen, you can see a list of devices backed up. Figure 10-33a shows that iPhone and iPad backups exist. Tap one to view a list of what's backed up and to manage the backup (see Figure 10-33b).

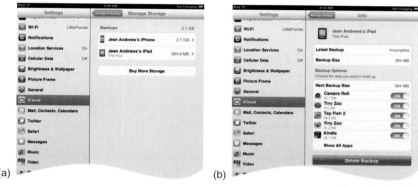

(a) (b)

© Cengage Learning 2013

Figure 10-33 Manage your backups kept in iCloud

Later, if you need to restore your data from iCloud backup, here are your options:

▲ When you are setting up a new iOS device, the Setup process provides a screen asking if you want to restore from backup. Tap **Restore from iCloud Backup**.

▲ If you lose the content and settings on a device, to restore from backup, connect the device to your computer. In the iTunes window, select the device in the DEVICES list. Right-click the device and click **Restore from Backup** (refer to Figure 10-27).

Apps, music, and books you have previously downloaded from iTunes can be downloaded again to this and other devices tied to your Apple ID. To automatically sync this content, tap **Settings** on the home screen and tap **Store**. On the Store screen (see Figure 10-34 for an iPhone), turn on and configure Automatic Downloads.

© Cengage Learning 2013

Figure 10-34 Decide how to handle Automatic Downloads

A+
220-802
3.5

10

A+
220-802
3.3

SECURING AN IOS MOBILE DEVICE

Smart phones and tablets are with us everywhere and most of us keep much personal and professional information on our smart phones. Here's a list of what might be stored on a smart phone and would be at risk if the phone is lost, stolen, or damaged:

- Data kept by apps can reveal much about our lives. Consider data kept on these iPhone apps: Email, Calendar, Call Logs, Voicemail, Text Messages, Google Maps, YouTube, Videos, Photos, Notes, Contacts, Bookmarks, and Web History.
- Videos and photos we have taken might be tagged with date and time stamps and GPS locations.
- Network connection settings, including Wi-Fi security keys, email configuration settings, usernames, and email addresses.

To protect this data, consider using passcode locks, locator applications, and remote wipes discussed in this part of the chapter.

PASSCODE LOCKS AND FAILED LOGINS

To protect your device in case it is stolen, you can set a passcode. For iOS devices, tap **Settings, General, Passcode Lock, Turn Passcode On,** and enter a four-digit code. When you wake up your iPhone or iPad, you must enter the passcode to proceed (see Figure 10-35). Notice in the figure that you can tap **Emergency Call** to bypass entering the passcode. This feature takes you to the keypad to make a call and protects you in the event you need to make an emergency call and don't want to take the time to enter your passcode.

© Cengage Learning 2013

Figure 10-35 Enter your four-digit passcode to unlock your iPhone

You can set the iOS to erase your data after it receives 10 failed logins (incorrect attempts at entering the passcode). This setting protects you from someone repeatedly guessing until she finally enters the correct passcode. After you have set a passcode, to set the device to erase data, tap **Settings, General, Passcode Lock**. You are required to enter your passcode to proceed. On the Passcode Lock screen (see Figure 10-36), tap **Erase Data** to turn it on and then tap **Enable**.

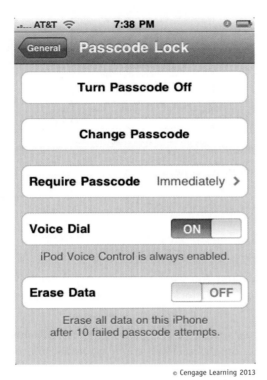

© Cengage Learning 2013

Figure 10-36 Set the iOS to erase your data after 10 failed logons

If your device is ever lost or stolen and the erase feature is used, you can restore your data from backup assuming you get your device back.

LOCATOR APPLICATIONS AND REMOTE WIPES

To cover the possibility that you might one day lose your mobile device, you can configure it to send its position to you. To do so, use the iCloud setting to turn on Find My iPhone or Find My iPad. How to do that was covered earlier in the chapter. If you lose your device, you can do the following:

1. Using a browser on any computer, go to **iCloud.com/find** and sign in with your Apple ID. If iCloud requests permission to install an add-on, allow the installation. Next, a map appears showing your device's reported position as a green dot on the map (see Figure 10-37).

2. Click the dot to see more options. The Info box appears, which is shown in Figure 10-37. If you see the device is close by, but you still can't find it, click **Play Sound or Send Message**, and have it play a sound. This sound overrides a low volume setting.

10

A+
220-802
3.3

Figure 10-37   Use the iCloud web site to locate a lost Apple device

© Cengage Learning 2013

3. If you still cannot find the device, you can have it display a message on-screen such as, "This device is lost. Please call me at 444-555-1234."

4. If you believe the device is stolen and you want to protect its contents, you can click **Remote Lock** to remotely set a passcode lock. Someone must key in this four-digit code to unlock the device.

5. If you decide the device cannot be found, you might want to click **Remote Wipe** to perform a remote wipe, which remotely erases all contacts, email, photos, and other data from the device to protect your privacy. Later, if you find the device, you can restore this data from backup.

Besides using a browser on a computer to find your device, you can also download the free app, Find My iPhone or Find My iPad, to another Apple device and use it to locate your lost device.

TROUBLESHOOTING IOS DEVICES

Common problems with iOS devices include the touch screen not working properly, iOS settings cannot be changed, buttons don't work, or an app does not work. For the iPhone or iPad, which use the iOS and a capacitive touch screen, recall that Apple says that the screen does not get out of alignment unless there is a hardware problem. Here are some tips to try when a touch screen is giving you problems:

- ◢ Clean the screen with a soft, damp cloth.
- ◢ Don't use the touch screen when your hands are wet or you are wearing gloves.
- ◢ Remove any plastic sheet or film protecting the touch screen.

For iPhones or iPads, you can sometimes solve an apparent touch screen alignment problem or other problems with the iOS by restarting, resetting, updating, or restoring the device.

A+
220-802
3.3

Try the first step that follows and if that does not solve the problem, move on to the next step. The steps are ordered so as to solve the problem while making the least changes to the system (least-intrusive solution). After you try one step, check to see if the problem is solved before you move on to the next step. Do the following:

1. *Restart the phone.* To restart the phone, press and hold the Wake/sleep button until the red slider bar appears and then drag the slider. Then press and hold the Wake/sleep button until the Apple logo appears.

2. *Reset the phone.* To reset the phone, press and hold the Wake/sleep button and the Home button at the same time for at least 10 seconds until the Apple logo appears.

3. *Update the iOS.* To update the iOS with the latest patches, first make sure the latest version of iTunes is installed on your computer. Connect the iPhone to your computer and select it in the DEVICES list. If possible, back up content and settings. Then click the **Summary** tab, and click **Updates**.

4. *Reset all settings.* If you have not already done so, back up the data and settings. Then to erase settings, tap **Settings**, **General** and **Reset**. On the Reset screen (see Figure 10-38), tap **Reset All Settings**.

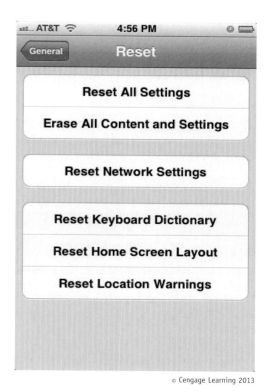

© Cengage Learning 2013

Figure 10-38 Erasing settings and content can sometimes solve problems with the iOS

5. *Erase all data and settings.* To erase all data and settings, tap **Settings**, **General** and **Reset**. On the Reset screen (see Figure 10-38), tap **Erase All Content and Settings**.

10

A+
220-802
3.3

6. *Restore the phone.* This process reinstalls the iOS and you will lose all your data on the device. The device is restored to its factory condition. Before you do this, try to back up all your data and settings. Then follow these steps:

   a. Make sure the latest version of iTunes is installed on your computer. Connect the iPhone to your computer and make sure it appears in the DEVICES list. Click the **Summary** tab and click **Restore**. You are given the opportunity to back up settings and data (see Figure 10-39). If you have not already done a backup, do so now.

   b. Don't unplug or interrupt the device during the restore. The iOS is reinstalled and all data and settings are lost.

   c. Next, restore your data and settings from backup. How to do that was covered earlier in the chapter.

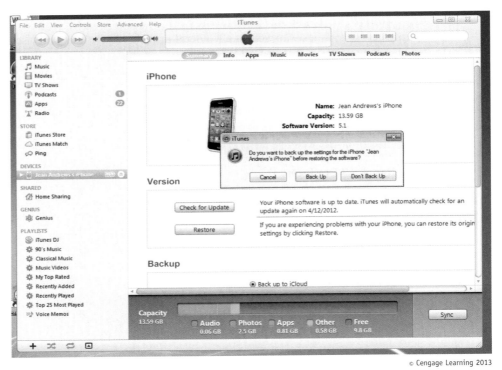

© Cengage Learning 2013

Figure 10-39 Back up data and settings and restore the device to factory condition

7. *Recover the device.* This process might work to restore the device to factory state when the restore process fails or you cannot start the restore process. The process does a firmware upgrade. All content and data are lost and the OS is refreshed. Follow these steps:

   a. Turn off the device. If you have trouble turning off the device, press and hold the Wake/sleep button and the Home button at the same time.

   b. While holding down the Home button, connect the device to your computer. If you see the device charging, wait a few minutes while it charges. Do not release the Home button while it is charging. When you see the Connect to iTunes screen, release the Home button.

A+
220-802
3.3

   c. Use the Start menu to start iTunes. iTunes should recognize the device and display a message saying the device is in recovery mode and ask if you want to restore the device. Follow the directions on-screen to restore the device to factory state.

   d. Restore data and settings using the most recent backups.

If the device is still not working properly, search for more troubleshooting tips on the Apple web site at *support.apple.com* or take the device to an Apple store for repair.

Hands-on | Project 10.1 Research Browser Apps

A smart phone or tablet comes with a built-in browser, but you can replace it with a third-party browser. Research browser apps and answer the following questions:

   1. List three browser apps that are popular with Apple devices using iOS. List one feature for each app that makes it stand out.

   2. The iPhone and iPad don't use Adobe Flash, and many web sites depend on Flash. What workaround app can be used with iOS so that the iPhone and iPad can view content on these web sites?

CONFIGURING, SYNCING, AND SECURING ANDROID DEVICES

A+
220-802
3.2

Because the Android operating system is open source, manufacturers can customize the OS and how it works in many variations. Therefore, it is not always possible to give specific step-by-step directions similar to those given for the iOS. In this part of the chapter, you learn about general procedures you can follow to support an Android device. And we give a few examples for specific Android devices so that you can see how the step-by-step directions might work on an Android device.

When you are assigned responsibility for supporting an Android device, begin with the user guide for the device, which you can download from the device manufacturer's web site. The user guide is likely to tell you the detailed steps of how to connect to a network, configure email, update the OS, sync and back up settings and data, secure the device, and what to do when things go wrong.

10

> **Notes** Most of us rarely follow step-by-step directions when learning to use a new device unless when "all else fails, read the directions." This part of the chapter can give you an idea of what to look for on an Android device, and you can likely figure out the steps for yourself.

Most of the settings you need to support an Android device are found in the Settings app. However, not all settings are there and the Settings app is not always easy to find. In addition, Android is not as intuitive as the iOS and relies more on third-party apps to do administrative chores than does the iOS.

On the other hand, Android is usually fun to use and support because it offers so much flexibility and the potential to customize. Once you get comfortable with Android, you can

A+
220-802
3.2

do amazing things with it. Technicians who love to tinker with devices tend to gravitate to Android, and those who just want a quick and easy tool to use without a hassle choose the iOS.

Now let's look at what to expect when supporting an Android device.

CONFIGURING NETWORK CONNECTIONS

To configure settings on an Android device, use the Settings app, which can always be found in the App launcher. For many Android phones, the App launcher is an app in the dock at the bottom of the screen (see Figure 10-40). Use it to access all installed apps, including the Settings app. For many Android tablets, the App launcher is the Apps icon in the upper-right corner of the screen (see Figure 10-41).

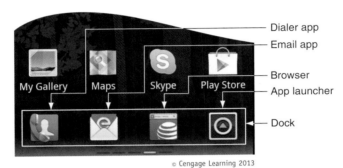

© Cengage Learning 2013

Figure 10-40 Up to four apps stay pinned to the dock at the bottom of the Android home screens

© Cengage Learning 2013

Figure 10-41 Use the Apps icon in the upper-right corner of a tablet to view and manage installed apps

Devices also have other methods that lead to the Settings app. For Android phones, tap the **Menu** button and tap **Settings**. For the tablet screen shown in Figure 10-41, tap the **Device admin** shortcut on the home screen. Figure 10-42 shows the Settings screen for one Android tablet.

To configure network connections using the Settings screen, tap **Wireless & networks**, as shown in Figure 10-42. Use the Wireless & networks screen to change these network settings:

© Cengage Learning 2013

Figure 10-42   In the Wireless & networks group of the Settings menu, change Airplane mode, Wi-Fi, Bluetooth, and VPN settings

▲ *Turn Airplane mode on or off.* Recall that airplane mode disables all wireless network antennas and is required in the United States during travel on airplanes. It's also convenient when you want to disable your device's data network access to conserve data usage or battery power when your battery is low. Some devices, such as Motorola smart phones, come preinstalled with a shortcut button on the home screen to toggle Airplane mode, Bluetooth, Wi-Fi, and GPS connections.

▲ *Turn Wi-Fi on or off and configure Wi-Fi access points*. Tap **Wi-Fi settings**. On the Wi-Fi settings screen, you can request to be notified of available networks, determine whether to auto-connect to Wi-Fi hot spots, determine when to disconnect from Wi-Fi, add a Wi-Fi network, and manage existing networks (see Figure 10-43). When you first attempt to connect to a secured Wi-Fi network, you need the security key.

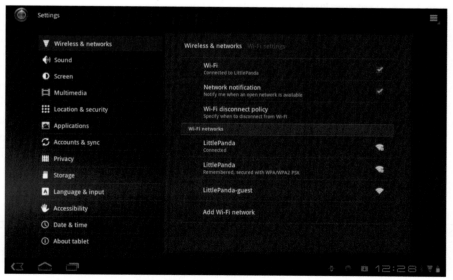

© Cengage Learning 2013

Figure 10-43   Configure Wi-Fi settings

10

**A+
220-802
3.2**

> **Notes** Searching for a Wi-Fi network can drain the battery power. To make a battery charge last longer, disable Wi-Fi when you're not using it.

◢ *Turn Bluetooth on or off.* To configure Bluetooth settings, tap **Bluetooth settings** on the Wireless & networks screen. On the Bluetooth settings screen, you can make the device discoverable by Bluetooth devices and pair with these devices (see Figure 10-44). You can also determine how long the Android device can be discovered.

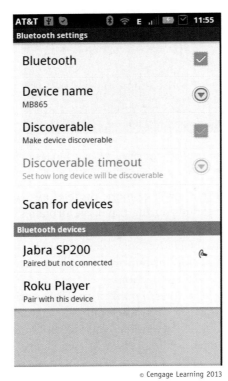

© Cengage Learning 2013

Figure 10-44   Configure Bluetooth settings and pair with Bluetooth devices

◢ *View cellular settings.* Figure 10-45 shows the top and bottom of the Wireless & network settings screen on an Android phone. To view settings for the cellular network connection, tap **Mobile networks**. Some systems offer the option on this screen to switch on or off the cellular data connection; this system does not. For this system, if you want to turn off cellular data and use Wi-Fi for data transmissions, first turn on Airplane mode, which disables cellular, Wi-Fi, and Bluetooth, and then enable Wi-Fi.

> **Notes** The advantage of disabling cellular data and using Wi-Fi for data transmissions is data transmissions over Wi-Fi are not charged against your cellular data subscription plan with your carrier. Also, Wi-Fi is generally faster than most cellular connections.

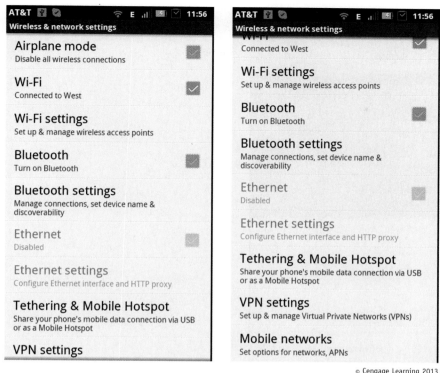

Figure 10-45 Top and bottom of the Wireless & network settings screen on an Android phone

▲ *Set up tethering.* To set up tethering so that your computer can use the cellular network that your phone is connected to, tap **Tethering & Mobile Hotspot**. (A tablet that does not have cellular capability will not have these last two options for Mobile networks and Tethering.)

CONFIGURING EMAIL

Because Google owns Gmail, Google makes it very easy to configure a Gmail account on an Android device. To set up a Gmail account, tap the **Gmail** app on the home screen and enter your email account and password. (If you don't see the app on your home screen, tap the App launcher, and then tap Gmail.) The app then gives you the opportunity to sync books, calendars, contacts, Gmail, and Google Photos with Google. Make your selections and tap **Done**. If you want to later change what type of data is synced, go to the Settings app, tap **Accounts & sync**, and select your Gmail account. The Data & synchronization screen appears (see Figure 10-46 for an Android phone).

Here are the steps to set up email accounts other than Gmail or any other type of account such as Skype, YouTube, Photobucket, Dropbox, or Facebook accounts:

1. Tap **Settings**, **Accounts & sync**, **Add account**. On the Setup accounts screen (see Figure 10-47a), select the type of account. For an email account, tap **Email**. On the next screen (see Figure 10-47b), enter your email account and password. Note on this screen that *Automatically configure account* is checked. Android can automatically configure several types of accounts. First try to set up the account with this item checked.

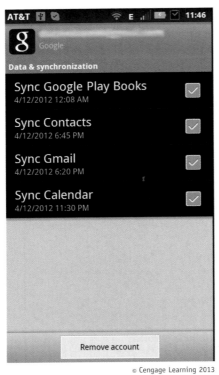

© Cengage Learning 2013

Figure 10-46   Sync content tied to your Gmail account

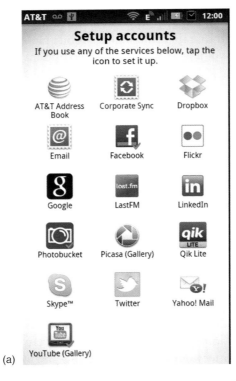

(a)

(b)

© Cengage Learning 2013

Figure 10-47   Android can automatically configure several types of accounts

A+
220-802
3.2

2. If you get errors using automatic configuration, then try again with **Automatically configure account** unchecked. You can then manually configure the account. When you manually configure an email account, you are given the opportunity to select the type of account (POP, IMAP, or Exchange), enter incoming and outgoing mail server addresses, POP or IMAP protocols, port addresses, and email encryption.

A+
220-802
3.5

SYNCING, BACKING UP, AND RESTORING FROM BACKUP

Syncing, backing up, and restoring from backup with Android is not quite as simple as it is with the iOS because Android offers more methods and options for these chores, and third-party apps are usually involved. In this part of the chapter, you learn to sync with online accounts (using third-party apps for syncing), sync all your apps to an app store, and back up any content to external storage connected to your device.

SYNC USING ONLINE ACCOUNTS

As you saw earlier, when you set up a Gmail account on your device, Google provides automatic syncing of books, contacts, Gmail, calendars, and Google photos (refer to Figure 10-46). You can also sync contacts and other data with other online accounts, including Facebook, Twitter, Dropbox, LinkedIn, and more that you have set up on your device (refer to Figure 10-47). With some online accounts, be aware that syncing might be automatic only from the online account, not the other way around.

USE THIRD-PARTY SYNCING APPS

For other content, including pictures, music and videos, third-party apps are normally used. Some Android devices come preinstalled with sync apps. Motorola's Phone Portal, for example, can sync music, pictures, and videos from a computer's iTunes program. Some apps require a USB connection to sync, and others sync wirelessly at set intervals. Some apps like SugarSync will sync entire folders in the background with no user intervention required, while others like Dropbox only sync files placed in the app's own folder. Some apps sync between a mobile device and computer, while others maintain those files in the cloud and the service is linked to the user's account.

SYNC APPS WITH YOUR APP SOURCE

Google Play maintains records of all apps for a particular Google account. A Google account is associated with an email address (Gmail or some other email address). To tie a Google account to your device, tap **Settings, Accounts & sync, Add account, Google Accounts**, and follow the directions on-screen. The process allows you to create a Google account if you don't already have one.

You can sometimes solve a problem with an app by uninstalling it and then installing it again. To uninstall an app, open the Settings app (refer to Figure 10-42) and tap **Applications, Manage applications**. Tap the app you want to uninstall and then tap **Uninstall**.

To update an app or restore an app you uninstalled, follow these steps:

1. On the home screen, tap **Play Store**. The Google Play screen appears (see Figure 10-48 for an Android tablet). Apps are tied to the Google account you used when you downloaded the app. If you have more than one Google account, tap the Menu icon on the far-right corner (for a tablet) or the Menu button (for a phone). Tap **Accounts** (see Figure 10-48) and select your Google account.

10

Download (to see all downloaded content under current account)

Search Google Play

Submenu under Google Play menu

Menu (to change the Google account and how updates are handled)

© Cengage Learning 2013

Figure 10-48 Manage apps you have downloaded from Play Store and search for more content

2. On the Google Play screen, tap the download icon (for a tablet), or tap **Menu** and My Apps (for a phone). On the next screen (see Figure 10-49), tap **INSTALLED** to see a list of apps. To update an app, select it and tap **Update**. To reinstall an app that has been uninstalled, tap **ALL** at the top of the screen. In the list of apps that you have previously downloaded, select the app and tap **Install**. The app installs again. Notice on these screens that you can control permissions assigned to each app, including how it can use storage, the network, GPS locator service, and other hardware controls.

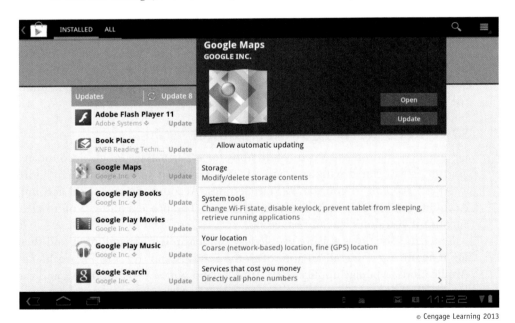

© Cengage Learning 2013

Figure 10-49 Sync apps with the app store from which you downloaded your apps

You can control how an app is updated. To do so, return to the Google Play screen and tap **Menu** (refer to Figure 10-48). Then tap **Settings**. The Settings screen appears (see Figure 10-50). To conserve battery charge and use of the cellular data network, check **Update over Wi-Fi only**. To manually control your updates, uncheck **Auto-update apps**. To manually update an app, go to the apps store, select the app, and tap **Update,** as shown earlier in Figure 10-49.

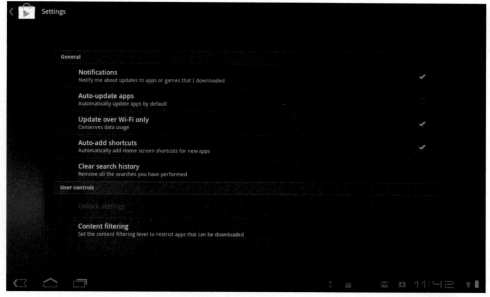

A+
220-802
3.5

Figure 10-50   Configure how to update your apps

© Cengage Learning 2013

In addition to the Play Store, each device manufacturer provides an app store, and you can purchase apps from other sites like Amazon.com. When you purchase an app from another source than the Play Store, make sure the site provides the opportunity to restore the app if that becomes necessary.

BACK UP TO A USB DEVICE OR SMART CARD

If an Android device has a slot for a smart card (for example, an SD card slot) or a USB port, most likely the manufacturer has preinstalled an app to back up your data to the smart card or USB flash drive. For example, Toshiba provides the File Manager app for this purpose. To use the app, follow these steps:

1. Tap **File Manager** on the home screen. The TOSHIBA File Manager screen appears (see Figure 10-51). The three storage devices listed at the top of the screen are Internal Storage (currently selected), SD card, and USB storage. Tap **Internal Storage** to select it.

10

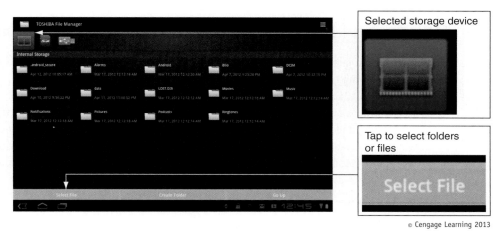

© Cengage Learning 2013

Figure 10-51   The File Manager app allows you to copy files and folders to an SD card or USB device

A+
220-802
3.5

2. Tap **Select File** at the bottom of the screen. New buttons appear (see Figure 10-52). Select the folders to back up or tap **Select All**. A red check mark indicates the folder is selected. Tap **Copy**.

© Cengage Learning 2013

Figure 10-52 Use the menu at the bottom of the screen to manage selected files and folders

3. Tap the device that is to receive the backup (SD card or USB storage). Then tap **Paste**. The files and folders are copied to the device.

Restoring data and settings from backup can be quite a production because no one app backs up all the data on an Android device. Basically, you have to go to wherever you have synced or backed up (an online account, app store, SD card, USB flash drive, or other location) and retrieve the contents from each location. The key to making this restoration process flow smoothly is to use apps with reliable syncing capabilities in both directions.

Hands-on | Project 10.2 Research Apps to Back Up Android Data

Research apps you might want to use to back up your data and settings on an Android device and answer the following questions:

1. List four apps available at Google Play that can be used to back up apps, contacts, pictures, music, and videos. Read a review or two about each app. Does the app require root access? (Root access requires that your device has been rooted so that you have administrator privileges to the Android OS.) What version of Android is required for the app? What are advantages and disadvantages of the app? How much does the app cost?

2. If you were to purchase one of these apps, which one would it be? Why?

A+
220-802
3.5

UPDATING THE ANDROID OS

Updates to the Android OS are automatically pushed to the device from the manufacturer. Because each manufacturer maintains its own versions of Android, these updates might not come at the same time Google announces a major update. When the device receives notice of an update, it displays a message asking permission to install the update. You can also manually check for updates at any time. To do so, go to the **Settings** app and tap **About tablet** or **About phone**. On the About screen (see Figure 10-53 for a phone), tap **System updates**. The device turns to the manufacturer's web site for information and reports updates available. Follow the directions on-screen to install these updates.

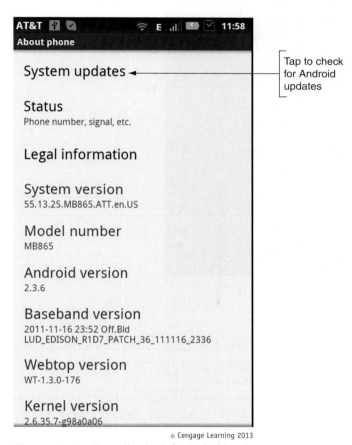

© Cengage Learning 2013

Figure 10-53 Manually check for Android updates

A+
220-802
3.3

SECURING AN ANDROID MOBILE DEVICE

The Android OS includes some security features and relies on third-party applications for other security needs. Here is an overview of how to secure an Android device:

▲ *Passcode protection.* To set a passcode for an Android, tap **Settings, Location & security**. On the Location & security screen (see Figure 10-54), tap **Configure lock screen**. On the next screen, you can set a Pattern, PIN, or Password that must be entered to unlock the device. A pattern is the most secure, which requires you to use your finger to connect at least four dots on the screen (see Figure 10-55).

A+
220-802
3.3

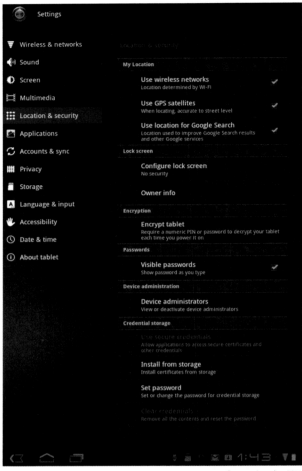

Figure 10-54 Secure a mobile device

© Cengage Learning 2013

▲ *Failed login restrictions.* Android automatically locks down the device after five attempts at the pattern. You are then given an opportunity to unlock the device by entering your Google account and password.

▲ *Remote wipes and locator applications.* The Android OS contains native code to remote wipe data from an Android device, but there is no native app on the device to access this feature. Microsoft Exchange server and similar systems implement this feature so that system administrators can wipe a device in an emergency to prevent the loss of corporate data. Google offers Google Apps Mobile Management software, which an administrator can use to secure Android devices used in their organization. This software includes the ability to remote wipe a device. Third-party apps can be used to locate a device. However, the app must be installed before the device is lost. Read several reviews about these apps before you choose one.

▲ *Antivirus protection.* Because Apple closely protects the iOS and iOS apps, it's unlikely an Apple device will need antivirus software. The Android OS and apps are not so closely guarded. Even so, Android devices don't normally get malware. Before installing an Android antivirus app, be sure to read reviews about it. Most of the major antivirus software companies provide Android antivirus apps.

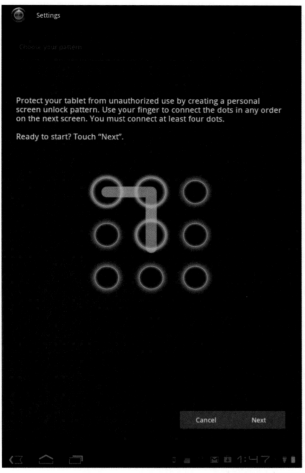

© Cengage Learning 2013

Figure 10-55 Create a pattern that must be entered in order to unlock the device

---

Hands-on | Project 10.3 Learn about Google Apps Mobile Management

Google has posted several videos to Youtube.com that you can use to learn about its products and services. Search Youtube.com for videos about Google Apps Mobile Management by Google. (To know if a video is by Google, look for *Uploaded by GoogleApps* on the Youtube.com web page below the video.) Answer the following questions:

1. What app should a user install on his device to use some of the features of Google Apps Mobile Management? What is the price of the software?

2. Can an administrator use the software to require that mobile devices must use a passcode? To lock a device remotely? To find a device when it is lost?

3. Which of the following mobile operating systems other than Android can work with Google Apps Mobile Management: iOS, Blackberry, Windows Phone?

4. Is it possible for a user to perform a remote wipe, or must it always be performed by an administrator?

10

**A+
220-802
3.3**

TROUBLESHOOTING ANDROID DEVICES

Follow these general tips to solve problems with Android devices. For more specific instructions, search the web site of the device manufacturer:

- ▲ You can forcefully reboot the device by pressing a combination of buttons on the device. Turn to the manufacturer's web site to find out this combination. As a last resort, you can open the back cover of the device, remove the battery, and then reinstall the battery.
- ▲ If you suspect an app is giving a problem, uninstall it and use the app store to reinstall it. How to do this was covered earlier in the chapter.
- ▲ Try installing Android updates.
- ▲ Take the device into Recovery mode. To do so, look for instructions on the manufacturer's web site. Most likely, you need to hold down a combination of buttons. Once there, Android presents a menu where you can reboot the system or restore the system to factory state. Try the reboot before you try the factory state, because this last option causes all your apps and data to be lost.

If you find you are unable to do all you want to do with your Android device (such as install a powerful app or download the latest Android release before your device manufacturer makes it available), you can root your device. **Rooting** is the process of obtaining root or administrator privileges to an Android device, which then gives you complete access to the entire file system (all folders and files) and all commands and features. To root a device, you download and use third-party software. The process takes some time and might even involve restoring the device to factory state.

The process of rooting might corrupt the OS, and after the device is rooted, installed apps that require root access can corrupt the OS. For some manufacturers, rooting will void your warranty, and some carriers refuse to provide technical support for a rooted device. Avoid it if you can; if you decide to root a device, do so with caution!

Hands-on | Project 10.4 Select a Mobile Device

Shop for a new smart phone or tablet using the iOS or Android. Be sure to read some reviews about a device you are considering. Select two devices that you might consider buying and answer the following questions:

1. What is the device brand, model, and price?

2. What is the OS and version? Amount of storage space? Screen size? Types of network connections? Battery life? Camera pixels?

3. What do you like about each device? Which would you chose and why?

Now let's turn our attention away from mobile devices and toward an entirely different topic, virtualization.

VIRTUALIZATION BASICS

In Chapter 2, you learned about using a virtual machine to hold an installation of Windows on a personal computer along with installed applications. In this chapter, we explore the many ways virtualization can be implemented, including using a virtual machine. **Virtualization** is when one physical machine hosts multiple activities that are normally done on multiple machines. Two general types of virtualization are server-side virtualization and client-side virtualization. The basic difference between the two is where the virtualizing takes place. Let's see how each can be implemented.

SERVER-SIDE VIRTUALIZATION

Server-side virtualization provides a virtual desktop for users on multiple client machines. Most, if not all, processing is done on the server, which provides to the client the **Virtual Desktop Infrastructure (VDI)**. See Figure 10-56.

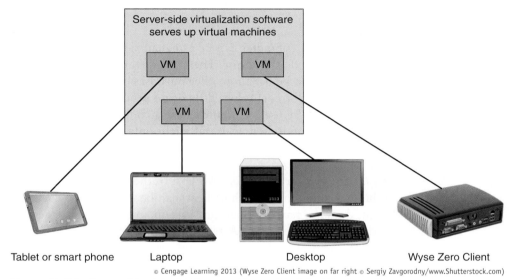

© Cengage Learning 2013 (Wyse Zero Client image on far right © Sergiy Zavgorodny/www.Shutterstock.com)

Figure 10-56 Server-side virtualization provides a virtual desktop to each user

The advantages or main purposes of using server-side virtualization are to:

▲ *Maximize a company's investment in hardware.* In recent years, processor computing power and hard drive storage capacity have exponentially increased compared to cost. Today, a server using the latest multi-core processor and hard drives can easily support multiple virtual machines on the same platform. This fact makes it more cost effective to run VMs on a single server rather than pay for hardware at each client computer. The trend, therefore, is to use virtualization with a high-power central server and inexpensive client machines that do very little processing, but are often reduced to merely sending commands to a VM running on the central server.

▲ *Centralize support for hardware, software, and users.* As the cost of labor increases, corporations can save money by centralizing technical support for hardware, software, and users. With virtualization, most hardware and software is installed at a central corporate office or even outsourced to another company, which means technical support is also centralized. Less onsite technical support is needed because a client computer needs less software installed and users can often be supported from a centralized help desk.

The disadvantages of using server-side virtualization are:

▲ *High-end servers are required and network load increases.* Therefore, the data center and network infrastructure are likely to need hardware improvements when implementing server-side virtualization.

10

◢ *User experience might suffer.* Remote users cannot work offline and are, therefore, totally dependent on the server and the network. What users can do at their local computers cannot be easily modified for unique user needs. Remote support rather than desk-side support is sometimes frustrating for users.

Now let's look at the types of clients and third-party services used with server-side virtualization.

CLIENTS USED WITH SERVER-SIDE VIRTUALIZATION

Using server-side virtualization, three categories of clients might be used, based on the computing power of the client:

◢ *Fat clients.* The client computer can be a regular desktop computer or laptop. In this case, the client is called a fat client. The main advantage of using fat clients is the personal computer can be used for other purposes than server-side virtualization.

◢ *Thin clients.* Because the client does little or no processing with server-side virtualization, a thin client can be used. A **thin client** is a computer that has an operating system, but has little computing power and might only need to support a browser used to communicate with the server. The main advantage of using thin clients is the reduced cost of the client machine.

◢ *Zero clients.* To even further reduce the cost of the client machine, a **zero client**, also called a **dumb terminal** or **ultra-thin client**, can be used. A zero client, such as a Wyse Zero Client, does not have an operating system and merely provides an interface between the user and the server. A zero client might contain little more than a keyboard, mouse, monitor, and network connection.

SERVER-SIDE VIRTUALIZATION USING CLOUD COMPUTING

Many small organizations that want to use server-side virtualization are turning to cloud computing services to reduce the cost of hardware, software, and technical support. **Cloud computing** is when server-side virtualization is delegated to a third-party service, and the Internet is used to connect server and client machines. Cloud computing can vary by the degree of service provided:

◢ **Infrastructure as a Service (IaaS).** Using IaaS, the cloud-computing service provides only the hardware, which can include servers, Network-attached Storage (NAS) devices, and networks. The organization is responsible for the operating systems and applications installed on the servers.

◢ **Platform as a Service (PaaS).** Using PaaS, the cloud-computing service provides hardware and the operating systems and is responsible for updating and maintaining both. The organization is responsible for the applications installed on these machines.

◢ **Software as a Service (SaaS).** Using SaaS, you guessed it, the service is responsible for the hardware, the operating systems, and the applications installed. These turnkey services are the most expensive, but for a small organization that does not have the technical expertise or other resources, this option is sometimes the most cost effective.

CLIENT-SIDE VIRTUALIZATION

Using **client-side virtualization**, a personal computer provides multiple virtual environments for applications. Client-side virtualization can be implemented using several methods, including these three, which are presented from the least amount of computing done on the client machine to the most computing done on the client machine:

▲ *Presentation virtualization.* Using presentation virtualization, a remote application running on a server is controlled by a local computer. You learned to set up these remote applications in Chapter 8 using Remote App and Desktop Connection. The user remotely controls the application running on the server and the application data is also stored on the server (see Figure 10-57).

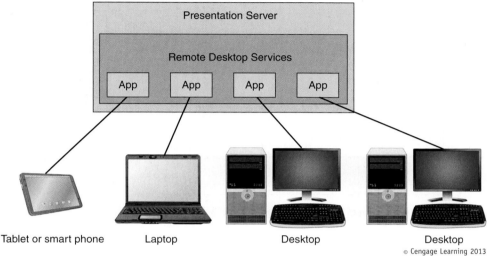

Figure 10-57 Microsoft Remote Desktop Services presents applications to the user at a local computer

▲ *Application virtualization.* Using application virtualization, a virtual environment is created in memory for an application to virtually install itself. An example of software used for application virtualization is Microsoft **Application Virtualization (App-V)**. The App-V software is installed on the client computer and is responsible for virtually installing an instance of an application whenever the user selects the application from a list provided by App-V. When the application installs and launches, it does not make changes to the Windows registry. An application managed by App-V can be permanently stored on the local hard drive or on an application server.

▲ *Client-side desktop virtualization.* Using client-side desktop virtualization, software installed on a desktop or laptop manages virtual machines. Each VM has its own operating system installed. In Chapter 2, you learned that Windows Virtual PC and Oracle VirtualBox are two examples of freeware that can be installed on a computer and used to manage virtual machines. This type of software is called a hypervisor or virtual machine manager (VMM).

Now let's take a closer look at different types of hypervisors and how each can be used to create virtual machines.

VIRTUAL MACHINES AND HYPERVISORS

Both server-side and client-side virtualization can be used to create a virtual machine (VM). The VM can exist on the server and be presented to a remote user (server-side desktop virtualization), or the VM can be created on the local machine to be used locally (client-side desktop virtualization). Software to create and manage virtual machines on a server or on a local computer is called a **virtual machine manager (VMM)** or **hypervisor**.

Now let's look at the different types of hypervisors, the hardware requirements needed for client-side virtualization, and how to secure a virtual machine.

10

A+
220-802
1.9

TYPE 1 AND TYPE 2 HYPERVISORS

Hypervisor software can be a Type 1 or Type 2 hypervisor. The differences are diagrammed in Figure 10-58.

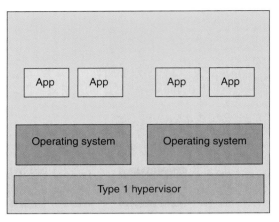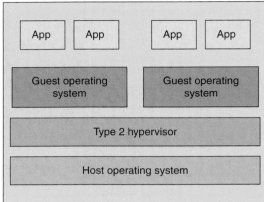

Figure 10-58 Type 1 and Type 2 hypervisors

© Cengage Learning 2013

Here is an explanation of the two types of hypervisors:

◢ A **Type 1 hypervisor** installs on a computer before any operating system, and is, therefore, called a bare-metal hypervisor. After it installs, it partitions the hardware computing power into multiple VMs. An OS is installed in each VM. Examples of Type 1 hypervisors are XenServer by Citrix, ESXi by VMware, and Hyper-V by Microsoft. Most server-side desktop virtualization is done using a Type 1 hypervisor.

Some Type 1 hypervisors are designed for client-side desktop virtualization on personal computers. For example, XenClient by Citrix installs on a personal computer and then you can install Windows or other operating systems in the VMs provided by XenClient. One major advantage of a local computer running a Type 1 hypervisor is added security because each OS and its applications are isolated from the others. For example, employees can install one OS in a VM for business use and another OS in a VM for personal use. The VM used for business can be locked down for secured VPN connections, and the personal VM does not require so much security.

> **Notes** To see some interesting videos of how XenClient by Citrix works and what it can do, go to *www.citrix.com/xenclient*.

◢ A **Type 2 hypervisor** installs in a host operating system as an application. Virtual PC, VirtualBox, and VMware Player are examples of Type 2 hypervisors. A Type 2 hypervisor is not as powerful as a Type 1 hypervisor because it is dependent on the host OS to allot its computing power. A VM in a Type 2 hypervisor is not as secure or as fast as a VM in a Type 1 hypervisor. Type 2 hypervisors are typically used on desktops and laptops when performance and security are not significant issues. Here are some ways that virtual machines provided by Type 2 hypervisors might be used:

A+
220-802
1.9

- Developers often use VMs to test applications. If you save a copy of a virtual hard drive (VHD) that has a fresh installation of Windows installed, you can easily build a new and fresh VM to test an application.
- Help desk technicians use VMs so they can easily switch from one OS to another when a user asks for help with a particular OS.
- Honeypots are a single computer or a network of computers that lure hackers to them so as to protect the real network. Virtual machines can be used to give the impression to a hacker that he has found a computer or entire network of computers. Administrators can monitor the honeypot for unauthorized activity.

HARDWARE REQUIREMENTS

When preparing to install a hypervisor and virtual machines, you need to be aware of the hardware requirements:

- *The motherboard BIOS.* The motherboard BIOS and the processor should support **hardware-assisted virtualization (HAV)**. For Intel processors, this feature is called Intel-VT. For AMD processors, the technology is called AMD-V. The feature must be enabled in BIOS setup. Figure 10-59 shows the BIOS setup screen for one motherboard where the feature is called Intel® VT. When you enable the feature, also verify that all subcategories under the main category for hardware virtualization are enabled.

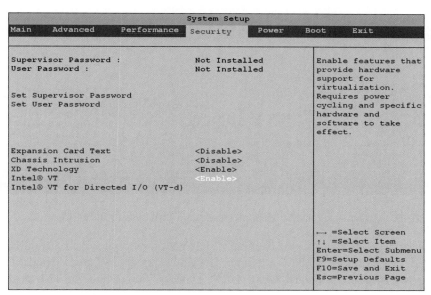

© Cengage Learning 2013

Figure 10-59 BIOS setup screen to enable hardware virtualization

- *Hard drive space.* See the requirements provided by the hypervisor manufacturer for hard drive space for the hypervisor. Each VM has its own virtual hard drive (VHD), which is a file stored on the physical hard drive and acts like a hard drive complete with its own boot sectors and file systems. You can configure this VHD to be a fixed size or dynamically expanding. The fixed size takes up hard drive space whether the VM uses the space or not. An expanding VHD increases in capacity as the VM uses the space. Remember that about 15 GB is required for a Windows installation. Therefore, you'll need at least 15 GB for each VM.

10

A+
220-802
1.9

▲ *Processor and memory.* All processors sold today support hardware-assisted virtualization. Plan on using at least a dual-core processor or better. A system needs lots of memory when running multiple virtual machines. Some hypervisors tie up all the memory you have configured for a VM from the time the VM is opened until the VM is closed.

When setting up a virtual machine, be aware of emulators that might be required by an application or user. A hypervisor emulates hardware and presents this virtual hardware to each VM, which can include a virtual processor, memory, motherboard, hard drive, optical drive, keyboard, mouse, monitor, network adapter, SD card, USB device, printer, and other components and peripherals. For example, all VMs have a virtual motherboard. When you press a key at startup to access setup BIOS on the VM under Windows Virtual PC, the BIOS setup main menu shown in Figure 10-60 appears. Using this virtual BIOS setup, you can configure the virtual motherboard and other hardware components in the VM.

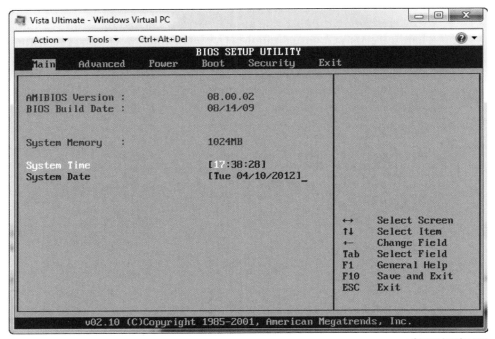

© Cengage Learning 2013

Figure 10-60   An emulated motherboard provides setup BIOS screens in the VM

A hypervisor offers a way to configure each VM, including which virtual hardware is installed. For example, when you launch Windows Virtual PC, the Virtual Machines window shown on the left side of Figure 10-61 appears. To configure a VM, select the VM in the right pane and click **Settings**. The Settings box shown on the right side of Figure 10-61 appears. You can use this box to install and uninstall virtual hard drives and other virtual devices in the VM.

Using Virtual PC, a VM must have Integrated Components software installed in the VM before it can share some hardware components with the host OS. This software is installed from the virtual DVD drive in the VM. After it is installed, the Integration Features selected in the Virtual PC Settings box become available. Notice on the right side of this box in Figure 10-61 that the VM can share audio, a printer, smart cards, USB drives, and other drives later plugged into the physical computer.

Also notice in the Settings box in Figure 10-61 that this VM has two hard drives installed. Hard Disk 1 is the virtual hard drive stored in the Win 7 VM.vhd file, and Hard Disk 2 is installed in the HDD4.vhd file.

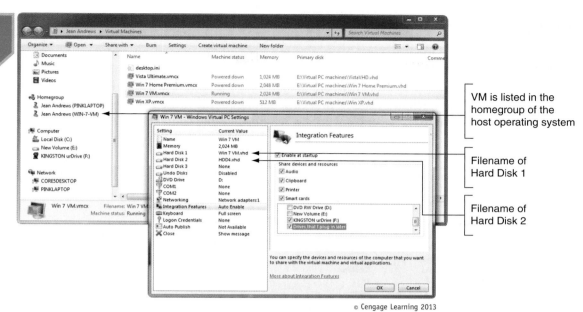

VM is listed in the
homegroup of the
host operating system

Filename of
Hard Disk 1

Filename of
Hard Disk 2

© Cengage Learning 2013

Figure 10-61 Emulated (virtual) hardware is installed in a VM under Windows Virtual PC

> **Notes** It's interesting to know that a Windows 7 system image and a Vista Complete PC Backup are each stored in a VHD file.

Recall that an .iso file holds the image of a CD. You can mount an .iso image file to the optical drive in a VM. To do so, first close the VM. Then select it in the Virtual Machines window and click **Settings** in the menu bar. The Settings box opens. Select the DVD Drive. Then on the right side of the Settings box, select **Open an ISO image** and click **Browse** to point to the .iso file (see Figure 10-62). Windows setup files can be downloaded from the Microsoft web site in an .iso file. When you mount this file to the VM, you can install Windows in the VM from this virtual CD.

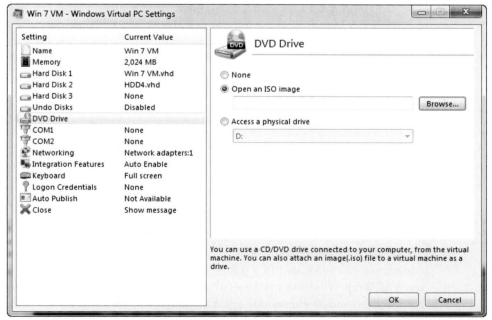

© Cengage Learning 2013

Figure 10-62 Mount an .iso file to the optical drive in a VM

10

A+
220-802
1.9

Also consider network requirements for the VM. A VM can have one or more virtual network adapters. A VM connects to a local network the same as other computers and can share and use shared resources on the network. Looking back at Figure 10-61, you can see the VM named Win 7 VM is running and is available in the Homegroup on this network. To change the virtual network adapters for this VM, first close the VM. Then select it in the Virtual Machines window and click **Settings** in the menu bar. The Settings box opens (see Figure 10-63). Select **Networking**, as shown in the figure. On the right side of the Settings box, you can control the number and type of installed network adapters up to four adapters.

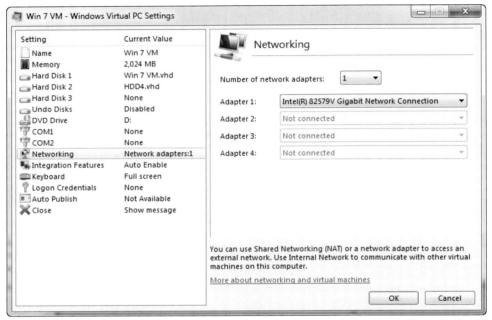

© Cengage Learning 2013

Figure 10-63   Emulate the network adapters in the VM

In one more example, Oracle VirtualBox can also emulate up to four network adapters in a VM. Figure 10-64 shows the Oracle VM VirtualBox Manager window on the left, which has two installed VMs listed in the left pane of this window. To manage the virtual hardware for a VM, first select it and then click **Settings**. The Settings box appears (see the right side of Figure 10-64). When you click **Network**, you can see the four tabs where each tab can be used to emulate a network adapter.

> **A+ Exam Tip**   The A+ 220-802 exam expects you to be able to explain methods used to secure a virtual machine installed on a client computer.

SECURE A VIRTUAL MACHINE

A virtual machine is susceptible to hackers and malware just as is a physical machine. Keep these points in mind when securing the resources in a VM:

◢ *Secure the VM* **within** *the VM*. When supporting a VM that has network and Internet connectivity or is located in a public area, be sure to configure Windows Firewall in the VM, keep Windows updates current, install and run antivirus software, and perform other security chores discussed in Chapters 8 and 9 to protect the virtual machine and its resources.

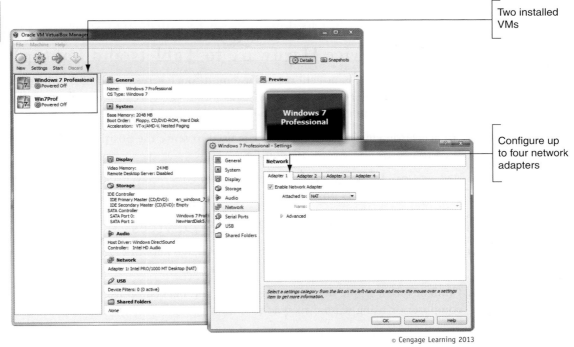

© Cengage Learning 2013

Figure 10-64 Configure up to four network adapters for a VM using Oracle VirtualBox

▲ *VMs should be isolated for best security.* One major advantage of using VMs on a desktop computer is that VMs running under a Type 1 hypervisor are isolated from each other. If one VM gets infected, the other VMs will not be affected.

▲ *Secure permissions to the files that hold a VM.* You can move a VM from one computer to another by moving the files that contain the VM. Be sure these files that hold the VM are secured with permissions that allow access only to specific local or network users.

Hands-on | Project 10.5   Set Up and Use a Virtual Machine

In Chapter 2, you installed Windows Virtual PC and used it to create a VM and install Windows 7. Install Windows Virtual PC on a second computer and move the VM you created earlier to this second computer. What files did you have to move? How did you configure Windows Virtual PC on the second computer to find and use the VM?

10

>> *CHAPTER SUMMARY*

Operating Systems Used on Mobile Devices

▲ Operating systems used on mobile devices include Android by Google, iOS by Apple, Blackberry by RIM, Windows Phone by Microsoft, and Symbian by the Symbian Foundation.

▲ Android is an open-source OS, and anyone can develop and sell Android apps or variations in the Android OS. Google is the major distributor of Android and Android apps from its Google Play web site.

◢ The iOS by Apple is used only on Apple devices, including the iPhone, iPad, and iPod touch. Apps for the iOS are distributed solely by Apple from its online iTunes App Store.

Comparing Mobile Device Hardware to Tablets and Laptops

◢ Smart phones and handheld tablets use multitouch screens and SSD storage, and they contain no field-serviceable parts. Because some tablets can make phone calls and send text messages, there is little distinction between a tablet and a smart phone.

◢ An accelerometer in a mobile device is used to sense the position of the device and can be used to change the screen orientation.

◢ A device can know its location because of its GPS receiver. Geotracking can be done as the device reports its position.

Configuring, Syncing, and Securing iOS Devices

◢ Using the iOS, the Settings app is used to manage network connections, configure email, manage content on the device, and configure many iOS settings.

◢ Content on an Apple device can be synced and backed up using iTunes to a personal computer or using iCloud to sync to online storage at icloud.com.

◢ iTunes installed on a personal computer is used to update the iOS and can restore the iOS to its factory state.

◢ iCloud can be used to sync content to all your iOS devices associated with an Apple ID. iCloud can also be used to locate a lost iOS device if the feature is enabled on the device.

◢ An iOS device can be secured using a passcode. In addition, you can use iCloud to perform a remote wipe to protect sensitive data.

◢ To troubleshoot an iOS device, you can restart, reset, update, erase, restore, and recover the iOS on the device.

Configuring, Syncing, and Securing Android Devices

◢ The Settings app on an Android device can be used to manage network connections, email, online accounts, updates to Android, and security.

◢ Syncing and backing up content on an Android device is done with online accounts, using third-party apps for syncing, syncing all your apps to an app store, and backing up content to external storage connected to the device.

Virtualization Basics

◢ Server-side virtualization happens on the server, and client-side virtualization happens on the client machine.

◢ Three ways to implement client-side virtualization include presentation virtualization, application virtualization, and client-side desktop virtualization.

◢ Client-side desktop virtualization is done by creating multiple virtual machines on a physical machine using a hypervisor.

◢ A Type 1 hypervisor installs before any OS is installed and is called a bare-metal hypervisor. A Type 2 hypervisor is an application that installs in an OS. A Type 1 hypervisor is faster and more secure than a Type 2 hypervisor.

>> KEY TERMS

accelerometer
airplane mode
Android
App Store
Apple ID
application virtualization
Application Virtualization
  (App-V)
Bluetooth PIN code
capacitive touch screen
client-side desktop
  virtualization
client-side virtualization
cloud computing
dock
dumb terminal
geotracking
Gmail
Google account
Google Play
GPS (Global Positioning
  System) receiver

gyroscope
handheld tablet
hardware-assisted virtualization (HAV)
HTC Sense
hypervisor
iCloud
Infrastructure as a Service
  (IaaS)
iOS
iPad
iPhone
iPod touch
iTunes Store
iTunes U
jailbreaking
Microsoft Exchange
Multimedia Messaging Service
  (MMS)
multitouch
open source
pairing

Platform as a Service (PaaS)
presentation virtualization
remote wipe
resistive touch screen
rooting
screen orientation
server-side virtualization
Short Message Service (SMS)
smart phone
Software as a Service (SaaS)
thin client
TouchFLO
Type 1 hypervisor
Type 2 hypervisor
ultra-thin client
Virtual Desktop Infrastructure
  (VDI)
virtual machine manager
  (VMM)
virtualization
zero client

>> REVIEWING THE BASICS

1. What is the symbol or icon that represents an Apple product? What is the symbol or icon that represents Android?

2. What are the last three releases of the Android OS in number and in name?

3. What company provides and oversees the Android marketplace? What is the web site of this marketplace?

4. List three Apple devices that use the iOS.

5. Who is the sole distributor of apps for the iOS?

6. What is one disadvantage to users when using an open-source operating system on a mobile device?

7. Which mobile device OS supports an SD card and USB port, iOS or Android?

8. Which programming language is used to write most Android apps? Apple requires that iOS apps be written in one of which three programming languages?

9. How can you configure a mobile device so it cannot connect to any network?

10. Which type of network connection requires that two devices pair before the connection is completed?

11. Which email protocol downloads email to be managed on the client machine? Manages email on the server?

12. Which email protocol uses port 110? 143? 993? 995?

10

13. Which security protocol is used to encrypt email?

14. Which email server uses ActiveSync to sync all email, contacts, and calendar updates on the server and client machines, including mobile devices?

15. What software must be installed on your computer before you can upgrade the version of iOS on your mobile device?

16. What are the steps to configure an iPhone so it can be located if it is lost?

17. How many failed logins on an iPad must happen before the device is locked?

18. Which procedure is the least-intrusive solution to a problem with the iOS, to reset an iOS device or to restore an iOS device?

19. When you attempt to set up an email account on an Android device using the automatic configuration feature and the setup fails, what do you do next?

20. List the steps to update the Android OS on a smart phone.

21. What are the three methods you can use on an Android to lock the screen? Which method is the most secure?

22. Which type of client-side virtualization creates a virtual environment in memory for an application to run on a client machine?

23. In Question 22, what Microsoft software can be used to create this environment?

24. List two types of hypervisors and describe their fundamental differences.

25. What are the three main ways to secure a VM?

>> THINKING CRITICALLY

1. Suppose you find an app that cost you $4.99 missing on your Android. What is the best way to restore the missing app?

   a. Go to backup storage and perform a restore to recover the lost app.

   b. Purchase the app again.

   c. Go to the app store where you bought the app and install it again.

   d. Go to the Settings app and perform an application restore.

2. Suppose you and your friend want to exchange document files on your Android tablet and her Android phone. What is the easiest way to do the exchange?

   a. Copy the files to an SD card and move the SD card to each device.

   b. Email the documents to each other.

   c. Each of you create a Dropbox account and use the dropbox to share the files.

   d. Pair the two devices using a Bluetooth connection and then share the document files.

   e. Set up a Google Docs account and share the account with your friend. Then copy documents to Google Docs that you want to share.

3. You have set up your Android phone using one Google account and your Android tablet using a second Google account. Now you would like to download the apps you purchased on your phone to your tablet. What is the best way to do this?

   a. Buy the apps a second time from your tablet.

   b. Set up the Google account on your tablet that you used to buy apps on your phone and then download the apps.

   c. Back up the apps on your phone to your SD card and then move the SD card to your tablet and transfer the apps.

   d. Call Google support and ask them to merge the two Google accounts into one.

>> REAL PROBLEMS, REAL SOLUTIONS

REAL PROBLEM 10-1: Use the Android SDK to Run an Android Emulator

This Real Problem is a challenging project and you might want to work with a partner so that you will have someone with whom to discuss solutions and share the work. Go to Youtube.com and watch some videos on downloading and installing the Android SDK and using it to install a virtual Android device using the Android Emulator. Then do the work to use the Android SDK and the Android Emulator to emulate an Android device. To prove you have accomplished this feat, take a screen shot of your virtual Android device running on your computer and email it to your instructor. Write a one-page report of your experience and include in it five or six tips that you think would help a student through this project.

REAL PROBLEM 10-2: Prepare for the A+ 220-802 Exam

This textbook and its companion web site together contain all the content you need to prepare for the A+ 220-802 exam. To find the online content, go to this book's companion web site at *www.cengagebrain.com*. See the Preface for more information. The online content mostly focuses on troubleshooting problems with hardware and includes how to:

◢ Troubleshoot problems related to motherboards, RAM, CPU, and power, including how to use a multimeter, power supply tester, loopback plugs, and POST card

◢ Troubleshoot problems with hard drives, including replacing the drive

◢ Troubleshoot problems with display and the video subsystem

◢ Troubleshoot wired networks, including using a punch-down tool, toner probe, wire strippers, and crimpers.

◢ Repair laptops, including replacing internal components

◢ Maintain printers and troubleshoot printer problems

Go online and read through the content. (If you like, you can download the content to your mobile device or computer.) Then answer the following questions:

1. What is the purpose of the dxdiag command?

2. How do you add Hibernate as an option on the Windows shutdown menu?

3. Explain the purpose of the PoE feature that a network adapter might support.

10

4. What does an extended series of beep codes at POST indicate?

5. What is one symptom that indicates a system has overheated?

6. Explain the purpose of loopback plugs and suggest one situation where you might want to use them.

7. Explain the purpose of a punch-down tool that a network technician might use.

8. When disassembling a laptop computer, explain one method to use to help keep screws and other small parts organized as you work.

9. What are two tools that can help prevent static electricity from damaging components as you work inside a computer?

10. What are the steps to clear a print queue using Windows 7?

APPENDIX A

Operating Systems Past and Present

As a PC support technician, you should be aware of the older and current operating systems and how they have evolved over the years.

DOS (DISK OPERATING SYSTEM)

In 1981, MS-DOS (also known as DOS) was introduced and quickly became the most popular OS among IBM computers and IBM-compatible computers using the Intel 8086 processors. DOS processed 16 bits at a time. Figure A-1 shows a computer screen using the DOS operating system. In those days, all computer screens used text and no graphics. As amazing as it might seem, old legacy applications that use the DOS operating system are still in use today. In fact, I still support one I wrote over 20 years ago that is used to track over a thousand entries in a huge annual horse show. The owners have the attitude, "If it ain't broke; don't fix it."

```
C:\>DIR \GAME

 Volume in drive C has no label
 Volume Serial Number is 0F52-09FC
 Directory of C:\GAME

 .               <DIR>        02-18-93      4:50a
 ..              <DIR>        02-18-93      4:50a
 CHESS           <DIR>        02-18-93      4:50a
 NUKE            <DIR>        02-18-93      4:51a
 PENTE           <DIR>        02-18-93      4:52a
 NETRIS          <DIR>        02-18-93      4:54a
 BEYOND          <DIR>        02-18-93      4:54a
         7 file(s)               0 bytes
                        9273344 bytes free

C:\>
```

Figure A-1   DOS provides a command-line prompt to receive user commands
© Cengage Learning 2013

DOS WITH WINDOWS 3.X

Early versions of Windows, including Windows 3.1 and Windows 3.2 (collectively referred to as Windows 3.x) didn't perform OS functions, but served as a user-friendly intermediate program between DOS, applications, and the user (see Figure A-2). Windows 3.x offered a graphical user interface, the Windows desktop, the windows concept, and the ability to keep more than one application open at the same time.

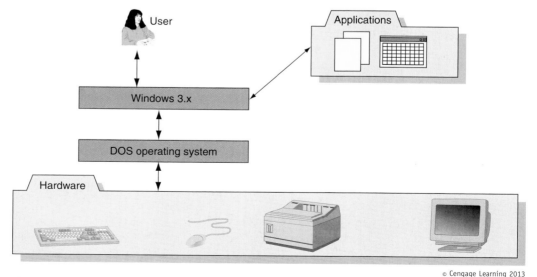

© Cengage Learning 2013

Figure A-2   Windows 3.x was layered between DOS and the user and applications to provide a graphics interface for the user and a multitasking environment for applications

WINDOWS 9X/ME

Windows 95, Windows 98, and Windows Me, collectively called Windows 9x/Me, used some DOS programs as part of the underlying OS (called a DOS core), and therefore had some DOS characteristics. However, these were true operating systems that could process 16 or 32 bits at a time and handle 16-bit and 32-bit applications.

WINDOWS NT AND WINDOWS 2000

Windows NT (New Technology) completely rewrote the OS core, totally eliminating the DOS core. Windows NT did all processing using 32 bits and was a major advance in OS architecture. Windows 2000 was an upgrade of Windows NT and offered several improvements, including a more stable environment, better network support, and features specifically targeting notebook computers. Microsoft didn't target Windows NT or 2000 to the home computer and game computer markets and did not make a commitment for Windows NT/2000 to be backward-compatible with older software and hardware. Therefore, Windows 9x/Me lived on until Windows XP.

WINDOWS XP

Windows XP is an upgrade of Windows 2000 and attempted to integrate Windows 9x/Me and 2000, while providing added support for multimedia and networking technologies. Windows XP is the first Windows OS to allow multiple users to log on simultaneously to the OS, each with their own applications open. Although Windows XP was first released with some bugs, the second service pack (Service Pack 2) resolved most of these problems. XP underwent three service packs. It is an extremely stable OS and was popular in both the home and corporate markets. The Windows XP desktop (see Figure A-3) has a different look from the desktops for earlier Windows.

© Cengage Learning 2013

Figure A-3   The Windows XP desktop, Start menu, and Windows Media Player on the desktop

A

The two main editions were Windows XP Home Edition and Windows XP Professional, though other less significant editions included Windows XP Media Center Edition, Windows XP Tablet PC Edition, and Windows XP Professional x64 Edition.

Because many people and corporations decided to not upgrade from XP to Windows Vista, Microsoft was forced to extend support for XP long past their initial timeframe. Microsoft no longer provides mainstream support to individuals for XP, but is still providing extended support to corporations until April, 2014. This extended support includes technical advice and releasing new security patches.

> **A+ Exam Tip** The only operating systems covered on the A+ exams are Windows XP, Windows Vista, and Windows 7.

WINDOWS VISTA

Windows Vista, an upgrade to Windows XP, was the first Windows OS to use the Aero user interface. The Windows Vista desktop shown in Figure A-4 uses this interface. Notice the Vista sidebar on the right side of the desktop contains some Vista gadgets. A gadget is a mini-app that you can add or remove from the sidebar by clicking the + sign at the top left of the sidebar.

© Cengage Learning 2013

Figure A-4 Windows Vista sidebar can be customized with Vista embedded gadgets or others you download from the web

Vista was not well received by consumers primarily because of the lack of compatibility with older hardware and software (called legacy hardware and software), the large amount of computer resources that Vista requires, and its slow performance. The first problem is partly caused by hardware manufacturers not providing Vista drivers for their devices that were originally sold with XP drivers. The second problem means that many low-end desktop and laptop computers can't run Vista. And the slow performance of Vista is partly due to the many unnecessary features (fluff) it offers; these features weigh heavy on system resources.

Vista comes in five versions: Windows Vista Home Basic, Home Premium, Business, Enterprise, and Ultimate. (Vista Starter is a sixth version available only to developing nations.) Also, Vista comes in 32-bit versions and 64-bit versions.

Vista underwent two service packs, and Microsoft no longer provides mainstream support for the OS. Microsoft is still providing extended support (advice and security patches) to corporations for Vista Business and Enterprise editions through April, 2017.

WINDOWS 7

Windows 7, the upgrade to Windows Vista, is the most current Windows desktop operating systems by Microsoft. Windows 7 solved many problems inherent in Vista: It performs better than Vista, is more compatible with legacy hardware and software, and provides a leaner and simpler user interface. Windows 7 introduced homegroups, the Action Center, and Windows XP Mode. Windows XP Mode is an environment useful for running legacy applications that work under XP but not under Windows 7.

WINDOWS 8

The next Microsoft desktop OS is code-named Windows 8, and is likely to be released by the time this book is in print. It has a tiled desktop designed especially for touch screens and a touch screen keyboard. Windows 8 is designed to work on a wide range of devices, from a powerful workstation to a smart phone. A smart phone is a mobile phone that has computing power, an installed operating system, and small applications called apps.

MAC OS

Currently, the Mac OS, which has its roots in the Unix OS, is available only on Macintosh computers from the Apple Corporation (*www.apple.com*). The Mac and the Mac OS were first introduced in 1984. The latest OS is Mac OS X (ten), which has had several releases. The latest release is called Mac OS X Lion. Figure A-5 shows the Mac OS X Lion desktop with a browser open.

> **Notes** Boot Camp software by Apple can be used to install Windows on a Mac computer as a dual boot with Mac OS X.

A

To keep from having to restart the Mac each time you want to switch from one OS to another, virtual machine software, such as VMWare (*www.vmware.com*), is used. The software creates a virtual machine (VM), which is a logical computer within a physical computer. The VM has its own virtual hard drive, and Windows can be installed in this virtual

Figure A-5   The Mac OS X Lion desktop and applications

© Cengage Learning 2013

environment on the VM's hard drive. A user can switch from the Mac OS to Windows by opening a VM window on the Mac OS desktop. You learn more about virtual machines in Chapter 2.

Currently, about 10 percent of personal computers sold today are Macs. Macs have been popular in the educational, graphics, and musical markets and are beginning to gain ground in both the corporate and home markets because Macs are stable and fun to use, costs are down, software is more available, and the iPad is acting like a magnet to bring more Macs into the corporate market.

> **Notes** You can learn more about the Mac OS by reading the content "Introducing the Mac OS" on this book's companion web site at *www.cengagebrain.com*. See the Preface for more information.

Linux is a variation of Unix that was created by Linus Torvalds when he was a student at the University of Helsinki in Finland. Versions of this OS are available for free, and all the underlying programming instructions (called source code) are also freely distributed. Like Unix, Linux is distributed by several different companies, whose versions of Linux are sometimes called distributions. Popular distributions of Linux include Ubuntu (*www.ubuntu.com*), Fedora (*fedoraproject.org*), RedHat (*www.redhat.com*), Puppy Linux (*puppylinux.org*), and Linux Mint (*linuxmint.com*).

> **A+ Exam Tip** The A+ exams do not cover Linux, the Mac OS, or server operating systems.

Linux is well suited to support various types of server applications such as a web server or email server. It is not as popular for a desktop OS because it is not easy to install or use and fewer Linux applications exist, as compared to those written for Windows or the Mac OS.

Linux is also used on netbooks because it requires fewer system resources than Windows. (A technician would say it has a small footprint.) Linux is an excellent training tool for learning UNIX.

A **shell** is the portion of an OS that relates to the user and to applications. The first Linux and UNIX shells consisted of commands entered at a command prompt. Two popular command-line shells for UNIX and Linux are the older Bourne shell and the newer Bourne-Again shell (BASH). But many users prefer a Windows-style GUI desktop. A typical Linux desktop is shown in Figure A-6.

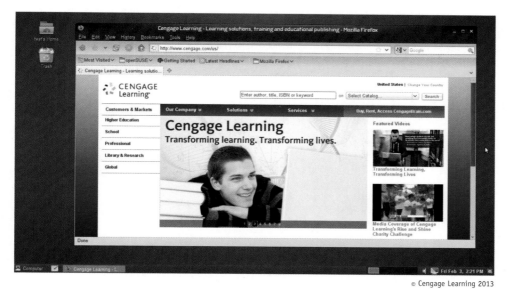

© Cengage Learning 2013

Figure A-6 A desktop using the Ubuntu Unity shell and Ubuntu distribution of Linux

> **Notes** You can find out more about Linux by reading the content "Introducing Linux" on this book's companion web site at *www.cengagebrain.com*. See the Preface for more information.

OPERATING SYSTEMS USED ON MOBILE DEVICES

A major evolution of operating systems is the operating systems used on smart phones, handheld tablets, or other mobile devices. A **handheld tablet** is a computing device that has a touch screen, installed operating system that can support simple or complex apps, touch-screen keyboard, and wireless capability. Some handheld tablets are also smart phones. The operating system for a mobile device is installed at the factory. Here are the more popular ones:

- ◢ Android OS distributed by Google (*android.com*) is based on Linux and is used on various smart phones and tablets. Currently, Android is the most popular OS for smart phones.
- ◢ iOS by Apple (*apple.com*) is based on Mac OS X and is used on the iPhone and iPad by Apple.
- ◢ Blackberry OS by RIM (*rim.com*) is a proprietary OS used on devices built by RIM.
- ◢ Windows Phone by Microsoft (*microsoft.com*) is based on Windows and is used on devices made by Dell, Fujitsu, Nokia, Samsung, and others.
- ◢ The Symbian OS from the Symbian Foundation (*symbian.org*) is popular outside the United States and is used on devices made by multiple manufacturers, including Nokia, Samsung, Sony, and others.

A

Windows Vista

This appendix covers the major differences between Windows 7 and Windows Vista. The content here applies to several chapters in the book. After you learn about Windows 7 in a chapter, turn to this appendix to learn how Windows Vista differs.

A+ Exam Tip The A+ 220-802 exam covers Windows 7, Vista, and XP. Use this appendix to study for the Vista portions of this exam.

CHAPTER 1: INTRODUCING WINDOWS OPERATING SYSTEMS

Following are differences in Windows 7 and Windows Vista that are associated with content covered in Chapter 1.

USER ACCOUNT CONTROL BOX

In Vista, you have little control over when the User Account Control box appears except to completely disable it, but for security purposes, that is not recommended. However, if you do decide to disable it in Vista, here's how:

1. In **Control Panel,** click **User Accounts** in the User Accounts and Family Safety group. In the User Accounts window, click **Turn User Account Control on or off.** Respond to the UAC box.

2. In the dialog box that appears (see Figure B-1), uncheck **Use User Account Control (UAC) to help protect your computer.** Click **OK.** Close all windows.

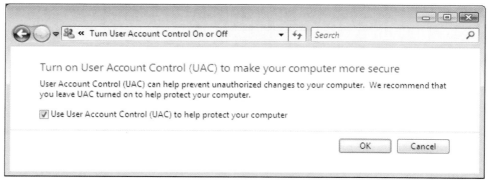

Figure B-1   Using Vista, you can turn on or off the User Account Control box   © Cengage Learning 2013

CHAPTER 2: INSTALLING WINDOWS

Following are differences in Windows 7 and Windows Vista that are associated with content covered in Chapter 2.

HOW TO PREPARE FOR AND INSTALL WINDOWS VISTA

Recall that you can no longer purchase Windows Vista. However, you might be called on to reinstall Vista on an existing system. For the most part, if you know how to prepare for and install Windows 7, you can also install Vista.

EDITIONS AND VERSIONS OF VISTA

The Vista editions are Windows Vista Starter, Home Basic, Home Premium, Business, Enterprise, and Ultimate. All the editions are included on the Windows Vista setup DVD; the edition installed depends on the product key that you enter during the installation. The major features for all editions are listed in Table B-1.

A+
220-802
1.2

Feature	Starter	Home Basic	Home Premium	Business	Enterprise	Ultimate
Aero user interface			X	X	X	X
BitLocker Drive Encryption					X	X
Optional dual processors				X	X	X
Complete PC backup				X	X	X
Encrypting File System (EFS)				X	X	X
IE parental controls	X	X	X			X
Network and Sharing Center	X	X	X	X	X	X
Scheduled and network backups			X	X	X	X
Tablet PC			X	X	X	X
Windows DVD Maker			X			X
Windows Media Center			X			X
Windows Movie Maker			X			X
Windows SideShow			X	X	X	X
Shadow Copy backup				X	X	X
Join a domain				X	X	X
Group Policy				X	X	X
Processor: 32-bit or 64-bit		X	X	X	X	X
Remote Desktop				X	X	X
Windows Meeting Space			X	X	X	X

© Cengage Learning 2013

Table B-1   Vista editions and their features

As you can see from Table B-1, all Vista editions except the Starter edition came in a 32-bit or 64-bit version. Table B-2 lists the maximum memory supported by each edition. The recommended hardware requirements for Vista are the same as those for Windows 7, which are listed in Table 2-3 in Chapter 2.

Operating System	32-Bit Version	64-Bit Version
Vista Ultimate	4 GB	128 GB
Vista Enterprise	4 GB	128 GB
Vista Business	4 GB	128 GB
Vista Home Premium	4 GB	16 GB
Vista Home Basic	4 GB	8 GB
Vista Starter	1 GB	NA

© Cengage Learning 2013

Table B-2   Maximum memory supported by Vista editions

INSTALL VISTA AND CONFIGURE THE SYSTEM

An in-place upgrade, a clean install, and a dual boot installation of Vista begin and proceed the same way as do Windows 7 installations. The steps are not repeated here. After the Vista installation, you need to perform the same chores as described in Chapter 2 for Windows 7. These chores are also not repeated in this appendix.

B

A+
220-802
1.2

Notes In Windows 7, you can view computers and their shared folders on the network by clicking Network in the left pane of Windows Explorer. In Vista, you can use this same method. In addition, you can click **Start**, **Network**. Windows Explorer opens showing the Network resources (see Figure B-2). Drill down to see these resources. The Network window on the Windows 7 Start menu is disabled by default, but you can add it using the Taskbar and Start Menu Properties box.

© Cengage Learning 2013

Figure B-2   Use the Network window to access resources on your network

CHAPTER 3: MAINTAINING WINDOWS

Following are differences in Windows 7 and Windows Vista that are associated with content covered in Chapter 3.

A+
220-802
1.7

CREATE AND USE BACKUPS IN WINDOWS VISTA

Vista handles backups differently than does Windows 7 for the Windows volume, user data, and restore points. These differences are covered next.

BACK UP THE WINDOWS VISTA VOLUME

The backup of the Windows Vista volume is called the Complete PC Backup. The Complete PC backup can be saved to a local device such as an external hard drive or to DVDs. Don't back up the volume to another partition on the same hard drive. After the initial backup is made, Vista will automatically keep this backup current by making incremental backups.

Notes Complete PC backup is not available in Vista Starter or Vista Home Editions.

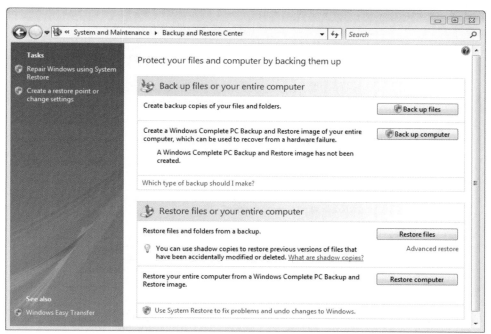

A+
220-802
1.7

Follow these steps to create the initial Complete PC Backup:

1. Connect your backup device to your PC. If you're using an external hard drive, use Windows Explorer to verify you can access the drive.

2. From Control Panel, in the System and Maintenance group, click **Back up your computer**. The Backup and Restore Center window appears, as shown in Figure B-3.

© Cengage Learning 2013

Figure B-3 Windows Vista Backup and Restore Center

3. Click **Back up computer** and respond to the UAC dialog box. Vista displays a list of available backup devices. Select the backup media and click **Next**.

4. In the next window, Vista Backup shows you the Vista volume it will back up and gives you the opportunity to select other volumes it finds to include in the backup. Make your selections and click **Next**.

5. In the next window, the backup tells you the maximum amount of space expected for the backup. If you are backing up to DVDs, the backup tells you about how many DVDs are required. Click **Start backup** to begin the backup.

To use the Complete PC Backup image to restore a corrupted Vista volume, boot from the Vista setup DVD, launch the Windows Recovery Environment (Windows RE), and select **Windows Complete PC Restore** on the System Recovery Options menu. Chapter 6 covers more about using Windows RE.

BACK UP AND RESTORE USER DATA

The Windows Vista Backup and Restore Center limits your decisions about which user files and folders on a Vista system you can back up. In addition, you are forced to back up data for all users.

To set up a backup schedule of user data and settings, open the Backup and Restore Center window, shown earlier in Figure B-3, click **Back up files,** and respond to the UAC box. Following

B

A+
220-802
1.7

windows let you choose where to save the backup, the volumes to back up, and the type of files to back up. The window that allows you to select the type of files to back up is shown in Figure B-4. The next window lets you set the backup schedule.

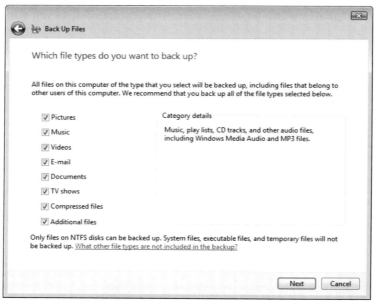

Figure B-4   Select the type of files to back up   © Cengage Learning 2013

To see the status of the last backup and change backup settings, click **Start, All Programs, Accessories, System Tools, Backup Status and Configuration**. The Backup Status and Configuration window opens, as shown in Figure B-5. If you change the settings, a new, full backup is created.

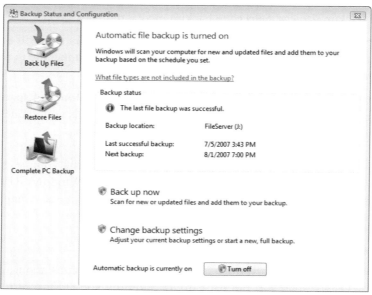

Figure B-5   Backup Status and Configuration window   © Cengage Learning 2013

To restore files from backup, on the Backup Status and Configuration window, click **Restore Files** and follow the directions on-screen to select a specific backup and specific folders or files to restore.

Because Windows Vista backup gives you so little control over the folders you choose to back up, many people turn to third-party backup utilities. If you use one of these utilities, besides the folders that contain your documents, spreadsheets, databases, and other data files, you also might want to back up these folders:

▲ *Your email messages and address book.* For Windows Mail, back up this folder: C:\Users*username*\AppData\Local\Microsoft\Windows Mail.

▲ *Your Internet Explorer favorites list.* To back up your IE favorites list, back up this folder: C:\Users*username*\Favorites.

BACK UP SYSTEM FILES

In Vista, System Protection creates restore points, and System Restore returns the system to a previous restore point the same as in Windows 7. The System Properties box for Vista is shown in Figure B-6. Make sure the drive on which Vista is installed is checked. To manually create a restore point, click **Create**. To apply a restore point, click **System Restore**. Incidentally, you can access this System Properties box in Vista by clicking **Create a restore point or change settings** in the left pane of the Backup and Restore Center window (refer to Figure B-3).

© Cengage Learning 2013

Figure B-6   Make sure System Protection is turned on

B

CHAPTER 4: OPTIMIZING WINDOWS

Following are differences in Windows 7 and Vista that are associated with content covered in Chapter 4.

WINDOWS VISTA SOFTWARE EXPLORER

Windows Vista uses the System Configuration utility to control startup programs just as does Windows 7. In addition, Vista offers Software Explorer, a user-friendly tool to control startup programs. Here is how to use Software Explorer:

1. To open Software Explorer, open Control Panel and click **Change startup programs**. The Windows Defender window opens. Under Category, select **Startup Programs** (see Figure B-7). A list of applications and services that are launched at startup appears.

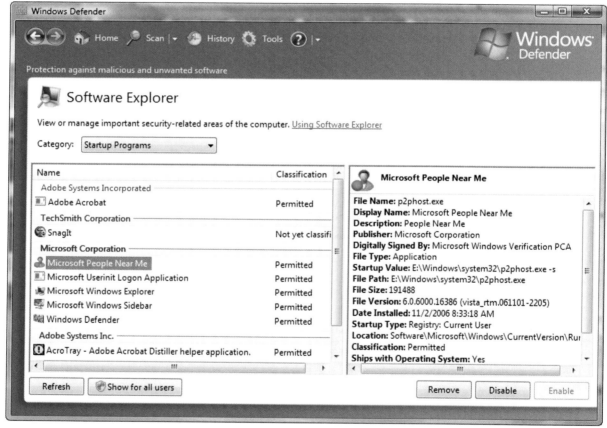

Figure B-7   Use Software Explorer in Vista to find out what programs are launched at startup

© Cengage Learning 2013

2. Select a program on the left to see on the right side how the program is launched at startup. For example, in Figure B-7, the selected program is launched by way of a registry entry. If a startup program is launched by way of a startup folder, the path to the folder is given instead of the registry key.

3. To temporarily disable the selected startup program, click **Disable** at the bottom of the window.

VISTA RELIABILITY AND PERFORMANCE MONITOR

The Windows Vista **Reliability and Performance Monitor (Perfmon.msc)** is an earlier version of three separate Windows 7 tools: Windows 7 Resource Monitor, Reliability Monitor, and Performance Monitor (Perfmon.msc). You can launch the Vista tool from the Computer Management Console or by entering **Perfmon.msc** in the Vista *Search* box. When you first open the monitor window (see Figure B-8), a resource overview appears that is similar to the Overview tab in the Windows 7 Resource Monitor window.

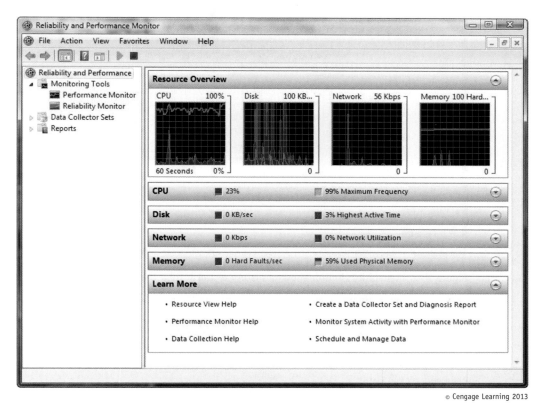

© Cengage Learning 2013

Figure B-8   Reliability and Performance Monitor window shows the Resource Overview screen

Here is how to use the Reliability and Performance Monitor window:

◢ In the left pane, click **Performance Monitor** to see a real-time view of Windows performance counters, which is similar in function to the Windows 7 Performance Monitor. Just as in Windows 7, you can add and delete counters and use data collector sets.

◢ In the left pane, click **Reliability Monitor** to see a pane that gives information similar to the Windows 7 Reliability Monitor. To get detailed information about a problem, click a day that shows an error, and then click the plus sign beside the error's category. For example, in Figure B-9, there was a Windows failure indicated by a red X. When you click the red X or the day the failure occurred, a list of events on that day appears under the graph. Click a plus sign beside the event to see details about the event.

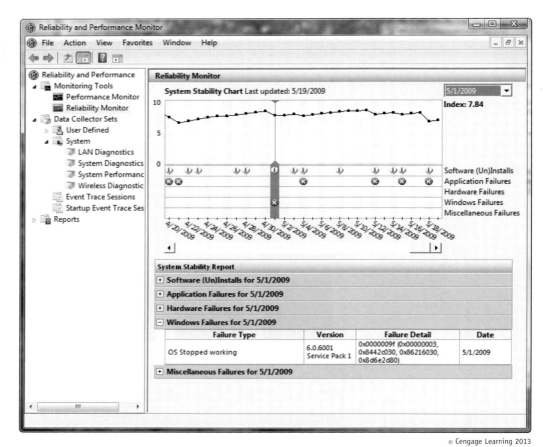

Figure B-9 Reliability Monitor shows a history of the system that can help identify problems with the stability of Windows

CHAPTER 7: CONNECTING TO AND SETTING UP A NETWORK

Following are differences in Windows 7 and Windows Vista that are associated with content covered in Chapter 7.

CONNECT TO A WIRED NETWORK IN VISTA

Follow these steps to connect a Vista computer to a wired network:

1. Open Control Panel, and click **Network and Sharing Center** in the Network and Internet group. In the Network and Sharing Center window (see the top part of Figure B-10), click **Connect to a network**.

2. When Vista recognizes available networks, they are listed in the Connect to a network box shown in the lower part of Figure B-10. If none are shown, click **Diagnose why Windows can't find any networks**. Then follow the recommendations that appear.

If you still do not have connectivity, follow these steps to verify and change TCP/IP settings:

1. In the left pane of the Network and Sharing Center, click **Manage network connections**. In the Network Connections window, right-click **Local Area Connection** and select **Properties** from the shortcut menu. Respond to the UAC box. The properties box appears (see the left side of Figure B-11).

A+
220-802
1.5, 1.6

© Cengage Learning 2013

Figure B-10   Vista Network and Sharing Center manages network connections

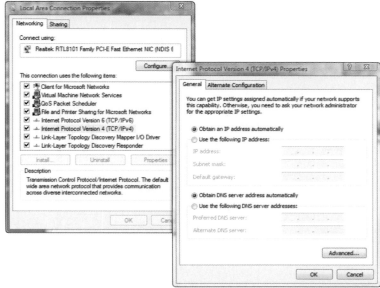

© Cengage Learning 2013

Figure B-11   Verify and change TCP/IP settings

B

2. Select **Internet Protocol Version 4 (TCP/IPv4)** and click **Properties**. The properties box on the right side of Figure B-11 appears. Settings are correct for dynamic IP addressing.

3. To change the settings to static IP addressing, select **Use the following IP address.** Then enter the IP address, subnet mask, and default gateway.

4. If you have been given the IP addresses of DNS servers, check **Use the following DNS server addresses** and enter up to two IP addresses. If you have other DNS IP addresses, click **Advanced** and enter them on the **DNS** tab of the Advanced TCP/IP Settings box.

5. You can also enter settings for an alternate IP address by clicking the Alternate Configuration tab of the Properties box.

CONNECT TO A WIRELESS NETWORK IN VISTA

To connect a Vista computer to a wireless network, follow these steps:

1. Using your mouse, hover over or double-click the network icon in your notification area. Vista reports that wireless networks are available (see Figure B-12).

© Cengage Learning 2013

Figure B-12 Windows reports that wireless networks are available

2. Click **Connect to a network**. A list of available networks appears (see Figure B-13).

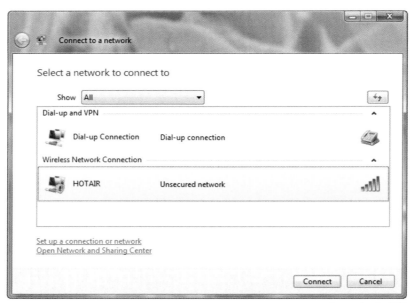

© Cengage Learning 2013

Figure B-13 Select a wireless network

A+
220-802
1.5, 1.6

3. If you select an unsecured network, Vista warns you about sending information over it. Click **Connect Anyway.**

4. Vista reports the connection is made using the window in Figure B-14. If you are comfortable with Vista automatically connecting to this network in the future, check **Save this network.** Close the window. If you hover your mouse pointer over the network icon in the notification area or double-click it, you can see the network to which you are connected (see Figure B-15).

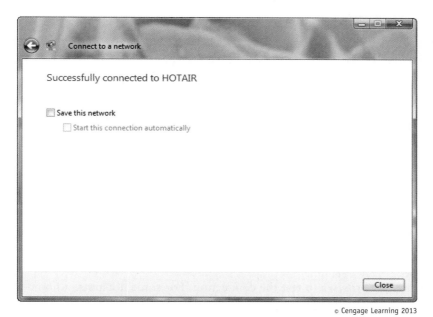

© Cengage Learning 2013

Figure B-14 Decide if you want to save this network connection

© Cengage Learning 2013

Figure B-15 Find out to which network you are connected

5. To verify firewall settings and check for errors, open the Network and Sharing Center window (see Figure B-16). Verify that Vista has configured the network as a public network and that Sharing and Discovery settings are all turned off. If Vista reports it has configured the network as a Private network, click **Customize** and change the setting to Public. In the figure, you can see there is a problem with the Internet connection from the HOTAIR network to the Internet.

B

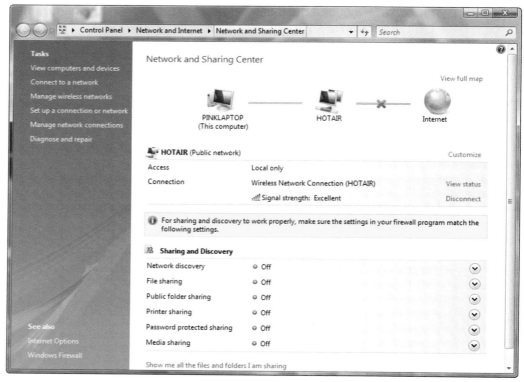

Figure B-16   Verify that your connection is secure

© Cengage Learning 2013

6. Open your browser to test the connection. For some hotspots, a home page appears and you must enter a code or agree to the terms of use.

CHAPTER 8: WINDOWS RESOURCES ON A NETWORK

Following are differences in Windows 7 and Windows Vista that are associated with content covered in Chapter 8.

SUPPORT AND TROUBLESHOOT SHARED FOLDERS AND FILES

The Network and Sharing Center works a little differently in Vista than in Windows 7. If you have problems accessing a shared folder or file on a network, follow these steps using Windows Vista:

1. Open the Network and Sharing Center (see Figure B-17) and verify the following:

   ◢ **File sharing** is turned on.

   ◢ If you want to share the Public folder to the network, turn on **Public folder sharing.**

   ◢ If you want the added protection of requiring that all users on the network must have a valid user account and password on this computer, turn on **Password protected sharing.**

   ◢ If you want to share a printer connected to this PC with others on the network, turn on **Printer sharing.**

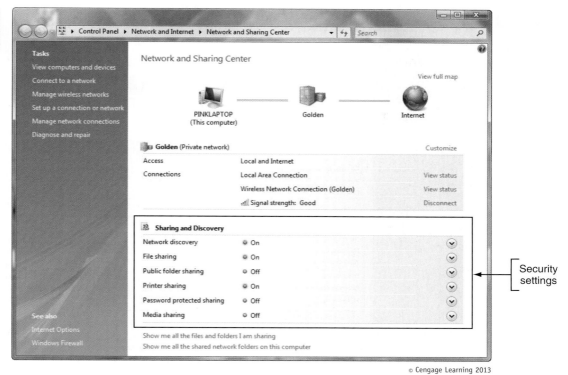

Figure B-17 Use the Network and Sharing Center to verify the computer is set to share resources

2. In the Network and Sharing Center, click **Manage network connections**. In the Network Connections window, right-click the network connection icon, select **Properties** from the shortcut menu, and respond to the UAC box. In the Properties dialog box, verify that **File and Printer Sharing for Microsoft Networks** is checked.

CHAPTER 9: SECURITY STRATEGIES

Following are differences in Windows 7 and Windows Vista that are associated with content covered in Chapter 9.

CONFIGURE WINDOWS FIREWALL IN VISTA

For Windows Vista, to see how firewall protection is set for a public or private network, use the Network and Sharing Center window. Follow these steps:

1. Click **Start**, right-click **Network**, and select **Properties** from the shortcut menu. The Network and Sharing Center window opens.

2. For the window showing in Figure B-18, the computer is connected to a wired and wireless network. The wired network is set to Private, and the wireless network is set to Public. Because the computer is connected to a public network, the Sharing and Discovery settings at the bottom of the window are set for maximum protection. To change the security setting for the Public network, click **Customize**.

B

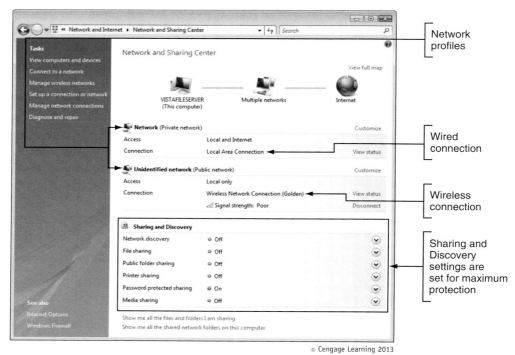

© Cengage Learning 2013

Figure B-18 Security is high when connected to a public network

3. The Set Network Location box appears (see Figure B-19). To allow for less security and more communication on the network, click **Private** and then click **Next**.

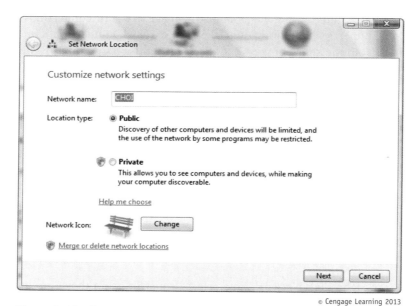

© Cengage Learning 2013

Figure B-19 Change the security settings for a network

4. Sharing and Discovery settings are now less secure, allowing the PC to be seen on the network (Network discovery), files on the PC to be shared with others on the network (File sharing), and printers installed on this PC to be shared (Printer sharing). These are the standard settings for a private network. To change a setting under the Sharing and Discovery group, click the down arrow to the right of the item and turn the item on or off (see Figure B-20).

A+
220-802
1.5

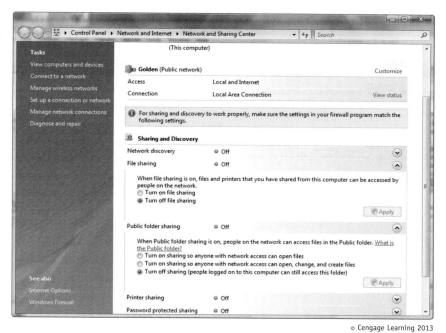

© Cengage Learning 2013

Figure B-20 Change the setting of an item under the Sharing and Discovery group

To see how Windows Firewall is configured for Vista, follow these steps:

1. For Vista, in the left pane of the Network and Sharing Center window, click **Windows Firewall**. The Windows Firewall dialog box opens (see Figure B-21). No matter what type of network you are connected to, Windows Firewall should always be turned on unless you are using a third-party software firewall instead of Windows Firewall.

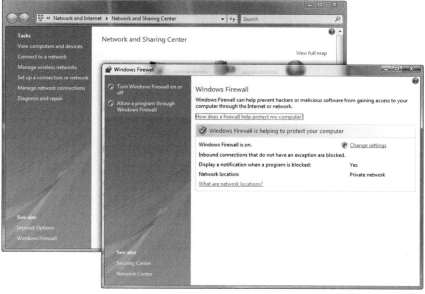

© Cengage Learning 2013

Figure B-21 Windows Firewall is turned on

2. To see the details of how Windows Firewall is working, click **Change settings** and respond to the UAC box. The Windows Firewall Settings box opens (see Figure B-22).

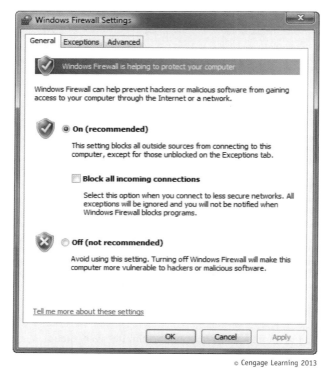

© Cengage Learning 2013

Figure B-22 Windows Firewall is on but not working at its highest security level

3. Notice the check box for *Block all incoming connections*, which controls communication initiated from another computer. For a private network, Vista does not check this box. When connected to a public network, the box is checked. To see what incoming connections are allowed, click the **Exceptions** tab (as shown on the left side of Figure B-23).

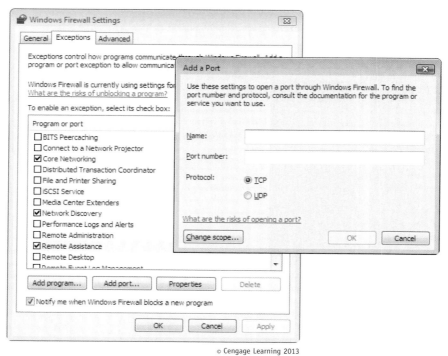

© Cengage Learning 2013

Figure B-23 Exceptions allowed for incoming connections can be made by program or port

A+
220-802
1.5

4. You can change individual settings on this Exceptions tab by checking or unchecking items. For example, notice in Figure B-23 that File and Printer Sharing is not checked. If you want to allow another computer to initiate communication with this computer to access a shared file or printer, check this item. Recall that a computer uses a port number to control incoming activity from client applications or programs on the network. This Exceptions box controls these ports. Each item in the list is associated with one or more ports, which are opened or closed based on the settings on this tab.

5. If you want to make sure a specific port is open, such as when you use a nondefault port for a program, click **Add port**. In the Add a Port box (see the right side of Figure B-23), enter a name for the port and the port number and click **OK**.

6. After you have Windows Firewall configured the way you want it, click **OK** to close the Windows Firewall Settings window.

Windows XP

This appendix covers the major differences between Windows 7 and Windows XP. The content here applies to several chapters in the book. After you learn about Windows 7 in a chapter, turn to this appendix to learn how Windows XP differs.

CHAPTER 1: INTRODUCING WINDOWS OPERATING SYSTEMS

Following are differences in Windows 7 and Windows XP that are associated with content covered in Chapter 1.

A+
220-802
1.1

DIFFERENCES IN THE WINDOWS XP DESKTOP AND THE WINDOWS 7 DESKTOP

The Windows XP desktop and Start menu is shown in Figure C-1. When you first install Windows 7 and Windows XP, only the Recycle Bin shows on the desktop by default. (Vista shows the Recycle bin and the sidebar on the desktop.)

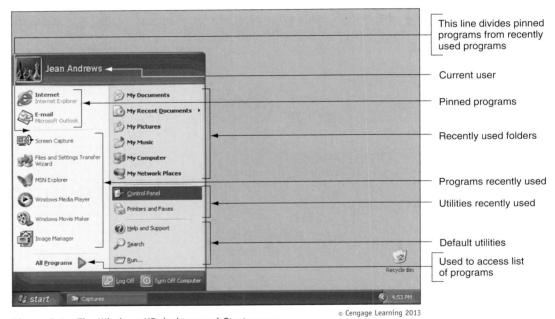

© Cengage Learning 2013

Figure C-1   The Windows XP desktop and Start menu

You can use the Display Properties box in XP to control the Start menu and taskbar. Right-click the desktop and select **Properties** from the shortcut menu. The left side of Figure C-2 shows the Display Properties box that appears with the Desktop tab selected. The right side of Figure C-2 shows the Desktop Items dialog box that appears when you click Customize Desktop. You can accomplish about the same things using the Windows 7 and Vista Personalization window and the XP Display Properties box, but they are organized differently.

When you first install Windows 7 and Windows XP, only the Recycle Bin shows on the desktop by default. (Vista shows the sidebar on the desktop.) In XP, you can add other shortcuts by using the Desktop Items box shown in Figure C-2. You can check My Documents, My Computer, My Network Places, and Internet Explorer to add these icons to the desktop. Also notice on this window the option to have Windows clean up your desktop by moving any shortcuts that you have not used in the last 60 days to a separate folder.

C

A+
220-802
1.1

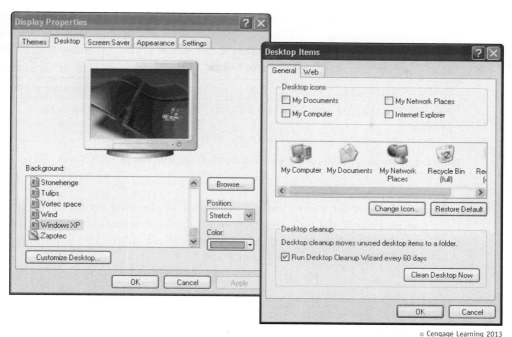

© Cengage Learning 2013

Figure C-2 Windows XP Display Properties window lets you change settings for your desktop

CHAPTER 2: INSTALLING WINDOWS

Following are differences in Windows 7 and Windows XP that are associated with content covered in Chapter 2.

A+
220-802
1.1, 1.2

HOW TO PREPARE FOR AND INSTALL WINDOWS XP

Windows XP comes in these editions:

▲ **Windows XP Home Edition** targets the home computer market. It supports the FAT, FAT32, and NTFS file systems as do all the editions of XP. It is a 32-bit OS and can support up to 4 GB of memory.

▲ **Windows XP Professional** targets the business market. Features not in the Home Edition include the ability to join a domain, Group Policy, Offline Files and Folders, Encrypting File System, Remote Desktop, Automated System Recovery, multilingual capabilities, and support for multiple processors.

▲ **Windows XP Professional x64 Edition** (formally called Windows XP 64-Bit Edition) is a 64-bit operating system and can support up to 128 GB of memory. (All other editions of XP are 32-bit and can support up to 4 GB of memory.)

▲ **Windows XP Media Center Edition** is an enhanced edition of Windows XP Professional, and includes additional support for digital entertainment hardware such as video recording integrated with TV input.

▲ **Windows XP Tablet PC Edition** is designed for laptops and tablet PCs.

Table C-1 lists the minimum and recommended requirements for Windows XP Professional.

A+
220-802
1.1, 1.2

Component or Device	Minimum Requirement	Recommended Requirement
One or two CPUs	Pentium II 233 MHz or better	Pentium II 300 MHz or better
RAM	64 MB	128 MB up to 4 GB
Hard drive partition	2 GB	More than 2 GB
Free space on the hard drive partition	1.5 GB (bare bones)	2 GB or more

© Cengage Learning 2013

Table C-1   Minimum and Recommended Requirements for Windows XP Professional

Next we look at the steps to install Windows XP. Because the OS is so old and can no longer be purchased, the only situation you can expect to encounter is reinstalling XP when the current XP installation gets corrupted or installing XP on a new hard drive that has replaced a failed drive in an XP system.

Notes For more detailed content on installing Windows XP, look on this textbook's companion web site for the content, "Installing Windows 2000/XP." See the Preface at the beginning of this book for how to access the web site.

Here are the general steps to install Windows XP:

1. As for any OS installation, back up data files and perform other tasks to prepare for an operating system installation. These steps are listed in Chapter 2 and are not repeated here.

Notes An error might occur during the XP installation if files on the hard drive are using a path and filename that together exceed 256 characters. To get around this problem, if you have a path (folders and filenames) that exceeds 256 characters, before you begin the installation move these folders and files to another media such as a USB drive or another computer on the network. Later, you can restore the folders and files to the hard drive. After the installation, you might find these folders and files still on the hard drive although filenames might be truncated.

2. Start the XP installation using one of these methods:

   ◢ For any edition of Windows XP, boot from the Windows XP setup CD. A setup menu appears from which you can start a clean installation of XP (see Figure C-3). Press **Enter** to start the installation.

Notes At the beginning of the Windows XP installation, if you need to use third-party drivers such as when your computer has multiple hard drives installed in a RAID array or uses SCSI or some SATA hard drives, press F6 when the blue screen appears. You can then install the XP RAID, SCSI, or SATA drivers that will be used by the XP setup process.

C

A+
220-802
1.1, 1.2

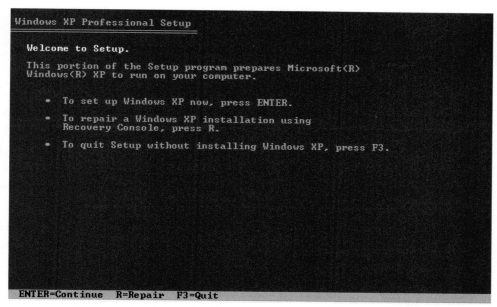

```
Windows XP Professional Setup

Welcome to Setup.

This portion of the Setup program prepares Microsoft(R)
Windows(R) XP to run on your computer.

    • To set up Windows XP now, press ENTER.

    • To repair a Windows XP installation using
      Recovery Console, press R.

    • To quit Setup without installing Windows XP, press F3.




ENTER=Continue   R=Repair   F3=Quit
```

Figure C-3   Windows XP setup opening menu   © Cengage Learning 2013

◢ If you can start Windows, use the following command for any 32-bit installation of
Windows XP, substituting the drive letter of your CD drive for D in the command line:

   D:\i386\Winnt32.exe

When you start the installation from within Windows, the Setup menu in Figure C-4
appears. Select **Install Windows XP**. On the next screen, under Installation Type, select
New Installation. The installation begins. (If you were upgrading an OS to Windows XP,
under New Installations, you would select Upgrade and then choose Express Upgrade or
Custom Upgrade.)

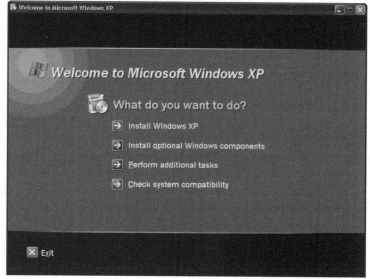

Figure C-4   Windows XP Setup menu   © Cengage Learning 2013

A+
220-802
1.1, 1.2

▲ When reinstalling Windows XP Professional x64 Edition, boot from the Windows setup CD. Alternately, you can start the installation using the following command line after Windows XP Professional x64 Edition has started:

```
D:\AMD64\Winnt32.exe
```

For 64-bit installations, the installation routine uses files stored in both the \AMD64 and \i386 folders.

3. Accept the End-User License agreement. Decide which partition and which file system to use for Windows. You can choose between FAT32 and NTFS. Choose NTFS unless the size of the volume is 2 GB or less. FAT32 does not use as much overhead as NTFS and is a better choice for these smaller volumes.

4. Select or assign values for your geographical location, your name, the name of your organization, and your product key. (The product key must be entered before the installation will continue.)

Notes If you have lost the Windows XP product key and you can start the old installation of XP, you can use a utility to find out the product key. Use a search engine such as Google.com to search for a key finder utility such as Magical Jelly Bean Keyfinder. Download and run the keyfinder, but be careful to only download from reliable web sites you trust.

5. Enter the computer name and the password for the local Administrator account. Select the date, time, time zone, and network settings. (Most likely you need to install Client for Microsoft Networks and File and Printer Sharing, and select dynamic IP addresses.) Enter a workgroup or domain name. Expect the computer to reboot three or more times during the installation.

Notes It is *very* important that you remember the Administrator password. You cannot log on to the system without it.

After you have installed XP, you need to do similar chores as you learned to do after installing Windows 7. Keep these differences in mind:

▲ *Windows XP uses the Network Setup Wizard.* To set up a new connection to the network, open Control Panel, and then click **Network and Internet Connections**. In the Network and Internet Connections window, click **Set up or change your home or small office network**. The Network Setup Wizard launches to step you through the process of connecting to the network.

▲ *Windows XP uses My Network Places.* To access the network, click **Start, My Network Places**. If you don't see network resources, try rebooting the PC. Use Device Manager to verify that the network card is installed and functioning with no errors. You might need to install device drivers for the network card or for the motherboard network port. To open Device Manager in XP, click **Start**, right-click **My Computer**, select **Properties** from the shortcut menu, and then select the **Hardware** tab from the System Properties window. Finally, click **Device Manager**.

A+
220-802
1.1, 1.2

> 🔮 **A+ Exam Tip** If you don't see My Network Places on the Start menu, you can add it. Right-click **Start** and select **Properties**. On the **Start menu** tab of the Taskbar and Start menu Properties box, click **Customize**. In the Customize Start Menu box, click the **Advanced** tab. Check **My Network Places** and click **OK** twice to close both boxes.

◢ *Windows XP uses the System Properties box to configure automatic updates.* Click **Start**, right-click **My Computer**, and select **Properties** from the shortcut menu. The System Properties box appears where you can see what service packs have been applied (see Figure C-5). Click the **Automatic Updates** tab to configure automatic updates.

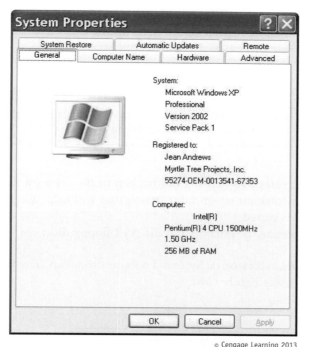

© Cengage Learning 2013

Figure C-5 Use the System Properties box to find out what Windows XP service packs are installed

◢ *Windows XP uses the Add or Remove Programs applet to install and configure XP components.* To install an XP component that was not installed during the installation, open the Add or Remove Programs applet in Control Panel. Click **Add/Remove Windows Components**. Check a component you want to install and click **Next**.

◢ *Windows XP uses the Files and Settings Transfer Wizard.* This tool is used to transfer user data and settings from one XP installation to another when a domain is not involved. Instructions to use the tool can be found in XP Help and Support.

◢ *Windows XP uses the User Accounts applet to create user accounts.* To create a new account in Windows XP, open the **User Accounts** applet in Control Panel and click **Create a new account**. Enter an account name and click **Next**. For the privilege level of the account, select either Computer administrator or Limited. Click **Create Account**.

CHAPTER 3: MAINTAINING WINDOWS

Following are differences in Windows 7 and Windows XP that are associated with content covered in Chapter 3.

A+
220-802
1.7

CREATE AND USE BACKUPS IN WINDOWS XP

Backup procedures in Windows XP vary significantly from those in Windows 7. In this part of the appendix, we look at how to back up the entire Windows volume, Windows system files, and user data.

WINDOWS XP AUTOMATED SYSTEM RECOVERY

You can use the Windows XP **Automated System Recovery (ASR)** tool, which is part of the Windows XP Backup utility (Ntbackup.exe), to back up the entire volume on which Windows is installed, most likely drive C:.

> **Notes** By default, Windows XP Home Edition does not automatically install the Backup utility. To install it manually, go to the \VALUEADD\MSFT\NTBACKUP folder on your Windows XP setup CD and double-click **Ntbackup.msi**. The installation wizard will complete the installation.

The ASR backup process creates two items: a full backup of the drive on which Windows is installed and an ASR floppy disk on which information that will help Windows use Automated System Recovery is stored.

Follow these directions to create the backup and the ASR floppy disk:

1. Click **Start**, **All Programs**, **Accessories**, **System Tools**, and **Backup**. The Backup or Restore Wizard appears (see Figure C-6).

Figure C-6   Backup or Restore Wizard

© Cengage Learning 2013

A+
220-802
1.7

2. Click the **Advanced Mode** link. The Backup Utility window appears (see Figure C-7). On the Welcome tab, click **Automated System Recovery Wizard**. Then click **Next**.

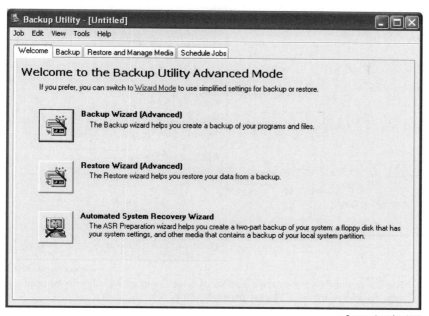

© Cengage Learning 2013

Figure C-7 Use the XP Backup Utility to create a backup of the Windows XP volume

3. Select the location of the backup and insert a disk into the floppy disk drive. This disk will become the ASR disk. Click **Next** and click **Finish**.

Notes The ASR process assumes you have a floppy disk drive. If your computer does not have this drive, you can use an external floppy drive. If you don't have either, it's possible to skip the step of making the ASR disk at the time you make the ASR backup. However, you must make the ASR disk later before you can perform the ASR restore. And, a floppy disk drive is required to perform an ASR restore unless you use third-party software to get around this requirement. For an example of this software, see the Acronis web site at *www.acronis.com*.

4. The backup process shows its progress, as seen in Figure C-8. When the backup is finished, label the disk with the name "ASR Disk," the date it was created, and the computer's name, and put the disk in a safe place.

You will learn how to use the ASR backup to recover from a failed Windows volume later in this appendix.

A+ Exam Tip The A+ 220-802 exam expects you to know how to create and use the XP Automated System Recovery.

BACK UP WINDOWS XP SYSTEM FILES

Windows XP offers two tools for backing up its system files: System Restore, used to create restore points, and the XP Backup Utility.

A+
220-802
1.7

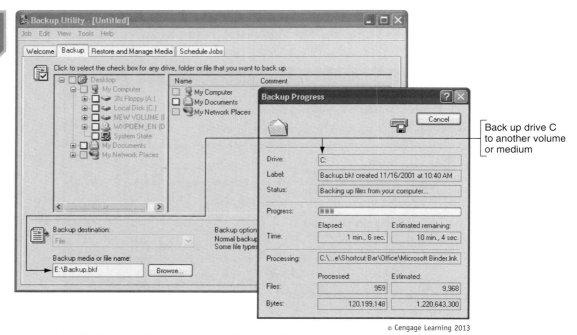

© Cengage Learning 2013

Figure C-8 The Backup utility can create a backup of drive C and an ASR disk to be used later for the Automated System Recovery utility

Use System Restore

Here is how to use XP System Restore:

◢ Click **Start,** right-click **My Computer,** and select **Properties.** The System Properties box opens. Click the **System Restore** tab (see Figure C-9). Using this box, you can turn on or off System Restore that creates restore points.

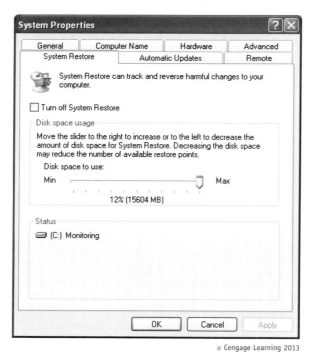

© Cengage Learning 2013

Figure C-9 Use the System Properties box to turn on or off System Restore that creates restore points

C

A+
220-802
1.7

◢ To manually create a restore point or apply a restore point, click **Start, All Programs, Accessories, System Tools,** and **System Restore.** In the System Restore dialog box, select **Create a restore point** or **Restore my computer to an earlier time.**

You can use the XP Backup utility to back up the system state data, which are the files critical to a successful operating system load. This backup includes all files necessary to boot the OS, the Windows XP registry, and all system files in the root directory of the Windows volume.

Back Up the System State

Here is how to back up the system state:

1. Click **Start, All Programs, Accessories, System Tools,** and **Backup.** The Backup or Restore Wizard appears (refer back to Figure C-6). Click **Advanced Mode.** On the Backup Utility window, click the **Backup** tab (see Figure C-10).

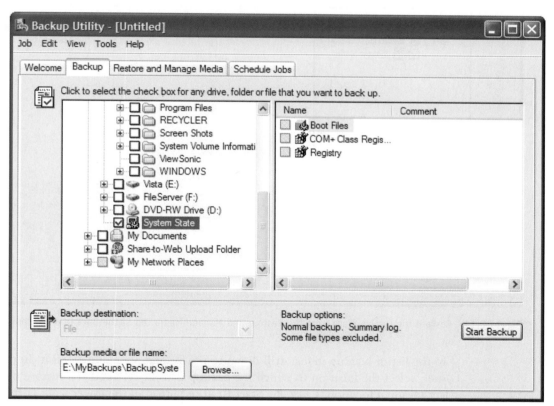

Figure C-10   Back up the Windows XP/2000 system state

© Cengage Learning 2013

2. Check the **System State** box in the list of items you can back up. Notice in Figure C-10 that the system state includes the boot files and the registry. It also includes the COM+ (Component Object Model) Class Registration Database, which contains information about applications and includes files in the Windows folders.

3. Click **Browse** to point to where you want the backup saved. You can back up to any media, including a second hard drive, USB drive, or network drive. Click **Start Backup.** A dialog box appears where you can decide to append the backup to the media or replace the data on the media with this backup. Make your selection, and click **Start Backup** again.

A+
220-802
1.7

> **Notes** When you back up the system state, the registry is also backed up to the folder C:\repair \RegBack. If you later have a corrupted registry, you can copy files from this folder to the registry folder, which is C:\System32\Config.

If Windows gives errors or the registry gets corrupted, you can restore the system to the state it was in when the last System State backup was made. To do that, open the Backup Utility window and select the **Restore and Manage Media** tab, which is shown in Figure C-11.

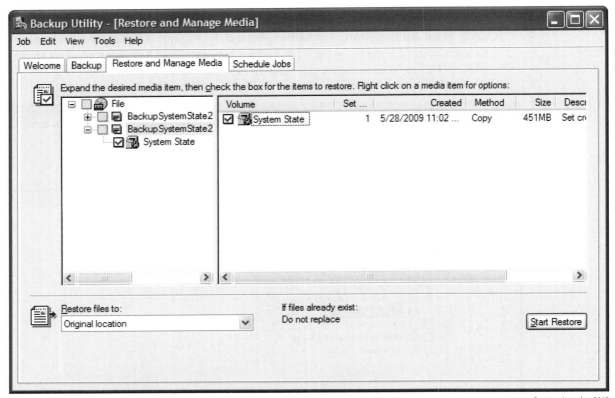

© Cengage Learning 2013

Figure C-11   Restore the system state from the Restore and Manage Media tab of the Backup dialog box

In the list of backup items, drill down to the System State and select it. In the lower-left corner, select the location to which the backup is to be restored. To restore the system state, select **Original location**. Click the **Start Restore** button in the lower-right corner. A warning box appears stating that you will overwrite the existing state. Click **OK** to start the process. Remember that you can restore the system state as a way of restoring the registry.

BACK UP USER DATA WITH WINDOWS XP

The Windows XP Backup utility (Ntbackup.exe) supports several types of scheduled backups:

▲ *Full backup (also called a normal backup).* All files selected for backup are copied to the backup media. Each file is marked as backed up by clearing its archive attribute. Later, if you need to recover data, this full backup is all you need. (After the backup, if a file is changed, its archive attribute is turned on to indicate the file has changed since its last backup.)

▲ *Copy backup.* All files selected for backup are copied to the backup media, but files are not marked as backed up (meaning file archive attributes are not cleared). A Copy backup is useful if you want to make a backup apart from your regularly scheduled backups.

▲ *Incremental backup.* All files that have been created or changed since the last backup are backed up, and all files are marked as backed up (meaning file archive attributes are cleared). Later, if you need to recover data, you'll need the last full backup and all the incremental backups since this last full backup.

▲ *Differential backup.* All files that have been created or changed since the last full or incremental backup are backed up, and files are not marked as backed up. Later, if you need to recover data, you'll need the last full backup and the last differential backup.

▲ *Daily backup.* All files that have been created or changed on this day are backed up. Files are not marked as backed up. Later, if you need to recover data, you'll need the last full backup and all daily backups since this last full backup.

The two best ways to schedule backups are a combination of full backups and incremental backups, or a combination of full backups and differential backups. When using a full backup and incremental backups to restore all the data, you must use a full backup and all the incremental backups since the full backup was made. When using a full backup and differential backups, you only need the full backup and the last differential backup.

For a business with heavy data entry, suppose you decide you need to back up every night at 11:55 PM. To implement this backup plan, you might decide to schedule two backups: a full backup each Friday at 11:55 PM, and a differential backup each Monday, Tuesday, Wednesday, and Thursday at 11:55 PM.

To schedule a backup, do the following:

1. Open the backup utility and click the **Schedule Jobs** tab, as shown in Figure C-12. Select a date on which you want to schedule a backup, and then click the **Add Job** button.

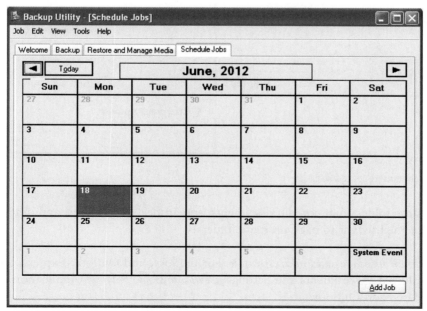

© Cengage Learning 2013

Figure C-12   The Schedule Jobs tab of the Windows XP Backup Utility window

2. The Backup Wizard opens. Follow the directions on-screen to make these selections:

▲ Chose to back up files, drives, or network data that you select.
▲ Select the drives, folders, or files you want to back up.
▲ Select the storage device and folder to save the backup.
▲ Assign a name to the backup file.
▲ Select the type of backup (Normal, Copy, Incremental, Differential, or Daily). Recall that a Normal backup is a full backup.
▲ Decide whether you want to verify the data after the backup and compress the data.
▲ Decide whether you want to append the data to an existing backup or replace an existing backup.
▲ To choose to perform the backup later, select **Later** and give the job a name, as shown on the left side of Figure C-13.
▲ Decide how often the backup will occur (see the right side of Figure C-13 where the backup is scheduled for each Monday, Tuesday, Wednesday, and Thursday at 11:55 PM.

3. When the wizard completes, it gives you an on-screen report summarizing information about the backup.

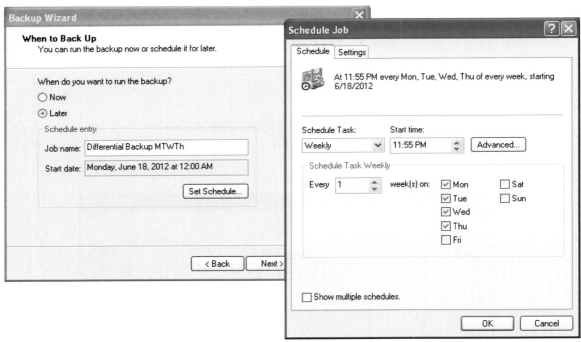

© Cengage Learning 2013

Figure C-13 Schedule repeated backups

Besides the folders that contain documents, spreadsheets, databases, and other data files, you also might want to back up these folders:

▲ *Email messages and address book*. For Outlook and Outlook Express, back up this folder: C:\Documents and Settings*username*\Local Settings\Application Data \Microsoft\Outlook.
▲ *Internet Explorer favorites list*. To back up an IE favorites list, back up this folder: C:\Documents and Settings*username*\Favorites.

A+
220-802
1.7

To recover files, folders, or the entire drive from backup using the Windows XP Backup utility, click the **Restore and Manage Media** tab on the Backup Utility window, and then select the backup job to use for the restore. The Backup utility displays the folders and files that were backed up with this job. You can select the ones that you want to restore.

CHAPTER 4: OPTIMIZING WINDOWS

Following are differences in Windows 7 and Windows XP that are associated with content covered in Chapter 4.

A+
220-802
1.4

TASK MANAGER IN WINDOWS XP

Windows 7/Vista Task Manager has six tabs: Applications, Processes, Services, Performance, Networking, and Users. Windows XP Task Manager does not have the Services tab (see Figure C-14). The Windows XP Users tab shows only when a system is set for Fast User Switching and lets you monitor other users logged onto the system. Figure C-14 shows the list of processes for a Windows XP system immediately after the installation was completed with no applications installed.

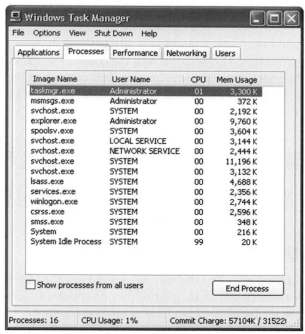

© Cengage Learning 2013

Figure C-14   This Processes tab of Windows XP Task Manager shows Windows processes before any applications are installed

WINDOWS XP PERFORMANCE MONITOR

Windows XP offers the Performance Monitor tool, also called the System Monitor. To open Performance Monitor, open **Control Panel**, and click **Administrative Tools** in the Performance and Maintenance group. Then double-click **Performance**. The Performance window is shown in Figure C-15.

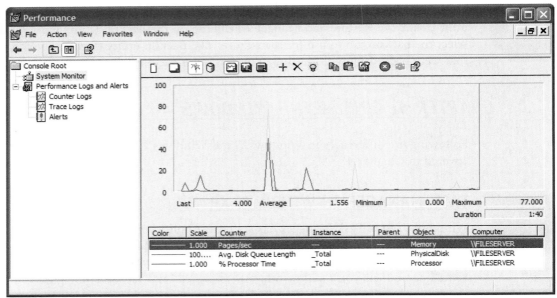

Figure C-15 Windows XP Performance Monitor (also called the System Monitor)

> 🔆 **A+ Exam Tip** The A+ 220-802 exam expects you to be able to use the Control Panel in Classic View.

When you first open the window, System Monitor is selected and shows a graph presenting data collected by counters. This window and the counters work the same as the Windows 7/Vista Performance Monitor window. You can drill down into the Performance Logs and Alerts group in the left pane to start and stop groups of counters that work similarly to Windows 7/Vista data collector sets.

CHAPTER 6: TROUBLESHOOTING WINDOWS STARTUP PROBLEMS

Following are differences in Windows 7 and Windows XP that are associated with content covered in Chapter 6.

WHAT HAPPENS WHEN WINDOWS XP STARTS UP

A Windows XP system has started up when the user has logged on, the Windows desktop is loaded, and the hourglass associated with the pointer has disappeared. Table C-2 outlines the steps in the boot sequence for Intel-based computers up to the point that the boot loader program, Ntldr, turns control over to the Windows core component program, Ntoskrnl.exe.

Step	Step Performed By	Description
1.	Startup BIOS	Startup BIOS runs the POST (power-on self test).
2.	Startup BIOS	Startup BIOS turns to the hard drive to find an OS. It first loads the MBR (Master Boot Record) and runs the master boot program within the MBR. (Recall that the master boot program is at the very beginning of the hard drive, before the partition table information.)

Table C-2 Steps in The Windows XP boot process for systems with Intel-based processors (continues)

Step	Step Performed By	Description
3.	MBR program	The MBR program uses partition table information to find the active partition. It then loads the OS boot sector (also called the OS boot record) from the active partition and runs the program in this boot sector.
4.	Boot sector program	This boot sector program launches Ntldr (NT Loader).
5.	Ntldr, the Windows XP boot loader program	Ntldr launches the minifile system drivers so that files can be read from either a FAT system or an NTFS file system on the hard drive.
6.	Ntldr	Ntldr reads the Boot.ini file, a hidden text file that contains information about installed OSs on the hard drive. For a dual boot, Ntldr displays a boot loader menu for the user to select an OS to load.
7.	Ntldr	If the user chooses Windows XP, then the loader runs Ntdetect.com, a 16-bit real mode program that queries the computer for time and date (taken from CMOS RAM) and surveys hardware (buses, drives, mouse, ports). Ntdetect passes the information back to Ntldr. This information is used later to update the Windows XP registry concerning the Last Known Good hardware profile used.
8.	Ntldr	Ntldr then loads Ntoskrnl.exe, Hal.dll, and the System hive. Recall that the System hive is a portion of the registry that includes hardware information used to load the proper device drivers for the hardware that's present. Ntldr then loads these device drivers.
9.	Ntldr	Ntldr passes control to Ntoskrnl.exe; Ntoskrnl.exe continues to load the Windows desktop and the supporting Windows environment.

© Cengage Learning 2013

Table C-2   Steps in The Windows XP boot process for systems with Intel-based processors (continued)

FILES NEEDED TO START WINDOWS XP

The files needed to start Windows XP successfully are listed in Table C-3. Several of these system files form the core components of XP.

File	Location and Description
Ntldr	◢ Located in the root folder of the system partition (usually C:\) ◢ Boot loader program
Boot.ini	◢ Located in the root folder of the system partition (usually C:\) ◢ Text file contains boot parameters
Bootsect.dos	◢ Located in the root folder of the system partition (usually C:\) ◢ Used to load another OS in a dual-boot environment
Ntdetect.com	◢ Located in the root folder of the system partition (usually C:\) ◢ Real-mode program detects hardware present
Ntbootdd.sys	◢ Located in the root folder of the system partition (usually C:\) ◢ Required only if a SCSI boot device is used

© Cengage Learning 2013

Table C-3   Files needed to boot Windows XP successfully (continues)

A+
220-802
1.3

File	Location and Description
Ntoskrnl.exe	◢ Located in C:\Windows\system32* folder of the boot partition ◢ Core component of the OS executive and kernel services
Hal.dll	◢ Located in C:\Windows\system32 folder of the boot partition ◢ Hardware abstraction layer
Ntdll.dll	◢ Located in C:\Windows\system32 folder of the boot partition ◢ Intermediating service to executive services; provides many support functions
Win32k.sys Kernel32.dll Advapi32.dll User32.dll Gdi32.dll	◢ Located in C:\Windows\system32 folder of the boot partition ◢ Core components of the Win32 subsystem
System	◢ Located in C:\Windows\system32\config folder of the boot partition ◢ Registry hive that holds hardware configuration data, including which device drivers need loading at startup
Device drivers	◢ Multiple files located in C:\Windows\system32\drivers folder of the boot partition ◢ Windows and third-party drivers needed for startup
Pagefile.sys	◢ Located in the root folder of the system partition (usually C:\) ◢ Virtual memory swap file

*It is assumed that Windows is installed in the C:\Windows folder.

Table C-3   Files needed to boot Windows XP successfully (continued)   © Cengage Learning 2013

THE BOOT.INI FILE

One key file used by Windows XP startup is Boot.ini. Recall that the **Boot.ini** file is a hidden text file stored in the root directory of the active partition that Ntldr reads to see what operating systems are available and how to set up the boot. You can view and edit the Boot.ini file, which might be necessary when you are trying to solve a difficult boot problem. Figure C-16 shows an example of a Boot.ini file for Windows XP.

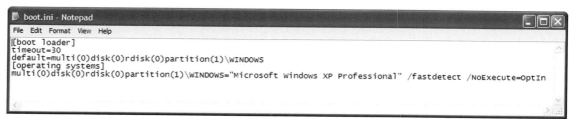

Figure C-16   A sample Windows XP Boot.ini file   © Cengage Learning 2013

Before you can view or edit the Boot.ini file using a text editor such as Notepad, you must first change the folder options to view hidden system files. To do so, open **Windows Explorer**, select the root directory, click **Tools** on the menu bar, click **Folder Options**, and then select the **View** tab. Uncheck the option to **Hide protected operating system files**.

There are two main sections in Boot.ini: the [boot loader] section and the [operating systems] section. The [boot loader] section contains the number of seconds the system gives the user to select an operating system before it loads the default operating system; this is called a timeout. In Figure C-16, the timeout is set to 30 seconds, the default value.

C

A+
220-802
1.3

If the system is set for a dual boot, the path to the default operating system is also listed in the [boot loader] section.

The [operating systems] section of the Boot.ini file provides a list of operating systems that can be loaded, including the path to the boot partition of each operating system. Here is the meaning of each entry in Figure C-16:

- ◢ *Multi(0).* Use the first hard drive controller.
- ◢ *Disk(0).* Use only when booting from a SCSI hard drive.
- ◢ *Rdisk(0).* Use the first hard drive.
- ◢ *Partition(1).* Use the first partition on the drive.

Switches are sometimes used in the [operating systems] section. In Figure C-16, the first switch used in this Boot.ini file is /fastdetect, which causes the OS not to attempt to inspect any peripherals connected to a COM port (serial port) at startup.

The second switch is /NoExecute=OptIn. This switch is new with Windows XP Service Pack 2 and is used to configure Data Execution Prevention (DEP). DEP stops a program if it tries to use a protected area of memory, which some viruses attempt to do.

Although you can change the Boot.ini file by editing it, a better way to make changes is by using the System Properties box. To access it, right-click My Computer and select Properties from the shortcut menu. Several of the startup and recovery options that you can change in this box are recorded as changes to Boot.ini.

A+
220-802
1.3, 4.6

TROUBLESHOOT PROBLEMS WITH XP STARTUP

When Windows XP startup fails, try to use options on the Advanced Options Menu, which can help fix problems with faulty device drivers or system services. To access the Advanced Options Menu, press **F8** near the beginning of the boot. The tools on this menu work as they do in Windows 7.

If the tools on this menu don't help, turn to the Emergency Repair Disk and then the Recovery Console. If XP still cannot start, use the Automated System Recovery to recover the XP installation.

WINDOWS XP EMERGENCY REPAIR DISK

A Windows XP emergency repair disk is a bootable floppy disk that can be used to boot the system bypassing the boot files stored in the root directory of drive C. If you boot from the disk and the Windows XP desktop loads successfully, then the problem is associated with damaged sectors or missing or damaged files in the root directory of drive C that are required to boot the OS. These sectors and files include the master boot program; the partition table; the OS boot record; the boot files named Ntldr file, Ntdetect.com file, and Ntbootdd.sys (if it exists); and the Boot.ini file. In addition, the problem can be caused by a boot sector virus. However, an emergency repair disk cannot be used to troubleshoot problems associated with unstable device drivers or any other system files stored in the \Windows folder or its subfolders.

You first create the boot disk by formatting the disk using a working Windows XP computer and then copying files to the disk. These files can be copied from a Windows XP setup CD or a Windows XP computer that is using the same version of Windows XP as the problem PC. Do the following to create the disk:

1. Obtain a floppy disk and format it on a Windows XP computer.

2. Using Explorer, copy Ntldr and Ntdetect.com from the i386 folder on the Windows XP setup CD or a Windows XP computer to the root of the floppy disk.

3. If your computer boots from a SCSI hard drive, then obtain a device driver (*.sys) for your SCSI hard drive, rename it **Ntbootdd.sys**, and copy it to the root of the floppy disk. (If you used an incorrect device driver, then you will receive an error after booting from the floppy disk. The error will mention a "computer disk hardware configuration problem" and that it "could not read from the selected boot disk." If this occurs, contact your computer manufacturer or hard drive manufacturer for the correct version of the SCSI hard drive device driver for your computer.)

4. Look at Boot.ini on the problem computer, and then obtain an identical copy from another known good computer (or create your own) and copy it to the root of the floppy disk.

5. If you can't find a good Boot.ini file to copy, you can use the following lines to create a Boot.ini file. These lines work for a Boot.ini file if the problem computer is booting from an IDE hard drive:

```
[boot loader]

timeout530

default5multi(0)disk(0)rdisk(0)partition(1)\WINDOWS

[operating systems]

multi(0)disk(0)rdisk(0)partition(1)\WINDOWS5"Microsoft
Windows XP Professional" /fastdetect
```

6. Write-protect the floppy disk so that it cannot become infected with a virus.

7. You have now created the Windows XP boot disk. Check BIOS setup to make sure the first boot device is set to the floppy disk, and then insert the boot disk and reboot your computer.

> **Notes** If you are creating your own Boot.ini file, be sure to enter a hard return after the /fastdetect switch in the last line of the file.

> **Notes** To learn more about the Windows XP boot disk, see the Microsoft Knowledge Base Articles 305595 and 314503 at the Microsoft web site *support.microsoft.com*.

If the Windows XP desktop loads successfully, then do the following to attempt to repair the Windows XP installation:

1. Load the Recovery Console and use the Fixmbr and Fixboot commands to repair the MBR and the OS boot sector.

2. Run antivirus software.

3. Use Disk Management to verify that the hard drive partition table is correct.

4. Defragment your hard drive.

5. Copy Ntldr, Ntdetect.com, and Boot.ini from your floppy disk to the root of the hard drive.

6. If you're using a SCSI hard drive, copy Ntbootdd.sys from your floppy disk to the root of the hard drive.

A+
220-802
1.3, 4.6

If the Windows XP desktop did not load by booting from the boot disk, then the next tool to try is the Recovery Console.

RECOVERY CONSOLE

Use Recovery Console when Windows XP does not start properly or hangs during the load. It works even when core Windows system files are corrupted. The Recovery Console is a command-driven operating system that does not use a GUI. With it, you can access the FAT16, FAT32, and NTFS file systems.

Using the Recovery Console, you can:

- Repair a damaged registry, system files, or file system on the hard drive
- Enable or disable a service or device driver
- Repair the MBR program on the hard drive or the boot sector on the system partition
- Repair a damaged Boot.ini file
- Recover data when the Windows installation is beyond repair

The Recovery Console software is on the Windows XP setup CD. You can launch the Recovery Console from the CD or manually install the Recovery Console on the hard drive and launch it from there.

To use the Recovery Console, insert the Windows XP setup CD in the CD drive and restart the system. When the Windows XP Setup opening menu appears (see Figure C-17), press **R** to load the Recovery Console.

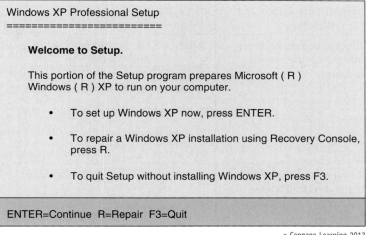

```
Windows XP Professional Setup
============================

  Welcome to Setup.

  This portion of the Setup program prepares Microsoft ( R )
  Windows ( R ) XP to run on your computer.

      •   To set up Windows XP now, press ENTER.

      •   To repair a Windows XP installation using Recovery Console,
          press R.

      •   To quit Setup without installing Windows XP, press F3.

ENTER=Continue  R=Repair  F3=Quit
```

© Cengage Learning 2013

Figure C-17 Windows XP Setup opening menu

You must enter the Administrator password in order to use the Recovery Console and access an NTFS volume. If the registry is so corrupted that the Recovery Console cannot read the password to validate it, you are not asked for the password, but you are limited in what you can do at the Recovery Console.

> **Notes** Here are two useful tips to help you when using the Recovery Console: To retrieve the last command entered, press **F3** at the command prompt. To retrieve the command one character at a time, press the **F1** key.

Many commands used at a command prompt window also work in the Recovery Console. These commands include attrib, cd, chkdsk, cls, copy, del, dir, disable, diskpart,

A+
220-802
1.3, 4.6

enable, exit, format, help, listsvc, md, more, rd, and rename. (The Windows 7/Vista Bootsect, Bcdedit, and Bootrec commands will not work in XP.) Table C-4 lists some additional Recovery Console commands.

Command	Description	Examples

Expand	Expands compressed files and extracts files from cabinet files and copies the files to the destination folder.	To extract File1 from the Drivers.cab file:
		
		 `C:\> Expand D:\i386\Drivers.cab -f:File1`
		
		 To expand the compressed file, File1.cp_:
		
		 `C:\> Expand File1.cp_`

Fixboot	Rewrites the OS boot sector on the hard drive. If a drive letter is not specified, the system drive is assumed.	To repair the OS boot sector of drive C: `C:\> Fixboot C:`
Fixmbr	Rewrites the Master Boot Record boot program.	To repair the Master Boot Record boot program: `C:\> Fixmbr`
Logon	Allows you to log onto an installation with the Administrator password. Use it to log onto a second installation of Windows in a dual-boot environment.	When logged onto the first Windows installation, use this command to log onto the second installation: `C:\> logon 2` If you don't enter the password correctly after three tries, the system automatically reboots.
Map	Lists all drive letters and file system types.	`C:\> Map`

Set	Displays or sets Recovery Console environmental variables.	To turn off the prompt when you are overwriting files:
		
		 `C:\> Set nocopyprompt=true`
		
		 To allow access to all files and folders on all drives:
		
		 `C:\> Set allowallpaths=true`
		
		 To allow copying any file to another media:
		
		 `C:\> Set allowremovablemedia=true`

Systemroot	Sets the current directory to the directory where Windows XP is installed.	`C:\> Systemroot C:\WINDOWS>`

Table C-4   Commands available from the Recovery Console

© Cengage Learning 2013

Unless you first use the set command with certain parameters, you are not allowed into all folders, and you cannot copy files from the hard drive to a removable media.

The **Fixmbr** command restores the master boot program in the MBR, and the **Fixboot** command repairs the OS boot record. As you enter each command, you're looking for clues that might indicate at what point the drive has failed. For example, Figure C-18 shows the results of using the Fixmbr command, which appears to have worked without errors, but the Fixboot command has actually failed. This tells us that most likely the master boot program is healthy, but drive C is not accessible. After using these commands, if you don't see any errors, exit the Recovery Console and try to boot from the hard drive.

A+
220-802
1.3, 4.6

© Cengage Learning 2013

Figure C-18 Results of using the Fixmbr and Fixboot commands in the Recovery Console

To exit the Recovery Console, type **Exit** and press **Enter**. The system will attempt to boot to the Windows desktop.

RESTORING THE SYSTEM USING AN AUTOMATED SYSTEM RECOVERY BACKUP

Recall that you can use the XP Backup or Restore Wizard to create an Automated System Recovery backup of the entire Windows volume. To restore the Windows volume to its state when the last ASR backup was made, do the following:

1. Boot the computer using the Windows XP setup CD.
2. A blue screen appears with the message "Press F6 to load RAID or SCSI drivers." If your system uses RAID, SCSI, or some SATA drives, press **F6**. If your system does not use these drives, ignore the message.
3. At the bottom of the blue screen, a message says, "Press F2 to run the Automated System Recovery process." Press **F2**.
4. The screen shown in Figure C-19 appears, instructing you to insert the ASR floppy disk. Insert the disk, and then press **Enter**. The entire Windows volume is reformatted and the volume is restored to the ASR backup.

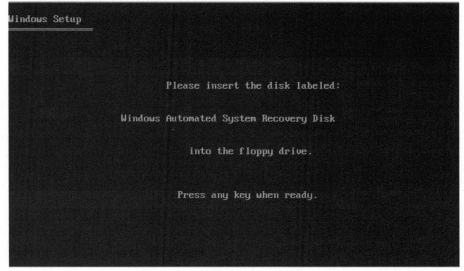

© Cengage Learning 2013

Figure C-19 Automatic System Recovery process must have the ASR floppy disk

CHAPTER 7: CONNECTING TO AND SETTING UP A NETWORK

Following are differences in Windows 7 and Windows XP that are associated with content covered in Chapter 7.

A+
220-802
1.5, 1.6

CONNECT TO A WIRED NETWORK IN XP

For Windows XP, to connect to a network or repair a connection, click **Start**, right-click **My Network Places**, and select **Properties** from the shortcut menu. The **Network Connections** window opens. See Figure C-20. To connect to a network, click **Create a new connection** in the left pane. To repair a wired network connection, right-click the **Local Area Connection** icon, and then select **Repair** from the shortcut menu.

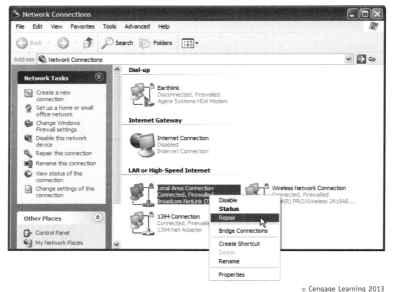

Figure C-20 Windows XP Network Connections window

© Cengage Learning 2013

You can also use the Control Panel to create and repair network connections. To open the Network Connections window, click **Network Connections** in Control Panel. To use a wizard to create a new network connection, click **Network Setup Wizard** in Control Panel and follow the directions to create the new connection.

VERIFY TCP/IP SETTINGS IN XP

To verify and change the TCP/IP settings for Windows XP, click **Start**, right-click **My Network Places**, and select **Properties** from the shortcut menu. The **Network Connections** window opens. Right-click the **Local Area Connection** icon, and then select **Properties** from the shortcut menu. Refer back to Figure C-20. The properties box opens. Select **Internet Protocol (TCP/IP)** and click **Properties**. Configure the TCP/IP properties the same as with Windows 7/Vista.

CONNECT TO A WIRELESS NETWORK IN XP

Here are the steps to connect to a public or private hot spot when using Windows XP:

1. Right-click **My Network Places** and select **Properties**. The Network Connections window opens. Right-click the **Wireless Network Connection** icon and select **View Available Wireless Networks** from the shortcut menu. The Wireless Network Connection window opens (see Figure C-21). Select an unsecured network from those listed and click **Connect**.

A+
220-802
1.5, 1.6

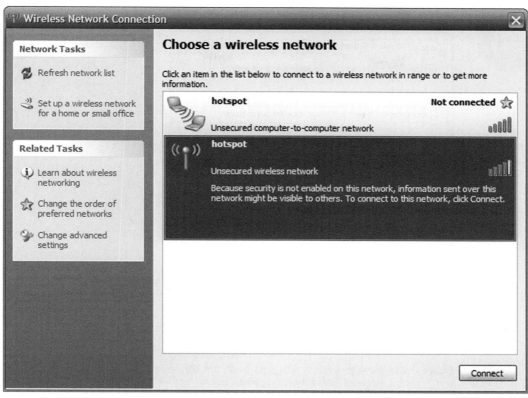

Figure C-21 Available wireless hot spots

© Cengage Learning 2013

2. When you select a secured network from the list, you must enter the key in a dialog box, as shown in Figure C-22.

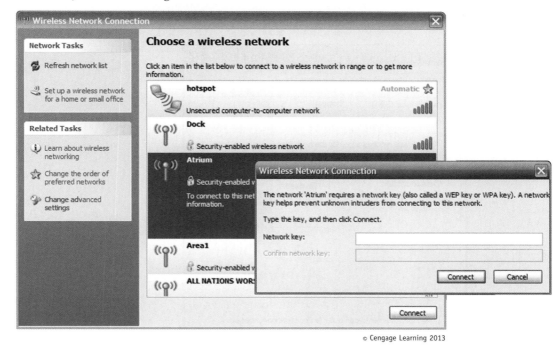

© Cengage Learning 2013

Figure C-22 To use a secured wireless network, you must know the encryption key

3. If you're having a problem making the connection and you know the SSID of the hot spot, you can enter the SSID. Click **Change advanced settings** in the Network Connections window. The Wireless Network Connection Properties dialog box opens. Click the **Wireless Networks** tab (see Figure C-23). Click **Add**.

A+
220-802
1.5, 1.6

© Cengage Learning 2013

Figure C-23   Manage wireless hot spots using the Wireless
Network Connection Properties box

4. The Wireless Network Properties window opens (see Figure C-24). Enter the SSID
of the network and make sure that Network Authentication is set to **Open** and Data
encryption is set to **Disabled**. Click **OK**. When a dialog box opens to warn you of the
dangers of disabling encryption, click **Continue Anyway**. Click **OK** to close the Wireless
Network Connection Properties dialog box. Try again to connect to the hot spot.

© Cengage Learning 2013

Figure C-24   Enter the SSID of a hot spot to which you
want to connect

CHAPTER 8: WINDOWS RESOURCES ON A NETWORK

Following are differences in Windows 7 and Windows XP that are associated with content covered in Chapter 8.

A+
220-802
1.8, 2.1

SHARE A FOLDER IN XP

To share a folder in Windows XP, follow these steps:

1. In Windows Explorer, right-click a folder and select **Sharing and Security** from the shortcut menu. The Properties box opens with the Sharing tab active (see Figure C-25). Click **If you understand the security risks but want to share files without running the wizard, click here.** The Enable File Sharing dialog box appears. Select **Just enable file sharing** and click **OK**. The Sharing tab on the Properties box now has the *Share this folder on the network* check box available, as shown in Figure C-25. You only need to enable file sharing once. After that, the check box is always available.

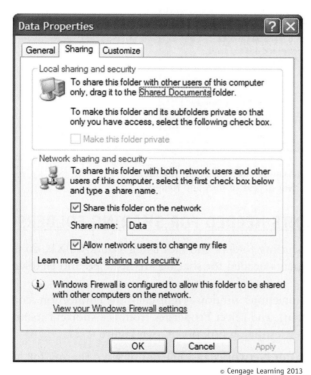

© Cengage Learning 2013

Figure C-25 A user on a network can share a folder with others on the network

2. Check **Share this folder on the network**. If you want to allow others to change the contents of the folder, check **Allow network users to change my files**. Click **Apply**, and close the window.

DISABLED SIMPLE FILE SHARING

Windows XP uses simple file sharing by default, which means you have no control over who has access to a shared folder or file. (By default, Windows 7/Vista does not use simple file sharing.) For Windows XP, to disable simple file sharing so that you have more control over access and can monitor that access, open the **Folder Options** applet in Control Panel and

A+
220-802
1.8, 2.1

click the **View** tab of the Folder Options box (see Figure C-26). Scroll down to the bottom of the **Advanced settings** list, uncheck **Use simple file sharing (Recommended)**, and click **Apply**. Close the window.

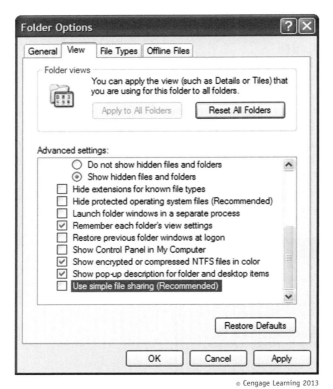

© Cengage Learning 2013

Figure C-26 Turn off Windows XP simple file sharing so that you have more control over access to files and folders

VERIFY XP COMPONENTS NEEDED FOR SHARING FOLDERS AND FILES

If you have a problem with sharing folders and files using Windows XP, do the following to verify that Windows components needed for sharing are installed and enabled:

1. Open the **Network Connections** window, right-click the connection icon (default name is **Local Area Connection**), and select **Properties** from the shortcut menu. The Local Area Connection Properties dialog box opens. See Figure C-27.

2. Verify **Client for Microsoft Networks** and **File and Printer Sharing for Microsoft Networks** are both checked. If you don't see these items in the list, click **Install** to install them. The Select Network Component Type box appears (see the left side of Figure C-27). Select **Client**, click **Add**, and follow the directions on-screen. When you're done, close all windows.

MAKE YOUR WINDOWS XP PERSONAL PROFILE PRIVATE

If you are using the NTFS file system with Windows XP, folders associated with your user account can be made private so that only you can access them. To make a user folder and all its subfolders private, in Windows Explorer, drill down to a folder that is part of your user profile under the Documents and Settings folder. Right-click the folder and select **Sharing and Security** from the shortcut menu. The folder Properties dialog box opens (see Figure C-28).

A+
220-802
1.8, 2.1

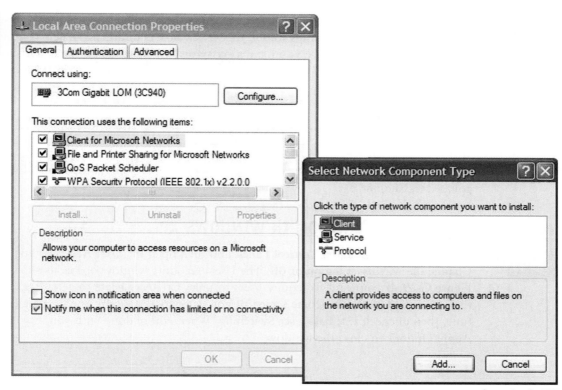

© Cengage Learning 2013

Figure C-27 Use the Network Connections applet to install a network client, service, or protocol for Windows XP

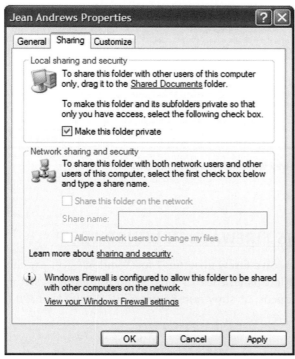

© Cengage Learning 2013

Figure C-28 A folder that belongs to a user profile in Windows XP can be made private

Check **Make this folder private** and click **Apply**. (If a folder is not part of a user profile in the Documents and Settings folder, this check box is dimmed.) When you make a personal folder private, be sure you have a password associated with your user account. If you don't have a password, anyone can log on as you and gain access to your private folders.

CHAPTER 9: SECURITY STRATEGIES

Following are differences in Windows 7 and Windows XP that are associated with content covered in Chapter 9.

HOW A USER LOGS ON IN WINDOWS XP

Using Windows XP, open **Control Panel,** and then open the **User Accounts** applet. Click **Change the way users log on or off**. The User Accounts window opens, as shown in Figure C-29. If you want to require users to press Ctrl-Alt-Delete to get a logon window, then uncheck **Use the Welcome screen**. If you want to allow only one user logged on at a time, then uncheck **Use Fast User Switching**. When you're done with your changes, click **Apply Options** to close the window.

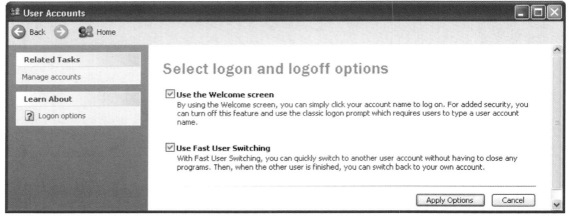

Figure C-29   Options to change the way Windows XP users log on or off

© Cengage Learning 2013

CONFIGURE WINDOWS FIREWALL IN WINDOWS XP

To view and change the Windows Firewall settings for Windows XP, use the Network Connections window. In the left pane, click **Change Windows Firewall settings**. The Windows Firewall window opens, as shown in Figure C-30. Verify that **On (recommended)** is selected.

A+
220-802
1.1, 1.4,
1.5, 1.6

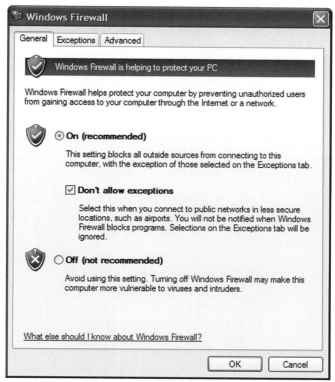

© Cengage Learning 2013

Figure C-30 Windows Firewall for Windows XP is set for
maximum protection

If you don't want to allow any communication to be initiated from remote computers, check **Don't allow exceptions**. This is the preferred setting when you're traveling or using public networks or Internet connections. If you are on a local network and need to allow others on the network to access your computer, uncheck **Don't allow exceptions**. Then click the **Exceptions** tab to select the exceptions to allow. For example, if you want to share files and folders on your local network, use the Exceptions tab to allow File and Printer Sharing activity.

Creating a Standard Image

To use the Windows Automated Installation Kit (AIK) to create a standard image, a system administrator uses one computer to set up the tools used to create the image (called the technician computer) and a second computer to build the image with all the Windows settings, drivers, and applications that will become part of the image (called the reference computer).

A+
220-802
1.2

This appendix contains the step-by-step process to create a standard image using the Windows AIK. For more information, see this link on the Microsoft web site: *technet .microsoft.com/en-us/library/ee523217(WS.10).aspx*. To create the image, you need two USB flash drives that are at least 8 GB in size and two computers. Designate one computer to be the technician computer and the other to be the reference computer. You also need a Windows 7 setup DVD. In these steps, we are using a 64-bit Windows 7 Professional DVD.

> **Notes** Before you begin creating a standard image, you might want to check out this video at the Microsoft Technet site: *technet.microsoft.com/en-us/windows/ee530017.aspx*.

PART 1: ON THE TECHNICIAN COMPUTER, INSTALL WINDOWS AIK

To install Windows AIK on the technician computer, follow these steps:

1. Go to the Microsoft Download Center (*www.microsoft.com/download*) and download the **Windows Automated Installation Kit (AIK) for Windows 7**, which is contained in an ISO file. At the time of this writing, the file is named KB3AIK_EN.iso. The download might take about two hours.

2. To burn the .iso file to a DVD, first insert a blank DVD-R into the optical drive. Right-click the .iso file and select **Burn disc image** from the shortcut menu. Follow the directions on-screen to burn the DVD.

3. Open the System window and find out if your OS installation is a 32-bit or 64-bit installation. On a separate sheet of paper, write the answer to this question:

   Are you using a 32-bit or 64-bit OS on the technician computer?

4. Using Windows Explorer, double-click one of the two setup programs on the DVD to install Windows AIK on your computer:

   ◢ If your OS is a 32-bit OS, double-click **wAIKX86.msi**.
   ◢ If your OS is a 64-bit OS, double-click **wAIKAMD64.msi**.

5. Follow the directions on-screen to install Windows AIK on your computer.

PART 2: ON THE TECHNICIAN COMPUTER, CREATE A BOOTABLE USB FLASH DRIVE (UFD)

Follow these steps on the technician computer to use Windows AIK to create a bootable UFD that contains the ImageX.exe program you will use to capture the image:

1. Click **Start, All Programs,** and **Microsoft Windows AIK**. In the Windows AIK group, right-click **Deployment Tools Command Prompt** and click **Run as administrator** (see Figure D-1). Respond to the UAC box. The Deployment Tools Command Prompt window opens.

2. Carefully enter one set of three commands to create an ISO folder on your hard drive with files in it that will later go on the bootable UFD:

   ◢ If the reference computer will hold a 32-bit installation of Windows, enter these three commands:
   - copype.cmd x86 C:\winpe_x86
   - copy C:\winpe_x86\winpe.wim C:\winpe_x86\ISO\sources\boot.wim
   - copy "C:\Program Files\Windows AIK\Tools\x86\ImageX.exe" C:\winpe_x86\ISO\

© Cengage Learning 2013

Figure D-1 Opening the Deployment Tools Command Prompt window

Notes Note the space in **Program Files** and **Windows AIK** in the path to the ImageX.exe file.

◢ If the reference computer will hold a 64-bit installation of Windows, enter these three commands:

- **copype.cmd amd64 C:\winpe_amd64**
- **copy C:\winpe_amd64\winpe.wim C:\winpe_amd64\ISO\sources\boot.wim**
- **copy "C:\Program Files\Windows AIK\Tools\amd64\ImageX.exe" C:\winpe_amd64\ISO**

3. Insert a USB flash drive in the USB port. Realize that all data on the drive will be deleted because you are about to format the drive. Open Windows Explorer and answer the following questions on a separate sheet of paper:

    ◢ What is the capacity of the UFD?
    ◢ How much of the UFD capacity is free space?
    ◢ What is the drive letter that Windows assigned to the UFD?

4. In the Deployment Tools Command Prompt window, enter the **diskpart** command. The Diskpart> prompt appears. Steps 5 through 13 use commands entered at the Diskpart> prompt.

5. To display a list of disks, enter **list disk**. A list of disks appears. On a separate sheet of paper, write the answer to this question:

    ◢ What is the number of the disk that is the UFD?

A+
220-802
1.2

6. Verify you have the correct disk because you are about to erase everything on it. For example, in Figure D-2, the UFD I'm using has a capacity of 29 GB and is Disk 2 in the list of disks. On a separate sheet of paper, write the answer to this question:

▲ Does the capacity and free space recorded in Step 3 match what you see listed for your disk?

```
Administrator: Deployment Tools Command Prompt - diskpart

C:\winpe_amd64>copy "c:\Program Files\Windows AIK\Tools\amd64\ImageX.exe" C:\win
pe_amd64\ISO\
        1 file(s) copied.

C:\winpe_amd64>diskpart

Microsoft DiskPart version 6.1.7601
Copyright (C) 1999-2008 Microsoft Corporation.
On computer: BLUELIGHT

DISKPART> list disk

  Disk ###  Status         Size     Free     Dyn  Gpt
  --------  -------------  -------  -------   ---  ---
  Disk 0    Online          500 GB    48 GB
  Disk 1    Online         1038 GB   195 GB
  Disk 2    Online           29 GB     0 B

DISKPART> select disk 2

Disk 2 is now the selected disk.

DISKPART> _
```

Figure D-2   Identify the disk number for your UFD   © Cengage Learning 2013

7. Enter the command **select disk** *number*, substituting the number you recorded in Step 5 for *number* in the command line. The UFD is now the selected disk.

8. To delete all partition information on the UFD, enter the **clean** command.

9. To create a new primary partition, enter the command **create partition primary**.

10. To select this partition, enter the command **select partition 1**.

11. To format the partition, enter the command **format fs=fat32 quick**.

12. To make the partition the active partition, enter the command **active**.

13. To exit the Diskpart interface, enter the command **exit**. The C prompt in the Deployment Tools Command Prompt window appears.

14. To copy the ISO folder and its contents to the UFD, use one of the following commands, substituting the drive letter of your UFD for D in the command line:

▲ If the reference computer will hold a 32-bit installation of Windows, enter this command:
  xcopy /s C:\winpe_x86\ISO*.* D:

▲ If the reference computer will hold a 64-bit installation of Windows, enter this command:
  xcopy /s C:\winpe_amd64\ISO*.* D:

The UFD is now ready to capture the standard image that you create on the reference computer. Figure D-3 shows the root directory and the Properties box of the UFD.

D

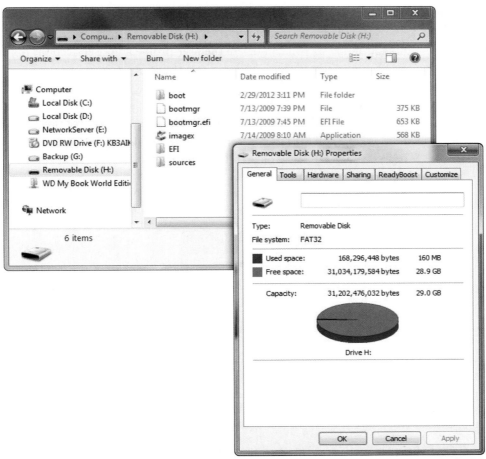

© Cengage Learning 2013

Figure D-3 Verify the files in the root directory of the UFD

PART 3: ON THE REFERENCE COMPUTER, INSTALL AND CUSTOMIZE WINDOWS 7

On the reference computer, follow these steps to install Windows 7 and all applications that go on the image:

1. Using a Windows 7 DVD or other media, install Windows 7. During the installation, enter a username, password, and other information as you would normally during a Windows installation. These items will later be deleted or cleaned from the installation. When asked for the product key, enter the product key as requested. If you are using a Volume Licensing version of Windows 7, enter the Volume Licensing product key. (You do not need to automatically activate Windows, but the product key is required.)

2. Install all Windows updates, device drivers, and applications that will be part of the image. Don't forget to install antivirus software. Configure all Windows settings as you want them in the standard image. Do not configure user settings because these settings will be lost when the image is cleaned.

3. Take care to verify you have all programs and settings as you want them because this is your last chance to change the image.

A+
220-802
1.2

PART 4: ON THE REFERENCE COMPUTER, CLEAN THE IMAGE

In the steps that follow, you use the System Preparation utility (sysprep.exe) to restart the system in audit mode so you can delete the user profile and user account that were created during the Windows installation. Follow these steps:

1. To launch Sysprep, click **Start**, type **C:\Windows\System32\sysprep\sysprep.exe** in the Search box, and press **Enter**. The System Preparation Tool dialog box appears. In the System Cleanup Action area, select **Enter System Audit Mode**. Check **Generalize**. In the Shutdown Options area, select **Reboot** if it is not already selected. See Figure D-4. When you click **OK**, the system reboots into Audit Mode, which automatically logs you in using the built-in Administrator account so that you can delete the user profile that belongs to the user account you were using earlier when you installed applications and drivers in Step 2 of Part 3.

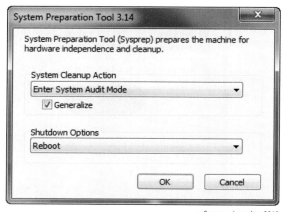

© Cengage Learning 2013

Figure D-4 Sysprep is ready to restart the system in audit mode

2. To delete the user profile you used in Step 2 of Part 3, click **Start**, type **user profile** in the Search box, and press **Enter**. In the User Profiles box (see Figure D-5), select the user profile. Click **Delete** and then click **Yes**. Close the User Profiles box.

© Cengage Learning 2013

Figure D-5 Delete the user profile created during the Windows installation

D

A+
220-802
1.2

3. Using Control Panel or the Computer Management console, delete the user account (see Figure D-6). Close all open windows.

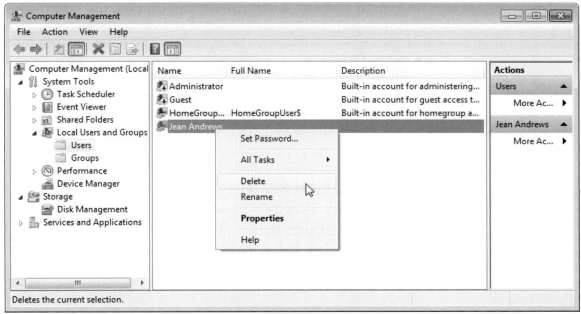

© Cengage Learning 2013

Figure D-6 Use the Computer Management console to delete the user account created during the Windows installation

PART 5: ON THE REFERENCE COMPUTER, GENERALIZE THE IMAGE

Next you use Sysprep again to remove any hardware-dependent information from the installation in a process called generalizing the image. Follow these steps:

1. On the reference computer, if the System Preparation Tool dialog box is not already open, launch sysprep to open it.

2. In the System Preparation Tool box, chose **Enter System Out-of-Box Experience (OOBE)**. Check **Generalize**. In the Shutdown Options area, select **Shutdown** (see Figure D-7).

3. Click **OK**. Sysprep generalizes the system and the computer shuts down.

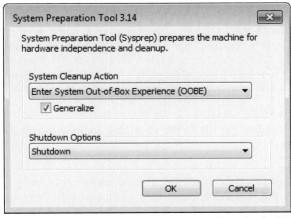

© Cengage Learning 2013

Figure D-7 Sysprep is set to remove hardware-dependent information from the Windows installation

PART 6: ON THE REFERENCE COMPUTER, CAPTURE THE IMAGE

The ImageX.exe program on the UFD is used to capture the image. It stores the image on the UFD in the file Install.wim. Follow these steps to capture the image:

1. Boot the reference computer from the bootable UFD you created earlier. To boot from the UFD, you might need to access BIOS setup and change the order of boot devices to list a removable device first in the list of boot devices. When you boot from the UFD, Windows PE is launched and provides a command prompt window showing the command prompt as X:\windows\system32>.

2. Next you need to determine the drive letter for the volume on the hard drive that holds the Windows installation and the drive letter for the bootable UFD. Most likely, the Windows volume will be D:. Do the following:

   a. Enter the command **Dir D:**. If you see the Windows and Program Files folder listed, you have found the Windows volume. If not, try a different drive letter. On a separate sheet of paper, record the answer to this question:

      • What is the drive letter of the Windows volume?

   b. Enter the commands **Dir E:**, **Dir F:**, or **Dir G:** until you find the drive that holds the imagex.exe file. This drive is the bootable UFD. On a separate sheet of paper, record the answer to this question:

      • What is the drive letter of the bootable UFD?

   In our example, we use D: for the Windows volume and F: for the bootable UFD, but your results might be different.

3. In the command prompt window, enter this command to capture the image on the D: drive to the F: drive when Windows 7 Professional is installed:

   F:\imagex /compress fast /check /flags "Professional" /capture D: F:\install.wim "Windows 7 Professional" "Windows 7 Professional Custom"

   Here is the command to use when Windows 7 Home Premium is installed:

   F:\imagex /compress fast /check /flags "HomePremium" /capture D: F:\install.wim "Windows 7 Home Premium" "Windows 7 Home Premium Custom"

4. The install.wim file is now stored on the UFD. This install.wim file can be 3 GB or higher depending on the space needed for installed applications. Shut down the computer and remove the UFD.

> **Notes** A problem arises when the install.wim file is larger than 4 GB because the FAT32 file system on the UFD cannot handle a file that large. In this situation, you have a couple of options. You can format the UFD using the NTFS file system. However, know that some computers will not boot from a UFD that is using the NTFS file system. Another solution is to use a second UFD that is formatted with NTFS. Boot from the FAT32 UFD, switch to the NTFS UFD, and save the image to this second UFD.

5. Most UFDs don't have a write-on label. To help you remember what's stored on the UFD, you can create a Readme.txt file in the root, and include in it a description of the contents of the UFD.

> **Notes** When you restart the reference computer, the Set Up Windows screen appears where you can configure the time, currency, and keyboard settings, enter a computer name, user account, and product key, and accept the licensing agreement as you normally would during a Windows installation. The Windows desktop then appears.

PART 7: ON THE TECHNICIAN COMPUTER, PREPARE A SECOND UFD TO USE WHEN DEPLOYING THE IMAGE

Use the technician computer to prepare the deployment UFD. To do so, you format a second UFD using the FAT32 file system and make the UFD bootable. Then you copy all files on the Windows setup DVD to the UFD along with the install.wim file you captured. Follow these steps to prepare the deployment UFD:

1. On the technician computer, open the Deployment Tools Command Prompt window. You will use this window to enter the commands in this section.

2. Copy the Install.wim file from the UFD you used to capture the file to the hard drive of the technician computer using this command: **copy H:\install.wim C:\install.wim.** Substitute the drive letter of the UFD for H in the command line. You can now remove this UFD from the USB port.

3. Insert a second UFD in a USB port. Format it with the FAT32 file system and make it bootable. To do so, follow Steps 3 through 13 in Part 2 of this appendix. Note that these steps use the following commands: diskpart, list disk, select disk, clean, create partition primary, select partition, format, and active.

4. Insert the Windows 7 setup DVD in the optical drive. Enter this command to copy all files from the setup DVD to the UFD: **xcopy /s D:*.* E:*.*.** In the command line, substitute the drive letter of your optical drive for D and substitute the drive letter of your UFD for E.

5. Use this command to copy the Install.wim file from the technician computer to the \Sources folder on the UFD, replacing the \Sources\install.wim file already there:

   Xcopy /r C:\install.wim E:\sources\install.wim

   Substitute the drive letter of your UFD for E in the command line.

6. Safely eject the UFD from the USB port. You might want to create a Readme.txt file in the root of the UFD with instructions and a description of the UFD contents.

To use the image on other computers, boot the computer from the UFD. Windows setup begins. Follow the instructions to install the OS. When the installation completes, all applications and Windows settings in the image are also installed. To make it easier to install the image on multiple computers, you might want to make several copies of the deployment UFD.

Keystroke Shortcuts in Windows

This appendix lists a few handy keystrokes to use when working with Windows, including the function keys you can use during startup. You can also use the mouse to do some of these same things, but keystrokes are sometimes faster. Also, in some troubleshooting situations, the mouse is not usable. At those times, knowing these keystrokes can get you out of a jam.

General Action	Keystrokes	Description
While loading Windows	F8	To display the Advanced Boot Options menu.
	Spacebar	To display the Windows boot menu.
Managing Windows and applications	F1	To display Help.
	Alt+Tab	To move from one loaded application to another.
	Ctrl+Tab and Ctrl+Shift+Tab	To move through tabbed pages in a dialog box.
	Alt+Esc	To cycle through items in the order they were opened.
	F6	To cycle through screen elements in a window or on the desktop.
	Win or Ctrl+Esc	Display Start menu. Use arrow keys to move over the menu. (The Win key is the one labeled with the Windows flag icon.)
	Win+E	Start Windows Explorer.
	Win+M	Minimize all windows.
	Win+Tab	Move through items on the taskbar.
	Win+R	Display the Run dialog box.
	Win+Break	Display the Windows 7/Vista System window or the XP System Properties window.
	F5	Refresh the contents of a window.
	Alt+F4	Close the active application window, or, if no window is open, shut down Windows.
	Ctrl+F4	Close the active document window.
	Alt+Spacebar	To display the System menu for the active window. To close this window, you can then use the arrow key to step down to Close.
	Alt+M	First, put the focus on the Start menu (use Win or Ctrl+Esc) and then press Alt+M to minimize all windows and move the focus to the desktop.
	F10 or Alt	Activate the menu bar in the active program.
	Ctrl+Alt+Del	Display the Task List, which you can use to switch to another application, end a task, or shut down Windows.
	Application	When an item is selected, display its shortcut menu. (The Application key is labeled with a box and an arrow.)
Working with text anywhere in Windows	Ctrl+C	Shortcut for Copy.
	Ctrl+V	Shortcut for Paste.
	Ctrl+A	Shortcut for selecting all text.
	Ctrl+X	Shortcut for Cut.
	Ctrl+Z	Shortcut for Undo.
	Ctrl+Y	Shortcut for Repeat/Redo.
	Shift+arrow keys	To select text, character by character.

General Action	Keystrokes	Description
Managing files, folders, icons, and shortcuts	Ctrl+Shift while dragging a file	Create a shortcut.
	Ctrl while dragging a file	Copy a file.
	Shift+Delete	Delete a file without placing it in the Recycle Bin.
	F2	Rename an item.
	Alt+Enter	Display an item's Properties window.
Selecting items	Shift+click	To select multiple entries in a list (such as file-names in Explorer), click the first item, hold down the Shift key, and click the last item you want to select in the list. All items between the first and last are selected.
	Ctrl+click	To select several nonsequential items in a list, click the first item to select it. Hold down the Ctrl key and click other items anywhere in the list. All items you click are selected.
Using menus	Alt	Press the Alt key to activate the menu bar.
	Alt, letter	After the menu bar is activated, press a letter to select a menu option. The letter must be under-lined in the menu.
	Alt, arrow keys, Enter	In a window, use the Alt key to make the menu bar active. Then use the arrow keys to move over the menu tree and highlight the correct option. Use the Enter key to select that option.
	Esc	Press Esc to exit a menu without making a selection.
Copying to the Clipboard	Print Screen	Copy the desktop to the Clipboard.
	Alt+Print Screen	Copy the active window to the Clipboard.

E

CompTIA A+ Acronyms

CompTIA provides a list of acronyms that you need to know before you sit for the A+ exams. You can download the list from the CompTIA web site at *www.comptia.org*. The list is included here for your convenience. However, CompTIA occasionally updates the list, so be sure to check the CompTIA web site for the latest version.

Acronym	Spelled Out
A/V	Audio Video
AC	alternating current
ACL	access control list
ACPI	advanced configuration power interface
ACT	activity
ADSL	asymmetrical digital subscriber line
AGP	accelerated graphics port
AMD	advanced micro devices
APIPA	automatic private internet protocol addressing
APM	advanced power management
ARP	address resolution protocol
ASR	automated system recovery
ATA	advanced technology attachment
ATAPI	advanced technology attachment packet interface
ATM	asynchronous transfer mode
ATX	advanced technology extended
BIOS	basic input/output system
BNC	Bayonet-Neill-Concelman or British Naval Connector
BTX	balanced technology extended
CAPTCHA	Completely Automated Public Turing Test To Tell Computers and Humans Apart
CCFL	Cold Cathode Fluorescent Lamp
CD	compact disc
CDFS	compact disc file system
CD-ROM	compact disc-read-only memory
CD-RW	compact disc-rewritable
CFS	Central File System, Common File System, Command File System
CMOS	complementary metal-oxide semiconductor
CNR	Communications and Networking Riser
COMx	communication port (x=port number)
CPU	central processing unit
CRIMM	Continuity Rambus Inline Memory Mode
CRT	cathode-ray tube
DAC	discretionary access control
DB-25	serial communications D-shell connector, 25 pins
DB-9	9 pin D shell connector
DC	direct current
DDOS	distributed denial of service
DDR	double data-rate
DDR RAM	double data-rate random access memory
DDR SDRAM	double data-rate synchronous dynamic random access memory

Acronym	Spelled Out
DFS	distributed file system
DHCP	dynamic host configuration protocol
DIMM	dual inline memory module
DIN	Deutsche Industrie Norm
DIP	dual inline package
DLP	digital light processing
DLT	digital linear tape
DMA	direct memory access
DMZ	demilitarized zone
DNS	domain name service or domain name server
DOS	denial of service
DRAM	dynamic random access memory
DSL	digital subscriber line
DVD	digital video disc or digital versatile disc
DVD-R	digital video disc-recordable
DVD-RAM	digital video disc-random access memory
DVD-ROM	digital video disc-read only memory
DVD-RW	digital video disc-rewritable
DVI	digital visual interface
ECC	error correction code
ECP	extended capabilities port
EEPROM	electrically erasable programmable read-only memory
EFS	encrypting file system
EIDE	enhanced integrated drive electronics
EMI	electromagnetic interference
EMP	electromagnetic pulse
EPP	enhanced parallel port
EPROM	erasable programmable read-only memory
ERD	emergency repair disk
ESD	electrostatic discharge
EVDO	evolution data optimized or evolution data only
EVGA	extended video graphics adapter/array
FAT	file allocation table
FAT12	12-bit file allocation table
FAT16	16-bit file allocation table
FAT32	32-bit file allocation table
FDD	floppy disk drive
Fn	Function (referring to the function key on a laptop)
FPM	fast page-mode
FQDN	fully qualified domain name

F

Acronym	Spelled Out
FRU	field replaceable unit
FSB	Front Side Bus
FTP	file transfer protocol
Gb	gigabit
GB	gigabyte
GDI	graphics device interface
GHz	gigahertz
GPS	global positioning system
GSM	global system for mobile communications
GUI	graphical user interface
HAL	hardware abstraction layer
HAV	Hardware Assisted Virtualization
HCL	hardware compatibility list
HDD	hard disk drive
HDMI	high definition media interface
HPFS	high performance file system
HTML	hypertext markup language
HTPC	Home Theater PC
HTTP	hypertext transfer protocol
HTTPS	hypertext transfer protocol over secure sockets layer
I/O	input/output
ICMP	internet control message protocol
ICR	intelligent character recognition
IDE	integrated drive electronics
IDS	Intrusion Detection System
IEEE	Institute of Electrical and Electronics Engineers
IIS	Internet Information Services
IMAP	internet mail access protocol
IP	internet protocol
IPCONFIG	internet protocol configuration
IPP	internet printing protocol
IPSEC	internet protocol security
IR	infrared
IrDA	Infrared Data Association
IRQ	interrupt request
ISA	industry standard architecture
ISDN	integrated services digital network
ISO	Industry Standards Organization
ISP	internet service provider
JBOD	just a bunch of disks

Acronym	Spelled Out
Kb	kilobit
KB	Kilobyte or knowledge base
LAN	local area network
LBA	logical block addressing
LC	Lucent connector
LCD	liquid crystal display
LDAP	lightweight directory access protocol
LED	light emitting diode
Li-on	lithium-ion
LPD/LPR	line printer daemon / line printer remote
LPT	line printer terminal
LVD	low voltage differential
MAC	media access control / mandatory access control
MAPI	messaging application programming interface
MAU	media access unit, media attachment unit
Mb	megabit
MB	megabyte
MBR	master boot record
MBSA	Microsoft Baseline Security Analyzer
MFD	multi-function device
MFP	multi-function product
MHz	megahertz
MicroDIMM	micro dual inline memory module
MIDI	musical instrument digital interface
MIME	multipurpose internet mail extension
MIMO	Multiple Input Multiple Output
MMC	Microsoft management console
MMX	multimedia extensions
MP3	Moving Picture Experts Group Layer 3 Audio
MP4	Moving Picture Experts Group Layer 4
MPEG	Moving Picture Experts Group
MSCONFIG	Microsoft configuration
MSDS	material safety data sheet
MUI	multilingual user interface
NAC	network access control
NAS	network-attached storage
NAT	network address translation
NetBEUI	networked basic input/output system extended user interface
NetBIOS	networked basic input/output system
NFS	network file system

Acronym	Spelled Out
NIC	network interface card
NiCd	nickel cadmium
NiMH	nickel metal hydride
NLX	new low-profile extended
NNTP	network news transfer protocol
NTFS	new technology file system
NTLDR	new technology loader
NTP	Network Time Protocol
OCR	optical character recognition
OEM	original equipment manufacturer
OLED	Organic Light Emitting Diode
OS	operating system
PAN	personal area network
PATA	parallel advanced technology attachment
PC	personal computer
PCI	peripheral component interconnect
PCIe	peripheral component interconnect express
PCIX	peripheral component interconnect extended
PCL	printer control language
PCMCIA	Personal Computer Memory Card International Association
PDA	personal digital assistant
PGA	pin grid array
PGA2	pin grid array 2
PII	Personally Identifiable Information
PIN	personal identification number
PKI	public key infrastructure
PnP	plug and play
POP3	post office protocol 3
PoS	Point of Sale
POST	power-on self test
POTS	plain old telephone service
PPP	point-to-point protocol
PPTP	point-to-point tunneling protocol
PRI	primary rate interface
PROM	programmable read-only memory
PS/2	personal system/2 connector
PSTN	public switched telephone network
PSU	power supply unit
PVC	permanent virtual circuit
PXE	preboot execution environment

Acronym	Spelled Out
QoS	quality of service
RAID	redundant array of independent (or inexpensive) discs
RAM	random access memory
RAS	remote access service
RDP	Remote Desktop Protocol
RDRAM	RAMBUS® dynamic random access memory
RF	radio frequency
RFI	radio frequency interference
RGB	red green blue
RIMM	RAMBUS® inline memory module
RIP	routing information protocol
RIS	remote installation service
RISC	reduced instruction set computer
RJ	registered jack
RJ-11	registered jack function 11
RJ-45	registered jack function 45
RMA	returned materials authorization
ROM	read only memory
RS-232 or RS-232C	recommended standard 232
RTC	real-time clock
S.M.A.R.T.	self-monitoring, analysis, and reporting technology
SAN	storage area network
SAS	Serial Attached SCSI
SATA	serial advanced technology attachment
SC	subscription channel
SCP	secure copy protection
SCSI	small computer system interface
SCSI ID	small computer system interface identifier
SD card	secure digital card
SDRAM	synchronous dynamic random access memory
SEC	single edge connector
SFC	system file checker
SFF	Small Form Factor
SGRAM	synchronous graphics random access memory
SIMM	single inline memory module
SLI	scalable link interface or system level integration or scanline interleave mode
SMB	server message block or small to midsize business
SMTP	simple mail transfer protocol
SNMP	simple network management protocol
SoDIMM	small outline dual inline memory module

F

Acronym	Spelled Out
SOHO	small office/home office
SP	service pack
SP1	service pack 1
SP2	service pack 2
SP3	service pack 3
SP4	service pack 4
SPDIF	Sony-Philips digital interface format
SPGA	staggered pin grid array
SRAM	static random access memory
SSH	secure shell
SSID	service set identifier
SSL	secure sockets layer
ST	straight tip
STP	shielded twisted pair
SVGA	super video graphics array
SXGA	super extended graphics array
TB	terabyte
TCP	transmission control protocol
TCP/IP	transmission control protocol/internet protocol
TDR	time domain reflectometer
TFTP	trivial file transfer protocol
TKIP	Temporal Key Integrity Protocol
TPM	trusted platform module
UAC	user account control
UART	universal asynchronous receiver transmitter
UDF	user defined functions or universal disk format or universal data format
UDMA	ultra direct memory access
UDP	user datagram protocol
UNC	universal naming convention
UPS	uninterruptible power supply
URL	uniform resource locator
USB	universal serial bus
USMT	user state migration tool
UTP	unshielded twisted pair
UXGA	ultra extended graphics array
VESA	Video Electronics Standards Association
VFAT	virtual file allocation table
VGA	video graphics array
VM	Virtual Machine
VoIP	voice over internet protocol

Acronym	Spelled Out
VPN	virtual private network
VRAM	video random access memory
WAN	wide area network
WAP	wireless application protocol
WEP	wired equivalent privacy
WIFI	wireless fidelity
WINS	windows internet name service
WLAN	wireless local area network
WPA	wireless protected access
WUXGA	wide ultra extended graphics array
XGA	extended graphics array
ZIF	zero-insertion-force
ZIP	zigzag inline package

F

APPENDIX
G

Entry Points for Startup Processes

This appendix contains a summary of the entry points that can affect Windows 7/Vista startup. The entry points include startup folders, Group Policy folders, the Scheduled Tasks folder, and registry keys.

Programs and shortcuts to programs are stored in these startup folders:

▲ C:\Users*username*\AppData\Roaming\Microsoft\Windows\Start\Menu\
Programs\Startup
▲ C:\ProgramData\Microsoft\Windows\Start Menu\Programs\Startup

Startup and shutdown scripts used by Group Policy are stored in these folders:

▲ C:\Windows\System32\GroupPolicy\Machine\Scripts\Startup
▲ C:\Windows\System32\GroupPolicy\Machine\Scripts\Shutdown
▲ C:\Windows\System32\GroupPolicy\User\Scripts\Logon
▲ C:\Windows\System32\GroupPolicy\User\Scripts\Logoff

Scheduled tasks are stored in this folder:

▲ C:\Windows\System32\Tasks

To see a list of scheduled tasks, enter the **schtasks** command in a command prompt window.

These keys cause an entry to run once and only once at startup:

▲ HKLM\Software\Microsoft\Windows\CurrentVersion\RunOnce
▲ HKLM\Software\Microsoft\Windows\CurrentVersion\RunServiceOnce
▲ HKLM\Software\Microsoft\Windows\CurrentVersion\RunServicesOnce
▲ HKCU\Software\Microsoft\Windows\CurrentVersion\RunOnce

Group Policy places entries in the following keys to affect startup:

▲ HKCU\Software\Microsoft\Windows\CurrentVersion\Policies\Explorer\Run
▲ HKLM\Software\Microsoft\Windows\CurrentVersion\Policies\Explorer\Run

Windows loads many DLL programs from the following key, which is sometimes used by malicious software. Don't delete one unless you know it's causing a problem:

▲ HKLM\Software\Microsoft\Windows\CurrentVersion\ShellServiceObjectDelayLoad

Entries in the keys listed next apply to all users and hold legitimate startup entries. Don't delete an entry unless you suspect it to be bad:

▲ HKLM\Software\Microsoft\Windows\CurrentVersion\Run
▲ HKCU\Software\Microsoft\Windows NT\CurrentVersion\Windows
▲ HKCU\Software\Microsoft\Windows NT\CurrentVersion\Windows\Run
▲ HKCU\Software\Microsoft\Windows\CurrentVersion\Run

These keys and their subkeys contain entries that pertain to background services that are sometimes launched at startup:

▲ HKLM\Software\Microsoft\Windows\CurrentVersion\RunService
▲ HKLM\Software\Microsoft\Windows\CurrentVersion\RunServices

The following key contains a value named BootExecute, which is normally set to autochk. It causes the system to run a type of Chkdsk program to check for hard drive integrity when it was previously shut down improperly. Sometimes another program adds itself to this value, causing a problem. For more information about this situation, see the Microsoft Knowledge Base article 151376, "How to Disable Autochk If It Stops Responding During Reboot" at *support.microsoft.com*.

◢ HKLM\System\CurrentControlSet\Control\Session Manager

Here is an assorted list of registry keys that have all been known to cause various problems at startup. Remember, before you delete a program entry from one of these keys, research the program filename so that you won't accidentally delete something you want to keep:

◢ HKCU\Software\Microsoft\Command
◢ HKCU\Software\Microsoft\Command Processor\AutoRun
◢ HKCU\Software\Microsoft\Windows\CurrentVersion\RunOnce\Setup
◢ HKCU\Software\Microsoft\Windows NT\CurrentVersion\Windows\load
◢ HKLM\Software\Microsoft\Windows NT\CurrentVersion\Windows\AppInit_DLLs
◢ HKLM\Software\Microsoft\Windows NT\CurrentVersion\Winlogon\System
◢ HKLM\Software\Microsoft\Windows NT\CurrentVersion\Winlogon\Us
◢ HKCR\batfile\shell\open\command
◢ HKCR\comfile\shell\open\command
◢ HKCR\exefile\shell\open\command
◢ HKCR\htafile\shell\open\command
◢ HKCR\piffile\shell\open\command
◢ HKCR\scrfile\shell\open\command

Finally, check out the subkeys in the following key, which apply to 32-bit programs installed in a 64-bit version of Windows:

◢ HKLM\Software\Wow6432Node

Other ways in which processes can be launched at startup:

◢ Services can be set to launch at startup. To manage services, use the Services Console (services.msc).
◢ Device drivers are launched at startup. For a listing of installed devices, use Device Manager (devmgmt.msc) or the System Information Utility (msinfo32.exe).

GLOSSARY

This glossary defines the key terms listed at the end of each chapter and other terms related to managing and maintaining a personal computer.

32-bit operating system   Type of operating system that processes 32 bits at a time.

6TO4   A tunnelling protocol in which IPv6 packets travel over an IPv4 network.

64-bit operating system   Type of operating system that processes 64 bits at a time.

802.11a/b/g/n   IEEE specifications for wireless communication and data synchronization. Also known as Wi-Fi. IEEE b/g/n standards are current, and IEEE 802.11a is outdated. Apple Computer's versions of 802.11 standards are called AirPort and AirPort Extreme.

accelerometer   A type of gyroscope used in mobile devices to sense the physical position of the device.

Action Center   A tool in Windows 7 that lists errors and issues that need attention.

Active Directory   A Windows server directory database and service that is used in managing a domain to allow for a single point of administration for all shared resources on a network, including files, peripheral devices, databases, web sites, users, and services.

active partition   The primary partition on the hard drive that boots the OS. Windows calls the active partition the system partition.

ActiveX control   A small app or add-on that can be downloaded from a web site along with a web page and is executed by a browser to enhance the web page.

adapter address   *See* MAC address.

administrative shares   The folders that are shared by default on a network domain that administrator accounts can access.

Administrative tools   A group of tools accessed through the Control Panel that you can use to manage the local computer or other computers on the network.

administrator account   In Windows, a user account that grants to the administrator(s) rights and privileges to all hardware and software resources, such as the right to add, delete, and change accounts and to change hardware configurations.

Administrators group   A type of user group. When a user account is assigned to this group, the account is granted rights that are assigned to an administrator account.

Advanced Options menu   A Windows menu that appears when you press F8 when Windows starts. The menu can be used to troubleshoot problems when loading Windows. In Windows 7/Vista, the menu is called the Advanced Boot Options menu.

adware   Software installed on a computer that produces pop-up ads using your browser; the ads are often based on your browsing habits.

Aero Peek   A Windows 7 feature that gives you a peek at the desktop when you move the mouse over the rectangle to the far-right side of the taskbar.

Aero Shake   A Windows 7 feature that minimizes all other windows except the one you shake.

Aero Snap   A Windows 7 feature that automatically maximizes a window when you drag it to the top of the desktop or snaps the window to the side of the screen when you drag it to a side.

Aero user interface   The Windows 7/Vista 3D user interface that gives a glassy appearance. *Also called* Aero glass.

AES (Advances Encryption Standard)   An encryption standard used by WPA2 and is currently the strongest encryption standard used by Wi-Fi.

airplane mode   A setting within a mobile device that disables all three antennas so the device cannot transmit nor receive signals.

alternate IP address   When configuring TCP/IP in Windows, the static IP address that Windows uses if it cannot lease an IP address from a DHCP server.

Android   An operating system used on mobile devices that is based on the Linux OS and supported by Google.

anonymous users   User accounts that have not been authenticated on a computer.

answer file   A text file that contains information that Windows requires in order to do an unattended installation.

antispyware software Software used to remove spyware and adware.

antivirus (AV) software Utility programs that prevent infection or scan a system to detect and remove viruses. McAfee Associates' VirusScan and Norton AntiVirus are two popular AV packages.

anycast address Used by routers. The address identifies multiple destinations, and packets are delivered to the closest destination.

App Store The app on an Apple device (iPad, iPhone, or iPod touch) that can be used to download content from the iTunes Store web site (*itunes .apple.com*).

Apple ID A user account that uses a valid email address and password and is associated with a credit card number that allows you to download iOS updates and patches, apps, and multimedia content.

application proxy A program that is intended to work on a client computer when the complete application is on a server.

application virtualization Using this virtualization, a virtual environment is created in memory for an application to virtually install itself.

Application Virtualization (App-V) Software by Microsoft used for application virtualization.

ATA Secure Erase Standards developed by the American National Standard Institute (ANSI) that dictate how to securely erase data from solid-state devices such as a USB flash drive or SSD drive in order to protect personal privacy.

Authenticated Users group All user accounts that have been authenticated to access the system except the Guest account. *Compare to* anonymous users.

Automated System Recovery (ASR) The Windows XP process that allows you to restore an entire hard drive volume or logical drive to its state at the time the backup of the volume was made.

Automatic Private IP Address (APIPA) An IP address in the address range 169.254.x.y, used by a computer when it cannot successfully lease an IP address from a DHCP server.

Backup Operator A type of Windows user account group. When a user account belongs to this group, it can back up and restore any files on the system regardless of its having access to these files.

basic disk The term Windows uses that applies to a hard drive when the drive is a stand-alone drive in the system. *Compare to* dynamic disk.

batch file A text file containing a series of OS commands. Autoexec.bat is a batch file.

bcdedit A command used to manually edit the BCD.

best-effort protocol *See* connectionless protocol.

biometric device An input device that inputs biological data about a person; the data can identify a person's fingerprints, handprints, face, voice, eye, and handwriting.

BitLocker Encryption A utility in Windows 7/Vista Ultimate and Enterprise editions that is used to lock down a hard drive by encrypting the entire Windows volume and any other volume on the drive.

blue screen error *See* blue screen of death (BSOD).

blue screen of death (BSOD) A Windows error that occurs in kernel mode, which is displayed against a blue screen and causes the system to halt. *Also called* a stop error.

Bluetooth PIN code A code that may be required to complete the Bluetooth connection in a pairing process.

Boot Configuration Data (BCD) file A Windows 7/Vista file structured the same as a registry file and contains configuration information about how Windows is started. The BCD file replaces the Boot.ini file used in Windows 2000/XP.

boot loader menu A startup menu that gives the user the choice of which operating system to load, such as Windows XP or Windows 7 which are both installed on the same system, creating a dual boot.

boot partition The hard drive partition where the Windows OS is stored. The system partition and the boot partition may be different partitions.

boot sector virus An infectious program that can replace the boot program with a modified, infected version, often causing boot and data retrieval problems.

boot.ini A Windows 2000/XP hidden text file that contains information needed to start the boot and build the boot loader menu.

booting The process of starting up a computer and loading an operating system.

bootrec A command used to repair the BCD and boot sectors.

bootsect A command used to repair a dual boot system.

Briefcase A system folder in Windows 9x/Me that is used to synchronize files between two computers.

cable tester A tool used to test a cable to find out if it is good or to find out what type of cable it is if the cable is not labeled.

capacitive touch screen A touch screen that uses electrodes that sense the conductive properties of skin. *Compare to* resistive touch screen.

CDFS (Compact Disc File System) The 32-bit file system for CD discs and some CD-R and CD-RW discs. *See also* Universal Disk Format (UDF).

Certificate of Authenticity A sticker that contains the Windows product key.

channel A specific radio frequency within a broader frequency.

child directories *See* subdirectory.

Class A A license leased for a range of IP addresses that defines a single octet, which is the network portion of the IP addresses in that license. The last three octets can be used for the host address or for subnetting the network.

Class B A license that leases the first two octets of a range of IP addresses, and these first two octets are used for the network portion of the IP address. The last two octets can be used for the host address or for subnetting the network.

Class C A license for IP addresses that leases the first three octets as the network portion of the range of IP addresses.

classful subnet mask A subnet mask that contain all ones or all zeroes in an octet, and the octets that contain all ones are the octets leased by the class license. For example, 11111111.11111111.11111111 .00000000 or 255.255.255.0 is the subnet mask for a Class C license.

classless subnet mask A subnet mask that can have a mix of zeroes and ones in one octet or can contain all ones in an octet that was not leased by the class license. For example, 11111111.11111111.11110000 .00000000 or 255.255.240.0.

clean install Used to overwrite the existing operating system and applications when installing Windows on a hard drive.

client/server A computer concept whereby one computer (the client) requests information from another computer (the server).

client-side desktop virtualization Using this virtualization, software installed on a desktop or laptop manages virtual machines used by the local user.

client-side virtualization Using this virtualization, a personal computer provides multiple virtual environments for applications.

cloud computing A service where server-side virtualization is delegated to a third-party service, and the Internet is used to connect server and client machines.

cluster One or more sectors that constitute the smallest unit of space on a disk for storing data (also referred to as a file allocation unit). Files are written to a disk as groups of whole clusters.

cold boot *See* hard boot.

compatibility mode A group of settings that can be applied to older drivers or applications that might cause them to work in Windows using a newer version of Windows than the one the programs were designed to use.

Complete PC Backup A Vista utility that can make a backup of the entire volume on which Vista is installed and can also back up other volumes. *Compare to* system image.

Component Services (COM+) A Microsoft Management Console snap-in that can be used to register components used by installed applications.

Compressed (zipped) Folder A folder with a .zip extension that contains compressed files. When files are put in the folder, they are compressed. When files are moved to a regular folder, the files are decompressed.

computer infestation *See* malicious software.

Computer Management (Compmgmt.msc) A Windows console that contains several administrative tools used by support technicians to manage the local computer or other computers on the network.

computer name *See* host name.

connectionless protocol A protocol such as UDP that does not require a connection before sending a packet and does not guarantee delivery. An example of a UDP transmission is streaming video over the web. *Also called* a best-effort protocol.

connection-oriented protocol In networking, a protocol that confirms that a good connection has been made before transmitting data to the other end. An example of a connection-oriented protocol is TCP.

Console A window that consolidates several Windows administrative tools.

Control Panel A window containing several small utility programs called applets that are used to manage hardware, software, users, and the system.

custom installation In the Windows setup program, the option used to overwrite the existing operating system and applications, producing a clean installation of the OS. The main advantage is that problems with the old OS are not carried forward.

data collector set A utility within the Windows 7 Performance Monitor and the Windows Vista Reliability and Performance Monitor that is used to create a set of counters to collect data about the system to measure performance. The results can be saved to a report for future use.

Data Sources Open Database Connectivity (ODBC)   A tool in the Administrative Tools group of Control Panel that is used to allow data files to be connected to applications they normally would not use.

default gateway   The gateway a computer on a network will use to access another network unless it knows to specifically use another gateway for quicker access to that network.

default program   A program associated with a file extension.

defragment   To rewrite a file to a disk in one contiguous chain of clusters, thus speeding up data retrieval.

degausser   A machine that exposes a storage device to a strong magnetic field to completely erase the data on a magnetic hard drive or tape drive.

desktop   The initial screen that is displayed when an OS has a GUI interface loaded.

device driver   A program stored on the hard drive that tells the computer how to communicate with a hardware device such as a printer or modem.

Device Manager   Primary Windows tool for managing hardware.

DHCP (Dynamic Host Configuration Protocol)   A protocol used by a server to assign dynamic IP addresses to computers on a network when they first access the network.

DHCP client   A computer or other device that requests addresses from a DHCP server.

digital certificate   A code used to authenticate the source of a file or document or to identify and authenticate a person or organization sending data over a network. The code is assigned by a certificate authority such as VeriSign and includes a public key for encryption. *Also called* digital ID or digital signature.

Disk Cleanup   A Windows utility that enables you to delete temporary files to free up space on a drive.

disk cloning   *See* drive imaging.

diskpart   A command to manage hard drives, partitions, and volumes.

distribution server   A file server holding Windows setup files used to install Windows on computers networked to the server.

distribution share   The collective files in the installation that include Windows, device drivers, and applications. The package of files is served up by a distribution server.

distributions   Versions of Linux or UNIX published by an individual or organization.

DMZ   Stands for "demilitarized zone" and refers to removing firewall protection from a computer or network within an organization of protected computers and networks.

DNS (Domain Name System or Domain Name Service)   A distributed pool of information (called the name space) that keeps track of assigned host names and domain names and their corresponding IP addresses, and the system that allows a host to locate information in the pool.

DNS client   When Windows queries the DNS server for a name resolution.

DNS server   A computer that can find an IP address for another computer when only the fully qualified domain name is known.

dock   The area at the bottom of the Android screen where up to four apps can be pinned.

domain   In Windows, a logical group of networked computers, such as those on a college campus, that share a centralized directory database of user account information and security for the entire domain.

domain name   A unique, text-based name that identifies a network. A fully qualified domain name is sometimes loosely called a domain name. *Also see* fully qualified domain name.

drive imaging   Making an exact image of a hard drive, including partition information, boot sectors, operating system installation, and application software to replicate the hard drive on another system or recover from a hard drive crash. *Also called* disk cloning or disk imaging.

dual boot   The ability to boot using either of two different OSs, such as Windows XP and Windows 7. *Also called* multiboot.

dumb terminal   *See* zero client.

dynamic disks   A way to partition one or more hard drives, so that the drives can work together to store data in order to increase space for data or to provide fault tolerance or improved performance. *Also see* RAID. *Compare to* basic disk.

dynamic IP address   An assigned IP address that is used for the current session only. When the session is terminated, the IP address is returned to the list of available addresses.

dynamic volume   A volume type used with dynamic disks by which you can create a single volume that uses space on multiple hard drives.

elevated command prompt window   A Windows 7/Vista command prompt window that allows commands that require administrative privileges.

email hoax   An email message that is trying to tempt you to give out personal information or trying to scam you.

Emergency Repair Disk (ERD)   (1) In Windows 2000, a record of critical information about your system that can be used to fix a problem with the OS. The ERD enables restoration of the Windows 2000 registry on your hard drive. (2) In Windows XP, a bootable floppy disk that can boot the system, bypassing the boot files stored in the root of drive C.

Encrypted File System (EFS)   A way to use a key to encode a file or folder on an NTFS volume to protect sensitive data. Because it is an integrated system service, EFS is transparent to users and applications.

Event Viewer (Eventvwr.msc)   A Windows tool useful for troubleshooting problems with Windows, applications, and hardware. It displays logs of significant events such as a hardware or network failure, OS failure, OS error messages, a device or service that has failed to start, or General Protection Faults.

Everyone group   In Windows, the Authenticated Users group as well as the Guest account. When you share a file or folder on the network, Windows, by default, gives access to the Everyone group.

executive services   In Windows, a group of components running in kernel mode that interfaces between the subsystems in user mode and the HAL.

extended partition   The only partition on a hard drive that can contain more than one logical drive. In Windows, a hard drive can have only a single extended partition. *Compare to* primary partition.

FAT (file allocation table)   A table on a hard drive or floppy disk used by the FAT file system that tracks the clusters used to contain a file.

FDISK   A Windows 9x/Me command used to create and manage partitions on a hard drive.

ferrite clamp   A clamp installed on a network cable to protect against electrical interference.

file allocation unit   *See* cluster.

file association   The association between a data file and an application that is determined by the file extension.

file attributes   The properties assigned to a file. Examples of file attributes are read-only and hidden status.

file extension   A portion of the name of a file that indicates how the file is organized or formatted, the type of content in the file, and what program uses the file. In command lines, the file extension follows the filename and is separated from it by a period, for example, Msd.exe, where exe is the file extension.

Files and Settings Transfer Wizard   A Windows XP tool used to copy user data and settings from one computer to another.

file server   A computer dedicated to storing and serving up data files and folders.

file system   The overall structure that an OS uses to name, store, and organize files on a disk. Examples of file systems are NTFS and FAT32. Windows is always installed on a volume that uses the NTFS file system.

File Transfer Protocol (FTP)   *See* FTP (File Transfer Protocol).

filename   The first part of the name assigned to a file, which does not include the file extension. In DOS, the filename can be no more than eight characters long and is followed by the file extension. In Windows, a filename can be up to 255 characters.

fixboot   A Windows 7/Vista command that repairs the boot sector of the system partition.

fixmbr   A Windows 7/Vista command to repair the MBR.

folder   *See* subdirectory.

folder attributes   The properties assigned to a folder. Examples of folder attributes are read-only and hidden status.

formatting   *See* high-level formatting.

fragmented file   A file that has been written to different portions of the disk so that it is not in contiguous clusters.

FTP (File Transfer Protocol)   The protocol used to transfer files over a TCP/IP network.

fully qualified domain name (FQDN)   A host name and a domain name such as *jsmith.amazon.com*. Sometimes loosely referred to as a domain name.

gadget   A mini-app that appears on the Windows 7 desktop or Vista sidebar.

gateway   A router, computer, or other device that connects networks.

geotracking   A mobile device routinely reports its position to Apple or Google at least twice a day, which makes it possible for these companies to track your device's whereabouts.

global account Sometimes called a domain user account or network account, the account is used at the domain level, created by an administrator, and stored in the SAM (security accounts manager) database on a Windows domain controller.

global address *See* global unicast address.

global unicast address A TCP/IP version 6 IP address that can be routed on the Internet. *Also called* a global address.

Globally Unique Identifier Partition Table (GUID or GPT) A partitioning system installed on a hard drive that can support 128 partitions and is recommended for drives larger than 2 TB.

Gmail An email service provided by Google at mail.google.com.

Google account An account that is up on the Google Play web site (*play.google.com*) and is used to download content to an Android device.

Google Play The official source for apps, *also called* the Android marketplace, at *play.google.com*.

GPS (Global Positioning System) receiver A receiver that uses the system of 24 or more satellites orbiting the earth. The receiver locates four or more of these satellites, and from these four locations calculates its own position in a process called triangulation.

graphical user interface (GUI) An interface that uses graphics as compared to a command-driven interface.

grayware A program that AV software recognizes to be potentially harmful or potentially unwanted.

Group Policy (gpedit.msc) A console available only in Windows professional and business editions that is used to control what users can do and how the system can be used.

Guests group A type of user group in Windows. User accounts that belong to this group have limited rights to the system and are given a temporary profile that is deleted after the user logs off.

gyroscope A device that contains a disc that is free to move and can respond to gravity as the device is moved.

HAL (hardware abstraction layer) The low-level part of Windows, written specifically for each CPU technology, so that only the HAL must change when platform components change.

handheld tablet A computing device with a touch screen that is larger than a smart phone and has functions similar to a smart phone.

hard boot Restart the computer by turning off the power or by pressing the Reset button. *Also called* a cold boot.

hardware address *See* MAC address.

hardware-assisted virtualization (HAV) Motherboard BIOS and processor support used by hypervisor software when it creates and runs virtual machines on a computer. The feature must be enabled in BIOS setup.

hardware RAID One of two ways to implement RAID. Hardware RAID is more reliable and better performing than software RAID, and is implemented using the BIOS on the motherboard or a RAID controller card.

hidden share A folder whose folder name ends with a $ symbol. When you share the folder, it does not appear in the Network window or My Network Places window.

high-level formatting A process performed by the Windows Format program (for example, FORMAT C:/S), the Windows installation program, or the Disk Management utility. The process creates the boot record, file system, and root directory on a hard drive volume or logical drive, a floppy disk, or USB flash drive. *Also called* formatting, OS formatting, or operating system formatting. *Compare to* low-level formatting.

high-touch using a standard image A strategy to install Windows that uses a standard image for the installation. A technician must perform the installation on the local computer. *Also see* standard image.

high-touch with retail media A strategy to install Windows where all the work is done by a technician sitting at the computer using Windows setup files. The technician also installs drivers and applications after the Windows installation is finished.

HKEY_CLASSES_ROOT (HKCR) A Windows registry key that stores information to determine which application is opened when the user double-clicks a file.

HKEY_CURRENT_CONFIG (HKCC) A Windows registry key that contains information about the hardware configuration that is used by the computer at startup.

HKEY_CURRENT_USER (HKCU) A Windows registry key that contains data about the current user. The key is built when a user logs on using data kept in the HKEY_USERS key and data kept in the Ntuser.dat file of the current user.

HKEY_LOCAL_MACHINE (HKLM) An important Windows registry key that contains hardware, software, and security data. The key is built using data taken from the SAM hive, the Security hive, the Software hive, and the System hive and from data collected at startup about the hardware.

HKEY_USERS (HKU)   A Windows registry key that contains data about all users and is taken from the Default hive.

homegroup   A type of peer-to-peer network where each computer shares files, folders, libraries, and printers with other computers in the homegroup. Access to the homegroup is secured using a homegroup password.

host name   A name that identifies a computer, printer, or other device on a network, which can be used instead of the computer's IP address to address the computer on the network. The host name together with the domain name is called the fully qualified domain name. *Also called* computer name.

Hosts file   A file in the C:\Windows\System32\drivers\ etc folder that contains computer names and their associated IP addresses on the local network. The file has no file extension.

HTC Sense   A comprehensive user interface that incorporates the older TouchFLO technology used by mobile devices.

HTTP (Hypertext Transfer Protocol)   The communications protocol used by the World Wide Web.

HTTPS (HTTP secure)   A version of the HTTP protocol that includes data encryption for security using the SSL or TLS security protocols.

hypervisor   *See* virtual machine manager (VMM).

iCloud   A web site by Apple (*www.icloud.com*) used to sync content on Apple devices in order to provide a backup of the content.

image deployment   Installing a standard image on a computer.

ImageX   A program included in the Windows Automated Installation Kit that is used to create and modify standard images.

IMAP4 (Internet Message Access Protocol, version 4)   A protocol used by an email server and client that allows the client to manage email stored on the server without downloading the email. *Compare to* POP3.

Infrastructure as a Service (IaaS)   A cloud-computing service that provides only the hardware, which can include servers, Network-attached Storage (NAS) devices, and networks.

inherited permissions   Permissions assigned by Windows that are attained from a parent object.

initialization files   Text files that keep hardware and software configuration information, user preferences, and application settings and are used by the OS when first loaded and when needed by hardware, applications, and users.

in-place upgrade   A Windows installation that is launched from the Windows desktop. The installation carries forward user settings and installed applications from the old OS to the new one. A Windows OS is already in place before the installation begins.

interface   In TCP/IP version 6, a node's attachment to a link. The attachment can be a physical attachment (for example, when using a network adapter) or a logical attachment (for example, when using a tunnelling protocol). Each interface is assigned an IP address.

interface ID   In TCP/IP version 6, the last 64 bits or 4 blocks of an IP address that identifies that interface.

Internet Options   A dialog box used to manage Internet Explorer settings.

Internet Protocol version 4 (IPv4)   A TCP/IP standard that allows for an IP address with 32-bits.

Internet Protocol version 6 (IPv6)   A TCP/IP standard that allows for an IP address with 128 bits.

intranet   A private network that uses the TCP/IP protocols.

iOS   The operating system owned and developed by Apple and used for their various mobile devices.

iPad   A handheld tablet developed by Apple.

IP address   A 32-bit or 128-bit address used to uniquely identify a device on a network that uses TCP/IP protocols. The first numbers identify the network; the last numbers identify a host. An example of a 32-bit IP address is 206.96.103.114. An example of a 128-bit IP address is 2001:0000:B80::D3:9C5A:CC.

Ipconfig (IP configuration)   A command that displays TCP/IP configuration information and can refresh TCP/IP assignments to a connection including its IP address.

iPhone   A smart phone developed by Apple.

iPod touch   A multimedia recorder and player developed by Apple.

ISATAP   Intra-Site Automatic Tunnel Addressing Protocol (ISATAP) in which IPv6 packets travel over an IPv4 network.

ISO Image   An International Organization for Standardization image that contains an image of a disc, including the file system used.

iTunes Store   The Apple web site at *itunes.apple .com* where apps, music, TV shows, movies, books, podcasts, and iTunes U content, can be purchased and downloaded to Apple mobile devices.

iTunes U Content at the iTunes Store web site (itunes.apple.com) that contains lectures and even complete courses from many schools, colleges, and universities.

jailbreaking A process to break through the restrictions that only allow apps to an iOS device to be downloaded from the iTunes Store at *itunes .apple.com*. Gives the userroot or administrative privileges to the operating system and the entire file system and complete access to all commands and features.

Jump List Appears when right-clicking an icon in the Windows 7 taskbar and provides access to some of the major functions of the program.

kernel The portion of an OS that is responsible for interacting with the hardware.

kernel mode A Windows "privileged" processing mode that has access to hardware components.

key fob A device, such as a type of smart card, that can fit conveniently on a key chain.

keylogger A type of spyware that tracks your keystrokes, including passwords, chat room sessions, email messages, documents, online purchases, and anything else you type on your PC. Text is logged to a text file and transmitted over the Internet without your knowledge.

Last Known Good Configuration In Windows, registry settings and device drivers that were in effect when the computer last booted successfully. These settings can be restored during the startup process to recover from errors during the last boot.

library In Windows 7, a collection of one or more folders that can be stored on different local drives or on the network.

lite-touch, high-volume deployment A strategy that uses a deployment server on the network to serve up a Windows installation after a technician starts the process at the local computer.

Lightweight Directory Access Protocol (LDAP) A protocol used by various client applications when the application needs to query a database.

limited account A type of Windows XP user group, also known as the Users group in Windows 2000. Accounts in this group have read-write access only on their own folders, read-only access to most system folders, and no access to other users' data. In Windows 7/Vista, a standard account is a limited account.

link In TCP/IP version 6, a local area network or wide area network bounded by routers. *Also called* local link.

link-local address A type of TCP/IP version 6 IP address that can be used for communication among nodes on the same link and is allowed on the Internet. *Also called* link-local unicast address or local address.

link-local unicast address *See* link-local address.

loadstate A command used by the User State Migration Tool (USMT) to copy user settings and data temporarily stored on a server or removable media to a new computer. *Also see* scanstate.

local account A Windows user account that applies only to the local computer and cannot be used to access resources from other computers on the network. *Compare to* global account.

local area network A network bound by routers or other gateway devices. *Also called* a LAN.

local link *See* link.

local shares Folders on a computer that are shared with others on the network by using a folder's Properties box. Local shares are used with a workgroup and not with a domain.

logical drive A portion or all of a hard drive extended partition that is treated by the operating system as though it were a physical drive or volume. Each logical drive is assigned a drive letter, such as drive F, and contains a file system. *Compare to* volume.

logical topology The logical way computers connect on a network.

LoJack A technology by Absolute Software used to track the whereabouts of a laptop computer and, if the computer is stolen, lock down access to the computer or erase data on it.

loopback address An IP address that indicates your own computer and is used to test TCP/IP configuration on the computer.

loopback plug A tool used to test a live network cable or port.

low-level formatting A process (usually performed at the factory) that electronically creates the hard drive tracks and sectors and tests for bad spots on the disk surface.

MAC (Media Access Control) address A 48-bit hardware address unique to each NIC card or onboard network controller and assigned by the manufacturer at the factory. The address is often printed on the adapter as hexadecimal numbers. An example is 00 00 0C 08 2F 35. *Also called* a physical address, an adapter address, or a hardware address.

malicious software   Any unwanted program that is transmitted to a computer without the user's knowledge and that is designed to do varying degrees of damage to data and software. Types of infestations include viruses, Trojan horses, worms, adware, spyware, keyloggers, browser hijackers, dialers, and downloaders. *Also called* malware, infestation, or computer infestation.

malware   *See* malicious software.

Master Boot Record (MBR)   The first sector on a hard drive, which contains the partition table and a program the BIOS uses to boot an OS from the drive.

master file table (MFT)   The database used by the NTFS file system to track the contents of a volume or logical drive.

Memory Diagnostics (mdsched.exe)   A Windows 7/Vista utility used to test memory.

Microsoft Assessment and Planning (MAP) Toolkit   Software that can be used by a system administrator from a network location to query hundreds of computers in a single scan to determine if a computer qualifies for a Windows upgrade.

Microsoft Exchange   A server application that can handle email, contacts, and calendars and is a popular application used by large corporations for employee email, contacts, and calendars.

Microsoft Management Console (MMC)   A Windows utility to build customized consoles. These consoles can be saved to a file with an .msc file extension.

mirroring   A Windows XP technique to provide fault tolerance whereby one hard drive duplicates another hard drive.

mount point   A folder that is used as a shortcut to space on another volume, which effectively increases the size of the folder to the size of the other volume. *Also see* mounted drive.

mounted drive   A volume that can be accessed by way of a folder on another volume so that the folder has more available space. *Also see* mount point.

mstsc   A command that allows you to start Remote Desktop Connection to remote in to your host computer using Remote Desktop.

multiboot   *See* dual boot.

multicast address   In TCP/IP version 6, an IP address used when packets are delivered to all nodes on a network.

multicasting   A process in which a message is sent by one host to multiple hosts, such as when a video conference is broadcast to several hosts on the Internet.

multiple input/multiple output (MIMO)   A feature of the IEEE 802.11n standard for wireless networking whereby two or more antennas are used at both ends of transmissions to improve performance.

Multimedia Messaging Service (MMS)   A technology that allows users to send text messages with photos, videos, or other multimedia content attached.

multitouch   A touch screen on a computer or mobile device that can handle a two-finger pinch.

name resolution   The process of associating a character-based computer name to an IP address.

NAT (Network Address Translation)   A protocol used to convert private IP addresses on a LAN to a public IP address before a data packet is sent over the Internet.

navigation pane   In Windows Explorer or the Computer window, pane on the left side of the window where devices, drives, and folders are listed. Double-click an item to drill down into the item.

nbtstat (NetBIOS over TCP/IP Statistics)   A TCP/IP command that is used to display statistics about the NetBT protocol.

neighbors   In TCP/IP version 6, two or more nodes on the same link.

netstat (network statistics)   A TCP/IP command that gives statistics about TCP/IP and network activity and includes several parameters.

net use   A TCP/IP command that connects or disconnects a computer from a shared resource or can display information about connections.

net user   A TCP/IP command used to manage user accounts.

network adapter   *See* network interface card.

Network and Sharing Center   The primary Windows 7/Vista utility used to manage network connections.

network drive map   Mounting a drive to a computer, such as drive E, that is actually hard drive space on another host computer on the network.

notification area   An area to the right of the taskbar that holds the icons for running services; these services include the volume control and network connectivity. *Also called* the system tray or systray.

Nslookup (name space lookup)   A TCP/IP command that lets you read information from the Internet name space by requesting information about domain name resolutions from the DNS server's zone data.

NTFS permissions   A method to share a folder or file over a network and can apply to local uses and network users. The folder or file must be on an NTFS volume. *Compare to* share permissions.

Ntldr   The Windows XP program responsible for starting Windows XP, called the boot loader program.

octet   In TCP/IP version 4, each of the four numbers that are separated by periods and make up a 32-bit IP address. One octet is 8 bits.

Offline Files   A utility that allows users to work with files in the folder when the computer is not connected to the corporate network. When the computer is later connected, Windows syncs up the offline files and folders with those on the network.

open source   Operating system or application where the source code is available for free and anyone can modify and redistribute the source code.

operating system (OS)   Software that controls a computer. An OS controls how system resources are used and provides a user interface, a way of managing hardware and software, and ways to work with files.

original equipment manufacturer (OEM) license   A software license that only manufacturers or builders of personal computers can purchase to be installed only on a computer intended for sale.

OS boot record   The first sector in the active partition. Windows XP uses this sector during the boot, but Windows 7/Vista does not.

packet   Segment of network data that also includes header, destination address, and type of data that is sent as a unit. *Also called* data packet or datagram.

pagefile.sys   The Windows swap file that is used to hold the virtual memory that is used to enhance physical memory installed in a system.

pairing   The process of two Bluetooth devices establishing connectivity.

partition   A division of a hard drive that can hold volumes. Using the MBR system, Windows can support up to four partitions on one hard drive.

partition table   A table at the beginning of the hard drive that contains information about each partition on the drive. The partition table is contained in the Master Boot Record.

patch   A minor update to software that corrects an error, adds a feature, or addresses security issues. *Also called* an update. *Compare to* service pack.

path   A drive and list of directories pointing to a file such as C:\Windows\System32.

peer-to-peer (P2P)   As applied to networking, a network of computers that are all equals, or peers. Each computer has the same amount of authority, and each can act as a server to the other computers.

Performance Information and Tools   A Windows 7 utility that provides information to evaluate the performance of a system and to adjust Windows for best performance.

Performance Monitor   A Microsoft Management Console snap-in that can track activity by hardware and software to measure performance.

permission propagation   When Windows passes permissions from parent objects to child objects.

permissions   Varying degrees of access assigned to a folder or file and given to a user account or user group. Access can include full control, write, delete, or read-only.

phishing   (1) A type of identity theft where a person is baited into giving personal data to a web site that appears to be the web site of a reputable company with which the person has an account. (2) Sending an email message with the intent of getting the user to reveal private information that can be used for identify theft.

physical address   *See* MAC address.

physical topology   The physical arrangement of connections between computers.

Ping (packet internet groper)   A TCP/IP command used to troubleshoot network connections. It verifies that the host can communicate with another host on the network.

Platform as a Service (PaaS)   A cloud computing service that provides the hardware and the operating system and is responsible for updating and maintaining both.

POP or POP3 (Post Office Protocol, version 3)   The protocol that an email server and client use when the client requests the downloading of email messages. The most recent version is POP version 3. *Compare to* IMAP3.

port   (1) As applied to services running on a computer, a number that a service or process on a computer uses to listen for activity. *Also called* a port address or port number. (2) A physical connector, usually at the back of a computer, that allows a cable from a peripheral device, such as a printer, mouse, or modem, to be attached.

port filtering To open or close certain ports so they can or cannot be used. A firewall uses port filtering to protect a network from unwanted communication.

port forwarding A technique that allows a computer on the Internet to reach a computer on a private network using a certain port when the private network is protected by a firewall device using NAT. *Also called* tunnelling.

port number *See* port.

port triggering When a firewall opens a port because a computer behind the firewall initiates communication on another port.

POST (power-on self test) A self-diagnostic program used to perform a simple test of the CPU, RAM, and various I/O devices. The POST is performed by startup BIOS when the computer is first turned on, and is stored in ROM-BIOS.

Power Users Group A type of user account group. Accounts assigned to this group can read from and write to parts of the system other than their own user profile folders, install applications, and perform limited administrative tasks.

Preboot eXecution Environment (PCE) Programming contained in the BIOS code on the motherboard used to start up the computer and search for a server on the network to provide a bootable operating system.

presentation virtualization Using this virtualization, a remote application running on a server is controlled by a local computer.

primary partition A hard disk partition that can contain only one volume. In Windows, a hard drive can have up to three primary partitions. *Compare to* extended partition.

principle of least privilege An approach where computer users are classified and the rights assigned are the minimum rights required to do their job.

privacy filter A device that fits over a monitor screen to prevent other people from viewing the monitor from a wide angle.

private IP address In TCP/IP version 4, an IP address that is used on a private network that is isolated from the Internet.

Problem Reports and Solutions A Windows utility that provides a list of current and past problems associated with a computer.

process A program that is running under the authority of the shell, together with the system resources assigned to it.

product activation The process that Microsoft uses to prevent software piracy. For example, once Windows 7 is activated for a particular computer, it cannot be legally installed on another computer.

Programs and Features A window within the Control Panel that lists the programs installed on a computer where you can uninstall, change, or repair programs.

protocols The rules for communication. For example, TCP/IP is a suite or group of protocols that define many types of communication on a TCP/IP network.

proxy server A computer that intercepts requests that a browser makes of a server and serves up the request from a cache it maintains in order to improve performance on a large network.

public IP address In TCP/IP version 4, an IP address available to the Internet.

pull automation A Windows installation that requires the local user to start the process. *Compare to* push automation.

push automation An installation where a server automatically pushes the installation to a computer when a user is not likely to be sitting at the computer. *Compare to* pull automation.

Quality of Service (QoS) A measure of the success of communication over the Internet. Communication is degraded on the Internet when packets are dropped, delayed, delivered out of order, or corrupted. VoIP requires a high QoS.

quarantined computer A computer that is suspected of infection and is not allowed to use the network, is put on a different network dedicated to quarantined computers, or is allowed to access only certain network resources.

quick format A format procedure, used to format a hard drive volume or other drive, that doesn't scan the volume or drive for bad sectors; use it only when a drive has been previously formatted and is in healthy condition.

radio frequency (RF) The frequency of waves generated by a radio signal, which are electromagnetic frequencies above audio and below light. For example, Wi-Fi 802.11n transmits using a radio frequency of 5 GHz and 2.4 GHz.

RAID (redundant array of inexpensive disks or redundant array of independent disks) Several methods of configuring multiple hard drives to store data to increase volume size and improve performance, or to ensure that if one hard drive fails, the data is still available from another hard drive.

RAID 0   Using space from two or more physical disks to increase the disk space available for a single volume. Performance improves because data is written evenly across all disks. Windows calls RAID 0 a striped volume. *Also called* striping.

RAID 1   A type of drive imaging that duplicates data on one drive to another drive and is used for fault tolerance. Windows calls RAID 1 a mirrored volume.

ReadyBoost   A Windows 7/Vista utility that uses a flash drive or secure digital (SD) memory card to boost hard drive performance.

Recovery Console   In Windows XP, a lean bootable command-line operating system on the Windows XP setup CD that can be used to troubleshoot an XP boot problem.

recovery image   A backup of the Windows volume.

registry   A database that Windows uses to store hardware and software configuration information, user preferences, and setup information.

Registry Editor (Regedit.exe)   The Windows utility used to edit the Windows registry.

Regsvr32   A utility that is used to register component services used by an installed application.

Reliability and Performance Monitor   A Vista utility (Perfmon.msc) that collects, records, and displays events, called Data Collector Sets, that can help track the performance and reliability of Windows. In Windows XP, this monitor is called the Performance Monitor or the System Monitor.

Reliability Monitor   A Windows 7 utility that provides information about problems and errors that happen over time.

Remote Admin   Gives an administrator access to the Windows folder on a remote computer.

RemoteApp and Desktop Connection   A tool used to install a remote application on a client computer using either an application proxy file or a URL to the server application.

remote application   An application that is installed and executed on a server and is presented to a user working at a client computer.

Remote Desktop   A Windows tool that gives a user access to his or her Windows desktop from anywhere on the Internet.

Remote Desktop Protocol (RDP)   The protocol used by the Windows Remote Desktop and Remote Assistance utilities to connect to and control a remote computer.

Remote Desktop Services   Software included in Windows 2008 and later that uses the RDP protocol to present a remote application and its data to the client. Prior to Windows 2008, the software was called Terminal Services.

remote network installation   An automated installation where no user intervention is required.

remote wipe   Remotely erases all contacts, email, photos, and other data from a device to protect your privacy.

resistive touch screen   A touch screen that has two sheets of glass covered with a resistive coating. When pressure is placed on the top glass, the glass bends and makes contact with the lower glass. *Compare to* capacitive touch screen.

Resource Monitor   A Windows tool that monitors the performance of the processor, memory, hard drive, and network.

restore point   A snapshot of the Windows system, usually made before installation of new hardware or applications.

retinal scanning   As part of the authentication process, some systems use biometric data by scanning the blood vessels on the back of the eye and is considered the most reliable of all biometric data scanning.

reverse lookup   To find the host name when you know a computer's IP address. The Nslookup command can perform a reverse lookup.

RFID badge   A badge worn by an employee and is used to gain entrance into a locked area of a building. A Radio Frequency Identification token transmits authentication to the system when the token gets in range of a query device.

root directory   The main directory, at the top of the top-down hierarchical structure of subdirectories, created when a hard drive or disk is first formatted. In Linux, it's indicated by a forward slash. In DOS and Windows, it's indicated by a backward slash.

rooting   The process of obtaining root or administrator privileges to an Android device which then gives you complete access to the entire file system and all commands and features.

rootkit   A type of malicious software that loads itself before the OS boot is complete and can hijack internal Windows components so that it masks information Windows provides to user-mode utilities such as Windows Explorer or Task Manager.

router   A device that connects networks and makes decisions as to the best routes to use when forwarding packets.

RSA tokens A type of smart card that contains authentication information.

scanstate A command used by the User State Migration Tool (USMT) to copy user settings and data from an old computer to a server or removable media. *Also see* loadstate.

screen orientation The layout of the screen that is either portrait or landscape.

screen resolution The number of dots or pixels on the monitor screen expressed as two numbers such as 1680 × 1050.

secondary logon Using administrative privileges to perform an operation when you are not logged on with an account that has these privileges.

sector On a hard disk drive or SSD, the smallest unit of bytes addressable by the operating system and BIOS. On hard disk drives, one sector equals 512 bytes; SSD drives might use larger sectors.

Secure FTP (SFTP) A protocol used to transfer files from an FTP server to an FTP client using encryption.

Secure Shell (SSH) A protocol that is used to pass login information to a remote computer and control that computer over a network using encryption.

Security Center A center in Vista where you can confirm Windows Firewall, Windows Update, anti-malware settings, including that of Windows Defender, and other security settings.

Server Message Block (SMB) A protocol used by Windows to share files and printers on a network.

server-side virtualization Using this virtualization, a server provides a virtual desktop or application for users on multiple client machines.

service A program that runs in the background to support or serve Windows or an application.

service pack A collection of several patches or updates that is installed as a single update to an OS or application.

Services console A Windows console used to control the Windows and third-party services installed on a system.

Service Set Identifier (SSID) The name of the access point for a wireless network.

setup BIOS Used to change motherboard settings. For example, you can use it to enable or disable a device on the motherboard, change the date and time that is later passed to the OS, and select the order of boot devices for startup BIOS to search when looking for an operating system to load.

shadow copy A copy of open files made so that open files are included in a backup.

share permissions A method to share a folder (not individual files) to remote users on the network, including assigning varying degrees of access to specific user accounts and user groups. Does not apply to local shares and can be used on an NTFS or FAT volume. *Compare to* NTFS permissions.

shell The portion of an OS that relates to the user and to applications.

Short Message Service (SMS) A technology that allows users to send a test message using a smart phone.

shoulder surfing Where other people secretly peek at your monitor screen as you work to gain valuable information.

sidebar Located on the right side of the Vista desktop and displays Vista gadgets.

SIM (Subscriber Identification Module) card A small flash memory card that contains all the information you need to connect to a cellular network, including a password and other authentication information needed to access the network, encryption standards used, and the services that your subscription includes.

simple file sharing A Windows XP technique to share folders or files with remote network users where you have no control over who has access to the shared folder or file.

Simple Network Management Protocol (SNMP) A TCP/IP protocol used to monitor network traffic.

simple volume A type of volume used on a single hard drive. *Compare to* dynamic volume.

slack Wasted space on a hard drive caused by not using all available space at the end of clusters.

smart card Any small device that contains authentication information that can be keyed into a logon window or read by a reader to authenticate a user on a network.

smart card reader A device that can read a smart card used to authenticate a person onto a network.

smart phone Primarily a cellphone and includes abilities to send text messages, text messages with photos, videos, or other multimedia content, surf the web, manage email, play games, take photos and videos, and download and use small apps.

SMTP (Simple Mail Transfer Protocol) The protocol used by email clients and servers to send email messages over the Internet. *Also see* POP and IMAP.

SMTP AUTH (SMTP Authentication) A protocol that is used to authenticate or prove that a client who attempts to use an email server to send email is authorized to use the server. The protocol is based on the Simple Authentication and Security Layer (SASL) protocol.

snap-ins A Windows utility that can be installed in a console window by Microsoft Management Console.

social engineering The practice of tricking people into giving out private information or allowing unsafe programs into the network or computer.

soft boot To restart a PC without turning off the power, for example, in Windows 7, by clicking Start, pointing to Shut down, and clicking Restart. *Also called* warm boot.

Software as a Service (SaaS) A cloud computing service where the service is responsible for the hardware, the operating systems, and the applications installed.

Software Explorer A Vista tool used to control startup programs.

software RAID Using Windows to implement RAID. The setup is done using the Disk Management utility.

spyware Malicious software that installs itself on your computer to spy on you. It collects personal information about you that it transmits over the Internet to web-hosting sites that intend to use your personal data for harm.

standard account The Windows 7/Vista user account type that can use software and hardware and make some system changes, but cannot make changes that affect the security of the system or other users.

standard image An image that includes Windows 7, drivers, and applications that are standard to all the computers that might use the image.

startup BIOS Part of system BIOS that is responsible for controlling the PC when it is first turned on. Startup BIOS gives control over to the OS once it is loaded.

static IP address A permanent IP address that is manually assigned to a computer.

striping *See* RAID 0.

strong password A password that is not easy to guess.

subdirectory A directory or folder contained in another directory or folder. *Also called* a child directory or folder.

subnet When several local networks are tied together in a subsystem of the larger intranet.

subnet ID Using TCP/IP version 6, the last block in the 64-bit prefix of an IP address.

subnet mask Using TCP/IP version 4, a group of four numbers (dotted decimal numbers) that tell TCP/IP if a remote computer is on the same or different network.

system BIOS (basic input/output system) BIOS located on the motherboard that is used to control essential devices before the OS is loaded.

System Configuration Utility (Msconfig.exe) A Windows utility that can identify what processes are launched at startup and can temporarily disable a process from loading.

System File Checker (SFC) *See* SFC (System File Checker).

system image The backup of the entire Windows 7 volume and can also include backups of other volumes. The backup is made using the Windows 7 Backup and Restore utility.

System Information A Windows tool that provides details about a system, including installed hardware and software, the current system configuration, and currently running programs. The program file is Msinfo32.exe.

System Monitor The Windows XP Performance Monitor.

system partition The active partition of the hard drive containing the boot record and the specific files required to start the Windows launch.

System Protection A utility that automatically backs up system files and stores them in restore points on the hard drive at regular intervals and just before you install software or hardware.

system repair disc A disc you can create using Windows 7 that can be used to launch Windows RE.

System Restore A Windows utility used to restore the system to a restore point.

system state data In Windows 2000/XP, files that are necessary for a successful load of the operating system.

system tray *See* notification area.

System window A window that displays brief and important information about installed hardware and software and gives access to important Windows tools needed to support the system.

systray *See* notification area.

tailgating When someone who is unauthorized follows the employee through a secured entrance to a room or building.

Task Manager (Taskmgr.exe) A Windows utility that lets you view the applications and processes running on your computer as well as information about process and memory performance, network activity, and user activity.

Task Scheduler A Windows tool that can set a task or program to launch at a future time, including at startup.

taskbar A bar normally located at the bottom of the Windows desktop, displaying information about open programs and providing quick access to others.

Taskkill A command that uses the process PID to kill a process.

Tasklist A command that returns the process identify (PID), which is a number that identifies each running process.

TCP (Transmission Control Protocol) A protocol in the TCP/IP protocol suite. TCP guarantees delivery of data for application protocols and establishes a session before it begins transmitting data.

TCP/IP (Transmission Control Protocol/Internet Protocol) The suite of protocols that supports communication on the Internet. Fundamentally, TCP is responsible for error checking transmissions, and IP is responsible for routing.

Telnet A TCP/IP command-line client/server application that allows an administrator or other user to control a computer remotely.

Teredo A tunneling protocol in which IPv6 packets travel over an IPv4 network. Named after the Teredo worm that bores holes in wood.

Terminal Services See Remote Desktop Services.

thin client A client computer that has an operating system but has little computing power and might only need to support a browser used to communicate with the server.

thread Each process that the CPU is aware of; a single task that is part of a longer task or request from a program.

TKIP (Temporal Key Integrity Protocol) A type of encryption used by WPA to secure a wireless Wi-Fi network.

TouchFLO A multi-touch technology developed by High Tech Computer (HTC) and widely used by mobile devices.

Tracert (trace route) A TCP/IP command that enables you to resolve a connectivity problem when attempting to reach a destination host such as a web site.

track One of many concentric circles on the surface of a hard disk drive or floppy disk.

Trojan A type of malware that tricks you into opening it by substituting itself for a legitimate program.

Type 1 hypervisor Software to manage virtual machines that is installed before any operating system is installed.

Type 2 hypervisor Software to manage virtual machines that is installed as an application in an operating system.

UDP (User Datagram Protocol) A connectionless TCP/IP protocol that does not require a connection to send a packet and does not guarantee that the packet arrives at its destination. UDP is faster than TCP because TCP takes the time to make a connection and guarantee delivery.

ultra-thin client See zero client.

unattended installation A Windows installation that is done by storing the answers to installation questions in a text file or script that Windows calls an answer file so that the answers do not have to be typed in during the installation.

unicast address Using TCP/IP version 6, an IP address assigned to a single node on a network.

unique local address (ULA) Using TCP/IP version 6, an IP address used to identify a specific site within a larger intranet. Also called a unique local unicast address.

unique local unicast address See unique local address (ULA).

Universal Disk Format (UDF) file system A file system for optical media used by all DVD discs and some CD-R and CD-RW discs.

upgrade paths A qualifying OS required by Microsoft in order to perform an in-place upgrade.

User Account Control (UAC) dialog box A Windows 7/Vista security feature that displays a dialog box when an event requiring administrative privileges is about to happen.

User group The group of standard user accounts.

user mode In Windows, a mode that provides an interface between an application and the OS, and only has access to hardware resources through the code running in kernel mode.

user profile A collection of files and settings about a user account that enables the user's personal data, desktop settings, and other operating parameters to be retained from one session to another.

user profile namespace The group of folders and subfolders in the C:\Users folder that belong to a specific user account and contain the user profile.

User State Migration Tool (USMT)   A Windows utility that helps you migrate user files and preferences from one computer to another to help a user make a smooth transition from one computer to another.

Virtual Desktop Infrastructure (VDI)   A presentation of a virtual desktop made to a client computer by a server that is serving up a virtual machine.

virtual machine (VM)   One or more logical machines created within one physical machine.

virtual machine manager (VMM)   Software that creates and manages virtual machines on a server or on a local computer. *Also called* hypervisor.

virtual memory   A method whereby the OS uses the hard drive as though it were RAM. *Also see* pagefile.sys.

virtual private network (VPN)   A security technique that uses encrypted data packets between a private network and a computer somewhere on the Internet.

virtualization   When one physical machine hosts multiple activities that are normally done on multiple machines.

virus   A program that often has an incubation period, is infectious, and is intended to cause damage. A virus program might destroy data and programs or damage a disk drive's boot sector.

virus definition   A set of distinguishing characteristics of a virus used by antivirus software to identify new viruses as they get into the wild. *Also called* virus signatures.

virus encyclopedia   A database about viruses that is kept on the Internet.

virus signature   *See* virus definition.

volume   A primary partition that has been assigned a drive letter and can be formatted with a file system such as NTFS. *Compare to* logical drive.

Wake on LAN   Configuring a computer so that it will respond to network activity when the computer is in a sleep state.

warm boot   *See* soft boot.

WEP (Wired Equivalent Privacy)   A data encryption method used on Wi-Fi wireless networks that uses either 64-bit or 128-bit encryption keys that are static keys, meaning the key does not change while the wireless network is in use.

Wi-Fi (Wireless Fidelity)   *See* 802.11 a/b/g/n.

Wi-Fi Protected Setup (WPS)   Designed to make it easier for users to connect their computers to a wireless network when a hard-to-remember SSID and security key are used.

wildcard   An *or ? character used in a command line that represents a character or group of characters in a filename or extension.

Windows 7 Enterprise   A Windows operating system that includes additional features over Windows 7 Professional. The major additional features include BitLocker Drive Encryption used to encrypt an entire hard drive and support for multiple languages. The edition does not include Windows DVD Maker. Multiple site licenses are available.

Windows 7 Home Basic   A Windows operating system that has limited features and is available only in underdeveloped countries and can only be activated in these countries.

Windows 7 Home Premium   A Windows operating system that is similar to Windows 7 Home Basic, but includes additional features.

Window 7 Professional   A Windows operating system that is intended for business users. You can purchase multiple site licenses (*also called* volume licensing) using this edition.

Windows 7 Starter   A Windows operating system that has the most limited features and is intended to be used on netbooks or in developing nations. In the United States, it can only be obtained preinstalled by the manufacturer on a new netbook computer. Windows Starter comes only in the 32-bit version. All other editions of Windows 7 are available in either the 32-bit or 4-bit version.

Windows 7 Ultimate   A Windows operating system that includes every Windows 7 feature. Multiple licenses are not available with this edition.

Windows Automated Installation Kit (AIK)   The Windows AIK for Windows 7 contains a group of tools used to deploy Windows 7 in a large organization and contains the User State Migration Tool (USMT).

Windows Boot Loader (WinLoad.exe)   One of two programs that manage the loading of Windows 7/Vista. The program file is stored in C:\Windows\System32, and it loads and starts essential Windows processes.

Windows Boot Manager (BootMgr)   The Windows 7/Vista program that manages the initial startup of Windows. The BootMgr program file is stored in the C:\ root directory and has no file extension.

Windows Defender   Antispyware utility included in Windows 7/Vista.

Windows Easy Transfer   A Windows tool used to transfer Windows 7/Vista/XP user data and preferences to the Windows 7/Vista/XP installation on another computer.

Windows Experience Index A Windows 7/Vista feature that gives a summary index designed to measure the overall performance of a system on a scale from 1.0 to 7.9.

Windows Firewall A personal firewall that protects a computer from intrusion and is automatically configured when you set your network location in the Network and Sharing Center.

Windows Preinstallation Environment (Windows PE) A minimum operating system used to start the Windows installation.

Windows Recovery Environment (Windows RE) A lean operating system installed on the Windows 7/Vista setup DVD and also on a Windows 7 hard drive that can be used to troubleshoot problems when Windows refuses to start.

Windows Vista Business The Vista edition designed for business users and includes support for a domain, Group Policy, and Encrypted File System, and does not include consumer features such as Movie Maker.

Windows Vista Enterprise The Vista edition that expands on Windows Vista Business, adding security features such as BitLocker Encryption.

Windows Vista Home Basic The Vista edition that is designed for low-cost home systems that don't require full security and networking features. It does not include the Aero glass interface.

Windows Vista Home Premium The Vista edition that includes more features than Windows Vista Home Basic, including the Aero user interface, DVD Maker, Media Center, SideShow, and backups.

Windows Vista Starter The Vista edition with the most limited features and intended to be used in developing nations.

Windows Vista Ultimate The Vista edition that includes every Windows Vista feature. Multiple licensing is not available.

Windows XP Home Edition The XP edition that does not include Remote Desktop, multilingual capabilities, roaming profiles, and support for high-end processors.

Windows XP Media Center Edition The XP edition is an enhanced version of XP Professional that includes support for digital entertainment hardware.

Windows XP Mode A Windows XP environment installed in Windows 7 that can be used to support older applications.

Windows XP Professional The XP edition that includes Remote Desktop, roaming profiles, multilingual capabilities and enhanced security features.

Windows XP Professional x64 Edition (formally called Windows XP 64-Bit Edition) A 64-bit operating system and can support up to 128 GB of memory. (All other editions of XP are 32-bit and can support up to 4 GB of memory.)

Windows XP Tablet PC Edition The XP edition designed for notebooks and tablet PCs.

wireless access point A wireless device that creates a wireless network.

wireless locator A tool that **can** locate a Wi-Fi hotspot and tell you the strength of the RF signal.

wireless wide area network (WWAN) A cellular network for mobile broadband devices.

workgroup In Windows, a logical group of computers and users in which administration, resources, and security are distributed throughout the network, without centralized management or security.

worm An infestation designed to copy itself repeatedly to memory, on drive space, or on a network, until little memory, disk space, or network bandwidth remains.

WPA (WiFi Protected Access) A data encryption method for wireless networks that use the TKIP (Temporal Key Integrity Protocol) encryption method and the encryption keys are changed at set intervals while the wireless LAN is in use.

WPA2 (WiFi Protected Access 2) A data encryption standard compliant with the IEEE802.11i standard that uses the AES (Advanced Encryption Standard) protocol. WPA2 is currently the strongest wireless encryption standard.

zero client A client computer that does not have an operating system and merely provides an interface between the user and the server.

zero-touch, high volume deployment An installation strategy that does not require the user to start the process. Instead a server pushes the installation to a computer when a user is not likely to be sitting at it.

INDEX

Note: Page numbers in **bold** indicate definitions.